CHURCHILL'S DOCTOR

A BIOGRAPHY OF LORD MORAN

by

Richard Lovell

Royal Society of Medicine Services Limited

Royal Society of Medicine Services Limited
1 Wimpole Street London W1M 8AE
150 East 58th Street New York NY 10155

British Library Cataloguing in Publication Data

A catalogue record for this book is available from the British Library

ISBN 1-85315-183-1

Phototypeset by Dobbie Typesetting Limited, Tavistock, Devon
Printed in Great Britain at Biddles Ltd, Guildford, Surrey

Contents

To Diana
and
in gratitude to AB Lloyd Baker, sometime form master
at Cheltenham College, whose teaching of English and
History was never confined by the set curriculum.

Foreword

Douglas Black

A good wine needs no bush. So all that need be said by way of commendation is that an adequate biography of Charles McMoran Wilson is long overdue; and that the need is now well satisfied by a book which is the fruit of years of study by a well-qualified biographer. Even within the narrow compass of a foreword, that may leave me room to express an independent view of Moran's contribution to the medical history of this century.

Moran could at the time extenuate his extended account of Churchill's illnesses as a contribution to history; and our country certainly benefited from the good medical care and general support which he gave to a man without whose leadership we might well have lost the war. Nevertheless, it is not for his contribution to general history that Moran is likely to be remembered—even the most competent medical attendants of the great still fall within the marginalia of history.

By contrast, his contribution to medical history was immense, and also highly individual. He made it not by outstanding clinical practice, nor by any major contribution to medical science; but by his timely and decisive impact on three institutions—St Mary's Hospital and Medical School; the Royal College of Physicians of London; and above all on the National Health Service at its inception.

Since I did not qualify at St Mary's, nor in London, nor indeed in England, it would be unwise of me to make extended comment on this account of Moran's contributions as physician and Dean to medical education at St Mary's, given by an author possessing all these advantages. The book describes in detail Moran's key role in the transformation of 'a badly organised medical school in decrepit buildings' into 'one of the finest medical schools in the country'. His interest in Rugby football, though it became a legend, was only a small part of the story—not for him Kipling's 'muddied oafs at the goal', he sought a combination of character and intellect, without which the School could not have flourished as it did.

As the sixth successor to Moran in the long line of Presidents of the Royal College of Physicians, I may be better placed to comment on his contribution to that College than I am on his period at St Mary's. As an active younger Fellow, he was constructively discontented with the lethargy into which the College had sunk, its remoteness from medical education and research, and its preoccupation with London medicine rather than with national medical issues—'They have made it a club, not a college.' His opportunity came, first as Treasurer from 1938 to 1941, then as President for the next nine years, probably the most momentous in the entire history of a College incorporated in 1518 under Henry VIII. His annual election to the Presidency was regularly challenged by conservative Fellows led by Lord Horder; but Moran enjoyed the support of the younger Fellows and was re-elected each year, sometimes by interesting margins. He was determined not only to bring new life to the college itself, but also to make it the recognised mouthpiece for consultant physicians, and to restore its influence, and that of other Colleges, in national medical counsels.

For the first of these objectives, he actively sought contacts with medical teachers, and with physicians outside London, initiatives which also contributed to his second objective, that of making the College representative of physicians in general. Later Presidents, most notably Platt and Rosenheim, have consolidated the process which Moran initiated, so that the College now has a very extensive educational programme; occupies new premises in which such activities can be undertaken; supervises the post-graduate training of physicians; has a voice in their appointment; and nourishes their continuing education after appointment. There is a close relationship with medical teachers—seven of the nine Presidents since Moran have occupied Chairs of Medicine. And the 'constituency' of the College is nation-wide—five of the same nine Presidents came from outside London. Of course, these things might have happened with time in any case; but Moran was the man who foresaw their desirability, and pursued change with the necessary determination and adroitness.

There was inevitable tension between Moran's ambition to make the College *the* recognised representative of physicians and the claim of the British Medical Association (BMA) to represent *all* doctors. At that time, general practitioners were dominant in the BMA to an extent which disposed physicians and other specialists to support Moran in his advocacy of alternative representation. Since then, there have been significant changes in the relationships between general practitioners and hospital doctors, with the formation of a Royal College of General Practitioners, and some increase in the influence of specialists within the BMA. A British compromise has been reached, with the BMA responsible for 'terms and conditions of service', officially negotiated with government, and the Colleges responsible for standards of training and practice. The arrangement works reasonably, so long as people have the sense to recognise the dangers inherent in excessive clarity of definition.

The BMA view of this tension, and its effect on the negotiations leading up to the National Health Service, is given in Volume II of the *History of the British Medical Association*, by Grey-Turner and Sutherland, which contrives to make only two references to Lord Moran. His struggles with the BMA may have given Moran the principal blind spot in his perception of what was needed in the national provision of health care. This was his tendency to underestimate the importance of general practitioners, whom he regarded, in a much-quoted phrase, as having 'fallen off the ladder'. He could not of course foresee the renaissance of general practice which was to end professional isolation (partly through the development of group practices, and of health centres, strongly advocated by Moran himself); introduce a proper training programme for entrants to practice; develop University Departments of General Practice, at the centre of a network of teaching practices; and make family practice a favoured career option among young graduates.

In his first Presidential Address to the College, Moran enunciated 'a working rule for my own guidance—that the interests of this College and the interests of the country shall be one and the same, and that where they are at odds the College must give way'. Faithfulness to this principle made him set the interests of patients above those of the official representatives of doctors, where there appeared to be a conflict; and that was the mainspring of his beneficent influence on the shape of the National Health Service. But he could not have exerted such influence had it not been for his careful cultivation of good relationships with men of political affairs, and the serendipity of his medical links with Churchill. He also had the breadth of mind to enable him to discern the worth of Bevan's intentions and ideas through the fog of political rhetoric, and so to avoid a damaging conflict between the medical profession and the government.

The Annigoni portrait of Moran which hangs in his College captures precisely the masterly combination of strategy and tactics which enabled him to do so much. What it perhaps shows less clearly is the strength of the idealism which inspired him, both for his profession and—more important still—for the health care of his fellow citizens. Of the Colleges, he said, 'We look to them to keep medicine a profession, and to see that it does not sink into a bureaucracy and a trade.' And the elitism of his vision of a consultant-led service was tempered by realisation that unless there is decent health care for all, there cannot be optimal health care for any.

Acknowledgments

For permission to use and quote from the Moran family papers I am indebted to the present Lord Moran. I gratefully acknowledge also his permission, and that of Constable Publishers, to quote from his father's two books: *The Anatomy of Courage*, Constable, London 1945 and *Winston Churchill, the Struggle for Survival*, Constable, London 1966.

I am grateful for access to archives at St Mary's Hospital to the Sector Administrator, A Macdonald; at St Mary's Hospital Medical School to the Dean, Professor Peter Richards; at the Wellcome Institute for the History of Medicine Contemporary Medical Archive Centre to the Archivist, Miss Julia Sheppard; at the Public Record Office, Kew to the Keeper of Public Records; at the Record Office, House of Lords to the Clerk of the Records; at the Countway Library, Harvard Medical School to the Archivist, Richard J Wolfe.

For help with library and record searches I am grateful to P Beaven (Ministry of Defence), the British Broadcasting Corporation Written Archives Centre, Donald Camm (University of Manchester), JA Allum, DN Cole and G Davenport (Royal College of Physicians), K Lockyer (St Mary's Hospital Medical School), A Macdonald (St Mary's Hospital), Miss Terry Parker (Royal College of Physicians), Miss J Pearce (Royal Army Medical College), AD Pickering (Pocklington School), Professor Geoffrey Rose (London School of Hygiene and Tropical Medicine), KR Douglas Scott (Australian Embassy, Rome), and JF Treble (Ministry of Defence).

I gratefully acknowledge permission from the Royal College of Physicians of London to use and quote from material in the archives of the College, including the Annals, Munk's Roll, the 1985 memorandum to Fellows on electing the President, the tape of Lord Moran being interviewed by Dr Charles Newman in 1970, Annual Addresses by the President, and pamphlets recording speeches at the Harveian dinner in 1945 and at the presentation of the portrait of Lord Moran in 1951. I am also indebted to the Royal College of Surgeons and the British Medical Association for permission for access to the papers and correspondence at the Royal College of Physicians of the Negotiating Committee and the Consultant Services Committee during the period leading to the formation of the National Health Service.

In addition to the above, I am grateful to the respective publishers for permission to quote extracts from the following books: Joan B Astley, *The Inner Circle*, London, Hutchinson & Co (Publishers) Ltd, 1971; Arthur Bryant, *Triumph in the West 1943-1946*, London, Harper Collins Publishers, 1959; AM Cooke, *A History of the Royal College of Physicians of London*, Vol. 3, Oxford, Oxford University

Press, 1972; J Colville, *The Fringes of Power*, London, Hodder & Stoughton Limited, 1985; M Foot, *Aneurin Bevan*, London, Davis-Poynter Ltd, 1973; J Peck, *Dublin from Downing Street*, Dublin, Gill & Macmillan Publishers, 1978; Mary Soames, *Clementine Churchill*, London, Cassell, 1979; AJP Taylor, *Beaverbrook*, London, Hamish Hamilton, 1972; F Watson, *Dawson of Penn*, London, Chatto and Windus, 1950. And I appreciate approval given on behalf of William Heinemann Ltd for the use of material in VZ Cope's *The History of St Mary's Hospital Medical School*, London, Heinemann, 1954.

I am also grateful for permission to quote extracts from *The Times* Newspaper, *The Lancet* and *St Mary's Hospital Gazette*, and for permission from the following to quote from letters of which they hold the copyright: The Clerk of Records, House of Lords for letters in their custody from Lord Beaverbrook; Dr AH James for a letter from Dr GWB James; Lady Soames for letters from Mrs (later Lady) Churchill. I have regretfully failed to trace copyright holders in the families of Dr John Ryle and Dr John Freeman whose letters in the Moran family papers I have quoted; to them I apologise.

In quoting from the papers of Sir Archibald Clark Kerr in the custody of the Public Records Office, Kew, Crown copyright is acknowledged, and in quoting from the Report of the Royal Commission on Doctors' and Dentists' Remuneration, Parliamentary copyright is acknowledged.

For permission to reproduce illustrations I am grateful to the present Lord Moran, The Wellcome Institute for the History of Medicine, St Mary's Hospital and Medical School Archives, the *Illustrated London News*, the Dean and Chapter of Canterbury, Karsh of Ottawa-Camera Press, *The Times*, and the Royal College of Physicians of London.

It would have been impossible to write this biography without asking questions of, and seeking recollections from, many people. In this regard I am grateful to the Editor of *Times Literary Supplement* for publishing a letter indicating my interest in receiving comments. In addition to acknowledging the help of the late Lord Moran's widow Dorothy, the present Lord and Lady Moran, and the Honourable Geoffrey and Mrs Jane Wilson, there are many, some no longer living, whose help—verbal, written or both—has been most generously given: Miss LB Appleton, Mrs Joan Astley, Dr TE Barwell, Colin Bingham, Hugh Bingham, Sir Douglas Black, Sir Christopher Booth, Dr Denis Brinton, Dr David Brooks, Dr WDW Brooks, A Montague Browne, Dr Howard G Bruenn, Dr WF Bynum, Lord David Cecil, Winston Churchill, Dr HD Cockburn, Dr J Cook, Dr AM Cooke, Rev HW Coffey, Sir John Colville, Dr EC Dax, Miss Marian Dean, Sir Edward Dunlop, Lord Franks, Sir Ronald Gibson, Martin Gilbert, Benjamin Glazebrook, Sir George Godber, Dr R Guest-Gornall, Sir William Haley, Mark Hamilton, Dr Michael Hamilton, Mrs Judith Harley, Dr John Havard, Colonel MVB Hill,

Dr J MacDonald Holmes, Mrs Mollie Holmes, Professor Sir Douglas Hubble, Dr TC Hunt, Sir Ian Jacob, Dr TA Kemp, Mrs TA Kemp, Dr Hugh L'Etang, Dr Stephen Lock, Lord Longford, Major General WD Mangham, Sir John Martin, Dr TR Maurice, Professor Gwyn Macfarlane, Mrs G Bartley McKean, Professor Sir John McMichael, Professor Sir John McNee, Miss Sheila Minto, Dr Charles Newman, JE Pater, Dr Oglesby Paul, Sir Stanley Peart, Lady Peart, Sir John Peck, Mrs Janet M Phillips, Professor Sir George Pickering, Lady Pickering, Lord Porritt, Dr David A Pyke, Mrs Wendy Reves, Professor Peter Richards, Lord Richardson, Lady Richardson, Dr R Geoffrey Rowley, Dr William Sargant, Dr Alvin Sellars, Lady Evelyn Sharp, Miss Julia Sheppard, Lord Shawcross, Dr Hugh Sinclair, Dr Walter Somerville, Dr Clive Sowry, AJP Taylor, Dr Thomas B Turner, Dame Janet Vaughan, Charles Webster, Dr RR Willcox, Dr Denis Williams, Sir Gordon Wolstenholme. To anyone inadvertently omitted from this list I can only apologise.

Sources of information bearing on the text are identified in the list of references. I would acknowledge how particularly useful the following publications were as sources of general background information:

in relation to St Mary's Hospital: VZ Cope's *The History of St Mary's Hospital Medical School* (Heinemann, London 1954)

in relation to medical practice in the 19th century: Jeanne M Peterson's *The Medical Profession in mid-Victorian London* (University of California Press, London 1978)

in relation to the First World War: BH Liddell Hart's *History of the First World War* (Pan Books, London 1972) and J Keegan's *The Face of Battle* (Penguin Books, Harmondsworth 1978)

in relation to the Royal College of Physicians: AM Cooke's *A History of the Royal College of Physicians of London, Vol. 3* (Oxford University Press 1972)

in relation to the Second World War: AJP Taylor's *English History 1914-1945* (Penguin Books, Harmondsworth 1970) and BH Liddell Hart's *History of the Second World War* (Pan Books, London 1973)

in relation to the National Health Service: JE Pater's *The Making of the National Health Service* (King Edward's Hospital Fund for London, 1981) and C Webster's *The Health Services since the War, Vol. 1* (HM Stationery Office, 1988)

in relation to Sir Winston Churchill: Mary Soames's *Clementine Churchill* (Cassell, London 1979), A Seldon's *Churchill's Indian Summer* (Hodder & Stoughton, London 1981), and Martin Gilbert's *Road to Victory* (Heinemann, London 1986) and *Never Despair* (Heinemann, London 1988).

Preface

To the world at large, Lord Moran was the doctor who looked after Winston Churchill and who precipitated a storm of comment when he published a book about his recently dead patient in 1966. But Moran contributed to his times and to posterity in several other roles. A few surviving soldiers of World War I, in their great age, remember him as a doctor who looked after them in a long posting at the front in France. To many people who paused to think of things like morale and leadership between the wars, he was the man who embodied the observations he made in France in lectures and later in a book called *The Anatomy of Courage*. To those concerned with medical education, he was the man who, on his return from World War I, rebuilt a medical school in London and sought to people it according to his very personal vision. To those involved in the politics of health, he was President of the Royal College of Physicians of London from 1941 to 1950, a period critical for the start of the National Health Service; to some in the British Medical Association at this time, he was Corkscrew Charlie.

When an octogenarian precipitates a controversy of the kind and size that Lord Moran did in 1966, all that went before may be dismissed if not forgotten. I set out to explore and record what went before because much of it seemed still to have relevance for education, the design of health services and for notions of leadership. I wondered too what light this exploration might throw on the affair of the Churchill book. Lord Moran taught me as a medical student that you cannot really understand people until you have unravelled what we doctors call, in the context of our patients, 'the past history'.

My personal contacts with Lord Moran were slight. As Dean of St Mary's Hospital Medical School, Dr CM Wilson, as he then was, interviewed me in 1935 when I applied for entry as a medical student. All I recall is his commenting that he had known my father, also a doctor, who died in 1919 after serving in France, and who had been a near contemporary of his at St Mary's. By the time I was a student in the wards, Dr Wilson had become an infrequent, although memorable, teacher. Returning to St Mary's after the Second World War as a medical registrar, I was occasionally involved with the care of one of his patients. And the last time I met him was following my appointment to the chair of medicine at the University of Melbourne in 1955 when he introduced my wife and myself to his friend Sir Thomas White, who was Australian High Commissioner in London.

When I began to explore the background for this biography in 1979, two years after Lord Moran's death, I wrote to his eldest son, John, who had succeeded to the title and who was serving as British

Ambassador in Lisbon. I called on him in the Spring of 1980, and from then on I had nothing but help and encouragement from him and his brother, Geoffrey Wilson.

The basis on which we proceeded was that I should see all of what John described as 'a fair quantity of unsorted letters and papers' on the understanding that, if I wanted to use any material and quote from it, I would obtain his permission. The caveat was entered simply, as John put it, because he did not know what was in the material. I was thus free to go through what turned out to be some twenty box files, ten old suitcases, many cardboard boxes and a few old trunks and laundry baskets, all bulging with papers—letters, newspaper cuttings, ephemera like old laundry bills, and apparently endless drafts of the book about Churchill. There were also records of patients in case-books and folders, and many papers concerning the activities of the Distinction Awards Committee in the early years of the National Health Service. All this was randomly distributed between a cupboard under the stairs in John's house in Wales and the basement of Geoffrey's house in Hampshire, and only a brief acquaintance with it was needed to realise that Charles and Dorothy Moran had thrown little away since they were married in 1919. I worked my way through this material during a period of study leave in 1981 and on subsequent regular visits to England. In 1984 the bulk of the archive was lodged by John in the Wellcome Institute for the History of Medicine in London. Additions were made in 1985 and 1990, and in due course I returned items that I had taken to work on in Melbourne.

Needless to say, I accepted the family's condition about the use of this material. Although in theory it would have been preferable, it was impracticable for them to go through all the papers and censor anything they did not want me to use. I therefore adopted a convention of sending John drafts of serial sections of the book, asking him to clear the family material I had used. Learning that he was a prize-winning biographer, I also invited him to make general comments. In the event, he cleared everything I had used and his comments as a first draft reader were invariably helpful. By proceeding in this way, the story as I have built it up from the records has been as uninfluenced by family bias as any work can be when a biographer and family members actually meet.

The other critical family contact that I had was with Lord Moran's widow Dorothy. She was in her eighties, considerably disabled physically and living in hospital, but her mind was alert and her memory only occasionally erratic. Like many old people, she responded readily and with pleasure to questions. I visited her twice and, between June 1980 and February 1982, we exchanged nineteen letters. She wrote graphically and clearly, and from her letters I was able to construct much of the background of my subject in his earlier and less public years. Dorothy died in July 1982.

In his two books, the *Anatomy of Courage* published in 1945, and *Winston Churchill—The Struggle for Survival 1940-1945* published in 1966, Lord Moran alluded to his diary. But he indicated in the prefaces to both books that he did not keep a diary in the ordinary sense of the word. In the First World War he scribbled in army notebooks, on the backs of orders and odd sheets of paper and in his Churchill years on the backs of envelopes and other scraps of paper. The scribblings in the army notebooks, and the elaboration of his thoughts in other notebooks formed the basis for the *Anatomy of Courage*. In his Churchill years, the earliest ordering of his thoughts from his jottings (some of which, often barely legible, were also scattered through the family papers) appeared in diary form in closely written loose-leaf manuscript books, which overflowed into collections of separate pages. Judging by the varied use of past, present and future tenses, and references under some dates to events that had not yet happened, these manuscript books cannot be regarded literally as a diary. Finally, in regard to the notion of a diary, the closest diary-like records from the Second World War onwards were unquestionably the letters written by Lord Moran to his family, many of which they kept. These have provided an invaluable resource for this biography.

As I worked my way through the family papers, five fragments of autobiographical material came to light. One was in the form of notebooks, handwritten in and soon after the First World War. Another fragment consisted of 17 handwritten pages concerning the 1920s and apparently written then. The other sets of autobiographical material consisted of type-written papers. The first, of about 1500 words, which could be dated to 1944, was an attempt at a first chapter of an autobiography which soon petered out. The second, of about 7000 words written in 1961, was an early version of a preface for the Churchill book. The third set of typewritten papers, about 5000 words, was written for, and used by, Maurice Wiggins in an article in the *Sunday Times Weekly Review*, 3 April 1966. I have used these freely.

Lord Moran's medical records and his notes concerning the Standing Committee on Distinction Awards during his chairmanship from 1949 to 1962 have needed special consideration. My principle has been not to divulge information about patients from the medical records that has not already been publicly mentioned by Lord Moran or others. Consequently I have given no details when clarifying Moran's involvement with Churchill before the visit to Washington in 1941.[1] The Distinction Awards papers contained comments made

---

[1]There have been conflicting published comments bearing on this. See Churchill, Winston S. *The Second World War.* Vol. 3. Cassell & Co Ltd. London (1950) pp 556. Moran, Lord. *Winston Churchill, The Struggle for Survival.* Constable, London (1966) p. 6,7. Colville I. *The Churchillians.* Weidenfeld & Nicolson, London (1981) p. 190.

in confidence about many named individuals, and I have regarded them in the same way as the medical records.

Three people in addition to John Moran generously gave of their time and expertise to comment on a draft of this book: Lord Richardson, Professor WF Bynum and Dr Stephen Lock. I am deeply indebted to them for their criticisms and suggestions. Responsibility for the final text is, of course, mine.

It would have been impossible to undertake this project without access to study facilities in England. For help with these I am particularly grateful to my late sister Joan, and her husband Gerald Ealand, who stored some of the material for me to work on at their home near Ledbury; also to Geoffrey and Jane Wilson for hospitably welcoming my wife and me to work on family papers at their home, to Professor Peter Richards, Dean of St Mary's Hospital Medical School who lent us a flat, and to King Edward's Hospital Fund for London for allowing use of their residential accommodation. At an early stage we were also indebted to Dr and Mrs J McDonald (Angus) Holmes for an invitation to visit them in Tuscany where they contributed many recollections.

Since the family papers were lodged with the Wellcome Institute for the History of Medicine in 1984 I have received invaluable help from the Archivist, Miss Julia Sheppard and I am particularly grateful to her for making study facilities available for me on my repeated visits to London.

Thanks to a grant to the Wellcome Institute from the Wellcome Trust I was able, in April 1990, to assist Mrs Penny Baker at the Institute with sorting and listing the family papers. Subsequently I have much appreciated Mrs Baker's help, particularly with the illustrations.

I undertook the initial research for this book as a special studies programme approved by the University of Melbourne in 1981, and I am glad to acknowledge the University's support in this and many other ways. Personal back-up was provided first from my own Department of Medicine, where I could always rely on Mrs Jackie Gilbert, and where I was helped with library work by Miss Talbot-Butt. Since 1983 the whole secretarial load has been cheerfully assumed as an extra burden by Mrs Susan Fitzpatrick at the Anti-Cancer Council of Victoria. To her indispensable help was added that of Mrs Mary Tuohey who typed the references.

Mrs Yvonne Rue, my publisher's house-editor, has been a tower of strength in the preparations for publication. I have also appreciated the support of Mr Howard Croft, Managing Director of the Royal Society of Medicine Services Ltd.

Finally, my wife Diana has, for over a decade, been the most candid, perceptive and constructive critic of my attempts to put this story together. With her insights into human nature, her contributions have been invaluable.

Portrait of 1st Baron Moran of Manton, painted in 1951 by Pietro Annigoni, which hangs in the Royal College of Physicians of London. (Reproduced by kind permission of the College.)

Chapter 1

Early Years

Charles McMoran Wilson, later Lord Moran, liked to recall that he came of turbulent stock. That at any rate was what he remembered his mother telling him. As she described it, Charles's father, when a young man, was breakfasting one day with his family at their home at Gortmore, near Limavady, in Co. Derry, Northern Ireland, when his brother James seemed put out by something that was said. Getting up from the table, James walked out of the room. He was not seen again, and later they learnt that he had emigrated to America. If service with the military were further evidence of a turbulent nature, there was also Charles's paternal great grandfather William Wilson (ca 1770-1857), who served as a trooper in the Louisa Cavalry of Muff, near Derry. Crossing the barrier between other ranks and officers, William, in 1808, married Elizabeth, daughter of Lieutenant John Lurting of Tamlaghtard. But there the military links ended, for Charles's grandfather, Alexander Lurting Wilson (1812-1883), who was the second son of the marriage, farmed some seventy-seven acres at Gortmore on a hillside with breathtaking views over Magilligan Strand, Loch Foyle and the hills of Donegal. Grandfather Alexander married Susan, daughter of Jacob Forsythe, also of Gortmore, and Charles's father, John Forsythe Wilson, born in 1850, was the youngest of their four children. Of the older ones, the daughter Jane married Hugh Cumming Fisher of the Northern Bank, Belfast; she died aged 40 in 1884. The eldest boy, William died aged 50 in 1896 and, like James who disappeared to America, he remained unmarried. Charles therefore had no substantial clan of uncles, aunts and cousins on his father's side.

John Forsythe Wilson grew up at Gortmore and from the ages of 14 to 16 went to the nearby Coleraine Academical Institution, a school maintained by the Irish Society and the London Clothworkers' Company. He then studied medicine at the Queen's College, Belfast, and in Dublin obtaining the degrees of MD, MCh, and LM in 1873. He spent his first years after graduation working for the New Zealand Government Emigration Service and travelled four times from Britain in sailing ships carrying migrants. Under sail, the voyage from Britain to New Zealand took about four months. A letter dated 21st December, 1877 from the New Zealand Undersecretary of Immigration, addressed to Dr J Forsythe Wilson as the late Surgeon Superintendent to the ship 'Huommi' stated:

'. . . On each of the four occasions that you have had charge of
an immigrant ship to this colony, the reports of inspecting
commissioners as to the medical arrangements of the ship show
that it has everything that could be desired, and if you decide to
bring out no more ships, the Colonial Government will lose the
services of an officer upon whom reliance could be placed.'[1]

In the autumn of 1877 Dr Wilson borrowed money and bought a
general practice in Skipton, a market town in the West Riding of
Yorkshire, and on 20th August, 1878, at the age of 27 he married.
His wife, Mary Jane Hanna, came from the market village of Clogher
in County Tyrone, where her father, the Reverend John Hanna, was
Presbyterian Minister. It was from this, Charles's mother's branch
of the family, that several names used later were derived. Mary's
mother Matilda was the eleventh and last child of the family of John
McMoran MD of the town of Monaghan. One of Matilda's brothers
was called Charles; and it was from McMoran that the title Moran
was later chosen.

Skipton has a fine wide street, dominated at the northern end by
a Norman castle and a substantial church. Beneath these, at 4/6
High Street, Dr Wilson settled when he took over the practice of
a Dr William Wylie, and it was to this house, known as The Doctor's
House, distinctive because it stands above its two-storey neighbours,
that he brought his young wife. The early years in Skipton were

*Figure 1. The old Doctor's House in the High Street, Skipton where Charles McMoran
Wilson was born. (The Wellcome Institute Library, London; CMAC PP/CMW/P.6)*

happy ones for the newly-weds. They were a young, cheerful and good-looking couple, and were taken up by the country families living round about. Despite his background it was noted that the doctor had no trace of Irishness in his speech. A year after Dr Wilson and Mary were married their first child Lorton Alexander was born (10th August, 1879). Then came a daughter Matilda (13th December, 1880) known as Maud, and two years later Charles (10th November, 1882). There must have been visits from Mary's family, for on 23rd June, 1884 William, second son of John Scott of Ashfield, Skipton, married Sina Hanna, Mary's youngest sister; and on 26th November, 1886 Mary's brother John Charles Hanna of Belfast married Mary Scott, fourth daughter of the same John Scott.

As an old man, Charles said he could remember little of Skipton, which he left at the age of five; he remembered the Dewhurst family, 'who were all very good at games',[2] and the Scotts. He wrote in some autobiographical notes:

'The practice prospered and three children were born in quick succession . . . And then he [my father] was put to bed with rheumatic fever, the first of four attacks that left his heart badly crippled. After that he had to struggle for the rest of his working life to educate the three of us and set us on our feet . . .'[3]

In June, 1886 the *Craven Herald* reported that Dr Wilson would leave Skipton shortly for the south of England, 'where it is earnestly hoped he will speedily recruit his strength and enjoy much better health than has been his lot whilst in Skipton' and, when he left, Dr Wilson received written testimonials from consultants in Leeds who had got to know him. F Pidgin Teale, Consulting Surgeon at the Leeds General Infirmary, affirmed: 'He combines experience, tact, kindness and good judgement, with a thorough knowledge of his profession, and of the advances that are being made in professional knowledge and practice'.[4] Clifford Albutt, Consulting Physician to the Leeds General Infirmary and later to become Regius Professor of Physic in the University of Cambridge, wrote: 'I have pleasure in cordially recommending Dr Forsythe Wilson for any public professional appointments. During Dr Wilson's residence in Skipton I met him repeatedly and found him not only a courteous intelligent man but an excellent and skilful practitioner of medicine. Dr Wilson is ranks above the average of his brethren and I much regret that the climate of the North of England was too severe for him.'[5]

Autobiographical notes continued the story:

'After 18 months of enforced illness, my father was faced with the expense of educating his three children, the eldest of whom was only eight years of age. The busy Skipton practice, scattered over the dales, had been too much for him, and he decided to buy a small practice in the village of Wolston in Warwickshire. There for six years he continued somehow to do his work.'

'Wolston [which is on the River Avon, about six miles from Coventry] was medieval then. The men went to work in the fields before I was up, and when I got about the village street was deserted save for a few women sitting on their doorsteps nursing babies. The silence that had fallen on everything seemed to belong to another time though I did not notice it then. I cannot put a face to any of the inhabitants nor can I remember the room where I slept. But I can see the outhouses and the animals as if it were yesterday, though it is nearly 80 years ago: the long ladder lying against the garden railings; the dirty brown blankets that were thrown over the cow-house to keep out draughts before a calf was born. I recall that I tried to penetrate the mystery of birth of a calf, but I could get nothing out of Hence the groom. I got a particular thrill from collecting the eggs from a hen-house. I wondered why some of them were warm.'

'My mother, a good natured, comely little woman, was not at all remarkable in any way, though she was saturated with a homely good sense. She could not see what my father saw in poetry, it seemed to her a lot of nonsense. However, in one respect she was anything but commonplace. She possessed a remarkable insight into human nature, and her 'spot diagnoses', as the family called them, of people she met for the first time, were generally pretty near the mark. She seemed to be able to guess what was in their minds, and often what they were up to and why. I sometimes fancy that she handed down to me her feeling for people.

'I cannot remember a time when my father was like ordinary people. He used to pause on the stairs to get his breath, and we children would wait for him at the top. It must have been a long time after this that I got it into my head that he could not last long. When I had said good night to him I would stand outside the door of his bedroom listening to his breathing. I was sure something would happen to him in the night.

'Perhaps it was his health that made him moody when he was vexed. At any rate, these moods might last for a day or two during which he hardly spoke, and the family existed in a kind of troubled suspense. Once when the grey horse got out of the stable and galloped on the lawn I thought in my childish way that he would never speak again . . .

'My father's Skipton practice had taken him into the Bronte country, and when I grew up I sometimes fancied that he had caught the dark thoughts of the people of the West Riding from Emily—her story of Wuthering Heights haunted him for a long time. However these moods settled on him only at long intervals; in between my father, in spite of constant pain from an ulcer in his stomach, was ready for adventure. I recall his zest for life, his childish eagerness to meet people. His family, as long as there is any record, had lived on the land, and he would always stop to admire a good crop or to sum up the points of a horse. Since he could not afford a pedigree animal he liked to pick up for his own use a horse of unimpeachable ancestry, but with some unattractive vice that brought it within his means. My mother was terrified of these high spirited beasts who were always up to mischief. On one occasion, I remember, we met an express train. The groom, scenting trouble, drew up, whereat my father, impatiently snatching the reins from him, used his whalebone whip to such purpose that the grey mare bounding forward, swerved away from the line and landed the off wheels of the phaeton up the bank on the verge. It seemed to me that we were about to overturn, but my father was not deterred. When we were passed and he had given back the reins to the groom he looked at my sister and then at me to see if we had been upset by the incident, and smiled his satisfaction that we thought it all good fun. Often the groom was left behind and my father would drive himself, flicking with his whip at the hedge while he declaimed to no one in particular verse after verse from Childe Harold.'[3]

Reflecting on his father Charles also wrote:

'He loved good painting; while still a student he saw a picture of a stone cutter by an artist called Walter, which he coveted, but could not afford to buy. Then an idea occurred to him and he exchanged a skeleton that he had kept from his anatomical studies for the stone cutter. He was an idealist and my mother felt that he had not got both feet firmly planted on the earth.

'Looking back I can see the two strains battling in me from the beginning. One of my father's ideas would take hold of me and just when it threatened to carry me off my feet would be pulled back by my mother's timely good sense.'[3]

A recurrence of Dr Wilson's rheumatic fever was a constant threat, and since it was held to run in families, Charles was affected by some of the anxiety:

'One day my mother found me with my legs in a bucket of hot water which seemed to ease the growing pains. She was certain after this that it was just a matter of time before I too got rheumatic fever, and though I was supposed to attend Priory Hill, a school about a mile from the village, I was allowed for most of the time to wander over the fields. My father was the more disposed to fall in with this plan because he did not take my abilities very seriously. My brother promised to be something of an infant prodigy—the hope of the house my father called him—and there would be plenty of time later to see if I had any wits. In the foolish fashion of those days I was not encouraged by my mother to mix with other boys in the village and I grew up a solitary dreamy little boy.'[3]

Charles recalled that the practice at Wolston was small, it was necessary to watch every penny, and they were encouraged to sit in the twilight for half an hour to save oil. The house in which they lived was also small, and right in the village. Nevertheless the low wages of the time enabled them to keep maids, a governess and a groom; the groom used to meet Charles, bringing a pony for him to ride home when school was over.

After about six years, when Charles was eleven, Dr Wilson, thinking he could undertake a bigger practice, decided to go to Barrow-in-Furness, a seaport on the coast of Lancashire. Barrow had grown rapidly in the nineteenth century with the development of a shipbuilding industry, and Dr Wilson built himself a house in Abbey Road, from which most of his patients were within walking or at least bicycling distance. He continued in Barrow for 15 years until he made the practice over to Lorton on his marriage in 1909.

Charles completed his primary or preparatory school education in Barrow, but no comment on this period remains. While his recollection of his childhood after an interval of 60 years was of time spent mooning in the fields, between the ages of nine and 15 he read many books. For Christmas 1897, when he was fifteen, he was given a little book, called *Books I have Read*, in which he wrote in a neat hand 159 titles and authors read between 1892 and 1898. Many of the books were by GA Henty, WHG Kingston, RM Ballantyne, Mayne Reid, J Fenimore Cooper and Sir Walter Scott. Against each entry, the column provided for remarks was filled, and prophetically perhaps, the first and only non-fiction title, read at the age of 14, was *The Jubilee Book of Cricket* by US Ranjitsinhji, and the remark was 'a good instructor and very interesting'. All the books listed were conventional ones, and for the most part the heroes in them reflected a time when Britain ruled the waves, the sun never set on the British Empire, and it was unthinkable that things would ever be different.

From Barrow-in-Furness, Charles's elder brother Lorton was sent to school at the Royal Medical Benevolent College, Epsom, in Surrey, where scholars of the foundation had to be sons of medical men, and Charles, when he was 14, was sent to boarding school with a similar scholarship scheme. Of this time Charles wrote in his old age:

'Like Winston [Churchill], I got no fun out of my school days. Perhaps I had not learnt in my solitary childhood to mix with other boys. I had been sent with the help of a scholarship to Pocklington, a Grammar School near York, but after two years I was allowed to leave before I had made a mark of any kind either in work or in games. I was not bullied, I was just ignored. It is more than sixty years since, but I can remember an epidemic of measles when the senior prefect came round the dormitory one night and spoke to the boy in the next bed, who told him that he had noticed that my eyes were bleary and that I should be the next to go down. ... "He would" ... the prefect said contemptuously. When he had left the room I pulled the bedclothes over my head and was miserable because they thought I was not like other boys. I must have been a sensitive child for one day in the holidays when I had eaten something that had disagreed with me, my father said cheerfully that I had inherited his tummy. I thought he must know and I went away and got on my bicycle and could hardly see for tears. It seemed to me a very dreadful thing to be so very different from other people. It may be that it was then that I decided, as Winston Churchill did at Harrow, that I would not always be a nonentity.'[3]

Charles was at Pocklington from Michaelmas Term 1897 to May Term 1899. Despite his unhappiness there, his father told him that he could not leave until he had taken the London Matriculation, which he sat at York, in June 1899 at the age of 16:

'The day after my return home my father summoned me to his study and asked me what I wanted to do for a living. "I want to write books" I replied. "I have no money" my father said "and writing is a precarious business. You had better write as a hobby and follow me into medicine".'[3]

Then came the results of the examination.

'So far my muted progress had impressed no one and the family did not hide their surprise when I passed the London Matriculation at the first attempt.'[3]

In October 1899, just before his 17th birthday, Charles registered as a medical student and went to Owen's College, Manchester, where his older brother Lorton was already studying medicine.

'I became a medical student at Manchester, sharing with another first year man two dark and dingy rooms in Akers Street, opposite the Church of the Holy Name. One night as I was about to go to bed I heard voices in the street; my friend was leaning against the

railings talking to a strange woman. When he saw me they moved
away, and though I sat up for a long time waiting for him he did
not come in. I suspected that she was a woman of the streets, and
was unhappy that he would come to some harm. Another time
when I returned to my lodgings about dinner time I found them
playing cards. They soon left and I opened the windows to get rid
of the smoke. I noticed during dinner that my friend could not see
what was on his plate and I realised that he was very drunk.'[3]

The solitary shy boy was moving awkwardly into manhood and a
wider world.

After completing the courses in biology and chemistry in
Manchester Charles moved to St Mary's Hospital Medical School
in London. Lorton continued in Manchester. He and Charles did not
get on very well together and this was one factor determining the
move. Charles had a great love and admiration for his father and
felt that Lorton added to his worries unnecessarily.[6] Charles simply
recorded:

'When I had been a year at Owens College, my mother persuaded
my father to allow me to join a London Medical School, St Mary's
and in a sense my life began there.'[3]

In going to St Mary's Charles was joining an institution that was
to influence him deeply up to the outbreak of the First World War
in 1914, and which he was to influence for more than a quarter of
a century after that war ended. Fifty years old, St Mary's was the
newest of the large voluntary hospitals responsible for the care of
the poorer citizens of London.[7] The term 'voluntary' indicated
freedom from State interference or control. Voluntary hospitals were
maintained by freewill offerings and contributions and by endowments, and St Mary's, like the other voluntary hospitals, was run
by socially important people sitting on its governing board. They
reflected the wish of the upper and upper-middle classes to provide
for their servants and poor relations an alternative system of hospital
care to that provided by the parish-based poor-law institutions.[8]

Charles entered St Mary's at the start of the academic year of
October, 1901. He was one of 48 new students,[9] 27 of whom were
born in the provinces, 12 in London and the rest in what were then
known as the British Dominions. Names among the students joining
St Mary's about that time suggest that it must have been quite
attractive to adventurous young minds. Alexander Fleming, who
won the senior entrance scholarship in natural science, joined at
the same time as Charles. As soon as Fleming graduated in 1908
he joined the focal point of research of that day, Sir Almroth Wright's
Inoculation Department, and he went on to be elected Fellow of the
Royal Society in 1943, and for his discovery of the action of penicillin

he shared the Nobel Prize for Medicine with Florey and Chain in 1945. Leonard Colebrook also entered with a natural science scholarship and became a pupil of Wright's. In the 1930s he made his name by using the then newly developed drug sulphanilamide to treat infections in childbirth. He was elected Fellow of the Royal Society in 1945. EH Kettle, who became a professor of pathology with an international reputation for his work on silicosis which ravaged the lungs of coal miners, was another entrance scholar destined to be elected Fellow of the Royal Society.

A student record card at St Mary's provides a bare account of Charles's undergraduate days. It was filled in by Mr BE Matthews, who was to be an important figure in Charles's life. Matthews, Bachelor of Arts of the University of Cambridge, was appointed Secretary of the Medical School in 1900 and held this post for 46 years, in the course of which Charles was only one of several whom he greeted as students and later served when they were on the staff of the Hospital and Medical School.

On the record card Charles is noted as entering the course for the degree of MB of the University of London. It was by no means the rule at that time to aim at a degree, for more easily obtainable qualifications such as the diplomas of membership of the Royal College of Surgeons and of licentiateship of the Royal College of Physicians, were accepted by the General Medical Council for registration as a doctor. Charles's father, no doubt conscious of the professional status that his own degree gave him, would have known that a degree was essential for anyone who might aspire to be other than a general practitioner. The record card also indicates Charles's future career as being probably in the Indian Medical Service, but too much should not be read into this. As was the case with the Emigration Service, which Dr Wilson had joined, so a term with the Army, Navy or Indian Medical Service provided a way to earn and save money that could be used to buy a practice. Charles could simply have been recognising that he would have no money behind him when he qualified.

Apart from being chided by Mr Matthews in 1902 for not attending instruction in the study of bones, Charles's card suggests uneventful progress leading to qualification in March 1908 with the diplomas of membership of the Royal College of Surgeons (MRCS) and licentiateship of the Royal College of Physicians (LRCP), and in November 1908 graduation with the degree of MB, BS of the University of London.

In the conventional British medical course in Charles's day, the first three years were spent studying pre-clinical subjects culminating in physiology, anatomy and pharmacology. The student then entered the wards and clinics of the hospital for another two or three years. In those last years in particular impressions were gained and attitudes adopted which lasted a lifetime. This was because high

on the list of those influencing the developing student were the heads
of the units or 'firms' to which the student was rostered as a 'medical
clerk' in a medical ward or a 'surgical dresser' in a surgical one.
These chiefs were remembered generally with respect, often with
real affection, very seldom with derision. Charles's first appointment
as a medical ward clerk was with Dr David Bridge Lees, then
approaching 60. He was a conscientious, painstaking and observant
clinician, of whose treatment of pneumonia by application of ice bags
to the chest, a posthumous comment was: 'Though students could
not always follow his reasoning, many of them were convinced of
the effectiveness of the treatment.' It was also said: 'He was a deeply
conscientious and religious man, the soul of honour in professional
matters and in everyday life', and 'He never made an enemy and
his friends and admirers comprised all he knew.'[10] Mr Herbert
William Page, on whose firm Charles was a surgical dresser, was
also approaching 60. He had been appointed to the staff of St Mary's
after serving as a surgeon in the German Army in the Franco-
Prussian War of 1870, and then as surgeon to the London and North
Western Railway. Page was to be remembered as a sound surgeon,
a good diagnostician, an excellent clinical lecturer, and an expert
in medicolegal matters. It was said that a speech from Page decorated
any occasion.[11]

Charles did his medical outpatient clerking under Dr Wilfred John
Harris, then in his early 40s and newly appointed to the Staff.
He was to play a critical part in Charles's life. Harris was born in
India, where his father was in the Indian Medical Service. His
medical studies had been at Gonville and Caius College, Cambridge,
and at St Mary's, and after graduation he had a blue ribbon career
with appointments at St Mary's and at the National Hospital for
Nervous Diseases at Queen Square. One of the outstanding
neurologists of his day, he was to be on the staff of St Mary's from
1905 to 1935, and to return to take charge of the neurology
department in the Second World War. In Munk's Roll, which
contains posthumous biographical notes on Fellows of the Royal
College of Physicians, Harris is described as 'above average height,
stoutly built but erect in carriage. In youth he played Rugby football
and at the end of his life liked to watch inter-hospital cup-ties at
Richmond. His oval, dark and rather handsome face was usually
impassive, but lighted up eagerly when explaining an interesting
point. His temperament was rather impatient, a fact which
sometimes acted to his detriment, but in later life the more genial
side of his character became more evident.'[12] Charles's surgical
outpatient appointment as a student was under William Henry
Clayton-Green who, like Harris, had just been appointed to the Staff.
Then aged 30, he also was to play a part in Charles's later career.
Clayton-Greene, whose medical course had been at Corpus Christi
College Cambridge and St Mary's, came to be regarded as the

outstanding surgical figure at the hospital during the first quarter of the century, dying in 1926 in his 50s. He was described as 'a wonderful teacher and brilliant operator who impressed the students by his forceful personality and his remarkably clear exposition of surgical principles. He had a very large practice . . .' Further: 'He was very forthright in his speech and spoke as he thought, but it was well said of him that to those who knew him intimately he revealed a charming personality and a loyalty nothing could shake. He was also quite frank in his dislikes.'[13] In respect of his younger mentors at any rate, Charles was thrown in at the deep end. Wilfred Harris and Clayton-Greene must both already have been exhibiting some of the characteristics of evolving medical prima donnas.

During his medical appointments Charles would also have clerked in the children's ward. This was under the charge of another person who was to influence his career. Sydney Philip Phillips was born in 1851 of Jewish parents and died 100 years later. A Londoner, he remembered as a boy fishing for tiddlers in the Westbourne Brook that ran through Paddington. His medical training had been at University College and he was in his middle 50s when Charles first met him. According to Munk's Roll 'Phillips was at his best when teaching at the bedside, impressing his words on his students by a mixture of gentle ferocity and caustic humour. His good natured, lovable perversity made him the centre of many anecdotes, which he himself was not at pains to discourage. He was a keen athlete and continued to take physical exercise and to swim till his eightieth year. He was a bachelor.'[14]

Charles left only brief written references to his student days.

'I had a certain aptitude for Rugby Football; I was elected Captain of the Hospital Fifteen and began to play for Middlesex in County games. More than a third of the students belonged to the Rugby Club and it dominated the life of the little community. I found that for the first time I had a say in things. I suppose that my yellow hair, which was the colour of a golden sovereign fresh from the Mint, made my face appear redder than it was and it went some way to atone for my irregular features. Anyway I found that I was no longer speechless when left alone with a nurse. London can be very attractive to a young man of seventeen, and I was in no great hurry to qualify.'[3]

There is little record of Charles's social life as a student. He and some friends joined a yeomanry regiment. Apart from a camp in the summer, this involved rigorous training with riding in London, when a sergeant instructor would put a sixpenny piece between the trainee's knee and saddle; it had to be in place after returning from a ride. He had two close friends. One was Archibald Hamilton, a big bluff Yorkshireman with a great sense of humour who became a general practitioner in Yorkshire. For years Charles used to stay with him and play golf. The other was Cyril (Gee-gee) Galpin, who was to captain the Rugby football team and who died quite young.

The St Mary's Hospital Gazette tells of Charles's exploits on the football field. He was mentioned as playing in the first XV in November 1902,[15] a year after he entered the medical school, and from 1904 onwards his performance was chronicled each year. Thus, in 1904: 'A very good forward, but very light, is a keen tackler, follows up well, and uses what weight he has';[16] in 1905: 'If heavier would be a grand forward. Very fast. His following up is of great service to his side. His tackling is very fine.'[17] In 1905 he was made Secretary of the Club and in 1906 the comment was: 'An excellent Secretary who has done great work in keeping the team together. A typical Irish forward, untiring and one of our few tacklers.'[18] Election as Captain of the first XV came in 1907. In that year he also played for Middlesex County[19] and he took the St Mary's team to play clubs in France for a week.[20] Looking back in 1965 on that French tour, Charles commented:

'I recall arriving in Paris with the St Mary's team and being met by the Consul. "I congratulate you" he said. "Why?" I asked. He explained that the previous week the United Services had arrived so tipsy that they had to be unpacked like sardines. I did not tell

Figure 2. The St Mary's Hospital Rugby Football Fifteen, with Wilson as Captain, visiting France in 1907. CMW seated centre of front row. (The Wellcome Institute Library, London; CMAC PP/CMW/P.4)

the Consul that at Havre the night before our match I deemed it
expedient to lock up in his bedroom one of the more virile of our
forwards. I thought that his impulsive affectionate temperament
might interfere with training.'[21]

The Gazette's comment for 1907 was: 'CMW has made a first rate
Captain on and off the field and is largely responsible for the
excellent work of the forwards. Good in the loose, tackles well, and
occasionally does good work in the scrum.'[22] In the following year
when he qualified: 'Superannuation cuts off the services of
Wilson.'[23]

One other of Charles's recorded activities in these undergraduate
student years was his interest in the St Mary's Hospital Gazette,
to which he was appointed Honorary Sub-Editor in October, 1905.[24]
The Gazette, like Rugby football, was to continue to be an important
component of his life. By the time he qualified at the age of 25 in
1908 Charles was, as he put it, on better terms with himself.[3] The
shy young boy was now a young man showing qualities of leadership.

Chapter 2

Disenchanted Young Doctor

In 1908 it was not necessary, as it became later, for a year to be spent under supervision in a hospital between passing the final examination and full registration as a legally qualified medical practitioner. The newly qualified doctor could go straight into general practice, where it was not even necessary to start by joining an older practitioner as an assistant. The new doctor could just put up his plate and wait for patients. But Charles's sights were set higher and despite his academically undistinguished progress through the medical course he was ambitious to win a resident appointment at his own hospital. Competition for these jobs, as house physician, house surgeon or resident obstetric officer, was intense, but in a London teaching hospital like St Mary's, where notice was taken of prowess in extra-curricular activities, it is questionable whether the captain of last season's Rugby team could have failed to be appointed. Be this as it may, the Board of Management on Thursday, 29 October 1908, having heard that Mr CM Wilson had satisfied the examiners and had been recommended for appointment, resolved that he be appointed House Physician for the regulation period of six months from 1 November 1908.[1]

Apart from the kudos that went with the appointment, the immediate implication for Charles was that he moved into the housemen's quarters. The stipend was negligible but the cost of living became negligible too for there was no more payment of rent for lodgings or of medical school and examination fees. The housemen's quarters were a row of bed-sitting rooms opening off a long dark corridor on the mezzanine floor above the main entrance of the original hospital block that faced Cambridge (now Norfolk) Place. The rooms were by no means poky, their windows looked out to Cambridge Place, their furnishings included a bed, a desk and an easy chair, and each room was heated by a rather smoky open fire. Meals were taken in a separate residents' dining room, and life 'on the house' was centred on this accommodation, the wards, outpatients and casualty departments and the operating theatre. Holidays, if any, were taken between appointments, and occasional time off in an evening or during a weekend was arranged with a colleague willing to provide cover.

The focal point of the professional life of the hospital was just inside the main entrance doors. Here, on the left, was a glass partitioned porter's lodge, where in the daytime the uniformed head porter, chest beribboned with campaign medals, took notice of, if he did not actually conduct, all that went on. He knew everybody—the visiting chiefs, the housemen and the senior students; indeed in some cases he had known their fathers or was to know their sons. From the entrance doors a short broad flight of steps led to a large hall and a grand staircase rising under a huge glass dome.

There were no internal telephones in the hospital. If one of the housemen were wanted in a ward, the sister sent a junior nurse to the porter at the front door who mounted the steps to the hall and in stentorian tones called the name of the wanted doctor. Thus a call such as 'Mr Wilson'—he always called new doctors Mister—would echo two floors up the well of the staircase and more distantly penetrate the residents' quarters and further afield. After hours the night porter would not shout but would materialise beside the houseman's bed, shake him awake, and convey the news which, with new patients in Casualty, usually included his estimate of the diagnosis and degree of urgency.

For each house physician the major events of the week were his chief's ward rounds. Charles's chief was Sidney Phillips. Twice a week, at two o'clock, white-coated groups of housemen and students of the firms whose chiefs' visiting day it was, gathered to meet the great men, who had signed the Attendance Book at the Praed Street entrance. By the end of the afternoon, after the ward round which combined patient care with bedside teaching, each houseman escorted his chief back to the entrance steps. These courtesies, formal though they might have appeared, did nothing but foster a close, virtually a family, relationship between many chiefs and their housemen.

Charles's performance as Dr Phillip's House Physician must have been satisfactory for at the end of April, 1909 he was appointed Resident Obstetric Officer for the next six months.[1] His friends Galpin and Hamilton were residents with him. Then, on completing his first year after graduation, Charles applied for the post of Medical Registrar. There was only one such job in the Hospital and it was traditionally the stepping stone to appointment as a member of the honorary medical staff. The duties were to see outpatients and all new patients admitted to the medical wards and to make decisions about them between the twice-weekly attendances of the members of the visiting staff. The appointment of the Medical Registrar was considered at the meeting of the Board of Management on 16 December 1909,[1] when two candidates were interviewed. One, Charles, simply had the qualifying degree of MB, BS. The other, Charles Singer, had in addition the diploma of membership of the Royal College of Physicians of London (MRCP), which was gained by passing a grilling postgraduate examination in internal medicine. In the event Charles was appointed for the regulation period of one year from 1 January 1910, on the motion of Dr Phillips, seconded by another senior physician Dr AP Luff. Charles wrote of this later:

'I had been a House Physician for a year when a vacancy occurred in the post of Medical Registrar at St Mary's. It seemed a forgone conclusion that Charles Singer, who later became the historian of English Medicine, would be appointed to fill the vacancy. But I had a hunch that he would not be altogether congenial to the physicians especially if they were given a reasonable alternative. My student career had been quite devoid of distinction, I had not gone up for any of the annual prizes, I had not even a reputation for industry. Besides I did not possess the higher qualifications which till then had been required by any candidate for such an office; in brief I was in no sense a "reasonable alternative". But I was appointed . . .'[2]

Charles was now a marked man, next in line for the Staff, with just a few years to pass while waiting for a vacancy. When he was reappointed as Medical Registrar a year later this perception was confirmed; and then, in October, 1911, nine months into his second year, he resigned. In his letter to the Board of Management he gave no reasons, and the Board simply minuted that Dr Wilson's resignation be accepted.[1] The vacancy was filled three months later by Alfred Hope Gosse, who as it turned out came to be the main competitor in Charles's early medical career. Charles left several accounts of his resignation, including one given to Winston Churchill during the Second World War:

'It was before the First War, when I held the coveted office of Medical Registrar at St Mary's Hospital. There was then only one registrar, and the occupant of the post was as it were, on approval for two years. If he passed the scrutiny, he was generally elected to the next vacancy on the staff and became a physician to the hospital, a full-blooded consultant. But, after a year in the office, I got it into my head—I was very young then—that some of my seniors were more concerned with their practices than with the students' training. It appeared a stuffy, material, and not very attractive existence, and I decided to send in my resignation. I did not give my reasons. It would sound priggish, I thought, if I tried to explain how I came to take such a suicidal step after all those years of apprenticeship.

As far as I can remember, I was not at all disconsolate that I had burnt my boats, irrevocably it seemed then. For some years my days had passed in the underground outpatient department of the hospital lit even at noon by artificial light. I worked in a small room, like the inside cabin of a ship; it had no windows, and got very hot, and was full of microbes and of the sour smell of the human body. Then in the late afternoon, exchanging my white overall for a morning coat, I would don my hat and wind my way in and out of the vehicles and vans crowding the goods yard of the Great Western Railway, which then separated the hospital from Harrow Road. For it was in that dreary street that I rented a single, shabby little room.

By coaching students for their final examinations I had been able to save a small sum of money, and that I planned to spend to travel—my resources would come to an end, I reckoned, in about a year.'[3]

Later, Charles described in more detail his work as a medical registrar and his growing disenchantment with the way his career was developing.

'It was my task as Registrar to examine patients when they were admitted into the medical wards and I became absorbed in problems of diagnosis. Some students disliked clerking in a medical ward, because little could be done for their patients beyond dieting and relieving them of pain. This was before the discovery of penicillin and the antibiotics, of insulin and liver extract and other remedies had converted medicine into a science, and the physician into a laboratory worker who would plan a series of controlled experiments before prescribing a new drug. Medicine was still an art. The great physician, like the great novelist, saw things which others somehow did not notice, his was an art of observation. But he did more than use his eyes. Often he made his diagnosis before touching his patients, before taking a single test. He did this by asking questions, which in sum made a pretty pattern of analytic reasoning. There were of course many uncertainties in medical diagnosis, then as now, so that to practise with the minimum of error called for judgement as from the bench, and that particular gift is given to only a few ... I was fascinated by this inquisitorial process.

Presently, however, I discovered that the physician's time is not all given up to academic medicine. In those days he was not paid for his hospital work, he had to make his living in Harley Street. From time to time I was asked by my chief to pin up a sheet of notepaper so that students crowding round could read that he had been called into the country and would not be able to take his class. There was some grumbling as his class scattered to the club, but it did not seem to trouble them that their seniors appeared to be more concerned with their practices than with their pupils.

One day a friend of mine asked me to see a patient in Kilburn. I was thrilled; it was my first patient outside the hospital, but when I came to explain to the relatives that I could hold out no hope of the patient's recovery, they at once demanded a second opinion. When Lord Dawson* arrived he made a perfunctory examination of the patient, accepting what I had found without troubling to confirm it, then we filed into a room where six relatives were already seated round a big dining table. Lord Dawson seemed to know without questioning what was passing through the head of each of the six. He did not touch on prognosis, he told them of the steps he proposed to take. He was in complete command of the situation. They sat at his feet, it was as if I did not exist. I learnt that the successful practise of medicine depends less on accurate diagnosis and more on a knowledge of human nature. I began to doubt whether I should find making a living in Harley Street as attractive as work in the wards.'[2]

It is possible to get an outside view of Charles at this stage in his career from the pages of the *St Mary's Hospital Gazette*. In February 1910, a month after starting as Medical Registrar, he was appointed Editor,[4] a position that had never been held by one as junior in the hierarchy of the hospital and medical school. The Gazette was mostly a serious publication concerned with all that went on at St Mary's. It made editorial comment, reported talks which were often given by distinguished outsiders to the Medical Society, and described sporting events in detail. The Gazette throws light on Charles from two angles. The first is through the editorial comments, which unfortunately were unsigned but which must have reflected Charles's thinking if they were not—and their style suggests they were—actually written by him. The other shaft of light comes from an open letter that was addressed to him.

So far as editorials are concerned, the creed in the prolix comment in the February, 1910 number must have been Charles's own: "That the games spirit is essential to the place. That Rugger is the only game with a hold on mens' imagination, and so the only means to that end. That we must rely on that spirit to wrap the place in the tradition and affection which are the precious fruit of a public school and alone bind a man to his school, when time has loosened all other bonds, and make him willing to work with the present for the future of the hospital. We are fortunate that those responsible are alive to this and working to that end.'[5] The May number, which recorded the death of King Edward the Seventh, devoted its editorial to the recent purchase of a new athletic ground at Acton. For this, Mr Clayton-Greene received an accolade. 'The secret of the influence of games on the school,' it was postulated, 'is not found in technical excellence, but in the spirit of unselfishness which must figure largely in any man who plays regularly for his hospital.'[6] The

---

*Lord Dawson of Penn, physician to the London Hospital.

editorial in June 1910, headed 'Democracy and Empire', was
introduced by quotations, one of which was from Gibbon: 'It is the
duty of a patriot to prepare and promote the exclusive interest and
glory of his native country.'[7] The editorial in July commented on
a domestic question entitled 'Hospitals and Democracy'.[8] The
organisation of medical practice was then a controversial topic, and
the flames of debate had been fanned by Bernard Shaw, a friend,
and in debate a sparring partner, of Almroth Wright. Shaw had
written *'The Doctor's Dilemma'* four years earlier, and in the
Introduction he had advocated a State medical service. On the control
of hospitals the editorial said: 'It is not our intention to enter into
the right or wrong of their control by the State. That this control
is coming there can be no manner of doubt.' There followed discussion
of some particular aspects of hospitals that would need safeguarding,
with stress on the importance of appointing people of the right
character to the staff. 'The influence of character on the medical
student' wrote the editor 'is not sufficiently realised. It determines
the tone of a school, and is very necessary in a profession in which
much is left to the individual sense of right or wrong.' All in all,
these pages contained ideas that were casting their shadows before
them. The writer showed at once political awareness, a radical
approach and a passionate desire to make St Mary's great, and all
this was against a background of belief in values that seem to have
come straight from GA Henty and the public school system which
Charles, like many in the Edwardian era, saw as the beau ideal.

In the July 1910 number of the Gazette there was a totally outside
view of Charles as he then was at the age of 28. In the two preceding
numbers he had written a sequence of signed articles, 'The Gazette,
a Retrospect', reviewing the Gazette's history and the policies of its
successive editors. The last of these articles brought the reader up
to the time of Charles's appointment as Editor, and it was
immediately followed by an addendum called 'The Retrospect
(completed by Another)', which was an open letter to Charles. The
identity of Another is unknown.

'You have with some audacity set out to estimate the exact value
of the work of your predecessors. It may be said at once that on
the whole you have evaded the traps which awaited clumsy feet,
though your second article was less penetrating than one might
have hoped for. To complete the Retrospect is only fair, for one
editor has escaped criticism, that one "CMW". I have said one,
but in reality there are two personalities who write under those
initials. With the first I have little patience. I dislike his crude
cynicism. He is nothing more nor less than the wild Irishman of
tradition, thirsty for controversy, daring, frivolous, often witty,
usually clever, yet in spite of his gifts, or perhaps because of them,
a little irritating. If this were all, the Retrospect might as far as

I am concerned remain unfinished. Irony might be beneficial, but on the whole this side of "CMW" is best left to time.

'The other gains somewhat by contrast. This second individual is, however, so genuine, so fraught with possibilities, that this is written in the hope that some—and we have in view the more serious section of the community—who have overlooked the second in their aversion to the first may be led to reconsider their judgment.

'If my criticism is really an appreciation it is because I am not here concerned with that Celtic constituent in "CMW" to which I have referred. Briefly, the rest of my discourse is addressed to your better self. . . . You have had for eight years a settled aim and a definite ideal. It is to make the school first by consistently backing and fostering the public school spirit. It is equally manifest in your work for the Rugby football club and for the GAZETTE. It is to the spectator a matter of surprise that with a craving for controversy and those other faults which by the charitable are ascribed to the "snap" of youth, are found a considered and comprehensive grasp of the problems which face the London Schools. But there it is. And it gives to your words a value which is beyond the reach of clever fooling. "You must realise the sources of entry or lose them." They are your own words, and you have taken them to heart. You have seen more than most of other schools, and you are intimately informed of every source from which students come to London schools, and of the causes which determine their choice of school. . . .

'You were educated at a "Soccer" school, you were quite light, and you played forward for the Hospital then as a Rugby power in very low water. And yet in spite of these apparently insuperable drawbacks you not only got on to a county, but stayed there. It is a small point, but is of some importance. It means that you are something more than an agitator, which is not a popular vocation, it means that you have the faculty of "getting there." And yet, though this achievement in the games world is eloquent tribute to your determination, it is not that which impresses me most in your athletic record, but the marked capacity for organisation and the astute management of men which you showed for several years in the direction of the Rugby club. You grasped the elementary fact on joining the school that it was the only form of athletics which appealed to hospital men, and so you threw up the game you knew and devoted yourself to one of whose technique you were ignorant, but of whose possibilities you were well aware.

'We have dwelt on this side of your career because it is the key to your work on the GAZETTE. Those who are deceived by the rather cheap cynicism you are pleased to indulge in miss the underlying enthusiasm for the school. It is good to meet one who is willing to risk something for the sake of an ideal, for ardent crusading makes enemies. . . .

'You aim at a school which shall be first. You know it is not a dream, but a possibility. It is to your credit that you see clearly the means to that end.

'It is the knowledge and the enthusiasm with which you spread it abroad which make us willing to forgive much. Your work is only incidentally concerned with games. You have persuaded many that character is the great recruiting sergeant for a school, that quantity follows quality. It is this which gives to your work the stamp of something beyond clever journalism, the brand of character.'[9]

Many might have let things rest at this stage but not Charles, who appended a footnote to 'Another's' comments:

'We have published this article because it is obvious that it is the opinions we have advocated and not the personality of the Editor with which our contributor is concerned. His article consists of two parts: the early portion is a direct attack on our frivolity, and is meant for the edification of the majority; the second part is more subtle, and is a concession to the fastidious minority. Here our style is deliberately assumed. Of course it is all very cynical to divide up your readers into the ignorant and the more favoured. As a matter of fact our correspondent is himself convinced, but has not the courage of his convictions. If his opinions are accepted and taken seriously, well and good. If they are ridiculed, then he takes refuge in the time-honoured trick that he is "getting at" the Editor. It is half-hearted support, but it is important that nothing should be left undone to drive home the fact that these views are not original, but are widely held. They are not a private fad, but a popular axiom. Our correspondent is good enough to credit us with much journalistic "nose". He has the gift of seeing the obvious. – Ed.'[9]

The July number of the Gazette was the last before the long vacation. At the next meeting of the Medical School Committee in October it was minuted: 'The Dean arranged to interview Mr Wilson on the subject of certain articles contained in the July 1910 issue which were severely criticized.'[10] Which these articles were was not divulged. Maybe Charles's views on 'Hospitals and Democracy' were seen by some as dangerously radical, maybe the article by 'Another' and Charles's riposte had undertones that are not appreciated today, maybe it was neither of these contributions that caused the criticism. The result of the interview was not recorded and Charles continued as a hard-working editor. Bernard Shaw's views were further considered editorially in the November issue under the heading 'The Attitudes of Socialism to the Medical Profession'.[11] Charles also tried his hand as a drama critic, reporting the Residents' Dramatic Entertainment, a play called *Jane*, in the January 1911 number. In doing this he deftly outlined his recollections of Irving and du Maurier, and incidentally revealed that he was no stranger to the theatre whose seats in 'the gods' were financially within the reach of most students. He handled the subject of women in a manner typical of one of his time and background: 'Of women I speak as one having no authority, and with a sense of awe with which we approach the Unknown.'[12]

Charles resigned as editor of the Gazette in March 1911, six months before he resigned from his appointment as Medical Registrar. The two events appear unrelated, but his final identifiable comment as editor shows that he felt impelled to defend freedom of editorial expression. He ended a note concerned with hospital journalism with the admonition: 'If a man shape his opinions to fact and not to persons he serves the interests of the community at the expense of his own. The path of least resistance is popular, but it does not lead to anything, and with that as Editor we have done.'[13]

Charles's later written comment on his resignation as Medical Registrar was brief:

'The staff were amazed, they decided I was an awkward, unaccountable fellow who would never fit in if appointed to staff. In those days anyone who aspired to be a consultant was supposed to have private means. My salary as Registrar was sixty-five pounds a year, but I had accumulated a little money by coaching students for their final examinations when my day's work was done. With this in the bank I left England and wandered in Egypt and Italy for a year.'[2]

Why Egypt and Italy? Charles later told his family that Almroth Wright had as a patient an American lady who had been ordered to spend the winter in Egypt—a prescription not uncommonly given to monied people. She wanted a young doctor who would be able to advise her if she were unwell. As Charles's widow told the story many years later:

'Sir Almroth thought of Charles who, like his father, was always ready for any adventure. So he went off to Egypt with Mrs Cords. As a fit and active young man, he was much in demand by the convalescents in Egypt. There was a race course and the British people were annoyed because the Germans always won. So they

clubbed together and bought a racing camel, and asked Charles
to ride it, which he did, and won, but could not stop the animal
and went a long way out into the desert until he was rescued. . . .
The prize for his race was two little silver donkeys which are now
on Geoffrey's mantel piece.

'After Egypt, and when Mrs Cords had gone home, he had a little
money in hand and he decided to spend it in Italy. So he went to
Venice and to Florence looking at pictures. . . . Someone gave him
an address in Florence, so he went there and found it was a young
ladies' finishing school. But he talked to the lady in charge and
quite won her over, so he was allowed to stay. He also went with
an American acquaintance to Monte Cassino, where he arrived
with his golf clubs.'[14]

Charles recorded giving Churchill an account of this visit to Monte
Cassino during the Second World War. The occasion was a visit to
General Alexander's* headquarters in Italy, in August 1944. The
morning had been spent visiting Monte Cassino, a monastery dating
from the sixth century AD that stands on an isolated hill dominating
the road and railway that join Rome and Naples. It had been the
scene of particularly tough fighting some months earlier, for the
allied forces could not advance northward from Naples to Rome until
Monte Cassino had been taken from the Germans. Standing in the
rubble of the monastery Charles had told Churchill that he had been
there before. Churchill's attention had been caught: 'You must tell
me, Charles, why you became a monk'. In the evening, when they
were alone, Churchill returned to the subject. Charles commented
elsewhere that this written account contained more than he actually
said, for Churchill was not a good listener, but it was what he would
have liked to have said:

'One day I met a professor from Yale University, who told me he
was going to Monte Cassino that afternoon. Whereupon I asked
if I could go with him. From the wayside station we climbed in
a creaking phaeton drawn by a dilapidated horse up what seemed
like the side of a mountain. At length the driver, who had been
encouraging his exhausted beast with curses and cracks of his
whip, stopped at the gate of the monastery and rang a bell so
violently that I felt abashed. A monk opened the door and spoke
in Italian to the professor. He led us to a cell on the other side
of the great stone building. That night I slept fitfully in my cell.
Leaving my bed in the small hours, I wandered out into the long,
deserted passages, until I found myself in a chapel where a monk

---

*General HRLG Alexander, Army Group Commander in Italy.

was at prayer. I do not suppose that it was a very long time until he rose to his feet. He left the chapel, and I followed him. He led me to a great terrace or battlement which looked down a wooded precipice into a valley far below. He had come to the monastery from Belgium to carve the screen in the chapel. Quite simply he told me, when I asked him, why he had given up the world. And then we stood in silence drinking in the utter peace of the place as the night left us.'[15]

This monologue evoked the comment from Churchill: 'You would have made a good monk.'

In 1913 after being away for some eighteen months, Charles headed for home.

'It happened that when I landed at Dover I ran into a certain Gordon Bryan who had been Surgical Registrar during my time and was now prudently taking steps to ensure his election to the surgical staff of St Mary's. He was so off-hand in his manner that it was obvious that I was no longer in the running for the Staff. Perhaps his bearing nettled me, anyway I began to think seriously about the problem. It looked pretty bleak. I found at St Mary's that the man who had been my chief rival had played his cards so well in my absence that he was regarded as a certainty for the next vacancy.

'The first step was to get a higher degree without which I could not be a serious candidate for the Staff. I had been so busy when Registrar that I had had little time for reading, and on my travels I had not opened a book. There was a lot of ground to cover. I decided to take a bed-sitting room in a slum off the Harrow Road and there I settled down to read. I read all day and half the night, only going for a little walk in the afternoon. I had a retentive memory and I was able to browse widely in the literature. Like Winston I do better when I have a target. I had to get the Gold Medal in the London University examination for Doctor of Medicine and I had to become a Member of the Royal College of Physicians at the first attempt; otherwise it would only be a waste of time to go up against Hope Gosse. It was an impudent gamble but it came off.'[2]

Charles's reading was guided by tutors from one of the business houses in London which, for a fee, coached people for exams of all sorts.[16] The MD examination was the hurdle that came first and on 7 July he wrote a gloomy account to his parents of his initial performance:

'Dear Dad and Mum,
I'm out of luck, knew everything today but felt seedy and headachy and consequently I wasn't alert and left out lots I knew. In morning

we had the commentary. I made correct diagnosis but on several points I missed putting down obvious deduction. In afternoon I misread one question and so omitted nearly half of it. I knew the whole question perfectly and gave the half I thought was wanted absolutely correctly. A good many read it like I did but the best would not and I shouldn't have made the mistake. Of course I'm through all right but had I been on form I could have done it all and in competitive things you cannot afford to drop even one point and I dropped more than one. However, it's all in day's work. Feel very weary tonight with aching legs. But this isn't astonishing as six hours on end concentrated work on milk diet is no joke. But I shall be all right tomorrow. I shall get through but don't think I can pick up now unless by a mistake. Don't mention anything of my not being fit to [Aunt] Maude. She took much trouble and it's bad luck.'[17]

Two days later, to his parents:

'It's not knowledge (I've known practically everything all along) but knack of concentrating knowledge. I could have written about two hours on each of three morning questions. I really only tumbled to trick at end of business.'[18]

After two weeks of waiting Charles learnt that he had won the Gold Medal, the first ever won from St Mary's in the subject of internal medicine in the MD. He had taken a temporary appointment at the London County Lunatic Asylum, at Hanwell, which was associated with St Mary's, and from there he sent a series of letters to his parents.

23 June 1913
'Dear Dad and Mum,
Many thanks for congratulations and letters and wire. I thought before event I had a very good chance though odds are against one. But had given up hope when things ran against me and my tips didn't come off. I thought I had not done quite well enough in medicine and not nearly well enough in pathology. So it was a pleasant and unexpected surprise. It is an asset in anything one takes up, a sort of trump card to play. I had made up my mind to get it if possible and was very sick I did badly in pathology. It would of course be a great asset if I went up for staff here. But I must say the game doesn't appeal at all. The men here (Mary's) were very pleased and especially Dicky Bird,* and the fact that I haven't kowtowed to staff makes it a popular win. . . '.[19]

---

*Dr Mitchell Bird, Medical Superintendent, St Mary's Hospital.

Later that day he added:

'I've just met a man who was Phillips's H.P. once and he told me
Phillips had told him 'I was streets ahead of anyone, no one
anywhere near' and that Phillips was extremely pleased and
thought it reflected favourably on him as I was his H.P.—since
writing and posting letter have seen all sorts of people at hospital
sort of triumphal progress! There is no doubt success is *the* modern
god. It hasn't come my way before but it's not unpleasant being
a sort of nine days wonder! You have to be labelled to be
appreciated—rather absurd.'[19]

In further letters to his parents Charles expressed mixed feelings
about competing for the next vacancy on the hospital staff, which
was due in two years' time. He wrote disparagingly of the intrigues
that were involved, describing them as too petty for words. 'Be sweet
to everyone and pick them to bits behind their backs is the motto.'[19]
Until Charles's gold medal there had been one obvious aspirant,
Hope Gosse, who had succeeded him as medical registrar and who
had the strong support of Dr William Willcox, a fairly junior but
increasingly influential staff member. Now Charles was in the
running, with the certain support of his old chief Sidney Phillips,
and when Wilfred Harris returned from his summer holiday Charles
learnt that he had his support also. Charles wrote to his parents:

'Harris was very candid about staff. He said it was no longer
necessary to collect proofs of ability but of industry and pulling
along smoothly! Every day more astonished by way people bow
down to success. It alters one's whole position at a hospital.'[20]

Charles wrote of other things that were on his mind. The firm
whose tutors had coached him offered him five guineas-worth of
books if they could use his name in an advertisement. 'It might not
do' he wrote, 'if I went up for staff. At the same time it's a pity to
throw away the five guineas. . . .'[16] Most pressing was the need to
decide on his next job. Harris told him that it was essential for him
to apply for the post of Casualty Physician when it fell vacant in
January (1914) if he wanted to win the staff appointment. But
Charles had another offer to consider. At one time as a student he
had shared digs with Godfrey Maurice whose family had conducted
the general practice in the country town of Marlborough since
1792.[21] Maurice, known to Charles as 'the Badger', had suggested
that Charles should consider becoming medical officer to the large
boys' school, Marlborough College, and he now invited him to come
for the weekend. Writing to his parents, Charles described the visit:

'I got down to Marlborough at 11.15 am and was met by Maurice.
He spent till about 7.00 pm (with intervals for lunch and tea) in

car covering 50 to 60 miles calling at many big houses seeing patients. In the evening went to a dance at his sister-in-law's. This brother was an engineer but married 1,600 a year and she wont live where he can work so he breeds pedigree cattle and is very good at it. About 20 there or more county people not locals very dull, rather bored.

'On Sunday we called on several outlying people and on some of his tough farmers going in car from place to place. Then we went up to Mrs Maurice's (senior) house and talked till 11 o'clock and then Badger and I talked till 2.00 am.

'I saw a good deal of Marlborough. It is a pleasant old world place. Their house is flush with the street as ours in Skipton but large rambling and full of old prints sporting tropheys open hearths etcetera. The sort of house you sit in the hall. Behind there is a fine, very large garden with fine views. The man servant who brought me tea in the morning had been in family for 35 years and rest in keeping. It would be pleasant if I lived there to have such a place and backing but of course without the Badger it would not be such an advantage. I met the school doctor a nice man and well up. The life would be I think monotonous.

'Expenses are allowed to mount up but it is a very good practice and they skim the cream of the county for miles doing 50 to 60 miles daily in cars.

'I shall have an uphill game at Mary's as Gosse is very popular. Pannett thinks I shall just get it*. He is very friendly. The Badger said I had not asked his advice but if I did he would advise me to go up to Mary's and not to Marlborough. He said very few got chance of being consultants and it ought to be taken. This really is very decent advice as it means probably £300–£500 yearly loss if I don't go to school as they do all operating there at present. Badger says they would not dare to put on Gosse but I'm not so sure. Shall try and convert Willcox and get Badger to get hold if possible of Clayton Greene. Nothing else can be done. If I get those two I should get it. At present both are friendly but more so to Gosse. He (Gosse) has entertained everybody at his club I hear. It's Mammon and the Medal. If Willcox would come over it would mean Luff and with Harris that's enough. I'm rather stale and need a holiday not so much for physical as mental grounds. Long grind plus reaction plus relaxing climate here have resulted in slackness but I must get MRCP next time then I can get a holiday.'[22]

---

*CA Pannett, surgeon (later professor of surgery) St Mary's Hospital.

After his visit, Charles opted against Marlborough and worked towards his next immediate hurdle, the passing of the examination for membership of the Royal College of Physicians.

The summer of the MD exam had been one of upheaval for Charles's parents, who were moving to retirement in Hastings, described in those days as a watering place noted for its mild climate on the coast of Sussex. His mother's health was indifferent and his father's gastric ulcer troublesome, and Charles was solicitous for them both and sent a series of admonitions:

'Don't on any account tire yourself packing. Tip servant well to do it.'[19]

'Mum should do nothing but sit about in sun and play croquet until she gets quite fit again. Nothing in house whatsoever.'[16]

Charles was still working at Hanwell and keen to contribute financially to his parents:

'My balance at bank is now £34 (£20 was paid out for MD fee). In September I shall get a cheque from here for about £47–£50 which will just about pay for MRCP fee in October. So I have £34 in hand towards paying off national debt!

'I enclose a cheque for £5/10s/0d. 10s to pay back borrowed 10s at Charing Cross. £2 for each of you and £1 for Cop. This to celebrate MD. To be spent on luxuries as you wish not on necessities or useful things but on pleasure pure and simple. If you would like £20 towards amount I owe it is quite easy for me to pay back that now and I could square up rest after MRCP in October.

'Don't economise as MRCP will be here soon and there will be after that no unproductive periods of not earning in digs. You may as well splash a bit as I am not economical and you'd spend it better than I shall and I shall always be able to make necessary fairly easily with work I've done behind me. So look up theatres etcetera and splash a bit!'[16]

The examination for membership of the Royal College of Physicians involved written papers, clinical and oral examinations. Soon after it started Charles got a bad cold, 'but, by 10 grains of Dover's powder, bath (very hot), hot bread and milk and sleeping under many clothes, checked it, also with Aspirin.'[23]

Then came controversy with an examiner.

27 October 1913
'Dear Mum and Dad,
Things went all wrong today. They gave me the Pseudo-Bulbar speech to spot and asked its causation. I told them it might be due to any bilateral lesion between cortex and pons and Hale White* said it could only be due to Internal Capsule. Went straight back to Harris and he of course said I was quite right. It destroyed all this case. It's really iniquitous they choose to examine in difficult Neurology—which they don't understand. I don't know whether they will pull me down over this. It's quite likely and they will never find out their mistake. However it can't be helped. You can't make old examiners understand Neurology. I gave my authority— author—which was foolish as no one likes to be ragged before another examiner. Indeed H. White was obviously not pleased at all. I am up again tomorrow and Wednesday. Nothing for it but to keep going. The day when it doesn't matter I'll let H. White have it straight. . . . Harris says it's dangerous to know more than your examiners. Iniquitous system! Much love C.'[24]

Soon it was all over. He passed the examination and in doing so completed what he had set out to do at the start of the year. With sights now firmly set on the staff appointment, the next stepping stone was the post of Casualty Physician. This job occupied about two hours each afternoon and involved seeing acutely ill patients of all ages who could not afford to see a general practitioner, or patients referred by an outside doctor for admission to the hospital. In November, it was announced that the appointment had gone to Charles.[25]

Then, totally unexpectedly, Dr Luff, one of the senior physicians on the staff, resigned.[26] Charles took the plunge and was one of four applicants for the vacancy; the others were A Hope Gosse, DW Carmalt-Jones and FS Langmead. Hope Gosse[28] was two years older than Charles. Born in what was then the British colony of South Australia, in the town of Wallaroo, where his father was a doctor, he had been sent to an English-type school, St Peters' College, in Adelaide and then to Cambridge, where he took an honours degree in the natural sciences tripos and rowed for his college, Gonville and Caius. He had done very well in the medical course at St Mary's and obtained the MRCP in the same years as Charles, but had not yet acquired an MD. Carmalt-Jones,[29] who was eight years older than Charles, had held junior appointments at St Mary's and at other hospitals in London and had worked in Sir Almroth Wright's department. At the time of his application he was Dean of the Westminster Hospital Medical School. Langmead[30] was three years

---

*Dr W Hale-White, physician to Guy's Hospital.

older than Charles, another of Sydney Phillips' old house physicians and already on the staff of two children's hospitals, Paddington Green and Great Ormond Street. The Medical Committee, on the motion of Dr Phillips, submitted to the Election Committee the names of Langmead and Carmalt-Jones indicating Langmead as the more eligible.[27] He was appointed. Carmalt-Jones later became Professor of Medicine in the University of Otago in New Zealand.

Neither Charles nor Gosse could seriously have expected to win in what was for them a premature contest. Gosse set out to fulfil his academic promise as a research assistant at the London Hospital with Sir James Mackenzie, one of the pioneers of modern studies of heart disease. Charles continued as Casualty Physician and in April 1914 also joined Wilfred Harris, in a newly constituted office of Clinical Assistant to the Nervous Diseases Department. The Spring of 1914 gave way to a summer that all later remembered as one with perfect weather. Then, as Charles carried on with his work at the hospital while his seniors took their long summer holidays, the lamps went out over Europe.

Addendum

A letter survives that was written by Charles when he had been a house physician for some three months. Addressed to his father at Barrow-in-Furness, it was written on a Sunday in February, 1909 on the backs of several printed hospital forms. It is rather rambling and concerned mostly with his views on surgery for the gastric ulcer with which his father was plagued; but it also gives insights into Charles's developing attitudes.

'Dear Dad and Mum,
Sorry tummy is so troublesome—Willcox here has something of a reputation as a Gastric specialist—But I think he only advises medical treatment in cases in which symptoms have been present for a comparatively short time. As far as operative treatment goes experience here indicates best results are obtained where there is much narrowing of pylorus and consequent obstruction.
We on our firm (Sidney Phillip's [sic] cases) don't have much experience of gastroenterostomy for GU as SP is conservative and against surgery. We have had two since I have been on. The first in a man of 25 was very sticky. He had persistent pain and vomiting and an enormous stomach. He was *very* thin and went out in about 30 days very fat, comparatively. The other was a woman of 50 just done. The after history varies and is not always a cure. You can tell nothing from published results as results are unconsciously cooked by keen people. The cases ought to be followed for a year or two to tell the exact benefit. On the side of the operation there is the chance of complete cure. Against operation the possibility of no benefit with all the discomforts of an operation and the natural reluctance to have a major operation if not forced to it. I do not think the immediate danger of the operation is a factor as bad results must be very rare if operation is done at time carefully chosen. That's a subject no two people agree on. Some think it much too radical for GU unless pain is unbearable. Some think it should be done as a routine if medical treatment fails. I've seen too little to give advice worth having. Nor do I think opinions much worth having.

The first would in your case advise against op: the second for an op. I don't think any particular symptom in your case would turn either school from their convictions, i.e. I don't think an examination or having history would influence them much.

Hamilton (H.P. to Willcox who is a junior physician here but in charge of wards for 6 months as Caley* has been away) tells me Willcox gets good results for medical treatment but mostly in early cases. I think Willcox would advise an op for you but as I said before I would not rely in this question on anybody's opinion but your own and of course if not convinced of value of operation I would always give non-operation the vote. Expect if I had a GU I should have an op because I should always be inclined to radical measures but I think there is much to be said on either side and I would not rush at an op after an attack of pain. I would consider it carefully in a period of good health comparatively. I would not make a decision either way except when you were free from pain and in fair trim. If you ever decided on an op I can recommend a surgeon and anaesthetist with utmost confidence. They do it here in from 20 minutes to 30 minutes. I suppose the nursing home would be only expense. If all goes well one month would be probable period in hospital. I thought these facts might be of some value. Sorry I can be of so little benefit in coming to a decision. But I think you will gather from what I have said the position of gastroenterostomy in treatment of gastric ulcer. Clayton-Greene our Dean and one of the junior surgeons whom I think is about best man on gastroenterostomy has asked me to dinner on Friday. Don't like these functions much as I am not keen on cards but am going. Did an empyema yesterday. I've had a fair number of interesting cases but I have made this so long I must stop.

Much love Charlie."[31]

---

*Dr HA Caley, physician to St Mary's Hospital.

Chapter 3

The Army in France 1914-1918

Within hours of the newspaper placards appearing on the streets on the fourth of August announcing that Britain was at war there was an exodus from St Mary's to join the forces. Charles, with conflicting emotions, found himself one of the few left. He wanted to join up for the same reason that so many young men of his day did—to go to France would be great fun. But the pleasant glow of anticipation was quickly replaced by anxiety that he might be too late and that the war would be over by Christmas. What was stopping him from simply writing a note to the secretary of the hospital and walking the length of Whitehall to enlist was that in a few months the vacancy on the staff would occur that he had been waiting and working for. He consulted his seniors. They told him that if he joined up he would only spend his days inoculating and vaccinating troops. He must do what he thought best. For a while he carried on, increasingly torn, and oppressed by the monotony of his job. His work at the hospital was over by four o'clock when he went to the Board Room for tea and a cigarette. By the time he had done an hour's coaching and taken an hour's exercise walking, the street lamps were lit and he was back in the two small dingy rooms in the lodging house in which he lived. August slipped away and then September. All the men for whom he had the least use had gone. By October he could bear it no longer and with self-recrimination at having, as he saw it, funked the consequences of throwing everything up, on 20 October he joined up.[1] On 25 October he was commissioned as a surgeon in His Majesty's Forces with the temporary rank of Lieutenant in the Army.[2]

When everything was arranged and he had only to get his kit, he took the train to Hastings to see his parents, very conscious of their local doctor's warning, 'If you go you'll finish your old people'. By now Dr and Mrs Wilson had settled into an agreeable life that included a little bridge circle and croquet that they played in a nearby park. Charles's father took the news philosophically and, having slept on it, decided that he himself must get some work to do. He asked Charles to get him a job in an asylum where there were not too many steps to climb, so, returning to London, Charles went to see the Superintendent at Hanwell. He believed that if his father were appointed he would not look upon the inmates as lunatics at all but would get to know them individually and be friends with them. Dr Wilson took a short course in psychiatry and obtained a job at Hanwell, which he kept through the war.[3] Charles's mother and sister Maud took rooms at Ealing. Mrs Wilson's health was failing and Maud, who was unmarried, gave up her work to look after her.[4]

Within days Charles was in France. He described his arrival:

'Towards the end of October I landed at Havre in the disguise of a temporary lieutenant in the RAMC [Royal Army Medical Corps] and went immediately to the office of the ADMS [Assistant Director of Medical Services] to report my arrival.

'It was a raw morning and I had not yet breakfasted but I had a feeling that if I delayed seeing the ADMS even for an hour I might miss a chance of going to the front.

'I found myself with about thirty other doctors in a big bare room without a carpet and with no furniture except a table and some chairs, a room not unlike a solicitor's office in a country town. It reminded me at once of the place in which candidates wait before an oral examination and there was the same subdued atmosphere of excitement and expectancy.

'The ADMS was out but a major in the RAMC sat at the big table writing. He wore a Staff hat which he lifted from time to time as if he was short of air; and every time he did this one noticed his bald polished head and the worried expression on his face.

'I felt sorry for him and thought of the type of student who retires into a corner with a text book between morning and afternoon papers of an examination and is quite overwhelmed by the amount he still has to read and by the possibilities of some damning error.

'When it was my turn to be questioned the major looked up in a confused way and said "Well?" Then remembering himself he asked my age, my medical qualifications, and next of kin and whether I could ride a horse or a motor bicycle. I replied that I was thirty, that I rode but had never in my life mounted a motor bicycle and no sooner had I said this than I began to regret my candour for from the roll before me apparently everyone else could ride both horse and bicycle and indeed appeared able to do everything and anything that could possibly be required at the Front.

'I wanted to tell this official that I had served in the Yeomanry as a trooper for six years, that I once played a lot of Rugby football and anything else which came into my head which might count for righteousness but there was no opportunity or perhaps it vanished while I was deliberating. However when asked my degrees I only confessed to the MRCS [Member of the Royal

College of Surgeons], thinking men with senior qualifications might be kept back for work at Base Hospitals. I did not know that if I had been Lister* himself it would have made no difference to my disposal. I knew nothing of the Army as yet.

'When everyone had been before the DADMS [Deputy ADMS] he placed his hat on the table, blew out his cheeks and taking a blue handkerchief from his sleeve mopped his head vigorously; then he rose and from the thirty doctors rapidly selected eight who apparently were to remain at Havre. The rest he ordered to report to the RTO [Railway Transport Officer] that night at 8 o'clock. I was in the party detailed for Rouen.'[1]

Rouen is on the River Seine between Paris and the English Channel, and Charles joined the 8th General Hospital there. He was still far from where the British Expeditionary Force (the BEF) was in action. This small professional army had been constantly on the move and repeatedly embattled since landing in France in the first weeks of August. First it had headed into Belgium to help counter the advancing German right wing. On reaching Mons it found the German strength was much greater than expected, and its retreat with the left wing of the French Army between 23 August and 6 September took it 100 miles southward to the River Marne. Here it fought with the French to contain the direct threat to Paris. The BEF then went north again, this time nearer the coast, to help stem the German thrust towards the Channel ports. The race to the sea, as it came to be called, ended on 15 October. There were now continuous Allied and German lines extending southward from the mouth of the River Yser, north-east of Dunkirk, to a point about 45 miles north of Paris and then extending generally south-eastward to the Swiss border. For the rest of the war it was on the upper part of the north-south component of this line that the British forces on the Western Front were to live and fight and die. The southern part of the British sector was in the ancient province of Artois in France, noted for its well watered pastures. The northern part was in Belgium, in the province of West Flanders, noted also for its agriculture and market gardens. If ever a soil could have been chosen rich in bacteria capable of causing disastrous wound infections and ready to be converted to mud, this was it.

Within a few days of the completion of the race to the sea, and just as Charles was joining up in London, the British took the offensive again and what came to be known as the first battle of Ypres started on 19 October. There was no breakthrough but the north-south line was left with a bulge projecting some five miles eastward from the town, the Ypres Salient. When this battle and the associated fighting south of Ypres round La Bassée and

---

*Joseph Lister (1827-1912). English surgeon and originator of antiseptic surgery.

Armentières ended on 22 November, little survived of the old British regular army.[5] Furthermore, a new type of warfare began. From the coast of Switzerland the opposing forces faced each other—and, though they did not know it, faced the first of four increasingly dreadful winters—in wet muddy trenches. So it came about that Charles's first medical experience in France was with casualties from trench warfare. Two weeks had gone by at the hospital at Rouen with nothing happening and then:

'We were sitting before a great fire in the mess of No. 8 General Hospital, Rouen; the servants were busy removing the dinner things and through the open door came a smell of cooking.

'For some time we sat in silence listening to the rain and the great gusts of wind that threatened any moment to blow down the big marquees in the grounds of the chateau, a big brick building which was reserved for the more serious cases. . . . Then there was the noise of an ambulance on the gravel and everybody got up and went out. . . . Ambulance after ambulance drew up in the darkness and stretchers were taken out, carried in and dumped down in crowded passages that connected the two wings of the building.

'The men seemed to have come straight from the trenches; there was mud on their clothes, on the stretchers and even on the blankets covering them and they took no notice of anything as they lay on their backs staring at the ceiling with a dull sleepy expression fixed on their grey unkempt and unshaven faces.

'And watching them I wanted more than ever to get away, if possible to a Regiment but failing that to a Field Ambulance.

'About midnight I went into the mess for a cigarette. There was no one there but Tomkins* who always had a night cap before turning in.

'I like Tomkins. He seemed cut out for this game and he too meant to get out of this place even if he had to make himself a bit of a nuisance in the process. "Pretty rotten aren't they?" he remarked. "I've never seen feet like that before. It looks to me as if most of them will have to come off". I sat listening to him. Evidently the conditions must be awful up there in the trenches for them to get into this state; as if it might be the Crimea with all that stinking gangrene.'[1]

After this first glimpse of war, Tomkins and Charles headed for bed in the neighbouring chateau in which they were billeted. In the

---

*A fictitious name.

hall they found cake and red wine left out for them, which they attacked willingly. Charles had a great apartment with an enormous bed under a canopy with red curtains. It was all very pleasant but, he reflected, it was somehow not quite what he had come for. The hospital was generally not very busy.

'Every day after tea most of the doctors who were not on duty went into Rouen. The trams passed the gate and ran frequently; if they heard one coming as they walked down the drive, they did not run for it, but waited for the next one. But Tomkins and I always walked both ways to keep fit; any day we might be sent up the line and we pictured the Front as a place where you slept in a ditch, when you could, a place where a flabby fellow would not last five minutes.'[1]

At last the day came. The Registrar of the hospital said that an MO was needed to go up to the Front that night and would Charles like to go? He reported to the RTO at 8.00 p.m.

'The journey from Rouen to the Front was like any other under army auspices, conducted throughout at the pace of a trotting horse but punctuated by an incredible number of stoppages for no apparent reason without a sign of any station and now and then a little spurt to raise hopes just to dash them to the ground. It was early in the morning of the second day when the train pulled up with a particularly vicious bump. "Lord, what a fug" I exclaimed, rubbing my eyes and beginning to wake up. I let the window down and put my head out.

'Troops were falling in on the down line, yawning and stretching their arms after a night in crowded trucks. From a board marked Steenwerk I learnt that this was the railhead. [Steenwerk is five miles west of Armentières].

'People had a glow on them and looking at the men my head was full of the Retreat and the tales we heard from the wounded frost-bitten patients in No. 8 General of the fierce struggle before Ypres.

'I climbed down and wandered about in the mud among the waiting lorries; by the gate I found a Ford ambulance which was to take me to the ADMS's office. There was not a breath of air; everything seemed damp and there were pools of standing water by the roadside and in the fields.

'"Is it always raining here?" I enquired of the driver. The fellow grinned "It don't do much else, Sir" he replied.

'There were soldiers billeted in the ugly villages through which we passed, mostly ASC [Army Service Corps] and a few gunners. In one longer and cleaner than the rest the sixth division had established its headquarters.

'The ADMS was out. A clerk turned up a Roll and said that I was posted to the 1st Royal Fusiliers and that the ambulance would take me to their headquarters at Armentières. He did not know if they were in the trenches or in billets. I was allowed to understand that the solution to that question did not interest him and I came away with the impression that I had asked a lot of foolish questions and had bothered him quite unnecessarily.

'Just beyond the village I heard guns, the battery sounded quite close. And presently there was a noise that might have been a Bosch shell though there was no smoke visible. I kept listening for the sound of approaching shells but did not feel rattled. I wanted to question the driver but did not like to expose my ignorance. He appeared to take no notice of these sounds, no doubt he was an old hand. . . .

'The car drew up at Chapel d'Armentières before a very modern looking house built of red brick which did not seem to have been knocked about. I went in to report my arrival to the Colonel with a sense of relief. I felt that even if I had missed the Retreat I should after all be in at the finish.

'It was something to get to the Front before the Hun handed in.'[1]

Charles was medical officer to the 1st Battalion the Royal Fusiliers, from shortly before Christmas 1914 until 21 February 1917*. He was not joining a group of novices but a battalion that still had a core of regular soldiers of the old professional army. They had lately been engaged in the last phase of the mobile fighting, which ended in the second half of October with the digging of trenches. The battalion's part of the line was in front of Armentières, 14 miles south of Ypres, and when the battalion was relieved on the 21 November at the end of the first Battle of Ypres, the diary recorded that, except for two days, it had completed 35 days continuously in the trenches. The weather had become dreadful, wet and cold, and at times the trenches were impassable with mud. While in December there was no fixed battle, there were always bullets and shells about, and even in that month 14 men were killed or died of wounds and 18 were wounded. Altogether at the end of December

---

*See p. 56 Note on Sources, for time with the Royal Fusiliers.

Figure 3. Picture of a Royal Fusilier taken from the Royal Fusiliers' Christmas card in 1916.

the battalion recorded 72 killed or died of wounds and 191 wounded since going into action.[7]

A pattern of life now developed, in which the battalion was in the trenches for between four to twelve days at a time. It would then be relieved by another battalion and settle in billets about two miles behind the front line, at Chapel d'Armentières, a small town on the edge of Armentières itself. Then it would be its turn for the trenches again. The front line that the battalion manned was quite straight and although there were casualties almost daily it was fairly quiet. Wet wintry day followed wet wintry day and, apart from those looking out, nights were spent as best they could be in holes dug in the walls of the trenches. For billets the officers and men were quartered in the small houses that made up the town, which had been much damaged in earlier fighting. While in billets, life was by no means all spent in rest and recreation, for there was cleaning up to be done and drilling. Also, since the only comparatively safe way to get to or leave the front line was to keep out of sight below ground level, once the line was established, 300-400 yard long communications trenches had to be dug and maintained.

As the regimental medical officer, Charles found himself responsible for the 1000 men of the battalion. He was attached to battalion headquarters, which consisted of the lieutenant colonel, who was the commanding officer; a major, an adjutant, who was a more junior officer; and a quartermaster, who dealt with stores and clothing. Additionally there were other ranks with administrative duties, cooks, cyclists and signallers. The main body of the battalion was divided into companies of 100-120 men, each commanded by an officer who, early in the war, was usually a captain. Charles's job was to see anyone who reported sick, to treat those who were only slightly ill or wounded and to send the others down the line to the Field Ambulance, where the medical resources were greater. He was also responsible for sanitary arrangements. One of Hill's* earliest memories of him was of finding him arguing with his commanding officer about the sanitation of the trenches, where excreta were floating about. Soon afterwards buckets arrived and were installed and strict instructions were given about their use. When the battalion was in the line the medical officer had to establish an aid post in some sheltered place, which might be a dug-out in a trench or among masonry in a shattered building. He had to attend to all casualties there or by going himself to the site of action, and stretcher-bearers were under his orders.[9]

Charles was introduced to the action that he had been striving to reach, when he was shelled for the first time on 20 December. At the start of the shelling he had taken the sick into the shallow cellar of the farmhouse in which he had his aid post a little way behind the front line. The cellar was hit and some of those around him were killed and wounded. He was, as he put it, not rattled, perhaps because the wounded gave him something to do and think about. At lunch immediately after this episode he noticed that the conversation was about hunting; the shelling was not mentioned; and he felt that he was listened to with a friendly interest that he had not noticed before. Evidently he had passed his test. But he was not without fear. He had to learn not to be at the mercy of his instincts, not to duck his head when a bullet pinged past and not necessarily to step into a ditch when a machine gun opened up. In the words of the time, he knew what it was to be windy.

Charles was very popular with the young officers because he came up to scratch not only in the line but also out of it where they spent much of their time riding horses.[8] They called themselves the Jockey Club. Early on they gave the doctor a horse described as 'rather hot', and having got him mounted two of them came up on each side and, beating its hind quarters, sent it galloping away. As with the camel in Egypt, it went far before it could be stopped. Charles, who was fond of riding, was elected an honorary member of the club. In the mess he drank only moderately, smoked a pipe as well as cigarettes, and he was much given to ragging the parson. He was struck by the way in which the officers in this typical line regiment spoke:

'[Their] conversational code was easily adapted to the new conditions. For if they chanced to refer to some incident where you

---

*Colonel MVB Hill. See Notes on Sources, p. 54.

had emerged not without credit you hastened to assure them that you were jittering with funk and that your teeth rattled. They knew the rules of the game and this only confirmed them in their opinion that you were a good fellow; then they went away and spoke of you to others as a gallant old quad or a good old thing.

'If you wished to express an opinion the recognized opening was "Of course I know nothing about these things but . . .". That made it all right. It was necessary too, if you shone in anything to appear quite unconscious of the part, though they always made for some mysterious reason an exception in favour of the horse. Everyone seemed to be an authority on the subject and even spoke dogmatically about it. They were reluctant to admit ignorance and the most unassuming fellow would imply that what he didn't know about a horse wasn't really worth knowing.'[1]

To begin with Charles found the men more difficult to understand:

'Whenever I imagined I was beginning to understand them something happened and I was utterly non-plussed. They are extraordinary people, I kept saying, just like children. And the officers smiled in a friendly sort of fashion because—as I see now—they felt I was quite unconsciously becoming a fusilier. While all the time I was greatly entertained by the kind of affectionate amusement with which the officers heard the doings of their men, however odd or even foolish—the invariable sign of a "good" officer . . .'.[1]

In fact, the men took to Charles less readily than the officers.[8] From the start he had a reputation for being very strict at medical parades and for sending back to the line scrimshankers who reported sick when there was nothing wrong with them. Evidently his reputation was well earned for it came to be noticed that when he went on leave the sick list doubled. Although he was very effective at keeping both officers and men in the trenches, some wondered if he overdid it and made one or two mistakes. Charles wondered too, and he wondered increasingly as the war went on. Indeed he referred again and again for the rest of his life to the dilemma he repeatedly faced—whether to send someone down the line with a label of illness or shell-shock or to send them back into action and risk being confronted with them soon afterwards dead or wounded. Thirty years later, in another war but in the peaceful atmosphere of Naples, he met a young subaltern who had lost three brothers and had been sent away for a rest: 'He is not broken yet but thank God it is not my job to return the poor devil to his unit. That is what the First War meant to me'.[10] The nature of the problem was brought home to him almost as soon as he joined the battalion, and he described the episode in the opening chapter of the *Anatomy of*

Courage. His hesitation in dealing with a sergeant who appeared no more than morose and out of sorts was followed within 24 hours by the man blowing his head off. Although his strictness made him at first less than popular with the men, they nevertheless respected him and this respect grew when he sent for one of the scrimshankers to accompany him to search for wounded in no-man's land after the battle of Hooge in the Ypres Salient in August 1915.[8] By then he had already been mentioned in despatches, the first of three mentions.

In his relationship with senior officers Charles showed characteristics that were to provoke comment again in the second war. He was a great talker and was full of original ideas and because of this he got on especially well with one known as 'Uncle Harper' who was the Brigade Commander. But closer to home, as MVB Hill, at one time his commanding officer, put it, 'he argued with the CO perhaps too much about tactics and what should be done from a military point of view. I dare say he was often right but what he suggested was not always possible so sometimes he was asked to keep quiet'.[8] Charles tremendously admired some of his commanding officers, and Hill became a life-long friend, but he was often highly critical of the more senior generals who determined strategy.

For Charles, apart from the Somme, the landmarks of the war were the winters. He saw the real enemy in the winter of 1914 to be exposure in the deep ditches in the clay soil of Flanders. And when, over Christmas, as the war diary put it, a kind of mutual truce appeared prevalent and 'there was no sniping etc. by the enemy',[7] Charles suddenly asked himself if the war was necessary. But it was to be some months yet before war ceased to have any elements that allowed him at times to regard it as a great adventure. The change was to come as the second winter approached.

The battalion continued in the first half of 1915 in the line opposite Armentières, where things were comparatively quiet. The losses were of some 10 a month killed or died of wounds and 20 wounded. Then, in June, the battalion moved northward and for the next twelve months fought in and around the Ypres Salient. This was when Charles started to keep his diary.[1] It soon became more than a simple record of events. The fly leaf of one of the field service correspondence books that he used is inscribed Sanctuary Wood—which is in the Salient—and has such headings as 'Patience', and 'Natural Courage Breaks Sooner or Later'. Here, right on the spot, experiencing continuous danger, discomfort and disaster, the psychologist and philosopher in Charles had taken over. He had become passionately interested in the nature of courage. Not only was the subject of the book he had longed to write determined, but at last he could fulfil his ambition to be a writer. As well as describing the men and events around him he recorded his own feelings. In the summer of 1915 when waiting in Sanctuary Wood to go into action at Hooge, he had a fever and learnt that illness may bring a man to the verge of defeat. A little later, after nearly a year with the battalion, while being shelled he experienced shivering that he could not control and for days he feared lest he should 'do something foolish when times were bad.'[6] By the second winter he understood the birth of fear. He was also experienced in monotony. At that time it did not disturb him in the sense that it did later when he began to see complaints about monotony as a sign of men who were not wearing well. In the first winter life had not appeared monotonous; it was novel and eventful and though nothing ever happened he kept thinking something would. By the second winter he had come to think of monotony as natural and even inevitable under circumstances 'when intelligent human beings were thrown into ditches that were mere stagnant drains in which the youth of England was rotting'.

'Strange as it may seem but that new life so different from anything we had experienced hitherto was not associated with a flood of new impressions. In fact the absence of any such reaction on the part of men, once curious and active, is one of the most constant phenomena of the trenches. . . . The most obtuse and those who count among the hopeful soon find one level under these sordid conditions. Men find their imagination is more dangerous for them than any Bosch. . . .'[1]

What was seen as the monotony of the life was accompanied by a sense of apathy. People got into the habit of just doing nothing. Behind the lines there were few books in the mess, not because they were hard to get but because people could no longer settle to read. In his twenty-six months with the battalion Charles read only one book, Conrad's *Mirror of the Sea*, which he came to know almost by heart. It met his mood.

Leave in England was generally granted for 10 days every four months, and Charles learnt how an acquired fatalism could be undermined by an urge to live when leave was in sight.

'At Ypres in 1915 I left the trenches with Weston to make our way to Poperinghe where the leave train would meander through the night to Boulogne. Our horses had been brought to the Asylum on the outskirts of Ypres. Ambling along we saw presently occasional shells falling on a village through which we must pass. We found ourselves standing in the middle of the road gaping at the familiar sight, then without a word and as if the horses had taken charge we took to the fields. When at last we pulled up our steaming horses we had made a wide detour; so completely had the desire to come through with leave in hand damped down our sense of humour; into our minds had crept an alternative.'[6]

The dead German at Armentières

Last night in the darkness two patrols met just beyond our wire. There were shots and the Bosch took to his heels save one big fellow who showed fight. A little later they dragged him into the trench where he was stripped of everything that might help in identifying his unit and left for dead. After stand to next morning he was found still breathing but when they brought him to the dressing station he was dead. They dumped him in an outhouse of the farm full of litter and all kinds of refuse. All day men of the resting Company came and looked through the open door at the dead Hun and some went in and cut off souvenirs from his clothing. When it was dark a fatigue party came and took him away to the field by the cemetery where they dug a grave and left him.

In a corner of the little French cemetery where the small wooden crosses contrasted strangely with the ornate monuments of civilian graves, a number of men were gathered round listening bare headed to the funeral service that was being read over one of their comrades who had been sniped that day. Now it is over and the men stand about in twos and threes and gradually melt away. I looked up. Three of us were alone in the gathering darkness. (then there were 3 of us alone, left) The adjutant spoke to the drum major and they went out of the cemetery

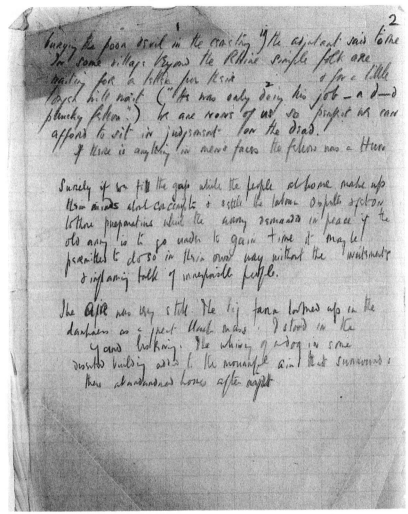

Figure 4. 'The dead German at Armentières'. Two pages, originally from an army field notebook, with an early draft of an episode included in The Anatomy of Courage. (Wellcome Institute Library, London; CMAC PP/CMW/I.1/6)

into the field and I followed them. The drum major read a few perfunctory sentences by the light of a torch and two men of the fatigue party who had been sent for lowered the Hun into the grave. Then we came away. ("Its all d __ d nonsense not burying the poor devil in the cemetery") the adjutant said to me. In some village beyond the Rhine simple folk are waiting for a letter from their [blank] and for a little longer will wait. ("He was only doing his job __ a d __ d plucky fellow"). We are none of us so perfect we can afford to sit in judgment on the dead.
NOTE: The next line and following two paragraphs were scribbled with a different pencil.
    If there is anything in men's faces, the fellow was a Hun.
    Surely if we fill the gap while the people at home make up their minds about conscription and settle the labour disputes and get on with those preparations which the army demanded in peace if the old army is to go under to gain time it may be permitted to do so in their own way without the incitements and inflaming talk of irresponsible people.
    The air was very still. The big farm loomed up in the darkness as a great black mass. I stood in the yard listening. The whining of a dog in some deserted building added to the mournful air that surrounds these abandoned homes after night.

Charles spent his leaves with his parents. It was common for those
going on leave to feel it was their last chance to get something out
of life, and in Charles's case this led him on impulse on the last day
of one of his leaves to look up the address of Mr Edmund Gosse in
the telephone directory and to appear unheralded and unknown on
his doorstep in Regent's Park. Gosse, then in his 60s, was a writer
and one of the outstanding literary critics of his day. Conducted by
the maid to the great man's presence, Charles told him without
beating about the bush that he was going to write a book and had
come for advice. Disappointingly Gosse displayed no interest in
Charles and what was happening in France, but he did spend half
an hour developing the theme that if Charles had anything to say
he ought to say it plainly, and that it must not be a fake, by which
Charles thought he meant he must not write a novel. The first advice
was probably salutary, for Charles, in his notebooks, was still
inclined to slip into the sort of purple passages that had coloured
his writings in the St Mary's Hospital Gazette. The second advice
may have determined that, as eventually written, the *Anatomy of
Courage* was not the thinly disguised autobiographical novel which,
at one stage, it might have become.

On 13 July, 1916, in high summer, the battalion was relieved in
the trenches of Flanders for the last time,[7] and on 24 July, after
a few days' training behind Armentières, it entrained at Bailleul
for the Somme, 60 miles to the south. When the battalion entrained,
the Battle of the Somme[11] was in its fourth week. The assault
on the German lines in this area had been planned as the main
aggressive action to be taken by the British and French forces on
the western front in 1916. The notion still existed that it should
be possible to win the war by punching a hole in the German lines,
sweeping through it and driving towards Germany itself, and one
of the reasons for choosing this particular part of the front for attack
was that the ground was not already pock-marked with shell-holes
and so movement through it should be possible. The German
commanders had different ideas. They believed that they had
no need to make a massive breakthrough into France, but rather
they would bleed the country to death by a sustained attack on a
part of the line that was so crucial that the French would be forced
to throw all they had into its defence. The Germans had chosen
Verdun for their purpose, 150 miles south-east of the Somme, and
had launched their attack there in February. The losses among the
French had been so large in the long battle that followed that, when
the allies attacked on the Somme on 1 July, the French contribution
was much smaller than originally planned. The Somme became
predominantly a British battle, to which were brought the new
armies of volunteers largely inexperienced in war.

The plan for the first day of the battle was for the infantry to
advance on a 15 miles front at walking pace, for the most part up

hill, behind a moving curtain of British shells. A sustained preliminary bombardment had been meant to kill the Germans in their forward positions, or at least to keep them in the deep dug-outs that they had prepared in the chalky soil, until the British leapt into their trenches. The aim of the bombardment was not achieved. The waves of British troops, walking in lines with about a yard between each man, were mown down by the Germans firing their machine guns from the higher ground. By the end of the first day 21 000 British had been killed or were missing, most of the fatalities having occurred in the first hour.[12] This was to remain the heaviest British loss on any day in the war. Virtually the only advance was on a six-mile front at the right hand end of the allied line, and through July the British gradually fought their way to the higher ground on this limited front. The whole area became a maze of trenches and shell craters, with tree stumps marking what had once been woods and rubble marking the remains of farmhouses and villages. The German resistance remained solid, the fighting was continuous, the losses on both sides were enormous. This was the situation when the battalion reached the Somme area on 25 July.

Charles presented his record of what went on around him in the next four weeks in a section of *The Anatomy of Courage*, headed 'How Courage is Spent', and the story may be unfolded from that and the battalion war diary. The days in the war diary and in Charles's record are close but not always in exact agreement, but, given the circumstances in which the records were kept, this is not surprising. The battalion spent its first two weeks in the area training, seeking to profit by the experience gained in the early days of the battle. Attacks were practised up hill against trenches dug in a chalky hillside in weather that was very hot and dry. On 8 August according to the war diary (7 August according to Charles),[6] the battalion moved into the front line, relieving troops in the 1500 yards of trenches between Delville Wood and Trones Wood. The first bad day was 10 August, when the war diary recorded: 'B Coy were shelled by our own 9.2s losing 23 casualties mostly however were buried and bruised but all suffered severely from shock. Lt W van Greeson showed great gallantry in rescuing buried men, also Cpl J Scott who was himself buried, when dug out he rendered great assistance in getting others out. Capt CM Wilson, our MO also distinguished himself at this time.'[7] There were other succinctly recorded brave and gallant acts on that day. On the following day: 'Bosch [sic] shelled us this afternoon from 3 to 5. Casualties were small. Captain CM Wilson again distinguished himself by rendering aid and evacuating Major Musgrove who was wounded by shell fire in a CT [communication trench] near Trones Wood when on his way to the front line.'[7]

The battalion was then engaged for five days in digging new communication trenches and jumping off trenches, in preparation for an attack by the whole division (some 12 000 men) directed towards what remained of the village of Guillemont, 1000 yards ahead. At this stage the battalion's casualties included its commanding officer, and Hill, by then a major and the second-in-command, took over. It was characteristic of him that he could not get to sleep at night until he had visited the whole of the battalion's section of the front line. At the same time it tells something of the battalion that during the battle there were no sick, for none would ask for an easy ticket to the rear.[13] The battalion took up its position for the attack on Guillemont on 17 August and at once was heavily engaged. Repeatedly under bombardment and uncertain what was going on, Charles attended to casualties with his medical orderlies and fretted in his aid post, which was a captured dug-out full of German ammunition. After five days, on 22 August in the afternoon, the battalion was relieved. It marched by platoons to a point behind the lines where there were cookers with tea and where the officers' horses and buses for the men had been sent to meet them. Watching the platoons coming slowly down from the front line, Charles noticed the absence of those who had been longest with the battalion: 'Most of the old hands had gone out, here and there was an old face, but the best go first.' He reflected that they had sat for days under heavy shelling without leaving their trenches, 'the supreme cold-blooded test of the war.' That night those who had come back slept at a place called Happy Valley.

The battalion was at rest for a week. There were rumours that they had to go back again. 'It seems' Charles wrote 'that a division is dipped twice into the Somme, with perhaps a week's rest in between. The second time it is kept in until it has no further fighting value.' Then, on the evening of 31 August, as the officers sat down to dinner, a runner arrived with orders for them to move. They set off within minutes and this time their destination was the Carlton Trench, which was on the other side of Delville Wood from their previous position. The battalion war diary outlines what happened:

'. . . on way up, a heavy gas barrage was encountered. Guides having taken us in an entirely wrong direction, it was 3.00 am before A & C Coys. reached their position in Carlton Trench, and 6.00 am when B & D Coys. arrived. All the men and most officers were considerably affected by the gas from barrage. In afternoon Bn. was withdrawn to trenches near Montaubon for rest.'[7]

Charles's description of this nightmare journey, 'an eight hour pilgrimage in the gas' as he calls it, covers three pages of *The Anatomy of Courage*[6]. On reaching Carlton Trench he found colonels of five battalions in one dug-out and men packed in the trench like herrings. Observing that it was clear that they were not

Figure 5. Medical Officer in the RAMC, 1914-18 War. (Wellcome Institute Library, London; CMAC PP/CMW/P.6)

wanted, he asked why they were there. Hill answered in one word "Wind". Orders came to rest everyone who was suffering from gas, and after two days in which their fate was uncertain the battalion was withdrawn. For them the Somme in its physical sense was over, but Charles was only one of thousands who lived with its scars on his mind for the rest of his life. As Medical Officer he had directly or indirectly been concerned during its period at the Somme with the battalion's 403 casualties, 52 dead, 345 wounded and 6 missing. Among the awards for the battalion's operations were one DSO and five MCs, of which Charles received one. For him the citation read:

'Temp Capt C McM Wilson, MD, RAMC.
'For conspicuous gallantry and devotion to duty during operations. He worked for over an hour digging out wounded men at great personal risk. He then returned to his aid post and attended to the wounded. Later, hearing that an officer had been wounded, he passed through a hundred yards of the enemy's artillery barrage, dressed his wounds, and finally got him into safety as soon as the barrage permitted. On other occasions he has done fine and gallant work.'[14]

A few days after being withdrawn from the Somme the battalion went on leave, but less than three weeks later it was in the trenches again, this time in the middle of the British part of the front between Bethune and Arras. It remained there through the winter, first at Souchez in the Vimy sector and then near Loos. To Charles this third winter seemed interminable 'The awful sameness of the days fastened on my mind, till I prayed that anything might happen; but nothing did happen, until at last I gave up anticipating anything.'[6] People had changed and Charles with the rest. For days after coming out of the Battle of the Somme his irritability was a nuisance to those around him. On looking back he saw that something had happened to him and that he was never quite the same again. He was aware of a decline in his morale. He had watched most of those in the battalion for whom he had the greatest admiration, 'those who were meant by nature to lead men', being struck down. Before his eyes the best of a generation had gone. He wrote in his diary: 'There is a limit to the number of good men any race can furnish', and 'The morale of all armies broke sooner or later.' He was depressed and he now knew very clearly not only how fear was born but also how courage was spent.[6]

The monotony of that third winter with its cold and mud and with the steady attrition of men was broken by one event which, although it lasted for little more than an hour, was accorded a chapter in *The Anatomy of Courage* and a nine-page account in the battalion war diary.[15] It was a raid on the German trenches in the vicinity of Loos on the night of 14/15 January, 1917, which involved first cutting the wire in front of the battalion's trench, cutting of a gap in the enemy's wire by gunfire, and then a quick bombardment of the trenches to be raided. In the dark, at 10.34 pm, four officers and 110 other ranks passed through their own wire and formed up in no-man's land. As they crossed to the German trenches, a tape was laid to indicate the way back. On reaching the German line the four bombing parties climbed into the trenches and set off in different directions. They were followed by four search parties, two grenade-carrying parties, connecting parties and Lewis gunners to guard the flanks. As the bombing parties moved along the trenches they were soon met by Germans and a bloody fight began, the raiding party throwing bombs down the steps of the deep dug-outs from which Germans were trying to come out. Three Germans were taken as prisoners just as the yellow signal for withdrawal went up. Back in their own trenches, when casualties were counted the raiding party was found to have had two men killed and 29 wounded. The raiders themselves brought all the wounded back. Very early the following morning a General arrived and disturbed the sleeping officers in their dug-out to tell them that he regarded the raid as a great success. Charles observed that they turned over and were asleep again almost before he had left the dug-out.

When Charles had learnt of the projected raid and that eight stretcher bearers were to be included in the raiding party, he elected to accompany them and consequently was left with a vivid memory of a trip across the patches of snow in no-man's land, of the friendly craters, of a brief sojourn in the German trench, and of the wounded who claimed his attention. His fellow officers were bothered about his sense of direction and from the start one of them was detailed to look after him. Even so his servant had to run after him because he had forgotten the white armlet worn by the raiders to distinguish them in trench fighting from the enemy.[8] In the report of the raid in the war diary many names were mentioned with commendation, including Charles 'for his courage in laying [sic] out in no-man's [sic] land near the German wire during the enterprise so as to be handy in case a hitch occurred in the removal of the wounded in which he very materially assisted. He then went to the Dressing Station at the head of Boyeau 51 and attended to the wounded.'[15]

After the raid the battalion moved out of the line and a month later, on 21 February 1917, Charles's service with it ended. By then he was almost, if not the last, of the officers who had been with the battalion in the first winter; there had only been four left when they went into the Somme. He left no record of his departure or of his postings and experience in the rest of 1917. He was first posted to the 73rd Field Ambulance,[7] but the official record which might have thrown light on subsequent moves has not survived the passage of time.[16] The fly leaves of the army correspondence books in which he elaborated the diary of his time with the Royal Fusiliers, however, show that by August 1917 he was medical officer in charge of the Bedford Yeomanry and in September 1917 he was with the 37th Casualty Clearing Station. While he was with the Bedford Yeomanry he had a chance encounter that was to prove significant for him after the war, both professionally and personally. One day when setting out on leave he obtained a lift in a passing car in which there were two muffled officers who asked him about his work. When the car reached Boulogne he asked the driver who the officers were and was told that one of them was Sir Wilmot Herringham.[17] Herringham was consultant in medicine to the headquarters of the British Expeditionary Force in France, in civilian life he was a senior physician at St Bartholomew's Hospital, and he had recently retired as Vice Chancellor of the University of London.[18]

At the end of 1917 Charles had a complete change when he was posted to the British medical base at Boulogne where, at No. 7 Stationary Hospital, he was set to work to find out how the wastage of men from mustard gas could be checked.[13] Poison gas had first been used on the Western Front by the Germans in a surprise attack in the Ypres Salient in 1915, when chlorine, which is intensely irritating to the respiratory tract, had been released down-wind from cylinders in the German trenches. Increasingly sophisticated gas masks and drills were developed to cope with the choking gases like chlorine which came to be used by both the opposing armies, and it was through gas of this sort that Charles wandered with his battalion on that night on the Somme while trying to find Carlton Trench. In July 1917, again at Ypres, the Germans produced another surprise, this time with mustard gas. Following contamination with this substance, in a period that varies from minutes to several hours depending on the concentration, an intense inflammation of the skin starts which progresses to blistering, as in a burn, and the eyes quickly become painful and acutely inflamed so that the lids are held tightly shut. Most importantly from the point of view of risk to life, the whole of the lining of the respiratory tract can be burned from the nose, throat and windpipe right down to the lungs, leading to death from bronchopneumonia.

Mustard gas was used extensively by both sides from mid-1917 onwards and the high casualty rate that it caused was a big threat to the allies, whose shortage of manpower had become so critical that every possible casualty had to be returned to duty. The problem was that what might be called the natural history of mustard gas poisoning was unknown, and there was a feeling that too many casualties were getting through the nets at casualty clearing stations and at the base hospitals in France and were being returned to England, never to be seen again by their units. This was the situation when Charles set out to study the mustard gas casualties admitted to No. 7 Stationary Hospital. As a co-worker he had James Macalister Mackintosh, then aged 27, who had been a medical student when war broke out and had given up his studies and served in France with a commission in the 6th Cameron Highlanders. After being wounded he returned to his studies and graduated, and when he started work at Boulogne he was a captain in the Royal Army Medical Corps. After the war Mackintosh was to have a brilliant career in public health, culminating in appointment to the chair in that subject at the London School of Hygiene and Tropical Medicine.[19] He had a great capacity for making friends, and Charles became and remained one of them.

The findings of the study which extended right through 1918 and continued in the early months after the Armistice, were published in January, 1920 in the *Quarterly Journal of Medicine* under the names of CM Wilson and JM Mackintosh.[20] Introducing their report the authors noted that the medical profession in general had not grasped the significance of this new weapon of war because work related to it had been regarded as secret. It was now clear that the sequels of gassing would persist for years and that treatment would not be confined to army hospitals, so that all doctors needed to know about it.

They also aimed to go beyond the narrow consideration of after-effects that would help in treating pensioners, and to provide data which would in due course allow the full story of mustard gas to be told. Although they did not say it in so many words, they were seeking to put mustard gas into perspective as a weapon of war for they believed that it might be used again, and that only if the ways in which it caused losses were understood could losses be minimised. The paper contained a descriptive analysis of a consecutive series of 1500 mustard gas casualties admitted to No. 7 Stationary Hospital between 1 January and 31 October 1918. 'We hope', they wrote, 'by a careful examination of a number of casualties that is sufficiently large to justify broad conclusions, to determine the exact place of the functional and organic results of mustard gas poisoning in the history of the subject, the proper relation of the part to the whole, so we may know, not what may happen after gassing, but what did happen, and in what proportion of cases it so happened.' Their first conclusion was that nearly one quarter of their cases exhibited a functional nervous disorder. By this they meant symptoms with no demonstrable underlying tissue damage, or out of proportion to initial or residual damage. There were four main functional disorders, intolerance of light as a result of which patients screwed up their eyes, inability to speak or ability only to whisper, persistent vomiting, and a disorder called effort syndrome, the main symptoms of which were inordinate fatigue and breathlessness on the mildest exertion. Their other main conclusion was that, of the organic disorders, the effects of gas on the skin, the eyes and the respiratory tract were, as anticipated, the most important. But most significantly, of these 1500 patients, only 24 died; the mortality in other words, was under 2%. And, lasting organic disabilities were relatively few.[20]

Over the 10 months in which Charles and James Mackintosh were making their observations, they were not detached observers for they were involved in the care of the patients they were studying. In the trenches Charles had a reputation for ruthlessness in dealing with soldiers endowed with lesser degrees of fortitude, but now, in his capacity as a doctor behind the lines, he gave similar care to those whose minds, as he said, had suffered hurt as he gave to those who were injured physically.[13] In later years James Mackintosh told how at one time a German aeroplane used to fly over Boulogne at night and drop bombs. There was a young man who was recovering from his gassing who was terrified by these planes. Mackintosh asked him one morning 'How did you get on last night?' 'Oh,' he said, 'last night was all right. You see there was a kind doctor called Major Wilson who came and sat on my bed and talked to me all the time so I didn't worry about it.' That, said Mackintosh, was the kind of thing Charles used to do.[21]

The involvement of the two investigators in the care of the patients led them, during the course of their study, to develop policies about treatment. They argued from their growing experience that, since in mustard gas poisoning the mortality is only 2%, the efficiency of this gas as a weapon of warfare must depend on the number of men gassed, and on the average length of time a man is incapacitated. They considered the casualties under two headings: gassed men who never left France but were returned to duty through convalescent camps, and the graver types of casualty who were sent to England as stretcher cases. They proceeded to record their experience with 559 cases admitted over five weeks when the deliberate policy was to curtail the period between gassing and discharge from hospital to convalescent camps. During those five weeks 2% were evacuated to England, 1% died and the rest were detained until they could march half a mile in their equipment to a camp. This test was passed within a month of gassing by 87% of all the admissions, and by over one half of the cases within 14 days. This led Charles and Mackintosh to a final comment: 'Bearing in mind that some of the less seriously gassed men do not reach the Base, but are retained in casualty clearing stations and corps gas stations, the fact that 87% of all who arrive at the Base can march within a month is a partial answer to the question of the efficiency of mustard gas in war.'[20]

Note on Sources for time with the Royal Fusiliers 1914-1917

Charles's story can be pieced together from several sources. For much of the time he kept what he used to describe as a diary, which consisted of scribblings in army notebooks and on the backs of orders, on odd sheets of paper and on old envelopes.[1] His avowed purpose was not to amuse others but, as he put it, to protect himself:

'It was at Ypres about the middle of 1915 that I began to keep a Diary. The long summer days found me idle and in a place like the Salient you must have something to do to keep normal. I often envied the other officers their daily round, the hundred and one duties in connection with their men. To do nothing, to be forever waiting is very difficult in trench life. There is time for reflection, and to begin thinking in this sort of existence is soon fatal.'[1]

Whatever his initial intention, some of the writing in the notebooks assumed autobiographical form, but by the time he came to publish his 'diary' 20 years later during the Second World War, it was presented in a totally different way, being scattered through the small book called *The Anatomy of Courage*.[6] Autobiographical material from these writings provides one source of information about his life with the battalion. The War Diaries of the battalion provide a second source.[7] They trace the battalion's fortunes for all but the first six months of 1916; the record for that period is missing. These diaries consist of daily pencilled entries, usually brief but containing at least references to place, weather, action if any and casualties. Charles appears in these pages from time to time. A third source of information has been Colonel MVB Hill, who is graphically portrayed under his own name in *The Anatomy of Courage*. Hill was a second lieutenant commanding a platoon when Charles joined the battalion. During the Somme battle, 20 months later, he was in command of it. In 1980 at the age of 93, on hearing of an intended biography, Colonel Hill offered to help by 'providing some tit-bits'[8] which he supplemented in a conversation in 1981.

Chapter 4

Reluctant Physician

On the 11 November 1918, following hard on the outbreak of revolution in Germany and mutiny in the German fleet, an armistice was signed. On the western front the advance of the allied forces, which now included troops from the USA, had pushed the Germans so far back through northern France and Belgium that, when the firing stopped at 11.00 am, they stood virtually on the line of the opening battles of August 1914. At sea the Royal Navy escorted 129 surrendered German submarines into Harwich and the main German fleet into the Firth of Forth. There was no particular reason to notice that, on Armistice Day, a lance-corporal of the 16th Bavarian Infantry reserve division was lying in a German hospital apparently blinded by the gas whose effects Charles and James Mackintosh were studying in Boulogne. His name was Adolf Hitler.[1]

Except that casualties stopped, the Armistice brought little immediate change in the lives of many in the forces. In Britain five million men had to be reabsorbed into civilian life, and a general election in December endorsed some popular but little thought-out ideas such as 'Homes fit for heros', 'Hang the Kaiser', and make Germany pay for what the war had cost. Meanwhile, Charles's commission to get the story of mustard gas casualties straight continued, and he was transferred to Cambridge, where treatment with oxygen of the after-effects of gas poisoning was being studied. There he shared lodgings with John Ryle, another temporary RAMC officer, who was to become a physician on the staff of Guy's Hospital. The work in Cambridge was being done under the direction of Joseph Barcroft, a leader in the great Cambridge school of physiologists. Barcroft was interested in the way in which oxygen was transferred in the lungs from the air into the blood, and how the red blood cells gave it up as they passed through capillaries in the tissues. By the time Charles arrived in Cambridge, Barcroft had had three glass cubicles built in which gassed patients could live while the concentration of oxygen in the air that they breathed was altered at will.[2] He had collected around him a small group of assistants, referred to as the Firm,[3] which was very much a family affair and which included a young science graduate, Miss Dorothy Dufton. By January 1919, Dorothy was writing to her mother: 'Major Wilson is very amusing, he's got an extraordinarily acute brain and he's a fearful cynic—but very good company and a stimulating conversationalist. I admire him for living up to his convictions.'[4]

55

Since the Armistice soon brought the project on gassed patients to an end, the Firm was not very busy and Cambridge was full of gaiety, with dances which Dorothy loved, and musical evenings at which she played the violin. 'I am having *such* dissipations!' she wrote to her mother, 'I don't know if it's the outbreak of peace or Bolshevism or what—but I've got a fever for getting the most out of life—which seems to be offering a good many excitements.'[5] The spring was frosty and Dorothy and Charles went for long walks and skated on the frozen fens, and then, on 25 March Dorothy wrote to ask her parents' permission to be engaged to what she called her medicine-man.[6] The Duftons gave their blessings. Dorothy was 24 and Charles was 36. Dorothy came from a close-knit family living in Leeds. Her father, Samuel Felix Dufton, was a doctor of science, and there was some surprise when he forsook the laboratory, where he was concerned with developing smokeless fuels, and became one of His Majesty's Inspectors of Schools in the West Riding of Yorkshire.[7] Dorothy had followed her father's scientific bent and had gone to Girton College, Cambridge, in 1913 to read Natural Sciences. In 1916 she graduated as a Bachelor of Arts and was awarded the first year's income of £160 from the Royal Society's Lawrence Fund to enable her to work on pneumonia produced by poisonous gases.[8] Her work prospered and in January 1917 she gave a communication at a meeting of the Physiological Society held at the King's College, London.[9] Her work also brought her an award of an MBE. When she met Charles she was planning to enrol as a medical student, but her engagement put an end to this ambition.

The day after they became engaged, Charles left Cambridge for the army hospital at Netley in Hampshire to be demobilised and a few days later Dorothy rejoined her parents at their home in Leeds, where she received a loving letter from Mrs Barcroft bemoaning the fact that, unlike her husband, she had not had an opportunity for a farewell embrace.[10] Dorothy also received a letter from John Ryle, now in London, with warm good wishes from himself and his wife:

'I am awfully glad to hear that freedom has come to our old Bolshevist at last. It was a great privilege to share rooms with him for that three months in Cambridge, and to find—after years in France which made me a little despondent at times about men's minds and faiths and energies—one who possesses, as you know better than I do, such gifts and humour and more than one kind of courage.

'It was a happy chapter altogether, and the gloom which we discussed so often will not be found in its re-perusal. The mists and floods of Cambridge will not linger in my thoughts so much as the sunshine of the past few days, and the kindly destiny it has

Figure 6. Portrait of Dorothy by Kay Vaughan, 1922. (Wellcome Institute Library, London)

provided for you two has almost inspired me with a faith in its academic atmosphere—which we were at such pains to deride.'[11]

During their engagement Dorothy and Charles wrote to each other frequently, and since Dorothy kept many of Charles's letters the story of the next three months can be traced from them. While waiting at Netley for his discharge, Charles's mind was still on his research on mustard gas. He wondered what the mechanism was that caused the early symptoms. Was it chemical poisoning or was it something else? In his first letter to Dorothy he raised some critical questions:

'If you meet Barcroft—don't bother to see him specially about it— ask him whether he thinks toxaemia seen in early stages of mustard gas poisoning was due to 1. the gas, or 2. to bacterial infection? And if to the gas, how long after gassing would the mustard gas exist in the body or exist as one of the two products of hydrolysis (ie) how long after gassing are chemical bodies there to poison? I think toxaemia was due to secondary bacterial infections but Barcroft may have views.'[12]

He was not getting on well with writing the actual paper. Not only did he find it hard to concentrate but he was gloomy and in a lonely way he dissected and questioned what was going on in the wider world where the peace treaties were being thrashed out.

'I went for a walk this afternoon and pondered a little on all sorts of things—there's no doubt you think more away from the towns and not working—on self deception as beautifully demonstrated by the *Daily Mail*'s "big four" in Paris: on our failure in Egypt and on a host of other things. And right at the end came to wonder what it is leads to right judgements of things and men?'[12]

Charles was discharged from the army on 4 April, as 'fit for general service' and destined 'for disposal',[13] and next day he headed for his parent's lodgings in Ealing, calling on the way at St Mary's.[14] Now he was free, his immediate aim was to pick up his career at the hospital and he foresaw hospital affairs keeping him in London for the next ten days. But he was unsettled and found himself, as he put it, out of conceit with his particular world.[15] He saw John Ryle and picked up the gossip and it bothered him particularly to hear that powerful people in the medical research world seemed to be using their influence to fill some newly created academic posts in teaching hospitals with laboratory people instead of people with clinical skills. At St Mary's no appointments had been made to the hospital's honorary staff during the war so that the lines for the physician's appointment were re-drawn as they were in August 1914. It would be Charles versus Hope Gosse, who in 1914 had been appointed assistant physician at the prestigious Brompton Hospital for Consumption and Diseases of the Chest and during the war had served in the RAMC in hospitals in Mesopotamia. Not only were the aspirants for the job the same, but so were the two factions on the staff.[16] Support for Charles stemmed from Wilfred Harris and

for Gosse from William Willcox, who, like his protegé, had lately
returned from Mesopotamia, where he had been a consultant to the
armies. Willcox, for all his aura of authority (he had come to public
notice for his identification of the drug hyoscine as the poison used
by Dr Crippen to murder his wife), was a slow hesitant speaker who
looked like a country squire, rode a horse in Hyde Park and hunted
in Leicestershire[17] and he was not one of Charles's favourite people.
After two days in London, Charles summarised his position to
Dorothy:

'I don't know about Mary's. What I can do I've done. The results
of independence have been, I think, largely lived down but I'm
up against intangible things.

'Willcox, quite apart from the election [to the forthcoming
physician's appointment], aspires to play a more prominent part
at Mary's, where he has never held the same position that he enjoys
in medico-legal circles and lately in military in Mespots. To bring
this about he seeks to weaken hold of people like Harris (who
dislikes him) over lay board. This he does by crafty inoculation
of their minds with creed that Harris is so prosperous he takes
no interest in the School etc. Some of these devious deeds are doing
me harm by weakening the position of my party. At one time
discoveries so unsavoury would have depressed me but the war
put that right. It was one of the great finds that men in bulk are
honest if stupid and that from the circles which are made up of
heads of things, a totally false impression is gained of human
nature.

'On the whole if it comes to a fight I think I should win, but there
will be a lot of dust. . . . Rotten game isn't it? Yet to avoid it is
the taking the veil business all over again. On the other side its
quite charming to find the unqualified or recently so bringing one
all the latest local Rugger gossip; whatever happens I'm the
member for the people at Mary's! Rather curious this considering
how I always lived by the sword at Mary's damning everything
that did not meet with the royal approval, as some petulant youth
put it.'[16]

The St Mary's appointment and the gas paper were not Charles's
only preoccupations. He was working on what he called his magnum
opus, which he had already discussed with Dorothy. From Ealing
he wrote to her:

'I toil in an uninspired sort of way at the gas paper; it hasn't the
attractions for me that "magnum opus" has. For one thing there
seems so little object in publication except for motives of expediency.

In case of "opus" have always wanted to point out the error of lumping everyone in France together and the injustice of method to the best people; to produce a suitable tribute to people who played the game is worth some trouble. But I'm not certain I have the necessary technique at hand to make the tribute fitting for their ways and the things they did.'[18]

The opus referred to was the autobiographical material that Charles had worked on during the war, which eventually saw the light of day 25 years later in *The Anatomy of Courage*. In these early months after demobilization, Charles not only retained his boyhood ambition to be a writer but rated this high among his priorities. Nevertheless, he found it hard at this time to be enthusiastic about anything, and even a visit to Twickenham to see New Zealand versus the Country at rugger did not dispel his gloom.

'Virile show much spoilt by free kicks for rule infringements . . . looks like being a vile Easter. Wish we could desert this climate. Every year I gravitate towards the sun as a deity. . . . I believe if we'd perfect days as happens once a month, I'd be a sunny optimist! Could one be a Bolshevist in eternal sunshine and blue up above?'[19]

Explaining in a letter to Dorothy's parents that the need to attend to hospital matters and difficulties in replacing his wardrobe accounted for his delay in visiting them in Leeds,[20] Charles next set off for St Leonard's to retrieve his civilian clothes that had been put into storage with his parents' furniture when he joined up in 1914. He ended his letter to Dorothy:

'I think a few good slaps with a wooden club down the fairway and a perfect still spring day with distant lap of waves below cliffs will be attractive after Praed Street.'[19]

Charles spent a week at St Leonard's basing himself on the East Sussex Club. After two days going through stored trunks and furniture his mood was still low, and he found that 18 holes of golf made him very weary. A dismal self-appraisal was sent off to Dorothy:

'At present there seems no sanity in friendship: twenty percent of men I know blindly believe I'm quite the sort of thing met once in a lifetime; forty percent hate me and rest vote on grounds that a man is worth supporting who will always fight the seniors and carry no airs with juniors.'[21]

The fairway and distant lap of waves below the cliffs must have worked their charm, for after a few days a sense of humour returned.

Complaining of the number of letters he had to write, Charles commented to Dorothy:

'How can anyone write or read or think in a club? Two specimens of the usual club breed are exchanging prejudices. X has just lamented that poor M should have chosen Primrose Day* for his demise. "He was always so keen on it." Y: "Primrose day seems to be dying out". X: "I'd like to know what is alive now". The waning interest in Primrose Day was to X a portent of crumbling civilisation.'[22]

A member of the club had befriended him and played golf with him.

'My Scot plays a steady pawky game with a favourite club on the tees. In the middle of the promising attack in a bogey competition he lent me the weapon. I didn't hit the ground but it parted into two pieces. My Scot took it well and took to driving with a mashie.'[22]

Charles also indulged in some self-analysis. Rugby football and everything that went with it continued to engross him, and in his first more relaxed mood he tried to explain his attitude:

'Heard today from man I once lived with who married maid with voice and brain. Dardenelles and dysentery have robbed him of much of his physical attraction but in the early days he was one of the young Greeks who in friezes gaze tranquilly into distance; his early expression may even have been the mask concealing very little but here at last is an instance of the happiest failure in detachment: I suppose to the end the business will be carried on in Rugger, young animal phase in which it began and has been since, quite free of any affair of the wits, or community of tastes; in the beginning instinct and now ossified by a sort of sentiment.'[22]

The week of peace and reflection at St Leonards would have been the first real holiday that Charles had had for over four years, and now for the first time he had someone with whom he could communicate on equal terms and without inhibition. By the end of the week he felt a fit of energy that he hoped would last and he set down for Dorothy his list of priorities:

'. . . I want regular work and something to contend with. I've been out at grass since Christmas. Now I must set out to tackle something or someone.'[18]

---

*Primrose Day 19th April: Anniversary of death in 1881 of Benjamin Disraeli, Earl of Beaconsfield, Leader of the Conservative Party in England.

First he must finish the gas paper. Then he must rub up his medicine for coaching students; he thought he was pretty rusty for he had read nothing medical for about five years—a common enough comment for a doctor to make who had been on active service through the war. Then he must find a flat to live in when they were married, which would be after June, when the outcome of the staff appointment at St Mary's would be known. As soon as the gas paper was out of the way, he would work regularly on the magnum opus, and if Dorothy would tackle the First Winter part of it, he said, he would make an effort to get it into final shape.

After a short visit to the Duftons in Leeds in late April, Charles went to live in digs, near his parents, in Windsor Road, Ealing and a few minutes on the train from St Mary's. He was uncomfortably placed, being as it were in, but not of, the hospital. His future hinged on his winning the appointment as a physician to outpatients, the vacancy for which was due to be advertised at the end of May.

By seeking to become a physician on the staff of a London teaching hospital, Charles was making a bid to join the élite of the medical profession. He was a typical starter for such a post, the son of a doctor, from a family with limited means and without connections in the higher ranks of society.[23] If he were to win, it would be entirely on his own merits, and he would have to face the years of financial stringency that were the lot of the young consultant in the days when hospital staff appointments were honorary. On this theme he wrote to Dorothy:

'I've promised to coach a man for MRCP: to act as assistant examiner for London MB about middle of May, which only means that you get cases together, and assist examiners, without examining (work usually done by registrars), but it brings in £15-20 and every little bit counts: and when in good temper go third on railways. Beyond that have done nothing so far to feather nest but am quite confident will raise wind somehow somewhere. With economy must aim at paying expenses first year, except furnishings. This is contrary to what everyone says can be done in consulting work when takings (nice word) all come in a few years after long wait but with a bit of effort it can be done I should think. But perhaps (is it well to admit it?) worth it, eh? That would leave our magnificent capital of £1500 less outlay on furniture as basis of fund on which eventually we shall see something of world. I'll end by being a financier which has hitherto not been among my failings. If I get no fixed part-time job it will mean using my wits more than I've done lately. What a game. Seems a far cry from Jermyn Street* ideal of other days.'[24]

---

*A centre of publishing houses.

A few days later there was more on the same subject:

'Great blow: find in BMJ* May 5 that I relinquished acting rank of Major on reposting, so drop over £200. Its amusing. I give up 500 patients [at Boulogne] for Springfield [at Cambridge]: to lose 10 shillings daily plus 6 shillings daily (difference between major and captain's pay) and now drop £200 odd: all of which not of my own willing but theirs. . . . One has to be a bit of a philosopher in life. However, though Cambridge was thoroughly bad move in every way but one, perhaps it was worth it, eh?

'The flat outlook is almost hopeless: if we are driven into Rooms you must have some lap game to play with as it would be a thin game sitting in digs on your lonesome.

'Phillips who was examining has taken to his bed so this [acting as an assistant examiner] may go west too. Also he was to propose formal motion that there shall be two vacancies and won't be able to. So its a sombre world. I have decided to give up *The Times* falling back on the *Express* of the home circle: a dreadful rag.'[25]

Dr Phillips's proposed motion that there should be two vacancies in the staff at St Mary's reflected a search for middle ground between the pro-Wilson and pro-Gosse parties. The letter continued:

'Sometimes wonder what paternal bird would think if he knew exact financial prospects his daughter is embracing. But its no good explaining, because its all intangible, a maze of ifs and contingencies. I don't find I worry about it but sometimes fear this is incorrigible self confidence, innate and acquired. I think it amuses me: certainly to tide over usual waiting period, which seems to offer not a penny anywhere save journalism and coaching, will require ingenuity.'[25]

Charles and Dorothy could not fix a date for their wedding until they knew the outcome of the staff appointment in June and whether, supposing Charles won it, he would be allowed leave for a honeymoon in July. Meanwhile, it was decided that they would be married in Leeds and they agreed that their finances could run to a honeymoon in Scotland.[26] After unsuccessfully canvassing the idea of being married in a registry office, Charles left the arrangements to the Duftons, commenting to Dorothy:

'People with life before them are apt to forget that to the elders small things take a significance and that way this business is done, which is of only a passing moment to us, may to them loom larger. . . .'[27]

*British Medical Journal.

As to his own family's involvement he wrote:

> 'The Mater says if it is to be a splash the Wilson clan ought
> to be represented. The Mater and Pater won't be able for
> journey. . . . My relatives are all in Ireland: if there's a beano I
> don't see how this clan (except my brother) is to be represented.
> We might publish in the [*Yorkshire*] *Post* that the Wilson family
> has no objection!'[28]

Charles continued to be concerned about his health, and like many
of his generation he blamed the war:

> 'I have got another of my vile colds and feel peevish and rotten.
> Wish I could get fit again, everything has been an effort for some
> months now.

> 'Suppose it is only inevitable payment after 2 years getting soaked
> and not changing with the battalion. Perhaps this summer will
> help matters. I loathe being unfit like an old woman. In France
> I never missed a day through illness.'[29]

A yearning for the sun was another continuing theme. A letter
headed Sunday started:

> 'The Mater and sister are churching and I've been working. Dull
> game. Full summer here: I'd like to sit in some old garden and
> dabble in books, with winters dedicated to wandering in Algiers,
> California or wherever the sun makes life genial.'[24]

As the date of the appointment at St Mary's approached, there
was a pressing need to finish the paper on mustard gas.[30] Charles
had no publications to his name and one was needed to offset what
he described as his frivolous habit of acting as a battalion medical
officer. Gosse had published several papers. It was not that the
magnum opus was taking up all his time, for, although Dorothy was
exhorted to be ultra-critical about it, Charles was becoming
disenchanted with it:

> 'On whole I came to conclusion that it missed being *the* war book
> through technical faults. Feel certain if my idea was carried out
> with proper technique it will be something not done so far and
> worth doing. But it is a business of many days.'[31]

Meanwhile the writings of others were a source of mutual interest.
Charles was reading William Wilberforce's *Cardinal Newman* in
the train south after his visit to the Duftons in Leeds,[32] and in their
letters to each other he and Dorothy compared the literary styles
of Walter Pater and Meredith.

On 30 May one vacancy for the staff position of St Mary's was advertised in the *Lancet*. Applications closed on 7 June and Charles learnt that they would be considered by the Medical Committee of the hospital on the 16th and that the actual appointment would be made by the Board of Management a few days later. Starting a letter to Dorothy on 2 June, 'I've always held the Napoleonic dictum that however probable is victory, it is well to anticipate defeat. . . .' Charles once more compared his position with that of Gosse:

'You must not run away with impression that I shall defeat Gosse through merit alone; perhaps it will be mainly result of superior strategy. Two things will get me home I believe: one, impression always prevalent at Mary's that if I wanted I could do things; two, war record.'[33]

At this stage Charles decided to invite one very significant person from outside St Mary's, Dr TR Elliott, to provide a testimonial for him. In 1913 Elliott had been elected Fellow of the Royal Society at the age of thirty-six for his brilliant work on the transmission of nerve impulses, and during the war he was the trusted adviser in France to the Medical Research Committee, which later became the Medical Research Council.[34] In that capacity he had been concerned with the mustard gas project and with Charles's transfer from Boulogne to Cambridge at the end of the war[25] and Charles saw him to be one of the key people in moves that were being made to develop academic medicine now that the war was over. Elliott's comments would certainly carry a lot of weight. So far as local sponsorship was concerned, it was customary for applicants for positions on the staff of London teaching hospitals to call on all staff members. Charles, moving his parents from London back to Hastings, coping with an invitation to take Dorothy to stay with the Maurices in Marlborough and involved with the final plans for his wedding, faced the first week in June without enthusiasm:

'Next week will be very unpleasant: a week of social penance calling on people who don't want to see me, a role I'm not exactly cut out for but I shan't be impatient with them. I feel exactly like your dog in pursuit of his tail because I've a hundred things to do and once one job is finished another waits and is overdue.'[35]

Then there was a rumour that two appointments would be confirmed, but this brought a new cause for anxiety, as Charles explained to Dorothy:

'Medical Committee decided yesterday to recommend Board to make two vacancies. They will do this. Then it is a fight for who is to be made the senior. This clears deck and means a sort of insurance that loser in fight will not be very much worse off than winner. I don't like compromises, but impatience is a poor thing and its necessary to get on Mary's to do anything in consultant work. I must be senior as I want to be Dean when Broadbent retires and as supernumerary my chances might be less. It won't be easy as my supporters think makes no difference who is senior and I can't explain my reasons, which would all sound to them impossibly ambitious, as Dean is generally and always at Mary's a senior, who has been on staff for about 10 years. . . .

'However, once at Mary's I'll make an attempt to pull School together and if I fail it will be a really good jumping off place for search for a better job.'[36]

At its meeting on 16 June the Medical Committee considered the applications of Charles and Gosse for the position of physician to outpatients, and the Committee's recommendations went to the Board of Management which met three days later, on 19 June in the afternoon. Charles and Gosse were interviewed by the Board and without further ado were told the Board's decision. Charles was appointed to the vacant post and Gosse to an additional one permitted by the by-laws. Charles ranked senior.

In a letter headed '6.40 pm', Charles wrote to Dorothy:

'It's strange affair, matrimony (or is it senility?—yes, 36). Here I am in digs alone an hour after result: I shall have two poached eggs on some toast with coffee at a Lyons shop as my dinner, write some letters, do a little thinking, and go to bed. There was a time when it would have been differently celebrated. I suppose it's last thing you might suspect but I've been as long as memory serves a perfect martyr to shyness! I've overcome it in ordinary everyday intercourse, but it still pursues me at committees, etc., unless I'm fighting something or someone, when it vanishes. I met Gosse in ante-room, and he told me I'd got it and he was to be additional, and so things being foregone I was very shy before committee! However doubtless one day they'll be surprised to find me in another role. They called us in in alphabetical order and read through our applications to us, and asked if they were correct, a procedure to let lay board have a look at us, which must have been entirely in Gosse's favour, for he was beautifully turned out in morning coat, etc., and I was in my Leeds costume, being too lazy to get into a morning coat on a hot day, though I went as far as unpacking it! Then after a pause they called me in and told me I was appointed. Harris got up and came across and shook hands, which was last public display of long-continued support. Then [Sir John] Broadbent did ditto, which left me cold. I did not feel slightest sense of triumph over him and his campaign, just a pity and contempt for anyone who in position of advantage sets out to stamp out a junior—and fails. . . .

'Galpin took me over to a squadron to get up in air, but owing to shortage of air mechanics, there was nothing doing. Then he got his gun and we wandered round grounds and links and he bagged two rabbits. I don't like seeing animals blotted: a curious feminine trait. Think it would be different if they stood an earthly. I'd not mind doing in a tiger who was out to do me in.

'Gosse told me he had his first patient today, a judge. Was in heart about it. I've no ambitions this way. His future is at the bedside

Figure 7. Wedding photograph, Leeds, 15 July 1919. (Wellcome Institute Library, London; CMAC PP/CMW/P.21)

and he'll be an immense success there—as a heart specialist. I hope if mine is to be ditto it will be a hospital bed and not the brass business of Mayfair.

'Now there's time to breathe and look round. Here's the opportunity, the picked place in the profession. I wish I could raise an atom of enthusiasm over it all. And I wish ever so much I'd left all scientific things alone and kept to writing and the control of men in which I think with the apprenticeship I've given to medicine I might now have done something.'[37]

So did the reluctant physician take up his appointment. One month later Charles and Dorothy were married at Mill Hill Chapel, Park Row, Leeds, according to the rites and ceremonies of the Unitarians.[38] Their honeymoon in Scotland is illuminated by a brief letter dated 30 July 1919 to Dorothy from Charles's father:

'Have you any rooms when you get back to London? Charlie is not very fond of long walks, but you seem to have changed his views on that matter. The Trossacks would be very nice to tramp through, but, as you say, the luggage is always a difficulty on a walking expedition.'[39]

Chapter 5

St Mary's Hospital

Charles's father was not the only one to post a letter to the honeymoon couple on 30 July. EH Kettle, the pathologist on the staff at St Mary's, wrote to tell Charles of continuing dissensions in the place. 'Fresh rows' he wrote, 'spring up like mushrooms, and I never know from day to day which of them hate each other.'[1] Morale certainly was at rock bottom, and few could have foreseen that what had become a badly organised medical school in decrepit buildings would before long change into one of the finest schools in the country.

The man at the helm during this change was Charles Wilson and to understand his achievement it is necessary to take account not only of the school itself but also of what had been going on in medical education in late Victorian London. When the medical school at St Mary's started in 1854, the physicians and surgeons taught all the subjects in the medical course except chemistry and natural philosophy—later to be called physics.[2] The appointments held by Dr William Broadbent reflect the versatility of that generation. On his path to an appointment as a physician in 1864, and later to a baronetcy and fellowship of the Royal Society, Broadbent at various times taught comparative anatomy, physiology, pathology and midwifery as well as medicine. But the days when Broadbent could comprehend all of medicine and the sciences on which it was based had already passed with the explosion of knowledge that had occurred before he died in 1907. By then the atom had proved not to be the ultimate unit of elementary matter, invisible rays called X-rays had been discovered which did not behave like light rays, and a new branch of science called biochemistry, which was concerned with living things, was taking shape despite notions reminiscent of the middle ages that attempts to understand biological phenomena were presumptuous and irreverent. Animal life had been shown to depend on photosynthesis in plants. And another new branch of science, microbiology, had developed, as a result of which a number of diseases were for the first time shown to be due to specific bacteria. It was small wonder the physicians and surgeons of the London teaching hospitals gradually retreated from their positions of omnipotence and allowed the appointment in their places of full-time teachers in pre-clinical subjects. Full-time appointments of lecturers in physiology, anatomy, pathology and bacteriology were gradually made so that the major pre-clinical subjects came to be headed by men with strong academic backgrounds who were dedicated to careers not only in teaching but also in research. The clinical

69

subjects—medicine, surgery and obstetrics—remained, however, entirely in the hands of the visiting consultants on the staffs of the hospitals.

This was the situation in 1910 when the largely autonomous London medical schools found themselves to be a focal point of interest to a Royal Commission appointed to review the working of the University of London. The chairman of the Commission was Richard Burdon Haldane, at the time Secretary of State for War, a statesman of great ability and a respected scholar. In reviewing the teaching of medicine, in which the university gave degrees, the Haldane Commission not only received submissions from London medical teachers but also sought and heard views from overseas. The most important of the overseas witnesses was Abraham Flexner who had been appointed by Andrew Carnegie's recently formed Foundation for the Advancement of Teaching to study medical education in the United States, Canada and Europe. In its report the Commission observed that the statement Flexner submitted and the evidence he gave in support of it 'contained a somewhat severe criticism of some aspects of teaching in the London medical schools. . . .'[3] The gist of his criticism was that, in contrast with what had happened in the pre-clinical subjects, no progress had been made towards formulating the concept of the clinician as a teacher. Clinical teaching in London remained an incident in the life of busy consultants appointed not by the University but by the hospitals. Furthermore there was no interaction between the fundamental scientists, with their burgeoning knowledge, and the clinicians who lacked the time, even if they had the training, which would enable them to bring to bear upon clinical problems the artillery which chemist and pharmacologist were forging.[4] While the London teaching hospitals were, according to Flexner, admirably designed for the care of the sick, they were not equipped and organised for teaching of university quality.

The Commission saw that the principle underlying Flexner's argument was that university teaching in clinical medicine, as in all other subjects, could be given only by men who were actively and systematically engaged in the advancement of knowledge of the subject they taught. To achieve this Flexner advocated the appointment of a new group of salaried university professors in the clinical disciplines. The Haldane Commission was a long drawn out affair, and it was a year after Flexner gave his evidence that the Commission heard at first hand from Friederick von Müller, professor of clinical medicine in the University of Munich, how such an arrangement worked in Germany. (When describing the capital and maintenance costs of his own medical school, von Müller managed incidentally to introduce the comment. 'You see that Germany not only spends great sums on the Army and Navy, I say for the prevention of war, but also much money for medical purposes, and therefore for the prevention of disease.')[5]

It was left to Sir William Osler, a Canadian who had come to the Regius chair of medicine in Oxford via the Johns Hopkins medical school, to introduce to the Commission an idea which, while falling short of the revolutionary notion of a complete university hospital advocated by Flexner, nevertheless allowed for the introduction of a few full-time university clinical staff into existing hospitals. Osler believed that what he called the Clinical Unit was the answer. A clinical unit would be under the complete control of the university, or under the joint control of the hospital and university, and it would be headed by a professor or director with charge of 60 or more beds and associated laboratories. The visiting honorary hospital staff would remain independent and would continue to teach in parallel.[6]

The Haldane Commission in its final report to parliament in 1913 favoured Flexner's and Osler's approach, concluding that there was a need to appoint and pay professors of the various branches of clinical medicine and surgery who would devote the greater part of their time to teaching and research.[7] The response of the Board of the Faculty of Medicine of the University of London in December 1913 was to emphasise what the Commission had indeed recognised, that everything in clinical education in London was not bad. The wealth of clinical material and the number of clinical teachers available were envied on the Continent and in America. The Board also noted the extraordinary sensitivity of any move that involved introducing university-appointed clinical professors into the proudly independent teaching hospitals. But despite their reservations the Board conceded that the University atmosphere would best be created with least disturbance by the appointment in each medical school of one or more professors of clinical subjects. In November 1913, without waiting for the university's response, the Board of Education, which held the government purse-strings, started to sound out the hospitals about the Commission's recommendations. The Medical School Committee at St Mary's expressed no great enthusiasm but was concerned that the hospital should be in a position to compete for clinical units if they were offered, and some preliminary steps were agreed upon.[8] The Committee, however, was overtaken by the long summer vacation and when it next met in October the country was at war and four years were to pass before university units and clinical professors again became agenda items.

Although negotiations over the Haldane Commission's recommendations lapsed during the war, the matter was not shelved by the Board of Education, whose Chief Medical Officer was Sir George Newman, a Quaker with a liking for resounding prose who, in his leisure, anonymously edited the Friends' *Quarterly Examiner*.[9] In July 1918 Newman's *Notes on Medical Education in England*[10] was published and in it he came down firmly in favour of clinical

units of the sort described by Osler. No sooner was the war over than
the Board of Education approached four hospitals about setting up
units with clinical directors in medicine, surgery and obstetrics.[11]
St Mary's was not among them. At this stage, in May 1919, Charles
felt so desperately that no one had things under control at St Mary's
that he intervened, undeterred by the fact that there was still a
month to go before his appointment to the staff would be considered
and that consequently he had no official status. He contrived that
a like-minded colleague, CA Pannett, who was a junior member of
the surgical staff, should see Newman. There was no obvious line
of communication between such a junior staff member and the Chief
Medical Officer, and the arrangement was made through Godfrey
Maurice who had a brother in the Department of Education. Charles
described what happened to Dorothy:

'The future of Marys seems to be in the lap of fools. Pannett saw
Newman, as I suggested to him, Maurice's brother arranging the
interview.

'Newman said treasury grant was not confined to any number
of schools such as four; the Professors of Medicine and Surgery
is *sine qua non* of a grant; that Mary's "must look slippy"
if it had a scheme in mind as other schools had theirs submitted
and now under consideration; that education authorities
must approve men suggested as Professors; that teaching
anatomy, physiology, chemistry physics and biology must be
also approved.

'So much for their demands. In what position are we able to meet
them, are we even willing to try and meet them? The self interest
of many of senior consultants is against appointment of Professors
because: (1) it means glorification of one of their number at expense
of rest; (2) sixty beds are minimum for each Professor which must
come out of the number they, the others, have for [the] 20 years
they spend on senior staff. There will be opposition and plenty of
it to reinforce habitual inertia and dislike of change. As to ability
to meet demands, presuming school decides to attempt to, there
are great difficulties: (1) finances—Treasury only pays 60% of large
expense incurred. No London School that is not run at a loss; no
endowments worth calling such ie a hand to mouth existence on
students fees and treasury grant; (2) our school buildings are simply
deplorable and want rebuilding; (3) any question of bringing in
an Outsider as Professor would raise storm. The logic is relentless;
I try to force it on them. They admit we cannot go on without grant;
that grant will soon be withdrawn if we don't toe the line as they—
education people—wish, in a word that the school must slowly die
unless we take up scheme.

'But in spite of all there seems little prospect of a move. There is no one with the drive to overcome the strong opposition. I have to work through Pannett. Think given two years I could pull show round but point is will we be given the time. It is an amazing position. See exactly what must be done and how to do it with minimum of friction but I ought to be 10 years older for job and must have time to get their confidence. Meanwhile there is a time limit and all sorts of things like problem, shall we take women, are settled by the most thoughtless set of muddle-headed old women you can imagine.

'This is for your eye and ear only . . .'[12]

The future of St Mary's as an undergraduate school, and the question whether or not a bid should be made for hospital units and clinical professors, were not the only matters troubling the waters at St Mary's. Sir Almroth Wright was creating his own area of turbulence. This larger than life figure had risen to fame by developing a vaccine for preventing typhoid fever.[13] He had convinced himself that the inoculation of killed bacteria, as in typhoid vaccination, would not only prevent but cure a large variety of other diseases and his mission was to convince others that this was so. The medical profession as a whole remained fairly skeptical but he was nevertheless able to gather round himself an enthusiastic group of young research workers. With a fellowship of the Royal Society and a knighthood awarded in 1906, he had made friends among powerful laymen and they had found money for him in 1907 to create, within St Mary's, an autonomous unit called the Inoculation Department. With the outbreak of the war in 1914 Wright, with his whole department, moved to Boulogne, where they tried to discover how to prevent and treat infection in wounds, which was the great killer of those whose injury was not immediately fatal. On his return from the war, Wright determined upon a grander concept than the Inoculation Department. He wanted to create an Institute of Pathology at St Mary's, and it was against this background that Charles, still awaiting his appointment, related to Dorothy what he had learnt had happened at a meeting of the hospital staff.

'Writing this while Phillips examines a nervous young lady. Withdrew as my presence may have exaggerated natural timidities.

'Last night's Staff Meeting was a stormy affair. Wright (Sir Almroth) began by outlining his scheme for a Path Clinical Institute in his wing of Mary's. Then they all attacked him and he being Irish, lost his temper. Then Pannett, when all were weary, brought up his scheme. Willcox and Broadbent* then countered with what I'd anticipated that Newman said: School was too small for units. Pannett then delivered my carefully prepared bomb, reading Newman's letter explaining his views and wanting units at Mary's!

'This flabbergasted meeting and took all wind out of Willcox's sails. Result was principle of unit was passed in excitement of moment! It will if it escapes death be a Path Professor but anyway once principle passes, it will be easier to introduce others and this will please Education authorities and give School a fillip.

'In last minute of meeting Clayton Greene, this supposed strong man of surgeons, got up and said if meeting was not already adjourned, he would like to suggest rebuilding of Mary's.

'Harris seconded and said if rest of staff would raise £10 000 he would give £1000. Such backing (for these two with another run Mary's) was enough and if money is forthcoming, we shall be able to make a public appeal with best chances of success.

'So on the whole meeting achieved much more than might have been hoped for. A committee of Pannett, C Greene, Harris, Wright and Willcox was appointed to report on Path Scheme. Pannett is secretary. He and I and Assistant Path man had a meeting after lunch today to fix the scheme as committee will meet on Monday without ideas.

'Unfortunately, thing being new, there is no model. I advised them to read Rockefeller Institute report for ideas. It's a very big place but must contain notions. This with Flexner's report is all we've got to go.

'Danger of this Path Unit is it means Willcox (now Sir William) will get in as Chemist and Wright as Path man which would damn any scheme and may bring Unit system into discredit at Mary's.

'Still things look a bit more promising. Newman's letter discrediting Willcox and Broadbent's speeches and Harris's demonstration of being in earnest by offer of finance were two turning points of meeting. Pannett's weakness has one advantage. He excites less opposition than most would in raising such

---

*Sir John Broadbent, physician to St Mary's Hospital and Dean of the Medical School.

controversial stuff. Next Friday they meet again. It will be fatal to me if Harris makes enemies (more than he already has) in these battles but it is absolutely necessary to school.

'I have told Pannett he must preserve peace between C Green and Harris on the subcommittee at all costs. Next thing that is coming up is women students. Harris is strongly opposed to them and thinks they freeze off male element!! That is grounds on which older schools won't have them. This is ungallant but amusing!

'I feel a bit more hopeful about the school today though there are a thousand and one chances of shipwreck before scheme gets to harbour. Still am more cheerful about it all but with conviction today that I'll not be here to see it. Don't take this too seriously and worry at all.'[14]

This was how things were when Charles won his staff appointment and took leave of absence to get married. It was summer time and he could be confident that nothing much would happen until October.

When Charles and Dorothy returned from their honeymoon in August they took rooms at number 65 Oxford Terrace, now Sussex Gardens, one block away from Praed Street and St Mary's. Dorothy then hunted for a flat and soon found one at 64 South Audley Street, near Grosvenor Square. It was on the fourth floor and above it lived a cook-housekeeper, so Dorothy had no kitchen. They lived there for the next two years.[15] Finances were tight because Charles at first had no private patients. The growth of his practice, and of his income, would depend on the number of patients that general practitioners chose to refer to him for his opinion as a consultant physician. Patients seen by consultants outside the hospitals that they visited as honorary members of staff fell into two groups. The first consisted of those who could afford a consultant's fee of between one and five guineas. The second consisted of clergymen and doctors and their families, and some from the ranks of the poor; these were quite numerous and were not charged a fee. The London consultant's potential parish was the whole of southern England, and patients would mostly come to see him in his consulting rooms in Harley Street or in its vicinity. But it was not uncommon for a consultant to be called by a general practitioner to a patient's own home, and invitations to consult in the country, at a fee conventionally calculated on the basis of a guinea a mile travelled, were particularly desirable as sources of income as well as status symbols.

In Charles's first few years in practice Wilfred Harris used to lend him his consulting room in Wimpole Street, and some of his earliest patients were referred to him for an opinion by Godfrey Maurice, then in the family practice at Marlborough. Three months after being best man at the wedding, Maurice, in the context of a referring letter, wrote: 'Ask your Missus if I may use her Christian name.'[16]

As a consultant building a practice, Charles had one particular advantage. In an age when many of the commoner diseases warranting a consultant's opinion were due to infections, like pneumonia, it was helpful both for diagnosis and for forecasting the outcome to know the number of white cells in the patient's blood. Dorothy had learnt to count blood cells in the course of her work with Barcroft and now she did blood counts on Charles's patients for him, sometimes accompanying him on visits with her portable equipment.[17]

Despite a negligible private practice, time never hung heavily from the moment Charles was back in London. In September he received a letter written on behalf of the medical school committee inviting him again to become editor of the *St Mary's Hospital Gazette*. 'You were so successful with it before' wrote the Dean, Sir John Broadbent, 'that I'm sure you will find no difficulty in running it once more.'[18] So, at the start of the academic year in October 1919, after an interval in which he had given up medicine, come back to it, gone to war and got married, Charles was back in the editorial chair. He continued there, at times sharing it, until 1931.[19] He signalled his return with a note in the October number written in a style reminiscent of the younger Charles:

'With this number, after a lapse of a whole decade, we sit again in the Editorial chair, well knowing that it is not the place of comfort, and not unmindful of ominous creakings and strange noises which that inhospitable seat gave forth when last we sat thereon. It is not possible, even if it were profitable, to recapture the abandon of those days. But the leopard does not change his spots, and if clamour for change is less raucous, the convictions are unaltered.'[20]

The main editorial comment was very differently composed. Entitled 'The Case for Change', it began by describing the situation at St Mary's as it was before the summer vacation.[21] There were two proposals, to rebuild the school and to establish a pathological institute. According to the editorial, the rebuilding was simply a necessary and belated attempt to make up leeway. As a scheme it lacked audacity, imagination and the quality of experiment that was needed for purposes of raising money. The creation of a pathological institute might ultimately provide an argument for the continued existence of the school, but the proposed directorate (no names mentioned) did not see its way to teach students and did not want them about the place. An institute was no substitute for other plans, and discussion of it must not replace the emphasis in discussion on needs related to teaching. Charles did not say plainly that the vital need was to seize the opportunity, while it remained available, to establish clinical units with professors of medicine and surgery.

Rather he said there was need to be open-minded about them; Newman's proposals had been very carefully thought out; no sound argument had been advanced against them; and clinical units were already being established in other hospitals, in some cases with imaginative schemes to open the way to youthful talent. The editorial ended on the theme that while the reputation of the hospital had been built by the seniors, its future depended on the juniors.

The October 1919 number of the Gazette contained another notable article, which, with hindsight, can be seen as more of Charles's writing on the wall. It was in the form of comments on an address given at the opening of the winter session of the medical school by Sir John Goodwin, Director General of the Royal Army Medical Corps. It was a critique of a health service, in this case a military one, in which the deficiencies in it were identified. One of the central points made was the need, in a reconstructed post-war Royal Army Medical Corps, to take account of merit:

'. . . it is well to recognize, now that the RAMC is in process of reconstruction, that if the call is made at some future time on any great scale, the mass of the profession will demand that the road is actually open to merit; that if nearly half a working profession are to become army doctors there will be a chance for all to rise by merit alone, whether they were in the Service before the war or only joined it for the emergency.'[22]

That an individual's merit should be the most important factor in deciding opportunities, responsibilities and the rewards that he should receive, was central to Charles's thinking, and it remained so. This tenet was to be critical years later in influencing the entry of consultants into the National Health Service, and in that context the term 'merit awards' was to be indissolubly linked with the name of Moran.

These two articles, 'The Case for Change' and the critique of the RAMC, marked the end of Charles's dalliance with the idea of writing a magnum opus on the Great War. He was looking ahead, not back, and very soon the leadership role that he had yearned for so long was his. Within four months of the publication of 'The Case for Change', on 29 January 1920, far-reaching steps were proposed by the Medical Committee[23] and approved by the Board of Management[24] of St Mary's. Clinical units were to be proceeded with, Charles was to be made responsible for their general organisation and administration, he was to be appointed sub-Dean, a small committee was to be appointed to organise in collaboration with him an appeal to the public for funds for the medical school, and he was to arrange for teaching in three neighbouring hospitals, the Paddington Infirmary, Paddington Green Children's Hospital, and the Maida Vale Hospital for Nervous Diseases.

Charles's attainment of this ascendancy at the end of January 1920, six months after his appointment to the staff, reflects the sense of purpose that he brought to the key committees when he started attending them at the beginning of the new academic year in October 1919.[25] He found the medical school committee a sleepy hollow. It was headed by Sir John Broadbent, who had served the place loyally during the difficult war years, but he was cautious and hesitant by nature[26] and if he had a vision splendid it was not apparent. The medical committee, prone as it was to internecine strife, had, during the summer, been concerned with yet another war, this time between Harris and Bernard Spilsbury, the pathologist, who soon afterwards moved to St Bartholomew's Hospital and a career in forensic medicine which made his name a household word in murder trials. Charles erupted into this scene all wound up and ready to go. Within weeks the medical committee received a report on *The System of Clinical Units*.[27] Produced by a sub-committee, it bears the hallmark of Charles's homework and it became his charter. It cited the Haldane report and Newman's memorandum, and pointed to the attraction that new posts in clinical units would have for young men awaiting staff appointments and to the difficulty St Mary's might have in retaining its good men without such posts. It emphasised the danger inherent in the Board of Education's belief that there were too many medical schools and it stressed that only a few clinical units would be funded and that other hospitals were a jump ahead of St Mary's. St Bartholomew's had already established a surgical unit and at Univesity College Hospital in January TR Elliott was to head a medical unit. Finally, the report said that the St Mary's medical school would shortly cease to exist unless the unit system were adopted and, at the same time the number of beds available for teaching was increased by amalgamation with neighbouring hospitals.

On receiving this report, the medical committee resolved on 8 December 'that the principle of "Clinical Units" be and is hereby approved'.[28] A sub-committee was formed to prepare a scheme that was to include affiliation with institutions in the district, including the 600 bed Paddington Poor Law Infirmary and Workhouse, which was about to be converted into a modern hospital. The new sub-committee got to work with great speed,[29] reporting back to the medical committee within a week. It was able to say that, after canvassing the staff, Clayton-Greene on the surgical side and Wilfred Harris on the medical side had indicated their willingness to be appointed whole-time directors of units. Their salaries would be £2000 a year and they would be debarred from private practice between 10.00 am and 4.00 pm on five days a week. CA Pannett on the surgical side and Charles and FS Langmead on the medical side had expressed willingness to be whole-time assistant directors at £750 per year, but Langmead's consent was conditional on his being able to retain his staff position at the Hospital for Sick Children at Great Ormond Street. The appointments of Pannett, and of Charles rather than Langmead, were recommended.

Meetings in those days handled few papers so that the report of this sub-committee was read to, and adopted by, the medical committee on 15 December,[30] and then, after the implications for funding by the hospital had been approved by the finance committee, it was presented to a meeting of the Board of Management on 18 December.[31] The board approved in principle the provision of the two clinical units and resolved that the scheme outlined in the report be proceeded with at once. So it was that Charles was given his charter by his peers and by the board of management. Things continued to move fast, and, without waiting for a formal response from Sir George Newman, the hospital appointed Wilfred Harris and Clayton Greene, and Charles and Pannett, paying them from the Hospital's own funds. Charles found himself in a full-time post at £750 a year and fulfilling his wish not to have to cast his bread upon the waters of Harley Street, although, while the unit scheme was in what was called its temporary stage he was allowed private practice outside the hours of duty.[33] The temporary nature of things must have been evident to all. For one thing, in the planning papers no reference had been made to the University of London, which would sooner or later be concerned about the terms and conditions of these appointments. Of more immediate practical importance was the fact that while the hospital had decided to carry the cost of the units in the current year, this was on the condition that, if approval and funding were not granted by the Board of Education, the whole matter would be reconsidered.[33] Nevertheless, two wards in the hospital were designated for each of the clinical units, another ward was converted into a clinical lecture theatre, a laboratory was made available and the directors of the units were given a room.[34]

As these events unfolded during February 1920, Charles cut all corners and, with the power given him the month before, went straight to the top, to one of the muffled figures in the back of the car in France in 1917, Sir Wilmot Herringham. Herringham, with Sir George Newman, had been entrusted by the University Grants Committee, in whose hands the funding of medical schools now lay, with visiting schools and determining how much each should receive. In response to his approach, in the first week in March 1920, Charles received a handwritten letter on eleven pages of folded notepaper. 'Dear Wilson', Herringham began, 'You must take this letter as private and unofficial'.[35] Then, quite simply, he outlined the position as he saw it. The Board of Education and the Treasury would regard clinical units as experiments, and their numbers would be based on educational needs, not on the number of medical schools, which were seen as private ventures that had sprung up for private ends. In regard to Charles's plea for St Mary's he wrote:

'You must remember that to say you have good teachers in any school is not to the point. Every school has good clinical teachers, and it is well recognised that London clinical teaching is up to its limits first rate. The clinical units were designed to supplement this by bringing in scientific physicians themselves original workers not by mere observation, as we all of us can claim to be, but by experimental research. In neurology Ferrier* and that school could claim to be of that calibre. Ordinary neurologists could not. Similarly with other branches. Plenty of people know a good deal about gout, but Garrod** stands alone in experiment.'

Herringham went on to say that the clinical unit scheme would be watched with very doubtful feelings by a good many people. 'There will', he said, 'have to be some justification for spending almost as much money on med. [sic] education in London, as goes to the whole of Edinburgh for all its Faculties together.' With regard to the plan for St Mary's, he said it was so novel and ambitious that no one could tell whether it could be carried out; he thought it too big for the school and also unwieldy. 'But,' he added, 'you may be able to work it.' He concluded 'I do not see, myself, why every school should expect or be expected to do the same thing. I look upon your attempt as an improvement on your ordinary clinical teaching, and I hope the Committee will consider it as grounds for raising the regular grant. But I can't say more than that at present.'[35]

Within 48 hours this thoughtful and slightly discouraging letter attracted a 15-page typewritten closely-argued defence of the plans for St Mary's. At the beginning, Charles introduced a new argument:

'Dear Sir Wilmot Herringham, Thank you for your letter. It is very kind of you to take so much trouble in explaining the whole position to me. Our efforts are naturally made on behalf of St Mary's, but their success or fortune has, we believe, more than local significance. That significance, as we see it, is simply whether, in the attempt to prevent reduplication of schools, the competitive element, which is the basis of all efficiency, is in danger of being lost. In other words, if the [London] schools are reduced in number from eleven to four, these four schools, however they were conducted, would have an assured entry, since there would be more than enough students for all of them, and no competitor from outside to take the place of any one of the four, if it became inefficient.'[36]

Charles ended the letter on a revealing personal note. After indicating the impossibility of the school being able to carry on its

---

*Dr D Ferrier, physiologist and physician to the National Hospital, Queen Square.
**Sir Archibald Garrod, physician to St Bartholomew's Hospital.

programme for more than a year without an additional grant, he wrote:

'Without such a grant, I should personally retain no hope of continuing the school on satisfactory and efficient lines, indeed I should devote myself entirely to gastro-intestinal research which I have for a long time meditated. To undertake extensive re-organisation on the top of five years in France is to make a serious gap in one's career. It means that in the seventh year after my membership [MRCP] I have still to be elected a fellow, and what is much more important, it means a serious distraction from the very arduous task of preparing the necessary technique for gastric research. But quite apart from St Mary's, I do not regret it, since I am firmly convinced that the question of medical education is the necessary preliminary to all other health schemes now in the air. Since my student days, I have nursed ideas on this subject, I believe they are sound, and that if they come to nothing, it will be due to my failure as an advocate.'[36]

With the clinical units launched, albeit with recognition from neither the Board of Education nor the University, and underwritten only temporarily by the hospital, life as a physician to outpatients and assistant director of the medical unit on £750 was now full of purpose, and Charles's position at the hospital was further strengthened in April, when he was appointed to the board of management. Dorothy must have been kept busy with her typewriter at 64 South Audley Street, for apart from his work in outpatients, his teaching and his politicking on behalf of the medical school, Charles embarked on three other enterprises: research, a consider-ation of the development of hospitals, and the sorting out of his ideas on shell shock.

Clinical research was laid down as one of the functions of members of the new clinical units. Charles got to work and by November 1920 the *Lancet* published a paper written with Dorothy as co-author entitled "The determination of the basal metabolic rate and its value in diseases of the thyroid gland'.[37] He also started a research project which led in the following year to a paper with CA Pannett as co-author, in the recently started *British Journal of Experimental Pathology*, on 'The influence of bile salts upon gastric function'.[38] This was his one excursion into the research field that he had mentioned to Herringham. These papers, with a third one published with his colleague in obstetrics and gynaecology, AW Bourne, in the *Lancet* in 1922 'On the relationship of the thyroid gland to the female pelvic organs',[39] all contained personally made carefully planned observations on patients, and reflected the application at the bedside of methods of the basic sciences which Flexner had identified as so conspicuously lacking in British medicine. After 1922 there was a gap of six years in Charles's listed publications and after that he wrote on medico-political matters and medical education. But taking into account his work on mustard gas and his by no means pedestrian publications in the three years after the war when he gave time to research, it is evident that he had ability as a researcher. As it turned out, his participation in research was short-lived, but by 1922 he had gained enough first-hand experience to speak with credibility among academics and to bring insight into the picking of academic staff for the medical school.

Charles's interest in health services and hospitals, already shown in the pages of the *St Mary's Hospital Gazette*, was now exposed in *The Times*. In April this reported that the newly-formed Ministry of Health was examining a proposal that local authorities should be given power to establish new hospitals when they were needed, and to co-ordinate the work of all hospitals within a given area.[40] The need, it was said, was to avoid a state of affairs recently described by the Chairman of the London Hospital: while 868 people were waiting to enter that hospital, where all the beds were full, there were 200 empty beds in the Whitechapel Infirmary across the road. In his first published letter to *The Times* on 5 May 1920,[41] Charles provided a table comparing the numbers of beds in London in general hospitals (1.125 per 1000 of population), in Poor Law Infirmaries (2.540 per 1000 population), in Fever Hospitals (1.182 per 1000 population), and in the few other categories. Acknowledging Mr Morris of the London Hospital as the source for his figures, he made a number of points. First, nearly half the beds in London were under the poor law. Second, the waiting lists at all the general hospitals were largely made up by patients awaiting surgical operations. Third, if the infirmaries with their empty beds were in a position to undertake surgical operations on the scale general in other hospitals, the problem of hospital accommodation would be solved without ambitious building operations. He argued that the transformation of Poor Law Infirmaries into modern hospitals would involve little increase in cost, and cited the arrangement already made and working well between St Mary's and the Paddington Infirmary. Charles's reasoned analysis led to an invitation in December to open a discussion on 'The future of the Poor Law Infirmary' at a meeting of the Harveian Society, whose membership comprised many of London's leading consultants. His paper, which was published in the *Lancet* in December 1920,[42] showed not just a parochial interest in London, but careful thought about the provision of hospital services in improving health care in England as a whole. Here again can be seen the development of ideas which were to become central to his thinking years later as he became engaged in debates on a national health service.

Despite having all these irons in the fire, Charles was stirred in 1920 by yet another issue. *The Times* of 2 September carried the announcement of the constitution of a War Office Departmental Committee on 'shell shock'.[43] The terms of reference were to consider different types of hysteria and traumatic neurosis commonly called 'shell shock', and to collate knowledge derived from the experience of the war 'with a view to recording for future use the ascertained facts as to its origin, nature and remedial treatment, and to advise whether, by military training or education, some scientific method of guarding against its occurrence cannot be devised.' Dorothy, years later, recalled what happened:

'I myself come from a very equable family, nothing really stirs them, but one day I came down to breakfast and found Charles in a towering rage. He had just seen in *The Times* the list of people who were appointed to a committee to deal with shell shock and he said that there was no one who had seen the inside of a trench. He resolved to write to *The Times* and a friend said "You are quite unknown—the only hope of getting it published is to write a very short letter." Charles was undeterred, wrote a long one and sent it in. Nothing happened for some time, then suddenly he found his letter, in full, on the centre page of the paper.'[44]

The actual conveying of this letter to *The Times* office in Printing House Square was undertaken by Dorothy, on her bicycle, immediately after she had typed it, for Charles would brook no delay. Charles's letter appeared on 22 September under the heading: 'Shell-shock—social significance of courage—character in action.'[45] He began by asserting that the facts about shell-shock were not pigeon-holed in archives; they were the perquisite of service in the trenches, and the committee's findings would merit consideration only in so far as it reached this first-hand experience. There were two steps in preventing shell-shock, elimination of unsuitable material by a process of selection, and the development of measures to fortify those who were selected. Charles devoted several paragraphs to factors to be taken into account in selection, and in this connection he observed that 'war has no power to transform, it merely exaggerates the good and bad in us.' Among factors contributing to a man's undoing in the trenches he stressed exhaustion of will-power, and he described a classification, based on a man's perception of fear and his reaction to it, that he had used to try to forecast what would happen to individuals as time went by. Even men who did not feel danger, men with what he called natural courage, would, he said, break sooner or later. The 'sticker' was one who managed to become insensitive and to give up thinking; the wise man lived for the hour. Finally, he questioned whether proposed methods for preparing the soldier's mind might not 'breed the habit of introspection which was the sure and certain herald of individual defeat.'

Charles was encouraged by the correspondence that followed his letter to send a second one, a column and a quarter long, which was published on 16 October.[46] He had something else to get off his chest. The headline this time was: 'Leaders and led—the nemesis of deception—peace lessons from war'. He sought to make points bearing on the prevailing industrial unrest. As prime factors in the decline in morale that had occurred in France as the war progressed, he identified misinformation—'the cooking of news before it was served up to the public at home'—and the 'heartbreaking inefficiency of the staff and generals with its resultant loss of life.' He argued that the only reason for men continuing was the immense toleration of the English—not Colonials, Scotch or Irish, but the English. With their capacity to live and let live he believed that the class antagonism that was becoming increasingly evident in post-war England was not inevitable. It was with these thoughts in his mind that Charles was invited to appear personally before the Departmental Committee on Shell Shock.[47] The prevailing industrial unrest was reflected in the opening remarks of the chairman, Lord Southwood: 'We have a small meeting today consequent on the fear of strikes and so on.' Lord Southwood referred to Charles's first letter to *The Times* and invited him to talk in a conversational way. What he had to say covered 25 pages of transcript and it was indeed conversational except where he was interrupted by questions. The main interest of the transcript lies in its demonstration that the basic ideas that appeared years later in *The Anatomy of Courage* were already etched in Charles's mind. It also reveals that Charles was not so good at free-ranging debate as he was at presenting a well-prepared argument.

Charles's second letter on peace lessons from war led six months later to his being invited to speak at the Royal Society of Arts on 'Some Effects of the War on Industrial Unrest'. The *Manchester Guardian* reported his paper under the headline: 'Psychology of unrest—"Greatest opportunity of the war" missed.'[48] Charles's first point was that no review of the existing discontent would carry people very far which did not clearly distinguish the case of the man who saw active service from that of the man who remained at home. Of the men who remained in England, one who did so involuntarily had been the target of abuse and felt a sharp sense of injustice, while one who had avoided active service was suffering from loss of self respect. In either event there was a morbid mental state less healthy and more dangerous to the community than that of the ex-soldier and these moods needed to be approached with sympathy and understanding. Charles went on to assert that men had been prepared by the war for an appeal based on something higher than self-interest. That was the greatest opportunity of the war, and it had not been taken by employers. The basis of contentment was not economic but moral. The captains of industry were, to the men, only leaders in name, and the men needed personal leadership based on the qualities they had learnt to recognise as the essential ones during the war. Charles and Dorothy both enjoyed the occasion of Charles's talk at the Royal Society of Arts, which included dinner in a flat above the lecture room.[49] They also enjoyed reading the correspondence that Charles received following his letters to *The Times* one of which was from Curtis Brown, the well known literary agent. He suggested that Charles should expand his ideas in a book of 75 000 words but when he heard what Charles's life was like, he agreed he would not be able to do it,[44] as indeed he was not—for 25 years.

Chapter 6

Dean of the Medical School

It was customary for the staff and lecturers of the medical school at St Mary's to meet in November, a month after the start of the academic year, to make a recommendation to the medical school committee about the deanship. At the meeting on 2 November 1920, Sir John Broadbent said that he did not propose to offer himself for re-election and Charles was nominated by ballot as his successor. At the meeting of the medical school committee which followed, the nomination was endorsed and Broadbent passed the chairmanship of the meeting to him.[1] As the new dean, Charles found himself in a remarkable situation. The office had always been held by senior members of the hospital staff, whereas he was 38 and had been on the staff for only 18 months. At the time he took over, the once prosperous medical school was generally described as a dump, the buildings were out of date, some had become derelict, and the school had an overdraft of £1113.[2] Charles inherited a room and an honorarium of 50 guineas per year. He also inherited BE Matthews, the school secretary who had admitted him as a student 19 years before, and an administrative assistant Miss LB Appleton. Matthews, now aged 56, had changed little with the passing years. He won the respect of generation after generation of the students by his integrity and impartiality, and so far as Charles was concerned, while he was retiring by nature and never volunteered an opinion, his advice when sought was always sound. 'His mind', Charles wrote later, 'recoiled from any kind of injustice or exaggeration or anything which fell below the most fastidious standards of the best kind of Englishman.'[3] Looking back on this time 40 years later, Miss Appleton recalled how the medical school put her in mind of a monastery. The staircases were stone and it was cold. Except in the dean's room, the heating came from ancient boilers in the basement which one of the tutors used to stoke. The dean's room had an open fire, and the new dean used to spend much time there talking with Mr Matthews. So far as the staff in the medical school office were concerned, the newcomer was soon discerned to be always considerate; you knew, Miss Appleton said, that you had a gentleman to work with. From the start there was one over-riding policy, which was that everything for the students had to be the best.[4]

Two weeks after his appointment as dean Charles called a special meeting of the medical school committee to deal with matters needing attention before the end of the year. One was the resignation of the lecturer in chemistry and another was Gosse's refusal of an invitation to accept the post of lecturer in pharmacology. A less weighty though doubtless to Charles an equally important matter was an application from the students to hold dances in the library at intervals of a fortnight instead of a month. It was agreed to meet the wishes of the students to the extent of allowing dances at intervals of three weeks. To Charles, these things were significant items of everyday housekeeping, but in the forefront of his mind were the three components of his grand design. The first was to win the battle for the school's continued existence, with which he linked the recognition and financing of the professorial clinical units; the second was to improve the quality of the students seeking admission; the third was the rebuilding of the school and its recreational facilities. The first task was urgent. As 1921 began the clinical units were still not recognised by the Board of Education,[5] and in March it was learnt that the King Edward's Hospital Fund for London, which was the main source of funds for the voluntary hospitals, had ruled that expenses in connection with clinical units should not be borne by the hospitals but by the medical schools. The St Mary's board of management promptly resolved that the units should cease to exist so far as their official relation with the hospital was concerned.[6] The only hope now was to win an outside grant. At this stage the students entered the fray. They petitioned the board of management to continue the units and the board resolved that the petition should be sent to Sir George Newman with a covering note in support from the secretary of the hospital. Many years later Charles recalled seeing Newman:

'I was Dean. He came round. Of course at that time I had got a fairly good head-piece. I knew every detail, absolutely to the last thing, and whatever he asked I threw at him, and I could see him saying to himself—"This fellow knows his business"—and after that I had no trouble with Newman at all, and he treated us very generously. Whatever his limitations were, we liked him at St Mary's. . . .'[7]

In some earlier autobiographical jottings, Charles placed the interview at the Ministry of Health:

'Sir George Newman, his secretary informed me, was very busy but could spare me five minutes on Wednesday at 11 o'clock. "And what can I do for you?" he asked. "Something, Sir George, which no one else can." Sir George smiled with a perceptible increase in friendliness. "These units are your doing, you have four schools running them who only half believe in them. If units were given to a school which really did believe in them, not only would that school make a success of them but the pace set would force the other schools to make a job of their units." Sir G leant back in his chair and folded his hands. All the units had been offered; he had made them do it. It was not necessary for me to open my dispatch case and produce papers which I had prepared to support my case. He talked on. An hour later Sir G. said suddenly, and rather archly—"How you are making me neglect my work," and resumed his role of the distracted servant of the state. Long before I found my way out of the innumerable corridors of the Ministry of Health I felt assured that Sir G. would not oppose my suit. There remained a more formidable obstacle, the second representative on the grants committee, Sir Wilmot Herringham. He was not going to be influenced by anybody, he was not in the least vain. He was a combative old gentleman and would give St Mary's marks for running units on their own. Sir G would put our case. I determined to leave Sir W to his eloquence.'[8]

By April 1921 the battle was all but over when the university grants committee offered £6000 a year to pay for the units.[9] A few people were bruised in the tidying up. There was a row between the board of management and the medical school committee over who should pay the expenses incurred by the temporary units, in the course of which the school committee, led by Charles, threatened to resign.[10] Also the university had refused to recognise Harris and Clayton-Greene as professors on the grounds that their posts had not been advertised and they were not full-time officers.[11] Consequently in May the medical school named representatives to serve with representatives of the University of London on a committee set up to recommend who should be appointed as full-time heads of the two units.[12] Charles was on the committee for the surgical appointment, which was deferred until the following year, when CA Pannett became professor of surgery. He was not, however, on the committee for the medical appointment for which his own name was to be considered. Following advertisement and the due processes of university and hospital committees, the appointment went to FS Langmead, who became professor of medicine and director of the medical unit in September. Charles was very disappointed.[13] He saw the appointment as a move of reaction against his own reforms, he believed that Langmead had no real interest in academic medicine,[14] and he would have liked to have been appointed himself. His name had certainly been in people's minds. Two years earlier, before his appointment to the staff, he had written to Dorothy: 'Phillips (senior physician at Mary's) said to Pannett I ought to be Professor of Medicine if one is appointed at St Mary's. I sat on the notion at once: it would raise all forms of envy. . . .'[15]

As things turned out, Langmead, who was a gentle kind man and well liked by his patients and by his students, did little to promote the new field of academic medicine. While he did not impede his young assistants from bringing laboratory methods to the wards, he did no research himself, and seemed to occupy much of his time writing summaries on his patients, which gathered dust in a corner of the new medical unit's laboratory.[16] In 1921 he must have been seen as totally unthreatening by his colleagues on the hospital staff. Charles never became an enthusiastic admirer,[17] but it is hard to see how he himself could have won appointment to the chair. It was characteristic of him that when he sought an objective he laid his plans with infinite care, but when this post was created he seems to have left things to chance. In fact both at St Mary's and in the wider world he had identified himself as a sponsor of the job rather than as a competitor for it. A paper by him appeared in the *Lancet* of 2 July, before the appointment formalities were completed, entitled "Clinical units, their purpose and achievement". It included a discussion of the unit concept and of the qualities to be sought in those who were to staff the new enterprises. 'We ask', Charles wrote, 'that these workers should pass tranquil days, a little away from the dusty paths of life, so that clinical medicine may receive a measure of the service that is freely given to the other sciences.'[18] To picture Charles, with his burning ambition for St Mary's, as being plausibly cast in this mould perhaps unduly extended the imagination of the assessors.

Charles's article on clinical units was long to remain one of the clearest of statements on the introduction of the university presence into the London teaching hospitals. Sir Clifford Albutt, Regius Professor of Physic at Cambridge, liked it greatly: 'Permit me to say', he wrote on 8 July, 'that I feel deeply indebted to you for so wise and even-handed a survey of the problem.'[19] Albutt's correspondence with Charles continued, with Albutt pressing on him his enthusiasm for bringing medicine and surgery together. 'Can you not', he wrote, 'persuade some of the "waiting" physicians to carry out his [sic] own surgery? They are all nowadays quite good surgeons when first qualified. Neither College can object.'[20] The publication of the paper in the *Lancet* also led to correspondence with TR Elliott from the medical unit at University College Hospital. In response to a letter from Charles, Elliott commented: 'Your letter gave me as much pleasure as your essay in the *Lancet* did. You state the ideals for which we should strive more finely and more clearly than any of us can ever feel about them. . . .' Elliott went on to comment on an assertion Charles had made that a good assistant in a unit could not be content to take his policy from his Director, and he added: 'That is the same thought which often fired you to explosions at Boulogne! Yet I suspect that you . . . would tyrannise over your juniors if you ever had a controlling post.'[21] Charles replied to Elliott's letter immediately:

'Dear Elliott,
'Lady Rhondda in her life of her father says that a man has three
personalities, one he shows to his superiors, one to his equals and
a third to his inferiors. In Lord Rhondda's case she says that the
first personality was thorny, he refused to acknowledge that
anyone was his superior unless he was proved so in character and
intellectual ability. To his equals he was friendly but critical. To
his inferiors he was sympathetic and charming. That prevented
him getting a chance till he was a dying man, and that has done
me down time and again. I have been in control in a small way
ever since school and I have as often had a solid backing when
I was up against authority, always holding that it was inartistic
to be other than one of the pack and that leadership should be felt
insensibly as due to greater efficiency in a particular individual
than expressed more crudely.'[22]

Charles went on to defend his comment that a good assistant in
a unit could not be content to take his policy from the Director on
the grounds that if the assistant had real capacity he might feel he
could do more unhindered. He then took Elliott up on his reference
to the Boulogne outbursts, which related in part at least to a clash
between Charles and a fellow RAMC officer who, in Charles's view
had run away from France and then treated his soldier patients like
dirt. 'Don't you see', he wrote, 'that it was not the small incident
or cause of the outburst that mattered there, but the fact that the
incident was working on a raw surface left by the trenches. . . . I
stuck Boulogne because you were out to get a job well done. . . .'[22]
A week later Elliott wrote again: 'I fear that I may have written
to you more emphatically than was my meaning, for your criticisms
of all things at Boulogne only gave me a stimulus or amusement,
and I always enjoyed them. Surely you never thought I was
querulous about that!'[23]
Charles's feelings about Langmead did not deter him from
accepting reappointment as first assistant and assistant director of
the now formally constituted medical unit[24] at the continuing
salary of £750 a year. Officially he was required to give the greater
part of his time to duties associated with the unit, but he was not
debarred from private practice, and the deanship had always been
seen as very much a part-time job.
Once clear where they were going, Charles and Dorothy moved
to 129 Harley Street, renting the two top floors and a consulting
room and shared waiting room on the ground floor.[26] Twice a week
Charles took an outpatient clinic at St Mary's, and since one was
on a Saturday morning, when few patients presented, he used this
clinic to follow patients who had been subject to special investigations,
and ones in whom he was specially interested.[27] His main responsibility for patients and for teaching the students was however

at Paddington Hospital, as the infirmary was now called. Of this he wrote to Elliott:

'Things at Mary's might be worse. They've let me take Paddington Infirmary and develop it, and here clerking under my tyrant sway quite prospers and we teach in new ways along new lines, while in matters of conduct we abolish altogether pomp and ceremony which prevents students really bringing their difficulties to a man, and there is no difference between any of us except that I have done more medicine than they and thought more about it perhaps, and nothing is done that might minister to the pedagogue's vanity. One mellows. I dislike my fellow consultant more and more as a class. I feel as able and more to get to know the average student as when Rugger captain. I like them and they like me. For the rest one reads more and builds up the little inner world which is a defence and a support against another world little to my own liking.'[22]

As a bedside teacher Charles could be brilliant, and his rounds that were open to any students who wished to attend were crowded. He never destroyed a student's self-respect by tearing him to pieces in front of the others, as some of his colleagues did. He never forgot that many of his students could not approach him in ability and he always gave them an opportunity to contribute in discussion, showed them where they erred, and taught them to think. He would quickly pick out the ablest of his audience and gave them the difficult questions.[28] He had a great facility too for drawing patients out when he taught at the bedside, speaking not only of their immediate symptoms but of their circumstances, home and background, so that their illness came into perspective. Charles had a knack of summing things up so that students were in no doubt that they were seeing a whole person, not just a case.

Early in his deanship, Charles made a quick visit to Germany to see at first hand how things were organised there. He and Dorothy, who spoke German, were introduced by an American friend to Professor Adolf Bickel, in whose flat they stayed in Berlin. Charles's impression was that everyone worked too hard, including the Bickel's two teen-age children, who were made to get up early in the morning to learn Latin verbs. He also made a prophecy. Referring in the Gazette to a German's reaction to the occupation by French and Belgian troops of the rich Ruhr valley, in order to collect reparations for the war by force, he wrote: 'Whatever might be the case before, France can now expect no mercy if Germany should, as she must, eventually recover.'[29]

As he became busier as dean, Charles's continuing occupation of a senior salaried post in the medical unit caused increasing unhappiness, particularly to the second assistant, AC Alport,[30] whom Langmead appointed in 1922. It is arguable that, as dean, Charles earned every penny and more of his medical unit salary and that it was statesmanlike of Langmead and the medical school committee to allow him the security which £750 a year afforded in those days. The issue was nevertheless divisive in the medical school, and it remained unresolved until 1935, when arrangements were made for the dean to be paid £500 instead of 50 guineas a year.[31] Charles then resigned from the medical unit and Alport was appointed assistant director in his place.

As the new academic session began in October 1922 Charles, in the annual Dean's Report,[32] could list several tasks already accomplished. He could point to the liaisons developed with Paddington Hospital, Paddington Green Children's Hospital and the Maida Vale Hospital, reminding readers that the particular attraction of London for medical students was the favourable ratio between numbers of students and numbers of beds available to them when holding their appointments as medical clerks and surgical dressers. He was also able to refer to the subsidy given by the university grants committee for the two professorial clinical units, and to St Mary's being one of only five schools funded for such units. At St Mary's units had been operating *de facto* for two years and the students liked them. The grant, he said, was a good omen for the future.

Charles also reported that, through Almroth Wright's new Institute of Pathology, students were able to undertake two-month

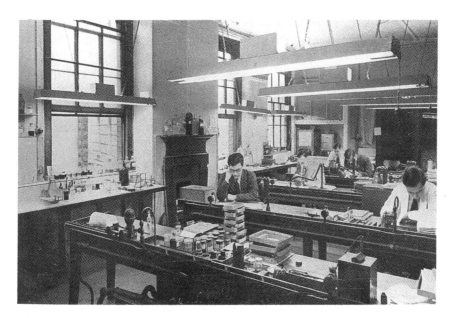

Figure 8. One of the laboratories in the Department of Pathology at St Mary's. (Reproduced by kind permission of St Mary's Hospital and Medical School Archives)

clerkships in pathology, bacteriology and pathological chemistry. In effect they carried out, under supervision, some of the routine investigational work of the hospital instead of just hearing about it. That Charles saw this as important is reflected in a comment that he wrote at about this time. To put it into context it needs to be appreciated that when he read a book and his interest was aroused he used to underline passages and make marginal comments in ink or with variously coloured pencils. Among the statements that he marked in a book called *Medical Education and Research* was one by James Ewing, professor of pathology at Cornell University Medical College: 'Not being familiar with the methods and limitations of laboratory technique, the practitioner acquires a confidence in the infallibility of diagnostic tests, of which the dead far outnumber the living.'[33] Charles's scribbled comment was: 'Perhaps we forget that it is as true that if only men with lab. [sic] training can do these tests only men of similar upbringing can use them.' The other action bearing on undergraduates that was recorded in the 1921-1922 Dean's Report was the building of a large pavilion costing nearly £3000 at the hospital's athletic ground at Wembley. And for postgraduates he reported a series of meetings, which he hoped would build up into an annual course, in which recent advances in diagnosis and treatment of disease were incorporated.

With these achievements behind him, Charles was ready to make his next move in his scheme to revitalise the medical school, namely to fill it with the best students and to provide them with the best of facilities. The selection of students was on the agenda at the meeting of the medical school committee on 7 November 1922.[34] It had been reported at the previous meeting that there had been no candidates for the two scholarships offered to students at Oxford and Cambridge, the so-called university scholarships. The question of increasing the value of these scholarships, one worth £100 and the other £50 a year, was raised and it was decided to find out the value of such scholarships offered by the other medical schools. At the November meeting this information was available and it was found that as a rule the university scholarships offered at St Mary's compared unfavourably with those offered elsewhere. According to the minutes, the dean then 'brought forward for consideration a proposal to use certain funds, known as the Pension Funds (at present paid over by certain members of the staff to the funds of the Medical School), for the purpose of providing two or more extra Scholarships to the value of £200 each, to be given by nomination to suitable candidates on the lines of the Rhodes Scholarships.' The dean's proposal embodied altering the basic principle that had hitherto governed the award of scholarships, that the award should be made according to the marks won in a competitive examination. Nevertheless, the committee expressed general approval of the idea and referred it for comment to a meeting of the staff and lecturers. That meeting not only approved the use of the pension money for the university scholarships but it went further. It recommended the abolition of two other, open, scholarships and their replacement by two scholarships, each representing a free medical education, to be offered to candidates on the basis of recommendations from the headmasters of selected public schools. Faced with these recommendations, the medical school committee on 5 December passed two resolutions.[35] The first was that 'the entrance scholarships of one hundred pounds and fifty pounds be forthwith abolished and replaced by two entrance scholarships, each representing a free Medical Education, which shall be awarded annually by nomination on the lines of the Rhodes Scholarships. The nominations to be made by the Medical School Committee from candidates sent up by the Headmasters of selected Public Schools.' The second resolution was 'That the existing University Scholarships be abolished and two University Scholarships of two hundred pounds each be awarded annually by nomination to members of a British or Overseas University, on the lines of the Rhodes Scholarships, provided that a sufficient sum of money is forthcoming from contributions to Pension Money by the Medical and Surgical Staff.' A proposal that the scholarship for a boy from Epsom College should be increased from fifty-two pounds and ten shillings to a level that would represent free tuition was postponed. These arrangements were described in the dean's annual report for 1922–1923: 'The examination system [for scholarships] has, after prolonged trial, been replaced by nomination. The former, with brilliant exceptions, failed to justify itself, and it will be interesting to see what type of man is attracted by a system which is moulded on the lines which the Rhodes Scholarships have made familiar.'[36]

In 1923 the new scholarships were advertised. A subcommittee consisting of Sir John Broadbent, the previous dean, JE Frazer, the professor of anatomy, and Charles was formed to examine nominations,[37] of which there were 12 from public schools and four from the universities.[38] Five of the public school nominees were selected for interview; history does not relate how the other four were handled but subsequent practice suggests that the dean at least would have interviewed all from universities in Britain. One public school scholarship went to J Ives from Wakefield Grammar School, the other was shared between GB Mitchell-Heggs from Nottingham High School (destined one day to be dean at St Mary's) and AW Littlewood of Trent College. The university scholarships went to AB Bourdillon of University College, Oxford, and PC Maclane of Queen's College, Oxford. Two years later, the medical school committee determined that those who were short-listed for scholarships but who did not win one, should receive a 10% reduction in their tuition fees.[39]

Another important change affecting student entry occurred at about this time. In April 1924 a large group of male students signed a petition begging that women students be no longer admitted.[40] Admission of women had been allowed during the war and had continued afterwards at the discretion of the dean.[41] The petition precipitated a debate in which feelings ran high and opinion was divided. Within one month Charles chaired three special meetings of the medical school committee that were called to discuss the matter, but his personal view was not recorded. Those opposing the admission of women claimed that men for the most part preferred to go to a school where women were not taken. This was of course in the Oxford and Cambridge collegiate tradition. It was also a view that had the weighty backing of Almroth Wright, who had written *The Unexpurgated Case Against Woman Suffrage* in 1913.[42] Wright had also engaged in a debate on this subject in the library at St Mary's with his friendly sparring partner, Bernard Shaw, before the war. Charles described the occasion:

'Shaw arrived in a blue reefer coat and red tie. When Shaw sat down I was sorry for Wright. I felt that he had been pulverized, but at the end of Wright's reply I blushed to think that Shaw, who was after all a guest, had been so mercilessly shown up. The devastating effect of such speech depends on the art of selection. Every single sentence was a direct hit; there was not a single word which did not contribute to the confusion of the enemy.'[42]

In the end, it was decided that the intake of women students should cease.[43] The matter was raised again in 1929 when the Senate of the University of London expressed the opinion that co-education was desirable. The school committee signified that 'it will be prepared to admit women students provided that all Metropolitan medical schools do the same.'[44] Another world war was to be fought before that came about.

As a sequel to the new scholarship arrangement, Charles set out to look for money to increase the number of awards that could be made. His success was such that by 1930 they numbered 15. By then these scholarships, identified officially as nomination scholarships, and by the ungodly as rugger scholarships, had become the focal point of a considerable dispute between St Mary's on the one hand and the big four among the other teaching hospitals—St Thomas's, St Bartholemew's, the London, and Guy's—on the other. The first public engagement in the dispute was a committee of the University of London in 1931.[45] By that time much else had happened, including the laying of the foundation stone of the new medical school. To understand Charles's position then, a number of threads in the story of the intervening years need to be picked up.

Chapter 7

Harley Street Years

Once the entrance scholarships had been organised, Charles directed his attention to the rebuilding of the medical school. After the war, in 1919, the board of management had accepted that some enlargement of the buildings was necessary and had looked at a proposal to add a storey to the museum.[1] This unambitious plan was nothing like what Charles believed was needed. Nor could it contribute to solving the accommodation problems of Almroth Wright's institute, which was renting unused ward space in the Clarence wing of the hospital. Over the next several years subcommittees concerned with rebuilding were formed, disbanded and re-formed. Limited funds were raised from among the staff and by appeal, but the project hung fire.[2] The overall need came to be seen to be not only for buildings for the medical school and the institute but also a building for a nurses' home, and for land to put all these buildings on. Seeking a bench-mark for the sort of money that had to be found, Charles could look to the happenings at University College Hospital. Having been convinced that the new clinical unit system must be enabled to succeed in at least one London hospital, the Rockefeller Foundation had given that hospital £835 000 for its medical school in 1920.[3] For Charles, and later as it turned out for the medical school at St Mary's, an important event occurred in the summer of 1924. It was the occasion of Charles's first meeting with the politician and newspaper magnate, Lord Beaverbrook. He had wrote an account of it in a notebook, probably in the early 1930s:

'I was sitting in my bath a little before midnight when the telephone bell rang. "Is that Dr Wilson?" "Hold on, Lord [Beaverbrook] wants to speak to you." "I want you" he said, "to come down to Leatherhead to see my son. They say he has got appendicitis and must operate at once. I'll send a car for you straight away." We [Dorothy and Charles] picked him up at the Hyde Park Hotel. Beyond Leatherhead we turned in by a white gate which showed up in the darkness and drove up a long drive (he told me later with gusto that the original design of the house and ground had made this drive to twist and turn to make it stretch out). The door opened into a big hall. There were men servants on the stairs like plants, too many of them. Facing one at the head of the first turn in the stairs a life size portrait of Lord B, hung on the wall. There was no escaping it. It was modern enough.

97

Lord B's face was meant to be painted. There were obvious difficulties and the painter had not been successful in overcoming them. It would be scrapped. But if by any chance it survived 100 years could one imagine it a family portrait? One couldn't. It was a face for Lowe to draw and call it a caricature. Lord B went to the telephone and rang up the local practitioner. "Dr Wilson is here, he'd better go on and examine Peter. It will save time. And you will bring the surgeon when he comes." The doctor agreed. And so Lord B got independent opinions. He wasn't the man to be defeated by medical etiquette. I found the boy sitting up with a normal pulse and temperature and with few signs but the history was enough. I said he had appendicitis and I had no doubt the surgeon would decide to operate at once when he had examined him. My verdict was received with a scowl. I saw I was there as a physician to check the surgeon's lust for cutting. And I had failed in my role. We waited in gloomy silence. The surgeon arrived and went up to the boy. He came from the same hospital as the practitioner, had been nominated by him and was an old friend. The practitioner had made him wise as to B's attitude to surgery. He came back. "Your son has an appendix but I don't think there's any need to do anything in a hurry. Things have quieted down" he said. B's face brightened. I was still in the house but as a harmless spectator. No one took any more notice of me. The surgeon gave us a lift to London. As it happened next morning about 4 am the boy had a sudden sharp pain and vomited. The practitioner hastily summoned the surgeon and he operated at once and he honestly admitted that the condition was worse than he had thought. From that time B became an ally of mine. He saw that I was prepared to stand by an opinion when it was not popular, that it made no difference what he, B, thought. I was concerned with the medical evidence. He lived among people who acted differently. From that hour he trusted my judgement in medical matters. This unfortunate man who could trust no one was faced that night by the necessity of accepting verdicts from strangers in a matter of life and death to him when he could not know the grounds on which that verdict was reached. His affection for his children was intense, it redeemed much that was less attractive.'[4]

Years later Beaverbrook reminded Charles of the episode and how, according to his recollection, Charles had determined the need for an operation by means of a blood count,[5] which Dorothy performed. Dorothy recalled Charles asking her apologetically to go with him to Leatherhead because he thought a blood count would be useful; she always kept her microscope, staining fluid and slides ready to take out in the car for calls such as this.[6] Charles and Dorothy were never sure why Beaverbrook called him in on that summer evening, but they surmised that he had remembered Charles's letters to

The Times after the war. Thereafter, up till the Second World War, Beaverbrook consulted Charles as a patient, and they remained friendly and in touch with each other until Beaverbrook died in 1964. There were many calls for help, particularly after Beaverbrook had a motor car accident just before Christmas 1928 and after he developed asthma in 1936.[7] Beaverbrook was always excessively health-conscious.[8]

Before long Charles's relationship with Beaverbrook changed from a purely professional one to include a social element, and he and Dorothy were invited to dine. Of one such occasion, Charles recorded:

> 'He asked me what I thought of the lighting arrangements at Cherkley. I said I thought lustres would have suited the room better. "You want tradition. Of course lustres have been used for this kind of room. I want something different. I'm going to clean out all these", pointing to some beautiful tallboys. "See this," and he pointed to an ugly table made of wood, "I have had it specially made." He was always altering the rooms, never at rest. He had no sense of beauty at all. The rooms gave one the impression that a secretary had telephoned Waring's to send a man and that the man had been told to get on with it. There were never any flowers in the house. He had a tame band which played after dinner. . . . The house, the servants, the band all gave the impression that they had been mobilised hurriedly by telephone regardless of cost. The place wasn't a home, didn't seem lived in, had no past. These were social offices, no more.'[4]

Dorothy recalled:

> 'I looked forward to invitations to Cherkley and if I could have sat silent to enjoy the conversation I should have been very happy. But I remember saying to a friend "I am an ordinary fairly intelligent woman, but I never feel so stupid as when I am at Lord Beaverbrook's dinner table". I don't know why it was, but I never felt really at ease with him."[6]

Beaverbrook never dined at Harley Street; indeed it was said that he never went out to lunch or dinner at all, asserting that if he were to do so he would get indigestion.[9] But what he did do was speak well of his doctor among his acquaintances, and it was probably in this way that Charles came to meet Lady Kenmare[10] whose son, Lord Castlerosse, was one of Beaverbrook's gossip writers.[11] Again, what started as a professional relationship developed into a social acquaintanceship, then into a lasting friendship, this time between Lady Kenmare and Dorothy. It was through this contact that Charles came to win his first large donation for the medical school. In 1928 he and Dorothy were invited to spend a holiday at the Kenmare's

home in Killarney.[12] Lord Kenmare, whom Dorothy found very
good-looking and charming, had a herd of dairy cattle, and with little
difficulty he got Charles talking about milk. Charles's briefing
must have been good because after he and Dorothy returned to
London Lady Kenmare sent them a quote from a speech of
Lord Kenmare's,[13] reported in the Cork Examiner,[14] to the effect
that physicians were agreed that there was no subject which was
of such vital importance to the health of the community as that of
obtaining a plentiful supply of pure, uncontaminated milk. There
were two other special memories of this visit. One was of Charles's
amazement at the smartness of the shoes in which Lady Kenmare
walked through the mud—most inappropriate, he thought. The other
concerned Lord Kenmare's prize bull. It developed a sore foot on the
day before it was to appear in a show. Charles prescribed soaking
in a bucket of hot water, and when on the next day the foot was
miraculously better, Charles's reputation was established. In the
following year when Charles and Dorothy's second child, Geoffrey,
was born, Lord Kenmare was asked to be a godfather, and he
was ever remembered by his godson for a later gift of a £5 note,
never spent and still treasured.[15] After their visit to Killarney,
Dorothy used to see Lady Kenmare often, and for the ambitions
which Dorothy shared with Charles for St Mary's, Lady Kenmare
came to provide a line of communication to people in high places,
including Buckingham Palace. The first line of communication to
be opened up resulted from Charles talking to Lady Kenmare about
St Mary's and finding he had enlisted a keen supporter who was
eager to help.[12] Lady Kenmare said she would interest her brother
John Baring, second baron Revelstoke, who was head of the family
business, Baring Brothers, and a director of the Bank of England.
She did this, and, after a talk with Charles, Lord Revelstoke, who
had also been Chairman of the Finance Committee of Guy's Hospital
and Treasurer of the Kind Edward's Hospital Fund, gave a dinner
for some of his city friends, invited Charles, and asked him to speak.
Revelstoke questioned Charles for three hours about medical
education, and before he left told him that he would be able to advise
a friend of his to leave £25 000 to the school.[10] When Revelstoke
died, he himself turned out to be the friend.[2] Charles wrote and told
Lady Kenmare how he had put his case.[16] The letter reads as
though he hoped she would use it to interest other people in his plans.
His opening assertion was that the only really hopeful method of
working for a healthier race was to increase the facilities in medical
schools for medical education and research. Under the voluntary
hospital system provision was not made for these, because money
coming to hospitals had to be spent on caring for the sick poor.
Failure to support medical schools had resulted in obsolete buildings
unsuitable for modern scientific work, lack of capacity to innovate,
and paucity of endowed scholarships which, because of the cost

of medical education, prevented many otherwise suitable recruits from taking up a medical career. Charles described the response:

'Lord Revelstoke made a prolonged investigation into the facts on which these statements rest and was eventually so struck by the disparity between the importance of medical education and research and the financial provision for them, and by the consequences to the country of this anomalous state of affairs, that he asked me to draw up plans for a fund to assist all the medical schools which he thought might possibly be run in conjunction with the King Edward's Hospital Fund. Finally he agreed that the time was probably not ripe for such a step. He felt that further work must be done in educating the country on the importance of medical education and research and he decided that the Royal Commission of 1913 was right in saying that all that could be done at the present time was to take one school and make a model of it to show what could be done by a medical school when it was no longer hampered financially. He therefore decided to make his bequest to the medical school at St Mary's in the hope that others would complete the scheme.'[16]

It is noteworthy that Charles had successfully advanced the same argument to Lord Revelstoke, the need for a model school, that had been put to the Haldane Commission and that had appealed to the Rockefeller Foundation in relation to University College Hospital. He did indeed mention the Rockefeller initiative in his letter to Lady Kenmare, and her brother would certainly have known about it, but Charles insisted that a scheme that would create an interest in medical education must be 'planned on English lines and supported by English people'.

Lord Revelstoke died on 19 April 1929 and Charles announced his bequest at a meeting of the medical school committee on 7 May.[17] A motion of thanks to Charles was passed. But this was only the beginning. At the next meeting of the committee on 4 June, Charles announced a gift of £63 000 from Lord Beaverbrook.[18] Several accounts exist of circumstances in which Beaverbrook made this gift.[19-22] They mostly mention a bun and a cup of tea, they all mention an envelope and a pencil, and they all involve an opening gambit by Beaverbrook to the effect: 'I hear you are rebuilding your medical school.' Cope's* account in his *History of St Mary's Hospital Medical School*, published in 1954, must be regarded as Charles's authorised version for he contributed to the writing of it.[23] Cope's account is as follows:

---

*VZ Cope, surgeon to St Mary's Hospital.

'Lord Beaverbrook had been a patient and was a personal friend of Dr Wilson, who had the gift of inspiring others with his own ideals. One day Lord Beaverbrook had asked to be allowed to pay a visit to St Mary's Hospital unattended and unknown, so that he might make his own judgement of the place. After going round the hospital wards he went down to the Outpatient Department. Going up to a small canteen which provides tea and buns for the patients he asked how much he would have to pay for a bun. "The price is three-halfpence, but if you can't afford it, you can have it for nothing" was the reply. He evidently thought well of the place for a few days later he telephoned Dr Wilson and asked him to come and see him. When the Dean entered his room he said: "I hear you are rebuilding your medical school. What do you need to complete it?" The Dean took out a pencil and envelope and said "Sixty three thousand pounds" whereupon Beaverbrook gave it to him in the form of a Covenant. It is obvious that the Dean must in previous conversation have convinced him that the encouragement of medical education of the best type was a project worthy of the strongest support.'[19]

As a nice variation in one of Charles's later versions, he 'took an envelope out of his pocket and borrowed a pencil from Max.'[22] And AJP Taylor, Beaverbrook's biographer, recounting the bun and tea episode in Beaverbrook's own words, has Charles entering at the end of it:

'When Wilson came in and greeted Beaverbrook, the old lady [serving buns and tea] was greatly distressed. She ran after Wilson whispering: "What shall I do? What shall I do? I've made a horrible mistake. Shall I apologise?" Wilson answered "Do nothing. You've got us our money."'[20]

In his history of the school, Cope was right in observing that the dean must have had previous conversations with Beaverbrook so that the opening gambit attributed to him—"I hear you are rebuilding your medical school"—is incongruous. Charles had in fact told Beaverbrook over a year before of his ambitions for the school, and had aroused Beaverbrook's interest sufficiently for him to have offered to visit St Mary's at that time. On 18 January 1928 Charles had written:

'My dear Lord Beaverbrook, it is very nice of you, offering to come to St Mary's tomorrow but I could not think of bothering you when you will be sufficiently harassed with preparation for your journey. It would only mean setting out on a cold journey tired out. And here the physician must keep the educational enthusiast in his place.

'At St Mary's we are scouring the country for men who are keen on medicine and fitted for it and we are endeavouring as far as our resources permit not to let their poverty debar them from going into medicine. I wanted you to come to St Mary's to satisfy yourself by questioning the scholars how far we succeed in this. It is a real beginning of an English Johns Hopkins which was recently described by a traveller in the States as the largest and most liberal-minded piece of individual charity that has ever been exercised. Ultimately to complete the scholarship endownment scheme and the rebuilding will cost a quarter of a million but the immediate necessity is to put up buildings at a cost of £100 000. The site which is larger than the existing site of the hospital and school and adjacent to it has been bought and paid for and the architect's plans are in our office. I have always dreamed of being able to interest some one in this scheme who can see its possibilities and who has the power which I haven't of making them practical business, and I hope this has not led me to bore you with it. I think it would grip the imagination of the people. I think this scheme will stand scrutiny. A contribution to the miners though indicated by the heart does not lead to the solution of anything, and properly organised businesses should surely provide for industrial research as part of overhead expenses. But the results of this scheme would multiply yearly.

'Now that I have got this off my chest I will not inflict it further upon you but if you trust my judgement to keep the physician's and the educationalist's role apart I would like to say this as a physician, that you have no more worlds to conquer in business and finance and that if you decide on some form of public service as the business of the next decade I believe real peace of mind is coming from building up a position in the affections of the people. It is worth doing and in saying this I am certain you know me enough to be confident that I am not using this argument as a back-door way of interesting you in St Mary's.

'Even if I have bored you with my scheme I have thoroughly enjoyed your illness! I have been into Aristotle and Socrates on happiness since I saw you and it is a good thing that you are going away or I might inflict them on you.   Bon voyage.'[24]

Charles's bait, the notion that Beaverbrook, by promoting an English Johns Hopkins medical school, might himself become a Johns Hopkins, was not taken, but Charles renewed his suit in the following year, encouraged perhaps by the fact that Beaverbrook had given £25 000 to charity as a thanks-offering for his escape in his car accident.[25] Following Revelstoke's death, Charles wrote again in May 1929, after a visit to Beaverbrook:

'I went over in the watches of the night the things I might have said to you but did not, and I feel I rather let the place down by the feeble way I put the case. I do not know if I only make matters worse by the enclosed pamphlet, but it is the only literature we have; I wrote it in popular form for the Queen! One of her ladies-in-waiting who was interested in our plans was anxious to have something to show her. I am afraid I am a rotten journalist but perhaps if there is any particular heading on which you wanted more facts you could refer to it without ploughing through my verbiage. I suppose the truth is that I am so keen on these plans that I get garrulous.'[26]

Charles then set out his case in much the same way as he had done before but in more detail. The cost of rebuilding the school would be £100 000. To endow fifty scholarships, £150 000 was needed, £50 000 for students entering from the universities and £100 000 for those entering from schools. According to his plan the entire annual entry would be made up entirely by scholars, but he again conceded that the first essential was to build. On this occasion Beaverbrook responded at once,[27] and Charles, after seeing him, wrote:

'It occurred to me after you left St Mary's that you might possibly wish to consult some more impartial authority than I can be as to the position and management of the school at St Mary's. Sir Wilmot Herringham of 25 Thurlow Road, Hampstead NW3, has inspected the school for several years for the University Grants Sub-Committee of the Treasury. Last time he was assisted by Sir Arthur Keith*. I am certain either of these would give you any information you would like to have.'[28]

Herringham, having told Charles that he was willing to speak to Beaverbrook in general terms, was pessimistic. 'You wont get anything out of that blackguard' he wrote. 'You've done your best and made your shot, and I should leave it at that.'[29] But Herringham was wrong, and when Charles called at Stornaway House on 23 May, Beaverbrook told him that he intended to give £63 000 to St Mary's.[22,30] The covenant was for payment to the hospital of £9000 a year for seven years from 25 May. The sum of £63 000, arrived at by Charles on the back of the envelope, would have resulted from taking £100 000 as the total needed for rebuilding, and subtracting Revelstoke's bequest of £25 000 and a further £12 000 for money already collected or expected.

---

*Sir Arthur Keith, conservator of the Hunterian Museum, Royal College of Surgeons.

What Charles never divulged about the meeting at Stornaway House was that, to the last, he had sought to get Beaverbrook to give his money for scholarships. Earlier in May Charles had been in touch with Montague Norman, who was governor of the Bank of England, about the global plans for building not only the medical school but also the pathology institute and nurses' home,[31] and after seeing Beaverbrook on 23 May Charles wrote to Norman:

'Although I was not successful when I saw Lord Beaverbrook last night in persuading him to give his money to scholarships and not to buildings, he said to me that if at any time in the near future we had sufficient money to put up the buildings without his assistance he would probably transfer his gift to scholarships. . . .'[30]

Charles gave Norman the impression that he might continue to try to induce Beaverbrook to change his mind but Norman poured cold water on the idea.[32] Charles replied saying he was bitterly disappointed and advanced further arguments for his scholarship scheme,[33] but to no avail. And so it was that Charles found that almost despite himself he had raised most of the money needed to rebuild his medical school.

It was characteristic of Charles that once he set himself an objective he was not to be deflected from it. He took stock, updated his case for raising an endowment of £150 000 for scholarships, and, after a few months, pressed it in new quarters. A gift such as this, Charles asserted, would create as much interest as Cecil Rhodes's gift to Oxford, but there were still no takers. In 1935 he had a final go at Beaverbrook, Dorothy writing to him, presumably at Charles's behest, after they had visited him.[34]
Her letter drew a rare written response:

'Dear Mrs Wilson,
'Thank you for writing to me so fully. I have read and followed every word of it. And I have known it well. That is the reason for my interest.

"I think your husband is a great figure—the greatest in London among professional men. I have been most anxious, again and again, to tell the public about him. But he always makes such a big objection that I cannot be bothered to fight for publication.

'Further, he is a very sensitive fellow. And easily hurt.

'And certainly he has sacrificed his own career. He ought to be in a lunatic asylum. He does not send any bills to his patients. They are all willing and anxious to pay. Some times they do not send for him because they are ashamed to do so.

'Your Charles is "a curious fellow". He will not mind that comment on him. These are the dying words of Bonar Law. He spoke them about me.

'As for the students at St Mary's I listened to Dr Wilson on Friday night. But I cannot see any use in subsidising any of them with scholarships.

'If I can find some way of helping the school I mean to do so. But his brats brought in from the provinces, with no particular ability, and no great prospect of doing any useful work, will not be benefited by making their lives easier during their school days.

'With kindest regards, I remain,
Yours sincerely,
Beaverbrook'[35]

Dorothy's championship of Charles's causes reflected the fact that he generally liked to play a lone hand, sharing his ambitions only with her. His activities were therefore directed to a large extent from 129 Harley Street, where the strands of public and private life were intertwined. In 1928 the landlord of number 129 died and Charles and Dorothy decided to borrow money[36] and buy the house rather than risk having to leave the flat that they had been living in.[37] Letting the flat and one downstairs room at the back, they occupied the rest of the building. A large front room off the entrance hall doubled as their dining room and as the waiting room for patients, so breakfast which, like all the meals, arrived at a hatch via a hand operated lift from the basement kitchen, had to be at 8 am sharp. Charles expected people to be punctual and was cross if they were late, and that applied to his family as much as anyone else. Half way up the stairs there was a small landing where the secretary, for many years Miss Wimbush, sat by the telephone exchange box, from which calls could be directed to different rooms. On the first floor was a big drawing room overlooking Harley Street, separated by folding doors from a back drawing room which served as Charles's consulting room. Here, where he had had bookshelves made for both sides of the open fireplace, and where a large window looked out over the mews, he and Dorothy sat in the evenings.

Charles never had a very large practice. He was really busy as a consultant only in the early 1930s when he became interested in the treatment of urinary tract infections, perhaps because he himself suffered repeated attacks.[38] He wrote two papers on a new treatment with what was called the ketogenic diet,[39,40] but when in 1935 this was displaced by the new sulphonamide drugs, his practice dwindled again[41] and he saw perhaps only three or four new patients a week.[42] Yet he was a good doctor, referred to by at least one general practitioner as superb because he was prepared to listen to what patients had to say,[43] and he could be marvellously comforting.[44] His reputation was in diagnosis[45] rather than treatment, which is not surprising since, before many of his contemporaries, he had realised that most of the favoured medications of the day were no more than nostrums.[36] The reason why Charles did not have a large consulting practice seems mainly to have been because he did not want one. He despised people who cultivated large practices,[46] ignoring perhaps the fact that some, by virtue of their high reputations, attracted many patients. What he wanted, and what he was interested in, was a few rich patients who would endow St Mary's, and powerful ones who would get things done.[47] One of the reasons why he was found acceptable by a number of such people was doubtless because of his view that, in general, people should not be stopped from doing what they wanted to do because of some ailment for which he could offer no effective treatment.

As well as appearing indifferent to the size of his practice, until the Second World War Charles showed little sign of an urge to earn money.[45] He didn't seem to understand money and it didn't interest him. Dorothy wrote the cheques, paid the bills and prepared the income tax returns.[15] In later years, money was a constant source of anxiety to him, not so much for himself but as a means for providing security for Dorothy, but in the 1920s and 1930s his life was the medical school,[45] and his personal fulfilment was in the work he did for it, in the success of the Rugby football team, and in a fairly simple home life with Dorothy and two boys. His attitude to money at this time was indeed extraordinary. His reluctance to charge Beaverbrook for his medical attendance after 1929 is understandable, though it led to bizarre situations, such as Beaverbrook handing Dorothy 400 one-pound notes, and observing teasingly but with some truth that with the way Charles went on she would be left penniless.[6] On another occasion, Beaverbrook sent a cheque for £1000 on account of fees.[48] Charles's readiness to reduce his usual fee of up to five guineas for a consultation if a patient was needy accorded with professional custom, but what seemed incomprehensible was that he failed to charge other patients who were well able to pay, notably some of Beaverbrook's friends, who at one stage wrote, four together, to protest that they had not been billed.[49] Dorothy, however, was an outstanding manager and dedicated to all Charles's enthusiasms so that although he was seen, in Harley Street terms, as a relatively poor man[50] with an income at best of about £4000 a year, number 129 was staffed with a married couple—Mr Warnes as chauffeur and Mrs Warnes as cook—as well as by a parlour maid and a tweenie.[51]

In many ways quite apart from his attitude to earning money, Charles was a very unpractical man. Before the first war, he had lived mostly on meagre funds in lodgings round Paddington, where landladies would have provided the basic necessities of life. Then, as an officer in the Royal Army Medical Corps, he was attended by a servant, and soon after he returned to civilian life Dorothy took charge and became his devoted guardian. Although he was at home on a horse and always retained an emotional attachment to childhood memories of Wolston, he was no country-man, and gardens, until he was an old man, were not part of his life.[15] His father never owned a car and for all practical purposes it could be said that Charles did not drive. However, on two occasions he had what Dorothy called delusions of grandeur about cars. The first was when he bought second-hand a very beautiful Rolls Royce of which Dorothy recalled:

> 'it was an absurd car really, a coupé-de ville where the driver sat [exposed] in front and the passengers behind. I never drove it and my father gave me a new little Morris Minor which I used all the time.'[52]

Dorothy's judgement on the purchase of the Rolls, a 20 horse power Sedanca-de-Ville which had been exhibited in Paris in 1926, was unduly severe because it was *de rigueur* for Harley Street consultants to have imposing cars. The possession of a Rolls or a Packard was visible evidence of success as a consultant. Charles's more real delusion about cars was when, after the Second World War, some doctors whom he was visiting in the Midlands persuaded him that if he bought a Bentley he could sell it at a profit a few years later. He bought one, but made no profit on it.

Despite the fact that Charles depended at times on a chauffeur, and for very many years on Dorothy, to drive him about, he was uninhibited in contributing personally to the driving process. He tended to give advice from the back seat; 'blow your horn', 'put out your hand' and 'get over to the left' were frequent instructions. Of other road-users, discerned to be hesitant or confused, he would exclaim, 'Infirm of purpose! Give me the daggers', or 'They're taking our water'. In contrast to the stern, ambitious, ruthless and reserved image that Charles projected at this time in his public life, at home he could be something of a wag, given to droll sayings that imprinted themselves on the minds of children. Outside the context of driving, 'All is lost!' and 'Once aboard the lugger and she is mine' were favourites. He was also given to mimicry, taking off great figures of the stage like Mrs Patrick Campbell, and he would amuse children, and tease Dorothy, by pretending to play a piano concerto for her on the dining room table.[53] But all these were very private things, and few outsiders had the chance to see him, as a secretary from St Mary's once did, having a boxing match at the top of the staircase in Harley Street, with the two little boys, John born in 1924 and Geoffrey in 1929.

There was relatively little social component in Charles's life in Harley Street before the Second World War. Dorothy was a light-hearted person with a great gift for friendship and a keen mind, and she was easily involved in a circle of friends and relations. She captivated some of Charles's friends too. But Charles with his Ulsterman's temperament, his shyness, and his monkish streak, which Churchill later discerned, found it hard to unbend. It is indeed difficult to identify him as positively enjoying himself in the years between the wars except in the context of St Mary's and its rugger team, and sometimes of his golf. For one thing, he tended to worry about his health. When he was first married he worried about having a gastric ulcer like his father, and his worry recurred over the years, and once after an attack of influenza, he developed asthma, but he recovered from it completely after a few weeks in a nursing home by the seaside at Broadstairs. He was also troubled from time to time by what he called his 'B. coli', with symptoms of kidney infection. Together with concern about his health, he was fussy about what he ate. Food had to be plain and he did not like sauces. What he really liked was what he called fresh vegetables, by which he meant ones cooked within half an hour of their being taken from the garden—a circumstance never achievable in Harley Street. Dinners were not things that he enjoyed. He kept no cellar and regarded himself as something of a connoisseur of water. 'That's good water' he would say. He limited his intake of alcohol to one glass of sherry in the evening before dinner, taken, he said, to stimulate the flow of gastric juice. But he smoked about 40 cigarettes a day up to the Second World War when he stopped and applied himself to his weekly ration of chocolate.

Of Charles's friends from student days, one, Archie Hamilton, who had become a general practitioner in Bradford, remained close and Charles would go away once a year, on his own, to Alnwick in Northumberland and play golf with him.[53] Golf remained throughout Charles's life a rather frustrating business. He approached it with exactly the same intensity of purpose and single-mindedness that he brought to any enterprise. He had learnt to play as a boy, bicycling over to the golf course on Walney Island from Barrow in Furness, but he never became more than moderately good and this bothered him, particularly because brother Lorton was, with no apparent effort, an outstanding player. He was inclined to look down on Lorton for being a general practitioner and not a consultant, regarding this as evidence of the same sort of infirmity of purpose that he attributed to his father-in-law, Felix Dufton, for being an inspector of schools when he possessed a doctorate of science. Both brother and father-in-law, according to Charles, had failed to aim at the top and that was a cardinal sin.

Charles's failure to reach the standard that he aspired to in golf was certainly not due to lack of effort. From Harley Street he went to a golf school in Regents Park and when that closed to one in Kensington.[41] Then he joined the Highgate Golf Club, and, finding it very crowded when he was free in the evenings, he persuaded Dorothy for a while to get up and drive him there to practise at 6.30 am. At the height of his endeavours, Warnes rigged up a platform against the back of number 129 Harley Street, and hung fine netting in front of the garage wall on the other side of a small courtyard. This saved the early morning expeditions and worked well until Charles wore a hole in the netting and a ball ricocheted back, narrowly missing his head.[54]

Of friends that Charles and Dorothy shared, TR Elliott and his wife were among the first. Elliott had met them independently before they themselves had met, Charles at Boulogne and Dorothy at Cambridge. When they were first married, Charles and Dorothy used to go to the Elliott's house and play tennis. While Charles's and Dorothy's friendship with the Elliotts was never very close, Dorothy felt that it was one that mattered a lot. Throughout their married life one of Dorothy's contributions to her partnership with Charles was to tidy up affairs and smooth ruffled feathers that he had disturbed. One of her first efforts was directed towards bringing Charles and Elliott together after the forthright exchanges that they had had in connection with the university appointments in 1921. In the course of a long letter that she wrote to Elliott a year later, in which she sought to repair the bridges, she gave a vivid sketch of the Charles that she knew:

'Unfortunately . . . the most sensitive and idealistic natures seem to hide under the most aggressive and prickly shells. And when that idealism is bruised and buffeted by an unsympathetic world it seems to hide deeper and the outside seems to bristle more than ever. Some day I would like to tell you the whole story of last year's visions and plans, not for Charles's own career as a Unit man, but for the future of Mary's and the greatness that might have come of it. And the personal defeat mattered nothing—but what mattered and hurt was the misjudgement of the people one hoped would have known him better. In that time of unhappiness I had great comfort in a small incident at Kings Cross. I was there one day with Charles and suddenly a porter stood still and stared and then his face lighted up and he came towards us. He had been a Fusilier and had known Charles in France. The battalion knew him as he is, his old Rugger team knew him, and the students today know him. I suppose that wherever he goes there will be factions—no one who is as intolerant as he is of incompetence—and particularly of incompetence that takes itself seriously, can help making enemies, but he has always very firm friends who will go through fire for him. And as for leadership—after all the truest leadership is based on idealism and unselfishness, and when these light the way, men, the pick of them, will follow. For it is in this that I think his greatest gift lies.'[55]

In concluding the letter Dorothy added:

'I feel it is presumptuous on my part to write all this to you—I wanted somehow to make you two understand each other and I seem to have developed an apologia.'[55]

As the years passed, Elliott and Charles came to have a great respect for each other.[47] Apart from the Boulogne experience of 1918 when Charles was working on mustard gas casualties and Elliott was there on behalf of the Medical Research Committee, they shared similar visions of the place of academics in clinical medicine and they were both architects in their own ways of the new era in their respective medical schools at University College Hospital and St Mary's.

Dr John Freeman and his wife Violet, who were near neighbours at 30 Devonshire Place, were other shared friends. From Almroth Wright's earliest days at St Mary's, Freeman had been one of his disciples and he had followed Wright to Boulogne and back. He supervised the routine bacteriology laboratory at St Mary's and was one of the pioneers of studies of allergic disorders such as hay fever.[56] He shared Charles's enthusiasm for the students' sporting activities, his special interest being the hospital's rifle club. He himself was a good shot and it was said that when Fleming qualified in 1906 it was Freeman who got him a job with Almroth Wright, for Fleming too was an excellent shot and Freeman wanted to make sure he was retained in the rifle club. Charles and Freeman used to speak and write to each other as man-to-man and, since Charles never had this sort of relationship with Almroth Wright, Freeman became something of a go-between when the competing interests of the medical school and pathology institute were in contention. Dorothy and Violet Freeman also saw quite a lot of each other in a neighbourly way.

Sir Wilmot Herringham, who had come into Charles's life in France during the war, and again over the establishment of the clinical units, became another shared friend. Charles was not given to according virtually unqualified praise to people but he came close to doing so in Herringham's case. In an apparently unpublished note that he wrote after Herringham's death in 1936, he described him as one who, by virtue of his broad scholarship, stood apart from the profession. 'While Herringham lived' he wrote, 'we were not allowed to forget that the heads of a learned profession should themselves be learned'.[57] Charles told how, with the end of the war, the death in action of his only son and the realisation that his wife's long and distressing illness could have but one end, the purpose was cut from Herringham's life. When on Osler's death in 1919 the regius professorship of medicine at Oxford was offered to him, he felt he was not fitted for the office and refused it. In 1970, when Charles was 87, he included comments on Herringham in an interview recorded on tape by Dr Charles Newman, the then Harveian Librarian of the Royal College of Physicians. With minor editing to avoid repetition, it may be transcribed as follows:

'Sir Wilmot Herringham was a very misleading figure. I knew him intimately. He was a first class scholar. He read his Greek with ease. All his tasks were intelligent. A man of great determination— lonely—his wife, a gifted creature, had died. Lone figure, when I knew him, living in Hampstead at the top of a house in a flat. There he stayed till about half past eleven when he made his way to the club—the Oxford and Cambridge Club—for lunch. Then he went back toward the evening to his place up in Hampstead. A great reader. A great friend of my wife. She used to drive him round the country. They were both interested in archeology. They used to go on those car trips . . . he always knew all the details of the places they went to. . . . He was one of the old brigade at Barts where people thought it was rather improper to practise. . . . They had private means. I don't think Wilmot Herringham ever had a patient in his life. They got on Barts, they had private means and that was the life they led. I think that applied to quite a number of them—except—Horder was an exception of course. . . . A very good administrator. Fearless. Knew principles. Not sure he was very good at handling people. . . .'[58]

Compassion for this lonely man, then in his middle 70s, led Charles to invite Herringham to dinner at 129 Harley Street in 1927.[59] Maybe some enlightened self-interest was involved too since Herringham was still a member of the university grants committee. Thereafter he dined at Harley Street, at times as often as once a fortnight, and the friendship continued until he died. This association with Herringham extended over the period of the fulfilment of Charles's work for the rebuilding of the medical school and of the nomination scholarship controversy. It is hard to believe these were not topics of conversation at dinner, but there is no clue in letters to his thoughts on them. Dorothy and Herringham became particularly attached to each other and he wrote some one hundred letters to her between 1929 and 1934. They were brief comments on everyday things and clearly she provided him with a welcome point of contact with a member of a younger generation who shared his love of beautiful things. When Herringham died, Dorothy wrote to another of her regular correspondents:

'He has been such a wonderful friend to me for the last seven years and I shall miss him sorely. I owe him such a lot and he has opened many windows on life for me, and has taught me to look with new eyes on books and poetry, and flowers and birds and trees, and pictures and buildings. He had a passion for beauty and was a scholar too.'[60]

The occasion of Herringham's first dining at Harley Street had a totally unforeseen consequence for Charles and Dorothy. It led to them coming to own one of the few portraits that exist of William Harvey, who in 1628 published to the world his discovery of the circulation of the blood. In 1980 Dorothy described how the purchase was made:

'I remember Sir Wilmot dining with us, when he had just been invited to give the [1929] Harveian Oration at the College of Physicians. He then said that he would talk about the life and times of Harvey and could not find out whether the family was armigerous or not. I said I could find out for him because my brother-in-law Charles's brother made a hobby of genealogy. . . . So I wrote to Lorton Wilson and he told me what books I should need and where I could find them, so I looked it up for Sir Wilmot. He wrote me a charming letter of thanks, ending, 'You seem a very idle young woman—come and help me.' I was thrilled to be invited to undertake any humble job of historical research, and the first thing I did was to copy all the wills of the Harvey brothers. That led me on to their families. One of the brothers, Eliab had a daughter or grand-daughter, Mary, who married Sir Edward Dering. Just at that moment I saw in *The Times* that a house with all its furniture and pictures in a picture gallery were being sold. I sent for the catalogue and there in the gallery was 'Mary Harvey, Lady Dering' by Lely. I went down to Maidstone to see her—a lovely picture that made me think of John's portrait of Suggia in the Tate Gallery. I then went round the house to see if there was a book or a silver spoon I could buy as a memento of the occasion, [and] when walking up the back stairs what should I see but a portrait of Uncle William. (I was familiar with Sir d'Arcy Power's book of Harvey portraits, so I recognised this one but it was not in the book). I came home and talked to Charles. For a long time he could not believe it, but finally said there were only two possibilities—if no one had spotted the connection, the picture was obviously worth very little, but if the connection was known it might fetch any price. At the end we decided that we could not afford more than £50 and I went to the sale. I was very excited, and had a puncture in a borrowed car on the way, and arrived just in time. The bidding was brisk up to £20 and then tailed away, and I bought the picture for £38.

'I paid the cheque, wrapped it in a rug and put in the back of the car. I took it to the Director of The Portrait Gallery (just opposite the RCP). He had it cleaned for me, and said that he was satisfied that it was a contemporary portrait and told me to insure it for some hundreds. I still have it in my room . . . but have sometimes lent it for special occasions. The last time was to Dr Lipscombe of Folkestone who had much to do with the local celebrations of the Harvey ter-centenary.'[52]

In the years between the wars, holidays were not among Charles's highest priorities, but several were memorable. An early trial of skiing at Pontresina with the Freemans ended with his colliding with a lady and breaking his leg. The guide skied down to the village with him on his shoulders. A conference at Bad Neuheim in 1933 led to Dorothy driving the very small Morris Minor, with John and the luggage in the back, through Armentières and other parts of the western front that Charles had known nearly twenty years before. In Germany there were lorry loads of youths wearing swastika arm bands, and Charles commented that the Jewish doctors expected at the conference did not turn up. But 'Charles had to go back to London' was a recurring theme in Dorothy's letters about seaside summer holidays, one of which was spent at St Briac in France, and one at Lady Kenmare's house at Walmer in Kent.[61] In the Easter holidays of 1934 Charles sent Dorothy and John on a cruise in SS 'Doric', and in a letter posted to reach the ship at Civitavecchia he entreated her not to spoil the trip by small economies and to be very careful about typhoid in Rome and Tangier.[62] In 1935 there was a visit to Ireland.[63] After that, holidays became equated with visits to the mill at Manton, just outside Marlborough. Access to the mill came about through Dorothy's inclusion in the long-standing friendship between Charles and Godfrey Maurice, who was making a distinguished career for himself in the Sudan Medical Service, contributing in the scientific field to knowledge of sleeping sickness[64] and in the literary field to *Blackwood's Magazine*.[65] Dorothy took to writing often to him, as she had done to Herringham, characterising him with a phrase borrowed from a play which she saw with Godfrey's widowed sister Cicely as 'a nice bronze Englishman'. With an eye to his eventual retirement, Godfrey, in 1934, bought Manton Weir House near Marlborough, and being concerned that if someone else bought the old mill adjacent to it they might spoil his privacy, he bought it as well.

Dorothy pressed Godfrey to let her have the mill to turn into a week-end cottage. It suited him well to have friends there and he told Dorothy she could live in it rent free as compensation for improving it and keeping it in repair.[64] It was one of those loose arrangements that so often come to destroy friendships, but to begin with it was a happy one. Dorothy went to work with enthusiasm and before long enlisted the help of Sir Edwin Cooper, the architect appointed for the building of the medical school.[65] She took him to the mill where, she reported to Godfrey, 'he put on an old Inverness cape and an ancient tweed hat and a pair of goloshes and banged on the walls and tested for damp and was most practical.' Warnes, whose capacity as a handyman was greater than his appreciation of cars—he had painted the silver headlamps of the Rolls black—was then sent to the mill and quite soon, at the cost of £100, transformed it into a charming riverside cottage.[66] Charles's commitments often kept him in London and the conversion of the mill into Mill House was very much Dorothy's enterprise. It was great for John, the older of the two boys, for Godfrey Maurice, when home on leave, made a good bachelor uncle. He reflected a way of life that had not been part of either Charles's or Dorothy's upbringing. For him shooting and fishing were part of the natural order of things and he introduced John to a whole range of country pursuits which he would not otherwise have experienced. Dorothy's letters of the 1930s to Godfrey Maurice, which he kept and which were later returned to her, give other glimpses of the family's life. In one letter Dorothy told him that she and Charles had had tea with Beaverbrook after visiting Winchester which they were considering as a possible school for John. Beaverbrook, she wrote, had scoffed and said 'Send him to a Board School and let him learn to mix with the people.' Dorothy added: 'Fleming—you know, the fellow at Mary's—who had the education of the very poor—is sending his son to Eton as he says that nothing matters except to be a good mixer—which of them is right?'.[67] In another letter she wrote: 'This is not a letter—its written in the only spare moment I've had in this most strenuous week end. Being Charles's chief of staff is an arduous occupation. . . . Time I picked Charles up and I believe I've forgotten the number of the house I was to go to'.

Charles's relatively quiet social life in the 1920s and 1930s was not just a reflection of rather tight finances. It suited him both temperamentally and because his work was all-absorbing. When in 1937 he was asked about his commitments as dean of the medical school, he replied that for the first 12 years of his appointment he had hardly done anything except work related to the rebuilding of the school and the interests of the students, and that included the week ends.[69] When he did relax at home in the evenings he liked to listen to the radio, particularly to programmes about sport, and he was often busy marking examination papers, for he examined in medicine at various times for the universities of Cambridge, Liverpool, Birmingham and London as well as for other medical licensing bodies. Although he tended to dip into books and annotate them in the margins rather than read them through, he gradually collected a considerable library. It started when they were first married, with the addition by Dorothy of two volumes of Chekhov to the well-worn copies of *The Darling and Other Stories* and *The Duel and Other Stories* which he had acquired in the last years of the war. He read *The Times* every day and Dorothy cut out pieces from it and a variety of other papers, particularly book reviews and descriptions of Rugby matches, which she thought would interest him and she pasted them into scrap books. Charles regarded playing cards and doing crossword puzzles as flippant pastimes, he never went to concerts and seldom accompanied Dorothy to the theatre, an occasion which she always enjoyed. Nor did he show any enthusiasm for going to church although he would attend on special occasions such as Armistice Sunday. Dorothy, on the other hand, took the boys to church regularly on Sunday mornings. She always wondered why he didn't like church for, as she put it, he knelt at his bedside every night of his life. Charles was never a clubbable man; when he became a member of the Athenaeum, in which senior academics and clergy tended to congregate, he used the place infrequently, complaining that it was full of bishops who never talked to him.[70]

Most of Charles's achievements resulted from his ability to influence people. He realised that what mattered was to pick those with or through whom he could work[71] and to talk to them. Before he could command audiences to address, he used the carefully written word, and his writings in the 1920s on poor law hospitals[72,73] and on clinical units[74] quickly brought him to the notice of the most influential men in medicine in England. At the head of them stood Lord Dawson of Penn of whom Charles wrote in an obituary in 1945:

'It will be a long time before any member of the medical profession will again influence opinion in England as Lord Dawson did between the two wars . . .

'He stood apart from others not so much because of his pre-eminence as a physician but rather because he possessed a gift which is more prized than any other by men of affairs: he knew instinctively what the average man was thinking and how he would react to some measure or action that had been taken by the official world.'[75]

And, using one of his favourite phrases, he credited Dawson with intuitive knowledge of 'what was happening in men's minds'. While Charles might well have claimed that he himself developed these capacities in considerable measure, Dawson differed from him in almost every other way. Outstandingly vigorous, good-looking, charming and self-assured, Dawson escaped from his practice during regular substantial holidays. His biographer, Francis Watson, described how there were house parties, yacht cruises, stalking and fishing trips. In the course of his professional duties, a special train would sometimes take him into the country on an important visit.

According to Watson: 'Dawson whole-heartedly enjoyed these pleasures while they lasted . . . he liked good living and good manners, and he continued to uphold them in a changing world', and the baffling quality in Dawson's life, Watson wrote, 'resided in the fact that by and large he was good, successful and happy. The coincidence of all three is phenomenal'.[76]

When Abraham Flexner revisited England after the war, in 1921, Dawson gave a dinner and invited representatives of the London medical schools to meet him, choosing not the senior physicians and surgeons but men he discerned to be the young hopefuls, of whom Charles was one.[41] Charles, having met Flexner and being already familiar with his writing, asked him to dine at Harley Street. He also invited Almroth Wright and Sir James Mackenzie, the doyen of British cardiologists. Dorothy wrote of the occasion: 'I always remember that dinner. Wright was a brilliant conversationalist and was at the top of his form. The practical Sir James got tired of it and I remember him striking the table and saying "Almroth you're talking through your hat and you know it."'[41]

In the Harley Street household, various people were identified from time to time as Public Enemy Number One.[77] Dawson sometimes rated a mention in this context, primarily as a figure to be tilted against. But there were no feelings of warmth for another prominent physician who, like Dawson, held royal appointments, Sir Thomas (later Lord) Horder. Horder, a St Bartholomew's man, was to contest the presidency of the Royal College of Physicians with Charles throughout Charles's tenure of that office, but they first crossed swords in a way that engendered bitter feelings in the 1920s, probably over a piece of apparatus called Abram's Box. In 1924 Horder, in an article in the *British Medical Journal*[78], showed remarkable credulity in discussing the possible diagnostic and therapeutic value of a magic box that had been promoted by an American called Abrams and this had led to tart comments, including ones in the *Lancet*[79] and the *St Mary's Hospital Gazette*,[80] and to Charles making what he later conceded was a silly jibe at Horder, accusing him of selling a story to a newspaper.[81] It was not until long after the battles for the presidency of the Royal College of Physicians were over, and Horder was dead that Charles found anything charitable to say about him:

'I probably saw him closer than most people because I was in his way. Horder was not a bad character really. The idea grew up in medicine that he was a pure mercenary . . . I don't think that was true . . . his son's memoir . . . quite revealing . . . he had another side to him . . . a keen gardener . . . an enormous success . . . there was a time in practice when he was *the* consultant . . . city people said: This man is not a bedside manner, he's a brain . . .'[82]

Chapter 8

Choosing People

At the meeting of the hospital's Board of Management on 30 May 1929 Charles occupied the centre of the stage.[1] While his report of Revelstoke's bequest to the medical school was not a surprise, since the school committee had been told of it three weeks before,[2] his announcement of Beaverbrook's gift came as a bolt from the blue. The two contributions totalling £88 000—equivalent to more than one million pounds in the 1990s—were recognised as the fruits of Charles's personal exertions and enterprise, as indeed they were. Certainly there had been a building and appeals subcommittee, and Charles, with the medical school's interests at heart, had been operating to some degree in liaison with it and with John Freeman and Almroth Wright, who were concerned with the pathology institute. The two buildings were to share the same site. But things had not been easy. Partly because they were sometimes competing for their separate projects among the same rich people in the higher echelons of society, Charles and Freeman got into a dreadful tangle. Dorothy, who usually went along behind Charles soothing people, compounded the problem on one occasion by joining Lady Kenmare in a separate initiative in the same scene. When one of the key figures to whom Dorothy, and thence Charles, had been led, proved to be one of Freeman's private patients, a furious telephone call from Freeman drew a three-and-a-half page closely typed explanation from Charles,[3] but Freeman was unappeased. He told Charles that his letter was right off the rails and that he was an impossible man to work with.[4] Intrigues about a hospital appointment, in which they were both also active at this time, drew another salvo from Freeman. He accused Charles of being an obstructionist. 'I don't think you are a villain' he wrote 'but you are an idjit [sic] and [underlined] a congenital grouser.'[5] However, within a few days, with the announcement of Beaverbrook's gift, all was happiness and light, and Freeman wrote:

'Dear Wilson, I see you have landed it rich again—hearty congratulations. Why didn't you tell me? . . . the Inoculation Department will have to pull up its socks.   Yours, JF.'[6]

Among the letters of congratulations Charles received, none would have pleased him more than one hand-written on note-paper of the Royal College of Surgeons from Sir Arthur Keith, who was on the university grants committee. Keith told him that

119

he would see that his fellow members on the committee appreciated Charles's efforts to the full.[7]

Seven weeks after the announcement of Beaverbrook's gift, the Board of Management authorised the appointment of an architect.[8] Sir Edwin Cooper, who was chosen, was then in his late 50s and had a list of fine public buildings to his credit, including the Marylebone Town Hall and the Gray's Inn Law Library. The choice of Cooper has been attributed to Charles[9] but it cannot have been his alone. It is indeed hard to be sure of the extent of Charles's influence on the building itself. As he and Dorothy grew older they were inclined to dilate with justifiable pride on what Charles had done for St Mary's, but at the time he shunned publicity, preferring to work behind the scenes and neither of them claimed later that he made any singular contribution to the planning of the lecture theatres and laboratories. What he did claim, and was given credit for, was his contribution to planning the amenities, outstanding among which was the handsome library. Cooper himself gave the wood for its pillars and walls.[10] There were few books to put in it at first but Charles said these would come later, and, when someone criticised the plans of the library on the grounds that it would be larger than that of the Royal Society, he was not at all bothered. Plenty of students, he said, would come and fill it.[11] Underneath the

Figure 9. The new St Mary's Hospital Medical School opened on 12 December 1933. (Reproduced by kind permission of St Mary's Hospital and Medical School Archives)

LIBRARY AND SPEECH HALL

Figure 10. St Mary's Hospital Medical School Library, designed by Sir Edwin Cooper. (Reproduced by kind permission of St Mary's Hospital and Medical School Archives)

library there was to be a fine swimming pool, and a lot of attention was to be paid to the students' restaurant, common room and adjacent gym and squash courts. The furniture bought for the common room was chosen by Dorothy and was in excellent taste. Some said the students would ruin it but Charles replied that if you gave students good furniture they would look after it and by and large they did. Tenders for the building were accepted in July 1930,[12] and the ceremony for the laying of the foundation stone was planned. Charles, true to form, went straight to the top and approached the Queen. Lady Kenmare wrote at the same time to the Queen's private secretary, Sir Harry Verney, who, replying that Queen Mary regretfully could not add to her engagements, suggested that one of the princes should be approached.[13] In the end, and again with Lady Kenmare's involvement, the Duchess of York was invited and agreed to set aside the afternoon of 30th June, 1931 for the event.[14] There could not have been a happier choice. The Duchess was to become the consort of King George VI and, when he died in 1952, the Queen Mother. The laying of the foundation stone marked the beginning of many decades in which St Mary's benefited from the lively interest of this greatly beloved lady.

Two months before the foundation stone was laid, the Court of the University of London made a grant of £10 000 towards the cost of the new buildings[15] and, one month before, the Prime Minister,

Stanley Baldwin, accepted the invitation of the chairman of the hospital's Board of Management, Lieutenant Colonel HE Verey, to speak. In his acceptance, hand-written from his home in Shropshire, Baldwin observed that providentially he had just got a new tail coat and, in undertaking to throw in a brief oration, he added: 'I couldn't give you £63 000 nor could the Beaver make my oration.'[16] In fact Beaverbrook could well have given the first part of it, for it was clearly based on a brief from Charles. The ceremony on 30 June 1931 was chronicled in the *St Mary's Hospital Gazette*:

'Cambridge [later Norfolk] Place, homing ground of staff and cars, orange peel and cats, was unrecognisable in the guise of a magnificent marquee, resplendent with gilded chairs and carpets, through which not even the most blatant orange peel nor the most insinuating of cats managed to intrude to ruffle the old street's borrowed plumes of glory.'[17]

The Times reported Baldwin's speech at length. The opening paragraph made the point that Charles had been emphasising from the time of his first approaches to Revelstoke and Beaverbrook. Medical schools, Baldwin said, depended for their income on students' fees and grants. For many years to come, all capital expenditure, and most of the cost of running the schools and of research, would continue to depend on gifts from the public. Later, mentioning Beaverbrook's gift, Baldwin remarked that he was glad 'to welcome him into the growing ranks of those men to whom the world has indeed been generous and who are seeking the right way in which the heart and the head may combine to make some return for that generosity.'[18] Beaverbrook was not there.[19]

Before the Duchess declared the foundation stone to be well and truly laid, first Charles and then Almroth Wright spoke. *The Times* did not record their addresses but Charles's manuscript shows that he started by paying tribute to the Duchess for the unflagging interest that she had shown in St Mary's since she had become president of the hospital. Having then thanked each major benefactor, he came to his peroration:

'The growing decrepitude of the old school buildings which date from 1850 will soon pass and in their place will rise up the beautiful building which Sir Edwin Cooper has designed for us. A beautiful environment fosters tradition and stirs up the spirit of service to an institution that is latent in youth. But the fame and fortune of a school are not built of bricks and mortar. They are in the keeping of its students. In the certain faith that education is the only remedy for our present distress I trust they may go forth from these walls in the fullness of time to spread respect for truth and in that manner may make their own contribution, however small, to the ultimate reign of reason.'[20]

The first part of this peroration reflected Charles's conviction that students, and above all students that he himself chose, were very important people, trustees for the future. His final sentence, read fifty years on, smacks of pomposity, but the genuineness of the sentiment he was conveying need not be doubted. England was in the middle of a deep world-wide financial depression, 'our present distress', and he believed that only educated minds would lead the country out of it. Charles could be remarkably persuasive as a public speaker with what was once described as his silver tongue and honied phrases. He took great trouble in writing out his speeches and then delivered them usually without a note, in what his family regarded as a rather special voice.[21] His voice was naturally sonorous, and he had a nice sense of words. At one time he considered taking a course of instruction in the art of speaking but, after one session, he decided he would not be helped. He realised he could already hold an audience. If he missed being always a top class orator it was because he tended to use long sentences in which parenthesis became piled on parenthesis, so that his audience had to pay very close attention to understand exactly what he meant.[22] He was at his best speaking in conversation and in closely reasoned pungent argument.

The interval between the laying of the foundation stone in 1931 and the opening of the new medical school building in 1933 saw the culmination of 'the great rugger scholarship row', which was the first of three occasions on which, in Dorothy's words, Charles was at war with public opinion. Ripples from the row spread so as to affect the plans for the opening and to influence some people's perception of Charles for the rest of his life. Those not associated with the London medical schools might find it hard to understand the passions that the affair aroused. The background lay in the fact that by the end of the 19th century, each London medical school had a special hallmark.[23] For St Mary's it was the enthusiasm of the students for sport, and high on the list of sports was Rugby football, which had become a clearly identifiable game at Rugby School in 1823, and had quickly been adopted by many other English public schools. As boys left school they formed clubs so that they could continue playing and one of the earliest clubs to be formed was at Guy's Hospital.[24] The St Mary's Hospital Rugby Football Club, founded in 1865, was also quite early. The game came to be regulated by a body called the English Rugby Union, which discouraged competitions between clubs that aimed at winning a cup. However, one of the few cup competitions allowed was the London Hospitals Cup, so the scene was set for strongly partisan feelings between the hospitals, feelings which permeated the medical staff, the general body of students, the nursing staff and everyone else associated with the hospital. By the time Charles became a medical student, St Mary's had been competing for the cup since 1875 but had won it only once, in 1900.[25]

If Rugby football had been important in the lives of Charles's student contemporaries, for none of them was it more important than it was for him: he associated his arrival at a state of manhood with his discovery that he was good at the game. But he would not have been unique in this experience, so there must have been something more than that to explain the intensity of his feelings about the game and his lifelong preoccupation—some might say obsession—with it. There are some clues in what he wrote and said on the subject. His writing in the *St Mary's Hospital Gazette,* before he temporarily rejected medicine and set out for Egypt and Italy in 1911, reflected his enchantment with the public school ethos which was such a feature of Edwardian life. It was perhaps odd that a youth, whose boarding school experience had consisted of two unhappy years at a small grammar school, should share the feeling so strongly, but share it he certainly did, and central to the public school ethos was the phenomenon of organised games.[26] It was believed that games not only kept boys fit but also instilled virtues in them—team spirit, manliness and bravery; games developed character; and they trained boys for leadership, particularly for leadership in war. In England there was a lively appreciation of the need for this as events leading to the first German war unfolded one after another.

Whatever underlay Charles's passion for Rugby football, the virtues attributed to it were clearly confirmed by his wartime experience. He mentioned football repeatedly in the evidence that he gave to the committee on shell shock in 1920. Defining shell shock as any sort of functional nervous disorder, and discussing ways of selecting in advance men who would not be prone to develop it, Charles asserted '. . . if you could get everybody playing rugby football, you would not have this thing to solve.'[27] Drawing again on his wartime experience, he laid things on the line in an editorial article in the *St Mary's Hospital Gazette* in 1922 entitled 'On the meaning of games to a medical school.' Rugby, he said, was a particular means of bringing out of a man the idealism in him— 'games prevent or delay a man becoming absorbed in himself' and 'a community may justly demand of its members that they serve not themselves only but the common weal. English institutions rely largely on games to bring about that end . . .' And, in conclusion, his up-dated credo: 'It is because games seek to implant above personal needs the idea of working for the School, that they bring with them a cleaner air. That, not the advertisement of athletic prowess in the papers, is the contribution they can make to the well-being of the school.'[28]

In accordance with this passionate belief, Charles set out to spread Rugby football through the school when he became Dean in 1920. While trying to improve the fixture list to ensure that the first XV played the better non-hospital clubs, he was proud to be able to say that the Rugby club at times ran seven or eight XVs. In other words, upwards of half the students played each week.[29] And he did not just run things from the Dean's office. He used to say that a good dean was a man who would referee the third XV rugger game on a wet November Saturday afternoon,[30] and this he sometimes did. His interest was not just in the first XV so that anyone with potential was encouraged. 'The second XV defeated King's second XV quite easily', he wrote to Dorothy who was staying in Devonshire in February 1926. 'I went down, and all the first [XV].'[31]

Despite his convictions Charles had to acknowledge sometimes that everybody cannot play Rugby football; that, he was forced to concede to the shell shock committee, was obvious. While therefore, what he really liked were intellectual Rugby players, he chose as students plenty of others with different athletic abilities, and many with none.[32] What he was ultimately after was what he called 'people who kept going',[11] and he was convinced he could pick them by taking careful account of what their schoolmasters and college tutors could tell him about them, and by interviewing them himself. In the Dean's Reports in the medical school handbooks that were published each year, Charles's very personal vision of the student body he wanted to create became clear for all to see. Year by year he referred to the consequences of introducing scholarships by nomination to replace those previously awarded by examination. In the 1924-25 report he recorded that there were nine candidates from Oxford and Cambridge for the university scholarships and 21 for those open to the public schools. He added:

'The success of the new system of awarding these scholarships has never been in doubt, and the competition is growing keener, so that the task of the selection committee becomes more difficult every year. This particularly applies to scholarships reserved for the public schools. It is not easy to discriminate in an entry that includes boys who have been heads of big schools, in the face of testimony from their headmasters that they stand out for all-round proficiency in a manner which they find difficult to parallel in their wide experience. They come to us with the stamp of leadership not only in the academic field but in those other activities where character as well as capacity counts. It is not difficult to see that a steady yearly stream of this kind of boy must have a profound influence upon the life and character of the medical school to which they go.'[23]

One of the scholars chosen that year, Denis Brinton—not a rugger player—was to succeed Charles as Dean 20 years later. As time went by, Charles was able to present a respectable list of academic distinctions won by scholars, and in his 1929-30 report, he took stock of the first 10 years of his work and unveiled his notion of what he called an Honours School:

'Throughout the decade since the war, behind every new venture at St Mary's, there is found the conviction that the type of student attracted to the School matters most . . .

'The introduction every year of a considerable number of . . . picked men means that at any one time they constitute a fair proportion of the total students at St Mary's.

'This picked fraction is increasing yearly. It provides already the effective nucleus of an Honours School, such as exists nowhere else in England . . .'[34]

He noted that the scholars of that year included past presidents of the Cambridge Medical Society, and of the Osler Society at Oxford, and the editor of the Cambridge Medical Society Magazine.

With his public reference to the creation of an Honours School of Medicine in this, the year before the foundation stone of the new medical school was laid, Charles really threw down the gauntlet. The recruiting policy and practice at St Mary's had been causing increasing dismay among some of the other London schools. It was being put about that St Mary's gave scholarships to students with indifferent intellects but ability at Rugby football. In other words, it gave rugger scholarships. Charles was the villain of the piece and his ingenuity was flattered by some splendid tales that have enlivened the reminiscences of generations of London-trained doctors. According to one, foreseeing a need for a new wing three-quarter, he did the rounds of the public school matches, picked his man, visited the changing room after the game, accosted him, persuaded him that he wanted to do medicine, and offered him a scholarship on the spot. According to another, he had had his eye on a Welsh student who he discovered to his dismay had elected to go to Bart's. Nothing daunted, it was recounted, Charles found out on which train the obviously misguided fellow would arrive at Paddington Station *en route* for his chosen medical school, intercepted him on Number One platform, and bore him triumphantly to St Mary's as his latest scholar. And so on. But the criticisms had more serious undertones and these surfaced in July 1931 just after the laying of the foundation stone.[35] Charles confronted the issue in his Dean's Report for 1930-1931. He wrote:

'During the summer two of the largest medical schools brought before the appropriate committee of London University a motion that nomination scholarships should be abolished. The motion was defeated. It was the last move in a campaign carried on for some years against the nomination scholarship scheme, which has been in use at St Mary's since the war.'[36]

Why, Charles went on to ask, are the schools so anxious that this scheme should be ended? The reason given, he said, was that too much attention was paid to athletes in making the awards. This was nonsense. The nominations were made by headmasters and college tutors. Would the medical school, he asked, have their cooperation if the system was merely used to secure athletes? And he went on to describe the outstanding academic records of the 1931 applicants from Oxford and Cambridge. The reason, he said, why some of the large London schools were so concerned with what he saw as the internal policy of St Mary's, was that men from Oxford and Cambridge who formerly would have gone to two or three of the larger schools were now going to St Mary's, where one third of the students were taking Oxford and Cambridge degrees. But it was not, he added, the number, but the kind of man, who was coming to St Mary's that was causing the heartburning. And the scholarship scheme was only one of the many reasons why they were coming. While other schools had been talking of football scholarships, St Mary's had been busy taking the lead in every movement that made for efficiency. There then followed, for the third year running in the Dean's Report, an essay entitled Choice of a Medical School, in which the claims for the excellence of St Mary's were set out, including its geographical situation with lodgings close by, the absence of dental students competing for patients in the wards (a dig at Guy's) the presence of two clinical professors with their units (only three hospitals had two units), and the limited student numbers which, with an entry of 50 a year, resulted in small groups clerking in the wards, and in the students having a good chance of winning a resident appointment at their own hospital when they qualified.

Charles's idea that the failure, in the university committee, of the motion for the abolition of nomination scholarships, was the last move against the scheme, proved to be wrong. He was soon engaged in two related controversies. By far the more threatening involved an accusation by members of the staff of some other London teaching hospitals that the St Mary's Rugby XV consisted of professionals and so was ineligible to compete in the Hospitals Cup. The other arose from criticism by the regius professor of medicine at Oxford of Charles's recruiting methods. Although news that trouble was brewing was hinted at in the Daily Mail in September 1932,[37] the row about the status of the St Mary's rugger team took place behind closed doors. William Sargant, who, with a distinguished record as an all-rounder at Cambridge, had won an entrance scholarship to St Mary's in 1928, and who later became physician in charge of the department of psychological medicine at St Thomas's, gave an account of how the matter came to a head at a meeting of the United Hospitals Rugby Football Club, with St Bartholemew's, St Thomas's and others threatening to withdraw from the cup competition.[38] Charles, as Dean, attended the meeting and, with what Sargant described as cunning clear-headedness, held his own despite abuse from the assembled students. He denied the accusations levelled at St Mary's and persuaded the meeting that they must be confirmed by an independent tribunal. He promised that St Mary's would withdraw from the cup if this verdict went against them. A tribunal of five was organised, chaired by Lord Ebbisham,[39] who was on the Council of Guy's Hospital and on the Grand Committee of St Thomas's. St Mary's took no part in determining the tribunal's membership.[40] The tribunal's unanimous decision was that there was no evidence of prominent Rugby football players having been induced illegitimately to join St Mary's[39] and, according to Sargant, at least two other hospitals were shown to have been offering scholarships attractive to Rugby players. It seems that the students and players were less concerned with this whole business than were their seniors. Sargant for one may have compounded the problem by assuring a friend from another teaching hospital that a £5 note was slipped into his boot every time he turned out for St Mary's.[38] This joke found its way to the tribunal and Sargant had to do some explaining. An attempt by St Thomas's to continue the vendetta came to nothing and for all practical purposes the tribunal's ruling brought the rugger scholarship row to an end.[41] The tidying up included the placation of the regius professor of medicine at Oxford, E Farquhar Buzzard, who in his student days was said to have given so much attention to football that he gained only a fourth class honour in the natural science school at Oxford.[42] But he did well as a clinical student at St Thomas's, and then gained a high reputation as a physician on the staff there, before being appointed to the regius chair in 1928. His quarrel with St Mary's was not with their success in obtaining what he conceded was the best type of student, but with the methods of advertising employed, which he said were undignified and excited the indignation of their rivals.[43] The methods in question are described in an exuberant letter which Charles wrote to Beaverbrook in 1931, thanking him for including the medical school in his will:

'Cambridge is the biggest single reservoir from which medical schools get recruits. The method of advertising used by the [London medical] schools was to say that the Session would open on such and such a date, and the fees were such and such. We invited the Oxford and Cambridge Medical Societies to come to St Mary's for a clinical evening, transported them, dined them, and got a dozen of the staff to demonstrate with cases, and sent them back convinced that we had the teachers. The first year about thirty accepted the invitation, last year from Cambridge alone 160 applied to come. Incidentally I took two pages in the Cambridge University Medical Society Magazine instead of the usual few lines to set out what were the advantages to Cambridge men of coming

to a middle sized school such as St Mary's rather than to Bart's
or Guy's.'[35]

Buzzard was moved to write in forthright terms about this to his
old friend John Freeman. Freeman, ever a doughty fighter, now leapt
to the defence of the Dean and the hospital. Surely, he said, Buzzard
was not referring to a rather stodgy paper that the Dean had written
in the Cambridge Medical Magazine at the editor's request. And
the motor bus and medical meeting business had been started by
the students. Freeman being tall and Charles being fairly slight,
the following passage contains an interesting nuance:

'Biggish men like you and me often think that small men are
pushing and bouncing too much—but we must be tolerant; the same
is true of the four big Hospitals I think—they mustn't shout
"advertisement" too readily.

'Look here Buzzard—strictly between ourselves and straight from
the shoulder—I believe the whole damned business has been the
wish of a few Senior Surgeons, chiefly from Thomas's and Bart's,
acting under jealousy—naturally masquerading as virtuous
indignation; and I believe they were set going by the incautious
remarks of a Mary's Surgeon who had only recently left our staff
and who has a personal feud against our Dean.'[44]

Within three months of this correspondence, by March 1933,
Buzzard and his fellow regius in Cambridge, Langdon Brown, were
ready to cooperate[45] and a note the following year shows that
Langdon Brown was giving all the help he could to Charles in his
search for the potential senior university scholar for that year.[46]
Throughout this whole affair, Charles was unwavering. He was
determined to continue to fill his medical school with 'people who
kept going', and he did not hesitate to chide some of his critics who,
he maintained, had caricatured as an irresponsible search for athletes
his attempts to attract the best students. Commenting on a report
made by the official inspectors of the school in 1932, Charles wrote:

'My school regrets that the Inspectors should appear to
countenance this attitude of mind by a quotation from the will
of Cecil Rhodes which is inaccurate. If that quotation "fondness
for success in manly outdoor sports such as cricket, football and
the like" were accurate, this single line, wrenched from its context
in this matter, conveys a wholly misleading summary of his ideals.
The relevant passage in the will is:

"My desire being that students who shall be elected to the
Scholarships shall not be merely bookworms, I direct that in the
election of a student to a scholarship regard shall be had to:

1. His literary and scholastic attainments.

2. His fondness for, and success in manly outdoor sports such as cricket, football and the like.

3. His qualities of manhood, truth, courage, devotion to duty, sympathy for, and protection of the weak, kindliness, unselfishness and fellowship.

4. His exhibition during school days of moral force of character and of instincts to lead and to take an interest in his schoolmates, for those latter attributes will be likely in after life to guide him to esteem the performance of public duties as his highest aim."

'My school does not believe that any attempt on the part of the London Medical Schools to attract men with these qualities would be a form of competition that we should all deplore.'[47]

All this—the story of his scholarship policy, the outcome of the tribunal and the complaint about his advertising methods—Charles set out in a long letter to Dawson on 9 March 1933.[45] By then he had apparently established a relationship that made him feel free to unburden himself to Dawson on a variety of topics, even such delicate ones as pertained to the *raison d'etre* of the Royal College of Physicians itself, over which Dawson presided from 1931 to 1938.[48] His object in writing on 9th March was to convince Dawson that there was now no reason, on the grounds of inter-hospital rivalries, why the King should not open the new medical school. All power in this matter lay with Dawson, on whom the King relied for both personal and political medical advice. Charles must have particularly enjoyed recounting his version of the sequel to the tribunal's findings, which, he said, he deliberately refrained from publishing because he was certain that the least said the soonest mended:

'The reaction came much sooner than I had anticipated. At St Bartholomew's one of their senior [physicians] laid it down that this attack on a smaller school was in his opinion discreditable. The echo of this word along the ramparts produced something like a sensation and some of the staff had to be revived with smelling salts.'[45]

History does not relate what Dawson, who later in life was determined not to write his memoirs on the grounds that he would have to leave out all the best bits,[49] thought of all this, but it is unlikely that Charles was able to tell one with his ear so close to the ground anything that he did not already know.

After all this, Charles must have been delighted when, in June, he received a hand-written letter from the Duchess of York, President of the hospital, from Glamis Castle, telling him that the King had promised to open what she called 'our medical school'.[50]

Surprisingly, for he had no particular link with St Mary's, Dawson now brought his mind and influence to bear in a most helpful way on the planning of the ceremony for the opening of the new buildings. Indeed he seems to have constituted himself as the chief of medical protocol for the occasion,[51] which was set down for 12 December 1933. He was concerned that while on the one hand it was right to give the University of London representatives priority, their numbers should be limited. 'We must be careful', he said, 'and not be overshadowed by the University.' The 'we' referred to the professional royal colleges and indicates the sense that they had of their importance in the world of the London medical schools. To them the University of London was a Johnny-come-lately. Dawson was concerned not only with precedence but also with ceremonial detail. Would the Chancellor or Vice Chancellor bring the Mace, and would the Vice Chancellor and Principal appear in robes? He ended a letter dealing with these matters on a light hearted note: 'One more suggestion, you might take Almroth Wright in the procession on a Sedia gestatoria preceded by trumpets—but we must not be flippant—good luck to you, D.' This comment probably reflected his knowledge of moves that Almroth Wright had been making to seek an honour and more recognition for himself at the opening, activities that had led to telephone calls to Charles from Sir Clive Wigram* at Buckingham Palace,[52] and the drafting of a letter to Sir George Newman asserting that the achievement of the building was almost entirely due to Charles, and could Sir George please straighten out the tangle.[53]

The opening took place on 12 December. The King was accompanied by Queen Mary, and on his arrival the Duchess of York, as President of the hospital, presented to him first the Earl of Athlone, Chancellor of the University, then Charles as Dean of the Medical School, and then Almroth Wright as Director of the Institute of Pathology.[54] During the ceremony Dorothy presented a bouquet to the Queen, Charles read an address, the Bishop of London offered up prayer, everyone sang 'Now thank we all our God', more people were presented, and the King and Queen then set out on a tour of inspection. As they went round, Charles maintained his usual rather low public profile, which belied the extent to which he, helped as always by Dorothy, had been involved in the detailed planning. For the rest of her life Dorothy retained vivid recollections of what she characterised as the awful goings-on.[55] First there was the affair of the trumpeter. Charles wanted a gorgeous ceremony. It had been arranged for the string band of the Royal Regiment of Artillery to play until the King and Queen arrived. Charles was determined that the proceedings should then open with a fanfare of trumpets. Through

*Sir Clive Wigram, Private Secretary to the King.

an old St Mary's man who was medical officer to the Life Guards, it was arranged that their trumpeters should attend. They arrived in their red rig, appropriate for duty in the presence of the Sovereign, but the King, espying them, said he didn't want them because on some occasion they had blown in his ear. Charles decided they should play at the end of the ceremony from some suitably distant point, and had them led away to a room and then forgot all about them. Then there was the wife of a member of the staff who, greeted by Charles on her arrival, announced in ringing tones: 'If I'm not in the front row I shall not stay.' And there had been a panic over carpets. The library in which the ceremony was to take place had an oak parquet floor. Dorothy was insistent that runners must be put down in the central aisle to prevent the noise of people's shoes. Floor coverings, she said, were also needed for the platform and the common room. Charles recollected that he had a patient, about to be discharged, who was in the carpet business, and introduced Dorothy to him. Nothing happened until the morning of the ceremony when Persian runners were delivered for the aisle, and a Chinese carpet for the dais; also a fine English needlework carpet for the common room which attracted Queen Mary's attention. A lover of beautiful things, she pointed at it and asked what it was. Dorothy, overhearing the question, wrote afterwards to the lady-in-waiting and the grateful patient soon received a royal visitor in his little shop off Praed Street. The King was less enchanted with the common room. He looked glumly at the furniture. Did Charles like it? he asked. Charles: 'Yes, it's very modern.' The King: 'It's horrible.' Before the ceremony the message had been received that careful thought should be given to what the King was to be shown, and Charles had sought advice from the Duchess of York. Don't show him buildings, was the reply, he likes medico-legal things like Crippen relics. In the event the King was shown a patient with leprosy and talked about it all through lunch.

In a more domestic way, the opening of the new school building was celebrated after Christmas, when Charles and Dorothy were entertained to dinner at Claridge's Restaurant by the members of the honorary staff of the hospital and the lecturers in the medical school. Apart from Dorothy, it was an all-male gathering and her inclusion as a guest reflected recognition of the fact that Charles operated in a very real partnership. The other guest was BE Matthews, who by this time had been secretary of the medical school for 25 years. Sir William Willcox, now the senior physician at St Mary's, presented Charles with a silver cup, a copy of the famous Fire of London cup, subscribed to by his colleagues.[56] A few weeks later, when the new buildings were inhabited, the Duchess of York again paid a visit. Dorothy was away and Charles wrote to her telling her that the Duchess had vetoed presentations, saying she would just stroll round people grouped on one side of the room. Charles wrote that after she had been received:

'. . . I then kept in the background and didn't see her again. I made myself useful talking to people and afterwards took Duchess of Westminster and Rothschilds a short round. . . . I think it went well. I felt I'd done the right thing in keeping in background.'[57]

To have the new medical school building and to people it with students of his own choosing were aims that had been central to Charles's life since the war. Now these aims had been fulfilled his mind ranged over a wider sphere than was encompassed by one institution. From his student days he had been ambitious to paint on a broader canvas. He had shown a particular interest in the organisation of health services, but in the 1930s his base in a medical school and in consulting practice was not a particularly appropriate one from which to seek a leadership role. Anyway, in so far as the general body of the profession was concerned, Dawson was still well entrenched in it as the expert. Charles was much better placed to seek to influence medical education, and this he now set out to do. In his whole-hearted support for the idea of introducing a university presence into teaching hospitals by creating professorial clinical units he had worked to a recipe provided by others. But in 1932 he made a contribution to thinking about medical education that, in its style, was all his own. It would be hard to claim originality for any ideas on this subject and he never did so, but at the time when he wrote an article which he called 'The Student in Irons'[58] he was not just climbing on someone else's bandwagon. What he said was in essence simple enough: that undergraduate medical students were so overloaded with fact that they had not time to think. The need for teachers to have time to think had been one of his arguments for creating professorial clinical units, and now he wanted to win the same time for students. His paper, with its eye-catching title, appeared in the *British Medical Journal* and, being Charles, and it being 1932, he expressed what he had to say in elaborate periods. He opened with the words:

'It is nowhere denied that we ask impossible tasks of students, who are bewildered by hours of listening, and that we stamp out the habit of reflection by a ceaseless drill.'

He saw as the root of the problem the development of modern laboratory aspects of medicine, as a result of which much had been added to the medical course while little had been taken away:

'Our educational roads are blocked by cars and lorries and great motor buses, by victorias drawn by high-stepping horses, and tricycles and old high bicycles, with here and there a sedan chair, all jumbled up anyhow and quite out of control.'

There followed what was essentially a criticism of teachers and teaching:

'In our fussy preoccupation with our pedagogic duties we have done grave hurt to those finer qualities that to a greater or a lesser degree are present in us all—the power to reason, the critical instinct, the overwhelming curiosity of all young things.'[58]

For all that Charles had something to say, and said it vehemently, the end of the paper was disappointing because the vigour and effectiveness of his criticism were hardly matched by his definition of what should be done. He advocated a periodical survey of the curriculum by a luminous intelligence, and identified for the next generation the task of discovering a new technique of teaching.

Charles's article provoked letters, spread through seven numbers of the British Medical Journal, in which many hobby horses were ridden. The first letter, strongly supporting Charles's thesis, was from one of the colourful characters in British medicine of those days, Professor Major Greenwood[59]—Major being his first name, not a military rank. Greenwood was at the forefront of those who had been introducing statistical methods into medicine. He was a Fellow of the Royal Society and broadly versed in scholarship, and, like Charles, with whom he was on easy terms as a correspondent, he had a contempt for pretentiousness and stupidity.[60] He was another prickly personality. John Ryle also joined in the correspondence.[61] In their post-war Cambridge days Ryle had identified Charles as 'our old Bolshevist'[62] and Greenwood evidently saw him as a kindred spirit, for two months after Greenwood's letter was published he wrote to Charles in somewhat revolutionary idiom.[63] The time, he believed, had come to strike. He and Charles should draw up an indictment of the medical curriculum. He had clear solutions to offer. He would drastically reduce preclinical studies and accept in their place an honours degree in any subject from a university; and he would abolish examination in all specialist subjects, and not allow anyone a licence to practise until they had done a series of approved appointments including one involving assistance to a panel practitioner—a general practitioner who accepted poor patients for a capitation fee under the National Health Insurance Act of 1911. Another world war was to pass before the idea embodied in his last suggestion—a pre-registration period between qualification and receipt of a licence to practise—became mandatory, and even then experience in general practice was not part of it. Greenwood ended his letter by commenting that what he had to say was extremely Bolshevist but 'unless we go to extremes we shall get nothing.'

Charles was evidently sensitive to being labelled Bolshevist, for in the following year he complained at a meeting of the Students' Representative Council of Edinburgh University, at which he spoke on 'Reform of the Medical Curriculum—Evolution not Revolution',[64] that he had been regarded as a natural ally by those who felt they could construct a model curriculum overnight; he wanted to make it clear that he believed in evolution, not revolution.[65] As things turned out, it was not until ten years later, when he was President of the Royal College of Physicians, that his chance came to lead in unshackling the students.

In writing 'The Student in Irons' Charles must have known that he was dropping a stone into a pool that was already disturbed. Maybe in timing his publication he sought to stake a claim to take part in the deliberations that he saw must take place. These included an enquiry into the curriculum, initated by the University of London chaired by Dawson.[66] Charles was not involved, nor was he asked two years later to join the curriculum committee set up by the General Medical Council, although the Registrar of that Council did ask him if he could spare eight reprints of 'The Student in Irons' for circulation to committee members.[67]

'The Student in Irons' brought one other private comment of note. TR Elliott gave it a place among a rare group of what he called very good papers, among which he had included Charles's earlier paper on clinical units.[68] Four years later, Charles tackled the subject of examinations in an article entitled 'Examinations as a Path to Freedom'.[69] In it he dissected exams and examiners. Commenting on the published evidence of the fallibility of the examining process, he remarked:

> 'The physician and surgeon teach as they examine, by the light of nature. They have never bothered their heads about the technique of either.'

He accepted exams as necessary but asserted that they could be made less harmful if they were applied by the right people, in the right form, for the right purpose. To have the right examiners was crucial:

> 'Our judicial system itself could scarcely survive the indiscriminate elevation to the bench of every successful lawyer. Yet we believe that each one of us who has been appointed to a teaching staff for quite another purpose is competent to examine, though we do not admit that the gift is bestowed until late in life, presumably as a kind of compensation for the failure of our other powers.'[69]

Charles's wit made him a devastating critic, but as in the case of 'The Student in Irons', so in 'Examinations as a Path to Freedom', one looks in vain for practical proposals on how we would solve the problems that he identified.

Charles's comments on examiners must have caused many chuckles but would have won him few friends among his seniors in London. Nevertheless it did not deter several institutions from inviting him to examine for them. Among students who were liable to meet him as an examiner, the cogniscenti believed that it was a good sign if he could be got talking about Rugby football. The minutes would tick by as he commented on a recent game. 'Look here' he would say 'you know your wing three-quarter is no good. You ought to bring this chap in.'[70] The cogniscenti were probably right. Charles would long since have learnt that those he would call intelligent examiners were generally able to decide whether a student should receive a pass mark after asking a few well chosen questions, and that however many more questions were asked the verdict would not alter. So an examiner might as well indulge his interests.

In his publications on medical education. Charles raised the question of the standards for admission of students to medical schools. In doing so, he was entering tiger country. With his dedication to the idea of creating an honours school of medicine, the fact that many students aimed to qualify by taking the easier and more quickly obtainable examinations for diplomas of the Royal Colleges instead of by obtaining university degrees, was deplorable.[71] Accordingly, St Mary's, led by Charles, decided that, from October 1935, only students qualified by their entrance exams to do university degree courses would be admitted.[72] The conflicting interests of the proud and ancient Royal Colleges with their conjoint qualifying diplomas, and the relatively new University of London with its qualifying degrees, had been exposed time and again in the previous 50 years, but that anyone should actually disturb the *status quo* was unthinkable. When Charles acquainted Dawson, as President of the Royal College of Physicians, with the intended entry policy of St Mary's, he received as petulant a response as could conceivably have been written by one so versed in diplomacy.[73] But St Mary's went ahead and experienced no shortage of applications from good students wanting to do medicine.

The publication of Examinations as a Path to Freedom in 1936 dates the end of Charles's contributions to changes in medical education, except for his work in 1942 on the report of the Royal College of Physicians' curriculum committee. By the end of the 1930s he was presiding over a student body largely of his own choosing, characterised by great *esprit-de-corps* and reflecting remarkably wide interests. Almost all enthusiams could be accommodated. Even a mountaineering club was allowable, but: 'Don't fall; it would be very bad for the name of the School.'[74] As the 1930s advanced, Charles's interest in St Mary's was undiminished, but he became an increasingly remote figure to the students. His visits to the medical school were brief; with 'Anthony Eden' hat on the back of his head, and dark overcoat unbuttoned, business was liable to be conducted in a passage. When he taught he still did so superbly, but his attendances for teaching were irregular and his ward rounds often perfunctory. It was as though he had picked his team—increasingly the hospital was staffed by his own scholars chosen in the 1920s—and he was content to delegate. Of his duties as a dean, he wrote at the time:

'I have no official hours at St Mary's as Dean. Anybody I see is by appointment. I go there daily, but I don't spend a large amount of time in office work. Apart from interviewing students, if a man has the power of devolution there is no reason why a Dean should spend much time in an office.'[75]

After listing six committees on which he had a place, he added:

'I have given up going to any of these committees except the Medical School Committee and the Medical School Finance Committee, of both of which I am chairman.'[75]

The one lot of students to whom he did not become remote were the rugger players. Individually or in groups they would be summoned to 129 Harley Street, where strategy and tactics of the game were discussed.[76] In 1937 Dorothy and Charles accompanied twenty of them to play a match at Torquay.[77] Charles decided that they should all stop on the way home at the Manor House Hotel on the edge of Dartmoor, and he paid the bill for this extra excursion.[78] But his passion for Rugby football did not extend to joining in the boisterous evenings that many players enjoyed. Neither the beer drinking, nor renderings of 'The Virgin Sturgeon' were to his taste. He would sit in a corner passionately discussing details of the afternoon's game, and then go to bed early.[79]

Charles's growing detachment from the medical school coincided with other calls on his time, and new horizons opened for him when, in 1935, he was invited to lecture to the cadets at the Royal Military Academy, Woolwich.[80] The letters on shell shock and leadership that he had written to *The Times* in 1920 had made a deep impression on a young army officer, Arthur Goschen, who had determined that, when he came to a position of command, he would invite the writer to address his men.[81] Goschen was now the Commandant. Charles's lecture was an outstanding success, and over the next few years invitation followed invitation for him to repeat his performance. By the time war broke out in 1939 he had talked once or more to the army officers of the London District, the Senior Army Officers' School at Sheerness, the Aldershot Command, the Staff College Camberley, and to the Royal Air Force Staff College

Andover. Through these invitations to speak—the lecture came to be called 'The Mind in War'—Charles met many senior officers, and he received many comments from them. One letter that he kept was from RV Pollock, Commandant at Sheerness,[83] saying that there had been more talk in the mess on the subject of his lecture than had ever been heard before. Pollock also told him of the discomfort of a senior guards' officer as a result of a remark that Charles had made about discipline. He had reminded his audience that, rather than being purposeful, discipline could in its extreme form become mindless. To illustrate the point he described how, after the brain of a frog had been destroyed by passing a nail into it, it was still possible to elicit from the animal a wide range of reflex movements. Pollock wrote that the guards' officer had been ragged unmercifully and had not forgiven a gunner who had searched the top of his head to see if the nail was still in it. Charles enjoyed these lecturing engagements. He was at home with his subject, and he spoke on it with humility born of bitter first hand experience. He wrote how, on one occasion at the RAF Staff College, in the middle of his lecture, he was suddenly seized with the incongruity of a middle-aged apothecary haranguing these young toughs on such a theme.[84] But while he knew that he was getting across to many of Britain's military leaders ideas that he believed were important, he was adamant that what he had to say should not be published.[85] He still wanted to write his 1919 *magnum opus*, but in his own way and in his own time, and the time was not yet.

There was a glimpse of another horizon when in November 1936, after much soul-searching, Charles found himself crossing the Atlantic on board the German liner 'Bremen', accompanying Beaverbrook, who wanted to see if the clear air of Arizona would help his asthma. The trip was expected to last several weeks, and payment, according to Beaverbrook, was to be 'delivered to your poor wife monthly during your absence, by my secretary'.[86] The trip ended abruptly with the crisis that led to the abdication of King Edward VIII, for by the time the 'Bremen' reached New York, Beaverbrook had decided to respond to the King's plea that he should return to London, and Charles was back in England in a fortnight. His daily letters, written, though unposted, to Dorothy, reflected Beaverbrook's continuing use of Charles as a confidant. Beaverbrook saw himself at this time as being on his way to retirement,[87] and Charles's comment was:

'B says he curses ER [Edward Rex] every morning he awakes: that he is bored to death with the whole business. But I cannot think he is other than pleased to have something to do.'[88]

Charles and Dorothy would have been less than human if they had not been disappointed at the failure of Charles's name to appear in the Honours List after the King had opened the new medical school in 1933. It is not hard to think of reasons for the delay. He had rocked too many boats for senior members of the medical establishment to feel comfortable with him. The rugger scholarship affair, his insistence that students aiming only at the conjoint diploma of the Royal Colleges should have no place at St Mary's and his attacks on the curriculum and the examination system, all contributed to his being viewed by many, even in his own hospital, with suspicion and by some with hatred.[89] The final arbiter where honours for doctors was concerned was Dawson.[90] Charles was given to soliloquies, and in one, on the ill-treatment of princes, he criticised the way in which doctors to royal households were chosen. He came to feel so strongly about the situation that he actually put his views in writing to Buckingham Palace.[91] Dawson, who by 1937 had been physician to four monarchs, naturally figured in both the soliloquy and the correspondence, as well as in a ditty that Charles used to recite:

> Lord Dawson of Penn
> Killed so many men
> That's why we sing
> God save the King[92]

Charles had reservations not only about Dawson as an ageing court physician but also because he questioned his sincerity. Describing to Dorothy the occasion of the re-election of Dawson for the last time as President of the Royal College of Physicians in 1937, Charles wrote:

> 'I sat next to Elliott who votes for Dawson. While I was talking to him over tea Dawson passed and said he was borrowing something that I said about Herringham for his presidential address. He mentioned 'my delightful account' but what he quoted was not recognisable. I can't really be agreeable to him. I'm not built the two way trick.'[93]

Despite these negative thoughts, Charles quite liked Dawson. He admired his political skills and he was no doubt pleased that Dawson had identified him as one of the young hopefuls, one of a group of a younger generation who could be expected to contribute to weighty affairs in medicine in their time.

When Charles's knighthood eventually came in January 1938 it led to an unusual event at 129 Harley Street. Charles arranged a party at which he surprised everyone by hiring two popular comedians, the Western Brothers. Lots of people came, there was champagne and dancing, and Dorothy found herself wondering afterwards why they did not do this sort of thing more often. The task of writing thank-you letters in response to congratulations coincided for Charles with the task of correcting examination papers, but he found time to draft at least quite long acknowledgments in some of which he described his motives for accepting the honour.[94-96] Indicating that he saw it as a chance to rehabilitate the family fortunes, and as making it easier for him to get things done in a broader sphere of medicine, he wrote to Beaverbrook:

'... I have slowly become persuaded—you told me this years ago—that to get things done in medicine one must be known as Dawson and Horder are known. I dare say I ought to have seen that long ago but doubt whether it would have made any difference if I had, because the opposition in certain medical quarters was kept up to the last. . . .'[96]

What he wanted to get done in medicine was set out in a letter to a senior civil servant, Sir Wilfred Eady. Dorothy and Lady Eady had got to know each other as mothers with boys of the same age at the Hall School in Hampstead, where the fathers had met at cricket matches and on sports days.[97] Charles wrote to Eady of his vision for the future of medicine:

'Ultimately the heads of Medicine will be whole-timers, who do not practise but devote their lives to research and teaching, Fellows of the Royal Society, living on State salaries, while Harley Street will be the middlemen, the distributors. But in the meantime those who want to shape the way the profession ought to be trained find it difficult to combine this with paying their way by seeing patients. At the bottom it is because I hope rather than expect that this business may help me to set aside a few years at the end, free from practice and the necessity to make money to pay educational bills etc. so that I may complete what I have only begun, that I get pleasure from this happening.'[94]

By the beginning of 1938, when Charles was busy writing these letters, he, like most people in Britain, saw that the likelihood of war with Germany was great. Thousands of air-raid casualties were expected from the moment war broke out and a scheme was needed to enable hospitals to cope with them. Eady was in charge of civil defence at the Home Office[98] and it was possibly due to his friendship with him[55] that in May Charles was appointed chairman of a committee to consider how best to plan a casualty hospital scheme for the London area. The Wilson Committee, as it was called, met over only two months and it developed a plan for dividing London and the surrounding country into 10 sectors, with one of the big teaching hospitals at the apex of each. Casualties received in these would later be despatched in convoys of buses to hospitals in the sector that radiated from the central hospital.[99] Charles was not particularly happy with this committee and the other members were not entirely happy with him. He characterised them as 'a group of flats with one E sharp', reflecting the presence among them of a distinguished civil servant, Evelyn (later Lady Evelyn) Sharp.[55] Many years later Lady Sharp recalled that Charles was one of the most charming and delightful men she had known, but she did not see him as the rough and tough fighter who she believed was needed at that stage.[100] Maybe she discerned the predominant temperament of the consultant in him rather than the practitioner, the advisor rather than the doer.

Chapter 9

Churchill's Doctor and President of the Royal College of Physicians

As the Wilson committee's deliberations ended in July 1938, an event occurred which determined the power base from which Charles was to operate for the next 12 years. He was elected Treasurer of the Royal College of Physicians. His interest in the College had been stimulated by Dawson, who, when elected President in 1931, had set out to explore ways of strengthening the College's waning influence on education, research and health.[1] Dawson had invited comments from Fellows of Charles's generation, and Charles had responded forthrightly with a letter saying that the only way in which the College could recover its influence was by furnishing something which other bodies could not give. It had to have a capacity to look further into the future than other medical bodies, and this could be achieved if Dawson chose his own lieutenants rather than letting them be chosen by the democratic method of election.[2] Dawson's presidency was marked by some invigoration of the College through the election of more Fellows (there were 419 in 1931 and 581 in 1938) and by including among them a broader representation of interests within medicine, but, for all Dawson's good intentions, the College's place in the counsels of state altered little.

Charles played no conspicuous part in College affairs during Dawson's presidency.[3] He did not speak at meetings for fourteen years after he was elected to the fellowship. From 1933 onwards he was just one among the large number of examiners appointed annually, and he served on a committee concerned with the examination for the membership. But unobtrusively he gave much attention to the way in which the College functioned. He shared Dawson's vision of its restoration to a position of power in the land, so that it would be consulted by, and would influence, governments. Charles was convinced of the wisdom of consultant physicians as a professional group, but he was bothered by the dominance in the College of Fellows from the staffs of the London teaching hospitals, and the small influence of Fellows from the provinces and the non-teaching hospitals. 'They have made it a club', he said, 'not a college.'[4]

By early 1938 Charles had put his thoughts about the College down on paper, as a typescript document of sixteen-and-a-half pages, identified on the front as *A Note on Policy* by Sir Charles Wilson.[5] This he circulated in March to a few Fellows on whose judgement he felt he could rely.[6] To be elected Treasurer in July, Charles had to be nominated by the College Council, which consisted of the President, senior College officers and 12 Fellows. That his name was put forward meant that he had already won support among a number of colleagues and this support must have reflected a response to the circulation of his Note. It was also probably not simply owing to chance that his election as Treasurer followed a change in the presidency of the College. In accordance with the custom of centuries, the first meeting of the year of the Fellows took place on the day following Palm Sunday, and Dawson, who had been re-elected president annually since 1931, was displaced. Dr Robert Hutchison, who won the election, came from Dawson's own hospital, the London, and, at the age of 67, was only seven years Dawson's junior. Having observed how the voting had gone in the previous year, Charles had expected a change, but thought the office would go to a younger man.[7] However, youth was not yet a characteristic of College officers. As Treasurer, Charles succeeded none other than his old chief Sydney Phillips, whose house physician he had been 30 years before. Phillips had been Treasurer since 1923 and was now 87 years old, with failing vision.[8] A friend, congratulating Charles on his election, hoped that he would retain his vigour as long as his predecessor, and that he didn't mind being described in a newspaper as ascetic in appearance; better, he thought than being described as bucolic.[9]

The *Note on Policy*, which put Charles in the ascendant, dealt first with the future of the conjoint qualifying diploma of MRCS LRCP. The rule, which had caused so much resentment a few years before when it was introduced at St Mary's, that students should read for a university degree rather than for the conjoint diploma, had quickly been adopted by other medical schools,[10] and as a result the College was threatened by loss of a substantial part of the revenue that it derived from examination fees. Charles pointed out critically that financial considerations were influencing the College's policy on education, and that the associated air of expediency chilled the younger generation and was injuring the College. He also pointed to the weakening of the long standing links between the medical schools and the College, links which he believed were important for the future of the College as a body concerned with education. The second part of the Note criticised the way in which College business was conducted. Agendas were too full and there was no time to debate things that were worth debating. College procedures were antiquated, designed for gatherings of 20 Fellows instead of the one or two hundred who might attend, and as a result the College was drifting away from education and it had no voice at all in research. Two different versions exist of the ending of the Note, one reproduced in the history of the College, the other originally circulated by Charles to a limited number of Fellows. The version in the College history ends by asserting that the laudable ambition that medicine should speak with one voice was an impracticable dream under existing conditions, but—and what followed comes as something of a non-sequitur—it would be a different story if the College were rebuilt on another site, closer to its sister College, the Royal College of Surgeons, so that the two Colleges, with the Medical Research Council, might form an Academy of Medicine to which the government of the day could turn for counsel and support.[11] The original version says nothing of this. It ends:

'The laudable ambition that medicine should speak with one voice is an impracticable dream (it is more important that it should have something to say). From time to time a President will arise from among us who by vigour of his personality and the variety of his contacts with public men can make his voice heard in many places where the point of view of the profession is seldom heard. When that happens it can only benefit the College, and spread its influence. But we must always come back to the proper business of this House of Learning which is education and research.'[5]

As with 'The Student in Irons', the reader of this version was left with a final thought hanging in the air, but the second sentence was, as it turned out, a singularly precise statement of Charles's personal intentions.

In March, as well as sending his Note to a selected number of Fellows, Charles sent a copy to the new President. Hutchison's response was that he thought it would not be judicious to circulate it to all the Fellows at present, that he intended to appoint a committee later in the year to go into the question of the machinery of the College, and that he hoped Charles would be on that committee.[12] Hutchison was bothered that if Charles's memorandum were circulated, it might look as if the President was not acting spontaneously. In October, the committee envisaged by Hutchison was appointed. It consisted of the College officers[13] so that Charles, by that time having been elected Treasurer, was on it. Charles now spoke repeatedly at the quarterly meetings of the College Fellows, called the Comitia, urging that the College should be more widely based and more representative of British medicine. These ideas did not go down well with some of the seniors, including Horder and the President, and the newly appointed Registrar, Letheby Tidy, a man for whom Charles made it plain that he had little regard.[4] He used to refer to him as Wetherby George, and it became part of the folklore of the College that the reason why the Treasurer precedes the Registrar in procession was that Charles, on being appointed Treasurer, refused to walk behind Tidy.[14] In fact the order of precedence was determined long before 1938.

Not only did Charles's criticisms of the College disturb some of the Fellows, but his mode of speaking at Comitia, often with one foot on his chair, also offended those with a strong sense of decorum, so that he had an uphill battle. But he had his friends and admirers, particularly among the younger Fellows, and the topics on which he spoke were important and it was he who, in October 1938, led the College to consider what action it would take on the outbreak of war.[13] September 1938 had brought with it the Munich crisis. Charles, depressed with thoughts of the implication of Chamberlain's policy of appeasement, hardly spoke to anyone for a week.[15] Had war come, he would have found himself Commandant of St Mary's, which, in accordance with the planning done by the Wilson committee a few months earlier, would, like the other teaching hospitals, have become a casualty clearing station.[16]

For the London hospitals, the Munich crisis had some of the benefits of a dress rehearsal. Following it, the organisation of the sector system proposed by the Wilson committee was elaborated, and a committee of Deans of the teaching hospitals started planning the details that would have to operate when war came.[17] In this plan, the Deans themselves were designated to be in charge of each sector, so that Charles became Group officer designate of Sector VI, at the apex of which was St Mary's. Although to Charles, as to so many in Britain, 1939 brought with it a realisation that another war with Germany was inevitable, life for the family went on as usual. His eldest son was in his second year at Eton, and Dorothy and the boys spent the holidays at the Mill at Manton.[18] Charles stayed in London, preoccupied not only with arrangements to cope with air-raid casualties but also with planning for the care of civilian sick and with the continuing education of medical students. No one was banking on a short war, and it was realised that lots of doctors would be needed. By the time Germany invaded Poland on 1 September 1939 and Britain declared war on Germany two days later, life had already re-ordered itself in a way that was dominated by the anticipation of air attacks. Gas masks were being carried in cardboard cases and the blackout plunged the country into darkness at night. One-and-a-half million souls—mothers with children under five, primary school children and teachers—had been evacuated from target cities, and another two million had moved out on their own initiative.[19] September 3rd found Charles at the headquarters nominated for Sector VI at Uxbridge, just outside London.

When the Prime Minister, Neville Chamberlain, announced on the wireless at 11.00 am on the 3 September that Britain was at war with Germany, no one quite knew what would happen next. Planning of air-raid precautions had been based on an expectation of attacks on cities by German bombers from the moment war broke out, and the Emergency Hospital Services had been designed so that 200 000 hospital beds could be available for casualties within

24 hours.[20] One estimate had been that 600 000 people might be killed and another 1 200 000 injured over 60 days.[21]

The headquarters at Uxbridge of Sector VI were in Cave House, an empty mansion set back from the road in a big garden.[22] Here Charles took up his post with his deputy, RM Handfield-Jones, a senior member of the surgical teaching staff at St Mary's. They were supported by an administrative assistant, a telephonist and two despatch riders and Dorothy was offered a full-time appointment as Charles's secretary at three pounds and two shillings a week.[23] As a Group Officer, Charles's salary was £1300 a year, plus allowances.[24] Charles's office was on the first floor, and when Dorothy tried through public service channels to reduce the noise made by people running up and down stairs, she was told that only ambassadors were allowed stair carpets. Living accommodation was found at the local doctor's house, Red Leys. When the doctor was called up and his wife moved, Dorothy brought her cook down from Harley Street; Mrs Law, the wife of the medical school Porter, who had been recalled to the navy, joined them and Red Leys became, for the time being, home. Not that Charles was resigned to spending the war as Group Officer to Sector VI. He lost no time in writing to Lord Gort* at the War office offering his services to the army but no opening was suggested.[25]

The end of 1939 and the early months of 1940 were difficult times for the whole medical profession. It was the period later called the phoney war when there was little action except at sea. Because the expected bombing did not happen, some 700 specialists, including those on the staffs of the London hospitals like Charles, found themselves spread through the sectors with little to do.[20] They had left their private practices, on which their usual incomes depended, accepting in most cases what were, by comparison, modest full-time salaries in the Emergency Medical Service (EMS). The only undoubted beneficiaries were the medical students in the clinical years of their course who were spread through the sectors with their teachers. Charles pointed this out in a letter to *The Times*:

'They live in the sector hospitals and their number in any one institution is small. The large class has gone. In its place there is intimate contact between student and teacher. The teacher is always in the hospital, the student shares his day. And when the work is done student and teacher go to the same building, they talk and play together, they live together, with incalculable gain to both.'[26]

---

*Lord Gort, Chief of the Imperial General Staff.

With his opening phrase in this letter, Charles won himself a place in the *Observer*'s Sayings of the Week: 'The violence of the hour is unfriendly to quiet thought.'

Those who were close to Charles in the planning and running of Section VI saw him as a good organiser.[27] When he gave up his appointment in 1941 the Group Officers of the nine other London sectors, his fellow Deans, signed a letter saying what pleasure it had given them to work with him as a colleague.[28] They acknowledged too that, as Chairman of the Wilson Committee, Charles was the real initiator of the arrangement for handling casualties. These arrangements had by then run smoothly over many months in the first blitz during which, in September and October 1940, London had been bombed on 57 nights by an average of 160 bombers.[24]

Given his ability to delegate work, Charles's job as Sector Officer was not onerous, and had it not been for his involvement with the Royal College of Physicians, time would have hung heavily on his hands. As it was, through the phoney war and the events of the following twelve-months—the fall of France, the Battle of Britain and the air raids of the 1940-1941 winter—Dorothy drove him to the College in Pall Mall almost daily. They moved their home in 1940 to what was known as The Garden Cottage on an estate at Harefield, close to one of the Sector VI hospitals, and stayed there until the end of the war. Compared with 129 Harley Street the cottage was tiny, but provided the essentials for living. Charles's salary as a Group Officer, and then at £1400 a year[30] as a Consultant Adviser to the Ministry of Health,[31] together with his stipend as Dean of the Medical School, enabled them to continue to meet school bills and to keep a living-in cook and a maid.

Like many who had survived the Western Front in the 1914-18 war, Charles hated loud bangs.[32] If duty demanded that he should be in London after dusk, when the bombing started, he would be there, but for the most part he and Dorothy would be back at the Cottage by 4.30 or 5.00 pm. If it was still daylight he would go for a stroll, often to scratch the back of Emma, a favourite pig, who lived about half a mile away, and in the evenings there was the wireless; life for most people in Britain in these years revolved around the 9.00 pm news. At this time, too, Charles began to work once more at converting his 20-year-old notes, and the lectures on morale and courage he had derived from them, into a book.[33]

At the Royal College of Physicians in 1940 the main consideration was the sort of health service that Britain should have after the war, a subject which was to occupy much of Charles's time for the next 10 years. At first sight it seems remarkable that, in this year when Britain and its Commonwealth and Empire were left alone to fight Hitler, when bombers came over nightly and invasion was threatened, the medical profession concentrated its attention on what was to happen after the war. The initiative came from the British Medical Association, and their proposal to set up a planning body at that time has been described as an exhibition of incongruous sangfroid.[34] But the fact that a debate about post-war affairs was engaged is not really remarkable. It was not a new debate: it had been progressing on and off for decades and was being resumed for very good reasons. Hitler had caused a revolution in the organisation of health care, apparent for all to see in the workings of the EMS and the medical services for the armed forces. The dislocation in the lives of many doctors and in the operation of hospitals was almost total, and the clock could never be put back.

The BMA's proposal to form a Medical Planning Commission to consider the effect of wartime developments on the country's present and future medical services came to the College in October 1940 at the height of the first blitz. The proposed membership of the Commission was 49, later to be about 70.[35] The College was invited to appoint only two representatives, which Charles was quick to observe was the same as the number sought from the Medical Women's Federation.[36] In sending the invitation, the BMA indicated that while it 'recognised the supreme position of the Royal Colleges in their scientific spheres and in their capacities as examining bodies', the Association claimed 'to represent the organised profession . . . in the field of medical politics'.[35] Charles saw danger and once more seized the initiative in the College by despatching a personal letter to a selected group of Fellows. Written from Sector VI headquarters at Uxbridge, and dated 28 October 1940, it was short and to the point.[36] He told them that the War Emergency Committee of the College, of which he was a member, had decided that the Comitia should be asked to decline the BMA's invitation on the grounds that such a commission was premature and that, when constituted, it should be an independent and representative committee set up by a Government body. Basically, Charles questioned whether the BMA, which was already committed to certain policies, should be allowed to plan for the future of the profession without any effective check by the Royal Colleges. If it were allowed to do so, it would mean that the Government would turn in future to the BMA, leaving the BMA to consult the College only if it wished to do so. The College would be practically eliminated as an adviser to the Government.

He concluded his letter:

'I am proposing at the Comitia that the College should set up a special committee to go into these matters and I hope that if it is at all possible you will be able to come to the Comitia on 31 October at 2.15 pm at the Royal Society of Medicine.* I do not think

---

*The college building in Pall Mall had been damaged by bombing a few days before.

it is an exaggeration to say that a step is being taken which will have very far reaching consequences both on the profession and such things as a State Medical Service, and also on the future of the College.'[36]

With this letter, lines of battle were defined on which the Royal Colleges, and the physicians in particular, were to confront the BMA over the next six years.

Charles's effort to get those to whom he sent his letter to attend the Comitia on 31 October was frustrated. His letter was written only three days before the meeting, and several replies reflected the uncertainties of communication and travel in wartime Britain. A Fellow from Buxton in Derbyshire, regretting he could not attend, wrote that the journey now often took eight hours and the trains frequently did not reach their London terminus at St Pancras, but disembarked their passengers at suburban stations.[37] Several of those who could not attend nevertheless took the trouble to write to Charles commenting on his letter. Throughout the debate over the following years, first about the College's participation in planning bodies and then about the design of a post-war health service, Charles took a lot of trouble to keep Fellows in provincial centres in touch with what was going on. As a result he also kept himself informed of the opinions of a much wider constituency of Fellows than those who could most easily attend meetings and incidentally he became able to rely on support from many Fellows outside London.

At the Comitia on 31 October, discussion on the War Emergency Committee's proposal that the BMA's invitation should be declined was inconclusive, but many letters written to Charles after this Comitia showed that he was being looked to for leadership by those who wanted the College to play an active part, but one independent of the BMA, in designing a new health service. To one of the younger Fellows, Harold Himsworth, who had succeeded TR Elliott at University College, Charles wrote on 20 November:

'As I see the situation the question is, will the BMA unaided be allowed to plan the future of Medicine? If it is, and if the College drifts on without an effort to help, then I think the College is done and I have no intention of going on as Treasurer. In my view, at the present time, the President should be daily in his office (it is nearly a whole-time job if done properly) and a real effort should be made to mobilise all the ability we have got in the College (there are nearly 600 Fellows) for the benefit of the country. I think everybody who is really anxious that this College should cease drifting ought to get together. If this is done, then I see no reason why the College should not take a really prominent part in shaping the future.'[38]

At the special Comitia on 10 December, Charles's motion for the appointment of a committee of the College to consider the future of the profession was successful but his proposal to send two Fellows with status only of observers to the BMA Commission failed. The Comitia, encouraged by Dawson and Horder,[39] resolved by 50 votes to 22, on the proposal of Sir William Willcox, that four representatives should be appointed to the Commission, with full powers to cooperate.[40] A few weeks later, the College's War Emergency Committee nominated Charles, Letheby Tidy, Charles's old companion of Cambridge days, John Ryle, and Harold Himsworth. Following this Comitia Charles received a letter which was of great significance for him not only for the immediate future but also for the longer term. It came from George Pickering, who, with Charles's strong support, had succeeded Langmead as professor of medicine at St Mary's, and it reported on a meeting of the Younger Fellows Club,[41] which consisted of Fellows under the age of 45.[42] Pickering set out a series of resolutions which had been passed about the functioning of the newly appointed College committee to consider the future of the profession. All the resolutions were in line with Charles's thinking, and the crucial one was to the effect that the Club considered Charles to be the most suitable chairman of the new committee and assured him of the members' full cooperation. If Charles had any doubts about his having a reasonable chance of becoming President at the election in four months' time, this letter must have gone far to dispel them. The young were on his side.

Most of the letters about College affairs that Charles received at this time were directed to 'Dear Wilson' by the older generation, and to 'Dear Sir Charles' by the younger one. They generally expressed approval of what he was doing and criticism of the incumbent President, but they reflected no particular intimacy. However, one of the few 'My dear Charles' letters to which the response was in terms of 'My dear Arthur', embodied a friendly warning. The Arthur concerned was Arthur Ellis, Professor of Medicine at the London Hospital. A man of Charles's age, Ellis was a Canadian who had settled in London after serving in France in the 1914-1918 war. Wise and warm-hearted, and noted for his humour and helpfulness,[43] Ellis, like James Mackintosh and Major Greenwood, seems never to have attracted from Charles the sort of barbed comment he made about many of his professional colleagues. Addressing his remarks to Charles as 'from one truculent one to another',[44] Ellis sought, a month before the presidential election was due, to warn Charles about the unfavourable reaction that he discerned among his colleagues to what was seen to be canvassing being conducted on Charles's behalf. The convention of the time was that aspiring Presidents did not canvass for votes. Ellis's warning appears to have been first given in conversation and to have been precipitated by the pro-Charles activities of the younger Fellows.

Charles set out his views in letters to Ellis written on two consecutive
days, both of which were long and contained closely reasoned
arguments.[45] He emphatically rejected the notion that elections in
the past had been free from lobbying and he asked how the right
man could be chosen without discussion between Fellows. 'Being
PRCP in the next few years is going to be a tremendous job,' he
concluded 'Are we going to decide who shall be the man responsible
for this task by becoming irritated because the zeal of a few of the
younger Fellows may have out-run their discretion?'

Ten days after writing these letters, and apparently after receiving
a reply from Ellis he wrote to Ellis again, summarising his ambition
for the College and reflecting his passionate belief that he was the
one to lead it forward.

'I want the College to have a Research Department comparable
to the Fullerton Fellowship of the Royal Society, with laboratories
on the premises etc. And I would make the Harvey Professorship
a very great honour. All this instead of hoarding funds.

'The library is full of treasures. I want the RCP to produce editions
of the medical classics, a real school of the history of medicine.

'I want the College to be moved so that Fellows meet daily over
luncheon and tea, for out of this contact must come a living
College—before the war I had taken steps with the Canadian High
Commissioner and was negotiating with him for the sale of our
present lease.

'I want the Government to turn to the College for advice as it now
turns to the Royal Society. If the College will give disinterested
advice gathered from its six hundred fellows, this should not be
difficult. For Wilson Jameson* will be friendly and Winston will
be sympathetic.

'I want this done and much more, and can see clearly how it can
all be done. What stands in the way? Probably the votes of about
twenty fellows, vaguely interested. And that is probably why one
feels a little impatient if all this should come to nothing because
someone has done some little thing which would have been better
done otherwise, or somebody has been too importunate in pressing
my claims.

'Is this so far bloodless revolution at the College to be accomplished
with the London Hospital looking on? I do not think that Fellows

---

*Sir Wilson Jameson, Chief Medical Officer of the Ministry of Health and Board
of Education.

there will allow themselves to be put off and stay in their tents because someone has been over-zealous, when the whole future of the College and perhaps the shaping of the practice of medicine in the future is in the melting pot.

'But the issue must be put to them and that is why your letter is so heartening.

'No more or I shall become a bore.'[46]

Whatever the convention had been about canvassing for votes in the past, it certainly went by the board right through the 1940s when Charles and Horder were the only serious rivals for the presidency. Their friends were assiduous in talking to all possible supporters, urging them to attend the April Comitia and vote. Wining, dining, the post and the phone were all used, and it was said to be difficult to walk down Harley Street without being accosted on this subject.[47]

On 7 April 1941 Charles was elected President of the Royal College of Physicians. This first contest, like several succeeding ones, was close and its drama was highlighted by the way in which elections were conducted. The voters were those Fellows of the College actually present at the meeting. The President completing his year of office first gave an address which included comments on every Fellow who had died in the previous 12 months. After the senior Fellow present had proposed a vote of thanks, the President took off his gown and, if he was seeking re-election, sat behind his ceremonial chair. If he was not seeking re-election he sat among the body of Fellows. Each Fellow then wrote on a slip of paper the name of one of his colleagues whom he wished to be President, and the slips were placed in silver urns passed round by College officers. The urns were then presented to the Senior Censor, who read aloud the name on every slip. If any Fellow had two thirds of the votes, he was elected, otherwise the two names having the highest numbers were balloted on.[48] On that Monday in 1941, Charles led Horder at the first count by 82 votes to 75, with another 66 votes being divided among four other individuals. The ensuing ballot must have seemed to both Charles and Horder to have taken a long time. Eventually the Senior Censor announced that Charles had 121 votes and Horder 109.[49] Charles came forward, first to be gowned, then to take the chair and receive the Caduceus—the silver rod which is the insignia of the President's office. He saw this election as the most significant event in his career.[50]

The closeness of the voting showed the extent to which consultant physicians, who saw themselves as the elite of the medical profession, were divided. In the development of a new health service, should they play their historic part as independent advisors to government, or should they work as a minority group within the BMA with its 40 000 members,[51] most of whom were general practitioners. Horder, who was opposed to radical change in the health service, was willing to go along with the BMA. Charles, who made no secret of his advocacy of a move towards what in the parlance of the day was called a state medical service, wanted developments to be strongly influenced, if not steered by, the consultants who were represented by the Royal Colleges, and above all by the Royal College of Physicians led by himself. The division in the College also reflected the personalities of the two main aspirants. Horder was widely considered to be the greatest clinician of his day, brilliant in diagnosis, wise at the bedside and with great humanity. He had earned the affectionate regard of generations of medical students at St Bartholomew's, and the respect of many postgraduates whom he had coached for postgraduate exams.[52] But there were question marks about his judgement in wider spheres. His credulous approach to some unorthodox treatments was unattractive to the up and coming generation of physicians who were intent on bringing rigorous scientific thinking into medicine. His son later commented on other characteristics which weighed against him[53]—that he was too much of a lone wolf and too single-minded a propagandist for his own ideas, and he was also impatient with the delays and manoeuvres that are necessary to get things done in the medico-political arena. Like Charles, he was also given to being caustically critical of colleagues. For his part, Charles, in addition to being politically astute, was manifestly dedicated to giving time to what many regarded as the top job in the medical profession. No longer would the College be a sleepy hollow. He himself would be there, concerned with its business, daily.[38] What he said and wrote left no doubt that he had defined a clear set of objectives. His aims were based on what, for some, was an appealing streak of idealism. And no one could have doubted his capacity for doing his homework meticulously and presenting arguments clearly. Nor could anyone have failed to recognise the driving force of his personal ambition to lead the physicians to influence the changes inevitable in medical practice after the war. But, and it was a big but, no one could deny that Charles had a penchant for being involved in controversy. Could one with such a penchant, and one who furthermore seemed positively to relish a fight, be trusted to lead the College at this critical time?

In the background to Charles's success at the election was another factor. It was no secret that for the previous 12 months he had been Winston Churchill's doctor, and to most people Churchill embodied all those things that explained Britain's survival through 1940 and would assure her survival during 1941. Charles's association with Churchill did not determine his election, but it must have been a factor which many weighed in the scales. As things turned out,

Charles's activities as Churchill's doctor and as President of the College were to become inextricably mixed.

Charles identified 24 May 1940 as the day on which he became Churchill's doctor, not, as he said, because the Prime Minister wanted one, but because certain members of the Cabinet decided that somebody ought to keep an eye on his health.[54] The appointment for Charles to see Churchill was made by Brendan Bracken.[55,56] On the outbreak of war, when Churchill became First Lord of the Admiralty, he had appointed Bracken, a long-time supporter and friend, as his Parliamentary Private Secretary,[57] and when Churchill became Prime Minister in May 1940, Bracken continued to perform the same duties for him, but without the title. Bracken was also a friend of Beaverbrook's. The two of them together with the first Lord Birkenhead had made up 'The Three Terrible B.s' whose personalities had so jarred with Mrs Churchill.[58] Like Beaverbrook, Bracken had become one of Charles's patients and then a friend. While Charles identified Bracken as the instigator of his relationship with Churchill[56]—and such an action on Bracken's part accords well with his continuing concern for Churchill's health as the war went on[59]—Beaverbrook evidently also joined in in persuading Clementine Churchill that a doctor must be appointed to keep a close watch and pay regular visits.[60]

Churchill had been Prime Minister for two weeks when Charles visited him on that May morning in the flat on the second floor of Admiralty House where the Churchills were staying until the residential part of Number Ten Downing Street, just across the Horse Guards Parade, became vacant.[55] Churchill, ever a late riser, was still in bed, presumably preoccupied with the retreat of the British Expeditionary Force in France and Belgium, and with the troops cut off on that day in Calais in particular.[61] Charles scribbled his first clinical notes in pencil on two sides of a sheet of paper.[62]

When Charles accepted the medical charge of Churchill, the name Sir Charles Wilson meant little to the world at large. A year was to pass before he was elected President of the Royal College of Physicians, and many might have expected one of the medical peers, Dawson or Horder, both well known to handle the illnesses of princes, and to have very large practices, to be called on.[63] The lot fell to Charles because, in his more limited practice he had cultivated powerful people like Beaverbrook, Bracken and Revelstoke, and people like that tended to rate him highly. Four years previously Beaverbrook had written to him:

'Now the good doctors in the world are few, and you are the best of all of them. The most honest, the most simple, the most clever and the most upright.'[64]

Apart from enjoying the long-standing respect of Beaverbrook and Bracken, Charles was also, in May 1940, in their minds. On 16 May he had written to congratulate Beaverbrook on his appointment as Minister of Aircraft Production[65] (to which Beaverbrook had responded saying he was disappointed Charles had not reproached him for taking such a risk with his health).[66] And on 23 May Charles had written to Bracken, with whom he was on 'Dear Brendan' terms.[67] The Director General of the Emergency Medical Service had just had a coronary thrombosis, and Charles sought to ensure that the shortcomings of possible aspirants for the job were taken into account. He did not apparently realise that Bracken's influence in matters of patronage was less than it was often supposed to be.[68]

In the first year of his commission to look after the Prime Minister, which involved making regular visits, Charles had a foretaste of the disruption of his life that the job later came to involve. In January 1941, in the run-up period before the critical College election, Charles called one morning at the fortified accommodation near Downing Street called the Annexe, and found Churchill with a heavy cold. The Prime Minister was intent on leaving at noon for Scapa Flow ostensibly to say farewell to Lord Halifax, the new ambassador to the United States, but probably with a real purpose of having a look at the Home Fleet, which was based in the Flow. Charles's advice that he should not go was rejected and, instead, at Mrs Churchill's instigation, Charles was included in the expedition. Within the hour, with a greatcoat lent him by the PM, but apart from that without even a toothbrush, he found himself sitting in a train at King's Cross station waiting to head north for an indefinite number of days.[69] His concerns with Sector VI, the Medical School, the College, his other patients and his domestic life were suddenly totally interrupted. Faced at Scapa with bitter cold, snow and sleet, Charles found it hard to share Churchill's enthusiasm. So did Harry Hopkins, Roosevelt's adviser and confidant who had come to England to see at first hand what was going on, and whom Churchill had included, apparently as inadequately clothed as Charles, in the party.[70] On the way home, Charles was invited to a small dinner given in the PM's honour by Tom Johnston, the Secretary of State for Scotland. Charles described how Hopkins, persuaded to say a few words, quoted from the Book of Ruth:

'Whither thou goest, I will go; and where thou lodgest, I will lodge: thy people shall be my people, and thy God my God'. Then he added very quietly: 'Even to the very end.''[69]

When he became better acquainted with his patient, Charles would not have been surprised, as he was on this occasion, to find Churchill in tears. General Ismay*, who was also present, found the moment deeply moving.[70]

---

*Major General Sir Hastings ('Pug') Ismay, Chief of Staff to Churchill and head of the office of the Minister of Defence.

Chapter 10

1941–Moscow and Washington

The meeting of the College which elected Charles President on 7 April 1941 not only appointed representatives to the BMA Planning Commission but also appointed its own Planning Committee, and it was a sign of the times that five of the 11 members were Fellows under 45 years of age.[1] Two sub-committees were formed, one on medical education and one on hospital services. Charles gave time to both, but his main concern in the summer of 1941 was to visit provincial medical centres to find out for the Ministry of Health what effect the war was having on the training of medical students. He was concerned with student numbers, their living and working accommodation, bomb damage to teaching hospitals and the effects of the calling up of teaching staff. In the course of this work he got to know, and came to be known by, consultants across the country to an extent hardly matched by previous college presidents. When he later became a controversial figure, controversy was therefore related not to some remote figurehead but to someone widely known at first hand.

Charles's notes on the student situation ended up being delivered by Dorothy's hand to the new Director of the Emergency Medical Service, Professor Francis Fraser,[2] Charles being then *en route* for Moscow on his second wartime journey. Russia, when invaded by the Germans three months before, had turned not only to the USA but also to Britain for materials of war, and British and American delegations had been organised to visit Moscow to find out what was needed. The British delegation was headed by Beaverbrook, now Minister of Supply, and Charles had been included to appraise Soviet needs for medical supplies.

The departure on this occasion was not a pier-head jump. Charles had time to delegate duties to College officers before he left on 22 September. He indicated that he expected to be back by the middle of October.[3] He also wrote to Bracken:

'I missed you on Saturday. I think that for many reasons it would be a good thing if something like this was given out in the Press:

"The Prime Minister has asked Sir Charles Wilson, President of the Royal College of Physicians, to accompany the British Mission to Moscow, in order to report to him on any medical help that should be given by this country."[4]

157

Figure 11. At sea, possibly in HMS 'London' on the trip to Archangel in September 1941. (Wellcome Institute Library, London; CMAC PP/CMW/P.70/2)

'I wonder if you could get this into *The Times*?

'There is such a very strong feeling throughout the country about helping Russia that I think it would do good if it could be said in the Press and possibly on the wireless that the PM was so keen on helping that even in medical matters he sent the President of the College. I saw the PM yesterday and in agreeing to let me go, he, off his own bat, said that it ought to appear in the Press. You will know when is the appropriate time for such a thing to appear,

I suppose when we are well on our way or when we arrive. I have left the best of the younger generation, one Brooks* by name, in charge of the PM. He is first-class and I should feel perfectly happy to leave him in charge of my own family. The PM is in quite good fettle but if any health emergency arises, then I ought to come back because it is half the battle for the patient to know his doctor well. You must see things through if the necessity arises.'

The outward and homeward legs of the journey from Scapa Flow to Archangel were made uneventfully in the cruiser HMS 'London', travelling at speed without escorts.[5] A snapshot shows Charles on deck looking totally unseamanlike, his inevitable black 'Anthony Eden' hat on the back of his head, and a duffel coat, done up with only one toggle, blowing in the breeze. The Archangel-Moscow sector was travelled by air and entailed being fired on by Russian anti-aircraft guns.

On all his other wartime journeys, Charles was with, but in a functional sense not part of, a group of people with a job to do. He was there to provide medical care in case of need. But on this trip he was included not for his clinical skills but as an equal worker among a small team of senior advisers which included General Hastings (Pug) Ismay, Chief of Staff to Churchill, and Mr Harold Balfour, Under-Secretary of State for Air, and their American opposite numbers led by Mr Averell Harriman.** And so Charles was kept busy, with planning to be done on the five-day outward voyage,[6] and a report to be written on the return trip.[7] Charles gave an account of the mission on the BBC soon after he returned.[8] He highlighted Beaverbrook's consuming passion for work; a 19-hour day allowed little time for sightseeing. He was impressed with the size of medical institutes that he was shown, one for blood transfusion, one for epidemic diseases and one for experimental medicine, and said that Russia appeared to be in the van of medical research. He ended his talk with a description of the dinner given for the Mission at the Kremlin:

'. . . as the hours went by, the toasts got less official, until at last someone drank to the two young pilots who had brought some of the Americans all the way from New York. Stalin had risen to previous toasts with a small glass of red wine in his right hand, and his left hand buried in his pocket. Now he rose and moving in his slow deliberate way half the length of the great table he came in front of it and clinking his glass with those of the pilots

---

*Dr WDW Brooks, physician to St Mary's Hospital and Surgeon Captain, Royal Naval Volunteer Reserve.
**Averell Harriman, President Roosevelt's special envoy to the United Kingdom.

he toasted them. It is what you would expect of him. He says what he thinks, his thoughts are on his face. . . . This toast was in tribute to youth, perhaps his summons to the idealism of young America.'[8]

Charles was not usually prone to such credulity.

Charles's return to England on 10 October had a greater sense of occasion than was the case with his later trips. There was a warm letter of congratulations from his father-in-law, Dr Dufton, who, with his wife, had been greatly cheered by a visit from Dorothy, and who reflected how proud and thrilled the boys must have been with his adventures.[9] And on 13 October a dinner was given at the Dorchester by the British and American delegates in honour of the mission leaders, Beaverbrook and Harriman. Charles collected 10 signatures on his menu, which, after two years of war, was still able to list a four-course meal starting with caviar and oysters.[10] A few days later Beaverbrook asked Charles to serve as chairman of a committee to handle the supply of medical goods to Russia[11] whose apparent needs, Charles had indicated in his report, were formidable. They included 850 000 pairs of forceps, 500 000 syringes, 10 million needles, 225 000 pairs of scissors and 250 000 rubber hot water bottles. 'But', added Charles, 'the army supplied is very large.'[7] A subtle change in relationships at this time led Beaverbrook to alter his mode of addressing Charles in letters. It was no longer Dear Sir Charles but Dear Charles.

In his new advisory role Charles found himself in touch with Mrs Agnes Maisky, wife of the Soviet Ambassador to London, who quickly involved herself in details.[12] In November she wrote to Charles asking about the power supply of the 64 X-ray units that had already been dispatched, and queried the number of forceps sent. Charles found out from the Ministry of Supply that 18 788 of the latter had gone, thereby clearing the British stocks.[13] A penned postscript to Mrs Maisky's letter told Charles that there had been 1 020 000 Russians wounded. Charles also found himself with a new link with Mrs Churchill who headed a Red Cross 'Aid to Russia' fund and who asked him to speak to Red Cross representatives about his visit.[14] And, like Mrs Maisky, Mrs Churchill also penned a postscript to her letter, telling Charles that at 10.30 am (the am was underlined) on the previous day, Winston was smoking a large, but not the very largest, cigar. Evidently there had been some collusion between the Prime Minister's wife and doctor in an attempt to change his smoking habits.

With his trip to Russia and his summer visits to the provincial medical centres behind him, Charles had a good account to give of his first six months in office to the Comitia of the College on 30 October.

His ability to speak cogently on complex issues, using few if any notes, was often remarked upon. However, it reflected no off-the-cuff mustering of his thoughts. Indeed he was not very good at spontaneously encapsulating his ideas. Loving words, he was liable to be carried away by them, and while this made his conversation sparkle, he must have realised it to be dangerous for critical pronouncements. Whenever he knew he was to speak, he took a lot of trouble in preparation, making notes on what he wanted to say and thoroughly honing not only the argument he wanted to advance but also certain key phrases. He put the notes aside before speaking. When, after a one-hour oration, he was once asked for the script, he replied that what there was of it was in Dorothy's handbag.

His rough scribblings for his report to Comitia on 30 October[15] flesh out the brief record in the College Annals.[16]

'I have been concerned for some time to find that this College is no longer consulted by the Government, that in the case of a recent important committee the Chairman was chosen after consultation with the BMA and without reference to the Royal Colleges. . . . As your President I am not disposed to accept this state of affairs. It is then a good omen that your President was asked by the Prime Minister to join the British Mission to Moscow to represent there the Government in medical matters, that he was invited on his return to discuss the medical conditions in Russia with members of the Cabinet, that his report was submitted to the Cabinet and that he was asked to broadcast to the Empire and to America.'[15]

A separate manuscript note read:

'What we ask is not I think un-reasonable. Other bodies have duties to perform in medical affairs which they and they only can carry out. We only ask that we should be consulted in these matters with which we are specially competent to advise.'[15]

In addition to telling the Fellows what he had seen in Russia, Charles brought them up to date with the business of the sub-committee on medical education. This sub-committee was to meet 16 times and produce a report in 1944. Charles was insistent that the report should be perfectly written. 'You know' he said to George Pickering, who drafted it, 'the people who will read this report are literary gents and you've got to get it so that literary gents approve it and don't turn up their noses at it.'[17] This was not too hard for Pickering, whose mentor had been Sir Thomas Lewis, Head of the Medical Research Council's unit at University College Hospital, who was renowned for his use of crisp biblical English.

The most significant discussion at the Comitia arose from the work of the sub-committee on hospital services. It reported its view, which today might seem platitudinous, that every member of the community should receive the best treatment available.[16] This thought, which coloured Charles's whole approach to a health service, was in his mind after his visits to provincial medical centres. He asserted that there was no fully qualified consultant obstetrician in the largest county in England.[17] Charles also commented that he had met Fellows who had expressed a wish that the College should give advice on all aspects of consultant services in a new health service, with its sister Colleges. The Comitia endorsed this view and nominated individuals to discuss closer cooperation with the Royal College of Surgeons.

As the months of 1941 passed, Charles's star was clearly in the ascendant. In his work there was a happy coincidence between his ambition to be known as someone of importance, his ambition to be involved in affairs of state, and his ambition for the College to regain its historic role as an adviser to Government. At home despite the war, his family life was free from worry. Dorothy and he had declined an offer from a Canadian, Dr Hurst, to take the two boys into their household on the other side of the Atlantic, and Geoffrey, now aged eleven, was at a boarding preparatory school. John, coming up to seventeen, with his ambition to join the forces still a shadow on the horizon, continued at Eton. School holidays were spent at the Garden Cottage at Harefield, the Mill at Manton having been requisitioned for the duration of the war. On his return from Russia, the Headmaster of Eton, CA Elliott, invited Charles to talk to the senior boys, the First Hundred, on his visit. He elected to speak on Leadership. John sat anxiously at the back, and was duly relieved by a very good performance. Thanking Charles a few days later, the Headmaster commented that what he had said about the Guards—he had presumably used his pithed frog analogy—had stimulated a very lively controversy.[18]

Not very far in the background was Dorothy, totally dedicated to help him. Despite his streak of idealism, capacity for leadership and the political astuteness that had brought him to his present position, he remained curiously unpractical. He had a reputation for doing things in foolish ways, for making loose arrangements and for upsetting people. But much was forgiven because his delightful wife charmed everybody, going along behind him and tidying everything up.[17]

In December 1941 Charles found himself detached for the third time in twelve months from his normal tasks. On 7 December Japan came into the war with an attack on Pearl Harbour, and Churchill, wanting to persuade the Americans, despite Japan's aggression, to give priority to defeating Hitler, decided to go and see Roosevelt.[19] On 12 December he embarked at Greenock for the Atlantic crossing in the battleship 'Duke of York'. The principal service members of the team were the First Sea Lord, the chief of Air Staff and Field Marshal Sir John Dill, who had just been succeeded by General Alan Brooke as Chief of the Imperial General Staff. Beaverbrook, who was Minister of Supply, was the only civilian principal team member.[20] Charles never explained how he came to accompany Churchill on this trip. Despite a plea from Mrs Churchill, supported by Bracken, Churchill had not taken Charles with him in August on his two-week voyage in HMS 'Prince of Wales' to meet Roosevelt in Newfoundland.[21] A clue to his presence on this occasion appears in his description of what happened on 22 December, the first night after the party arrived in Washington. In his book Charles described how, at nearly midnight, when he had gone to his room at the Mayflower Hotel, he received a message that the PM wanted to see him at the White House, where Churchill was staying. Charles waited in Churchill's bedroom. When Churchill came in:

'"Is there anything wrong?" I asked "The pulse is regular", he said with a whimsical smile. He wanted to know if he could take a sleeping pill. . . . I could see he was bottling up his excitement.'[22]

Churchill's immediate reference to his pulse (and this is the first clinical note in Charles's book) could mean only that Churchill's pulse already had significance for both of them. But Charles did not explain its significance to the reader any more than he explained the significance of the episode that he described two days later, after Churchill had spoken at the Christmas tree ceremony in the grounds of the White House:

'When the PM came in from the balcony he told me he had had palpitations during the ceremony; he made me take his pulse. "What is it, Charles?" "Oh, it's alright" "But what is it?" he persisted. "A hundred and five" He was a little taken aback. "It has all been very moving", he lisped with excitement. . . .'[23]

Charles, of course, knew that, while palpitations did not usually indicate serious heart disease, they often caused anxiety, and called for repeated reassurance.[24] He, and anyone else close to Churchill who knew of the problem, must have been acutely aware that if a rumour got about that Churchill had any sort of 'heart trouble', it would not only give aid and comfort to the enemy but it might also diminish Churchill's influence with Roosevelt. Hence, Charles's attendance during a visit to America was prudent. If Churchill was bothered by his pulse, he could turn to Charles, rather than risk spreading rumours by seeking medical help in Washington.

The decision that Charles should accompany Churchill came to be more than vindicated when Churchill developed a problem of a very different sort after Christmas. In his book, Charles described what happened under the date 27 December:

'The PM seems so preoccupied with his mission of good fellowship to America in general and to the President in particular that I decided not to bother him by calling this morning. When I got back to the hotel at ten o'clock, after a stroll through the streets, I found an urgent message. I was wanted at the White House. Would I go at once. I took a taxi.

'"I am glad you have come" the PM began. He was in bed and looked worried. "It was hot last night and I got up to open the window. It was very stiff, I had to use considerable force and I noticed all at once that I was short of breath. I had a dull pain over my heart. It went down my left arm. It didn't last very long, but it has never happened before. What is it? Is my heart all right? I thought of sending for you, but it passed off."

'There was not much to be found when I examined his heart. Indeed, the time I spent listening to his chest was given to some quick thinking. I knew that when I took the stethoscope out of my ears he would ask me pointed questions, and I had no doubt that whether the electrocardiograph showed evidence of a coronary thrombosis or not, his symptoms were those of coronary insufficiency. The text book treatment for this is at least six weeks in bed. That would mean publishing to the world—and the American newspapers would see to this—that the PM was an invalid with a crippled heart and a doubtful future. And this at a moment when America has just come into the war, and there is no one but Winston to take her by the hand. I felt that the effect of announcing that the PM had had a heart attack could only be disastrous. I knew, too, the consequences to one of his imaginative temperament of the feeling that his heart was affected. His work would suffer. On the other hand, if I did nothing and he had another and severer attack—perhaps a fatal seizure—the world would undoubtedly say that I had killed him through not insisting on rest. These thoughts went racing through my head while I was listening to his heart. I took my stethoscope out of my ears. Then I replaced it and listened again. Right or wrong, it seemed plain that I must sit tight on what had happened, whatever the consequences.

"Well," he asked, looking full at me, "is my heart all right?"

"There is nothing serious," I answered "You have been overdoing things."

"Now, Charles, you're not going to tell me to rest. I can't. I wont. Nobody else can do this job. I must. What actually happened when I opened the window?" he demanded "My idea is that I strained one of my chest muscles. I used great force. I don't believe it was my heart at all." He waited for me to answer.

"Your circulation was a bit sluggish. It is nothing serious. You needn't rest in the sense of lying up, but you mustn't do more than you can help in the way of exertion for a little while." There was a knock at the door. It was Harry Hopkins. I slipped away. I went and sat in a corner of the secretaries' room, picking up a newspaper, so that they would not talk to me. I began to think things out more deliberately. I did not like it, but I determined to tell no one. When we get back to England, I shall take him to Parkinson*, who will hold his tongue.'[25]

Given the symptoms Churchill described, Charles had no alternative but to diagnose a coronary attack of some sort, and to confront the fact that, whatever an electrocardiogram might show, the conventional treatment was rest in bed for six weeks. His decision to sit tight and tell no one was brave and correct. Charles's experience would have taught him that patients who had unrecognized heart attacks, and who carried on normally, sometimes made uneventful recoveries. All alone and very quickly, he had to balance the equanimity of his patient, and an appreciation of political considerations, against his own professional reputation. Before this event, and subsequently, Charles never hesitated to consult over Churchill's medical problems with the best specialists he could find, and he chose well. This time the need for complete secrecy meant that he was on his own, and the next few days brought anxiety to patient and doctor alike. On the day following the episode, when Churchill left the White House to take the train to Ottawa, Charles recorded:

'The PM asked me to drive with him in his car to the station. As we drove out of the grounds he opened the window of the car. He was short of breath. "There seems no air," he said, "in this car. Is it a stuffy night Charles?" And then he put his hand on my knee. "It is a great comfort to have you with me" he said. He has used these words twice in four days; the first time was before the heart attack. This is something new; it has not happened before.'[26]

In Ottawa on 29 December, Charles described the busy programme, adding:

'There was still dinner at Government House to be got through, and then a reception. However, so far nothing untoward has happened. Whenever we are alone, he keeps asking me to take his pulse. I get out of it somehow, but once, when I found him lifting something heavy, I did expostulate. At this he broke out:

---

*Dr John Parkinson, physician to the London Hospital and the National Heart Hospital.

"Now, Charles, you are making me heart-minded. I shall soon think of nothing else. I couldn't do my work if I kept thinking of my heart." The next time he asked me to take his pulse I refused point blank. "You're alright. Forget your damned heart."

He won't get through his speech tomorrow if this goes on.'[27]

Churchill returned from Ottawa to Washington on New Year's Eve and on 4 January flew south to Palm Beach in Florida, where he told the Cabinet in London he was resting for a few days on Charles's advice.[29] It was his first holiday for nearly three years.[30] He acknowledged that he had had a rather strenuous time—intense, laborious and exhausting were other adjectives he later applied to it.[31] Charles saw Florida as giving the PM time to work off steam, which he evidently did. While after a few days he had not forgotten what he called his 'pump', he had given up feeling his pulse.[32] After a week at Palm Beach the party returned to Washington, and Churchill then set off home to England from Bermuda in a flying boat. His entire party could not be fitted in and he suggested to Charles that he should return by sea. Charles was appalled. Medically he would be responsible if anything happened to Churchill in the air. He would also be in difficulties if he returned to England a week or more after the PM, for he had met criticism of his absence as President of the College by arguing that looking after the PM's health was even more important than doing the job as President. Charles responded by breaking without ceremony into a meeting of the Chiefs of Staff and making it plain that he could not agree.[33] In an earlier typescript he recorded making it plain 'that if it was necessary to persist in that plan the Prime Minister would have to make other medical arrangements.'[34] Whatever arguments he used, they were effective for on the following day he left Bermuda with the Prime Minister and his immediate entourage in the flying boat RMA 'Berwick'. Medically the flight was uneventful.

Why Charles, in writing his book published in 1966, never alluded to the background to Churchill's comment, made on his first night in Washington, that his pulse was regular, is curious. The explanation probably lies in the manner in which Charles's book was written. Although it was not published until 1966, an early typed version of the first part of it was completed by 1954.[34] In this, the story started with Churchill boarding the 'Duke of York' on 12 December 1941 to go to Washington. In the 1960s a publisher's reader pencilled a comment on the title page asking how the author got involved with Churchill. In the book the introductory pages before the events of 12 December 1941 were therefore later additions made by Charles in his late seventies, when he may well have forgotten the medical details of the early years of his association with Churchill. Charles never submitted a draft of his book to a medical reader, so that the apparent incongruity of recording Churchill's comments on his pulse and palpitation was easily missed. The same factors may have contributed to Charles's statement in his book that before the Washington visit in December 1941 Churchill was fit and well and did not need him.[35] While this was generally true, Churchill did from time to time present him with complaints some of which led to consultations with specialists, who in due course received copies of *Marlborough*.[36] Like Charles himself, who regarded his care of Churchill as his contribution to the war effort, others whose professional help was sought also refused to charge a fee. All in all, Churchill's comment that during 1941 Charles had become his constant medical adviser[37] summed up the situation well.

During his six weeks away with Churchill, on this the first of a long series of overseas travels, Charles made no complaint of time hanging on his hands. The novelty of the surroundings in which he found himself, and his involvement in activities in his own field, are reflected in some manuscript diary entries.[38]

On 24 December in Washington:

'Walked from Mayflower to Academy of Science for conference of doctors. Bush, a layman, dominated the party. He described the new machinery for securing that when anything was found out there should be no delay in applying it.

'I had meant to go to the White House for the Christmas Tree celebrations in the garden but was detained by the Beaver who had a sore throat . . .'

On 25 December:

'Its a lovely day, blue sky and for the first time a fresh keen air. When I went to the White House this morning I found myself walking a great pace. It was a day to be alive.

'When I saw the PM this morning he said that he was going to Ottawa in a few days and asked me to go with him. He added that he wasn't afraid of being ill but that he must keep fit for his job and it was a comfort to have me.

'The Embassy telephoned inviting me to dine tonight with Halifax and to go on with about thirty other people to a film but I had to decline as three of us have been asked to have our Christmas dinner with the Roosevelt family at the White House. Roger Lee, the President of the American College of Physicians had asked me to stay with him at Boston for Christmas. I should have liked to see Boston but I thought it was better not to run away just now.'

On 31 December in Ottawa:

'I talked to about sixty staff officers on morale. When I had done Ralston, the Defence Minister, took me aside. Are you busy? And when I said I was not, he said. Then come with me and led the way into a small room where I had to go through the performance again, verbatim, to a stenographer. "You see" he said, "there's nothing in writing on the subject. Its what the boys want". We left Ottawa at 3 pm arriving in Washington next morning.'

On Thursday 1 January 1942 in Washington:

'A quiet day with time to look round. Many things unlike England. There is no blackout to speak of, though the White House is no longer flood lit. The New York Times has 43 pages of good stuff but what is said could be said in much less space. When you order roast beef a big plate is completely covered with a thick but tender slice of meat. By the time I've disposed of it I've only room for an ice . . . Tomorrow, if all is well here, I must go to New York to talk.'

On Friday 2 January in Washington:

'Left Mayflower 9 am so that I might call at the White House before leaving for New York. An embassy car took me to the Washington Air Port, about half an hour's drive. We left 10.45, travelling at 9000 feet at 259 miles per hour, helped by a tail wind of 76 miles per hour: the fastest time the company has done since 1933. A little bumpy towards the end of the journey. Each passenger was offered thin slab of Wrigley's chewing gum. Arrived N. York 12.11. The fact that I give all these details is significant. The air is still a novelty to us whereas standing at the Washington Air Port planes went off every few minutes to various parts of America, like Victoria Station at a busy hour. Lunched with Pope (?)*. At 4.30 I met the National Committee on Morale, about sixty present. I talked and then they asked questions. A lean angular spinster rose: "England", she said, "had been just on the edge of Europe all these centuries, and could not expect America to have so high a morale. Hitler invading wasn't real to America. At a meeting at Chicago, the day after Pearl Habour, someone had suggested peace. It had been more loudly applauded than any other remark." Another speaker asked what effect the foreign ingredients of the USA would have on morale. I gave some kind of reply but wondered what was the real answer . . . The lean angular lady rose again. "You British" she said, "come of the same stock but we Americans come from

---

*Pope—unidentified.

many sources; if we sought shelter in a Tube we should sleep in different postural positions and get our elbows into each other." I wondered where this discussion was going to stop. At night I talked with the New York Academy of Medicine, perhaps 700 doctors. I gave them an hour on morale and it seemed to go well. I slept in Wardwell's* house, leaving the airport next morning at 9.8 am, travelling at 4000 feet at 176 miles an hour arriving 10.33 (in Washington).'

On Saturday 3 January in Washington:

'After luncheon I called on Brigadier General Osborne who advised the American army on all matters concerned with morale. He explained to me what they were doing already to find out the soldier's attitude to various things . . . Osborne began to talk about a 'psychological' offensive against Hitler. I explained that was not my line of country. I was only concerned with those things which helped to keep a man in the line. Ah he said, you mean you are interested in combat morale. He rang a bell. Major . . . he said when a man answered. Major . . . is in charge of combat morale. When he appeared I learnt on questioning him that he had never heard a shot fired in anger. He was the son of a solider who had been in charge of combat morale in the last war—a charming example of continuity in a young country.'

The manuscript diary entries[38] covering the week in Florida include:
On Monday 5 January:

'. . . there is a great bunch of bananas hanging in a kind of conservatory. You pull one off and eat it when you feel inclined. The sea is warmer than anything we know at home and just after we had finished bathing a shark appeared to provide a little local colour and when I was taking a short cut I was warned to avoid the long grass because there were rattle snakes in it.'

On Thursday 8 January:

'After an early tea I started with Martin** to go by car to Miami . . . one street of luxury shops, another of luxury hotels, and as we passed we saw a beggar arrested. There is a certain beauty of sky and palms, a kind of cunning in the lay out but all is impermanent.'

---

*Wardwell—unidentified.
**John Martin, Churchill's Principal Private Secretary.

On Friday 9 January:

'Worked all morning on my book [*The Anatomy of Courage*]'

Madame Balsan, former Duchess of Marlborough, was a visitor and Charles recorded:

> 'During luncheon Madame Balsan said: "Winston looks very well. This is due to Sir Charles Wilson. He is President of the Royal College of Physicians but he has given up everything to do this." I think the PM was rather surprised at this pronouncement. It had never been put like this before. Perhaps he took things too much for granted.'

While still in Florida Charles received a telegram asking him to make available the talk he had given at the New York Academy of Medicine for publication in a journal called, *Medical Economics.* He noted with surprise that the telegram contained 130 words, and added:

> 'I wonder do other people who speak get pleasure from this sort of stuff. I do. It's not vanity, but a great longing for reassurance that your speech wasn't a flop.'[38]

Being included with Beaverbrook, Sir Dudley Pound*, Sir Charles Portal** and Colonel Hollis*** in Churchill's flight home across the Atlantic put Charles well in the limelight.[39] The whole episode was newsworthy, for crossing the Atlantic in a flying boat at that stage in the war was a hazardous thing to do. Charles had recognised this, and before take-off he did what he had done twice before battle in the First World War: he made a will. On a sheet of Bermuda Government House notepaper he wrote a note leaving everything that he had to Dorothy, addressed the envelope to himself at the Royal College of Physicians and endorsed it "To be opened by Lady Wilson in my absence."[40] It was not until some time after their return that Churchill and Charles learnt how hazardous the flight had been. Their course had carried them too far to the south, within minutes of flying over German-occupied Brest. Then, having turned north just in time, they were reported to British Fighter Command as a hostile bomber. Fortunately they were not intercepted.[41]

---

*Admiral of the Fleet Sir Dudley Pound, First Sea Lord.
**Air Chief Marshal Sir Charles Portal, Chief of Air Staff.
***Colonel Leslie Hollis, a principal assistant to General Ismay in the office of the Minister of Defence.

The newspaper reports of the trip brought Charles letters from a number of acquaintances from his distant past. One letter, addressed to 'My dear Doc', by an officer of his old battalion, implored him to make use of his access to high quarters to have trenches dug to enable the Home Guard, who were, it was said, themselves too old to dig, to defend East Anglia from invasion. 'Try to imagine', he was exhorted, with reference to the Somme, 'what our position in Trones Wood would have been worth if someone had not prepared that dug-out for us.' The threat of invasion was still in people's minds, and this letter to Charles ended on a heroic note: '*Moriturus* (about April) *te saluto*.'[42]

At Comitia at the end of January 1942 Charles reported on his visit to America, on the medical contacts he had made, and on his lectures on morale.[43] One person he saw as particularly important in American medical circles was Dr Roger Irving Lee, whose invitation for Christmas in Boston he had been unable to accept. Charles set about trying through him to develop a more intimate relationship between the American and London colleges. At a personal level things were set in train for Dr Lee to be elected an Honorary Fellow of the Royal College of Physicians. At the same time, Charles wrote to Lee expressing his consistently stated view that it was the College and no other body that should be the authoritative British voice on clinical medical matters in England:

'I found that when I was in America that English scientists who are only remotely connected with medicine have been the means by which our experiences in clinical matters in the War have been conveyed to those in America who are interested. In short, that medical matters in England are transmitted to America very largely by members of the Medical Research Council. The Medical Research Council is a most efficient body with a most efficient Secretary, but it was set up to deal with research and I believe clinical matters ought to be dealt with by the two Colleges [of physicians and surgeons].'[44]

Dawson wrote to welcome Charles on his return from Washington.[45] Very conscious of this elder statesman's attempts to influence medical affairs,[46] before leaving for Washington Charles had written him a forthright letter reiterating his conviction that the government should be advised directly by the Colleges on consultant services and other matters within their competence:

'I have therefore made up my mind to go ahead on this policy. I think it is evident that it has overwhelming support both in London and in the Provinces, and in the last resort, if anybody questions this, I shall call a special Comitia, and if, by any chance, I am wrong and they do not agree with me, I shall resign.'[47]

It was not only to Dawson, to his opposite number in the United States, and to the Fellows of the College that Charles proclaimed his view of the College's advisory role. Hearing towards the end of March that, without having consulted the College, the Minister of Health was about to announce the terms of reference and membership of a committee to enquire into the organisation of medical schools (later called the Goodenough committee after its chairman), Charles wrote complaining to the Prime Minister.[48] Churchill responded through his Principal Private Secretary, John Martin, indicating that he had asked the Minister of Health to see Charles.[49] By the time Charles saw the Minister a few days later, the formation of the committee had been announced, but the Minister promised to talk over the question of medical consultation with the Chief Medical Officer to the Ministry, Sir Wilson Jameson.[50] Charles had ended his letter to the Prime Minister with a criticism of the way in which the government was receiving medical advice generally:

'There are eight or nine medical men advising Government departments (some of whom are nearer 80 than 70), unconscious of each-other's doings and often giving contradictory advice, without anyone coordinating their efforts.'[48]

Charles returned to this theme in a letter to John Martin immediately after seeing the Minister. Having referred to their conversation about the Goodenough committee, Charles wrote:

'I did not raise the much more important question of any attempt to co-ordinate the advice given by various medical men to various Government Departments, because this has really nothing to do with the Ministry of Health. I can imagine no more difficult undertaking than to persuade the various Government Departments to subordinate themselves to the Ministry of Health. They are much more likely to accept a co-ordinating man whose reign would, they hope, be temporary, whereas if they are to be under the Ministry of Health it would be for all time. I doubt whether much more can be done at the present time than for a notice to appear, say in *The Times* that so-and-so had been appointed to co-ordinate the medical work of the various Government Departments. The co-ordinator would then have to work out his own salvation and his strength would entirely depend upon his own tact and upon the general feeling that the Government was behind him. I do not know whether the Government is prepared to take such a step, if not, there seems little alternative except to drift on until some particular result of the lack of co-ordination forces this question into a public issue which I do not think would be very long.'[50]

It is hard to see this proposal as other than a solicitation by Charles of an appointment for himself as a sort of national medical overseer.

Furthermore, in addressing his remarks to the Principal Private Secretary, Charles must have hoped that his views would reach Churchill. This was in character. From Charles's point of view the matter was straightforward. He believed the medical advisory system at a national level was wrong, he believed he knew the remedy, and he believed that, given authority, he could apply it. Armed with these convictions, he by-passed the senior people with whom decision-making in such a matter did not ultimately lie, and took his case directly to the level where there was power to act. A few days later he was pressing the case on Bracken who had raised with him the question of the Prime Minister recommending him for a further honour. He wrote of 'putting medical things right . . . during my years as President'.[46]

The idea of the creation of a medical overseer got nowhere, but Charles's pressure for the College to be consulted by all departments of the government eventually led to his having talks with Sir John Anderson, the Lord President of the Council, who, as Chairman of the Home Affairs Committee, relieved Churchill of much work that was not directly concerned with the military conduct of the war. Anderson's conclusion was that the situation of which Charles complained resulted from several factors, one of which was the changing policy of the College itself, which had depended on the personalities of successive presidents. But in Anderson's view the situation was due much more to the development of a strong medical organisation under the Ministry of Health, which had been established in 1919, and the increasing prestige and usefulness of the Medical Research Council.[51] Charles had to be satisfied with Anderson's assurance that he would, subject to the Prime Minister's approval, have further talks with the Minister of Health and Secretary of the Medical Research Council to encourage them to take a lead in consulting the College. The fact was that the College's broad influence on the government had passed to others. For too many years the College had been a sleepy hollow. Vigorous younger bodies had been found more useful by modern governments. Charles's interviews with John Anderson ended his attempts to restore the College to a position of global influence in medical affairs. What he could do, and proceeded to do, was to ensure that its voice was heard where no one could deny its expertise: medicine at the consultant level.

While Charles was making this bid for himself and the College in Whitehall, he was also discreetly chancing his arm in another contest. The Regius professorship of medicine at Oxford fell vacant and he became a candidate. Where the initiative lay is unclear. With his interest in young people, Charles would have liked to be head of a university college and he may have seen this as a stepping stone. In any event the appointment would provide a prestigious base from which he could pursue his ambition to influence a new health service, as well as an assured income for several years. As the deliberations over the appointment progressed, Charles told Dorothy that he gathered they did not want a 'dominant gent',[52] and he would not be heartbroken if he were unsuccessful,[53] which he was.

One of the people in the manoeuvering over the Oxford appointment was the newly appointed Registrar of the College, Dr Harold Boldero. Seven years younger than Charles, Boldero's background was Charterhouse, Trinity College, Oxford, and the Middlesex Hospital, where he became Dean in 1934. He had many of the qualities that Charles liked, including a good record of service in the First World War and a combination of administrative and academic abilities, but the fact that he had played hockey rather than Rugby football for England made him less than totally noteworthy in Charles's estimation. Charles had got to know Boldero as a fellow medical school dean, the acquaintanceship was extended socially, and Dorothy soon came to support Boldero and his wife in the latter's long illness.[55] Boldero made an excellent Registrar, taking over much of the load of the day to day running of the College.[56] He was as stern a critic as Charles, but much more tactful, and had impeccable manners and a strong sense of what was right and honourable. Charles recognised his capacity as an organiser but regarded him as being full of prejudices of what he called the public school variety.[54] Perhaps he discovered Boldero's habit, which was not exceptional in men of his generation and background, of registering his opinion of people by little marginal private signs, such as 'HO' which meant humble origin. For all Charles's criticisms—and few who came within arm's length of him were spared critical dissection—Charles accepted Boldero as a nice man[54] and relied heavily on him. Boldero, for his part, regarded Charles as a very ruthless and critical person, but one whom he admired nevertheless.[57]

Of no less importance in Charles's life as President of the College was the Secretary, Miss Ina Cooke. Outstanding in her job, and with a first class mind, Miss Cooke feared nobody, Charles included. With her Charles established a *modus vivendi* which allowed business to be done, but without cordiality. Miss Cooke and Boldero, on the other hand, worked admirably together; they were both traditionalists.[57]

In March 1942 Charles was re-elected President of the College with 127 votes to Horder's 27,[58] and he was able to report that notice was being taken of the College.[59] He and Mr Ernest Rock Carling* had been asked by the Ministry of Health to survey consultants in England and Wales. He took on another enterprise, as an occasional

---

*E Rock Carling, surgeon to the Westminster Hospital and consultant adviser to the Ministry of Health.

member of one of the most famous programmes ever broadcast by the BBC, the Brains Trust, in which five people from widely differing backgrounds answered questions sent in by listeners.[60] The deep timbre of Charles's voice was easily recognised by those who knew him, for as a doctor he was not identified by name. An old friend commended him for never 'humming and hawing' but chided him for not joining in the laughter of the group. His association with the Brains Trust proved to be brief, for he was not very reliable in his attendances. Sometimes he would disappear without notice on what turned out to be a trip with Churchill, and sometimes he simply forgot to turn up. Left to himself, he created an aura of helplessness and would bombard Dorothy in what were often daily letters with questions such as how best to get back to Harefield from the College in her absence.[53]

The subject of morale, and his book on it, continued to be much in Charles's mind and conversation at this time.[62] His talks in America had brought several congratulatory letters, and in April the Commander in Chief of the army in England, General Bernard Paget, invited him to accompany him on a visit to a battle school in the north of England where a large group of senior officers was to gather.[63] Charles's letter of thanks to Paget after the visit[64] led to more correspondence in which Paget told him he thought he should be appointed as the controlling head in this field, to co-ordinate studies and their application in the three services.[65] The actual writing of *The Anatomy of Courage* was now well advanced. As early as September 1940 Charles had sent a typescript to Sir Arthur Quiller-Couch, a writer who used the pseudonym 'Q', whom he admired.[66] Q had thought it ought to be published at once, but Charles was set upon including more material from the new war, including naval and air force experience. In May 1942 he sent an expanded version to Desmond MacCarthy, a well known literary critic, and asked him for his comments. It was delivered to MacCarthy when he was visiting Lady Desborough in Hertfordshire for the weekend. Both he and his hostess, two of whose sons had been killed in the First World War, read it and wrote letters of encouragement.[67,68] MacCarthy did more. He went through the draft carefully and suggested a good many corrections which, while mostly small, contributed to the elegance of the final version. From then on Charles consulted him freely.[69]

Chapter 11

His Itinerant Patient

The world at large remained ignorant of Churchill's coronary episode in Washington for twenty four years, until Charles described it in his book in 1966. But the word that Churchill's heart was 'not too good' quickly reached several key people in London, Churchill himelf mentioning it.[1] It was taken into account when, three weeks after the Prime Minister's return from America in January 1942 the Japanese threat to Singapore led to a proposal that he should fly out to India and the Middle East. It figured again in discussions in March when Churchill suggested he should go to meet Stalin.[2] When June came, and Churchill's concern about ensuring agreement with the Americans on the timing of the Second Front in western Europe led him to return to Washington, Charles's advice was clear: there would be a real risk in undertaking the trans-Atlantic journey without a medical attendant.[3]

Charles described as fragmentary his notes on this second visit to Washington, which involved an absence of 10 days. The journey was made both ways by air in reasonable comfort and there were no medical problems. Time hung heavily enough for Charles to record some disenchantment with his lot:

'There are great changes imminent in the health services of our country and as President of the Royal College of Physicians I ought to be at home trying to shape them. So I asked if I might telephone to the Registar of the College from the White House about some rather important matters which he had brought to my notice. Now apparently I went on for some minutes, anyway Martin rather pompously said he was responsible for looking after the taxpayers interests and that my call had cost £33. He made rather heavy weather about it and as the said taxpayer is getting my services year after year gratis and as my own practice has in consequence vanished and as my expenses go on I did not feel in a mood to argue the point but straightaway sat down and wrote him a cheque for the amount, which he having consulted the PM proceeded to return to me. Perhaps the PM felt a little penitent over Martin's business like zeal in protecting the national finances at any rate when we got home he wrote me a letter (dated 29 June): "Thank you so much for your great kindness in coming with me to Washington at such short notice and, I fear, at no little personal inconvenience. It was a great comfort to have you there and I am more than grateful.

I was almost sorry not to be able to provide you with some work.
But your presence kept marauders away.'''[4]

The sense of vexation expressed in Charles's note was to recur over
the years. When he accompanied Churchill overseas he was not
involved in the affairs that made the journeys necessary. The things
that occupied his mind were going on at home in London, and no
one in the entourage that travelled with the Prime Minister had
reason to be interested in them. Medico-political manoeuvring over
a new health service was removed from the concerns of the soldiers,
sailors and airmen who were travelling for one purpose only. The
service chiefs and their staffs were extremely busy on these travels
and their little socialising was with their American opposite
numbers.[5] Charles, except when Churchill had need of him, was,
by contrast, essentially a passenger. Hence, not surprisingly, in
loneliness and boredom he reflected on the growing implications for
himself of his attachment to the Prime Minister. On the one hand
was his belief that looking after Churchill without charging him
a fee was his special contribution to winning the war. He must have
enjoyed the kudos too, as well as the chances that he had, as a
frustrated writer, of observing and analysing those who were making
history. On the other hand unpredictable absences from London
made his personal way of conducting College business difficult, and
there was the problem of a diminishing income through the loss of
his private practice which he saw to be the result of his absences—
visits to Moscow once and Washington twice in the space of nine
months. To the extent that one of the things general practictioners
ask of their chosen consultants is that they should be always
available, Charles was right, and since his pre-war practice was
relatively small he was specially vulnerable. But this was not the
whole story. Charles had never been enchanted with the notion of
earning a living from private practice. Now resident outside London,
busy with the College, and later having 129 Harley Street damaged
by bombing, the sustaining of his practice was not a priority. One
with different ideals could have exploited most profitably the fact
that he was Winston Churchill's doctor.

Charles must at this time have pondered other implications of his
relationship with his patient, for circumstances were forcing him
to make some complex judgements. Churchill's health was a matter
of confidence between himself and his doctor. However, knowledge
that Churchill had had some heart symptoms was shared by senior
members of the government and their personal staff and Charles
was drawn into discussions about what the Prime Minister should
do on health grounds. In July Churchill told Charles that he was
again thinking of visiting Cairo,[6] where he wanted to examine the
possibility of changing the army command in the Middle East. At
the time Charles was seeing Sir John Anderson about the College's

role as an advisory body to the government.[7] On July 9 Charles sent Anderson a hand-delivered note which showed his appreciation of the dilemma in which he found himself:

'I saw the PM this morning and he said (without my raising the subject) that he was still thinking of undertaking the journey we discussed and that he might set out in a few days. I said I was against it on health grounds, because of the heat. He then said "what is wrong with me?" I said he had had a threat of embarrassed circulation in Washington and that in view of that, Parkinson and I were against his taking any steps which might throw any additional strain on the circulation; that if he were careful he would have no bother. It was left at that. I said it so that I don't think he was alarmed at all. But if it should prove impossible to dissuade him on other grounds, then, I think, I should have to tell him of the coronary thrombosis threat. I am very much against this if it can possibly be avoided because it will weigh on his mind.

'I was a little puzzled when I saw you, how you would be able to contrive to limit his activities without his becoming aware that his health had been discussed. It will be even more difficult now when I have had to come out against the journey. I need not say how difficult my position would be if he discovers that I have been discussing his health. Can this be avoided? He will be on the alert now. I mean he would readily think I might be behind any opposition to his going which may be advanced on other grounds.'[6]

Later in the day on which he sent his letter, Charles received a hand-written response from Anderson assuring him that there would never be any allusion to Churchill's health, but he would press more vigorously other grounds that existed for objecting to the journey. He expressed his sympathy for Charles in the responsibility he was carrying.[8]

By 29 July clearly neither Charles's advice nor the other grounds for objecting had prevailed. Churchill told the Cabinet of his intended visit[9] and, a day later, decided to extend it to meet Stalin. He assured the cabinet that he would take his medical adviser with him.[10] His responses were tested in the laboratory to simulated flying at 15 000 ft and were judged satisfactory,[11] and shortly after midnight on 2 August Charles was airborne with him once again, leaving a crescendo of activity in College affairs. The report of the Medical Planning Commission (in effect the BMA and the Royal Colleges) had been received by the Comitia on 30 July[12] and on the next day Charles had been to see the Minister of Health, Ernest Brown, to discuss the formation of yet another committee which the

Minister was proposing.[13] Charles expressed reservations to both the Minister and to Dr George Anderson, Secretary of the BMA, about joining any new committee on health services whose composition was not discussed in advance with the BMA and the Royal Colleges. In his letter to Anderson Charles suggested that he could invoke powerful support. 'I need not tell you', he wrote, 'that we shall have support higher up, and if that fact affects your conclusions I shall be happy to convince you on that point with further evidence.'[14] There is nothing to suggest that 'support higher up' indicated any assurance of support from his patient, who was occupied with a crucial phase of the war. Probably Charles would have pointed out his relationship with the Lord President of the Council, on whom Churchill relied in home affairs. Charles added in his letter to Dr Anderson: 'I tried to get you on the telephone but failed, and I'm afraid I shall not personally be available for some little time, as I shall be out of London, but Boldero, Registrar of the College, is very wise in his judgement and I have complete confidence in him. He knows the situation and will act for me until I am able to take this matter up.'[14]

'. . . a rather feckless way of sending him over the world when he is approaching his seventieth year' was how Charles summed up the means of travel for the Prime Minister on his next trip.[15] He was referring to the unheated draughty American Liberator bomber in which Churchill and his party took off from Lyneham in the small hours of 2 August, heading for Gibraltar. Those on board included Sir Alexander Cadogan, Permanent Secretary to the Foreign Office,[16] and Dr Roland Wingfield, who was responsible for the oxygen equipment. In the after cabin there were two shelves on which Churchill and Charles lay. Charles, a sound sleeper, passed the night in comfort.[15] Once the coast of England was left behind, Churchill also, 'fortified' as he put it, 'by a good sleeping cachet',[17] forgot his discomfort and slept soundly. After a day at Gibraltar, the party flew through a second night, arriving over the Nile as dawn broke.[18] 'Vanderkloot has brought it off', Charles recorded with relief, referring to the American pilot of the Liberator, after they had landed near the Pyramids and driven into Cairo.[15] They had, after all, had a long flight, at times over enemy-held territory. General Alan Brooke, the Chief of the Imperial General Staff, who flew in a few hours later, learnt from Charles that he was a little worried about Churchill's pulse[19] but by both their accounts he was well, and Charles marvelled at his stamina:

'He is in great heart. No longer is he compelled to deal with great events by correspondence; he is 'the man on the spot'. Twice he has said this to me. A great feeling of elation stokes the marvellous machine, which seems quite impervious to fatigue.'[15]

For the next week Charles stayed, as did Churchill, at the British Embassy. Churchill wanted his doctor to be close at hand, for on his arrival he asked his host, Sir Miles Lampson, the Ambassador, that Charles should be substituted for the Adjutant General in the house party.[20] Unlike Churchill's, Charles's bedroom was not air-conditioned:

'My bedroom is on the wrong side of the house and without a fan gets very hot so that I generally wake in the morning damp with perspiration. But the days are pleasant. The evenings like a lovely summer day in England with a breeze from the Nile to temper the heat. In the evening we dine on the balcony and sit afterwards in the gardens where it is quite cool beneath the stars.'[21]

During this week the army command in the Middle East was re-organised. When Churchill visited the Eighth Army at Alamein, Charles accompanied him and registered a series of new faces among the senior service people,[22] but Churchill made no call on him and the largest single part of his notes on this week concerned Field Marshall Jan Smuts, Prime Minister of South Africa, whom the Prime Minister had invited to Cairo.[23] Having discerned that when the rest of the party went off to bath and change for dinner, Smuts sat alone on the lawn, Charles decided one evening to change early and join him. He recorded a wide ranging conversation, which inevitably included his own preoccupation with the mind in war.[24] He couldn't quite fathom Smuts, who intrigued him as a soldier who 'collected facts like a man of science'.[15] But he was glad Smuts had come, for he thought he would fortify and comfort Churchill in the difficult decisions he was having to make. On his return to South Africa, Smuts sent Charles a telegram: 'Please continue your efforts for Prime Minister's health. I feel he cannot continue at the present pace without breakdown. Grave national responsibility rests on you for Leader's health. All good wishes.'[25]

Smuts's exhortion reached Charles when he returned to Cairo after the next leg of the Prime Minister's trip, which involved four days in Moscow. Churchill had bad news for Stalin, and wanted to give it to him face to face. The Russians had been pressing for a major assault by British and American forces on the west coast of Europe so that Germany would be forced to transfer troops from the Russian front. Churchill had to tell Stalin that it was impossible to open up this Second Front in 1942. The bitter pill was to be sweetened with the news that, in October, British and United States forces would land in French North Africa, and these alternative operations would relieve some of the pressure on Russia.

Churchill's Liberator was the first of the aircraft carrying his party to land at Moscow on Wednesday 12 August, after an overnight stop at Teheran. Among those who met the plane was Sir Archibald Clark

Figure 12. Cairo, August 1942. Left to right, back row: Air Vice-Marshal Sir Arthur Tedder, General Sir Alan Brooke, Admiral Sir Henry Harwood, General Sir Claude Auchinleck, Lieutenant General Sir Archibald Wavell, Sir Charles Wilson, Sir Alexander Cadogan. Front row: Field Marshall Jan Smuts, Winston Churchill, Sir Miles Lampson, RG Casey. (Crown copyright) (CMAC PP/CMW/P.71)

Kerr, the British Ambassador.[26] Perhaps because the arrival of the aircraft carrying Churchill's senior advisers—Brooke, Wavell*, Cadogan, Tedder** and Jacob***—was delayed for 24 hours, the Ambassador found time to identify, and later to write a pithy comment on, each member of Churchill's personal party, which consisted of Commander CR (Tommy) Thompson RN, his personal assistant; Leslie Rowan, one of the Private secretaries; Pat Kinna, one of the clerks from Number Ten Downing Street; Inspector WH Thompson, Churchill's private detective; and Sawyers, his valet. He identified Charles as 'the PM's doctor with whom I established instant harmonies'.[26]

Between their arrival in Moscow on the Wednesday and their departure on the Sunday, Charles's notes concerned Churchill's

---

*General Sir Archibald Wavell, Supreme Commander in South East Asia.
**Air Vice Marshal Sir Arthur Tedder, Commander in Chief of the Desert Air Force.
***Colonel EIC Jacob, a principal assistant to General Ismay in the office of the Minister of Defence. Later, as Lt-General Sir Ian Jacob, Director General of the BBC (1952-1960).

reactions to his four evening meetings with Stalin. The first was on the Wednesday. Charles heard Churchill, Clark Kerr and Harriman discuss it when they returned at about 11.00 pm from the Kremlin to State Villa Number Seven, outside Moscow, where the Prime Minister's personal party was staying. Charles had evidently been pessimistic about this trip to Moscow, but those at the meeting felt things had gone well and Harriman told him his fears were groundless.[27] In the early hours of the morning Charles took the weary Churchill, who had been on the aerodrome at Teheran at 6.00 am, to bed. As he undressed, he told Charles the journey had been worth it.[28]

After lunch on the next day, Thursday 13th, Charles was surprised when Churchill said he would like to go for a walk in the wood in which the villa stood, because he hardly ever walked for the sake of exercise.[28] Such conversation as Charles recorded on the walk was of Churchill's optimism that now he had broken the bad news to Stalin the rest should be plain sailing.[28] Charles had another walk on that day, in the garden, with Clark Kerr. In the morning when he called, the Ambassador had found Churchill in a querulous mood, to be attributed, he thought to too much Caucasian champagne on the previous night. He asked Charles about his patient's 'black bile' and Charles said he could not account for it but it was a 'frequent manifestation'.[26] Charles waited up again that night for Churchill to come back from his second meeting with Stalin, and recorded Churchill as returning downhearted and dispirited.[29] It had been as if the previous day's meeting had never taken place. Stalin had made insulting remarks about the British Army, and said Britain had broken its word about a Second Front. Churchill was in two minds whether to stay on in Moscow and go to the dinner to which Stalin had invited him on the next night.[30,31] There was some discussion of this with Cadogan who then left and Charles accompanied Churchill to his bedroom, where the Prime Minister continued to unburden himself while he was undressing.[31]

There were a number of guests for lunch at the dacha on the following day, Friday 14th, including Brooke, the American Ambassador, Averill Harriman and Clark Kerr. The last observed that the PM was again in a bad mood and concentrated his ill humour on him. 'The wise doctor' he noted, 'telegraphed silent messages of sympathy and encouragement to me across the table.'[26] After lunch, Clark Kerr had first a walk in the garden with Cadogan. Then he wrote, 'I had a little walk with the doctor who seems to me to be the wisest man of the whole bunch. My opinion of him gets higher and higher. He was obviously concerned and he seemed to want to talk, but he didn't. He asked me a lot of things about myself, which I tried to answer faithfully. All the time I felt that he had a piece to say but couldn't bring himself to say it. I must have another talk with him tomorrow.'[26]

Charles was one of the over one hundred people[26] who went to the banquet at the Kremlin that night. He gave no account of his neighbours and he sat too far away from Stalin and Churchill to hear what they said. Churchill, who did not enjoy himself,[32] left abruptly after nearly four hours, without it being clear that he would see Stalin again.[33,34] Charles followed Churchill and Cadogan in another car back to State Villa Number Seven, where, on arriving, he was told that the Prime Minister wanted him. He found him with Rowan and Cadogan sitting at a long table, arguing about a proposed communiqué describing the results of the PM's visit.[34] 'The matter under discussion was so plainly secret' Charles recorded 'that I rose to leave. "Don't go, Charles" the PM interjected, and went on talking.' The argument was vigorous. Charles had never seen anyone talk to Churchill as Cadogan did. Charles commented in his manuscript that he 'gradually realised that Cadogan was very drunk',[35] and Cadogan himelf acknowledged how 'fortified by too much vodka', he reacted strongly to the Prime Minister's comments on the communiqué.[36] Cadogan was not alone in being fortified. All who wrote about the banquet referred to the interminable toasts. Brooke had shuddered at the idea of having to dodge the effects of vodka, and regarded the affair as a complete orgy.[37] There is no reason to suppose that Charles had been other than his usual abstemious self, and when Rowan and Cadogan left the room, for the third night in succession he went after Churchill to his bedroom. His graphic description of the scene which followed shows not only Churchill but, most unusually, his doctor also, unburdening himself:

'He [Churchill] had flopped into an armchair and sat staring at the carpet. When he noticed me he said: "Stalin didn't want to talk to me. I closed the proceedings down. I had had enough. The food was filthy. I ought not to have come."'[34]

Charles's account in his manuscript includes here a passage omitted from his book:

'There was a pause during which I mentioned I had said so in Cairo. The PM impatiently: "That was on medical grounds". I said No, I felt Stalin only wanted the goods and as they could not be delivered I thought he would be rude about our army and that the PM would resent this. And that's what he was.'[38]

Both versions continue:

'The PM got up, pacing the room in nothing but his silk undervest, mumbling to himself. At last he pulled up before me:

"I still feel I could work with that man if I could break down the language barrier. That is a terrible difficulty."

'He wondered whether he should make another attempt. He might be snubbed. I said he must risk that. It wasn't a question of whether Stalin was a brigand or not, but if we did not work in with him it would mean at least a longer war and more casualties. But the PM wasn't listening. He said he wouldn't go near Stalin again. He had deliberately said "Goodbye" and not "Good night." If there was any fresh move, Stalin must make it. He wouldn't. He got into bed, put on his black eye-shade and settled his head in the pillow. I turned out the light. When I left the room I looked at my watch. It was a quarter to four. The night was nearly over. I could not sleep; the consequences of leaving Moscow like this with Stalin and the PM at loggerheads frightened me.'[34,38]

This is the first indication that Charles was ever other than a passive listener when he escorted Churchill to his room and Sawyers, his valet, helped him prepare for bed. One must suppose that, in presuming to press a line of action affecting the conduct of the war, Charles felt very strongly. Certainly he had discussed the Moscow visit with Averill Harriman, who was Roosevelt's Special Representative in the United Kingdom, before setting out. Perhaps what he said to Churchill in the privacy of his bedrooms was what he had been unable to bring himself to say to Clark Kerr earlier in the day. There is no suggestion that Charles was acting on behalf of anyone else, and it is clear from the invitation he received to sit in on a very sensitive discussion earlier in the evening, that Churchill was willing for him to know what was going on. Charles's anxiety did not disappear in what remained of the night, and in the morning (Saturday 15th) he took his concern to Clark Kerr:

'August 15. After breakfast I ran into Read* [sic], one of the Embassy people, on the drive. I said to him I'd like to see his master [Clark Kerr], but hesitated to ring him up.

'Read said at once. "He said to me only this morning that you were the best diplomatist of the lot. I'm sure he'd be very glad to see you. He's with Alec [Cadogan] now".

'They came up the drive, the Ambassador puffing his pipe, and passed us by.

'When I saw there was no chance of getting him away from Cadogan I went into the house and wrote to him. I confessed my fears, prayed him to forgive my butting in but I had wondered if it would be possible to put into Stalin's ear:

*JL Reed, Second Secretary at the British Embassy in Moscow.

1.   That the PM must not leave Moscow without seeing Stalin.
2.   That the PM had said after their first meeting: "I'd like that man to like me" and after dinner "I feel I could work with that man if I could break down the barrier of language."
3.   That Stalin must be made to understand the PM's success or failure in Moscow with the Russians would not influence the electorate in the United Kingdom; only continued defeats could weaken his position.
4.   That the PM's only interest was to defeat Hitler: that was an obsession with him.

'On the other hand it would help if the PM could be persuaded:

1.   That a quarrel with Stalin meant larger British casualties.
2.   That Stalin coming to the door to see the PM off was without precedent.
3.   That they both wanted to come together but something was keeping them apart.
4.   That it was up to him (the PM) with his vast experience to handle the situation so that this was brought about.

'When I had finished the note I was on the point of tearing it up. It seemed cheek. Read passing through the room at that moment settled the matter and I gave it him and watched him through the window hand it to the Ambassador.

'About an hour afterwards Clark Kerr came up to me. "I'm more hopeful", he said, "he listened and said to me at the end "It was my fault" (ie at the dinner).'[38]

Whether Charles wrote out a reasoned argument in this way is doubtful.[36] Clark Kerr, in his account,[26] did not mention receiving a letter, and John Reed, wrote soon afterwards to a friend that '. . . the PM's doctor (who I think, is more of a travelling conscience than a medical adviser) button-holed HE and implored him to intervene.'[39] Clark Kerr, according to his own account, found a terrific flurry at the dacha when he arrived at about 11.00 am, the PM having decided to leave. Cadogan asked him (Kerr) to have a shot at changing his mind. The soldiers were with the PM and it seemed to Clark Kerr that the best place to hang about was among the raspberry bushes. 'There', he wrote, 'I found the wise doctor. He wasn't after raspberries as I was. He was after me. Happily we were able to have a longish talk.'[26] And he went on to describe Charles's account of his bedtime conversation with Churchill, and the points of his written argument. It would, of course, have been entirely in character for Charles to have jotted down the headings of his argument on any handy bit of paper, to marshal his own thoughts. But his handwriting was such that they would have been almost undecipherable to anyone but himself.

While this was going on, Churchill had sent for Colonel Jacob to discuss the previous night's stormy meeting with Stalin and was having second thoughts. Jacob had suggested to Churchill that he should meet Stalin again, alone, and with a better interpreter.[33] Clark Kerr, having persuaded Churchill to take a walk with him in the grounds of the dacha, also vehemently argued for another meeting[26] and Churchill at last agreed. He would see Stalin again. He did, on that evening. He spent seven hours with him and left well pleased.[40] Charles had no opportunity to see him to bed afterwards for he did not go to bed. On returning to the dacha at 3.30 am he held court while he was undressing, had a bath and then set out for the airport *en route* for Teheran and Cairo.

In retrospect Charles can be seen as only one among a number of people who sought to ensure that Churchill paid that last visit to Stalin. The interest in the episode lies in its illustration of the depth of Charles's concern about a lack of accord between Churchill and Stalin, as well as the rapport that he had established with his patient.

On returning to Cairo, Charles once more became just an observer of men and affairs. He accompanied Churchill on another 24 hour visit to the Eighth Army in the desert and then wrote a pen portrait of General Bernard Montgomery, who had taken command. He contrasted Montgomery's habit of going out among his men with his own First World War experience when, he recalled, he saw his Divisional General only once in two years, at a horse show.[41] An outsider's view of Charles at this time is given in a letter written by Alexander Cadogan. Back in Cairo after visiting Montgomery, Churchill was evidently in great form. Ragging everyone, one of his principal butts at dinner was Charles, whose views on military psychology as, according to Charles himself, on most other things, did not greatly appeal to the Prime Minister. When Charles developed 'gyppy tummy', Churchill went about saying 'Sir Charles has been a terrible anxiety to us the whole time, but I hope we'll get him through!'[42] Charles, brilliant in conversation in some situations, was temperamentally unsuited to shine when Churchill was at the head of the table—not that he was alone in this regard, for no one was really encouraged to do more than listen.[43]

In Cairo Charles contacted medical colleagues who were serving in the Middle East. One was GWB James, who in peacetime was Honorary Physician for Mental Diseases at St Mary's, but in 1942 a Brigadier in the Army Medical Services. When Charles retired from the staff of St Mary's five years later, James wrote to him:

'My best memories of you will always be war ones. The first was one cold day in January or February 1915 or more likely 1916.

I waited (on a motor bicycle) to let a weary looking battalion pass a cross road not far from Poperinghe. At its tail there you were swinging along rather sadly and looking very thin. How delighted I was and I remember lunching with your HQ later in the week. We were both "out" of the line.

'And more exciting still was your chat with me at the Embassy in Cairo in 1942. You have no idea what a tonic that visit was and how it relieved one's awful nostalgia for home. We had had two very bad and sad years then.'[44]

Charles arrived back in England with Churchill on 24th August, after an absence of three weeks. His life again became dominated by College affairs, and with routine visits to Number Ten Downing Street. 'Turning Point' was the title he gave to the chapter in his book which covered the last four months of 1942, reflecting Churchill's comment to him 10 years later that these were the most anxious months of the war.[45] Churchill at this time was assailed politically at home, the Battle of Alamein was fought, the landings in North Africa became a reality, and the Allied shipping lost to U-boat attack reached its peak.[46] During this time Brendan Bracken was worried about the Prime Minister; he wondered if he was sleeping all right[47] and exhorted Charles to keep an eye on him.[48] After the first week of the Battle of Alamein, in October, when things seemed to hang in the balance, Brooke too was worried. 'Is the PM all right, Charles?' he asked when Charles saw Churchill about a sleeping pill.[47] But Charles was not worried. In accordance with his perception of staying power and of factors that influence it, he was keeping an eye on his patients' reserves—applying, as he saw it, the fruits of his studies in the earlier war:

'It is true that whenever I appeared at No. 10 there seemed to be some fresh burden on his mind, but he met these calls with such abounding energy that I felt his reserves had hardly been touched.'[45]

Charles had burdens of his own to carry in the last months of 1942. His private burden was his health. Like his father, he was prone to dyspepsia, and he now had a bad flare-up of symptoms which he feared might be due to an ulcer. He knew of course that that diagnosis implied treatment involving four or more weeks rest in bed. On X-ray examination no ulcer was seen and so he kept going,[49] following a strict diet consisting of eggs, fish, milk puddings and toast for the main meals, and taking milk, biscuits and antacid powders at two-hourly intervals between meals. Notes kept by Dorothy through November and December show that he continued to suffer frequent pain, which sometimes woke him at night. However, he stuck meticulously to the diet, knowing that, short of a long spell of rest, there was nothing else for him in the 1942 medical armamentarium. The thought that he might be defeated by his own physical frailty at the peak of his career must have been galling. Dorothy's notes, while primarily a log of treatment, give an idea of his activities:

* Tuesday Nov.24—Not v. well am took eggs and milk to College for lunch with HEAB [Boldero]. Committee afternoon.
* Wednesday Nov.25—8.00 am—Milk and toast. Went to College etc. 12.30 milk, 2 eggs, toast and butter. RCS [Royal College of Surgeons] committee pm v. difficult.
* Thursday Nov.26—8.00 am—Milk, boiled egg, toast. Went up by train. Milk, eggs and toast for lunch. Special Comitia at College, went well.
* Monday Nov.30—9.30 am—Breakfast of boiled egg, milk, toast and butter. 11 am slight discomfort—biscuit and powder. 1 pm— Brains Trust lunch (fish).
* Saturday Dec.5—8 am—Breakfast. v. dyspeptic. Decided to leave out elevenses and bedtime 'snacks'. At Harefield all day—rather tired and depressed part of time. John arrived pm. Cheerful in the evening.
* Wednesday Dec.9—Morning at Harefield. Milk & boiled egg for lunch. Then London—College—milk at 4—Brendan—College— Milk at St Mary's at 6—met John. Dinner GWR fish & Potato.
* Thursday Dec.10—Day in London—on milk with scrambled egg for lunch. Long interview Univ. London so late back. Worked at papers all evening.
* Friday Dec.11—Went up by early train—said he was slightly uncomfortable in train. Went to No.10 then College all day, came back at 7 with HB [Boldero].[50]

Charles's public burdens at this time were carried as President of the College, where, in the last months of 1942, several sensitive matters had to be dealt with. These did not concern the war so much as planning a new post-war society. A great national social planning session was under way, and nothing could deflect Charles from the course he had set for the involvement of the College. 'You've got Comitia kicking lustily with life instead of being dead from the feet up', wrote one Fellow in November,[51] in a letter in which he also deplored the fact that Charles's Russian and American journeys had robbed him of the 'fun' of examining with him in Liverpool.

As Charles had foreshadowed just before leaving for Cairo in August, the September Comitia came to grips with the report of the BMA's Medical Planning Commission, the membership of which had caused such dissension among the Fellows in 1940. The report dealt with the basics of a new health service, and Charles played the part of an impartial chairman as he led Comitia through the business paper dealing with it. At Comitias in October and November, following the publication of the Goodenough report on medical schools, he steered the Fellows through a debate on this equally hot topic, making a personal contribution which reflected his mastery of facts and figures about student enrolments and examinations. Charles's own views on a future health service were set out in October in a BBC broadcast in its Swedish programme. He saw a single hospital service being developed to replace the existing arrangement in which there were both municipal hospitals supported by public funds and separate voluntary hospitals dependant on charitable benefactions, and he stressed that the new system would stand or fall by the calibre of the specialists who would staff the new hospital service. He saw an end to the situation in which, in many hospitals, all the work was done by general practitioners, and he looked to a redistribution of specialists and consultants to cover the whole country. He also looked forward to bringing together general practitioners to work in health centres. He wanted to see the end of the sort of solo general practice that he remembered his father conducting.[52]

Although they did not cure his dyspepsia, two nice things happened in December. He found time to write to Desmond MacCarthy again reminding him of his offer of further help with his book. His trips to Washington and the Middle East had given him many hours in which to work on it and it was practically finished, but he had a list of questions. Was the Preface, which MacCarthy had suggested, all right? What about the chapter on 'Exposure'? And what about a new chapter he had written on 'Thoughts that Fester in the Mind and Bring Defeat'?[53] The other nice thing that happened was the arrival of a letter from his patient asking if he was agreeable to his name being submitted to the King with a recommendation that he be made a Baron in the New Year's Honours.[54] Apart from the personal gratification which must have come with the realisation that this honour was above that of the baronetcy usually bestowed on presidents of the Royal College of Physicians, the honour had important political implications for Charles. It gave him a seat in the House of Lords where, as in the House of Commons, the papers and bills leading towards a national health service would be debated. No longer would the medical voices there be only those of the aged Dawson and the very conservative Horder. Among the many congratulatory letters Charles received when the Honours List was published was one from Beaverbrook exhorting him to take part early and often in debate.[55] Another from a close colleague who had anaesthetised a member of the Churchill family recalled being subjected by Churchill to a concentrated and rapid cross examination on the dangers of anaesthesia which lasted for 45 minutes. If, he wrote, Charles was confronted with this situation any time he ordered a dose of medicine, his reward was not too great.[56]

Figure 13. Broadcasting to Sweden, November 1942, on his vision of a new health service. (Wellcome Institute Library, London; CMAC PP/CMW/P.7)

But Charles had little time to deal with his mail. Plans were well advanced for yet another meeting between Churchill and Roosevelt, and on 12 January the PMs personal party was again airborne, this time heading for Casablanca, with Charles, not having decided on his title and designation as a peer,[57] still travelling as Sir Charles Wilson. A meeting had in fact been suggested some weeks earlier. Charles had been dead against it but the deciding factor then had been that Churchill had not wanted to go.[58] The medical concern continued to be the risk of a coronary thrombosis and the possibility that this might be brought on by flying. Mrs Churchill discussed with her daughter Mary whether Churchill should be warned; they thought he should not be.[59]

Charles's dyspepsia was still troubling him, and having found that Allen and Hanbury's baby food gave him relief, he arranged for a stock of it to accompany him on the trip.[49] Both he and Churchill recorded the discomforts of the 10-hour flight, in which they were alternately too hot or too cold.[49,60] Charles was again the only passenger other than the Prime Minister who could lie out straight on a mattress, qualifying, he supposed, on age. He was now 60. But a hot sun, blue sky, and oranges with leaves attached, soon worked their magic, albeit temporarily, for time soon hung heavily. On the third day Charles noted:

'The worst of these trips is that I am the only member of the whole party who has nothing to do; I am here only as an insurance against emergencies. I rise at 8 am and after breakfast write the book [*The Anatomy of Courage*] till lunch. Then if there is any sun I sit in it and do a little more book. After tea, my daily walk. Then a bath and dinner at 8.30. Bed at 11.00 pm. The PM often dines with the President, which means a quick meal with Tommy [Thompson] and Martin [Private Secretary]. If the sun comes out you feel it is at least a pleasant break in the winter, and if its chilly as it is today you feel its dull in every way and College matters stay in your head.'[49]

College matters certainly obtruded on this occasion. A telegram arrived from Boldero, the Registrar, asking Charles to return to London for the Comitia due to be held in two weeks time. Charles spent an hour tramping up and down weighing the pros and cons:

'At this time of year air travel is very uncertain, you may get held up for days at Gibraltar by fog. I might be away a week or ten days. On the other hand, if the Comitia becomes fractious they'll soon begin to say that the President is always away and that in these days when the medical services of the country are being reorganised in the most drastic fashion the President ought to be on the spot to put the view of the College. There has been a good deal of talk of this kind and there is a Presidential election in about two months' time. I have found out that there is an aeroplane returning with two brigadiers which would arrive back in time for the Comitia. But once I begin holding their hand at the College they will always be sending for me. I believe I ought not to leave here. If I do the PM will inevitably start a temperature and get in a flap.'[49]

After this cogitation, Charles telegraphed Boldero saying he could not return. The plane in which he would have travelled crashed and the two brigadiers were killed. Charles was given to writing captions at the top of his manuscript pages. At the top of the page describing this episode he wrote 'RCP want me to return, I refuse and so save my skin.'[49] The event underlines that wartime flying, which Churchill himself undertook so frequently, was hazardous. Those who indulged in it were undoubtedly on active service, and the bonds forged between such an unlikely pair as Churchill and Charles, bonds which lasted for a quarter of a century, were partly the result of the shared dangers and excitements of their wartime flights.

Roosevelt arrived in Casablanca on 14 January,[61] and two days later Charles recorded something of a family gathering:

'The President dined with us this day. Randolph* began arguing about Flandin** and defending him and got very excited, raising his voice and monopolising the conversation. Harry Hopkins got fed up with him. Randolph protested he wasn't excited and the PM told him he was never anything else. The PM eventually told him to shut up, and turning to Harry's boy who is in the American army he asked him about his experiences. I was sorry for the PM. After dinner some black man in the American army came and crooned for the President.'[62]

Three weeks later, Cadogan was also to reflect unfavourably on Randolph Churchill in his diary, describing him as a dreadful young man who had been an incubus on the party ever since Casablanca.[63] Charles came to have a very poor opinion of Randolph, particularly because he believed he showed no consideration for his father's well-being, often keeping him up far into the night playing bezique when he needed rest.[64] For Charles playing cards was a frivolous pastime anyway.

The Casablanca conference broke up after 12 days. On 24 January the soldiers, sailors and airmen headed for home, and what Charles described as 'our little family party' set off by road across the desert to Marrakesh[65], one of the most beautiful of places

---

*Randolph Churchill, only son of Winston Churchill, serving in the army during the war.
**Pierre Flandin, Foreign Minister in Vichy government in France.

which Churchill, who had been there before, described as 'the Paris of the Sahara.'[66] For 24 hours the party included Roosevelt, and Charles described how, over dinner, the President and Churchill made affectionate little speeches to each other.[67] Churchill recalled the dinner as being very jolly, with songs being sung.[66] Hard though he found it to fill his time in the days at Casablanca, Charles's records give the impression that he was beginning to feel himself one of the family of those close to the Prime Minister. The working members of the entourage certainly did anything they could to seek to include him in the few off-duty activities which their busy programmes allowed.[62] Churchill kept asking him what title he proposed to take, a walk along the beach at Casablanca provided time for a chat with the Chiefs of Staff, and he was on first-name terms with Harry Hopkins. The conference organisers arranged for him to drive one day 155 miles to Fez with someone he described as a Foreign Office fellow, and they lunched with a Moorish merchant:

'I was not very skilled at eating a chicken without a knife and fork, whereupon mine host, noticing my plight, pulled off some bits from a fat bird and dumped them on my plate. . . . Perhaps Arab hospitality was too much for me, anyway I had a lot of pain on the return journey.'[62]

Leaving Marrakesh after 48 hours, Charles was well occupied for the next week, for the party kept moving, first to Cairo, then briefly to Turkey, then back to Cairo after a stopover in Cyprus, and then to Tripoli before flying home from Algiers. The Prime Minister's Liberator, in which they flew, had at last been made more comfortable.[68] At Nicosia in Cyprus, Cadogan, whom he had got to know during the Moscow trip, persuaded him to go sightseeing, and, with the Head of the Museum of Antiquities as guide, they climbed innumerable steps up a hill 2400 feet above sea level:

'Long before I got to the top of this small mountain I had discovered the representative of the FO was much fitter than the champion of medicine. I was glad the view of Cyprus at the top justified a long pause before we began the descent.'[69]

His thumb-nail sketch of Cadogan was not included in his book:

'Cadogan always attends these conferences in grey flannels and a black coat. I should take this as a subtle compliment to his Prime Minister's sartorial eccentricities if I had not learnt that the Permanent Secretary of the Foreign Office would bend his knee to no man. He has all the coolness and nonchalence of the English of the books. I imagine he contrives to combine in his person all the things for which the Foreign Office is criticised by the vulgar. I do not say that this is necessarily against him. In his cups he gets more emphatic and even less pliable.'[69]

Among the senior service officers, Brooke was one whom Charles came particularly to admire. He was getting to know him better on this trip. On returning to Cairo from Nicosia Charles recorded that he went shopping with the CIGS and 'bought a rubber hot water bottle for 75 piastres, blades, and also 12 yards of velvet at 140p per yard=1680p=£16.16.0.'[70] Four days after having slept in a train which provided Churchill's accommodation in Turkey, Charles found himself sleeping in one of three caravans outside Tripoli where Churchill again visited the Eighth Army. The other two caravans were occupied by the Prime Minister and Alexander, whom Charles also much liked and admired as a brave man and with whom he kept up after the war. On this occasion Charles became a victim of the army's hospitality:

'We dined last night in a big tent. Alex poured me out a tumbler of Chianti which I swallowed as a good guest with dire consequences; as I picked my way in the dark through some kind of vegetation to my caravan I was seized with an unusually severe attack of belly pain; it was dark enough to cover antics. I pulled up for a moment and then went after Alex who was acting as my guide.'[71]

The following day in Tripoli Charles accompanied the Prime Minister on his inspection of the troops. He had a chance to talk with the Commanding Officer of the Highland Division, General Wimberley:

'I led him to talk on morale on which he had strong views. He thought a bit of tartan was worth most things put together in building up morale, pride in their forebears and in their clan. He had thought on the matter and what he said had the truth in it.'[71]

But for Charles the high spot was the inspection of the New Zealand Division under General Sir Bernard Freyberg. Like John Masefield viewing the ANZACs* in the First World War, he discerned in these troops an appearance of physical perfection that made them different from the youth of other countries.[72] In his manuscript notes Charles associated his description of Freyberg and his men with a section of reflective writing, some of which he incorporated in *The Anatomy of Courage*.

---

*Australian and New Zealand Army Corps.

Early on the morning of 7 February 1943, after a delayed take-off from Algiers owing to magneto failure in the Liberator—an event which again underlined the hazards that they were sharing—an eight-and-a-half hour flight brought Churchill and his party back to England.[73]

Chapter 12

More of the Travelling Circus

Despite his stomach trouble, Charles was none the worse for his North African adventures, and he plunged into activity as soon as he returned in February 1943. The Garter King of Arms was pressing him for a decision on the title he would take as a peer.[1] After many changes of mind, and with euphony as a consideration, he decided he would be Baron Moran of Manton, Moran coming from the McMorans (originally McMorrans) on his mother's side of the family, and Manton being where Dorothy had converted the mill near Marlborough into a holiday cottage. This decision led to an unhappy estrangement. His old friend who owned the mill, Godfrey Maurice, had been among the first to congratulate him on his barony, asking through his usual correspondent, Dorothy, if Charles would 'transmit the infection to his offspring, as the louse did in typhus'.[2] He was now furious. Four generations of Maurices had been doctors in Marlborough, Manton Grange had the family crest on it, and Charles had chosen Manton as his designation without consulting them. Even Dorothy was unable to heal this breach, though she herself continued to keep up with one of Godfrey's sisters.[3]

Another letter greeting Charles was from Birmingham University inviting him to be an external examiner for 1943 at a fee of £60[4], and Charles wrote a letter to *The Times* welcoming a munificent gift to medicine from Lord Nuffield*. He returned to the theme of the letters he had written to *The Times* 20 years before, after the first war. Lord Nuffield, he said, had done more than affirm his faith in a scientific approach to the problems of life:

'Many will remember that in the life of the trenches in the last war a few simple demands were made of all men. If they were not met, the defaulter became an outlaw. The first virtue was unselfishness. When the Armistice was signed those who came back from France and Flanders wanted to build a new Jerusalem. But they found selfishness and apathy in high places, they found no plans of any kind for a fuller life for the people, their hopes went sour and the disillusionment of that generation weakened the purpose of the country for two decades. We may take heart that there are tokens of a different spirit at the present time.'[5]

*Lord Nuffield, industrialist and philanthropist.

This letter brought Charles a message from Lord Dawson, who had taken to sending him friendly little cards commenting on his activities. They usually contained one or two pithy sentences and were subscribed 'No answer yrs D.' On this occasion Dawson's accolade described Charles's letter as 'so apt in its occasion, so ahead in its vision and so attractive in its expression.'[6]

A week after returning to England, Charles had the Prime Minister on his hands with pneumonia, which, in those days, was a serious condition, exhausting for the patient and stressful for the relatives. As Charles noted, it was, broadly speaking, the heart and not the lungs that decided the issue in the elderly.[7] He called in a genial expert in chest diseases, Dr Geoffrey Marshall of Guy's Hospital and, as usual, his choice could not have been better. The patient's heart caused his doctors no anxiety, but the preparation of a bulletin did. Early in the illness it was judged that a public statement was called for. John Peck, the Private Secretary at Downing Street, described its preparation:

'The intercom bell. I was on duty, "John, will you come in." The Prime Minister was sitting up in bed, looking sulky. Lord Moran was up against the opposite wall, trying to look at ease and master of the situation, and giving the impression of trying to stop a very aggressive terrier from nipping his shins. A row of some magnitude was evidently in progress.

'Lord Moran had told the PM that he would have to issue a bulletin, and Mr Churchill had instantly demanded to see it. As Moran had not yet drafted it he was at a disadvantage so he sat down with pencil and paper and wrote it out. The Prime Minister said that it was an alarmist statement which would cause confusion and despondency and was in any case untrue. He would write an accurate one himself. He thereupon sent for his shorthand typist and dictated his own bulletin. On seeing it in type he was hugely pleased with his first effort in this new genre, but Moran said it was inaccurate and misleading and he could not possibly sign it. Temper, obstinacy and deadlock.'[8]

The deadlock was resolved in the end through the mediation of John Peck who proceeded on the basis that it was for the doctor to say what was the matter and for his patient, the Prime Minister, to pronounce on the political implications of the way the doctor put it. By early March Churchill was well enough to go to Chequers, where Charles continued to visit him. One of the nurses who looked after him, Doris Miles, recollected the convalescent Prime Minister, walking round in his bath towel, going through speeches he was preparing with Charles or Lord Cherwell (the Prof*),[9] another example of the doctor fulfilling more than a medical role. Churchill's recovery was a great relief to many people and some of the credit, including a congratulatory note from Horder,[10] came to Charles.

The presidential election at the Royal College of Physicians on 19 April occurred without drama. Charles received 78 votes to Horder's 17.[11] Two particular abilities had by now helped him to make his mark among the general body of Fellows. One was his capacity, in his annual addresses, for illuminating the medical scene and for imparting his vision of the future. In 1943 he highlighted the requirements for the successful development of a new health service. People at the top should have wisdom and not just a reputation for past political aptitude. There must be the best possible working conditions for the rank and file of the profession, by which he meant the extension of something like the collegiate atmosphere of teaching hospitals into new general practice health centres. And an efficient hospital service must be based on a proper geographical distribution of consultants.[12] Another of Charles's abilities was what one senior Fellow called, in a letter of appreciation to Charles, his 'weaving of the story of our Fellows who have passed away'.[13] It was customary for the President, in his annual address, to say something about each Fellow who had died in the previous year. Charles, it was observed, performed this function virtually without a note. His comments were based on diligent homework and his apparent spontaneity reflected his retentive memory. He was also at an advantage because he knew many of the Fellows personally, and not only those in London, for he had met many others on his travels round England and Wales on behalf of the Ministry of Health. When a Fellow whom he did not know died, he certainly knew who to telephone to ask about him. His insights into the lives of the recently deceased were often both penetrating and, to his audience, sometimes surprising. His critical habit of mind and his disbelief in the precept *de mortuis nil nisi bonum*—speak nothing but good of the dead—sometimes landed him in trouble. It was said that some members of the staff of Guy's Hospital never forgave him for the intimate portrait that he sketched of his old friend John Ryle but, on the whole both what he had to say and the elegance with which he said it were highly regarded. Charles's contributions to College affairs at this time were, of course, influenced by the fact that he had a great deal of time to think. He could not spend all the many hours on his travels with Churchill, when he was left to his own devices, revising and adding to *The Anatomy of Courage*. That task took up less and less of his time. College affairs and particularly the College's contribution to the planning of a new health service were what those travelling with him

---

*Professor Frederick Lindemann, later Viscount Cherwell, whom Churchill consulted on scientific matters. Often referred to as 'the Prof.'.

discerned as his main preoccupation.[14] And when he thought about a new health service for Britain, he pondered more than the immediate future. Here was someone with time to think and who in all things stressed the importance of looking far ahead. What mattered he used to say, was what would happen in fifty years time.[15]

Charles had barely resumed his home routine when his patient decided to go to Washington again. Churchill was concerned that a discussion already planned for the allied military commanders in America might result in the main emphasis of military operations being changed from Europe to the Pacific, and he proposed that the British commanders present should have his personal support.[16] After some prevarication the decision was made to go by sea, and Charles found himself leaving London by train on 4 May bound for the 'Queen Mary', which was lying in the Clyde. Churchill credited Charles with the decision that he should not fly after his pneumonia,[17] and Charles was certainly involved at that time in discussions about the design of a specially pressurised cabin which might be fitted into an aircraft so that worries about the effect of altitude on the Prime Minister's circulation could be overcome. He felt, however, that he really had little say in the decision to go by sea: 'It was the PM himself who weighed the pros and cons. I was never allowed to touch the scales.'[17]

Captions at the head of Charles's manuscript pages give highlights of the trip from his point of view: 'Our travelling circus grows'; 'On tipping'; 'Bugs in the Queen Mary'; 'On secrecy'; 'I get my B. Coli back'.[18] The travelling circus had indeed grown. The PM's special party of 14 was part of a large party of 70 which was supplemented by 16 Royal Marine orderlies and 16 WRNS cypher officers,[19] so that the intimacy of the earlier expeditions was lacking. Security involved each individual having to decide what story to tell their friends and relations to explain their absence,[19] but Charles had no convincing cover and the professional circle in which he moved naturally assumed that when he disappeared he was with his patient.[20] Charles's notes on 'Tips' throw light on his status among his travelling companions:

'The Ministry of War Transport guides and shapes our generosity on tips. Gratuities are to be settled in one block payment. £150 is the minimal and £200 the desirable sum to be raised and we are all grouped according to the standard of accommodation provided for us and perhaps (though this is not mentioned) by the W.T.'s [War Transport] idea of what might reasonably be expected of us having regard for our supposed worldly circumstances. The £10 class is very select and only the PM, Harriman, the Beaver and Lord Leathers* qualify. The three Chiefs of Staff, Wavell,

*Lord Leathers, Minister of War Transport.

Somerville*, Air Chief Marshal Sir R Pierse, Pug [Ismay], the Prof (Lindemann) and myself fall into the £6 group. The rest are divided up into three classes, £2, £1 and ten shillings.'[18]

Charles found the 'Queen Mary' very comfortable. He reflected that, on the eastward trip over the Atlantic, when the ship carried 15 000 troops, seven or eight officers would sleep in his cabin. The troops, he discovered, had left their mark behind them:

'. . . the part of the ship used for us is scoured and scrubbed but those who travel in the rest of the ship are less fortunate and Lady Beveridge has I gather been eaten by bugs.'[18]

Lady Beveridge was accompanying her husband**, who, five months before, had produced the blueprint for rebuilding Britain after the war.[21] One of the assumptions was that a comprehensive health service available to all would be provided, divorced from any insurance contributions.[22] Charles met the Beveridges at lunch at the PM's table on the third day out. He noted that the atmosphere was correct without being unduly cordial,[23] and that Churchill's thoughts were far away.[24] Returning to his cabin after lunch, Charles found that he had a temperature and it was soon plain that his old trouble, pyelitis, due to the microbe *Bacillus coli*, had come back. He was confined to his bunk for the rest of the trip, and the ship's doctor treated him with large doses of a sulpha drug. Whether or not he benefited is not clear, but the treatment dramatically reduced the white blood cells in his blood which form part of the body's normal defence mechanisms, and this led him to reflect:

'I sometimes say to Jane [Charles ordinarily called Dorothy Jane], if the public knew how dangerous it is to be ill they would never dare to contract diseases.'[23]

Charles remembered Churchill visiting him, clearly upset at his physicians's plight and concerned that Dorothy should not be made anxious. As soon as the 'Queen Mary' reached New York Charles was taken off on a stretcher and found himself in a spacious private room at the Presbyterian Hospital, where he was at once worried about the cost. In accordance with medical convention, the urologist who looked after him did not charge him, but his room cost him £5 a day and that did not include the nurses' fees. He described his total account as a formidable affair, and commented, apropos the order

*Admiral Sir James Somerville, Commander-in-Chief Eastern Fleet.
**Sir William Beveridge, Chairman of the Interdepartmental Committee on Social Insurance and Allied Services 1941-42.

of tipping on the 'Queen Mary', and the fact that Harriman had organised his medical care in New York, 'I think I was included in the Harriman class.' While he was in hospital, Leslie Rowan telephoned him from the White House to tell him that Churchill had telephoned Dorothy twice.[23]

Apart from money, the new health service at home was much on Charles's mind as he lay in bed. At the College, a few days before he left on this trip, he had reported to the Fellows the progress being made with drawing up a geographical list of consultants and specialists in England and Wales. The task was being undertaken by a series of local committees each under the chairmanship of the vice chancellor of the local university, because, as Charles had told the Fellows, the only criterion for admission to the list at the time was the consent of the profession in the neighbourhood.[25] Things were different, he found, in the USA.

'By my bed there is a book, about the size of Who's Who; this volume contains the name of every specialist in the United States. To get into the book you have to satisfy a Board you are a consultant; have been trained as such, and so forth. The public use this book and if you are not in it you are sunk. I looked my man up at once. How differently we do things in England. Anyone there without any training can take a room in Harley Street until the address, the adventurer's patter and the credulity of the public bring him practice.'[26]

After a week, Charles travelled in comfort to Washington, escorted from the hospital to a Pullman coach in the train by the ADC to the local US Admiral. In Washington he stayed at the Statler, where, on most days, be breakfasted, lunched and dined. Time again hung heavily and he reflected how strange it was that, never having given a thought to food before the war, he now lingered over the menu.[27] The PM took a fatherly interest in his health and commented, like an expert, on his appearance.[27] He continued to have a fever and recorded little that was going on around him, but he was well enough to go to a large lunch party at the White House, where he sat next to General Stillwell, known as Vinegar Joe—'a sour, dried up little man' who was, according to Charles, critical of the British.[28] Charles did not record discussing morale and leadership with him. Charles also went to a dinner given by Major General MacCready, 'a pundit in the Supply world':[27]

'There were no American men there but five American wives of Englishmen. They happened all of them to be intelligent and that means the dinner party "went"! Women at such functions dictate the level of conversation. The men can only toe whatever line they draw. I gave up giving dinner parties in London because of the women. Dudley Pound brought me back in his car.'[27]

Charles's comment on women at dinner parties reflected the fact that he was fundamentally shy and so bad with them, not encouraging them to talk but rather tending to lecture them and hold forth. This shyness caused him to have real limitations as a host because only experienced and self-confident women could hold their own with him. With them he could be very good.[29]

This trip ended with what had become a customary shopping expedition, on this occasion for groceries and stockings, of which there were no silk or nylon ones. The girl at the information bureau recommended Rayon. Then, after what had been a dismal three weeks away from home, Charles left Washington on May 26th in a flying boat with Churchill and his personal retinue. After a fuelling stop in Newfoundland, they flew to Gibraltar, the PM being on his way to North Africa once more. At Gibraltar Charles decided that, with a recurrent temperature, he might be a nuisance if he continued. Churchill insisted that he should go home and get fit[30] and so, after spending an afternoon worrying about abandoning his patient, he embarked in a small plane for England. It was a melancholy night flight. The floor of the aircraft was taken up by a young soldier with a brain tumour, lying on a stretcher, whose loud irregular stertorous breathing made the night seem interminable.[30]

Anxious as he was about the cost of his illness in New York, Charles's dejection would hardly have been helped by finding a letter from the Treasury awaiting him at home. It informed him that the Foreign Office had advised that a year before, when accompanying the Prime Minister to Washington, he had made a telephone call from the White House to Dorothy. He was now asked for a cheque for £9.18.9d in payment.[31]

While Charles was in hospital in New York at the beginning of May, a landmark was passed in the war with the surrender of the last Axis forces in North Africa.[32] Another landmark was passed in June when more ships were built than were sunk in the Atlantic.[33] Post-war planning now had a sense of immediacy in it, and, as Charles settled down on his return from Washington, his activities reflected this. He was incredibly busy. From the President's room in the bombed College building overlooking Trafalgar Square, he corresponded on a series of complex and often inter-related matters with the presidents of the sister Colleges, vice chancellors of universities, deans of medical schools, the General Medical Council, the BMA and the Ministry of Health. At the same time he remained closely in touch with his constituency. In responding to letters from Fellows, he lost no opportunity for informing them of his ideas, not only on the philosophy of a new health service but also on the strategy he was developing. The assumption in the Beveridge report that there would be a comprehensive health service was one on which Charles would choose his time and place to speak publicly. Meanwhile he continued his moves to ensure that, when negotiations between the government and the profession began, the BMA alone should not speak for all the doctors, and in particular not for consultants.[34] Charles knew that he had powerful support for this stance, not only in the College but also from universities,[35] and he was able to show how, by thinking ahead, he had already placed the College in a strong position. In a letter to a Fellow, following the setting up by the BMA in March of a committee to consider the way in which the consultations with the government should be conducted,[36] he described how, immediately after becoming President, he had set about trying to organise consultants into one solid bloc. He cited drawing up the list of consultants, his visits to all the provincial teaching centres, and the steps to speak with consultants outside these centres. He had indeed been living up to his maxim that you must look ahead.

Of course this had not all been plain sailing. The General Medical Council, the BMA, and some vice chancellors had questioned the right of the Colleges to draw up the list of consultants,[37] and someone with less determination than Charles might have given in. As it turned out it was this task, bringing as it did the Colleges, the vice chancellors and the Ministry of Health together, that put the Colleges in a commanding position for future negotiations. Another factor was also determining that a prominent place would be taken by the Colleges in the forthcoming debate. Years of thinking in the BMA and, although it was not widely known, in the Ministry of Health too, had led to fairly similar conclusions about the need for a comprehensive health service. The assumption in the Beveridge report that there would be a comprehensive service was, therefore, not novel for the profession, and the questions were about ways of achieving the objective rather than about the objective itself. Clearly the debate was going to be difficult. One reason was that the administrative machinery of the BMA made it an awkward negotiating body.[38] Another was the widespread suspicion of the Ministry of Health in the minds of most doctors,[39] a suspicion that was aggravated now by a proposal that, in a new health service, general practitioners should be employees of local government authorities. In this situation, containing as it did the seeds of confrontation between the BMA and the Ministry, the Colleges were in a unique position. Their entry into negotiations was legitimised by their being the representatives of the consultants. But, in addition, as relative newcomers to medical politics, they were in a position to adopt what a historian of the National Health Service later described as a more objective and moderate approach.[38] With the initiative Charles had taken in the Royal College of Physicians, this was the position that the Colleges now assumed.

Charles chose the occasion of the debate in the House of Lords on 1 June, on the medical aspects of the Beveridge report, to make his

his maiden speech.[40] He spoke on a motion by Lord Derwent to the effect that the medical plan in the report did not appear to be designed to further the interests of British medicine or the population. Derwent was flamboyantly negative in his speech, using phrases such as 'State lackeys' as he conjured up a picture of the likely lot of the doctors. Lord Dawson followed him, complaining of haste and bustle and counselling gradual change. Charles then rose and said he would set out to explain to those who were not doctors what he believed to be the essential minimum of any plan for reforming the health services. He described a central administrative machinery, the conditions under which the rank and file of the profession should work, the staffing of hospitals, and the identification and distribution of consultants.[40] This was in fact a recapitulation of the points he had made in his broadcast to Sweden a year before but had not yet presented to a wide audience in England. His speech brought him many congratulations, among others from Mrs Churchill, who wrote that she had heard from several people that his speech was admirable. She liked its form and the policy it advocated; she had been told he had a beautiful voice and she referred, as others did, to the fact that he spoke without a note. 'As I fear you must have been feeling extremely unwell', she added, 'it is all the more remarkable, and shows what "Morale" can do. By the way, when is your book coming out?'[41] To the laymen who made up the majority of his audience, Charles came across as an eloquent speaker and an independent and dispassionate thinker; 'statesmanlike' was an adjective applied to him.[42]

Two months later Charles made his second contribution in the House of Lords, this time on a non-medical topic on which he was well qualified to speak. There was a debate on post-war educational policy,[43] and on the question of the supply of teachers Charles said there should be some method of finding out during the war the men who should be recruited as teachers afterwards. He introduced the House to one of his favourite themes, that war was a final test of character. He believed that there should be some record of those who passed the test and that teachers should be recruited from among their ranks. There were no recorded comments on his performance on this occasion, perhaps because, by the time the debate was reported in *The Times*, he had disappeared. He was in the 'Queen Mary' once more, as a member of the Prime Minister's party which was heading for Quebec to confer with the Americans following the successful allied invasion of Sicily.

The travelling party had increased in size yet again, and a lot of hard work was involved in its organisation. Joan Astley, one of the organisers, gave a vivid account of the arrival at the Chateau Frontenac in Quebec; some members looked as if they wished they had never come, the usual complainers looked for someone to complain to, and a few stood waiting for the commotion to subside:

'Lord Moran had lost his hat and I joined rather half heartedly in the search. As physician-extraordinary to the Prime Minister, he had no particular niche, was as absent-minded as an absent-minded professor, and managed to lose something at each conference.'[44]

This was widely attested. On later trips with the Prime Minister he took to bringing his golf clubs—not that he had much chance to use them as everyone he might have played with was so busy.[45] He was forever losing them, and by the end of the war, some members of the Prime Minister's ancillary staff were unofficially detailed to ensure that he was in the right place at the right time, and to gather up the pieces of luggage and equipment he was all too apt to leave behind.[46] The young man of 1917 who had forgotten to take his identifying arm band on a trench raid, and whose fellow officers had detailed one of their number to make sure he didn't get lost in no man's land, hadn't changed.

The British party arrived in Quebec on 10th August[47] and Churchill left the next day, with his daughter Mary, who was acting as his ADC,[48] to stay with Roosevelt at his home, Hyde Park, on the Hudson River 400 miles away. Mrs Churchill, who had accompanied her husband to Canada, remained resting in the Citadel, the Governor General's summer residence where the Churchills were staying. According to her daughter, Mrs Churchill was in a state of physical and nervous exhaustion after the strain of the last four years;[48] she was also one who never really fell under Roosevelt's spell[49]—an observation echoed by Charles, who noted that she had once told him she did not like any great man except Winston.[50]

While Churchill was at Hyde Park, the British and Americans conferred and Charles, left to his own devices, was lonely:

'Chateau Frontenac. In this vast hotel full of soldiers, sailors, airmen and oddments, both British and American, I don't suppose I speak a dozen words during the day. Breakfast alone in the big restaurant at 8.30; work in my room at the book till 1 o'clock, when I lunch, again by myself. Then I go for a tramp, then tea (alone) and I dine in solitary state, retiring to bed at 9 o'clock. The rest of the party is in conference all day with the Americans and they come into meals late and feed with them. I suppose were I a gregarious beast I'd not be eating alone. In three quarters of an hour before dinner people foregather for drinks, but since my trouble with my belly I keep off alcohol when I can so I don't join them.'[51]

The monotony was occasionally broken:

'Once as I sat at my small table the CIGS came in to dinner late and asked if he might join me. He had been all day in conference and said he was weary and—so unlike his steady Ulster self—down about things. He is very reserved and normally keeps his thoughts to himself but I think today the cup which has gradually been filling overflowed. He complained that the PM flitted from one subject to another, that he never disposed of anything. Temperamentally of course they are poles apart. The Ulsterman matter of fact, sticking to the point at issue, not much in love with words, meaning always just what he says. Winston flying off at a tangent as some idea takes hold of him, and always talking.'[51]

Writing his book later, Charles condensed the reference to Alan Brooke's worries, and added:

'But are his critics measuring the Prime Minister by the right yardstick? His claim to a place in history does not rest on his strategy. His gifts are of a rarer kind.'[52]

In this sort of environment, any doctor who was a sympathetic listener would have been a shoulder to be lent upon and Charles was well equipped to fulfil this role. A few days later, General Marshall* was confiding that, from time to time, he had an irregular rhythm of the heart called atrial fibrillation, and Charles hoped he would keep on his feet for he had and retained a very high regard for Marshall.[53] Mackenzie King, the Canadian Prime Minister, consulting him professionally,[54] opened the way for a correspondence which continued on and off for years. Charles of course was not only readily available to be lent on, but he also had an attractive aura as a confidant. It could have been no secret that important people like Beaverbrook and Bracken, who were sometimes in the travelling party, had, like Churchill, used his professional services. Charles for his part was deeply interested in people. Indeed one of the rewards that came to him from his travels with Churchill was the opportunity to observe and draw out not only the Prime Minister but most of those who came within his orbit. His concern with morale was a good talking point. He learnt of General Marshall's heart irregularity during a 24-hour trip up the St Lawrence in a river steamer, when he was enjoying a talk with him on that subject:

'Marshall the most benevolent old gentleman is quite ruthless when it comes to scrapping an incompetent commander, they seem to be getting rid of a considerable number of duds in the American army. I said to him if we have a general who makes a bog of

---

*General George Marshall, Chief of Staff to the United States Army.

things we promote him. Marshall answered "We don't think of the general, we think of the division he commands."'[53]

Charles made another note bearing on his relationship with the service officers at this time:

'These trips expose character. As an odd number who cannot promote or demote anybody I'm in a peculiar position among this crowd of service people. War is their great opportunity and most of them feel this. The real Sahib is very friendly and pleasant; indeed if you made a list of the folk who go out of their way to be pleasant to me, well knowing it can profit them nothing, you would get probably the pick of the people. By this test Marshall (USA Chief of Staff) comes out first with the Mountbatten* fellow a bad last. He seems a horrid, pushing go-getter. On the whole the party comes out of this test with flying colours, there are some able staff officers (Head** etc) who interest me.'[55]

Charles was not the only one to be critical of Mountbatten, but apart from General Marshall, who qualified his opinion later,[56] he seems to have been alone in speaking ill of Pug Ismay[57] whom he described disparagingly as the perfect oil can[58] and whom he regarded as a worldy courtier, not a real soldier.[29] The aversion between Charles and Ismay was probably mutual,[59] with Ismay, who was very outgoing, regarding Charles as an austere old stick, and not one of the chaps.[14]

Churchill's return after four days at Hyde Park did something to relieve the monotony. Charles was included as a guest at two formal dinners at the Citadel, and when Brendan Bracken arrived he had someone to chat to.[60] As the conference proceeded, Churchill complained of feeling tired[61] and Charles, watching him, was concerned that he was unduly depressed.[62] A few days' rest was planned and two days after the conference ended, on 26 August, Charles accompanied Churchill and his immediate family group to a comfortable log cabin in the Laurentian mountains, 60 miles from Quebec. Charles was introduced to the art of casting a fly for trout but even landing a three-and-a-half pounder failed to induce any passion for the sport.[63] Not that he despised it. One pleasurable happening in Quebec had been the arrival of a letter from his elder son John, for whom he recorded his hope that he would be 'good at something solid with fishing and writing for his leisure hours.'[60] It was very much a family holiday party in the log cabin, with moments of intimate conversation with

---

*Acting Vice-Admiral Lord Louis Mountbatten, Chief of Combined Operations.
**Brigadier Antony Head. Became Secretary of State for War in 1951.

Mrs Churchill,[64] and moments of hilarity, with Winston singing at lunch,[65] and adventurous expeditions:

'(31.8.43). Last night the PM would go on talking till nearly midnight, then we embarked in a small motor boat which took us down the lake (six miles long) to a spot where our cars were waiting. (So like the PM to wait to the next morning before taking to the water. The wind came down the lake and caught the breath). We eventually got to the cabin on the Montmorency River at 2.00 am. This morning we rose early and in 2½ hours were in Quebec. The PM broadcasts at 12.50 and then we lunch with Mackenzie King and his cabinet. Tonight we leave for Washington.'[66]

After a luxurious train journey—Charles had a bathroom all to himself—Churchill's party arrived in Washington in the afternoon of 1 September:

'I drove with Winston, who contrived to pick up a cold on the Lake in the middle of the night, to the White House and the President gave us (WC and self) tea on the balcony. He made an iced drink with great attention to detail.'[66]

Churchill stayed in Washington for five days, during which he learnt of Italy's surrender, and he and Roosevelt started planning for a tripartite meeting with Stalin.[67] Charles filled some of his time accompanying Mrs Churchill and Mary on visits to the Lincoln and Jefferson memorials.[66] Then, on 5 September while in the train to Boston with the Prime Minister, who was to make a speech at Harvard, Charles found himself again running a temperature.[68] After returning to Washington two days later he took the opportunity to visit the surgeon, George F. Cahill, who had looked after him in May, and in whose judgment he had complete faith. In this case the judgement was that nothing more could be done.[69] Then, after being once more reduced by boredom to writing comments about the menu at the Statler ('This hotel is like the Strand Palace only more expensive'), Charles set out with the Churchills on 11 September for home. He had forecast an earlier return and was concerned about missing meetings at the College.[70] Telegrams and telephone calls crossed the Atlantic, and one of the latter attracted another note from the British secretariat at the White House. Martin apologised for interrupting a 21-minute conversation which cost $147, observing that if it had been a private call the charge would have been higher.[71] The first leg of the journey home took Churchill and his party to Hyde Park, where they spent a day.[72] Then, on 14 September, they boarded the battleship HMS 'Renown' in Halifax.[73] Six days later they were back in London after an absence of seven weeks.

Chapter 13

Frustrations, conflicts and hard decisions

On his return from Quebec Charles learnt that Lord Dawson was likely to become president of the BMA. The news awaited him in a letter from Dawson himself, who added a postscript saying that he hoped his acceptance would aid cooperation with the Colleges.[1] Charles for his part addressed the Fellows on the need to work in harmony with the Association, and he sought interviews with Dawson, Dr Guy Dain, who was chairman of the BMA Council, and with Dr George Anderson, the Secretary.[2] In many respects the Secretary of the BMA was the most powerful person in the organisation and Anderson was a man whom Charles respected.[3] Within weeks of Dawson's succession, Anderson was taken ill[4] and he died two months later. Perhaps the ensuing relationship between the BMA and the Colleges would have been different if he had lived. Be this as it may, one thing was now abundantly clear. Charles had come back from Quebec more convinced than ever that he should carry the flag in the development of the new health service. In October he wrote of his ambition to Beaverbrook,[5] who had returned to office in the government as Lord Privy Seal at the end of September.[6] Beaverbrook, responding to Charles's congratulations, had asked him about his attitude to Beveridge, Dawson and the BMA.[7] Charles thought for two-and-a-half weeks before replying.[5] Beveridge, he then said, had made a stir largely because of the poor showing of the recent Ministers of Health, Ernest Brown and Walter Elliott, who, according to Charles, did not know the first thing about the intimate structure of the health machine as it was, much less about it as it should be:

'Some day it will be seen that a medical Woolton* or Leathers is essential, who knows details and who has the confidence of the doctors.'[5]

As to Dawson, he wrote:

'He is an old man, in sight of the 80s, a kind of medical Queen Alexandra, reluctant to leave the stage. He talks in a series of catch words and has no real power of thinking on anything. My relations with him are excellent but he is too old to be of any use in setting up the new service.'[5]

---

*Lord Woolton, Minister of Food.

The BMA he considered 'no better and no worse than any other trades union'. It represented what he called the rank and file of the profession, while the Colleges represented the consultants and specialists. Both organisations should reflect a common front, but this was not easy. Charles then referred to the maldistribution of consultants, and about complex surgery being done by general practitioners with no special training. He looked ahead to identifying consultants on the basis of prescribed courses of training, as, during his illness in New York, he had learned they were identified in America. Then came his punch lines:

'In short at the present time the medical profession wants radically reforming. If this were done every person throughout the land would be able to get the opinion of a trained man in whatever branch it was needed. I need hardly tell you of the difficulties that exist in carrying out reforms which will vitally affect the incomes of all doctors. An atmosphere is produced like that between the North and South of Ireland in which one's best friends accuse one of wobbling the moment any statesman-like action is taken which seems to threaten their interest. Any Minister of Health who can solve this health problem on these lines will be very unpopular with the profession. But he would give to the government a constructive piece of legislation which would be remembered when a good deal which now seems important is forgotten. At the end of the job, if he were a doctor, he would find it impossible to return to practice because he wouldn't get any, but he would be able in his retirement to feel that he had probably done more for the country in a couple of years than most cabinet ministers do in their lifetime.

'But the only doctor with enough administrative experience and in a position to do this is myself. And I would far rather act as your Chief of Staff. Why not take it on?'[5]

Beaverbrook's acknowledgement was speedy, brief and enigmatic. He called Charles's letter a stick of dynamite and said he had 'de-dynamited' it.[8] After that, the line went dead so far as letters were concerned although it is hard to believe that there was not further conversation on the topic.

Charles was, at this time, himself a pawn in a power game being played by others. The Regius professorship of physic at Cambridge was vacant, and HA Harris, the professor of anatomy there, had been pressing Charles intermittently through 1943 to indicate that he would be interested in the appointment.[9] The chair was proving hard to fill and in November Harris once again pressed Charles to declare his interest.[9] Harris wanted him to repeat his performance at St Mary's and 'put the Cambridge medical school on the map'. Charles, aware that this approach did not have the support of the major local power brokers, refused to be drawn. Not that he had lost his interest in medical education. In a letter to *The Times* he put forward the idea, not calculated to appeal to many members of a heavily treatment-orientated profession, that the profession's first function was the preservation of health and not the cure of disease.[10]

During October, knowing that he would be travelling again sooner rather than later, he put the finishing touches to *The Anatomy of Courage*. He checked some facts bearing on morale in pilots with Sir Charles Symonds,[11] consultant adviser in neuropsychiatry to the Royal Air Force, and on morale at sea with Dr Desmond Curran,[12] a consultant psychiatrist serving with the Royal Navy. He wrote too to his old friend from the Royal Fusiliers, Colonel MVB Hill, who was a practising solicitor, asking him to check the typescript for possible libels.[13] One matter saddened him. Churchill had once volunteered to write a preface, but when he dipped into the book he grumbled that the picture Charles had painted might injure recruiting, and, besides, he had no patience with all the 'damned psychological nonsense'.[14] So no more was said of the preface. However, Churchill relented so far as to suggest that Charles should take his book to Macmillans, the publisher, and this Charles did. He made his way to their office armed with a big bundle of typed sheets in cloth covers:

'I was received by Donald Macmillan*, the senior partner in the firm. He took my bulky parcel and deposited it at one end of a long refectory table, he then led the way to the other end where he invited me to be seated and for half an hour he proceeded to talk about Churchill. My book was not mentioned.'[14]

The days went by and Charles anxiously watched the posts, but hope was deferred. Two weeks later, still having heard nothing, he left Plymouth with the Prime Minister's party in HMS 'Renown',[15] heading for a meeting with Roosevelt in Cairo and then for a tripartite meeting with Stalin and Roosevelt in Teheran. As 'Renown' approached Gibraltar, Charles wrote the first of the many letters[16] that he was to send to Dorothy and his sons on this trip. He had been a little queasy in the heavy weather on the first day out but now, after consuming tea with the scarce wartime commodities of good jam and chocolate bicuits, and looking at everything on board from the point of view of his son John, who, having left school, was serving as an Ordinary Seaman in HMS 'Belfast', he reflected that if the seamen fed as well as the passengers, they would burst. He asked Dorothy to deal with a number of College affairs. This was an administrative channel which he found convenient on his travels

---

*It would have been Daniel Macmillan.

THE PREMIER ON HIS WAY TO NORTH AFRICA FOR HIS MEETING WITH MR. ROOSEVELT
AND THE GENERALISSIMO : A GROUP ON THE QUARTER-DECK.
This photograph was taken during the Premier's voyage by warship to the place, "somewhere in North
Africa," where the five-day conference with Mr. Roosevelt and Marshal Chiang Kai-shek was held. The
group shows (l. to r.) Section Officer Mrs. Oliver, W.A.A.F., formerly Miss Sarah Churchill, who acted
as A.D.C. to her father, Mr. Churchill, Major Desmond Morton, M.C., his special assistant, Admiral of
the Fleet Sir Andrew Cunningham, First Sea Lord, and Lord Moran, Mr. Churchill's personal physician.

*Figure 14. On board HMS 'Renown' on the way to Cairo and the Teheran conference,
November 1943. (Reproduced by kind permission of* The Illustrated London News*)
(CMAC PP/CMW/P.72)*

but its use did nothing to endear him to the very efficient Secretary
of the College, Miss Cook. Would Dorothy please warn Lord Astor*
that there was doubt about his keeping a luncheon engagement;
would she advise the senior examiner in the Birmingham Medical
School to have a reserve examiner on call; and would she make
tentative arrangements for a committee meeting at the College to
be postponed. Churchill's departure had not been announced, and
Charles had no idea when he would be back. 'At present' he wrote,
'my man shows no intention of returning before peace . . .'[16]

Charles's 'man' had come on board with a heavy cold and fever
attributed to his inoculations,[15] despite which, Charles wrote
disapprovingly:

'Himself and Himself Junior [Randolph] are playing bezique.
Yesterday afternoon they played four hours and went to bed on
top of this at 5 am!'[16]

---

*Lord Astor, proprietor of *The Observer*.

But Charles wrote to Dorothy mostly not about Churchill but about *The Anatomy of Courage*. He had the typescript with him and from it he was preparing a series of articles which he hoped would be accepted for publication by *The Times* or the *Sunday Times*. Gil Winant, the American ambassador to Britain, was on board, and had asked if he could read the typescript. As Charles wrote his letter, Winant was half-way through it, and enthusiastic. Charles greatly liked and admired Winant, who had been a pilot in the First World War, and he told Dorothy how encouraging Winant's enthusiasm for the book was after Churchill's and Bracken's failure to get on with it. Charles's next letters were from Malta, where Churchill took to his bed in the Governor's Palace with his still feverish cold.[17] After being called before breakfast to visit his patient, Charles spent a morning sight-seeing in Valetta[18] and in the afternoon Brooke and Alexander gave him a lift when they drove together round the island—an unattractive way of seeing it, he wrote.[19] Winant had now finished the book:

'He is very appreciative and discerning. He thought at first that [the section headed] Moods should come out because it was a break from scientific detachment to a personal account, then he said he was wrong because it brought assurance to the reader that the author had himself been through the mill and was not in London concocting it all.'[20]

Then, as Churchill's party boarded 'Renown' to continue their voyage to Alexandria, the unbelievable happened. A letter from Dorothy brought news that Macmillans would not publish *The Anatomy of Courage*. Charles's immediate reaction was characteristic. The news was a blow but it made him more determined than ever to get it published. He wrote to Dorothy:

'These things stir in me some basic fighting instinct and I'll not let them beat me. . . . This book has become part of me, my apologia . . .'[20]

A week later, Charles wrote from Cairo:

'I got your letter and John's last night just as we were setting out to dine with my man's great friend (who gave me his photograph at Christmas) [Roosevelt]. I am worried you've been so upset about the book. As you know I get worried and irritable about little things but never over a big issue and I look at the book as a big issue in my life.'[21]

The only doubt that Charles mentioned to Dorothy was whether the chapter on Moods might be too strong meat for the ordinary person,

but he felt he had thought this through so often already that he was
not inclined to alter it. The next step was to approach a new
publisher, but Charles's instinct was first to talk to Churchill about
it; however, he added, for the moment the Prime Minister was
'irritable (not with me) and on edge.'[21]

During the five days in Cairo, which the party had reached on
21 November, Charles continued to work on the separate articles
he was hoping to have published. He was distanced from meal-time
talk on the prosecution of the war:

> 'My man is inclined to have a single person to dine with him and
> we are all cleared off to a second mess which is very dull. I have
> been out very little. To the town twice. Once for lunch with S
> [Smuts?] at club. Once today to lunch at Embassy. And I dined
> with his great friend [Roosevelt] last night. That's the sum of
> it.'[21]

The dinner referred to was given by the American Ambassador in
Cairo on the occasion of Thanksgiving Day. Charles, writing to John,
described how:

> '. . . my man and his great friend made very moving speeches of
> which the substance was their gratitude to Providence that the
> other was in power at such a time. The two speeches were made
> sitting down as is always done with his friend. We had soup and
> turkey, pumpkin tart and fruit. There were 18 of us.'[22]

Charles went on to comment to John on some of the people he had
been meeting. At the lunch at the British Embassy he had
sat between the Ambassador and Arthur Tedder, Air Commander-
in-Chief, Middle East, whom he had ragged about recent happenings
in the area, saying they had missed his strategic advice. The
battalion medical officer of 20 years ago had not lost his propensity
for advising the military on the conduct of their business.

In his letters, Charles found it hard to take the requirements of
security and censorship very seriously. He generally referred to
Churchill as 'my man' and to Roosevelt as 'my man's great friend',
and he now referred to Harold Macmillan* as 'namesake of man
who refused my book (his brother)'. But, at the same time, he put
names to Harriman, Hopkins, Sarah Churchill** and many others.
In his letters he was also prone not only to name, but to write candid
comments on, people he was meeting. Thus to his son John:

---

*Harold Macmillan, Minister resident at Allied Headquarters, North West Africa.
**Sarah Churchill, second daughter of Winston and Clementine Churchill, who
sometimes acted as ADC to her father.

'I find ambassadors or such as I have met intelligent and easy to get on with. Our man here [Miles Lampson], our man in Moscow [Clark Kerr], Winant, I seem to know pretty well. Tedder and Marshall I like too but I can't stand Mountbatten'.[22]

Perhaps with a twinge of conscience about security and envisaging the delivery of his letter to an Ordinary Seaman in a mess deck in HMS 'Belfast', he ended this particular letter with a postscript:

'You must tear this up. It is most indiscreet. No announcement of any kind so don't mention me.'[22]

The postscript was somewhat paradoxically juxtaposed to some fatherly advice in his letter, the last paragraph of which began:

'Be very discreet in what you say, very diligent and uncritical . . .'

The advice went on:

'Life consists in a long series of experiences and one gets to look back on some that were not very comfortable at the time. I always regard the time I spent with the Royal Fusiliers as one of the best times of my life though we were grossly uncomfortable at first and often very insecure. To make the best and get the best out of each place is a great art. I haven't always possessed it. People are always interesting and most jobs worth doing involve managing them or at any rate knowledge of them (eg writing books). You'll get to know all sorts. It's no use only knowing a small section. Try and get people you meet to show you their best; an art I was woefully deficient in. The art of listening sympathetically brings out a lot I often miss.'

He ended his letter:

'Might be Lord Chesterfield* instead of—
                           Daddy."[22]

Of the two outings in Cairo that Charles mentioned, one was to see Mme Chiang Kai-shek** professionally:

'I treated her as man to man, saying that most of her complaints were the way she was made and I couldn't help her in that. We

---

*Lord Chesterfield (1694-1773), statesman, diplomat and wit who set out his philosophy in *Letters to His Son*.
**Mme Chiang Kai-shek, wife of the generalissimo of the Chinese Forces in World War II.

got on very well. She told my man I asked "wonderful questions"
which I suppose means that she felt I had got to know quickly her
past.'[22]

Charles's services were rewarded with a gift of a carved ivory
tablet which Miles Lampson, the British Ambassador, told him was
of the best period of chinese ivory carving, about 1620. His
other outing was a visit to the Egyptian Minister of Health,
made at the suggestion of the ambassador. By his own account,
Charles told the minister of the shortcomings of Egyptian hospitals.[22]
In the eyes of his erstwhile colleague on the Medical Unit at St
Mary's, AC Alport, who was professor of medicine at Cairo
University, he should have done more,[23] although anyone
acquainted with Egyptian hospitals at that time might well ask what
the itinerant president of the London College of Physicians could
have achieved.

Churchill and his party flew from Cairo to Teheran on Saturday
27 November. The four-day conference which followed included
sessions attended by Churchill, Roosevelt and Stalin, consultations
between the service chiefs of their three countries, working lunches,
and dinners given in turn by Roosevelt on the Sunday, Stalin on
the Monday, and Churchill on the Tuesday which was his 69th
birthday. Charles found himself staying with the First Secretary
of the British Embassy, Adrian Holman and his wife. Clark Kerr
and Alexander Cadogan were fellow guests.[24] On his arrival in
Teheran, Churchill, who seemed otherwise quite well, had lost his
voice, and Charles was summoned repeatedly to spray his throat.
The problem, Charles commented, was 'simply the nuisance of being
voiceless in Gaza (or was it eyeless?)'.[25] In his book Charles wrote
mostly of what he gleaned about the conference from conversations
with Harry Hopkins, Brooke and Clark Kerr.[26] He attended
Churchill's birthday dinner, sitting at the long table set for thirty-
four, between the Americans General Arnold and Averill Harriman
and opposite Brooke.[27] With greater, and for him unusual,
enthusiasm Charles also wrote to Dorothy of a very pleasant dinner
party with the three Chiefs of Staff at the Holman's.[28] Charles was
late, having been called to spray the Prime Minister's throat and
the evening started gloomily, the service chiefs being at one in calling
the conference a waste of time. However, the dinner was small and
friendly; Portal, the Chief of Air Staff, a man of whom Charles had
a very high opinion, did conjuring tricks; and Charles was clearly
delighted to be asked to sum up a discussion on whether Germany
would break at the top or at the bottom.[28]

Apart from these social events, Charles once more had a lot of time
on his hands. He went on writing the newspaper articles, assured
Dorothy he was feeling very well, and sent her a stream of messages
about college affairs:

'Hal's [Boldero's] letters very brief and inadequate. Don't grumble at him, he can't help it, but let me know what happens about GMC [General Medical Council] meeting. What's happening at the BMA? and Anderson and Dawson? Is there any talk about the White Paper and the negotiating committee?'[28]

As during the visit to Moscow, Charles again took to seeing his patient to bed, an occasion which usually marked for Churchill the end of a long formal dinner followed by talk extending into the small hours of the morning. At this stage of the trip Charles was involved in two memorable bed-time sessions. One, on the night of Monday 29 November, followed the dinner hosted by Stalin. At about midnight Charles went to the Legation, where Churchill was staying, to see if he needed anything.[29] He found Churchill, Clark Kerr and Anthony Eden* together, glasses of whisky in their hands and, joining them, he became the recorder of a discussion the tenor of which was Churchill's concern about the menace of a post-war Russia. When the others left, Charles took Churchill's pulse, and finding it was 100 told him it was 'due to all the stuff he drank and he ought not to go on at this rate'. Churchill retorted that it would soon fall.[30] Then, as he prepared for bed, he conveyed to Charles a presentiment of catastrophe:

'I believe man might destroy man and wipe out civilisation. Europe would be desolate and I may be held responsible.'[30]

And again:

'Stupendous issues are unfolding before our eyes, and we are only specks of dust, that have settled in the night on the map of the world. Do you think, he demanded abruptly, my strength will last out the war? I fancy sometimes that I am nearly spent.

'He said no more as he got into bed. I hung about for a few minutes and then asked him whether he wanted his light put out. He did not answer. He was already asleep.'[30]

Charles himself lay awake for a long time after he went to bed, anxious as he had been in Moscow, when be believed Churchill would depart unreconciled to Stalin. Reading years later of this episode of late night gloom, it may be wondered whether Churchill was portraying visions not only of an aggressive post-war Russia but also of an age that might follow the development of the atom bomb. Eighteen months were to pass before he told Charles about that.[31]

---

*Anthony Eden (later Lord Avon), Minister for Foreign Affairs.

The other bed-time session led to Charles heading a page in his
manuscript book 'I have a row with PM over Mosley*.'[32] On the
Tuesday evening, when Churchill's birthday dinner guests had gone,
Charles followed him to his room in case, as he put it, he was the
worse for wear.[32] A storm quickly came up over a telegram
Churchill had received from Clement Attlee who was deputising for
him in London. This was one of a series of telegrams about Oswald
Mosley that had passed between Churchill and the cabinet since he
had left England. Leader of a small fascist group in England, Mosley
had been detained since the outbreak of war under a regulation
known as 18b which allowed detention without definite charges
being laid, and without trial. Reports that Mosley's health was
impaired had led to the proposal that he should be released, and
this had raised the question whether regulation 18b should now be
completely abolished and everyone detained under it released. The
matter had become a subject of controversy in the cabinet.[33]
Charles described the ensuing scene:

'He [the PM] was pacing up and down the bedroom with quick
strides. He turned to me. "The government are going to go out
over Mosley, Bevin** is kicking." There followed a great diatribe
over their folly and stupidity. Much about Habeas Corpus. "Where
is Eden?" he said with great impatience, "I want Eden." I had seen
him talking in the banqueting room so I told Kinnear [a sergeant
on Churchill's staff] to tell him the PM wanted to see him. He
delayed coming upstairs for a few minutes. "Where is
Mr Eden." the PM shouted, "tell him I want to see him at once
on most urgent business, and less talking there" he said sharply
to a little group at the head of the stairs (Tommy [Thompson],
Martin [the PM's Private Secretary] and self). I looked at my
watch. It was 12.30. I went to bed.'[34]

Next morning, he heard from Martin that Churchill was in good
spirits. A telegram from the Chief Whip and the statement made
on behalf of the government had satisfied the House of Commons
although not the Trades Unions. Despite this evidence that the pot
was simmering down, Charles felt impelled to confront Churchill
with his views on the decision to release Mosley:

'Up to now whenever the PM has opened up about Politics I've
dried up partly because I feel he has already so much on his plate
I ought not to add to it unless some useful purpose is served and
partly because my instinct warns me that if I'm to see this job

---

*Sir Oswald Mosley, leader of the British Union of Fascists 1932-1940.
**Ernest Bevin, Minister of Labour and National Service.

through the fewer arguments we have the better. But at last the guard I've kept on my tongue slipped. I felt his arbitrary moods would do him harm, that in this kind of question he was out of touch with the people. I hate to see him undermining the hold he has on the country.

'I said I usually stuck to my last and confined any views I brought to him to medical matters but would he listen to me for a few minutes while I put a point of view to him. I said I thought a mistake had been made. It was a logical step to release all political prisoners who had not had a trial. After all it was the rights of the individual against those of the state that we were fighting for. But to release Mosley alone was a different matter. And when the PM blew up I said he had not the right to resign whenever he wished as in peacetime. He denied this hotly. "I shall resign when I like". I said he could not govern England without Labour, it would impair unity and interfere with production. At this he shouted he could get on quite well without them. He would not get rid of them but they could go if they wanted. If the public held such views he'd no further use for them. He had never paid much attention to public opinion. If he had in the last 12 years he would not now be in a position to help as he was. Public opinion was stupid but he would say nothing against the people, who were sound and would come to sensible conclusions! I was a Fascist. I explained that I had never met anyone I was less attracted to than Mosley. That's it, you want to imprison someone you don't like. If he, the PM, were at home this wouldn't have happened. He would make one of the best speeches of his parliamentary career on this theme. Several times I made to withdraw but he called me back to shout some new contradiction. I left him with the strong sense of conviction of the corrosion of absolute power. He doesn't want to hear views contrary to his own. I felt very sad. I want to get back to my own job, but I must not hand in. I must see this job through.'[34]

What led Charles to embark on this discussion is unclear. He must have known it would provoke a storm. Pent-up frustration with his role of being seen but not heard probably played a part. The unexpected rejection of his book by Macmillans must still have been rankling. And maybe the reprimand from his cross patient on the previous evening had disturbed his equanimity more than his description of the occasion suggested. Whatever the reason, the argument that he precipitated was based on a misconception. He was evidently unaware that Churchill's personal attitude to the Mosley affair was close to his own, and that five days earlier Churchill had telegraphed Herbert Morrison, the Home Secretary, stating his personal conviction that Regulation 18b should be abolished, but adding that he would not press his view for to do so would have put him at variance with the views of his cabinet colleagues at home in London who had to deal with the matter.[33]

Flying back from Teheran to Cairo on 2 December, Charles noted the menu—turtle soup, roast duck, pears and cream—and added:

> 'A good deal has happened since we lunched on this aircraft five days ago. I hope the PM will have a long sleep when we have finished luncheon; he is very tired.'[35]

The return to Cairo on 2 December heralded several days when Churchill was undecided about his travel plans—he fancied a few days so-called holiday in Italy among other things—and Charles was increasingly concerned about engagements to which he had committed himself at home.[36] He sent a wire to cancel his appointment to examine at Birmingham,[37] but he badly wanted to take the chair at a committee meeting at the College in the following week when the possible formation of a section of paediatrics was to be discussed. He was anxious to show his readiness to meet the wishes of physicians who specialised in children's diseases, and indeed to suggest that other specialist sections of the College should be formed which the parent body would treat 'as England treats its Dominions'. Apart from anything else, he saw this as good electioneering for the next presidential election was only three months away and he was in danger of being seen as an absentee President. He didn't want to miss examining in Cambridge either, partly, again, because he would meet some 10 Fellows of the College and the opportunity would be provided for more electioneering. There would also be a chance to size up the position with the regius professorship[36] and a fee of £25 was a consideration.[38]

Once again, Charles was spending most of the day in his bedroom, writing, and lunches and dinners were unexciting, Churchill usually being with Roosevelt on these occasions.[39] Socially the monotony was broken for Charles when he was included in a big dinner given at the British Embassy for President Inönü of Turkey and his Foreign Minister. Charles, who sat opposite the Turkish President, once more found himself at home in the company of the diplomats:

> 'I missed my vocation by going into medicine. Our ambassador in Ankara was deeply impressed by my grasp of essentials . . . Knatchbull Hugesson like Clark Kerr in Moscow thinks I'm a very wise person, which is something after recent blows about book.'[38]

In the face of his worries, Charles was glad to find himself in Churchill's good books. On his return to Cairo the Prime Minister was smitten by diarrhoea, and he attributed his quick recovery to Charles's treatment. The argument over Mosley had not undermined their relationship. People close to Churchill recognised that if they held their own in argument with him, they earned his respect,[40] so it is not surprising that, a few days after the dispute Charles wrote to Dorothy:

'I think . . . my stock with the PM is higher than it has been. I had a tiff with him over Mosley, when I spoke my views plainly and he didn't like them. But things medically have gone well. Sulphaguanidine cleared up his diarrhoea like magic. Last night after dinner at Embassy he suddenly said—Lord Moran took his gun and put it to his shoulder (making appropriate gestures) and fired and the enemy (bug) was immediately put to flight.

'Another time during a big luncheon party he said apropos of nothing but with a quizzical expression—"when Lord Moran is irritated he has a powerful kick. The other day he [Moran] told me [Churchill] I might know something about strategy and politics but I knew damn all about medicine". Which is all to the good. He gets more and more self centred and *this trip has not been in a good temper*, but I think if I said I could not come [on] these trips he would be sorry. I've no use for Eden at all . . .'[38]

As each day of December 1943 passed and the prospects of being home for the College committee meeting and for examining at Cambridge diminished, Charles continued to be a prey to indecision. On the one hand the advantages of returning at once were clear. On the other hand, if he waited and came back with Churchill by sea:

'that . . . would be best opportunity to tackle him about book and even to get him if possible to read it. Further he feels if I finish with him a little better disposed than if I leave him. I fancy second view will prevail . . .

'I shall have a day in my room today. PM has functions or away. I'm quite well . . .

'I had fixed some dress material at Teheran for you and then we were whisked away before I had a chance of collecting it so, as things are absurdly expensive here now, I don't think I'll bring you anything this time. I think this is sensible thing to do though I'd have liked to give you something as solace for your uncomfortable vigil. All my love C.'[38]

Also as the days passed, Charles became increasingly concerned about his patient. Churchill, in retrospect, described how at this time he became conscious of being very tired, to the extent that he no longer dried himself after his bath, but lay on the bed wrapped in his towel until he dried naturally.[41] Charles observed that at times he seemed almost played out:

'I went to his bedroom tonight and found him sitting with his head in his hands. "I have never felt like this before" he said, "Can't you give me something so that I won't feel so exhausted?"'

'Nevertheless, he still talks of going to Italy when he leaves here. At this time of the year the climate there is vile, and Alex's tent is no proper resting place for a man who is tired out. I feel so certain that he will get harm if we go to Italy that I've written to Smuts in the strongest possible terms. He is the only man who has any influence with the PM . . .'[42]

Charles drafted the letter to Smuts on Wednesday December 8 in his room at Casey Villa, where he was staying.[43] He recalled Smuts's earlier expression of concern that Churchill's health might not last out, and how he, Charles, was not really worried at that time. Now, after thinking it over, he had concluded that he ought to explain the present position. He referred to the threatened coronary thrombosis in Washington after Pearl Harbour, and how he had felt that if news of it got about in Washington, Churchill would be looked upon as a semi-invalid. He described how, as a minor complication, Churchill had been threatened with becoming conscious of his heart and worrying about it, and how he (Charles) had taken steps to allay his fears and apprehensions. Churchill had had two or three little incidents since, always on extra exertion; their significance was uncertain but they were very suspicious. Charles then referred to Churchill's pneumonia earlier in the year and to the risk of fresh chest troubles if he visited Italy in the cold and wet; but that was only a chance:

'What is more important is a review of the general position. I have been less certain lately that he will see the war through at this present pace. He complains of feeling tired, of his age and of the racket and wear and tear of such things as the Turks and other important decisions. Twice in the last week he has had a pulse of 96 (normal 72) *before leaving* his bed in the morning. Yesterday, after saying to me that he felt v. tired and down, he went to bed at 3 am. I am afraid of nothing except his heart. If that lasts, he will last. There is no medical remedy, if he goes on racing the machine it may give in. In advising at all we have to realise that he would be miserable if he did not make major decisions, that he would never consent to abdication, all that can be done is to persuade him to give moderation a chance in all things, what he has never yet done. There is nobody around him or in Cabinet who has any influence on him, I believe you are the only person he listens to. I think he has a feeling that I know my job and will tell him what he does not like when necessary . . . but at best if I have any influence, it cannot be used often, and may be ineffective when used.'[43]

Charles went on to summarise his own clash of interests:

'A minor conflict is that I am PRCP and that almost at once the Ministry of Health is bringing out a White Paper setting out a comprehensive medical service for Great Britain. I asked John Anderson not to let it come out till we got back. We were six weeks in Canada and USA, then six weeks at home, and then we left again on November 12 for apparently another six weeks away. It is very difficult to do my job at home under such conditions, and as head of the medical profession for the time being I have responsibility for after war arrangements which seems to be in direct conflict with my duty to the PM. He says I am a comfort to him in these gatherings. I suppose a kind of mental assurance for he is very imaginative. But any use I am can easily be exaggerated. Ought I to do a job for which I was elected as President, or ought I to go on being out of England for six weeks at a time, at decreasing intervals. More important, can anything be done to ease the PM's burden.'[43]

Charles continued:

'I have just seen him (noon) and his diarrhoea has returned. I shall be glad when I get him safely on the ship on return journey.'[43]

He ended his letter by saying he would be available at any time to clear up any points with Smuts. His only commitment was to see the Egyptian Prime Minister in the evening about health matters.

Charles did not record a conversation with Smuts following the delivery of his letter, but Smuts may have taken note of it for that evening he drew Brooke aside and told him he was not at all happy about the condition of the PM and was beginning to doubt if he would stay the course.[44] Charles had no real conviction that, should Smuts press counsels of common sense on Churchill, the Prime Minister would be persuaded to be sensible.[42] He doubted too if even Smuts could alter the PM's plans to go to Italy. Nevertheless, Charles must have felt better after sharing his worries with an elder statesman for whom he had great admiration.

The day after he wrote his letter to Smuts, Charles sent Dorothy another section of *The Anatomy of Courage* to be typed as an article for the newspapers.[45] In his covering letter he said Churchill wanted him to go with him on his holiday. Charles identified the place not by name but by alluding to one of his First World War decorations, the Silver Medal for Military Valour which was bestowed from Italy. The holiday plan would involve his missing examining in Cambridge, and a Brains Trust session also now looked uncertain:

'When I think of Birmingham and Cambridge and Brains Trust I feel I'm paying a considerable price for this business. I get very fed up with it at times. Whole days in bedroom except meals. I said to Martin today "it's curious that if that was England with blue sky and hot sun we'd gloat in the perfect day, here we only grouse at the flies."

'I had a successful interview with Egyptian PM yesterday (lasting 1 hour): the Finance Minister was also present. Webb J. [Webb Johnson, President of the Royal College of Surgeons] would have made a lot of it. Tonight I call on Mrs Casey* at 6 pm. She's able and asked me to look in at 6 pm and I'm doing this out of politeness.

'My man is tired which is not to be wondered at as things have been hectic for him. I sometimes think I ought to get more kick out of these journeys where historic things happen than I do. Partly I suppose I have a very uninteresting role to play. Partly I think war is always on my mind and partly its the nature of the beast.It was nice to get your long letter today with the poem, which was pleasant. The captains and the kings depart [The Conference was over] and we are left. I suppose I ought to rush round some more mosques.

'This doesn't sound a very cheerful epistle to send to a lady in a damp cottage in a wet December whose days are not very entertaining but I'm quite well, only moody! I'd give all these journeys for a good peace time game at Twickenham.

'If the old man's heart gave way suddenly I might be left with the memory of these journeys and not much else! I'd like to get a settled job after the war. I somehow feel that Provost Eton and Trinity are not real possibilities. Yet I should not like to govern somewhere out of England with Geoffrey at Eton and RJM [John] back on leave. I wish very much war was over. All love.   C.'[45]

A postscript in the margin of the letter added:

'Winant bid me farewell with a tremendous handshake. He likes me.'[45]

Two days later, Charles noted:

'Better news this morning, Italy, thank God, is off, at any rate for the present. Tonight we go by air to Tunis and then on by car

---

*Mrs RG Casey, wife of the Minister of State resident in the Middle East.

to Carthage to stay with General Eisenhower*. I have never before been so blunt with the PM, rating him for his folly, but I take no credit for the change in plans. He knows without my help that he is at the end of his tether . . .'[46]

Charles went on to comment that, whatever the strain, it was always broken by convivial nights, and in his manuscript book he wrote a comment which shows his understanding, albeit with disapproval, of Churchill's drinking at this time:

'I do not doubt that some of this drinking is to find some escape from the burden of responsibility and even to seek an antidote to the mere physical strain of feeling rotten . . .'[47]

The conviviality referred to was sometimes rather one-sided. Charles recorded trying to contribute to one of these occasions:

'Last night at the Embassy we sat at the dinner table from 8 pm till 11.50 pm. Mountbatten's eyes closed and opened spasmodically. I looked down the long table at the faces of the soldiers and sailors. They seemed only half awake. I was sorry for Winston: surely someone ought to show some interest in the drawn-out monologue. On the spur of the moment I blurted out: "Do you remember Landor's lovely lines?" Winston glared at me. He hates being interrupted. "What are they?" he snorted. I wanted to get under the table. "What are they?" Winston shouted with growing impatience. I could think of no way to escape.

'"There are no fields of amaranth on this side of the grave; there are no voices, O Rhodope, that are not soon mute, however, tuneful; there is no name, with whatever emphasis of passionate love repeated, of which the echo is not faint at last."

'I scampered over the lovely vowel sounds. Winston (with great contempt):
"I call that pure defeatist stuff."
I would not give in. I tried Milton:
"While the still morn went out with sandals grey."
"He was on the wrong side in the Civil War," Winston growled.
I gave up.

'After leaving the table we spent another hour and a half in the drawing-room. The servants talked in whispers. No one kept quite

---

*General Dwight D Eisenhower, Commanding General of the US forces in the European theatre of operations.

awake. At last, in a lull in the conversation, the PM was heard to make the same remark he had made three hours before. We were where we began.'[46]

At 1.00 am on Saturday 11 December, Churchill left Cairo by air for Tunisia. He still aimed to visit Italy, and Tunisia was planned as a brief stopover on the way.[41] Arriving over Tunis soon after daybreak, the plane was diverted to an airfield 40 miles away from the intended one, and as the Prime Minister sat in the cold wind on his official boxes that had been unloaded onto the sandy ground, Charles noted that his face shone with perspiration.[48] When Churchill disembarked two hours later at the right airfield, and was being driven to General Eisenhower's villa at Carthage where he was to stay, he confessed to Eisenhower that he was at the end of his tether.[49] After lunch he went to bed. Charles gave an account of the following weeks in letters that he wrote almost daily to Dorothy. What he wrote to her of his patient's illness formed the basis of the account that he gave years later in his book on Churchill. But the letters tell a much more personal story too: of his reaction to the responsibility that fell on him as a doctor; of his frustration at being marooned in North Africa; of his longing to have Dorothy with him and of his sense of deprivation at the prospect of missing Geoffrey's school holidays and John's impending leave from his ship. In the background was his deep concern at being unable to control things at the College.

So far as Churchill's illness was concerned, Charles found the first 24 hours worrying because he could not make a diagnosis. Confronted with what is described medically as a PUO—pyrexia of undetermined origin—he made the appropriate moves. He sent for a pathologist, Colonel Pulvertaft*, to do laboratory tests, and he arranged for a chest X-ray to be taken.[50] Meanwhile, pending the arrival of two nurses, he shared the night watches with Churchill's personal detective:

'Last night I got Inspector Thomson to sit outside his door and I went to bed at 1 o'clock. He [Thomson] came for me at 2 am and I sat with him 2-3 am. Then he went to sleep and the temp is now 100. . . . Its devil of a nuisance (1) to have fever as yet undiagnosed and no symptoms, (2) to know how much to tell Mrs C and cabinet, (3) his pulse 2-3 am was shabby. He has felt strain of conference enormously, on top of this had severe diarrhoea and a heavy cold and now this.

---

*Lt Col R Pulvertaft, Assistant Director of Pathology, Middle East Forces, and Professor of clinical pathology, Westminster School of Medicine.

'However my nerves are excellent in those crises and I take charge which is as well as there's no one to fall back upon here. If Mrs C. telephones you be guarded. Say I'd written he was seedy but had not said anything more.'[50]

By the next day it was clear that his patient had pneumonia[51] and Charles arranged for two specialists to join him, Brigadier DE Bedford* from Cairo, who in peacetime was consultant for heart diseases at the Middlesex Hospital, and Lieutenant-Colonel Buttle, an expert on the use of M & B. Meanwhile, that night, Churchill's heart gave cause for concern and on the following morning Charles told Harold Macmillan that he had thought his patient might die.[52] To Dorothy, Charles wrote:

'My man's pulse between 2 & 3 am got bad. Yet fact that I might be faced with returning alone without him to face and explain to public did not fizz on me in slightest. Yet I never stop worrying about John. Isn't it funny how we are made. At present his condition isn't at all bad.'[51]

Then the specialists started to arrive:

'Bedford arrived yesterday and Scadding** (lung specialist) also. All this [was] as well, as Attlee called would I like Marshall sent out. I said no! I sent Mrs C. message this morning explaining everything and said "If I myself were ill in London I would not change this team." Last night at 6 pm before Bedford's arrival he suddenly began Auricular Fibrillation. But on digitalis Pulse of 120 has this morning fallen to 96. He has a largish patch of Pneumonia and congestion (due to heart) at other base. I thought Bedford too optimistic in bulletin but I have covered this with message to Mrs C. and Attlee. We shall say nothing of fibrillation to press and public but have told Cabinet and Mrs C. I am more happy about him today.

'Yesterday I was doubtful if he would come through and I saw myself arriving alone at Paddington with Mrs C. reproachful and public incensed! However my nerves are excellent and though outlook yesterday was sombre I believe he'll come through if no further complications and no recurrence of fibrillation.'[53]

---

*Brigadier D Evan Bedford, Consulting Physician, Middle East Forces and Physician to the National Heart Hospital.
**Lt Col JG Scadding, officer-in-charge of a medical division, Middle East Forces, and physician to the Brompton Hospital.

Charles now realised that he would be stuck for several weeks in North Africa. He foresaw at least another two weeks in Carthage and then a period of convalescence would be needed. Churchill talked of bringing Mrs Churchill out[53] and Charles wondered if Dorothy, perhaps with Geoffrey, might come out too. He was evidently reluctant to raise the matter at this stage with his patient and suggested that Dorothy, who was in touch with Mrs Churchill, might mention it to her. However, events overtook them:

'I fear it must have been a blow to you that our return will be postponed as it was to me. Mrs C arrived yesterday by air, not at our suggestion but on her own. It is instructive that Cabinet opposed her coming out on grounds it was joy riding! Which is not very helpful for my getting you out. About this I gather (1) John gets leave: I stupidly cannot lay my hands on date. You must be home for this and spend what money is necessary to give him an enjoyable holiday. (2) GH's [Geoffrey's] return to Eton. These two events govern even the remote possibility of your coming out and look to me not very favourable for any chance of this. Beaverbrook will probably fly out here about Dec 26 or so which is no good for John's leave. Mrs C's plane was not heated. Travelling by air is very uncomfortable in winter. I'm almost reconciled to not attempting to get you out in view of GH's return Eton and John's leave. I hate missing their holidays and also missing chance of giving you a pleasant change but don't know how to get over these two hurdles (GH and John), I'm very fed up at events and see now we have another fuss over Liverpool, Jan. 20. I think he aims at getting back 1/6 of GH's age after that date. But this is very fluid.

'Last night he had second attack of auricular fibrillation in night. I think he will come home alright. (Pneumonia is about better and Temp. normal) but situation is full of worries and I find incidentally that getting up 2 am-3 am every night and coming back to bed with a brain working continuously is bad for sleep. But I am very well if fed up ... We're not very comfortable here and fed abominably (American and bad at that) but I'm very well. Only between being late for White Paper, cutting exams, possibly scratching Liverpool, disappointing you missing boys etc etc with endless worries here (Sarah. Randolph. Mrs C. private messages to cabinet etc etc) I feel fed up and in toils of a commitment I cannot cut. More and more I seem to be committed to waiting on him hand and foot most of year and neglecting my other things RCP and domestic which I hate doing. There are two strong wills here his and mine and I try hard to prevent them clashing. He feels very grateful to me that illness has been marvellously managed with science (blood count etc etc) and foresight and is almost affectionate at times but is constantly thoughtless and self-centred. Macmillan (Harold) having read Parts I and II [of *The Anatomy of Courage*] (he took Part III away with him) said it was interesting but added "It rather frightens me." This, a man in Guards last war, wounded 3 times! Before he read it he rather took attitude—My brother is hard pressed, short handed and we have commitments to text books etc etc . . . but I don't know if he also feels its too strong meat for public. Have I produced a book very well done but too strong for ordinary consumption?'[54]

There was one cheerful item in the postscript to this rather dismal letter, a reference to an achievement by Geoffrey at school:

'You can't tell how delighted I was about GH. It's splendid. Once he knows what is necessary to get a 1st, he's got the hang of things . . . CIGS will take this tomorrow.'[54]

It may be imagined how joyfully Charles would have written this postscript, for he was not only himself ambitious. The boys too should excel in whatever they did. There was no question of their being sent to an indifferent school. They went to the best, and they were expected to aim for the top. In fact Charles couldn't understand anyone aiming for less. He was wont to point, in his own family, to his brother Lorton as a cautionary example of someone who had as a young man preferred golf to work (becoming a scratch or plus 1 player) and so spent his life as a general practitioner in Barrow-in-Furness instead of becoming a distinguished consultant. Aiming at the top applied to everything. At one stage when John, at Eton, became involved with the beagles, his father's reaction was to ask why he did not set out to become master of the hounds. It had to be explained to him that the mastership involved bringing the pack home for the holidays.[55]

By Christmas eve it was clear that Dorothy would not be brought out:

'I failed to fix up you and GH. It's as much a disappointment to me as to you and I kick myself for mentioning it before making certain I could bring it off. I think Mrs C tried but he is in a curious mood. She said apropos of nothing "I (Mrs C) would not be out here if Winston were not ill", forgetting Quebec. PM said "you've seen cable about John (which said) John is at sea and 'Belfast' will not call at English or Scottish port for two weeks and more probably three weeks (cable dated December 23). He won't be available till 14 January at earliest and you can go home then if I'm not returning" PM said. So I think John also won't come out. I have made up my mind to be back for 19 January. I doubt whether he will be back then but I'll just fly back. Inwardly I get a good deal fed up with C family. They disregard everything where their own

family is concerned, Sarah and Mary come with them: Mrs C arrives
with multitude of evening clothes etc. whereas we are not
changing. R [Randolph] is always with us instead of with his
unit.'[56]

Lonely, with little to occupy him on this Christmas eve, Charles also
poured out to Dorothy his concern about the College and about his
own future. April would soon come, and with it once again the
presidential election. On the whole he believed he would not be
turned out. Churchill had sent for the White Paper on the health
service and would show it to him. When knowledge of this spread,
it might do something to counter the criticism that Charles was too
much away from London. After all, Charles reflected, no other
President had been in such a position to influence things. He included
in his Christmas Eve letter a message for Boldero, making it clear
that the impending discussion of the possibility of moving the College
from its present site must be deferred until he returned: 'This at
last resort is Orders and if they are not obeyed they can get a new
PRCP . . .'[56] The date of his return remained uncertain, and Charles
thought that factors other than Churchill's health would determine
it:

'History plays curious tricks and his judgement and character are
very different from public estimate. He wants to come home with
Rome in his pocket and is going to delay out here until end of
January if there is any chance of this. It would quiet criticism of
Leros and last two months ineptitude. I sometimes wonder if I'm
wise going on with these trips instead of making an outstanding
success of RCP and cashing in PRCP in practice.

'Ah my dear I feel very much the monotony of your existence and
the new disappointment and I've done my damndest to bring it
off. But these things pass and I see here that with all our faults
we are altogether superior to C menage and that we are very
fortunate in having good boys. One day if there is any money I'll
try and let you see something of the world.'[56]

On Christmas Day Charles consoled himself by picking up his pen
at intervals and writing another long letter to Dorothy.[57] Much of
it again was a commentary on College business which Dorothy would
pass on to Boldero and to such other people as she might think
appropriate, for Dorothy and Charles were so close to each other
in their thinking that the presidency had become something of a
partnership. The day started with an episode at holy communion
that was later recorded in several diaries:[58,59]

'At 8 am I went with Mrs C. to early service with Coldstreams in a dilapidated fort. As service was ending a white dove which had probably been sitting on a beam fluttered down and perching quite near us, looked down on us. A private behind me said "that must mean something, perhaps peace".'[57]

Churchill was now much better and appeared for Christmas dinner in the middle of the day:

'PM in great form. Proposed health of Bedford and me (M & B). I replied that when in difficulty we had another consultant at hand, himself (much appreciated by everyone who knows his interfering nature).'[57]

In the afternoon Charles went for a walk for an hour with General Alexander, and in the evening he had a talk with Macmillan about *The Anatomy of Courage*:

'Harold Macmillan tackled me tonight and returned book. He said "I think I understand why my brother refused this book though I've not communicated with him. 1) We have only 25% of paper and we use that to keep our textbooks going and occasionally to try out new young authors; 2) I think he may have been frightened a little. There are a hundred possible libel actions in it. After the war Yes but now? It is a brilliant book. I read it with emotion. I knew the characters" and so he returned it saying lots and lots of firms would publish it straightaway. "I shall read it again when its published with interest".'[57]

After Christmas, Charles judged that his patient was well enough to fly to Marrakesh to convalesce. Beaverbrook, who had now joined the family party, provided some companionship:

'Yesterday afternoon we went by car into Atlas mountains about one and a half hours there and ditto back. Very good looking scenery, lower slopes dotted with black goats, tops of mountains snow, and road clinging to slopes with hairpin bends, an engineering feat. On return Max asked me to go a walk and we went into native quarter where in a great square we saw a man telling Romances while squatting on ground around him a crowd of Arabs listened intently, a little farther on a snake charmer, and again four Arabs playing musical instruments, like a market square but with many little groups round Arabs entertaining them by stories, music etc.

'Max friendly but cryptic as usual. Evidently thinks I must go on doing this job and after war get (vaguely) some 'professor's job'.

Did not mention finance. Asked me if I liked flying. Did you touch on this? Wants Brendan to get new and bigger job. Ministry of Health or Chancellor of Exchequer. Fantastic. He is very tactful with C family but what his real feelings towards C are I would not like to say.

'Today we're going to picnic somewhere. It's on cold side but good air after Cairo.

''Belfast' was *not* hit in convoy in which 'Scharnhorst' was sunk. They have apparently not been molesting these convoys for a considerable time and this was a surface vessel attack on Convoy. It's a big experience, a naval action in twilight of Arctic Circle, and I have no doubt if John comes through this war all right it will have an altogether beneficial effect on his character and do much to counter those Max Beerbohm*, Noel Coward**, film tastes which were so evident.

'I'm writing against time as we came in from picnic in Atlas Mountains about 5.45, then I had to go to PM and get a bath before Com. Thomson who shared my room last night giving his to General Montgomery, who goes home tonight. He came picnic with us. He's a showman and conceited but I think he has regard of troops. He said his "padres were more useful to him than his artillery". PM has read Vol. 1. Says it held him, was very interested ("did *not* have to read it from duty") and well written with great literary art. But (there is always a *but*) he was not sure it would not frighten people (ie like Macmillan). He knows nothing of matter. Perhaps other two volumes will alter his opinion. All for publishing it after war but not sure about now.'[60]

As in Carthage, so in Marrakesh, Charles's thoughts continually returned to College affairs. The White Paper arrived and he was very pleased when Churchill gave it to him to read and told him he wanted him to confer with Willink, the Minister of Health, about it. Charles suggested to Dorothy that this fact should be conveyed with caution to what he called the right people.[61] But it would not do if everybody, including Horder, knew he was going about saying he had seen the White Paper. He added:

'But if Hal [Boldero] digested [the] above surely it can be vaguely put about that RCP gains enormously in having such influence in highest quarters. Or is it safer with such bunglers to wait till I get back to do it.'[61]

---

*Sir Max Beerbohm, author and cartoonist.
**Noel Coward (later Sir Noel), actor, playwright and composer.

The sense of frustration behind these comments must have been great. There was Charles, more involved in politics than ever before, having to endure idleness in the African winter sunshine while Horder, still his rival for the presidency, remained on the spot in London, and the in-fighting had to be left to the admirable and loyal, but politically much less sophisticated, Harold Boldero. Then, suddenly, things looked better. A signal from the Admiralty indicated that John was due for a fortnight's leave before joining the officer's training course at HMS 'King Alfred', and there was no objection to his visiting Marrakesh. Churchill agreed that he should come[62] and Charles's next letters were devoted to instructions about the clothes he should bring. Charles was very anxious that the young ordinary seaman he was introducing to this unusual house party should fit in comfortably. He would be in mufti and it really did matter that he should conform, meaning he should wear a tweed jacket and flannels in the day-time and be able to change into a suit if the occasion demanded it. On 10 January John, who had flown out in a Transport Command plane, arrived at the Villa Taylor, where the Churchills and their immediate entourage were staying.[63] It was lunchtime and the rest of the party were out on a picnic so father and son could do as they wished. After they had had lunch on the veranda Charles ordered a car and, together with Mrs Churchill's secretary and a Royal Marine disguised as a GI, they went to visit the bazaars in the town. On their return at teatime John was introduced to the Prime Minister. Sitting next to him that night at dinner, Ordinary Seaman Wilson, attired in his dinner jacket, had to tell the story of the sinking of the 'Scharnhorst'. Writing to Dorothy Charles noted that the PM had talked till 1 am; first Mrs Churchill had given up, then Charles, but John stayed till the end.[64] Picnics in the hills and the long leisurely dinners, which occupied much of Charles's and John's time in the next few days, gave John a glimpse of his father among the Churchills. He saw him as a figure somewhat apart; a Roundhead among the Cavaliers was how he later characterised him.[65] Charles, for his part, was able to tell Dorothy how easily and well John fitted in with the Churchill family party.[64]

On 14 January Charles set out for home, accompanying Churchill by air to Gibraltar. John travelled in another plane. At Gibraltar the Prime Minister had a choice of flying on or sailing in the battleship 'King George V'.[66] In the event the party embarked in 'King George V' in the small hours of 15 January. At 5.30 pm on the previous evening Charles penned a hasty note to Dorothy:

'. . . Am bringing 200 oranges if I succeed in getting them back which I have no doubt I shall. I tell you this in case you want to make preparations for making marmalade. I bought them yesterday . . . they ought to be used at once.'[67]

Chapter 14

Self Perceptions

HMS 'King George V' reached Plymouth late on the night of 17 January 1944, and an overnight train journey brought Churchill's party to Paddington Station at nine o'clock on the following morning.[1] Dorothy met Charles and John, who retrieved the luggage and the crates of oranges while Churchill was being greeted by the cabinet and the media. Dorothy then drove them straight to the College, from which Charles had been absent for over two months. Now that he was released from what he described as the antechamber of the councils of war,[2] there was an abrupt change in the tempo of his life. He picked up the reins at the College quickly for, as he told the Comitia 10 days after his return, he had been in almost daily touch with the College officers while he was away.[3] He was indeed a major user of the courier service which catered for the Prime Minister's needs.[4] When the Comitia met on 27 January, the proposed form of the new health service could not usefully be debated because, although Charles had read the White Paper, it had still not been published. He foreshadowed that it would be considered by a special meeting later in the year. The planning of consultant services was the main subject of his address, and there was a new sense of urgency about what he had to say, for, with the end of the war in sight, many doctors in the forces were asking what demobilisation held in store for them.[5] In his address Charles said that the time was coming when there would be a consultant service; most consultants would join it; they would really be employees of the hospitals, and the old system of visiting honorary staff would go. Consultants, Charles said, would wish to be represented centrally and whatever body represented them would have to be elected by the consultants themselves.[3]

Charles's prediction of the imminent demise of the old honorary system produced no outcry in the Comitia. This was surprising because, for many consultants, giving their services without fee to patients in voluntary hospitals was an article of faith, and the whole teaching hospital system was based on the honorary concept. Perhaps Charles, whose address to this Comitia was one of his most persuasive, managed to temper what must have been bad news for many by showing how determined he was that the Colleges should mould the consultant services.

In passing, the Comitia on 27 January noted the death of Dr George Anderson,[3] the secretary of the BMA, and when Charles took the chair two weeks later at the meeting of the Central Medical

237

Academic Council he was confronted by Anderson's successor, Dr Charles Hill.[6] Hill was already known to him as the BMA's deputy secretary and as the principal draughtsman of the report published by the Medical Planning Commission in 1942.[7] The meeting left him unimpressed. On the following day he wrote to Leonard Parsons, a physician and one of his confidants in Birmingham, that he was disappointed with the attitude of the BMA at the meeting: 'I was determined', he wrote, 'not to believe (until I proved it) that Hill is unreliable—he is.' He was critical too of Guy Dain, the chairman of the BMA council: 'Dain is honest and courageous but I am doubtful if he has the first class ability which a statesman needs . . .'[6]

Parsons, in his reply, exhorted Charles not to be downhearted.[8] Parsons believed Charles would get what he wanted; he did not believe Dain and Hill were antagonistic. Dain, he said, was a good debater, and Charles's speech had contained one or two points which he seized on. Hill he described as an able person known to be a good drafter of resolutions. Parsons felt that Charles was over-reacting, but Charles was not comforted, and, although he continued to admire Dain's honesty and courage,[9] he never had a good opinion of Hill. As for the new President of the BMA, the ageing Dawson, Charles's tolerance was sorely tried. After a round table meeting to discuss relationships between the BMA and the College, he wrote to Dawson:

'Your memorandum is meant I think to indicate what is in your mind rather than what actually took place at the conference.'[10]

The long-awaited White Paper on a National Health Service was published on 17 February.[11] Its stated aim was to ensure that every man, woman and child could rely on getting the best medical and other facilities available, and that their getting these facilities should not depend on whether they could pay for them. Charles made his first public response to the White Paper when it was debated in the House of Lords a month later. He found the purpose and aims unexceptionable but criticised several aspects of the proposed administration.[12] In his stance he had the support of most of the Fellows of the College for at the Comitia on 3 April he was re-elected President with 92 votes compared with Horder's 19.[13] The Comitia considered the White Paper in July, when discussion of a motion by two senior Fellows expressing misgivings about the government's proposals was deferred until October.[14] Meanwhile much of Charles's time at the College continued to be occupied with defining and discussing questions about consultants.[15]

Undoubtedly, at this time, Charles saw himself as what he called the 'leader of the profession for the moment' and, in that capacity, as having a heavy responsibility thrust upon him. This was evident in correspondence with Robert Barrington-Ward, the editor of *The*

Times, at the end of June. Following the publication of the White Paper there had been a good deal of public bickering among doctors. On 21 June Charles sent a letter to *The Times* in which he asserted the need for unity in the medical profession.[16] He started by making a point that he was to return to time and again, that it was the will of the people expressed through the government of the day that there should be a comprehensive health service to include the whole population, and that that decision must be accepted because it was a political and not a medical issue. Then he referred to impatience that was becoming evident with what appeared to be the doctors' intransigence. The profession, he said, was not opposed to the aims of the White Paper, but only to some of the means that had been suggested to carry out those aims. He instanced failure to relate reward of doctors in the service to professional success so that the keen and the slovenly would profit alike. And he asserted that doctors believed they could not do their best work serving, as proposed, under local authorities. He gave historical examples to support this assertion. The editor's office asked Charles to shorten his letter,[17] whereupon he wrote a personal letter of greater length to Barrington-Ward.

'June 25th 1944

'My dear Barrington-Ward

'On Wednesday I sent a letter to *The Times* and last night, on my return from Cambridge, I found the reply I enclose. I am sending you my letter because even if you don't publish it I'd like you to know the points it tries to make.

'The structure of the profession—the conditions under which doctors live and work—is being radically changed at a time when almost everyone who will have to work the new service is with the forces and cannot be consulted. That seems to me to throw a heavy responsibility on our shoulders.

'Unfortunately it happens that where gifts of administration and presentation are concerned, the White Paper has caught us in a lean time. The lieutenants on whom in the ordinary way I should rely to help me to put the position before the public just do not exist. The Regius Professorship of Physic at Cambridge is vacant. Hill, a demagogue, has just succeeded Anderson as secretary of the BMA. He has a gift for drafting documents, considerable readiness of speech and a slick cleverness, but his mind is without depth or balance—not a wise man. At present he has not a large following but on the other hand he has no rival in his organisation.

Bone*, Dain, Peter Macdonald** are all over 73 and they are the office holders of the BMA. Dawson was elected President of the BMA for one year on the sudden death of their President. It has not worked; he is too old (he is now in his eightieth year) and they find him a source of embarrassment. His rather woolly letters with their cliches leave Hill impatient; indeed in the manner of his kind he makes no secret of the fact that he has little use for his President. There is no one in the House of Commons except Graham-Little*** who is anathema to almost everyone in the profession. In short there is no one who has any following to back up any effort that may be made to steady opinion.

'The results are obvious enough. There will always be a selfish section, I suppose that is true of most professions and there is a larger number of thoughtless doctors who give no time or consideration to these problems which indeed they dub contemptuously as the political side of medicine. And these two sections have done great harm by ill-considered and selfish demands. There has been no one to tell them plainly that doctors like other parts of the community must make their contribution to social betterment, that they cannot hold up a Government measure merely because if passed it would mean change in their lives and a break with habit. I have kept my peace so far because it is of some importance to preserve some kind of unity in the profession and in particular to try and keep the Royal Colleges in some kind of step with the BMA. But I think the time has come to say what I do say in my letter about Health Centres and the 100% issue.

'On the other hand advantage has been taken of this short-sightedness on the part of some doctors to misrepresent the attitude of the profession generally, to discredit it as parochial and selfish. This matters the more because in reality the interests of doctors and of the country are the same. If we are right in our fears the country will suffer as much as the medical profession. I have tried in my letter to bring home to the public what those fears are. The Government is proposing a medical service (it will by general consent become a whole-time service in something like fifteen years) and we fear that the quality of a man's work may suffer in a service, particularly in a service without promotion. We fear the effect on the type of man taking up medicine.

---

*Dr TW Bone of Luton.
**Dr Peter Macdonald of York
***Sir Ernest Graham-Little, MP for London University and physician to the Skin Department, St Mary's Hospital.

'The vast majority of doctors feel they cannot do their best work under local authorities. It is like asking Ulster to come under the South of Ireland. They show what they are afraid of when they go on to say "If we must be under local authorities let there be only twelve or thirteen large areas in England each based on a University so that the University atmosphere may prevail and not that of local politics". Everyone agrees that this is right (even the Ministry in private conversation) but the Ministry will not back these large areas because it means a battle with the dispossessed local authorities (145 in number) who would be superseded by such a decision.

'You will see how fundamental are these objections to the underlying proposals of the White Paper and yet how difficult it is to bring them home to the laity. That was why I wrote. I would gladly re-write the letter if I knew how to make my points more tersely. Perhaps I was wrong in feeling that there is more excuse for anyone who is long winded if he is speaking as head of the profession than for an individual expressing a personal view on an isolated aspect of the White Paper. I had 1 & 1/2 hours talk with Dain (Chairman of the BMA Council) at Birmingham a week ago, and a whole morning's discussion with Charles* who is I think the wisest man at the Ministry of Health. They did not know that I was writing to *The Times* and are in no way responsible for anything I say. I only mention them because my effusion was drawn from me by representation from more than one quarter that there was a good deal of irresponsible stuff going about, and that as leader of the profession for the moment it was my duty to steady things. Anyway if you feel after consideration that my screed is too long, I think we had better just drop it.
Yours sincerely.'

'A small point: unless my mathematics are wrong Dawson's letter contained 991 words and mine 976!'[18]

Charles's original 'letter to the editor' was then published, and he wrote again to Barrington-Ward:

'Thank you for being lenient to my inordinately long epistle. There was some evidence from the letters that I have had that the silent vote of the profession was waiting for something a little more detached than they had had. It requires a wise man to get the best out of people and I hope we shall find him.'[19]

---

*Dr John Charles, Deputy Chief Medical Officer, Ministry of Health.

Away from the College, Charles's patient continued to occupy his attention. Churchill, despite the burdens that he was carrying made a generous gesture to his physician at this time. Soon after their return from Marrakesh, Charles had received a letter from Mrs Churchill in which she referred to his having asked her if the Prime Minister would attend a luncheon given by the College. Mrs Churchill was able to say that Winston would like to do so. She added that she had been a long time finding out because it had been 'rather difficult to engage Winston's attention'.[20] In the same letter Mrs Churchill also asked if Charles could spare his book because Winston would like to continue to read it, and she too, having started it, would like to finish it. She ended by thanking Charles for his masterly handling of the situation during their recent travels. The luncheon was arranged for 2 March at the Savoy, Charles presided, and Churchill was the principal guest. *The Times* reported the tribute which Charles paid to his patient:

'When the surge and thunder of the Prime Minister's vast vocabulary are heard no more, history will recount how he spread abroad a sense of purpose and direction which gave men hope when there was really none. More than once I have been with him when news of shattering reverses was brought to him, and in my heart I have come to think of him as invincible.'[21]

These Churchillian periods were recognised as such by the Prime Minister. The audience could see, he said, that he and Charles divided their labours; Charles instructed him in the art of public speaking and he taught Charles how to cure pneumonia. Churchill also spoke of the government's plan for the new health service, making the point that in ordinary times of peace it would rivet and dominate the attention of the whole country.[21]

The records of many of those who were close to Churchill during the first six months of 1944 contain references to his tiredness.[22] Charles left no comment on this, but he did, on medical grounds, oppose what Brooke called the Prime Minister's 'attempts to start off wandering again',[23] attempts which Brooke opposed on military grounds. By now Churchill was well aware that his advisers took account of Charles's opinion on matters such as travel which might affect his health. These consultations required discretion. As Churchill was sickening with his pneumonia at Carthage in December 1943, Brooke had tried to persuade him not to go to Italy:

'I was beginning to make a little progress, and then foolishly said: "And what is more, Moran entirely agrees with me". He rose up on his elbow in the bed, shook his fist in my face and said: "Don't you get in league with that bloody old man".'[24]

In April 1944 Charles's finances were once more a source of worry to himself and his friends, and his friends did something about it. Beaverbrook sent him a cheque, which, after some indecision, he accepted, writing '. . . I know quite well I have done nothing to justify your generosity and that it is just your kindly consideration of my chaotic finances.'[25] And Bracken, who owned the monthly medical journal, *The Practitioner*, arranged for Charles to be offered the editorship[26] at a salary of £1000 a year.[27] Charles accepted the offer on the understanding that he would not have to begin for six months, until October. But it is hard to believe that he convinced himself that he would be able to cope with the ties and the load of work that the job would involve.

In April the three years' work on medical education done by the College's planning committee came to fruition. The report[28] was written by George Pickering, who, from the chair of medicine at St Mary's, continued unobtrusively to be one of Charles's strongest supporters at the College. Charles spoke of the main features of the report in a fifteen minute talk on the BBC on 2 May.[29] He told his listeners that the three main reforms proposed would do more for the health of the people than all the measures in the White Paper put together. These reforms were first that the field from which medical students were selected should be widened by making all university education free; second, unnecessary detail should be eliminated from the curriculum; and third there should be a compulsory resident period in a recognised hospital for one year at the end of the medical course. The first and last of these represented fairly advanced thinking in 1944.

With the landings by the allied forces in Normandy on D-day, 6 June, Charles felt an urgent need to have *The Anatomy of Courage* published. He wrote to Beaverbrook:

'Things have been going so quickly in the military line that I think if I don't get the book out I shall miss the bus. After the German War is over there may be a great reaction against war books of any kind, so that I fear I should get a move on.'[30]

On 26 July he sent the typescript to the publishing house of Constable.[31] This time, he heard within a month that it had been accepted.[32] Meanwhile he had been on the move again.

The prelude to Churchill's Italian journey in August involved an exchange of salvos between doctor and the patient about the need for Churchill to take the yellow anti-malaria tablets mepacrine (Atebrin). Charles had a presentiment that there would be trouble. He also by now had plenty of experience in handling his patient:

'I wanted to avoid, if I could, a pitched battle with the PM. After all, he has enough trouble, without my adding to it. He will always listen to advice if the reasoning seems to him sound—it is futile, of course to lay down the law—though I am careful to administer it in small doses and—this is important—I only give him the draught when we are alone.'[33]

In his book Charles gave an entertaining account of the battle, how he advised Churchill of the importance of his taking mepacrine in Italy and how Churchill reacted by phoning Buckingham Palace, from where the answer came back that the King hadn't taken anything at all when he visited Italy.[34] On this Charles commented:

'Winston is just incorrigible. He has only to press a bell to bring into the room the greatest malarial experts in the world; instead he turns his back on science and asks the King whether he ought to take mepacrine when in Italy.'[34]

Churchill also sent a Top Secret signal to General Alexander, who rubbished the idea of taking mepacrine and affirmed that neither he nor his staff took pills.[34] But Charles was totally prepared. Briefed by Major-General Biggam, the professor of tropical medicine at the Millbank military hospital in London, he was able to tell Churchill that experience in New Guinea between September 1943 and February 1944 had been that of 98 050 troops 3140 had been battle casualties and 47 534 had been evacuated sick; 28 909 of the latter had been evacuated because of malaria, more than nine times the battle casualties. Since then, in the campaign in New Guinea, with the use of mepacrine, the death rate from malaria among Australian troops had been reduced to one tenth of the normal rate for that region.[35] Churchill's response was immediate:

'Telephone message from Prime Minister to Lord Moran: In view of your salvo, all surrender unconditionally and hoist the yellow flag.'[36]

An unsigned later note in Charles's papers contained the comment that General Alexander's observations were in conflict with his own orders, the orders of the War Office, the experience of his chief consulting physician in Italy, the experimental evidence, and the official handbook issued to all officers in the Mediterranean Command.[37]

The Italian journey extended from 10 to 29 August.[38] The trip was made in the comfortable special York aircraft with the personal entourage, on this occasion consisting of Charles, Brigadier Jacob, Commander Thompson, Leslie Rowan, John Peck, Sawyers the valet, and a detective. Charles reflected how much safer their travels by air had become now that they flew over friendly territory. Churchill was on the move during most of the time they were away, and felt

Figure 15. Standing beside Churchill on a visit to the Vatican where Churchill had an audience with the Pope, August 1944. (Crown Copyright) (CMAC PP/CMW/P.73)

greatly restored by the change and movement and warm weather. Charles was with him except for two days when the Prime Minister went by sea to observe the landing of the allied forces in the south of France, and for one day when he visited the front line in Italy.[39] In his book Charles revealed little of himself over these few weeks except by introducing an account (already quoted) of his first visit to Monte Cassino 33 years before. His concern to keep in touch with doctors serving in the forces led him to visit the British 92nd General Hospital, where he talked to army medical officers, many of whom had come from a distance to find out what was happening at home in medical matters. Charles noted in his manuscript book:

'A considerable proportion of them had been plucked at a moment's notice from their practices which they had built up laboriously over the years and they were concerned [about] what was happening. Would they have to begin all over again? They asked all sorts of questions. I suppose they are merely a cross section of this army with their worries and domestic anxieties. It doesn't affect me in this way. War seems to fall like a curtain between me and the past and I do not expect things will be the same again in my lifetime. Sometimes I do wonder if I shall ever get back to my practice and if I don't what will happen. When you are young if you know your job and have a medical degree there is no real cause for concern but when you throw up your practice for half

a dozen years in the 60's most folk will think you have retired
and it may be less simple to begin again. But these thoughts only
come at long intervals and they don't stay; they are not a long
drawn out gnawing anxiety eating away at your peace of mind.
I suppose its simply a question of the way you're made.'[40]

The arrival back at Northolt aerodrome on the evening of
29 August provided a moment of unexpected drama. The York taxied
up to the group of people including Mrs Churchill, the Chiefs of Staff
and news correspondents, who had gathered to welcome the Prime
Minister. Out came Charles, who ran across to the car in which
Mrs Churchill was sitting.[41] Churchill had developed a high
temperature two hours before the plane landed. He was driven
quickly to London, where he was put to bed in the Annexe. Charles
arranged for nurses to move in and once more for Dr Geoffrey
Marshall to provide a second opinion. Within three days, with
M & B, Churchill's temperature was normal, and plans that had
already been made for him to confer yet again with Roosevelt were
not changed, for Charles thought that he would be able to meet the
schedule and leave on 5 September to cross the Atlantic by sea.

When Charles set out with Churchill, as planned, on 5 September
from Addison Road station in London to board the 'Queen Mary' at
Greenock, the medical back-up included not only himself but
Mrs Pugh, one of the nurses from St Mary's who had looked after
the Prime Minister before, and Brigadier Lionel Whitby,[42] a
pathologist whose studies on the early sulphonamide compounds had
contributed to the introduction of M & B 693 for clinical use just
before the war.[43] The mild attack of pneumonia that Churchill had
just had was known to few people, and the British Secretariat in
Quebec, for which the party was bound, were instructed that the
presence of Whitby and Mrs Pugh should not be disclosed.[42] On the
train journey north to Greenock Charles had Dorothy and their
14-year old son Geoffrey with him for company. Their plans for a
holiday in Scotland had been disrupted by Charles's comings and
goings, but thanks to Churchill they were now able to start off in
the PM's train. Charles could not have known, when he left them
on the deserted platform at Greenock, how little he was to see of
them in the next six months.

Added to Charles's continued concern about Churchill's heart,[44]
passing fevers, to which the Prime Minister was prone, had now
become a worry, lest they should herald another attack of
pneumonia. In the 'Queen Mary' en route for Quebec, Whitby restored
morale by finding a normal blood count during one such episode,[45]
and in Moscow a month later, during another episode, Charles was
moved to send a message to Cairo asking the doctors whom he had
brought in in consultation 10 months before in Carthage, and two
nurses, to stand by,[46] for he knew how vulnerable to criticism he

would be should Churchill again become seriously ill while travelling.[47] When they reached Quebec Churchill, despite his illnesses, generally appeared no more than older and tireder, but Charles and many others observed a striking change in Roosevelt when they reached Quebec:

'. . . he seemed to me to have lost a couple of stone in weight—you could have put your fist between his neck and his collar—and I said to myself then that men at his time of life do not go thin all of a sudden just for nothing.'[48]

The travellers reached Quebec on 11 September,[49] and they re-embarked in the 'Queen Mary' nine days later in New York.[50] In Quebec Charles stayed as Churchill did at the Citadel, the residence of the Governor-General, the Earl of Athlone, and life was unexciting.[51] After the inevitable banquet given by the Athlones on the night of their arrival, Charles found himself caught:

'When they had all gone the PM, who rested for two hours in the afternoon, was most reluctant to go to bed and in default of anyone else more militarily minded carted me off to the Map Room. However I slipped away to bed not long after midnight.'[52]

Apart from some golf Charles's days followed the now familiar pattern:

'The golf saves the trip. The Athlones, Roosevelts and [Churchills] have so far been feeding apart and the soldiery etc. are down in the Hotel [Chateau Frontenac] so that our mess is not very entertaining. I breakfast in bed and work all morning in my room and unless there is a function at night I turn in very early.'[51]

After the banquet, Charles noted only one other evening function on this trip, and from his point of view it was extraordinary:

'September 13, 1944. There was a men's dinner at the Citadel tonight; the President, the PM, Morgenthau [Henry Morgenthau, US Secretary of the Treasury], the Prof [Lord Cherwell], Admiral Leahy [Fleet-Admiral William Leahy, US Chief of Staff to C-in-C— the President], Leathers [Lord Leathers, Minister of War Transport], Ross McIntire [Admiral Ross McIntire, Personal physician to President Roosevelt] and I were all seated at a round table. How to prevent another war with Germany was the only subject of conversation.'[53]

Charles made notes of the dinner-table conversation, during which, according to him, the Americans maintained that Germany should not be allowed ships or the yards in which to build them, and Morgenthau wanted to close down the industrial heartland of the Ruhr. Germany should be made to return to a pastoral state. Charles later recorded this conversation in his book on Churchill,[53] but omitted the final comment written in his manuscript book:

'It is this kind of discussion which is so disquieting. Those taking part in it are plainly not big enough to think the thing out as far as that is possible and their mental processes when exposed in this fashion are anything but impressive. The dinner went on from 8.15 to 11.30 so we did not go to Mackenzie King's reception at the Frontenac after all.'[54]

Although unrecorded by him, Charles also attended a large dinner on the following night, which was noted by a fellow diarist, Jock Colville, then aged 29, one of the Prime Minister's secretaries whom Charles sometimes referred to as the understrappers. Colville, whose background included the Diplomatic Service and a period as a fighter pilot in the RAF, wrote:

'At dinner Lord Moran gave me a dissertation on the poor use we have made of our great scientific brains and resources during this war. Though Moran is vain, egotistic and exceedingly indiscreet, his judgment of people is often shrewd, though by no means always. He has a low opinion of Anthony Eden, simply based on his handling of the Turks in Cairo (and also of Pug). I cannot quite make up my mind if he is right about Eden. He is certainly wrong about Pug.'[55]

Back in London at the end of September Charles was soon faced with a conflict of interests and loyalties. On 12 October a special Comitia would meet to discuss the White Paper on a national health service. This Comitia was to consider two resolutions already proposed by Fellows which were critical of the government's plans. If ever Charles would need to use his influence in debate, this was the occasion. But no sooner was he back in London than Churchill found it imperative to go to Russia.[56] He wanted to see Stalin about the part Russia would play in the war against Japan, and about settling the future of Poland. It was therefore with misgiving that late on 7 October, 10 days after his return from Quebec, Charles joined Churchill, Ismay, John Martin and Commander Thompson at Northolt to fly via Naples to Moscow. Charles recorded how, as they approached their first stopover at Naples early next morning the PM sent for him:

'The man who called me had been put in charge of the oxygen cylinder. He said the PM had been having oxygen throughout the night although we had been flying no higher than 3000 feet, adding that the PM had asked him to take his pulse. I found Winston dozing. The mask had fallen off his face into the bed, the oxygen was hissing out while he held his cigar, which was still alight, in his hand.'[57]

On reaching their quarters in Moscow there was some light relief:

'This is a big house, but has only two bath rooms, one of which is reserved for the PM. My bedroom has four great windows overlooking the pinewood, they are all open. When we got here this morning there was no Sawyers. He had stayed behind to look after the luggage and did not turn up for an hour and a half. Presently I heard the PM's voice calling "Sawyers, Sawyers!" I went to his room and found him sitting in his bath with his hand on one of the taps. "Where is Sawyers?" he demanded petulantly. "I can't get the bath hot enough". There were six taps, two were obviously for the shower bath, but why six? They were labelled in Russian. I deliberated and at last turned a tap. A great gush of icy water came out with great pressure, hitting the PM in the middle of his back. He gave a shriek. I went off to look for help. Everything else rather palatial.'[58]

In addition to making copious notes of conversation outside the conference rooms, Charles had opportunities on this visit to be a tourist:

'Thursday October 12. This afternoon I went with the CIGS to a 16th century monastery, now uninhabited, where Stalin's first wife is buried. The CIGS is a keen sightseer. I like him more as I see more of him. He lives for the day when he can get out of uniform and resume his country pursuits, especially photographing birds. He is full of a new camera he has been given. He hates the war and all its ways, a little unusual for the senior soldier of his country in a world war.'[59]

Charles also recorded visiting Leningrad, walking through the Kremlin and attending the ballet. In his writings, he tended to use descriptions of outings such as these to indicate his association with a particular individual, creating the impression of an intimate outing à deux, whereas they were often substantial expeditions in which he was invited to take part.[61] He was rarely a lone sightseer.

The only medical alarm on this trip was when Churchill briefly developed a fever,[46] but Charles's concerns about leaving the college turned out to be justified for when he returned to Moscow on 14 October from his 24-hour visit to Leningrad, he found disquieting mail from London. There had been a long debate in the

Comitia two days before, and the motion on the White Paper put
forward by the College officers had been lost:

'That means that, in my absence, my Government at the College
has been defeated. There can be no doubt that my frequent
absences from England, at a time when the medical services are
being transformed, are exciting more and more criticism. Many
Fellows of the College feel that I am so much away that the College
has not taken a proper part in countering Willink's proposals. I
am always abroad, they say, when it is being discussed at the
Ministry. There is a feeling, too, that I might be behind the White
Paper and that I may indeed have inspired it. It is natural that
this should be said, because I am always travelling with the PM.
We are bound to talk it over, people say, and it is inevitable, since
the White Paper is anathema to most of the profession, that I am
the target for adverse criticism. While many doctors are saying
these things, a good many laymen are beginning to blame me
because I allow the PM to go on these journeys. If I took a stronger
line, they say, he would stay at home.

'It is rather distracting, steering a course between my two
conflicting loyalties, but it is plain that I must not abandon
Winston, whatever happens at the College. After all, it is my job;
the PM has enough on his plate without my adding my little
worries. I am only sorry for Dorothy. She has to sit at home and
watch the storm gathering. She asks: "Can anything be done?"
And the answer is, "Nothing".'[62]

Charles was back in London on Sunday 22 October[63] and took the
chair at the Comitia four days later.[64] The motion that had been
passed two weeks before in his absence was that the College did not
believe that the proposals in the White Paper would lead to the
improvements in the health services that the government expected;
the proposals would lead to a whole-time State Medical Service, the
doctor-patient relationship would be changed to the detriment of the
patient, and voluntary hospitals would disappear.[65] Charles opened
the discussion by saying that he had not had time to talk to many
Fellows about the meeting held while he was in Moscow, and he then
spoke at length on the medical-political scene. Following his address
he was for the first time vigorously criticised for his interpretation
of what the College really felt. The attack was led by a formidable
adversary, a senior Fellow close to his own age, FMR Walshe*.
Walshe, like Charles, had a gift for words. He also had a quick mind,

---

*Dr FMR (later Sir Francis) Walshe, physician to the National Hospital, Queen
Square.

and an ability to muster trenchant and stinging arguments in debate.[66] A good deal of emotion was released in the ensuing discussion, which ended with Charles explicitly accepting that the motion that had been passed was the policy of the College. Charles was then out of the firing line for three months, until the Comitia next met in January. But if he was looking forward to a peaceful Christmas, he was disappointed. On Christmas Eve he was sitting by the fire after tea in the cottage at Harefield when the telephone rang. It was one of the secretaries at Chequers who said the PM wanted to speak to him:

> 'The PM said "I'm off to G." I asked when? "Tonight" he answered. When he had rung off I asked Jane (Dorothy) where G was. She suggested Gibraltar. "We must know because of clothes" she said. "There's nothing for it but to drive over to Chequers and find out something definite".'[67]

On that morning the black-out restrictions on the use of car headlights had been removed so Dorothy and Charles, instead of groping their way, swept along lanes that were thrown up brilliantly before them for the first time in over five years. 'G.' turned out to be Greece, which, Charles commented, sounded fun. And so, at Northolt in the small hours of Christmas morning, he boarded the Prime Minister's new luxurious American Skymaster. The party was made up this time of Churchill, Anthony Eden, Pierson Dixon (Eden's Principal Private Secretary), Colville, Tommy Thompson, two typists—Miss Layton and Miss Holmes—a detective and Sawyers.[69] After a brief stop at Naples they landed late on Christmas afternoon outside Athens, and were transferred by armoured cars and then by launch to the cruiser HMS 'Ajax', which was lying off shore. For the next few days Charles resumed his role as a chronicler, this time of what was later described as one of the most bizarre and dramatic episodes of Churchill's life.[70] Churchill's avowed intention was to 'square the Greek entanglement' which involved reconciling the official Greek government in exile in London and the left-wing organisation which had been conducting guerrilla operations during the recently ended German occupation. Troops of this organisation were now sporadically shelling Athens where, despite the presence of the British liberating force, street fighting between Greek factions was still going on. Not only was gunfire audible; it was close by, and shells straddled 'Ajax' as the Prime Minister and his party, including Charles, were waiting to go ashore to a conference on the afternoon of Boxing Day.[71] There was still sporadic shooting when Charles accompanied the Prime Minister ashore on the next day.[72] Churchill was nevertheless set upon reviewing the positions of the British occupying troops, and he was also determined that Charles should see the Acropolis:

Figure 16. With General HRLG Alexander in Athens, December 1944. (Crown copyright) (CMAC PP/CMW/P.74)

'We were sitting at luncheon with the Ambassador and his wife when there was a knock at the door. It opened and a para-troop officer saluted and stood to attention. "I have come" he said, "for Lord Moran". It was all like an incident in one of Sean O'Casey's plays, where some wretched man is taken for a ride and bumped off. Alex turned to me: "Where are you going, Charles?" "The Acropolis, I suppose" "Can I come with you?" No armoured car was waiting, but a local touring car. We were apparently to see the Acropolis with an armed escort of two paratroop officers. When we got to the Parthenon Alex went to speak to a machine gun section stationed in a position to command the entrance. One of the paratroop officers came to me. "It's a lovely spot" he said. "We have got all Athens in our arc of fire." As we left, Alex said: "I propose we send the car away and walk. I want a little exercise. What about it, Charles?" Halfway to the Embassy, Alex stopped. "Do you see that little temple there?" pointing to a small building about a quarter of a mile from the road. "I have never been there; let's go and have a look at it." We started off, but one of the paratroop men came up. "I don't think, sir, you ought to go there. There was a man killed there this morning; there are some snipers overlooking it." "Oh, nonsense" Alex broke in, "if we go that way"—pointing to a short detour—"it's quite all right." Our guard made one more attempt a little further on to dissuade Alex, but to no purpose. We loitered in the little temple for some time.'[73]

On 28 December the party set off for home. Before the plane took off from Hassani airfield outside Athens Charles opened a suitcase and took out a pullover which he was surprised to see was not his. Thinking he had inadvertently packed a pullover belonging to the officer whose cabin he had used in HMS 'Ajax', he asked Admiral Mansfield, who was seeing the Prime Minister off, to return the garment as soon as possible to the ship. It was not until after take-off that Charles, taking a closer look at the suitcase, realised he had given away Harold Macmillan's favourite pullover.[74]

Dorothy was with Mr Churchill to greet the travellers when they landed at Bovingdon airfield outside London on the afternoon of 29 December.[75]

Chapter 15

The Anatomy of Courage and a New Diary

Charles's manuscript book was largely a record of his travels, with notes on conversations and thumb-nail sketches of the individuals he met. However, in January 1945, after his return from Athens, several entries reflected his activities at home.

> '*January 1*—Danced the year out at the Coxs. Geoffrey got early into his first boiled shirt and dinner jacket (borrowed). Between us we got his black tie into shape. What fun it is growing up.'[1]

The remainder of Monday's entry was a diatribe about Sir Alfred Webb-Johnson, President of the Royal College of Surgeons, with whom Charles found collaboration exceedingly difficult. The two Colleges, of physicians and surgeons, had long been coming together to manage the conjoint qualifying diploma of LRCP MRCS. Now they shared an interest in planning the consultant services, and in the possibility of both Colleges occupying a new common site. As personalities, Webb-Johnson, who was outgoing, dogmatic and companionable, and Charles, were poles apart. Webb-Johnson loathed Charles, and Charles had no time for him.[2] After they had met on 1 January, Charles noted:

> 'At the Committee of Management, Webb-Johnson, not propitiated at all by his Baronetcy, was at his most mulish self. What an oaf the fellow is . . . It's very difficult to work with people like this and yet never more necessary with the negotiations with the Minister of Health about to open. I came home in the fog, moody and inclined to wonder why I should have to conduct our battle with the Ministry with two such allies as Alfred and Charles Hill of the BMA.'[1]

Another entry in the manuscript book concerned Mrs Churchill, who had been invited to visit Russia in recognition of her efforts in having raised six million pounds for the Aid to Russia fund. She would be away a month:

> '*January 2*—Mrs C is always either up or down. She telephoned me when the pendulum was at the top asking me to go with her. "I'll never forgive you if you fail me" she said lightly, "we'll have a whale of a time . . ." Now when I say I'm not certain I can get away she isn't a bit pleased. It is devilish awkward being away for

months at a time. College matters get neglected and my income from practice has fallen from £5000 to £70 . . . I don't think the PM has the least idea I used to practice as a physician before these journeys made my GP supporters look elsewhere when they needed a second opinion. But I've taken a job and must go through with it now.'[3]

This entry ended on a more cheerful note:

'Tonight Geoffrey's reports (from Eton) came. I read and re-read them three times before bed-time, each time getting a bigger and bigger kick out of them.'[3]

On 9 January Charles called on Churchill in the morning and was called back to see him at 5.15 pm at the Annexe because he had a cold. Having asked Sawyers to leave the room, Churchill told Charles about a planned trip, this time to Yalta in the Crimea.[4] So Charles was for once forewarned of his next absence from London.

The following page in the manuscript book bears the heading: The Provost of Eton. My disappointment:

'*January 13*—John writes Henry Martin has been appointed Provost of Eton . . . I wanted this job desperately. But I don't suppose my name even came up and if it did I'm sure it wasn't considered for a moment. I have come to think that Eton is for the intelligent boy a marvellous training. I'd love to introduce some of the first hundred to the great world. To get them to talk, there in the Provost's Lodge under the Gainsboroughs.* I have spent so much of my life in the rather squalid atmosphere of the competitive life that I have a deep yearning to end my days in lovely old buildings surrounded by young people. I'm only really happy with them. I know too I could have done the job . . .'[5]

Charles's yearning to end his days in an academic environment surrounded by young people had persisted through the war years. The Regius chair at Oxford having eluded him, and the Cambridge one not going his way, he really did want the Eton appointment.[6] The fact that statutes determined that only an Etonian could become Provost seems to have passed him by. While Charles was in Moscow in October Dorothy had solicited Brendan Bracken's interest and he had pointed this out.[7] Charles had also unfolded his plan to Colville on the flight home from Athens on 29 December.[8] Since the appointment was made by the Crown, Charles asked him whether he should go straight to Churchill and ask for it, and Colville had

---

*Charles got it wrong. They were Romneys.

said no. He was sceptical about Charles's protestations that the proposal was being forced on him by friends, and he noted in his diary, but without giving reasons, that Charles would be in every way unsuitable. Whether Colville's judgement was right, or whether Charles's own perception that he would have done a good job was right, was not put to the test. He never, in his old age, became head of an academic institution.

When the College met on 17 January after an interval of three months Charles ran into more trouble. The College Council presented a document entitled *New Machinery for New Tasks*. From its style it was evident that Charles was the author.[9] The paper sought to meet criticisms that the College had not done enough in the public arena. It began with the theme on which the Fellows had heard Charles speak before, the abdication by the College, before and early in the war, of any part in the government of the profession. It then outlined what had been done since, it summarised the resolutions bearing on a national health service which the College had passed in the previous two years, and it added a new resolution, that the College did not desire to oppose the government's intention to make a comprehensive medical service available to the entire population. The discussion ended with the Comitia congratulating the Council on its report,[10] but not before blood had been spilt. It was the opening passage that caused the trouble:

'*January 17*—A bad day. The Special Comitia summoned to discuss Willink's White Paper fell foul of the first two paragraphs of Council's paper which they thought implied criticism of Dawson and Hutchison when President. I think there was something in this. It was all true, but Englishmen hate personal criticism and when it appears to be lacking in generosity their hatred boils up. The result was the report on a record of 3½ years far-sighted planning came in for nothing but abuse. . . . Geoffrey Evans* began, Horder carried on and finally Walshe said the College was on the wrong track in these political activities. We ought to return to our real task, the promotion of knowledge. In the end these passages were referred back to the Council but not before the faction, which is out for my blood, had had a field day. Lord Horder spoke six times: he complained of bad taste in these paragraphs. We could hardly have been punished more effectively than by being admonished by Lord H. on taste.'[5]

Entries over the following days record a controversy in a different quarter, a battle of wills over the management of Churchill's laryngitis. During one consultation:

---

*Dr Geoffrey Evans, physician to St Bartholomew's Hospital.

'. . . Sawyers arrived with a jug full of hot water and Friar's Balsam. The PM began inhaling it. After five minutes he pushed it away and lit a big black cigar. I said to him you aren't very logical . . .'[11]

But the week was not a complete write-off. On the Saturday Dorothy and Charles went to Teddington to see St Mary's play Coventry, who up till then had not been beaten:

'The hospital halves and three quarters are all very fast and have football in their heads. It's a lovely sight, like good polo. . . . In the end we won comfortably by 8-3.'[12]

Any hopes that Charles may have had that things at the College would quieten down after the stormy special Comitia were quickly dashed. For some time the Royal College of Surgeons had been pressing the physicians to join them in building on a common site at Lincoln's Inn Fields,[13] and this was to be discussed at a Comitia on 25 January. In the early part of the month letters supporting the idea appeared in *The Times* from Dawson and from members of what emerged at the 17 January special Comitia as leaders of an anti-Moran group. These letters drew a response from Charles, published under the heading 'Views of the RCP', in which he questioned the wisdom of the proposal to move the College. Geoffrey Evans, Horder, Tidy and Walshe promptly wrote pointing out that Charles's response could not represent current opinion for the College was yet to meet to discuss the matter.[13] Against this background of public discord on what was really a domestic issue, the special Comitia met and Charles made an opening statement. Vehement criticism followed, but on this occasion there was also vehement defence of both Charles personally and his policy.[14] These two January Comitias showed that Charles, by being away from London so often in the last six months, had lost the close touch with his constituency that was necessary if he was to lead the Fellows along the way he had foreshadowed when he originally had been elected. Yet exasperatingly, with the question of his re-election coming up again in two months, he had to go away once more, for two days after the second Comitia the PM decided he would take the first good weather to fly to Malta on his way to Yalta.[15] As a result Charles would miss negotiations that had been arranged at the Ministry of Health.

Charles's account of the Yalta conference, which involved the Prime Minister, Roosevelt and Stalin, each with a large supporting staff, constituted the longest wartime chapter in his book on Churchill.[16] The Prime Minister's personal party, which left on the evening of 29 January,[17] included Churchill's daughter Sarah. 'Oh Lord! There we go again', she thought[18] when, an hour after take-off, Charles was roused by Sawyers with the news that Churchill had a temperature.[19] At Malta in the morning Charles arranged for a blood count to be done while Churchill stayed on board the aircraft. The result did not suggest an impending attack of pneumonia, and the anxiety was soon over. When, at 11 pm, the patient, now on board HMS 'Orion' and feeling better, started to play bezique with Harriman, Charles crept off to bed.[20] Charles found Malta very tranquil after the alarms and excursions of the College and set to work to tidy up his last year's presidential address and to prepare his next one.[21] He was disappointed to find that only Cadogan had read his *Sunday Times* articles on *The Anatomy of Courage* and asked Dorothy to send him copies so that he could pass them round.

From Malta the party flew to the Crimea, where their journey ended with a long drive over bad roads to the Black Sea resort of Yalta. The conference ran from 3 February and the return journey included a three-day stay in the back-up ship 'Franconia', off Sebastopol, and brief visits to Athens, Alexandria and Cairo.[22] Charles as usual made notes on the scenes and conversations outside the conference rooms. Although he was accommodated with Churchill and his small personal staff in the Vorontzov Palace, bedtime sessions with the Prime Minister were not a feature of this trip. And the only strictly medical call on Charles's time must have taken him back to his First World War days, for the Prime Minister and other members of the British delegation, as well as the Americans, were bitten by bed bugs. Fortunately the Americans had sanitary squads with them and Charles was able to enlist their help.[23]

On reaching Yalta, Roosevelt's health was once more commented on among the British. He appeared to be in a sorry state,[24] and people kept asking Charles what might be the cause.[25] None of Charles's writings indicate that he and the President's doctors exchanged confidences about their patients. Dr Howard G Bruenn, who looked after Roosevelt from March 1944 until his death a year later, had no knowledge of Churchill's health during the war years,[26] and all that Charles knew at this time of Roosevelt's health was what he had learnt from his Boston friend Dr Roger Lee just before leaving London. Lee had written telling him that Roosevelt had had heart failure eight months previously.[27] From what Charles observed now, he doubted if the President was fit for his job at the Conference.[26] On the second day at Yalta he noted in his manuscript book:

'There was a good deal of talk last night about the afternoon conference at the President's House. Everyone thought the President had gone to bits physically. But it was not only his physical deterioration that was noted. He intervened in the discussion very little, his mouth drooped and he seemed to have little grip of things. He has always been short of knowledge about the subject under discussion but his shrewdness has covered this up. Now, they say, the shrewdness is gone and there is nothing left.'[28]

By contrast with Roosevelt's situation, there was no suggestion in Charles's notes that his own patient was in less than good health; when, on the last day at Yalta, Charles found him moody, it was the President's health, not his own, that occupied Churchill's mind.[29]

During the Yalta conference there was plenty of time for sightseeing, not only for Charles but also for the service people, for the conference was essentially political and the military hung about waiting for calls which never came.[30] So Charles moved round in a group which included the chiefs of staff and other senior officers, with most of whom he was by now well acquainted and on easy terms. At Yalta Charles also came to know Sir Edward Bridges, who, as Secretary of the Cabinet since before the war, had become one of the most significant figures in the machinery of the wartime government. Bridges had not previously been a member of one of Churchill's overseas expeditions, and on the day after they arrived at Yalta, Charles noted:

'I had a talk with Bridges this afternoon. He does not exactly radiate geniality and when I used to run into him at No. 10 I thought he took unnecessary pains to frown on a stranger. But I find this is all a mask. His uncompromising integrity, his dislike of intrigue of any kind and his rugged honesty are known to everyone. But what I've seen since we left England is quite new to me and I suspect to many others. He is like a school boy in his eagerness and his unspoilt pleasure in sightseeing. He got out of bed at 5 am in the aeroplane to see the isles of Greece. I've seen a good deal of him and I like what I've seen. He has a good headpiece and thinks for himself.'[23]

Later in the week Charles recorded a conversation that he had with Bridges over lunch. The topic was the art of selecting men:

'I said the first essential was to be interested in people. The PM for example knew nothing about the people who served him because he was not interested in them. He liked having old faces about him but never gave a thought to what will become of them in life, what they are like, how they are made up. When people spoke of doctors with a flair for medicine they only meant doctors who noticed things other people had missed. That was the secret of the gift for the measurement of men; he saw and heard what others had not observed or heard.'[31]

Bridges, according to Charles, said he was interested in all this because one of his new duties as head of the Civil Service was to pick the right men for certain posts. Charles continued:

> 'I said if he wanted to learn about the art of choosing winners he ought to begin now. He had to overcome the Englishman's distaste for pulling people to pieces. He must learn that Alexander was a lovable fellow but only a third rate general, . . . that 'Pug' Ismay was an adroit courtier but a hypocrite . . .'[31]

Given the freedom from reserve with which Charles illustrated his thesis, the Secretary of the Cabinet could understandably have been led to agree with Colville's comment that Charles was extraordinarily indiscreet.[32]

Clark Kerr was another old acquaintance whom Charles met at Yalta, and when the ambassador gave him an account of the speech that Stalin had made when proposing the Prime Minister's health at a dinner after their arrival, Charles scribbled down Clark Kerr's words as he spoke.[33] Charles made no secret of his recording of the passing scene, and he was interested in the expectations that others had of writing up their experiences. On the day on which he visited Balaclava someone commented (Ismay in one of Charles's notes,[34] & 'one of the secretaries' in another[35]), that Maurice Hankey, who had been secretary to the Committee of Imperial Defence in the First World War, then Secretary to the Cabinet until Bridges's appointment in 1938, had sought permission to publish his diary. This had been refused on the grounds that if the secretary of the Cabinet or anyone else were allowed to publish what he had heard in an official capacity, no Cabinet minister would feel safe.

> 'Whereupon Portal asked Bridges, "How far could I publish a book? For example, could I print Stalin's remarkable speech at the beginning of the Tehran conference?" Bridges thought not. Anyone in the inner circle could get £25 000 any day for his Memoirs. Portal made no bones to me about his intention to write a book after the war. He had plainly kept the necessary documents and diary. The CIGS too told me his first work after the war must be to arrange his notes and papers. He too, the most reticent of Ulstermen, had a book up his sleeve.'[35]

At this time Charles does not appear to have decided what his own role would be as a post-war memoir writer. But he was unremitting in his note taking. During his three-day stay on board the 'Franconia' after the Yalta conference his writings covered eight-and-a-half closely written pages of his manuscript book. Annotations at the tops of the pages reflect the entries, many of which were records of Churchill's conversation: PM's relief conference is over; PM on Greece; PM on Stalin (his word is his bond); PM on Jack Lawson (of Labour Party); PM on religion; PM regrets passing of ritual; PM on Max; and so on.

On leaving the 'Franconia' Churchill's party flew to Athens and there Charles saw at last the fruits of his note-taking labours begun 30 years before in the Ypres Salient—a bound copy of *The Anatomy of Courage*:

'Found the Mosquito had brought the mail to Athens and it was waiting for us at the embassy. There at last was the book, bound and ready to be launched on its precarious voyage. The binding, print and paper were better than I had expected. How many years has it been on the stocks?

'Strangely enough though I have wanted to do this job well more than I have ever wished to bring off anything else in life, now that it is done [and] I ought to be on tenter hooks how it will be received, it is hardly in my mind at all. The thing is done and can't be undone. What fun it has been in writing! What a constant source of comfort and interest when things weren't going too well in the competitive world in which I live. It has been my child and now it has thrown off parental control and must face the world on its merits, if it has any.'[36]

In his book, interspersed with diary entries written in dug-outs and in billets behind the lines in France and Flanders between 1914 and 1917, were Charles's reflections which had given rise to his main conclusions: courage is a moral quantity; courage is an act of renunciation which must be made not once but many times by the power of the will; courage is will-power. And, most importantly, courage is seen as capital, men start with different quantities of it and when it is spent they are finished. Rest can restore some of the capital, but in war of the kind that Charles knew so well men wore out like clothes. Perhaps not surprisingly, given these conclusions, there was no indication that *The Anatomy of Courage* was a topic of conversation at the dinner given for Churchill at the British Embassy on that evening. After all, Churchill was impatient with 'all this psychological nonsense'; the picture painted of what goes on in a soldier's head would discourage the young soldiers; it might affect recruiting; if a soldier did not do his duty he ought to be shot.[37] Rather, the page in Charles's manuscript book describing the evening was headed 'The PM's conversation wears us down.'

'The PM was in terrific form after dinner (8.45 pm-12.45) and we had a long sitting. But people are no longer accustomed to these drawn out sessions. Ismay was practically asleep from 11 onwards. Martin's face for the last hour gave no sign that he was listening. The Air Force ADC confessed at the end that he could hardly keep awake. And so forth. Yet here was the big man of the conflict talking (practically a monologue) for nearly four hours on every subject without any reserve, an entertainment and an experience which millions in GB [Britain] would give their right hand to add to their memories, and nearly everyone wanted to go to bed and wondered how much longer he would go on and whether they could decently break up the party.'[36]

Charles could not have been sure of it, but this was the last of those wartime evenings when he sat for hours with the captains of war as part of the travelling Prime Minister's captive audience. The evening ended, as others had before, with a departure for an airfield, this time *en route* for Cairo and home, where Charles was able to read how *The Anatomy of Courage* had been received. The two extracts published in *The Sunday Times* in January had brought him letters of congratulation, as well as a cheque for £500, and now the book itself was widely reviewed. It contained 'descriptions which can be set beside the best passages in war literature'. It was 'profound and well written', and one passage on Death was 'not unworthy to be compared with Bacon and Browne in its quiet reflective dignity'.[38] These were heartwarming terms indeed for one who had always wanted to be not a doctor but a writer. At a more personal level, Charles received a note from Brendan Bracken which epitomised the sentiments of many thoughtful people in Britain as the European war was drawing to a close and a weary country with empty coffers was faced with implementing the Beveridge plan. A lot of courage would be needed in the years ahead.[39]

The letters that Charles wrote to Dorothy from Yalta showed that he was anxious, and he brought his worries home with him. The presidential election at the College was due again in a few weeks, and his latest absence had provided yet more ammunition for his critics. It occurred to him that some further public recognition, perhaps another honour, for his continuing services to the Prime Minister would silence a good deal of the criticism but it was hard to see how this could come about.[40] He was also uneasy about John, whose ship, he thought, might be sent out east to join in the battles yet to be fought with Japan. Planning far ahead as usual, Charles had decided to try to secure a career for John in the diplomatic service after the war, and as a first step he wondered about pulling strings to have John sent to study languages in order to become an interpreter.[41] As things turned out, these problems solved themselves. On 26 March Charles was re-elected President with 127 votes to Horder's 60[42], and John was not posted to the far east.

On 12 April Roosevelt died, and Charles heard of this in the small hours of the next morning, when the *Daily Mirror* roused him from his sleep to ask him if he had seen the president professionally, to which the answer was no.[43] Later in the day he was asked to write something personal about Roosevelt for *The Sunday Times*, and he noted: 'I said I would think it over but on reflection I decided to refuse. I fancy people might think I was advertising my fine acquaintances.'[43]

Charles took a firm line at this time on professional publicity. In May, learning that an article entitled 'They Reach the Top', which included references to himself as well as to Horder and Webb-Johnson, was being written for a weekly journal, he intervened and had the references to himelf withdrawn. He told the editor that he believed that publicity of this kind was harmful to the best interests of the profession.[44] Charles also continued to stand firm on another matter which he saw as one of principle. Sir Edward Bridges, having telephoned and asked him to call on him at the Treasury, told him that the Prime Minister had been concerned about the time he spent abroad away from his work. He knew that Charles got a salary of £1200 per annum as a consultant to the Ministry of Health, for which he was not able to do very much. Taking this into account, the Prime Minister had suggested that the income might be made up to £2000 or £2500 a year for five years. The stipend would come from public funds and would not be subject to income tax. Charles's immediate reaction was that he didn't like the idea and he telephoned Bridges on the following day and confirmed his decision. He agreed that Bridges should tell Churchill he was touched by his suggestion but was against it.[43] A few weeks later Churchill himself tackled Charles about this. Charles had paid him a routine visit at the Annexe and Churchill, as he often did when Charles called, made some comments on matters that were in his mind, on this occasion problems with de Gaulle*, and Stalin's recent attitude:

---

*General Charles de Gaulle, leader of the Free French Forces.

'. . . Then he said suddenly "Bridges tells me you wont accept what we propose. You must. This is a public matter. It doesn't come out of my pocket." I asked him if I might put my case and he said no, but I did. I told him I didn't want any reward, that it was my war job and that this would spoil the flavour of it for me. Then, when he was obstinate, I told him that I had had to give up practice for five years on account of these journeys (I might have said practice had given me up), it only meant I must do some money grubbing after the war. I had gone to Ayr to see a patient and had been given a cheque for four hundred pounds. Like some of the lawyers a doctor in the public eye could, if he wanted, make a lot of money in a short time. "If you are given that for going to Scotland what ought you to be given for going to Moscow", he retorted. Then I saw he was tired of the subject and was eying his papers so I took my departure—but not before he said Stalin had suggested July 15 for a meeting. . . . "Where is it going to be?" I ventured. "Berlin" he answered at once, "probably in a suburb. You'll come, won't you? There'll be plenty of bugs there."'[45]

This conversation took place just after the war in Europe had ended. The time of the announcement of the day on which victory was to be celebrated had been uncertain because of the wish for coordination between Britain, the United States and Russia. When in the later afternoon of 7 May Charles called at the Annexe to learn from the secretaries' room, no precise information was to be had and he was beset by a new anxiety. Believing there would be a cease-fire that night, and not wanting John to be mixed up in a scrap a minute after midnight, he asked Commander Pym, who was in charge of the Map Room, about HMS 'Oribi'. Pym told him that the ship might be despatched to Copenhagen to try to take over two German cruisers before the Russians captured them. So he went home uncomforted.[46] Later he heard that victory was to be celebrated on the following day, 8 May, and on that afternoon he took Dorothy and Harold Boldero to the Library of the House of Lords to hear the Prime Minister's broadcast. When the speech was over, a peer next to Charles remarked that there was no allusion in it to God. Charles reflected that there was no doubt in Winston's mind to whom the credit was due.[47] Charles then joined in procession with his fellow peers to Westminster Abbey, where a thanksgiving service was held. He found it neither impressive nor moving, but with his eyes about him as usual, he observed:

'. . . [that] once when the Dean prayed that God would grant that we should "care for him who shall have borne the battle and for his widow", a Roman matron facing me bent her head and I knew again what victory has meant for many.'[48]

The victory in Europe brought little immediate change in Charles's life. He realised, as others did who were close to Churchill, that the Prime Minister was very tired, and this was not simply because, with Mrs Churchill away visiting Russia, it was after 3 am before he went to bed.[49] The fact was that enormous problems still confronted him including the settlement of Europe, the continuing conflict with Japan, and doubt about Russia's intentions.[50] But Charles thought the most perplexing matter for him was the general election which he would have to contest in July, and he was concerned that Churchill was too weary to think out a policy for the reconstruction of the country after the war. Furthermore, he observed:

'To have had arbitrary powers for five years to speak for Britain without anybody's leave or question, and then to wait cap in hand on the doorstep, irks him.'[49]

Charles stuck to his policy of not adding to Churchill's burdens by arguing with him, but when the PM sent him the part of the Conservative election manifesto that dealt with the new health service, with a covering note from Leslie Rowan asking for his comments as soon as possible, he entered the fray. Charles found the document full of platitudes:

'So I sat down and wrote a short criticism ending sardonically "I trust and believe the PM will carry even his present Minister of Health on his back to Victory." After lunch I took it to the Annexe' . . . He [the Prime Minister] read what I had written in grim silence, my quips did not seem to amuse him. "The doctors aren't going to dictate to the country, they tried that with Lloyd George."* I didn't answer. I wondered who had put this sort of stuff into his head. Then he folded up my short memorandum and handed it to Assheton [Chairman of the Conservative Party] who put it into his pocket. So my wisdom and my remarks about Willink passed into an official file.'[45]

When Churchill challenged Charles and asked him how he would alter the manifesto, Charles said that health centres ought to be in it. As he had said as long ago as 1942, in his broadcast to Sweden,[51] he believed one of the weaknesses of British medicine was the solo general practice. To remedy the isolation of general practitioners he wanted them to be grouped in health centres in which each doctor would have a chance to develop special interests

---

*David Lloyd George, British statesman who introduced the National Insurance Act of 1911.

and in which basic facilities for investigation, like blood tests, would be available. He saw health centres as an extension of the collegiate atmosphere of the teaching hospitals. As the British Medical Association had dug in against his zeal for these centres, he thought he ought to warn the PM what might happen, but he had exhausted his attention. The Prime Minister, he remarked, was in a bad temper.[45]

Six weeks after the war ended, St Mary's Hospital celebrated its centenary, and Charles was cast in one of the leading roles in an attempt to raise funds for the reconstruction and extension of the hospital buildings.[52] Charles was not optimistic about the fund-raising:

> '*Tuesday 26 June*
> This week St Mary's is busy celebrating its centenary. The occasion is seized to raise funds, all the celebrations are designed to that end. An appeal for two million pounds has been launched. The times are against us, the future is too uncertain to tempt men to divest themselves of what wealth they retain; the taxation too strips them of any feeling that they ought to support charitable objects. But penicillin is a godsend. Men, who might argue if I support St Mary's other institutions will fall on me, can subscribe out of gratitude to Fleming or as a thanks offering for its services to wounded soldiers, without feeling they have no answer when other hospitals assail them.'[53]

The appeal opened with a concert at the Albert Hall with Yehudi Menuhin and the London Symphony Orchestra conducted by Paul Paray. The Hall was sold out, Lord Camrose* paid all expenses, and the appeal received £5000. Charles's diary note was headed 'Jane [Dorothy] speaks to 6000 people in the Albert Hall and brings the house down.' It was Dorothy's task to thank Menuhin and Paray and others who had performed without recompense. Charles wrote:

> 'She is so in tune with what Menuhin said through his fiddle that her little speech seemed not so much a break in the music as part of it. She stood very still and spoke very quietly and said: "Perhaps they will accept this very inadequate tribute of our gratitude not only for what they have given us tonight but for an even greater service to this distracted and angry world. In the midst of the shabby utility of war they have kept alive for us the things of beauty and loveliness, the eternal things of the spirit, which transcend all bitterness and faction." '[54]

---

*Lord Camrose, proprietor of *The Sunday Times* and *Daily Telegraph*.

It was Charles's turn to perform on the following night, at a dinner at the Mansion House at which Brendan Bracken, who had recently become First Lord of the Admiralty, was the principal speaker. Bracken was weary with electioneering and not in good form, and when Charles followed him with a carefully prepared speech, he found that his 'mild quips fell off the target like blunt darts'.[54] He was much more comfortable on the next day, when the Queen, who was President of the hospital, spoke in the medical school library, and he replied. He was followed by Almroth Wright, now 84, who spoke without a note and, Charles thought, spoke well. That day ended with a ball at the Dorchester run by the students. Charles rescued his white tie and tails for the occasion from a box in the garage where they had been for six years, and an ounce of caviar which Dorothy had kept in the refrigerator since his return from Yalta was auctioned for £13. The next day, a little wearily, he pulled himself out of bed to call on Churchill.[55]

Polling day for the general election was a week away (5 July) but the result would not be known until three weeks later when the votes of the men and women in the services from all over the world had been counted. Charles had added his voice to the voices of others pressing the Prime Minister to take a holiday in France in the interval. Before leaving to accompany him, Charles had one more task to perform for the St Mary's centenary programme: to broadcast an appeal on behalf of the hospital.[56] In his five-minute talk he concentrated on the question why listeners should help St Mary's specially. He gave two reasons. Two doctors, he said, working in one laboratory of the hospital had saved more lives in the armies in the field than anyone else in the world; and he cited Almroth Wright's typhoid inoculation and Fleming's penicillin. This was a dramatic statement which many who knew about these things regarded as acceptable, although it can have done nothing but aggravate the sense of injustice felt by Howard Florey and his team at Oxford who had been responsible for the long struggle that led to the development of a method for preparing penicillin in quantities needed to test its clinical usefulness.

Churchill's week's holiday in France was a prelude not only to the declaration of the results of the general election but also to a conference to be held in Berlin. The holiday was spent near Hendaye at the Chateau Bordaberry, thanks to the hospitality of its owner, Brigadier-General Raymond Brutinel, a Canadian who had managed to remain in France throughout the German occupation.[57] Charles was once more a member of the small family group made up by Mr and Mrs Churchill and Mary, with Tommy Thompson and Jock Colville, and a supporting staff that included Sawyers, three detectives and two typists.[58] Charles as usual recorded Churchill's moods and details of his conversation. The General, like Charles, proved to be a good listener and the two of them would sometimes sit for hours over lunch, listening to a flow of reminiscences and comments long after Mrs Churchill, Mary, Tommy and Jock had left the table.[59] Charles was not such a good listener in the evenings for he tended to be overcome by sleep especially if he had played golf while Churchill painted during the day.[60] Charles was concerned at this time with the effects of the stresses and strains of the last few years on this one man, just as in the First World War he had been concerned with how men of a whole battalion were wearing.[61] As a listener and occasional prompter he was conducting what was known, in the language that came out of the war, as debriefing, so that in addition to relaxation from painting and bathing in the sea, Churchill obtained the benefit that comes from unburdening the mind. Not that he would have seen it in quite that light. Indeed Charles's only altercation with him during this holiday arose one evening after Mrs Churchill and Mary had gone to bed, when Churchill asked Charles about advances in medicine. After speaking of curing disease, Charles rashly remarked that doctors were going to find out more about how the mind worked:

'The PM said at once "As long as you keep the psychiatric stuff out of the army I don't mind." I allowed his antiquated attitude to everything psychological to irritate me into an argument. Perhaps the fact that he had once offered to write me a preface, and had never brought himself even to read my book, though it's always lying about his room, contributed. Anyway, we were soon at it hammer and tongs . . .'[60]

Much of Charles's time at Hendaye must have been occupied with writing notes, for there was a great deal of talk and the record of it covered 12 pages of the manuscript book. The picture portrayed was of Churchill unwinding, on the one hand not wanting to do anything,[62] and on the other stamping repeatedly into the secretaries' room from habit to see if any news had come in.[63] But, Charles commented:

'The German war is over, nothing is coming in from the east or at any rate nothing which No. 10 deems worth forwarding. . . . Well, it is a belated rest and too short at that. . . . Tomorrow we start off for Berlin.'[64]

Charles flew with the Prime Minister from Hendaye to Berlin for the conference at Potsdam on 15 July and he flew back to England with him 10 days later. Staying on the outskirts of the city in a substantial house built of stone that had survived the bombing by the allies, Charles continued to write assiduously. Whereas before Hendaye his manuscript book had had gaps in it, now he kept a strictly daily record. He referred to this record-keeping in a letter to Dorothy at the end of the conference:

'I've written 16 000 words for diary since starting off for Hendaye. Don't know how far it is of ephemeral interest only. It takes a good deal of time. I jot down anything I think at all worthwhile as soon after it happens as possible otherwise it vanishes rapidly out of my mind.'[65]

Mostly he described what he heard about the political manoeuvring that was going on among the Big Three. There were no significant calls on his medical skills and his manuscript book gave few personal insights, but, to read between the lines, a closer personal relationship seems to have developed at this time between himself and Churchill, perhaps promoted by the time spent together during the Hendaye holiday. There were again bedtime sessions when anxieties about the election results surfaced,[66] and one evening Churchill invited Charles to dinner with the Edens. Churchill warned him that they had just heard that Eden's son had been killed in an air crash. Charles, despite the poor opinion he held of Eden, paid tribute to the quiet dignity with which he and his wife behaved throughout the evening, and wondered if he could have matched it immediately after hearing that John had been killed.[67] In another gesture of intimacy, the Prime Minister, when sitting on the balcony of their house after a conference session said to Leslie Rowan, his private secretary, 'Charles might like to see these', whereupon Rowan handed Charles two typewritten résumés of sessions that Churchill had had, one with Stalin and the other with Truman*. In the latter session Charles saw a reference to a secret weapon that the allies had up their sleeve, but it was not until later in the week that Churchill, binding Charles to secrecy, told him that it was the atom bomb, which had just been exploded successfully in the desert in Arizona.[68]

Churchill hosted the final banquet of the conference on 23 July.[69] There were 28 people present. It was left to Stalin and Truman to pick their representatives and both chose their chiefs of staff and other officials. Churchill extended his group to include three Field-Marshals and members of his personal entourage—Ismay, Tommy and Charles. This selection, Charles observed, involved the omission of two Cabinet ministers, Lord Cherwell and the Solicitor-General. Charles sat next to Admiral King, the American Chief of Naval Operations, with whom he chatted on a variety of topics. He had met him before and always liked him despite his lukewarm attitude to the British. Towards the end of the meal, the guests started signing one another's menus:

---

*Harry S Truman who had become President of the United States when Roosevelt died on 12 April 1945.

'There was a shortage of fountain pens and the borrowing and general movement seemed to break the icy formality and generate a very friendly spirit. The CIGS brought his card to me. "You must sign when we've travelled together so many times." Very unlike his reserved Ulster nature with its dislike of gush to make any such observation, and I was very pleased by his friendliness for I have a high regard for him . . .'[70]

On Wednesday 25 July Churchill and his party flew back to England in order to hear the election results on the following day. Charles drove to the aerodrome with Bridges, and, passing Russian soldiers tramping about in fields of corn as they guarded the route, they reflected how this showed a difference between the Russians and the British.[71] The British would take a chance of some German having a pot shot at the PM rather than tread down the corn. Somehow, on this drive, they came to discuss Mountbatten and Charles learnt that the opinion of the Secretary of the Cabinet about him—a pestilential fellow, he called him—was both forthright and coincident with his own. Charles was to reflect on this conversation before very long, when he came to think seriously about what to do with what he now called his diary.

Charles's expectation of the results of the election was no different from that of others close to Churchill. The Prime Minister would be returned to power, perhaps with a small majority, and based on this belief Charles left half his luggage in Berlin.[71] On the Thursday morning he went to the College to see Boldero about the comitia, which was not a threatening one, to be held on that afternoon. He then went out for a hair cut and, walking back to the College along Pall Mall at 1.15, he met Jock Colville, who told him there had been a landslide.[72] It was already known that several of Churchill's ministers were out, including Bracken and Macmillan, and it looked as if Labour might get a big majority. After the Comitia, when the fellows were having tea, Dorothy brought Charles the three o'clock results that had been given on the wireless, and a little later the four o'clock results confirmed the rout of the Conservative Party.[72] Charles was now confronted with handling a situation closely akin to a bereavement. Churchill had suffered a loss and Charles's job was to help him. After tea at the college he walked down to the Annexe. Churchill was engaged so he wrote him a note, and the message came back that the PM would like to see him. Saying what he could to comfort him, Charles added that if Churchill went abroad for health or other purposes he would like to go with him as he had done during the war.[73] This was a thoughtful remark, for with his loss of office as Prime Minister, Churchill's personal support system had vanished. His private office, with the secretaries, who had made up his 'secret circle', were at once at the service of his successor, Clement Attlee. Two of his detectives left to take up other duties, and Tommy Thompson went too. And for the first time in over five years, no boxes of official papers arrived to demand his attention.[74] His change in circumstances could hardly have been more dramatic. Charles paid him weekly visits, dealing with anxieties as best he could. Aneurin Bevan had become Minister for Health and was pledged to introduce the new health service. Would there, Churchill asked, be private practice? And would Charles be able to look after him?[75] Then there was talk of a holiday in a few weeks time in the south of France. Churchill thought that if he was ill, Charles could fly out to him; the government would surely arrange that.[76]

Charles himself coasted along through the weeks of August. He took Dorothy to hear the King's speech in the House of Lords at the opening of the new parliament and noted the passing scene:

'Just before the arrival of the King and Queen, Horder entered. If I'd been in his place I'd have crept to a seat—if there was one— in the back row. But my Lord Horder is made of sterner stuff. Slowly he passed along the Government bench, stopping to talk to Addison, Nathan and someone to whom I could put no name. For five years he has had no say in things. Now he will have another fling . . .'[77]

Dawson had died in March and Charles reflected on the report in the papers that he had left £139 000 in his will:

'He wasn't mercenary; publicity and power appealed to him more than acquisition of wealth. No doctor in his day (probably this is true of all time) had more of both.'[78]

The end of the war in Europe brought other official and ceremonial occasions, like the thanksgiving service at St Paul's, about which Dorothy conversed on the following day at luncheon at the Ritz with the Dean of the cathedral.[78] Life for Charles and Dorothy had never been quite like this before. In the new peacetime world they had become people of note, and Charles was aware that he himself had changed. One day, in the House of Lords, a stranger came up and spoke to him about *The Anatomy of Courage*:

'My little book seems somehow to have broken down barriers which in my life have separated me from strangers and acquaintances, and I can see how much I have missed all this time through being a bad mixer . . .

'Until my book appeared nobody seemed interested in my views on any subject save medicine—I could always earn a few guineas by selling my professional opinion. Now all this is changed. I have made friends who speak the same language and don't bother me about their damned colons. It's a bit late in the day—I was born in 1882—but anyway I've made a fresh start and there may be a few years left.'[79]

Charles's family also noticed a change in him. Whereas before the war he had seemed to be not in perfect health, to have little social life, and to have been preoccupied with St Mary's, his horizons seemed now to have broadened and he was more at ease.[80] Nevertheless, as peace became a reality with Japan's surrender on 15 August, Charles was beset with doubts about what the future held for him. In a note in his manuscript book dated 28 August 1945, under the heading 'How the Election Result has Affected Me', he wrote:

'Since the election something seems to have gone out of my life. It's not that I am sorry for Winston. If he is to preserve the legend that has grown up during the war of another Chatham* he ought to devote the rest of his life to writing and leave politics to others . . . Desmond MacCarthy quoted today a letter of Chekhov: "There is a sort of stagnation in my soul. I explain it by the stagnation in my own personal life. I am not disappointed. I am not tired. I am not depressed, but simply everything has become less interesting."

'The truth is I have always hoped Winston would give me some job which would take me out of medicine. I was very vague what kind of job I wanted. Jane argued: how could Winston know I wanted to give up medicine; he would never dream I would accept anything that would mean the end of my professional career. I knew this was reasonable but all the same I went on hoping . . .'[81]

Charles was diverted from making an immediate decision about his future when Churchill made plans to take a holiday in September in a house on Lake Como in Italy, which was in the military zone under Alexander's command. On hearing indirectly what had been arranged, Charles telephoned Mrs Churchill and asked her if Winston was quite happy going off to Italy without him:

'She said at once she was sure he was, that he was very well and that I need not worry. But that night after I had gone to bed she telephoned: she had mentioned what I had said to Winston and he had rather jumped at the idea of my going with him. It would be a great comfort to her too. I was rather taken aback. I don't

---

*William Pitt, Earl of Chatham (1708-1778), British statesman.

think I ever imagined he would let me go now the war was over but I said "Good, I'll find out from Mrs Hill what time we must be at Northolt." It was a long time before I could get to sleep. I thought I was demobilised at last and could get down to the business of building up my practice again—I haven't any at present and I wasn't quite sure when these journeys were going to end. Would he wander as much as ever, on one pretext or another and if so was I to go with him? Besides Jane badly needs a holiday and I had hoped to take her to Harlech before she begins moving house and the winter closes down on us.'[82]

Charles left on the very next day, flying with Churchill, and Sarah who had been given leave from her unit, in Field Marshal Alexander's Dakota—'Not quite the luxury of the Skymaster but very comfortable'.[82] He spent three weeks with Churchill, staying in what the latter described as one of the most pleasant and delectable places he had ever struck.[83] The house was by the lake and every arrangement had been made for their convenience. The small party was completed by two young officers from Churchill's old regiment, the 4th Hussars, assigned by Alexander to see that all went well. Churchill painted, there were picnics and Charles played some golf but mostly he spent his days writing. He was preparing letters for the medical journals on the subject of demobilisation, an address that he had been invited to give at the Royal Free Hospital, and letters on College business. He also had his diary to write.[84] Alexander paid a brief visit but otherwise they were a small isolated group relaxing in great comfort. There was one six-day period without papers, telegrams and letters and the absence of news was scarcely noticed.[85] Charles listened to Churchill pouring out his reminiscences and, from time to time, egged him on. There were long monologues over dinner and there were again bedtime sessions when Charles went to Churchill's room to settle him for the night.[86] There was generally at least one call for Charles's professional help on Churchill's travels and on this occasion it was the discovery of a hernia which was handled by a prompt consultation with the consulting surgeon to the army in Italy.[86]

Charles's writing during these three weeks filled many more pages of his manuscript book, and on one of these pages he indicated what he had in mind as the purpose of this self-imposed task. Churchill was re-reading the minutes he had sent out to the Chiefs of Staff, cabinet and others while he was Prime Minister:

'. . . "You'd like to read them, Charles." I jumped at the offer. I kept feeling the picture I am leaving to the children in this diary is not fair to Winston. Inevitably all his little frailties are stripped bare on these journeys until you may begin to wonder why he is where he is. . . . Here was a chance to give the other side of the picture.'[82]

The party broke up on 19 September when Sarah returned to her unit and Charles flew home, leaving Churchill to extend his holiday with a visit to the French Riviera. Charles left with some relief, not having shared Churchill's view of their idyllic surroundings on Lake Como; to him it was 'heat, mosquitos and endless talk'.[84]

Chapter 16

Public Figure

A warm invitation from Mrs Churchill for Charles and Dorothy to lunch with her greeted Charles on his return from Lake Como. Mrs Churchill had been comforted by Charles's report on Churchill and she said that if only her husband was not set upon by Lord Beaverbrook, he might remain serene.[1]

For Charles the latter months of 1945 ended one of his great enterprises, the deanship of St Mary's Hospital Medical School. A week after his return from Lake Como, on the evening of 26 September, the customary meeting of the staff and lecturers considered the nomination of the Dean for the following year. Charles left the room before this item was discussed, and on the following day he received a letter telling him that it had been resolved to nominate a new dean, that one nomination, of Dr Denis Brinton, had been received, and that it had been approved unanimously.[2] This letter, which also contained expressions of appreciation for Charles's outstanding services over 25 years, came from 119 Harley Street, five doors along from number 129, to which Dorothy and Charles had now returned, and it was signed by the chairman of the meeting who was none other than Charles's competitor for the prized appointment to the hospital staff in 1919, Hope Gosse. Charles's forecast about Gosse at the end of the First War[3] had been right; he had been a great success as a heart specialist.

The future of the deanship had been under discussion for many months. Charles's brief and infrequent visits to the medical school had been criticised, and, while reasons for his recent absences were appreciated, to many they were symptomatic of his attitude in the last years before the war, when he had given decreasing time to medical school affairs and to teaching. There was a widely held feeling that the post-war situation called for someone to spend a lot more time in the place.[4] Charles was well aware of the discussions. On one of his wartime visits to Cairo he had invited Denis Brinton, the physician for nervous diseases at St Mary's, who was serving as consultant neuropsychiatrist to the Royal Air Force in the Middle East, to see him. The message that Brinton got was that Charles wanted him to be his successor.[5] Brinton had figured in Charles's long-term planning on earlier occasions. Charles had selected him when he was an undergraduate at Oxford for one of the earliest entrance scholarships, despite the fact that Brinton had only played rugger twice in his life. Then, after Brinton graduated in 1925 and had an ambition to be a surgeon, Charles told him that the idea was hopeless. Arthur Porritt, Brinton's contemporary, was aiming at surgery, and, according to Charles, would one day be President of the Royal College of Surgeons. He would beat Brinton everywhere. But, Charles said, Wilfred Harris, the neurologist, would soon be leaving the staff. 'You go to the National [Hospital for Nervous Diseases]' said Charles, 'and we'll be ready for you in six years.' And so it was.[5] Brinton was appointed as neurologist on the staff of St Mary's when Harris retired in 1935, and Porritt became President of the Royal College of Surgeons in 1960.

When it came to the decision about the deanship it turned out that Charles very much wanted to continue as dean and he was furious when he was not re-elected.[6] There followed a prolonged estrangement between himself and his successor, who until then had been his blue eyed boy.[5] The situation was aggravated when the method of selection of students for entry into the school was changed. No longer were reports of heads of Colleges and schools, together with the dean's intuition, the determinants. Brinton delegated the interviews of applicants to several small committees. He was no less interested than his predecessor in the selection of students and in their progress. Indeed, when he retired, he travelled the world to see how they had fared. But to Charles the changed method of selection was anathema. Two days after learning that his deanship was over, he reiterated his conviction in his invited inaugural address at the Royal Free Hospital. A dean, he said, had the task of selecting the entry. 'Give me the choice of the school entry and anybody else can have all the rest.'[7] When, three years later, the status of the medical school was altered under a new Act of Parliament, Brinton wrote to invite Charles to become a vice-president of the new school council. Charles declined, saying that the council would be concerned with the policy of the school; it was a policy with which he disagreed, and he was anxious that knowledge of his disagreement should not become public.[8] No one was enjoying this persisting umbrage which was socially embarrassing, for both the Morans and the Brintons had a boy in the same house at Eton and found themselves together on school visits, and anyway many people at St Mary's, including Brinton, would have valued Charles's counsel. At last, as was so often the case when something unfortunate happened, Dorothy intervened. Brinton was suddenly bidden to tea at 129 Harley Street. Dorothy poured out two cups and then excused herself. Brinton and Charles were alone, and when they parted friendship had been restored.[5] Brinton was greatly relieved, for Charles's friendship and support had meant a lot to him and he tremendously admired what Charles had done for the medical school.[9] The friendship ran onto no more rocks, and years later, when Dorothy was gravely ill, Brinton was one of the people to whom Charles turned for help. But, despite this personal rapprochement, Charles continued to distance himself from

St Mary's. He could never agree that the new process for selecting students was right, and when in 1952 AG Cross, another of his scholars, succeeded Brinton as dean, he hammered his point home again: 'Get the boys of first class ability at any price if you can. But for the rest, go for character.'[10]

Charles had another cause for sadness, when he realised that the true history of his beloved medical school was not being written. In 1950 Carmalt-Jones, who had retired from the chair of medicine at Otago, consulted him about material he was collecting for a history.[11] The enterprise, of which Charles was critical, came to nothing, perhaps because Zachary Cope was also at work on a volume which was published in 1954 as *The History of St Mary's Hospital Medical School*.[12] Cope sought little help from Charles for his book, on which Charles commented that he wished that the author, instead of writing it all like a *Times* obituary, had done it with the discernment and critical faculty of the historian.[13] Charles now doubted whether the true history would ever be written, but did not seem to have reflected that without the records in his possession of his dealings with people like Herringham, Newman, Lady Kenmare and Beaverbrook, any story would be incomplete. For, over many critical years, the story of the medical school was the story of Charles himself, a story which, in its entirety, he had shared with no one but Dorothy.

In October of 1945 there were several significant dinners. The first called for no particular effort on Charles's part for it was a dinner given by the Lord Mayor at the Mansion House to meet the senior officers of HM Forces,[14] and Charles knew many of the guests. At the second dinner, the Harveian Dinner of the Royal College of Physicians, Charles was the host, and he fielded a remarkable team of speakers. Attlee, as Prime Minister, proposed the toast of The College, to which Charles replied. Then John Parkinson, who had given the college's prestigious Harveian Oration earlier in the day, proposed The Guests, and both the Archbishop of Canterbury and Ernest Bevin, who was Minister for Foreign Affairs, replied.[15] In a series of speeches that were all urbane and witty, Charles's contribution was judged by Mackenzie King, who was one of the guests, to be outstanding.[16] His main theme was the question whether personal qualities that command success were the same in both politics and medicine, and he concluded, after an entertaining examination of the matter, that on the whole they were. He then devoted a peroration to the country's debt to the fallen in the war. It was a risky thing to do, for it would have been so easy to be trite, but he judged the occasion, and chose his words admirably. He told the story of one of his ex-students, Surgeon Lieutenant Peter McRae RNVR:

'He came to us from Christ's Hospital, a frail boy, and had become one of the great athletes of his time. What endeared him to us was the kick he got out of everything in life, his quiet gusto. Early in the war he joined the Navy and when his ship was sunk in Northern waters by a torpedo, he swam to a Carley float and climbed on to it. He looked round and said: "I think there are too many of us on this float" and slipped off into the great seas and was not seen again. Captain Oates walked out into the Arctic blizzard and into immortality. This boy, like thousands of others, went without trumpets. His story is not known.'[15]

Charles then ended with the same exhortation he had used in 1919:

'We have been saved from utter ruin by our children. These boys who have gone were the flower of our race. I do not trust myself to speak of what we have lost. But if they did this for us, surely, we shall do this for them, that we shall go forward into the future without bitterness and without faction, working together as one people for the betterment of all mankind.'[15]

Charles returned to this theme of working and living together five years later, at an invited address in Canterbury Cathedral at a service for the commemoration of the science and art of healing.[17] After recounting achievements of medicine in tackling diseases of the body, he said he could recount no tale of triumph when physicians tried to follow the working of the mind. He believed people had not organised the art of living together because of this gap in knowledge, and failure to acquire the art was the crucial problem confronting society.[18] These thoughts were eloquently elaborated to an immense congregation, estimated by Dorothy at 2000, as Charles spoke without a note from the middle of the steps just below the high altar.[19] Spontaneous though his address may have seemed, he had taken a great deal of trouble over it. He had, as Dorothy put it, been broody with his sermon for days before, and when trying the loud speakers before the service he had found that, to be intelligible, he had to speak at about half his normal rate, so he had to cut what he wanted to say. Dorothy, at any rate, enjoyed the lunch associated with the event. She wrote to John:

'We were bidden, he and I, to lunch with the "Red Dean" Hewlett Johnson. The Deanery is a lovely old house, very much damaged by bombing but now in process of repair. In the study into which we were shown was a portrait of Lenin which someone must have presented. H.J. has a fine face and looks magnificent in his robes with two little well-scrubbed matching fair-haired boys as his cope-bearers. I sat next to him at luncheon, with Lord Harris, the Ld Lieutenant (son of the cricketer) on my other side. The Dean was very easy, intelligent and amusing, Lady Harris on the other side is a staunch conservative lady and deplored his politics openly.

The Dean-ess is very young, attractive, an artist. She must be 30 years younger than he is.'[19]

Dorothy added that the speech had made a great stir and that the *Observer* had asked Charles to write a leader.[19] Read years later, detached from the atmosphere of the occasion, and uninfluenced by Charles's diction, which could be superb, the address has remained as thought-provoking as Charles's earlier writings on the narrower theme of medical education. Again it is the vivid description of a situation and the stimulation of ideas about it that stand out. This ability to expand fascinatingly on a topic, to conjure up a vivid word picture—often a critical one—of a person or situation, made Charles an admired conversationalist who could hold the attention of a dinner table for minutes on end. But his inclination to leave his listeners hanging in the air, with a brilliant analysis of a problem but without leading them on to solution, drew criticism in the highly politically-thinking circle close to Churchill.[20] Politicians are, after all, concerned primarily with solutions, and this was well illustrated by a short note in Charles's records typed with the large-lettered type used in the Prime Minister's office, and headed 'Prevention of another war.'[21] It was evidently written at the time of the extraordinary dinner in which Charles was included on 13 September 1944 in Quebec, when the sole topic of conversation was what to do with Germany after the war.[22] Charles made three points in the note: disarmament alone was not enough since it could not be enforced in the long term; whatever steps were to be taken to prevent a third war needed to be taken before a new generation which had forgotten the lessons of the present war got into the saddle; and 'you may prevent the German manhood of tomorrow making war, you will never prevent them wishing to make war.' In red ink at the end of the note are scrawled the words: 'Lord Moran. But what do you recommend?' followed by Churchill's initials and the date 17-9.[21]

The third notable dining engagement in October 1945 was with a small medical group to talk with the new Minister for Health, Aneurin Bevan.[23] This was an early incident in a story extending over the next three years during which Charles gave his time almost exclusively to shaping the new health service. But before starting on that he was called to make one more overseas journey, to examine Rudolf Hess at Nuremberg. Hess, who had been Hitler's deputy, had flown alone from Germany in 1941 and landed by parachute in Scotland. He was detained in England for the rest of the war and was now arraigned with the other leading Nazis as a war criminal. His sanity was in question and doctors from Britain, the USA, the USSR and France were sent to Nuremberg to advise on his fitness to stand trial. The British medical group sent to examine him consisted of Charles, George Riddoch, who was head of the neurology department at the London Hospital, and JR Rees, consulting psychiatrist to the Army, who had had responsibility for Hess's case from 1941 to 1945.[25] The three doctors flew from Hendon on 12 November and returned four days later.[26] They spent some time questioning Hess, and Charles and a Russian physician made a physical examination. Charles found himself in contention with both Riddoch and Rees over writing their report, and the British, Russian and French experts also differed in their opinions. They all agreed that Hess was suffering from lack of memory but did not agree on how far this might prejudice his defence.[27] The failure of these experts to agree was not surprising because they would have had to rely heavily on documents held by Rees, covering the years of Hess's detention in England, and Rees told Charles that the Foreign Office had ordered him not to let the dossier out of his possession.[26] At the time Charles was most impressed with the comment of the American, Colonel Schroeder, whom he considered the only doctor present, excluding the Russians, whose experience qualified him to speak with authority on disorders like Hess's. The fact that Schroeder also had experience of the criminal law and of the procedure of courts also influenced him.[26] And, according to Charles, Schroeder's personal opinion was that Hess was insane. In the event, Hess stood trial and was sentenced to life imprisonment; he died in prison 43 years later. For once Charles rendered an account for a fee for his services. It was for two hundred and fifty guineas.[28]

In the five immediate post-war years only sporadic calls were made on Charles by Churchill who, out of office, was busy writing his *History of the Second World War*.[29] He usually saw Churchill at 28 Hyde Park Gate, the Churchill's London house, or at Chartwell, their home in Kent. Once Churchill visited 129 Harley Street, where Dorothy and Charles saw themselves as only camping after the war. The ex-land army girl, who was acting as parlour maid, had not been warned of the visit and on opening the front door uttered an appalled 'OW'.[30] There were occasional echoes of the close associations that Charles had had with Churchill at Hendaye and Lake Como in 1945. He advised Churchill to spend the worst of the British winters in a warm climate, and in 1947 Churchill returned to Marrakesh to write and to paint, while Mrs Churchill remained at home. One day after Christmas Churchill phoned Charles. He had developed a cold and a temperature, and Charles was left in no doubt that he was wanted.[31] Brendan Bracken procured a plane and Charles, regardless of a crisis that was looming in the health service negotiations, took off forthwith accompanied by Mrs Churchill and Dorothy, so honouring the pledge he had given Churchill on the evening of his electoral defeat two years before. The relief party arrived on 3 January 1948, as Churchill's daughter Mary put it 'to supervise, pet and scold him.'[32]

There proved to be no serious health problem, and there was plenty of opportunity to recall old times, and Charles and Dorothy stayed until 18 January.[33] Three months later, in April 1948, Charles was again on the move with Churchill, this time at the instigation of Churchill's son-in-law Duncan Sandys, who was promoting the concept of unity in Europe.[34] Churchill was committed to go to The Hague for a meeting of leading statesmen who were campaigning for institutions for European cooperation,[35] and it was suggested that Charles should accompany him to represent medicine. Charles was adamant that if he went it would be because of his connection with Churchill and not with an implication that he favoured the idea of a united Europe.[34] Churchill suggested that Charles should also accompany him to Oslo after the meeting at The Hague, saying that the King of Norway had said he would be glad if he would do so. Charles wrote from Oslo of this curious episode, starting with an account of the travel plans:

> 'Winston left it too late to book a passage by sea, if he ever meant to mix in with the multitude, so he chartered a Dakota and the Government paid for it from The Hague to Oslo because they feel he is doing good here, but not from England to The Hague because they feel presumably that is not doing good—anyway to their party prospects. So like English politics!'[34]

Charles enjoyed The Hague, where he stayed in an hotel with many of the delegates. He joined the cultural section at the conference because he believed he had no qualifications for the other two sections, which were political and economic, and he wrote comments on several of the contributors. He saw a good deal of Bertand Russell* without being at all impressed—'I fancy its better to read his books and forget the man.' 'Charles Morgan'**, he said, 'exudes a fastidious intolerance.' The person he really liked was the Poet Laureate, John Masefield:

> 'I only knew Masefield slightly before The Hague. I got to know him there. He attracts me very much. Old, very wise, very tolerant, exquisitely polite to nonentities and to famous alike, everything he said sounded from the bench, after a long life of trying people and events. Moreover like Winston without any effort he uses the only right word, you never think he uses it to impress you but only because it is the only word. He is an admirer of Winston's. "Abundance" he said quoting Dr Johnson, "is a sign of genius". I shall use this in my book. It is the right quotation to do WC

---

*Bertrand Russell, English philosopher.
**Charles Morgan, English author.

justice. We (delegates) were only allowed £1 daily in currency but hotels were paid. Last day but one he [Masefield] asked me to share a taxi to Amsterdam. I thought it extravagant but not too much for three hours alone with him. We did the main museum. He has an intense love of beautiful things, which only leaks out, he is very silent going round. Then he makes a casual remark which shows how much he sees. Then we went by mistake to a museum of decadent modern things and I had to lead him away bleeding. Then he asked me if I could bear to go to the Marine Museum. He loves ships and here with the models before him he knows how they have been modified since Greek times. He knows every rope in these sailing ships. Coming home he urged me to write about Winston. He likened him to Lincoln . . .'[34]

While the conference at The Hague was impressive for the intellectual calibre of those who attended, Oslo provided other interests. It was a new experience for Charles to live in a palace with a royal family, albeit a very democratic one headed by the elderly King Haakon, and Charles was unusually enthusiastic about this part of the trip. When it was time to leave, the King gave him a signed photograph of himself and, on a more mundane note, Charles recorded that Winston did the tipping at the Palace, giving £50 in all.[34]

Another call from overseas by Churchill for professional help came on the morning of 24 August 1949. Churchill was staying with Beaverbrook at his villa near Monte Carlo[36] and, while playing gin rummy at two o'cock one morning,[37] he suffered a mild stroke which caused a lack of sensation in his right arm and leg.[38] On being telephoned Charles flew out at once. The symptoms passed in a day or two but the question of issuing a bulletin arose, for Charles had been spotted by the press at the aerodrome,[39] and an engagement for Churchill in Strasbourg had had to be cancelled.[36] Charles, acutely sensitive to the implications for his patient of any suggestion that he had had a stroke—apart from anything else there was the possibility of a general election at the end of the year—was determined that nothing should be said, and he had his way. 'Tell them [the press]', he told Beaverbrook, 'that I am your guest for a few days, that I've brought my golf clubs. We'll produce him in a day or two, and that will convince them there is nothing wrong'. It was put about that Churchill had caught a chill while bathing,[36] and the real nature of the illness remained a closely kept secret.[37]

The infrequent medical calls on Charles over these years were not the only contact with the Churchills. Dorothy and Charles were included in Winston's birthday parties[40] and Mrs Churchill invited Dorothy to lunch when Charles was away.[41] Also enquiries would come from Hyde Park Gate about obscure drugs and curious remedies with which Mrs Churchill seemed to be fascinated.[42] In the spring of 1949 Dorothy, writing to John, who had been posted to the British Embassy in Ankara, described a visit to Chartwell with Charles and their younger son Geoffrey, who had just been given a commission in the Royal Horse Guards, known since 1690 as the Blues:

'We spent (we three) the day yesterday with Winston and family at Chartwell—a very happy and amusing day. Sarah [Churchill] asked for a lift and we took her down—she had been travelling all night from Swansea where she had been on tour with a play called "The Horse on the Sands" which I gather from Mrs C deals with homo-sexuality [sic]!

'Winston, who caught cold on the Queen Mary, was in great form in spite of sniffles. He said that the Boston speech had worried him very much—in fact he admitted that he had been in "a foul temper" for days beforehand. And, said he—making a pumping gesture at the side of his chair—"I pumped and pumped and all I could raise was a little muddy water". Then he went on. "It was like walking on a narrow ridge—on the one side were platitudes and on the other indiscretions—and it was easy to fall off into either." In the end I think he was very pleased with it. He was so sweet and affectionate—and patted Daddy's leg—and drank to the downfall of Horder! [The presidential election at the college was due on the following day]. We walked round the garden—inspected the new cascades and the black swans and the Jersey cows—and all went back to tea. Winston is going to give us each a copy of the American edition of the next two books—and he is going to send you a copy for President Inönü [of Turkey] with a note to you, asking you to deliver it personally. We are going on Wednesday to the Keswick Hotel, Keswick, Cumberland for a week. I hope it will be a good holiday for Daddy . . . Winston was v. impressed with G's [Geoffrey's] commission and kept murmuring "A cornet in the Blues—a cornet in the Blues".'[43]

Politically in the early post war years, apart from the health service, Charles was interested in conscription. He believed that its continuation in peacetime was wrong and that there should be a strong professional army instead.[44] He was also concerned about the effects on their morals of plunging young conscripts into the barrack room in peacetime when they would have endless time on their hands. He spoke about that with the Archbishop of Canterbury, Geoffrey Fisher, at the Victory Parade, and the Archbishop referred to the conversation when he wrote to Charles a year later inviting him to join a small group of people to discuss the matter, and specifically to press for a drastic revision of the wartime system of sex education.[45] The Archbishop pointed out that such sex education as there was in the forces emphasised prophylaxis against venereal diseases, and carried with it the assumption that the risks of acquiring what was colloquially known as v.d. would be incurred. Fisher wanted to suggest to the Minister for War that the approach should be changed towards what he called positive moral education.[46] Charles's demurred because he felt that to tackle the Minister about conscription on moral grounds would not go to the root of the matter. He told the Archbishop that he had already pressed on the Prime Minister, Mr Attlee, the need to reconsider the whole question of peacetime conscription and he believed that his advocacy would be weakened if he were associated with what he regarded as the secondary question of sex education.[47] Charles's opportunity to argue publicly against conscription came on 3 June 1947 in the debate in the House of Lords on the second reading of the National Service Bill. In support of his argument he cited figures from the Army Medical Department demonstrating a high rate of venereal disease in the British Armies in the various occupied territories, the highest rate being 228 per 1000 men in Japan, and he related this to absence from home and boredom. But the majority opinion in the debate was against him.[48]

Through this time, Charles received many invitations to speak, and he was particularly glad to respond to invitations from schools. He was at this time on the council of Cheltenham College. He liked to talk about what he saw as challenges to be met. Dread of responsibility was one of his themes, which he illustrated by referring to his opposition to pressure from the cabinet for the despatch of more consultants from England during Churchill's illness at Carthage in 1943:

'Of course I knew that if he had not recovered I should have been for it. For fifty or sixty years ago, when the German Emperor of that day was supposed to be suffering from cancer, he called in an English throat surgeon, who decided he had not got cancer. But when he died of that malady, the German profession became very vocal and there was a great hubbub. Even now, books that have a large circulation are written explaining for the benefit of his descendants that [the doctor] Morrell Mackenzie was a nitwit and a man of no character. I knew that if I returned to England alone I should be another Morrell Mackenzie.'[49]

Charles linked dread of responsibility with fear of public opinion, a fear which he suspected began at school. Decay in the pride of craftsmanship was another thing that he discussed in post-war Britain:

'This is not, of course, a new complaint, for when I was a school boy—and that is quite a long time ago—any boy who did his work properly and mastered his job was called a swot and held of no account. Two wars cured us of that nonsense. We came to dislike a man who did not know his job, because it meant more casualties. But I am not sure that we have not had a relapse. Playing in the semi-final of the Parliamentary Golf Handicap—I like to tell you it was the semi-final because that was the apex of my athletic achievements—I put down a new ball at the first tee at Walton Heath, and when I took it out of the hole on the first green after four immaculate and, for me, very unusual, shots, it was split up the middle, so that you could see its inwards.'[49]

As a remedy for the decline in pride of craftsmanship, Charles pointed to the importance of people finding out what they were best fitted to do and then doing it. In that direction lay a contented work force. Here, yet again, Charles was reflecting the thoughts on society that he had distilled from his experience in The First World War and had first expounded in 1919. But his talks were not just sermons. He larded what he had to say with well-tried asides. Some came from his times with Churchill:

'Mr Churchill once said to me: "Two things have vanished in my lifetime—the teaching of the classics is a great loss, the loss of a discipline common to all civilised countries." I asked him what was the second thing that had gone, and he said: "The horse of course".'[49]

Other asides reflected the party politics of the times:

'An aged friend of mine, a crusty old Tory, invited me to go and see the pictures of Picasso. And as we wandered round the walls on which hung his enigmatic canvasses, from time to time he gave a snort and at last he said with great feeling, "Well, after all, what can you expect from a Labour government?"'[49]

Apart from journeys primarily related to Churchill Charles made two other trips overseas soon after the war. One, in 1949, was all fun,—an invited visit to French spas.[50] The other was at the end of 1948, when, with Dorothy, he visited Turkey for the British Council. Their four-day schedule allowed some sight-seeing, and they were able to meet John in Ankara, but most of their time was taken up with the leading medical personalities. Charles gave lectures in Istanbul and in Ankara on the new British health service, and the officer of the British Council in Turkey was enthusiastic about his performance.[51] While he was in Ankara Charles, accompanied by his son, also called on the President of Turkey and gave him a personal letter from Churchill, then Leader of the Opposition.[52] Charles commented in response to the President's question that Churchill was not too happy in opposition when great events were taking place. John noted:

> 'My father also said that it was a great mistake for a man who was tired and too old to remain in power as he was no longer able to be effective. He said that, for example, Mr Roosevelt at Yalta had been so tired and so ill that he did not know what was going on and made disastrous mistakes for which we are paying dearly now.'[52]

For Charles and Dorothy, money remained tight, but because Dorothy was such a good manager, and partly too because the situation was the same for many other professional people, their difficulties were not obvious. Charles continued to complain that his unpredictable absences during the war had resulted in the disappearance of his practice and that he was now regarded as having retired,[53] but he still took no steps to correct the impression, and he continued to speak disdainfully of people who made a lot of money through private medicine—medical grocers he called them.[6] To his colleagues it was obvious that what he had to offer was limited, for he had long been divorced from the day to day management of illness. He was seen as a doctor who, for nearly a decade, had had only Churchill as a patient; hence the remark by FMR Walshe, when a bacteriologist was mentioned as a possible successor to Charles as President of the College: 'What, exchange a President with one patient for one with none?'.[54] In fact, Charles continued to have a few patients referred to him,[55] and as before the war they tended to be famous and successful people and Charles continued to be erratic in charging them. Distinguished statesmen were put in the same category as clergy and members of medical families, and despite protestations were not billed. Captains of industry chided him, as Beaverbrook had done. One wrote: 'I suppose it is because you are a millionaire that you never think of sending me an account.'[56] By contrast, a member of a foreign royal family sudenly received an account for 300 guineas for services rendered over 12 years.[57]

By the end of the war Charles had come to bear a grudge, not against Churchill but against the government, for the way in which he considered he had been treated financially, and he came to question whether he had been wise to refuse the proposal put to him by Sir Edward Bridges, just before the war ended, that he should

accept an income from public funds for five years.[58] But he had
made up his mind that that matter had been ineptly handled.
Arguing that several members of the government had been insistent
that he should travel with the Prime Minister, he had expected some
other form of recognition:

> 'If I had been a general who had lost a battle or two or had muddled
> my way from Rome to Florence, no doubt they would have made
> me a director of the Suez Canal instead of offering me a tip.'[59]

That outburst, directed by Charles to Attlee's Principal Private
Secretary, Leslie Rowan, in 1946, was prompted by an invitation
from Attlee to lead a team to investigate German medical war
crimes. Ten three-day trips to Paris were foreshadowed and the
honorarium offered was 10 guineas a day and a subsistence
allowance of 45 shillings a night.[60] At that time a common fee for
one consultation occupying under an hour in Harley Street was five
guineas. Charles was no happier when a further one pound and 10
shillings a day as a tax-free entertainment allowance was offered
by the Treasury. He commented to Rowan: 'I received fifty guineas
a day for five days for going to Nuremberg. Perhaps with so much
pocket money I might get into trouble in Paris.'[53]

By 1947 Charles had concluded that there was no alternative to
writing and lecturing to supplement his income.[61] Patients were too
few and far between, and while the loss of his stipend as dean of the
medical school had been offset, thanks to Brendan Bracken, by his
appointment as chairman (instead of Editor, as originally suggested)
of the *Practitioner*, this brought in only £1000 a year. Nevertheless as
early as 1946 he declined an offer from the United States, prompted
by Randolph Churchill, who was lecturing there, to tour for three
months and speak on what the American entrepreneur concerned
described as 'your government's move in the field of socialised
medicine'.[62] That was not what he wanted to talk about. He wanted
to lecture on his wartime journeys with Churchill,[63] but there were
no offers for that topic. So far as writing was concerned, he was
beginning to conceive of a major work on Churchill, although any financial reward for that seemed far in the future. Meanwhile, he resisted
pressure to write newspaper articles. In 1948 he wrote to John:

> 'Mummy and I dined not long ago with Max [Beaverbrook]. I
> usually find him impossible to talk to but we were alone (except
> for a lady from Bermuda). I got going and the evening was a great
> success. . . . Max asked me to write about Churchill in the *Evening
> Standard* and made no bones that financially it would pay me very
> well to do so. He told me that if he had to choose between Horder
> and Charles Hill of the BMA as a doctor he would choose Charles
> Hill. I replied that I had never hitherto suspected him of suicidal
> tendencies.'[64]

Relief from their tight financial position and security for the immediate future came in 1949. First Charles was invited to take the salaried position of chairman of the newly created committee designed, under The National Health Service, to identify consultants for merit awards. Then Churchill again pressed him to accept some recompense for his services, and this time Charles agreed to do so, judging that Churchill was at last well off.[65] Churchill made two seven-year convenants, to operate during his life-time, so that both Charles's sons should receive £300 a year,[66] and a few months later, after his stroke in Monte Carlo, Churchill executed another seven-year deed in favour of Dorothy for £500 a year.[67] And so relief for the time being came to the family fortunes and Charles was, as it were, retained by his patient for future professional services.

Chapter 17

The National Health
Service Crisis

Charles came to be remembered for three main things, the re-making of the medical school at St Mary's Hospital, the fashioning of the National Health Service, and his association with Winston Churchill. His contribution to St Mary's was over by the end of 1945, although he continued on the staff for another two years and he was seen at Rugby football matches for many years after that. Immediately post-war, his time was mostly absorbed by negotiations on the health service, and while the finale of that drama was on 5 July 1948, the day on which the new service began, a more significant day was eighteen months later when on 3 April 1950 he stepped down from the presidency of the College. That day was the end of an era so far as he was concerned.

For his activity in influencing the shape of the National Health Service, Charles's main base was the President's room in the Royal College of Physicians overlooking Trafalgar Square, and his public platforms were the Comitia of the College and the chamber of the House of Lords. The main actors with him from the medical profession were Webb-Johnson, President of the Royal College of Surgeons and Charles Hill, Secretary of the British Medical Association (BMA). The gulf between Charles and Charles Hill, as with Webb-Johnson, remained unbridgeable. Hill persisted in seeking to have the BMA negotiate for the whole medical profession, while Charles remained determined that consultants should speak directly to the government with their own voice through their own Colleges—of physicians, surgeons and obstetricians and gynaecologists. That the Colleges had some independence in negotiation had been acknowledged by Willink, the then health minister, in January 1945 when he had agreed to a request from Charles that representatives of the Royal Colleges should be summoned to meetings of the official negotiating committee directly and not through the BMA.[1] This was a small point gained but there was no change in the attitude of Hill and the BMA leadership. Hill, recalling these times later, asserted that he had appreciated Charles's devotion to the Royal College of Physicians and consultants generally, but he did not understand Charles's habit of looking far ahead, and the way in which he regarded each prospective move in terms of its distant repercussions.[2] Hill also said that he found Charles's enjoyment of personal diplomacy both unfamiliar and unwelcome, though he appeared more tolerant of the same propensity in Webb-Johnson, who, unlike Charles, was in the habit of dropping in at Hill's office every week or so to talk.[3] Even if personal diplomacy had not been Charles's way of operating, by 1946 his experience had given him strong reasons for pursuing it. In negotiations over the 1944 White Paper, and over the so-called Willink plan that was derived from it in 1945, Charles had felt himself threatened with being squeezed out. When the question of the regional organisation of a service was discussed, the Ministry of Health and the BMA had appeared to him unwilling, when arranging meetings, to take account of his enforced absences with Churchill. He had complained to Sir Arthur Rucker, deputy secretary at the Ministry:

'I don't believe those whom I represent would be satisfied with a substitute unless some very good reason could be given. After all, when I go abroad, I imagine it is the wish of the Cabinet that I should do so and I do not believe they would wish me to be disenfranchised from such important negotiations except for some very cogent reason.'[4]

And from Yalta in February 1945 Charles had written to Boldero:

'. . . In short I am dissatisfied with the Minister because he has taken no notice of my representations that Regions should not be discussed in my absence: that he is in reality only considering the BMA. And I'm fed up with Hill because he is really responsible for going ahead while I'm away. . . . Don't run away with the idea that I'm in a temper. Willink and Hill are taking no notice of the RCP over Regions and over arrangements for meeting. And I'll take the risks involved in bringing them to their senses . . . I believe the RCP will back my attack . . . I have Bridges here, the Secretary of the Cabinet, and I'll discuss the above with him. I think Willink and Hill have underestimated what the RCP can do.'[5]

Another main medical actor in the drama of those years was Sir Wilson Jameson, chief medical officer at the Ministry of Health from 1940 to 1950. He had been a professor of public health before he had gone to the ministry and remained widely trusted by all factions in the medical profession throughout the sometimes bitter debates of the time.[6] Charles had no problems dealing with him. He thought him a typical civil servant and very unimaginative.[7] The name obviously missing from the list of actors was Dawson who died in March 1945. Towering above all these, and the person with whom Charles's relationship was to become crucial, was Aneurin Bevan,[8] the Minister of Health in the Labour government that was elected in July 1945. Bevan was one of eight children surviving out of 13 born in a four-room home in a mining town in South Wales. He worked in the pit from the age of 13 until he was 20, when he moved to a job at the pithead after developing a disability called miner's nystagmus, which affects the eyesight. He had then gone into mining politics, and in 1929, at the age of 32, had been elected to parliament.[8] In 1945, still in his forties, Bevan was an experienced politician, and well known as eloquent, energetic, left wing and very much his own man. As an MP living in London, his horizons had broadened, and some of the people among whom he moved were far from the left politically. Like Charles, he had become familiar at first hand with talk at Beaverbrook's table at Cherkley, where, in the 1930's, he would somtimes dine two or three times a week and argue with such fellow guests as Brendan Bracken. Bevan enjoyed Beaverbrook's company at this time, and his champagne, and Bracken nicknamed him the Bollinger Bolshevik.[9] Charles saw a good deal of Bevan over the three years during which the details of the NHS were finally negotiated, generally calling on him in Whitehall. On one occasion Bevan visited Charles in Harley Street and the two men dined alone. Bevan had had a cold and John made him a whisky toddy; he greatly liked it and asked for another.[10] The occasion of this *tête-à-tête* may well have been what Charles described to Bevan's biographer, Michael Foot, as his own initial advance to the minister. Foot quoted a conversation in which Charles said to him:

'The Service was inevitable . . . so it at once became important, if doctors were to have any say in things, that Bevan, as Minister of Health, should look upon them as allies and seek their advice.

'I felt that we should have a much greater say in things if we could establish a friendly approach to the Minister, for he had a way of dividing the world into those who were for him and those who were against him.'[11]

The BMA leaders also began with a friendly approach,[12] when, in October 1945, Charles Hill arranged a small private off-the-record dinner at the Cafe Royal to enable those he described as 'leading the profession in the negotiations ahead' to meet the new Minister.[13] Those invited were Dain and Souttar* of the BMA, Charles, Webb-Johnson and JB Miller.**

After the 1945 general election, Bevan took over responsibility for preparing the bill to create the comprehensive health service that the electorate so evidently wanted. His advisers already knew from months of discussion what aspects of the 1944 White Paper and the 1945 Willink plan bothered the doctors. So the new minister was

---

*Sir Henry Souttar, Consulting surgeon to the London Hospital.
**Dr JB Miller of Bishoprigs.

not starting from scratch. Overall, indeed, he faced a situation in which there was much common ground between the Ministry of Health, the BMA and the Royal Colleges.[14] From the doctors' point of view the new element was the Labour Party's declared policy that the medical profession should be organised as a national, full-time, salaried pensionable service.[15] No one knew how far Bevan would adhere to this. The fact that there was already a good deal of common ground allowed Charles to concentrate on a few specific issues related to consultant services, for which he continued to assume the role of spokesman. He carried no particular flag on other issues, but rather, through personal diplomacy, he sought to smoothe the way so that the deadlines set politically could be met. The need to respect the wishes of the people expressed at the 1945 general election was a sentiment that he was to voice repeatedly.[16]

So far as the Royal College of Physicians was concerned, immediately after the Labour election victory there was a lull in discussions about the health service.[17] Bevan was mastering his brief and negotiating with his colleagues in the cabinet.[18] During this lull, the College again considered moving to a new site and linking itself more closely with its sister Colleges. However, in October the Comitia voted by a large majority to remain in Pall Mall, and to maintain the College's name and identity.[19] Charles strongly advocated this. The College's decision inevitably added to the tension that existed with Webb-Johnson, who favoured a closer relationship between the Royal Colleges, but Charles's credit among the physicians did not suffer and, in the presidential election six months later, in April 1946, he received more than twice as many votes as Horder.[20]

The National Health Service Bill was published on 19 March 1946. Three months earlier a paper outlining the proposed scheme had been sent by the minister to many interested medical and para-medical bodies.[21] Charles, asking about the extent to which the proposals were to be regarded as confidential, was told that Bevan held that the first publication must be to Parliament. He was only speaking of the proposals before that to a few selected experts so as to benefit from their advice in settling how he would present his scheme.[22] In the interval between sending out the paper and presenting the bill to Parliament, Bevan met many groups, including the medical negotiating committee, and at these meetings he stuck to his policy; he listened to comments but he would not negotiate.[21] The national health service proposed in the bill, and summarised in the accompanying White Paper,[23] was to be conducted through three main channels. The hospital and specialist services would be the direct responsibility of the minister, but administered on a new regional basis by new regional bodies. The new health centres (the concept of which Charles had so consistently supported) and various local domiciliary and other special clinic services, would be the direct responsibility of local authorities. And for the provision of general practitioner services, new local executive councils would be formed.

When Bevan took over in July 1945, one of the central unresolved problems he had inherited was the organisation and administration of hospitals. Bevan's prescription was that all hospitals, local as well as voluntary, should be taken into national ownership and the new regional bodies should administer them.[18] This radical proposal engaged the attention of the Comitia on 15 April 1946, which re-elected Charles to the presidency for the sixth time. Early in the discussion Charles reiterated his point about the government's mandate. If, he said, Comitia wanted to alter the bill, which was being sponsored by a government with a huge majority, what they must do was to try to put forward reasoned amendments.[16] The College council had proposed that the College approve the transfer of the ownership of hospitals provided the composition of the regional boards was satisfactory, but the Comitia passed a more cautious resolution, that the College 'approves the central direction and coordination of the general policy of hospitals, provided the composition of the regional boards is satisfactory'.[16]

As it turned out, the first parliamentary debate on the bill was not in the House of Commons but in the House of Lords, on the day following the discussion in the Comitia. Charles opened the debate by calling attention to the government White Paper, and moving that the House, while regretting any measures which might impair the efficiency of the general practitioner's service, welcomed proposals for the better coordination of the hospital services of the country.[24] Charles came to the debate not only knowing the feelings expressed in the College the day before, but also aware that the BMA council had criticised many features of the bill as soon as it was published, including the divided administration of the service, ministerial appointment to committees and the take-over of hospitals. With regard to general practice, the BMA considered the proposed control of the distribution of doctors to be unnecessary and undesirable, the abolition of the sale of practices unnecessary, and the idea of a basic salary unjustified.[25]

Charles spoke mostly about hospital services. He first emphasised the need for drastic reorganisation. Of the total beds in voluntary hospitals he pointed to the high proportion that were in small hospitals, and of the total beds in municipal hospitals, one fifth were in institutions that provided little but food and shelter; many of them, he said, might have stepped out of a reforming novel by Charles Dickens. He described the financial difficulties of the voluntary hospitals, aggravated by bombing and the lack of expenditure on them during the war. Large calls on the Treasury were inevitable, to an extent that meant some public control. Should the control be by local authorities or by the minister working through regional bodies? Doctors dreaded being put under local authorities. No statesman, he said, would dream of putting hospitals under local authorities until the whole local government system had been reformed. Charles came down firmly in favour of the proposed national ownership of hospitals.

Speaking briefly about general practice, Charles said he was satisfied that there was fairly general disquiet among general practitioners about the future, for one reason: the trend of the government's proposals might lead to a whole-time service. Was a whole-time service good for the profession and good for the public? His answer was that he was unable to say what would be the effect of a whole-time service on the practice of medicine, but he believed some form of incentive was needed to maintain efficiency.[26] To anyone familiar with his view of the army medical service, derived from his First World War experience and his observations in the Second War, his stressing the need in any form of service to build in incentives would have come as no surprise. Charles ended by saying that the bill was the product of all parties working over a number of years and that when it became law the whole medical profession would unite to try to make it work.

Horder, the other consultant from the medical profession who spoke in the debate, found much to criticise in the bill.[26] He claimed that the Colleges of surgeons and obstetricians had dissociated themselves from the proposals to transfer the ownership of hospitals to the nation. Since there was no public knowledge of the attitudes of these two Colleges, this was an odd announcement from one who was a member of neither. Horder then added that the Royal College of Physicians had voted on the matter on the day before, but, evidently having scruples about revealing the proceedings of his own College, he said he could not reveal the results. It seemed that their lordships were being invited to conclude that the physicians were of the same opinion as the surgeons and obstetricians, and Charles, who had not claimed to be speaking for his College, was put in a position in which he could hardly remain silent. He intervened and quoted the Royal College of Physicians' resolution approving the central direction and coordination of hospital policy provided the composition of the regional boards was satisfactory. This incident led to an unpleasant episode at the Comitia a month later, when consideration of the NHS bill was resumed.[27] Walshe attacked Charles, alleging that he had represented his own views in the House of Lords debate, not the views of the Comitia. Charles proceeded not only to defend his own actions but criticised Horder vehemently for acting improperly in the debate. He said that a senior member of the House of Lords had come up to him after the debate, saying he was sorry for what had occurred and that it was alien to the spirit of the House. Further hard words were spoken before the Comitia agreed to consider the business before them.

Despite this, the Comitia on 16 May was productive. Charles, as had become his custom, encouraged younger Fellows to speak, and in his opening statement stressed that Bevan was reasonable so long as you could persuade him that you were trying to improve the bill. The Comitia passed a series of motions by a large majority approving the principles of the bill's proposals for reorganising the hospital service, and emphasising the crucial place of the regional boards and the need to allow hospitals as much independence as possible in administration. The *Lancet*, whose editor Dr Theodore Fox was a Fellow of the College, published an annotation indicating a belief that this meeting would prove a turning point because, for the first time, one of the principal organisations of the profession had made a public statement on the NHS which emphasised support rather than objections.[28] The outcome of the college meeting was certainly a triumph for Charles's efforts to orientate his colleagues towards trying to improve the bill.

In the House of Commons, debate on the second reading of the NHS bill began at the end of April, the committee stage extended through May and June, and the third reading was in July.[29] Disquiet among doctors over this period came to focus on two particular matters. One was that the bill gave too much power to the minister to determine details of the service by regulation. The other, all the more threatening because of the first one, was Bevan's remark in the second reading debate that the profession was not yet ripe for a full-time salaried service. Many were convinced, and with reason, that the government intended to impose such a service.

The bill came to the House of Lords for its second reading after the summer recess on 8 October. Charles spoke along the same lines as he had done in April,[30] but now he felt able to assert that the hospital provisions of the bill had been sympathetically received by the vast majority of those who worked in hospitals. He was pleased that the government had indicated that there would be an investigation of the remuneration for consultants and specialists. A committee had already considered the remuneration of general practitioners. Touching also on the need to ensure, within the service, that leisure would be assured for able men to do research, he managed to introduce one of the sayings with which he delighted his audiences. Leisure, he said, had gone out of the learned professions; committees, which were the drowsy syrup of the democratic state, ate up the spare time of specialists. With regard to general practitioners, Charles again pointed out that their disquiet was based on their concern that there would be a whole-time service, and again he said he had no certain answer to the question whether this was necessarily bad; again he emphasised the importance of incentive to keep men keen.

Later in October, when the bill went through the committee stage in the House of Lords, Charles took part in the debates and proposed some amendments on administrative processes in hospitals.[31] When Lord Llewellin moved an amendment to provide that general practitioners in the new service should be paid by capitation fee except in exceptional cases, rather than by salary, Charles no longer equivocated. He spoke in support of the amendment, Horder did also, and the amendment was carried. However, the matter came back to the House of Lords for further consideration in November,[32] for the Commons had disagreed with the Lords' amendment on the grounds that it was inexpedient to lay down the method of remuneration by statute. In the interval the government had given an assurance that salaries would be only a minor part of general practitioners' remuneration and that capitation fees would be the main part. On behalf of the government the Lord Chancellor moved that the house 'doth not insist' on the Lords' amendment, whereupon Horder and Charles both expressed reservations but accepted the Lord Chancellor's motion.[32] The legislative process had now run its course, and on 6 November 1946 the bill received the Royal Assent.

With the National Health Service Act on the statute book, and a starting date given as 1 April 1948,[33] Bevan was ready to discuss with the medical profession regulations under which the service would operate. The profession's negotiating committee, set up in 1944 after the publication of the coalition government's white paper, was made up mainly of nominees of the BMA and the Royal Colleges. Its chairman was the elderly Guy Dain, chairman of the BMA council, who had served on the council since 1921. Webb-Johnson was vice-chairman, and Hill was its secretary.[34] Charles was on the committee as one of the members nominated by the Royal College of Physicians, and he was also a member of the nine-man sub-committee which was, in effect, the committee's voice.[35]

While Bevan was ready to start negotiations, the BMA reserved its position. It conducted a plebiscite of the whole profession, asking doctors whether they wished the negotiating committee to enter into discussions on regulations with the minister. By early December the result was known; overall, 55% of doctors said no. The council of the Royal College of Physicians, on the other hand, resolved unanimously on 5 December that it desired the negotiating committee to enter into negotiations.[36] Furthermore, the council agreed that, if the negotiating committee ceased to exist, the College would still be prepared to discuss with the minister matters that were within its competence. There was no question of their shutting the door. The council of the Royal College of Surgeons, by a majority, also declared in favour of negotiations, but doubt was thrown on how Webb-Johnson would act following what Charles described as a noisy meeting of 150 surgeons very strongly in favour of not negotiating.[37]

These divisions in the profession led to intense activity behind the scenes in the last part of December and in the first week in January 1947. Charles set out his perception in a letter that he wrote on 7 January to his colleague Dr TL Hardy in Birmingham.[38] Hardy, as a member of the College council, had been at the council meeting on 5 December that had passed the resolution in favour of negotiation. He was about to attend a meeting of the profession in Birmingham and he wrote to Charles on 3 January asking to be brought up to date.[39] Charles replied that 'strictly for your own ear and on no account to be transmitted to the meeting' he would like to tell him what had been happening. He said that when the bill became law, he had tried to get the Presidents of the three Colleges to write a letter to the press in favour of negotiations. The ministry had liked the idea but Webb-Johnson would not sign it. The next step was a proposal that the minister should make a statement to the profession. The three Presidents had met the minister and Webb-Johnson had devised a message, and the Presidents and the minister had agreed that Charles should sound out Hill whether the *British Medical Journal* would send such a message to the profession without comment. Charles told Hardy that he had found Hill entirely in favour of this step and they had discussed what concessions were necessary to make such an appeal from the minister effective. Charles reported back to the ministry, but a day or two later the minister, being furious about a leading article in the *British Medical Journal*, felt he could no longer take the agreed step. The next move came when Webb-Johnson saw the minister. He did not tell Charles he was doing so, but showed Charles a letter he had written to Bevan pleading for action along the same lines that Charles had been advocating. Bevan said he thought the letter should be signed by the three Presidents. This was done, and Bevan replied to the questions in the letter. Charles told Hardy that the Presidents' letter and the minister's reply would appear within the week in the *British Medical Journal*, and that he considered that, in his reply, Bevan was forthcoming. He also told Hardy that he did not want him to mention the conference that had taken place behind the scenes, and particularly his seeing Hill, as that would put Hill in a difficulty with his supporters.[38]

The Presidents' letter and Bevan's response to it were published in the *British Medical Journal* in January. The Presidents set out the contentious points which were leading to an impasse between the government and the medical profession, and Bevan's reply was sufficiently conciliatory to lead the BMA to resume negotiations.[40] The complexity of the paths trodden by the main actors in the drama leading to the exchange of letters reflected many factors. There was not simply a difference of opinion between the Colleges and the BMA. The Colleges themselves were to some extent divided, and Webb-Johnson found his electorate harder to handle than Charles found his. Furthermore Charles and Webb-Johnson regarded themselves as free to communicate with the minister independently of each other and did so.[37,38] Charles indeed felt constrained in speaking with the minister in the presence of Webb-Johnson, for, as he explained to Bevan, everything that was said in Webb-Johnson's

Figure 17. With Lord Webb-Johnson at Canterbury Cathedral for a service for the commemoration of the science and art of healing, September 1949. This photograph appeared on the front of the Canterbury Cathedral Chronicle. *(Reproduced by kind permission of the Dean and Chapter of Canterbury) (CMAC PP/CMW/H.3)*

presence would, by going to the council of the Royal College of Surgeons, also reach the BMA because Dain was a member of that council. The BMA could then, Charles asserted, counter any moves suggested.[37]

The intervention of the Presidents of the Colleges with Bevan was a landmark in fashioning the NHS because it ended an impasse. Charles would have liked to have been seen as the prime mover but Webb-Johnson at this stage was no less enterprising as a conciliator.[39,41] The Presidents' actions, however, brought sharp criticism from BMA circles, which Hill did nothing to counter. The criticism came to be focused particularly on Charles, perhaps because he most forthrightly and publicly defended what had been done. In his annual presidential address to the College three month's later, in March, he said of the BMA:

'The extremists were in control. The Council of the Association was gradually purged of its more moderate members. Soon the brakes were taken off, the machine got out of control. Those at the wheel shut their eyes and waited for the collision. At that moment the three Presidents jumped on the running board, jammed on the brakes, and contrived to steer the great lumbering skidding machine round the corner. If you think my picture too highly coloured, I must quote one of the pundits of the Association, "The letter of the three Presidents was", he said, "a godsend".'[42]

Charles did not quote a personal letter from another practitioner who wrote 'I am glad that you will not live to see the result of your sins'.[43] Despite the sense of betrayal among some doctors that resulted from the Presidents' letter,[44] when opinion came to be tested at the March presidential election at the college, Charles was re-elected for the seventh consecutive year with 123 votes to Horder's 70.[45]

Through 1947 Charles continued to play his part as a member of the negotiating committee, remaining highly critical of how the BMA members handled things. He had encouraged the younger physicians, those who were members of the College but not yet Fellows, to take part in College business. Meetings of members were arranged, at which he presided, and at one of the early meetings in 1947 he arrived late, saying he had had a terrible afternoon at the negotiating committee.[46] If Hill and Dain had spat in Bevan's face, they couldn't have done more harm, he said. They would get nothing from him by treating him with abusive language. Explaining his own position, Charles said that it might be thought that, as Churchill's friend and physician, he would get nowhere with Bevan as Churchill and Bevan were political enemies and hated each other. But he, Charles, found Bevan a fair-minded man, open to reasoned argument and capable of compromise, even against his political principles. Personal letters exchanged by Charles and Bevan at this time, in relation to Bevan having to take time off work due to illness, certainly reflect a friendly relationship between the two men.[47,48]

While in terms of medical politics most of 1947 was fairly quiet for Charles, the winter brought another crisis. At a meeting of the negotiating committee with the minister at the beginning of December, nearly all the points of difference were raised again.[49] Charles returned from his visit to Churchill at Marrakesh to find a crescendo of criticism directed against the Act itself and against the compliant attitude of the consultants.[50] The general practitioners, according to the *British Medical Journal*, must lead the opposition.[51] The BMA organised another plebiscite, this time to determine the numbers of doctors in favour of accepting service under the Act. The vote was to be taken in February 1948, and a special representative meeting of the BMA was scheduled for 17 March. Critical for Charles's thinking was that five days after that, on 22 March, he would again be up for re-election as President of the College, and Horder would make a tremendous effort to displace him. Even before this series of events unfolded, another bridge had to be crossed. On 29 January the Comitia was to discuss the unharmonious December meeting of the negotiating committee and Charles's freedom of action would inevitably be influenced by the line that the Comitia adopted. At that Comitia he first waited to see if common ground would emerge in the discussion, but the debate was slow to get going and he soon took the lead.[52] With emotions running hot, he said, it was hard to know how to do anything helpful. The minister had made concessions on points brought up by the consultants, but the general practitioners remained unhappy, particularly on their rights to buy and sell practices and to choose their area of practise, the need for remuneration by capitation fee and not by salary, and the right to appeal to the High Court in matters of dispute. How, Charles asked, could the College help the general practitioners? By way of answer he introduced a resolution previously agreed to by the College council which simply left all options open. No position was to be taken up on that day. Then, after the planned February plebiscite and the special representative meeting of the BMA on 17 March, a special Comitia would be held to determine what action could most usefully be taken in the interests of the public and the profession as a whole. The motion was passed by a large majority. That evening, Dorothy wrote to John in Ankara:

'Daddy faced 200 yelling Amalekites this evening, but made straight out of thin air one of the speeches of his life and routed the enemy, finally carrying his crucial motion with only five votes against him. People have been ringing up all night to tell us what a performance it was (Daddy was out to dinner). He finally returned very much buoyed up and in tremendous form.'[53]

The BMJ lost no time in condemning the College's resolution as evasive, indecisive and lacking in courage,[50] but Charles had won what he wanted, which was wide room to manoeuvre.

At this stage the government took the unusual step of arranging a debate in the House of Commons about the Act despite the fact that parliament had already passed it.[54] This was intended as part of a campaign aimed to secure the participation of doctors in the service which was due to start in five months time, the 'appointed day' having been postponed to 5 July. But Bevan's speech, described as one of the most coruscating he had ever delivered,[55] did nothing to promote harmony with the medical profession, and at the end of February the BMA's plebiscite showed only 4735 doctors approving of the Act in its current form and 40814 disapproving.[56] Given these results and the rough words of the minister, nothing but aggravation of this second impasse could be expected from the special representative meeting of the BMA on 17 March.

Owing to his foresight, Charles was now in a commanding position. Outside the profession he was not seen to be closely involved with what many saw as a battle between the government and the BMA, so he was regarded as a possible mediator,[57] and the College had not tied his hands. Free to pursue his own line of diplomacy, he went into action. On 10 March he had an interview with Bevan. His account of what transpired was set out in handwriting on two-and-a-half foolscap pages.[58] Charles started by saying that the general practitioners were afraid that a whole-time service might be brought in overnight by regulation. The minister had given assurances that this could not be done but he would be the first to admit that these assurances were not binding on his successor. What was wanted was an amending Act to lay down that a whole-time service would not be brought in without the sanction of parliament. The minister was sympathetic, but such an amending Act might not appear until after 5 July, the appointed day. However, he would make a statement that he would bring in such a bill.

The note continued:

'The Minister and I then discussed the timing of his statement. He proposed the third week in April because he wanted things to settle down after the March 17 BMA discussion.

'I said I was concerned how to satisfy moderate opinion until the 3rd week in April. He agreed that I should make a statement to the Comitia on March 22 asking the Comitia to entrust me with powers to explore the situation and that I had good reasons for believing that if this were done, I should be in a position at the Comitia on April 29 to make a statement conveying reassurances to practitioners who feared that a whole-time service might be brought in by regulations. I think I should be able to satisfy practitioners that this would not be done.

'I discussed with the Minister whether I was at liberty to say what had happened with any of the opposition. He replied yes, but not to Horder. He feared that if the statement became generally known, his announcement in April would be an anti-climax.

'He told me that Horder had seen Addison* but that when Addison had asked how much he should tell Horder, Bevan replied "Little or nothing".

'Bevan said that a notice would go out to GPs setting out terms of remuneration etc; and a few days later notices would be sent to 13 million people, asking them in effect to choose their doctor.

'These three events:

'1. Bevan's reassurance about amending Bill
'2. Notices to doctors re remuneration
'3. Notices to the public, would be sent out in quick succession

'Bevan said that he could do nothing about the basic salary because it would not go through with his own supporters. He anticipated that as time went on GPs would be much less belligerent [sic] but he agreed that it was important that they should not go into the service disgruntled. He said his information from the Party and the Party in the country was that there ought to be no concessions given to the doctors. He agreed this hostility was mainly to the BMA.

'He proposed that the three Presidents should write him a letter asking for this amending Bill, the exact timing being a matter for future discussion. He did not wish to make an announcement until after the BMA meeting.'[58]

The Minister of Health and the President of the Royal College of Physicians having plotted this scenario, a great deal now turned on Charles being re-elected President on 22 March. On 13 March Dorothy wrote to John:

'The campaign is in full swing and spirits go up and down—there are all kinds of movements and cross currents and negotiations

---

*Lord Addison, the eighty-year old leader of the Labour Party in the House of Lords and an ex-Minister of Health.

open and underground. On the whole Daddy is cheerful but it is a delicate and anxious and wearying time for him. However there is only a week till polling day. After that on Thursday 25 I'm going to take him to the Dormy House at Brancaster—on the Norfolk coast near Hunstanton—for the week-end. Hal is coming too and they will play golf a little together. Let's hope that Daddy will still be PRCP.'[59]

Five days later Dorothy wrote again:

'Daddy is working terribly hard and is caught up in this campaign. It is very tricky with feelings everywhere at white heat, and TH [Horder] leading the extremists and stirring up passions. I shall be glad when it is over—he will have a gruelling day on Monday. Non-teachers [physicians from non-teaching hospitals] in the morning, election with his obituaries in the afternoon, and if he survives that, a comitia to discuss the profession and the Act at 4.30; and a dinner at night. He is dining at the Mansion House tonight which will take him out of it all for a bit.'[60]

Few Fellows who attended the Comitia on Monday 22 March would ever forget the tension of that election. Charles used to do the arithmetic before important College votes. He knew enough about the active Fellows to have a good idea where their allegiances lay and he listed them in columns, for him or against, and added up the totals. He estimated that if more than 300 Fellows attended, he would be in danger.[61] Three hundred seats were put out, many more than were usually needed, and when Charles saw that these were not enough, he knew it was going to be a near thing. Horder's, and no doubt Charles's, supporters had, as Charles put it, been out into the highways and byeways and collected backwoodsmen, many of whom had not attended the College for years. Even Boldero was caught out for once. It was the custom of the College that every attending Fellow should be handed a florin, and the supply was not enough; more coins had to be sent for.

Charles declaimed the obituaries with his usual verve and then he disrobed and the age-old voting procedure began. The silver urns passed up and down the rows and the Fellows placed their slips of paper in them, each with one name on it. The names were then called out one by one by the Senior Censor. Charles's total came to 155 votes, Horder's 122, and 60 more votes were shared among eight other names. Charles had failed to obtain two-thirds of the votes so that a second ballot had to take place with votes going only to Horder or himself. The urns went round again and the names in the second ballot were read out. It was clearly going to be neck and neck and Boldero hastily looked up the by-laws to see what would happen if there was a dead heat.[62] After about 150 votes had been counted, Horder got ahead. Five Horder votes were called in succession and things looked bad for Charles. But, when all votes were counted, Charles had 171 and Horder 165. Charles had won by six votes in a total of 336.[63]

The election seems to have been drama enough in one afternoon for some Fellows, for only 180 attended the special Comitia after tea. Horder was among the absentees, and he did not attend the dinner in the evening. Charles felt sorry for him, for at 77 the presidency was the one professional prize left to him, but he was convinced that Horder's attitude to the health service was completely wrong.[61]

As agreed in January, the special Comitia discussed what could most usefully be done now that the result of the plebiscite was known and the BMA had met. Charles was facing his last hurdle. Would the decisions about to be made allow the plan he had agreed with Bevan on 10 March to unfold? He was satisfied that he had Bevan's promise to bring in an amending Bill to make it impossible for the government to create a whole-time medical service by regulation, but he could not divulge this.[64] According to the plan, the College must ask Bevan to act. The Comitia had before it resolutions from three sources,[65] the College council, Dr Arthur Thomson of Birmingham, and Dr Geoffrey Marshall of Guy's Hospital, whom Charles had consulted over Churchill's pneumonia. Seventeen Fellows spoke in what became a complicated debate, for the council's and Thomson's resolutions contained several clauses with much in common. In the end the council's resolution and two of the three clauses in Thomson's resolution were accepted with only minor amendments. In effect what was agreed to was an affirmation of the College's desire for unity in the profession, and an expression of belief that this could be secured if the minister made it clear in an amending Act that a whole-time salaried service would not be brought in by regulation. This having been decided, Marshall's resolution, which called for rejection of the Act in its present form, was not put. Charles had won. He rounded off the discussion by obtaining agreement that the afternoon's proceedings should not be made public until the other Royal Colleges had been approached, and that the actual publication of the resolutions that had been passed should be postponed until the time was opportune.

There was a late night at 129 Harley Street after the College dinner in the evening.[62] Boldero and Lionel Whitby, who had accompanied Charles to Quebec with Churchill in 1944, looked in, and one whom Dorothy described as 'a nice Dr Hewer from Bristol' stayed the night. News of the closeness of the vote in the election, which some said was more exciting than the Grand National, was soon public knowledge and there were many telephone calls, including ones from both Winston and Mrs Churchill.[61] Next day Charles described himself as 'just ticking over', and Dorothy was glad she had arranged for them to leave on Thursday for the long Easter weekend at

Brancaster. Although the College's resolutions were conveyed informally to Bevan,[66] they were otherwise kept remarkably secret for some days. Then, on 4 April, Charles wrote formally to the minister. Bevan responded on 6 April saying that he hoped the terms of the statement that he would be making in the House of Commons would be satisfactory to Charles and to the vast bulk of the medical profession.[67] By this time the College's resolutions had been made public and had been welcomed in the press. There was backing too from William Gilliat who had succeeded Eardley Holland as President of the Royal College of Obstetricians and Gynaecologists, and qualified backing from Webb-Johnson, who also pressed Bevan to modify the planned method of remuneration of general practitioners.[68] Even a BMA spokesman was guardedly welcoming, although Charles took such exception to a letter from Guy Dain in the *British Medical Journal*[69] that he wrote a very blunt personal letter to the editor reminding him that he, Charles, had neither revealed the fact that the BMA headquarters had been in on the three Colleges' letter in 1947, nor had it been pointed out publicly that one of the chief difficulties in getting a proper atmosphere for the Negotiating Committee was the fact that Hill was a candidate for Parliament for another political party. There was a limit, Charles said, to forebearance at the College.[70]

As planned, on 7 April Bevan made his conciliatory statement in the House of Commons.[71] He announced proposals designed not only to remove the doctors' fears that a full-time salaried service might be introduced by regulation, but also to remove their objections to the £300 basic payment proposed under the health scheme. In the House of Lords, Lord Addison made a statement similar to that made by Bevan in the Commons. Lord Salisbury said the opposition hoped the proposals would lead to agreement, and Lord Samuel, for the Liberals, congratulated the President of the Royal College of Physicians for doing so much to settle the controversy. Charles, to whom Addison had shown Bevan's speech,[64] then rose and warmly welcomed the government's statement, saying that the minister had boldly met the doctors' main fears, and he trusted that Bevan would be rewarded by the loyal support of all reasonable members of the profession. Charles was indeed well pleased with what Bevan said, and wrote and told him so. Bevan, in response, told Charles that his speech in the Lords was 'the most helpful thing said by any doctor in the whole of this business'.[72]

In a letter in which Charles described these events to John,[64] he wrote that this was an interesting example of months of restraint and silently submitting to criticism and even abuse, and then intervening at exactly the right time when there were forces in the Cabinet pressing on the Minister. He quoted Lady Jowitt, wife of the Lord Chancellor, as telling Dorothy that he had saved the government, and he quoted the French Ambassador as greeting him at a dinner party with 'Ah, the peacemaker'. There is no doubt that Charles saw himself at this stage as the peacemaker, and while it may be hard to apportion responsibility for the behind-the-scenes initiative that led to the three Presidents' letter in January 1947, Charles was unquestionably the effective President in overcoming the impasse in March 1948.[73,74] But it would be an oversimplification to see him as having intervened and settled the dispute out of hand, for the Minister already had his own plans for dealing with the situation.[75] Charles's intervention was nevertheless a most welcome bonus and a real contribution to the final fashioning of the National Health Service.

When Charles wrote to John in April, it was all over bar some shouting. Another plebiscite showed that since February 8000 general practitioners had relinquished their opposition to entering the service and in May the BMA's objection was withdrawn.[76] The new health service started on the appointed day, 5 July 1948, and in December the amendments to the Act which Bevan had promised reached the Statute Book.[77] Meanwhile Horder joined in founding the Fellowship for Freedom in Medicine,[76] an organisation which failed to thrive, to carry on a campaign against the service, and in BMA circles Charles acquired the nickname 'Corkscrew Charlie'. This stemmed from his work behind the scenes for an accommodation between the BMA and the Ministry of Health, and while it was intended to characterise what his opponents saw as his deviousness, it of course delighted his admirers and would-be emulators,[78] who saw his activities as manifesting outstanding political skill. Charles himself remained unaware of the nickname for many years.[79]

The last two years of Charles's presidency contained nothing of the drama of the middle years. College business was dominated by matters affecting consultants in the new service. In the 1949 election Horder was again the runner up, but this time was well behind with only 123 votes to Charles's 201.[80] Before this election Charles let it be known that he intended this to be his last year as a candidate,[81] but the process of withdrawal from office, when it came, was not smooth. At the end of the year Dorothy started to turn out a lot of things that had collected in Charles's room at the College, and reflected that after nine years they would miss the College a lot, as a platform, an office and a restaurant in that order.[82] Then, in February, Charles decided he would stand again.[83] He had been pressed to do so by friends and supporters who feared that the candidate who was likely to reflect continuity of his policy, Lionel Whitby, might not beat Horder.[84,85] Charles managed to persuade himself that he had not actually undertaken to stand aside but rather had given a warning that people should start thinking about a successor. The state of uncertainty did not last long. Charles invited Dr Theodore Fox, editor of the Lancet, to lunch with him. Fox was a person whom Charles probably respected more than any other medical man. The regard seems to have been mutual, and such that after the lunch Fox felt able to write Charles a very candid letter.[86] He accepted that if Charles did not stand again there was a risk of losing much that Charles had gained for the profession. He conceded that the argument of expediency was strong. But Fox said that he kept returning to the fact that if Charles stood again it would involve his going back on a clear declaration of intent made before the last election, that might well have won him some votes. If, Fox said, Charles decided to stand again, he would not lose any of his respect or affection, but he would lose the respect of many who knew him less well. Fox's advice prevailed. Charles wrote to a close colleague who was among those pressing him to stand again:

'... it is not really considerations of the odds that discourage me, but rather the fact that some of my best friends, such as Fox of the *Lancet* take the line that I gave an undertaking.'[87]

As the day of the election approached, Charles circulated a personal note to selected Fellows.[81] He confirmed that he would not be standing. He reiterated the need for consultants to speak for themselves independently of the BMA, and pointed to the maiden speech that Charles Hill had made on his recent election to Parliament in which he had advocated narrowing the margin of remuneration between general practitioners and consultants. Finally, he declared his intention to vote for Russell Brain as his successor, and in doing so pointed to one of the most respected and scholarly physicians in London, an outstanding neurologist and long a member of the staff of the London Hospital as well as the Maida Vale Hospital, where Charles would first have made his acquaintance in the early 1920s. The election day, Monday 3 April, found Charles in his usual eloquent form. He began his Presidential Address:

'Fellows of the College, once I wrote a little book full of extracts from a war diary that I kept with no thought of publication, and when I came to read my book I was a little put out to find in print the intimate metabolism of my own mind. For some years now I have spoken in these addresses of so many Fellows that I seem to have drawn aside a curtain, laying bare a view of life, my sympathies and my prejudices, a testament of faith.'[88]

This was indeed so, for in his obituaries Charles not only held his audience by portraying recently dead Fellows with brilliant brush strokes, but also with background strokes reflecting something of his own philosophy. On this, his last occasion for declaiming obituaries, he had seven Fellows to commemorate. He had most to say about his prickly old friend and self-acknowledged fellow Bolshie, Major Greenwood, with whom he had continued to exchange prickly

Figure 18. Portrait of Charles in July 1949. (Photograph by Karsh of Ottowa.
Reproduced by permission of Karsh of Ottawa—Camera Press) (CMAC PP/CMW/P.10)

and Bolshie letters virtually up to Greenwood's death. His friend
would probably have relished Charles's opening observation that
Greenwood had inherited a little reluctantly the uncommon christian
name of Major 'but by way of compensation his father handed down
to him an unusually exact mind'. And he would not have disapproved
of Charles's comment on his shy humanity, when Charles told how
he used to visit an old neighbour, who was ninety years of age, once

a week, 'to cheer her up by playing a card game that nobody else understood'. Then came a final admonition about the BMA. Charles had not been unscathed by the acid references to the College and to himself that had appeared in the columns of the *British Medical Journal*:

'It is obvious that these methods of controversy do not benefit a learned profession—they should cease. I do not pretend that they do not hurt. . . . Meanwhile I trust that until wiser counsels prevail the College will be careful not to elect anyone as President who has one foot in Tavistock Square [the BMA's headquarters] and the other in Trafalgar Square. In that position of unstable equilibrium a man cannot hope to stand effectively for all the College cherishes.'[88]

Acknowledgement of the support he had had from Boldero and the College secretary, Miss Cook, rounded off his address, and suddenly it was all over. Charles removed his presidential robe and sat among the general body of Fellows. The silver urns circulated, Russell Brain led in the first ballot, and in the second he received 233 votes to Lionel Whitby's 105.[89] For the first time since 1941, Horder was not the runner-up.

Chapter 18

Gracious Living

On 4 April 1950, the day after Charles stood down from the Presidency of the College, he and Dorothy sailed for America in RMS 'Caronia'. In the previous November he had accepted an invitation from the President of the American College of Physicians, Dr Reginald Fitz, to give his College's annual convocational lecture in Boston and to speak at its scientific meeting.[1] Before they sailed, Dorothy wrote proudly to her mother[2] that on that morning they had read a leading article in *The Times* headed 'Lord Moran'.[3] In it a tribute was paid to Charles for having to a large extent guided the main body of consultants in suggesting, and striving for, modifications in the plans for the NHS. A man of his temperament, observed the leader, was bound to stir up opposition, and a man of his character was bound to thrive on difficulties and struggles, but it was to be noted that, through the annual election of the President of the Royal College of Physicians, Lord Moran and his policy had been confirmed year after year for over nine years, which was the longest term for a President for over 100 years. On the following day Charles and Dorothy must also have been delighted to receive an affectionate cablegram addressed to them both from Mrs Churchill saying that she and Winston had read the article with pleasure and wishing them a happy journey.[4]

Charles's immediate reaction to Dr Fitz's invitation had been to seek funds to top up those offered by the American college so as to cover the cost of taking Dorothy with him and of showing her something of America. A commission from Lord Camrose to write one or two articles for the *Daily Telegraph* on his impressions of the United States resolved the problem, although this led to embarrassment later when Charles, having accepted some dollars in advance, produced nothing. Camrose, who knew Charles quite well, was not at all put out and refused Charles's offer to refund the amount.[5] Charles's search for supplementary funds also led him to explore the possibility of undertaking a lecture tour while in America.[6] He was advised that the time for planning was too short and that, although he might want to talk about his wartime journeys with Churchill, American audiences would still want lectures on medicine in Britain and the National Health Service.[7]

When Charles and Dorothy arrived in New York they spent a few days at the St Regis Hotel. Charles had been asked by the *Practitioner* to make a courtesy call on the journal's representative in America, Paul Elliott Smith. Charles was also invited to lunch in New York by the Chairman of the Board of Editors of *Life*, Daniel Longwell,[9] who had been alerted to his visit by Walter Graebner,[10] the London representative of Time-Life. Graebner and Charles had coincided as visitors to Churchill at Marrakesh in 1947.[11] Charles must have been identified as a potential author of interest, but his letter of thanks for the lunch did not refer to his own literary aspirations but rather to Churchill's approach to writing. As publishers, Time-Life were already committed to Churchill as an author.[12]

For the meeting of the American College of Physicians in Boston Charles and Dorothy stayed with Charles's friend from wartime days, Dr Roger Lee and Mrs Lee.[13] Charles had had second thoughts about the scientific session that he was to address. He had first offered 'some subject connected with the stomach'.[14] It is hard to think what aspect of this topic he had in mind for he was now far removed from modern ideas on the working of the gastro-intestinal tract. He actually spoke on 'Wear and Tear',[15] drawing on thoughts that he had long mulled over when writing *The Anatomy of Courage*. At the convocation ceremony, after becoming the first recipient of an honorary fellowship of the American College,[16] he spoke on The Royal College of Physicians, and intrigued his audience by producing a gold headed cane that he had brought with him from the London College's library.[17] This walking stick first appeared on the medical scene in 1689 in the hands of John Radcliffe, physician to William and Mary and to Queen Anne, and it had become, over several centuries, something of a symbol of a physician's equipment. It was observed with admiration by his American audiences that for both his talks he spoke without a note.[18] A few days spent at Government House, Ottawa, where his wartime friend Alexander, now a Field Marshal and Viscount, was Governor General, rounded off the trip.[16]

Flying back to London from Montreal, Charles and Dorothy may have reflected that this was the first occasion in many years when the real journey's end would not be the College in Pall Mall but home. Not that Charles was immediately to be out of sight or out of mind at the College. On his return he found that the Fellows had made an unusual gesture. It had never been the custom to have a portrait painted of every President. Indeed only two Presidents had been hung on the College walls in the previous 50 years.[19] Now 364 Fellows subscribed to the painting of a portrait, and Charles was unashamedly proud of the fact. He was given the opportunity to choose the artist, so he and Dorothy set about looking for what he described as someone who does a portrait and not just a photo.[20] By October they had made their choice[21] which was determined by their liking of a small portrait of Lady Howard de Walden by an Italian who was little known in England at this time, Pietro Annigoni. Dorothy addressed enquiries to friends in Florence where Annigoni lived. The replies were not reassuring. They warned her that Annigoni was very careless with his clothes and would probably turn up in his scruffy painting overalls. However, Dorothy recalled that when Annigoni next visited England:

'I asked him to lunch and he came at exactly the right day and time and was smartly dressed. We then had lunch together. He had no English and we had no Italian, however, we struggled along all through lunch and I saw him watching Charles's face. At the end I asked him if he would like to paint him. He said he would but must make some conditions. Charles must go for a sitting whenever he asked, and he said he was a slow painter and would probably need a lot of sittings.

'Charles said "I shall only be painted once so I am willing to make any necessary sacrifice in order to help".'[22]

Upwards of 40 sittings extended through the early months of 1951 and Annigoni later described them.[23] In those days he was able to communicate with most of his English sitters in French, which Dorothy spoke but Charles did not. Dorothy, accompanying Charles for the first sitting, explained that Charles would like to be shown as strong and lively. This was not easy, for while each session began with Charles sitting up proud and strong, within a few minutes he would fall asleep and Annigoni would have to make a noise to wake him up. Across the language barrier the only opinion that Annigoni felt justified in forming about Charles was that he was rather vain, perhaps because he almost always arrived at the studio with a scrap of paper on which Dorothy had written in French some comment that Charles wished to make about his nose, his mouth or an eye. Annigoni made gestures intended to say 'Don't worry, just wait and everything will be all right'. And in the end, so far as Dorothy and Charles were concerned, everything was indeed all right. They so liked the portrait that when Charles's successor Russell Brain told Dorothy that the Fellows would like to spend the sum left over from the portrait subscription on a gift for her, she said she would like a copy of the portrait rather than the suggested jewel or silver salver. She was thrilled when, eventually, Annigoni painted the copy himself.[24]

The presentation of the portrait was made to Charles on 10 July 1951 in the library of the College, at a dinner attended by Churchill, who was still Leader of the Opposition in the House of Commons. Mrs Churchill sent Charles a note (they were now on Dear Charles, Dear Clemmie terms) apologising because she would not be there, but undertaking to see that Winston arrived in good time.[25] Russell Brain, in proposing Churchill's health, reminded the guests that Churchill was the only Honorary Fellow of the College. Churchill replied, talking mostly in light vein from skimpy notes.[26] But he ended with a graceful tribute to Charles in which he acknowledged his First World War record, his sharing some awkward moments in their Second World War air travels together, and his part in leading the College in a policy of cooperation over the National Health Service.[19] Charles's reply was longer, more polished and more solemn. A major theme in it was a biographical sketch of his father and a tribute to him as a remarkable man 'for whom the door of opportunity never opened'. Charles, like Churchill, had reached a stage in life when he wanted to inscribe his own historical record. Most significantly, on that evening Charles also went on to give notice publicly and in Churchill's presence that he aspired to write about his patient. Expressing his delight that the College had chosen its most distinguished Fellow to make the presentation of the portrait, Charles said:

'The undertones of history fall a little faintly on the ear, but there is a feeling, a very general conviction, that when we are all gone, Mr Churchill will live on as the Chatham of our age. One of my forebears, William Hazlitt, the writer, wrote a fine chapter on Chatham, and it would be fitting if one of his descendants were allowed to add a postscript on Mr Churchill.'[19]

This reference by Charles to William Hazlitt must also have intrigued some of his listeners. Charles sincerely believed, without apparently any solid evidence, that his ancestry included this distinguished literary critic and essayist. His ancestor was in fact a Haslett of Clooney, in Ireland, a different branch of the family from William Hazlitt. (Charles was also inclined to believe, and sometimes he made play with the notion, that William Harvey too was one of his ancestors.) Arising from these foibles Charles's younger son had been given the second name of Hazlitt.[27]

Annigoni's portrait of Charles became the one of outstanding interest in a row hung in the Royal College of Physicians. His sparring partner FMR Walshe is said on first seeing it to have muttered 'Toad of Toad Hall'. In a more considered view it reflects a compounding of tenseness, brooding and a hint of puckish humour, rather than the strength and liveliness requested by the sitter. In Dorothy and Charles's last years their copy hung in their small rather dark living room, together with their portrait of William Harvey, unseen by any but their immediate family.

The final honour bestowed on Charles by the College was his appointment to give the Harveian Oration in 1952. Many physicians famous in their day had given this lecture aimed to commemorate the discoverer of the circulation of the blood. It was given in Latin until 1864, when Robert Lee started in that tongue but found himself having to finish in English. Charles chose to speak on 'Credulity',[28] a topic which gave him plenty of scope. He could not resist the temptation to include some comments on the theme on which he had addressed remarks to Buckingham Palace 20 years before, the ill-treatment of princes. He spoke without notes, such ones as there were being as usual in Dorothy's handbag. When Fox asked him for a copy of the oration so that it could be published in the *Lancet*, Charles said he had dictated it soon after he had given it but needed a few days to correct it and get it into shape.[29] Eventually it appeared in the *Lancet* in January 1954, when it evoked a tart comment personally addressed to Charles by a doctor associated with royalty who felt greatly disturbed at having, in his view, been labelled as a quack.

As the 1940s ended and the 1950s began, Dorothy and Charles, who was approaching seventy, realised that the pre-war menage at 129 Harley Street could never be restored. Maintaining a house like that depended on servants and even if they could be afforded they were almost impossible to find. Despite Dorothy's managerial skills, life was stressful. 'You need strong nerves in this house' remarked one of her post-war cooks.[30] Recognising these difficulties, and that with the dwindling practice a consulting room would soon be no longer needed, Charles and Dorothy planned to move. Dorothy hankered for somewhere in the country, not too far away, where they could see family and friends, and where they might eventually settle.[31] It so happened that this was also a time of change in the life of Hal Boldero, who, like Wilmot Herringham in the 1920s and Godfrey Maurice in the 1930s, had come to have a special place in Dorothy's affections. Not only had her involvement in College business during Charles's wartime travels brought them together, but she had also supported Hal through his wife's long and tragic illness, and through the accidental death of his elder son during military training. Dorothy shared with Hal, as she had done with Wilmot Herringham and Godfrey Maurice, an enjoyment for the civilised things of life, and she and Charles were post-war weekend visitors to Hal's country house Wassall, at Rolvenden in Kent. When Margery Boldero died in 1950, Hal's own health was poor and he decided to sell Wassall and join with Dorothy and Charles in buying a country house which he could share with them. The idea was that after Hal's death, his share of the house would come to Dorothy and Charles and in return Dorothy would make a home for his remaining son Ned. By March 1951 Dorothy was writing to John to tell him that they had found a house near Uckfield in Sussex that was easily run yet had a graciousness that made it more than a cottage.[32] Marshalls Manor was, for Sussex, off the beaten track. Standing in three acres and originally 14th or 13th century, it had been added to, and now had seven bedrooms. One of its most attractive features was a large drawing room looking out over the garden. The purchase was completed by the summer, and Dorothy was able to conjure up for John a picture that was to become a treasured part of her life for many years to come:

'I am sitting in the swing sofa after tea. Desmond [MacCarthy, who, with his wife was one of their first guests] is a few yards away, deep in a book. Daddy is in the house and I hear the wireless in the distance, relaying the test match. Marjorie Napier [another guest] is unpacking, and Hal and Ned are in the old orchard, demolishing the old wire fruit cage, which we shall erect elsewhere.'[33]

The garden was entirely the province of Dorothy and Hal who both enjoyed working in it. Charles, who was never known to lift a trowel in his life, centred his activities in the house, writing, reading, listening to sport on the wireless and above all talking. He liked to have what he called 'booky' people as guests and especially, as time went by, people who shared his interest in the Second World War and with whom he could discuss his own story of Churchill.[34] But in the first few years, most of the names in the visitor's book were those of relations.[35] Dorothy's brother Geoffrey Dufton and his wife Nan appeared early, and Charles's sister Maude, who lived at St Leonards-on-Sea, came regularly. Maude used to infuriate her brother by greeting him with 'How's the physic, Charlie?' John, who in 1948 had married Shirley Harris of Bossall Hall in Yorkshire, and who was posted in the diplomatic service to the Middle East, brought his growing family to stay when they were on leave, and the name of Jane Hebblethwaite from nearby Binsted, who married Geoffrey in 1955, also began to appear in the book.

People from the diplomatic world were also occasional guests in the early years. The Israeli Ambassador, Mr Eliahu Elath and his wife; the New Zealand High Commissioner, Sir Frederick Doidge and his wife; and the Australian High Commissioner, Sir Thomas White and his wife and daughter Judith were visitors in 1953. The American Ambassador, Mr Withrop Aldridge and his wife and daughter Mary were guests in 1954. The Whites became particular friends, Lady White sharing interests with Dorothy in the Red Cross and Sir Thomas appealing to Charles both as a man of action and a man with a fondness of words. In the First World War, White had been a pioneer aviator with the Australian Flying Corps in the Middle East. Captured by the Turks, he escaped and then wrote a book about his adventures in which he included several of his poems.[36] General Sir Bernard Freyberg was another guest in the category of brave men. He and his wife came for a weekend in 1954. Freyberg, a New Zealander, had won a Victoria Cross in the First World War and had commanded the New Zealand troops in North Africa in the second. Charles had first made his acquaintance when visiting the army in the desert outside Cairo with Churchill in 1942,[37] and had met him again when Churchill inspected the New Zealand division in Tripoli in February 1943. Freyberg was something of an enigma to Charles, who was fond of quoting Lord Gort, another VC, who, when asked if he ever felt fear replied that all animals felt fear. Freyberg, Charles fancied, might be the one exception to that generalisation.[38]

Consistent threads run through the thank-you letters that guests wrote to Dorothy after their visits, and in their memories years later. Above all there were Dorothy's charm as a hostess and Charles's conversation. When he got going he was like a waterfall,[39] and people would sit at the dining room table from breakfast until lunchtime, so that the meal could not be cleared, as he reminisced and speculated. In the evenings visitors were sometimes taken to nearby Glyndebourne to see an opera. Charles, it was noticed, was never bothered if they were one ticket short as he seemed to prefer to sit outside in the garden. In an evening at home, Hal Boldero, if there, would look after drinks before dinner and Dorothy would preside in the drawing room after dinner, when there was more conversation until Dorothy led the way to bed.[40] All who knew Dorothy and Charles well through the 1950's recognised that Marshalls brought them both much happiness, and they blossomed there.

Chapter 19

Work and Play—Merit Awards and Writing

In February 1945 the wartime coalition government appointed a committee under the chairmanship of Sir Will Spens, Master of Corpus Christi College, Cambridge, to advise on the payment of general practitioners in a national health service. When the committee reported in 1946 to the Labour government, Charles pressed for the payment of consultants to be handled in the same way rather than informally, as had been suggested.[1] This was agreed to and in May 1947 another committee under Sir Will Spens was formed with Charles as a member. Another member was Sir Horace Hamilton, a senior civil servant who had been Permanent Under-Secretary of State at the Scottish Office. The committee's report,[2] in May 1948, contained a section which started Charles and Hamilton on a collaborative enterprise lasting 10 years. It concerned the way in which one consultant should be distinguished from another for remuneration. The report said that distinctions should be made. It noted that there was far greater diversity of ability and effort among specialists than admitted of remuneration by some simple scale applicable to all, and that specialists must be able to feel that more than ordinary ability and effort received an adequate reward; age and length of service should not be the sole factors in determining pay. The committee recommended that the differentiation of individuals for what it called 'exceptional reward in respect of outstanding professional ability' should be in the hands of a predominantly professional body, as detached as possible from individual hospitals and particular localities. It recommended that one-third of all specialists should receive a distinction award; 4% should receive one of £2500 a year, thus doubling their salary; 10% should receive one of £1500 a year and 20% one of £500. The scheme proved acceptable to the government, it was adopted, and in 1949 a Standing Advisory Committee on Distinction Awards was created to administer it.[3]

Charles was recognised as the architect of the scheme,[4] which exactly reflected the views he had formed while in the RAMC in the First World War.[5] Promotion by seniority alone was an idea repugnant to him. The only danger that he saw was that the scheme might not be well administered,[6] but he was very clear about the part the chairman of the committee would need to play and equally clear that he was the one person who could do the job. In September he wrote and told Bevan so,[7] and in October Bevan invited him to take it on,[8] telling him at the same time that Hamilton had been offered the vice-chairmanship. Charles received the letter just as he was leaving with Dorothy for Turkey and Baghdad but, with the prize within his grasp, he demurred. The proposed honorarium of £2000 a year was insufficient, given that he thought of the chairmanship as full-time. He was worried, too, that the appointment was offered for two years and not five.[9] Before posting his letter to Bevan, he called on Bridges, who was still Secretary to the Cabinet, to ask him if he thought the committee would be likely to continue or whether it might be brought to an end on a political change, and Bridges expressed a personal opinion that he need not be anxious on that score.[10] Charles's concern about the short term of the appointment was based on the fact that he was still seeing some private patients. He argued that if he gave up his practice for two years he could never return to it and would be left with no income. He needed a greater assurance of security. Could he come and see Bevan when he returned from Baghdad in November? The answer was yes, he could, so the announcement of the committee was held up. Charles eventually accepted the chairmanship in December with his difficulties unresolved but expressing willingness to leave the final decisions to Bevan.[11] Eventually it was agreed that the appointment would be for three years, and the salary would be 3000 guineas in the first year, 2500 in the second and 2000 in the third.[12]

Through the 1950s, chairing the distinction awards committee was Charles's major interest apart from his writing, and his main source of income. From the start he put his own stamp on the job. Just as when he was appointed dean at St Mary's in 1920, he had a very personal vision of what he wanted to achieve and, furthermore, the committee's work was not the primary interest of any other member apart from Hamilton. His team was remarkable for its over-whelmingly medical nature. Eleven members were nominated by the royal colleges and Scottish royal corporations, one by the Medical Research Council, and one by the Universities' Committee of Vice-chancellors and Principals. It was a committee of senior consultants and specialists who were to judge their peers and successors. It was devoid of BMA influence, although the association's advice was sought,[13] and Hamilton was the only civil servant on it. Many of the members knew Charles already and Hamilton was an ideal number two, for his efficiency made up for Charles's intolerance of administrative detail. Meticulous, imperturbable and the soul of discretion, Hamilton came to be known and respected by many of the doctors whom he met year after year, and as Charles came to know him he found him congenial and wise.[14]

Most of 1949 was spent developing an operational plan and contacting the many people whose advice would be needed. Charles emphasised the committee's conviction that, while it had the entire responsibility for selecting people, consultation with local and regional bodies, as well as with the central colleges and faculties, was vital. To chairmen of medical committees of teaching hospitals he wrote:

'We are convinced that your help is essential, because without it the whole task of selection for awards would have to be performed centrally, and you will agree that the selection of one third of the total number of consultants in the country, by a remote central body without local knowledge, would be unlikely to give satisfactory results.'[15]

The lines of communication having been opened, the visitations from the committee began. Outside London the visiting party often consisted just of Charles and Hamilton. They would set out in the autumn by car, with Dorothy driving, starting at Ipswich.[16] One trip would take about three weeks, and altogether three months of each year were set aside for visiting.[17] While every minute of Charles's and Hamilton's time was spent meeting people, Dorothy would read, knit and visit museums and cathedrals.[16] The style of the operation necessary to contact local opinion varied from centre to centre. In some regions Charles and Hamilton visited all the main hospitals and Charles spoke to gatherings of specialists and then invited questions. In other regions specialists would gather in one place for an evening meeting. In London the three Royal Colleges gave detailed help and further information came from advisers spread through specialties and local areas. These advisers, to whom Charles turned for what he called 'constituency opinion',[18] came from a great variety of hospitals and universities, and what they seemed to have in common was that Charles liked and trusted them.[19] Despite the shroud of secrecy that was meant to envelop the whole process, news that someone was an adviser sometimes got around. The wife of one of them found that, before a visit from Charles was due, certain doctors and their wives would entertain her and her husband vigorously. After the visit they were dropped again.[20] Different centres also varied in the way in which names were brought forward for consideration, and Charles encouraged each centre to work out its preferred method, be it through an elected committee or through more direct personal communications.[17] Inevitably the sifting was not only formal. At one meeting the superintendant of a large psychiatric hospital complained that psychiatrists were neglected in the distribution of awards. Before dinner that evening Charles went up to a doctor he knew who had been at the meeting and asked him about the speaker who had complained. 'You visit his hospital and you know him well', he said, 'what do you think about him?' 'He is an excellent administrator' the doctor replied, 'and his hospital is well known for the decoration of its wards and the quality of its cuisine.' 'Come' replied Charles, 'You know what I'm after. I'm not interested in his ability to choose cooks. Let me put it another way. Would you call him if your wife had a psychiatric illness?'[21] There was a strong impression that Charles always regarded a reputation for clinical acumen as the main criterion for giving an award and if this was associated with breadth of interest, and ability to communicate, so much the better. Asked by non-medical people how they could choose a good doctor, Charles's advice was 'Engage him in general conversation'.[22]

None of the major enterprises on which Charles embarked during his life were free from controversy, and the distinction award scheme was no exception. As things were getting going in 1949 he wrote to John:

'I'm in the midst of the awards business. . . . Picking 1/3 of all consultants and leaving 2/3 out in the cold . . . arouses primitive instincts, and there has been a good deal of criticism and some abuse. It is a difficult job but worth doing as it provides an incentive.'[23]

Led by FMR Walshe in the columns of the *British Medical Journal*,[24] many writers certainly inveighed against the scheme, one of the main questions being whether merit and distinction could really be measured for grading salaries. Charles kept quiet and got on with the job. He was as confident that he could measure merit in consultants as he had been that he could measure character in a battalion at war and in aspiring medical students at St Mary's. And he had done his arithmetic.[25] One third of consultants would have an award, and the remaining two-thirds knew that they had a 50% chance of receiving one sooner or later, so that so long as the administration proved acceptable it was unlikely that consultants would reject the scheme. This proved to be the case and, as the scheme started to operate, it became widely accepted and criticism diminished. After three years, Dorothy mentioned in a letter, sent when Charles was on one of his awards visits, that she had met a leading radiologist at a sherry party who had told her that three years before he was the only member of a committee of specialists who supported the scheme; a year before, the vote was fifty-fifty; and at a recent meeting, when someone proposed that the awards should be abolished, there was a howl of derision.[26]

All who came closely into contact with Charles in the 1950s seem to have been impressed with how intensely he worked on the distinction awards.[27] Dorothy wrote to John:

'Daddy is in Liverpool today for an awards meeting. He is working frightfully hard at it. A few days ago he started at 9 am and was still talking at 12.15 am when I interrupted and said no one could be at his best after 15 solid hours. He seems very well on it.'[28]

Charles's thoroughness was particularly visible when he and
Hamilton were on tour. His little black books became a familiar
sight.[29] Against long lists of consultants were concise comments in
Charles's handwriting, bearing on reputation and esteem. They were
completely candid, many of them laudatory, others damning such
as: 'Experimental physiologist. Does not start to be a doctor'.[30]
Perhaps it was because of Charles's manifest thoroughness and of
people's perception that he was being fair that his colleagues on the
committee allowed him to conduct affairs very much in his own style.
His reduction of both committee meetings and circulated papers to
a minimum[4] partly reflected his attitude to confidentiality, as he
explained to Robert Platt, who succeeded Russell Brain as president
of the college in 1957:

> 'One of my difficulties as Chairman is that while I want to let
> members of the Awards Committee know as much as possible of
> the evidence and even something of the sources from which I get
> it, I have on the other hand to realise that these opinions are given
> to me in confidence and quite apart from ethical reasons I should
> not get this evidence if people did not feel confident that I should
> not land them in difficulties at their school or with their colleagues
> generally.'[31]

Later in the same letter, in which an individual consultant's name
was under discussion, Charles added:

> 'It is essential for the Awards system to enjoy the confidence of
> the consultants and I never attempt to press a name against what
> I must take as the responsible voice of a school. After all, our terms
> of reference are not only to reward professional distinction but also
> to serve as a means of remuneration, which clearly implies the
> consent of the governed. For no Ministry could support a system
> of remuneration which was not agreeable to the consultants in
> general.'[31]

Charles's broader philosophy also prevailed, that awards should
remain confidential to avoid invidious comparisons being made
between individual members of the profession.[32] Even the
publication of statistical information would, in his view, provide
ammunition for mischief makers.

Later examination of the judgements made in the early years of
the committee[4] showed that the distribution of awards across the
country was uneven, the highest rates being in the London teaching
hospitals and the Oxford region. The distribution among different
specialties also varied, with a high proportion of neurologists receiving
awards and low proportions of psychiatrists and anaesthetists.
Whether or not this reflected the distribution of consultants with

particular merit in the 1950s is a matter of speculation. The extraordinary feature of the operation was that, despite its sensitive nature, once it got going, Charles attracted little personal criticism and appeared to make no enemies.[33]

Charles's work on the merit awards coincided with the beginning of his second book. In August 1948, with his work on the Spens committee completed, Charles wrote to an old acquaintance who had made a comment on *The Anatomy of Courage*:

> 'At present I am writing another book on the memoir line but whether I shall be able to publish it in my lifetime is pretty dubious.'[34]

Dorothy had given Charles a ticket for the Olympic Games for his birthday and he was attending the games in the afternoons after writing all morning.[35] College affairs, until he left the presidency in 1950, and his new involvement with the distinction awards, were in a sense distractions from what he had wanted to do ever since leaving school, which was to become a writer. During the previous year, when he believed he would have to rely on lecturing and writing to earn a living, he had toyed with the idea of a book with several contributors.[36] Desmond MacCarthy might write on Churchill as an author, Harold Nicolson* on Churchill as a speaker, and Edward Bridges on Churchill in cabinet and at conferences. Charles himself would write the body of the book. He speculated that MacCarthy would play, but he was doubtful about Nicolson, and very doubtful about Bridges, and he did not pursue this idea.

Once Charles started writing, he worked fast,[37] and by the summer of 1949 he had written what he called Book 1, on the wartime conferences, and Book 2 on Churchill's fall from power. There were still sections to be filled in in both books, and he was dissatisfied with Book 1 because it was too disjointed. He envisaged writing a third book, which would contain a series of essays, and, in addition to polishing what he had written, he started working on these in the latter part of 1949. There would be essays on Winston and Roosevelt, Winston and Stalin, Winston's oratory, Winston's conversation and Winston's health. He also planned to write a page or two on Winston's character, to come just before the end, 'in the manner in which Boswell's life of Johnson ends.' (Boswell described how he sought, in a few pages, 'to collect into one view the capital and distinguishing features of this extraordinary man'.[38]) In a letter from 129 Harley Street in December 1950, written to wish John and his family, now in Tel Aviv, a happy Christmas, Charles reported progress, at the same time conveying a snippet of personal advice:

---

*Harold Nicolson, author and critic, formerly in the Diplomatic Service.

'Shirley spends tonight here and flies to you tomorrow. It will be a very happy Christmas for you, to have the family around and all the interest of new surroundings and new work. I believe you will make your mark in Tel Aviv if you can manage to listen in silence to the Ambassador's outbursts, and don't follow my example of talking too freely. I learned long ago personal remarks always get back to the people concerned, and often mean a lot of extra work in conseqeunce to get anything done.

'My "awards" are now done for the year and I shall have a breather until about February. So I turn to my book and feel that by say June next the whole book shall be in type. No doubt it will be a good deal altered after that, but the main structure will be built, perhaps 100 000 words, perhaps 130 000. *The Anatomy of Courage* was about 70 000. I see no prospect of publishing it then. In fact I doubt if it can be published in Winston's lifetime. But he is 76. There is mounting evidence here that Winston's long directives and memoranda are wearing down his reading public . . . I begin to think it's impossible to combine two purposes, 1. to bolster up his conduct of war for posterity by numerous directives etc, 2. to produce a work of art. There may be before he has finished a reaction against war books of this kind which might tell against mine. But I think a personal portrait of Winston might escape the reaction. The more I work at book of course the more chapters like Teheran and Yalta become reasoned accounts of policy whereas in my original script it was all utterly personal observations, but they needed the serious framework I'm giving it and I'm dropping more of the personal stuff.

'Camrose's dinner was perfectly done in a lovely setting. But what made it good was the fact that nearly all the men were able. Donald Somerville (who was Attorney General in last Conservative Government) was very down on Harold Nicolson for his chapter on Curzon*: he felt he had abused his position, working under him. I always have a kind of feeling of this sort about Winston. I shall have to be very careful. But until book is finished it is impossible to gauge whether any verdict on him is sufficiently favourable. Alexander, Max Beaverbrook and Pug Ismay come out badly in it.

'The thaw has put an end to some vile weather. I did not go out of house in four days, but sat here working on the book.
'*Sunday Times* asked me to contribute 200 words on a book in last year. I didn't take much trouble over it. David Cecil**, I find since,

---

*George Nathaniel Curzon, Marquis of Kedleston, English statesman and Viceroy of India, 1898-1905.
**Lord David Cecil, professor of English literature, University of Oxford.

says exactly opposite things about same book, Boswell's *Diary*. I confess I dipped into it rather than read it, but I don't agree with Cecil's praise.

'Winston is at Marrakesh as guest of Time and Life, with Lord Cherwell (very sour with a duodenal ulcer), General Pownall (who checks the military stuff in [Winston's] book) and a few others. Between racehorses and his special Skymasters Winston's life now runs in lines of comfort, all due to proceeds from book. I hope you and family will have a very happy Christmas . . .'[39]

Charles's qualms, mentioned in this letter, about what he was writing and the possible time of publication, were not new. From the time in 1946 at Yalta, and then at Hendaye, when he made systematic records of what was going on, he was concerned about questions that would arise should he publish what he then called his diary.[40] Two things in particular bothered him: revealing remarks made in confidence, and giving a distorted picture of Winston. Would the picture he painted be fair?[41-43] He stated his dilemma in an entry dated 10 Nov 1946 in his manuscript book, under the heading 'My doubts whether any Memoirs I could write would be fair to Winston, any more than Boswell's *Life of Johnson* was fair to Johnson:

'Charles Morgan, in a review of CE Valliamy's *Ursa Major*, says that the success of Boswell's *Life of Johnson* was due to its "accurate vitality"; the dialogue was "almost certainly faithful". It was the truth but not the whole truth. That is the explanation why Johnson, who seen through Boswell's eyes seems so full of faults, so brutal and insensitive, so narrow and so full of prejudices, was regarded by his contemporaries as a genuinely great spirit. Boswell gave us not Johnson but Johnson playing the part of Johnson. Like all great talkers he emphasized those aspects of his style which produced most responses. He had a streak of brutality but he exaggerated it to make the groundlings shudder. He exaggerated his successful mannerisms. Evening after evening he had to rebuild a legend. That's why Boswell seems to be making him forever play to the gallery.

'People say to me from time to time that I ought to write my memoirs: they almost seem to suggest that if I don't, if I fail to make use of opportunities no one else had during the war of studying Winston, that I am robbing posterity through idleness of something they can get from no one else. But the more I look through what notes I have kept the more I doubt whether I ought to use what I learnt on our travels, at any rate in our lifetime. I was a silent member of a travelling circus and as the years went by I fancied people like the CIGS and Bridges came to trust my discretion and said things to me they would certainly have kept to themselves if they had doubted my discretion. Moreover I was with them often when they were off-guard, when they were weary and when events had lent an edge to their speech. Examples hurry through my head. Brooke entered the dining room at the Chateau Frontenac Hotel at Quebec after a long day of conferences and of bickerings. He was tired and out of spirits. The PM would flit from subject to subject, never finishing anything; he had always been like that but had got much worse. It was getting more and more difficult to get anything done. Then there was the outburst during dinner at Teheran when the three Chiefs of Staff agreed they were wasting their time and blew-up together, the first and last time this happened. And Bridges' acid comment on Mountbatten. And Brooke on Alex. But quite apart from any question of betraying trust I question whether any portrait I may paint of Winston could be a faithful likeness. I saw him in his bedroom when he was out of temper and more than a little shop-worn. He spoke his mind without restraint or form of discipline. It seemed to help him to blow off steam. At such moments he tore away any curtain that concealed the real Winston. You got him "neat" and undiluted. But it was only one Winston and not I think the man at his strongest and best. I saw nothing of the Prime Minister dominating his Cabinet in a way to make Bridges marvel at his ascendancy, I saw nothing of the adroit debater in conference whose vast experience and skilful speech often dominated the councils of the Big Three as at Potsdam and elsewhere. I saw nothing of his mastery of the House of Commons. What I did see was the way he dominated everybody.'[43]

Despite all Charles's hesitations, there were some things on which he was quite clear when he took up his pen. The first was that people whose opinions he respected, including GM Trevelyan*,[44] John Masefield,[45] Mackenzie King[46] and Smuts[47] were at one in urging him to write about Churchill. Mackenzie King indeed, with whom he was on friendly terms, strongly urged him to publish during Churchill's and his, Charles's, lifetime.[46] Churchill might, Mackenzie King wrote, puff and pout for a bit about comments he might not wholly like, but he would come to see that his qualities of greatness had received an emphasis they might otherwise have missed. Secondly, Charles was adamant that what he wrote would be written for posterity.[44] He would produce 'a work of art which will be read after we are gone'.[48] And, thirdly, he would write without a thought as to what could or could not be published at once.

*GM Trevelyan, historian and Master of Trinity College, Cambridge.

It would be time enough to think about that when the writing was complete.[48]

As Charles worked his way through his first draft, he alluded repeatedly to these matters, and to them he soon added another. 'I always kick myself' he wrote to John 'for living decade after decade without bothering about the art of writing though it's the one thing that really interests me'.[48] Loving words, Charles realised that he was undisciplined in their use when it came to writing. As when he spoke, his sentences tended to be complex and he had a liking for the purple passage. Desmond MacCarthy had helped him with The *Anatomy of Courage* and Charles now turned to him again.[47] MacCarthy re-ordered sentences in early drafts, and made incisive comments, like a tutor correcting a student's essay. Thus, apropros a reference by Charles to Karl Marx, the pencilled comment was 'Karl Marx is neither a Russian writer nor imaginative—safer to say "Russian Writers"'; and, elsewhere 'You must not under-rate Winston as a writer'.[49] When MacCarthy died in 1952 Charles missed him greatly. Charles also sought help from John right from the start. He exhorted him to say exactly what he thought, what parts of the text were best, what were worst, and to make verbal criticisms.[48] John's earliest comments on the batches of typescript that came to him in the diplomatic bag in the Middle East were concerned with the balance of the picture Charles was painting. It was most important, he told his father, that he should give a balanced impression of Winston, and he criticised him for assuming that the reader knew the great man of 1940, and for concentrating on his dark side. He cautioned him, too, about making judgements, in the light of the limited information then available, about how much responsibility Winston should bear for the disastrous Yalta and Potsdam settlements. 'I think you'll find it hard' he wrote, 'to see yourself whether the balance is right—you'll be too soaked in it.'[50]

Charles made no secret that he was writing a book. In January 1951 his fellow ex-College-President in Boston, Dr Roger Lee, wrote to say he was delighted that he was getting on with it, and that he was confident Charles could chart the perilous course between dullness and libel suits.[51] Four months later he told FW Hodson of *The Sunday Times* about it. Hodson expressed deep interest and the hope that Charles would not forget his newspaper when the time came for publication.[52] Charles replied that he was concentrating on doing the thing properly and not giving a thought to publication. He added:

'It is obviously not easy to produce a book of permanent value, judging by what has been done so far, and that is the challenge I am trying to meet. It is easy to report events, but to bring people to life is another matter. If I were to illustrate what I am saying

I should turn to the two pages which Cunningham* devotes to the Teheran Conference. It is difficult to believe he was there as one of the actors.'[53]

Although Charles would write to people and talk with people about his task, and refer to some of his material in speeches, he was determined to publish nothing at this stage. When he was invited to give the Founders' Memorial Lecture at Girton College in February 1951, for which he chose as the topic The Doctor's Dilemma, and the editor of the *British Medical Journal* asked him if he would make his lecture available for publication[54] Charles explained that he had asked the Mistress of Girton that there should be no publicity:

'The reason is that I wanted to illustrate my theme, where necessary, with my war experiences, and though there are not very many of these, the people concerned don't like them in print. I want to be free really to talk off the record.'[55]

The years 1950 and 1951 were good and productive ones for Charles. He no longer carried the cares of the College, the distinction awards committee provided an outside interest and occupation that he found congenial, he shared as much as he wanted to of an interesting social life with Dorothy, his sons were progressing in their careers, and he felt reasonably secure financially. By the end of 1951 he had put down on paper practically all the story that he wanted to tell. Then, quite suddenly, his life changed again. On 27 October 1951 the Conservative Party won the general election, Churchill returned to office, and Charles was once more close to the political centre.

---

*Admiral of the Fleet Sir Andrew Cunningham, later Viscount Cunningham of Hyndhope.

Chapter 20

Affairs of State

In the weeks before the general election in October 1951, Charles saw Churchill regularly, but at first it was the King's* illness rather than his own health that Churchill wanted to discuss.[1] The anticipated election was sometimes touched on in their conversations, but Charles was given no encouragement to air his views on the health service. When, on 20 September, Churchill asked him to come over from Marshalls to see him at Chartwell, and Charles said he had brought a few notes on the health service, Churchill put them in his pocket without reading them.[2] Charles was concerned at this time about general practitioners.[3] The specialists in the health service were fairly content but the general practitioners were not. Charles believed their pride in their job had gone. He believed that the decline in their status was not solely due to the health service, but stemmed from the technical advances in medicine and the increased specialisation that had been going on for many years. Patients increasingly considered that GPs were safe only for handling minor maladies. Nevertheless he felt some responsibility for what had happened, he wanted to help, and he had a remedy to propose. General practitioners must be allowed to follow their patients into the hospitals, from which they had been largely excluded as consultant services had developed:

> 'In my heart I knew that without this reformation of general practice there would be no peace and contentment among doctors. I wanted to give up the rest of my life to a crusade to open the doors of the hospitals, for the benefits must be incalculable. . . . I knew in my heart that I could do it and that no one else could.'[3]

Here was Charles once more in his most ambitious mood. The distinction awards system for consultants was becoming a routine, and he believed he had all but finished his book. After all, Winston, who was approaching his 77th year, could not live for ever. What better than for Charles, who was approaching his 69th year, to crown his own achievements by refining the operation of the NHS? He believed that doctors attributed everything they disliked in the health service to him,[4] and perhaps he could put things right. A month before the election, with this sort of ferment in his mind, he

---

*King George VI.

raised the question of the next Minister of Health with Churchill. During a conversation apparently initiated by Churchill, Charles suddenly warned him against appointing a certain person as Minister. The person was possibly Charles Hill, but Charles mentioned no name in his account of the episode. Charles was very worked up, bubbling over as he put it, and in retrospect shocked at his violence and want of reason. Churchill said he had no intention of giving the person concerned any appointment in the Ministry of Health, and according to Charles, 'He added in a kindly way: I've never seen you so upset before, Charles. You mustn't let anything I say upset you.'[5] Over the period of the election itself, no more seems to have been said, athough Charles was in demand to cope with a number of his patient's symptoms.[6] Comfort and reassurance were his watchwords as, at the sort of short notice he had become used to during the war, he accompanied Churchill on an electioneering trip to Huddersfield. In the train, Winston asked him to vet his speech.[7]

Two weeks after the election, at which Churchill was returned to power, Charles had a more serious confrontation. It was all the more extraordinary because it was a political one precipitated by Charles himself at the end of a professional visit. Charles deeply regretted that Churchill had appointed Harry Crookshank* as Minister of Health. He had had it in mind that Churchill might have consulted him about the appointment, and even have asked him to undertake the task.

'When I had done I rose to take my leave and then, in the impulse of the moment, I said to him: "I wish you had made me Minister of Health." I think the most I expected was that he would say: "I wish I had known this before." What he did say was: "I'm surprised. I never dreamt of such a thing. Really I don't know what people would have said if I had made my doctor Minister of Health. I confess I am a little shocked. You have had no experience in politics. Why, we might not even agree with your policy".

'I cannot say now why I had not the sense to see that nothing was to be gained by prolonging the argument. Perhaps I was nettled by the line he had taken. I think we both lost our tempers.'[3]

According to his account, Charles then proceeded to tell Churchill how, in travelling with him during the war, his practice had disappeared, that this was the first time in 11 years that he had

---

*Captain Harry Crookshank, previously Secretary to the Treasury and Postmaster General.

bothered him with his private affairs, and that Churchill might not be there at all but for him. As soon as he said this Charles realised he should not have done so. 'Ah', came the response, 'because you saved my life you want me to make you Minister of Health.' On this note, the interview ended, and feeling sore and humiliated Charles went out to the car where Dorothy was waiting for him and told her what had happened. They drove through the Park in silence. The following week went by very slowly. Charles found it hard to settle to anything. He watched the post and as the days passed he became more and more certain that his relationship with Churchill was over, and people would want to know why he had ceased to be his doctor.[3] But this was not the end. Dorothy, performing her familiar function of pouring oil on waters that Charles had troubled, wrote a note to 'Dearest Mr Churchill' asking that Charles should be forgiven for losing his temper and saying some very foolish things.[8] Characteristically, for Churchill's magnanimity was one of his salient features,[9] Charles was forgiven. Churchill never referred to this incident, but he did once tell Colville how much it had distressed him.[10]

If Charles had lingering doubts whether he was still the Prime Minister's doctor, they were soon dispelled, for within a month he was having to prepare for another transatlantic journey. And, so far as the health service was concerned, he had an opportunity to express his opinions publicly and to advocate his remedies in a debate in the House of Lords on 26 March 1952.[11] He prepared his argument carefully and spoke for 35 minutes. He wrote in advance, expressing his views, to the editors of *The Times*, *Daily Telegraph* and the *Guardian*[12] all of which papers gave him good coverage, and the day after his speech he sent a summary, to Churchill,[13] who acknowledged it and passed it on to the Minister of Health.[14] The Minister's response, forwarded to Charles by Churchill a month later, included a comment agreeing that the closest possible association between general practitioners and the hospital service was desirable and saying that discussions about this were under way.[15] It was several years before Charles again engaged in battle over the health service.

Churchill's latest Atlantic journey was prompted by his determination to meet President Truman.[16] The outward trip was to be by sea but there was a possibility that the return might be by air, and Charles sought to prevent this. He wrote to Sir Alan Lascelles, the King's private secretary:

'If the Monarch can influence Winston—no one else can—to return from America by ship and not by air, it would be helpful.

'For one thing, to cross the Atlantic by air in one's seventy-eighth year cannot be anything but a medical gamble. For another, the mere respite from the rehabilitation of the country's finances, gained by another few days at sea, may in itself help to keep him going.'[17]

Charles ended his letter:

'In any case keep my name out of it with Winston, as he gets enough blunt advice from me direct, and might get restive if he thought I was no longer content with direct action.'[17]

The reply from Lascelles was concise. He would do all he could but if Churchill had made up his mind he doubted if the archangel Gabriel would turn him.[18]

Churchill's party boarded the 'Queen Mary' at Southampton on 31 December 1951. The entourage echoed times past, and included Eden, Ismay and Cherwell, all of whom were now in the Cabinet. Charles reflected that it was 10 years since he first travelled with Winston in the 'Queen Mary', and that they might be back again in the war:

'. . . the PM is still talking and there, opposite him, is Pug, still listening to him with his mouth open, as if he would not miss a syllable, uttering the same throaty, gurgling sounds of mirth. Pug, anyway, has not changed. Everything else seems different. The indomitable spirit of the PM of those years, battling against a deadly threat to the world's freedom, is now struggling only with the humiliations of old age and with economic problems that are quite beyond his ken.'[19]

By the end of the visit, Charles's comment was less severe. The old appetite for work might have gone but he judged that Churchill was still better informed than any of his ministers on the armed forces. He fought obstinately in Washington over details of the Atlantic Command. 'No other man' wrote Charles, 'could have achieved so much when the Americans were disposed to give so little.'[20]

This sort of comment reflected the fact that, while Charles did not take part in the conferences, he was present at informal conversations to a greater extent than had been the case during the war when military secrecy guarded people's lips. There were no separate messes[21] and he was now on first name terms with Anthony Eden and many of the other main actors. He dined with Churchill once and lunched with him twice during the crossing, and in Washington he stayed at the British Embassy and in Ottawa at Government House. Apart from a reference to working on his book in the ship, there was no hint of his having time on his hands. He liked the British ambassador, Sir Oliver Franks, was glad to be

included in a dinner given by Dean Acheson*, and commented that
when Marshall came to lunch he was most affectionate.[22] In
Ottawa, he told Dorothy, Alex said he would like to see more of him.
He also met General Sir Gerald Templer in Ottawa and wrote:

'Templer, who goes out to command in Malaya said to me: I like
meeting you; you always say something I remember. Whereupon
he repeated remarks I'd made when I met him first, lecturing for
him when he had Eastern Command. He isn't a flatterer. I seem
to interest everyone except WC! He is friendly but [has] no idea
I have anything exceptional in my head.'[21]

The most significant personal happening for Charles on this visit
was his meeting with people at the top of the American publishing
world. As well as meeting Daniel Longwell of *Life* again,[23] he met
Henry A Laughlin of Houghton Mifflin and Company, and his wife,
at the home of Bernard Baruch with whom Churchill stayed in New
York.[24] Houghton Mifflin were the American publishers of
Churchill's *History of the Second World War*[25] and *Life* was
concerned with the serialisation.[26] Charles told Laughlin about his
own book, and on his return home (they travelled by sea at the end
of January)[27] he received a letter from Laughlin[28] expressing
Houghton Mifflin's interest in publishing it when the time came,
and asking if he, Laughlin, could talk this over with Charles during
his visit to London in July. Charles responded with a welcoming
letter in which he foreshadowed that he would in due course be
discussing serial rights with *Life*[28]. And so, at this early stage,
Charles established communication not only with potential
American publishers, but ones who had already invested in
Churchill's writings. How far in the future the publication of
Charles's book lay, he had no means of telling. But it must have
seemed sooner rather than later when, three weeks after returning
from America, he had, as he put it, to practise his calling.[29] On the
evening of 21 February 1952 he was telephoned directly by
Churchill, and when he reached Downing Street Churchill told him
that, an hour before, on waking from his afternoon sleep, he had
taken up the telephone and could not think of the words he wanted.
Charles explained that some small vessels in his brain had gone
into spasm, contracting so that the circulation to the speech centre
had been diminished. Together they went and told Mrs Churchill
about it.[30] When Charles called on the following morning, he found
his patient had had a good night and was in a mood to regard the
incident as closed. But Charles had come to a decision. He saw
himself as having taken great risks in the past, in letting Churchill

*Dean Acheson, President Truman's Secretary of State.

carry on in Washington after his heart attack in 1941 and, again, after his stroke in Monte Carlo in 1949. This time he would really try to get him to reduce his work load, but what he first needed to know was whether Churchill's duties as Prime Minister could be cut. Without delay he told Jock Colville, who was back as one of the Principal Private Secretaries, and who was also devoted to Churchill, what had happened.[31] Two hours later they together saw Lord Salisbury, a member of the Cabinet whom Charles greatly respected, and in the afternoon they saw Lascelles at Buckingham Palace. Salisbury suggested that Churchill might go to the House of Lords, remaining as Prime Minister, with Eden leading the House of Commons.[32] But, talking this through with Lascelles, the feeling was that even the Queen, who had been on the throne for only two weeks, would be unable to persuade Churchill to make the move.

Charles, who had initiated these discussions, explained to Lascelles that, as Churchill's doctor, he was in a difficult position in speaking to a third party. If he could not help his patient, he must see that nothing that he said did him hurt.[33] In saying this he was stating two of the basic ethics of medical practice, to try to do good for your patient, and never to do harm. Charles's perception of what was best for Churchill at this stage was that he should cut down his work.[34] The discussion with Lascelles ended with a decision that the small group should keep their counsel until pending debates in the Commons, and the budget, were over.[35] Then Charles would deliver a medical ultimatum.[36] Charles saw Churchill daily for the next few days. He did not add to his concerns by discussing his future, and the gamble that nothing would happen, and in particular that the episode on 21 February would not be followed by a massive stroke, paid off. Five days after that episode Churchill replied effectively to a vote of censure in the House of Commons,[37] and on 5 March made a speech introducing the defence estimates. Colville suggested to him that he should leave the latter task to the Secretary of State for War, whereupon Churchill turned on him in a flash; 'Have you been talking to Charles?' he said, and somehow Jock had to brazen it out.[38]

Once these events were over, Charles decided to warn his patient, and to convey his message on paper so that Churchill might absorb it.[34] He told him that the 'little disturbance' when he went to the telephone on 21 February, the mistiness of vision he had had in the previous year, and the 'blocking of the little artery' in Monte Carlo in 1949, all pointed to 'some instability of the cerebral circulation, which must be increased by excessive mental effort'. Charles's advice was that 'if it were possible to lighten the load, without giving up being Prime Minister, which on medical grounds would not be wise at the moment, then you ought to be able to carry on more or less indefinitely.' Charles ended by saying that he had told Clemmie his view. On the following day, Clemmie telephoned to say that Winston was not angry when he got Charles's letter, he just swept it aside.[39] A few days later Churchill told Charles he had got his letter and added: 'I don't want you to worry. You really needn't. One has got to die sometime'.[39] Years later Charles called the two chapters in his book which covered the fifteen months to June 1953, 'Muddling Through', and 'A New Lease of Life', and these headings are consistent with the notion that, in this period of his Indian summer, Churchill's performance did not fall far short of his expectations.[40] Charles saw him regularly, but there were no major medical problems, and Churchill started 1953 with a visit to North America, this time leaving a protesting Charles behind.[41,42] Charles said he was unhappy that he should go so far afield without medical aid, to which Churchill replied that he would take a chance as the visit was not official.[43]

Chapter 21

One-patient Doctor

By 1953 Charles had been in the House of Lords for 12 years. He belonged to no political party and he spoke only on subjects on which he could claim some expertise. Now, however, he gave his mind to a topic which was remote from his usual interests. There was a proposal for the creation of a limited number of Life Peers, people who would not transmit their peerages to their heirs,[1] and Charles was opposed to the idea. Having done some homework, and helped by Dorothy, who spent a happy morning in the London Library,[2] he acquired statistics showing that one-fifth of the members of the House were, like himself, what he called Lords of first creation who had not inherited their peerages, and that this group spoke disproportionately often. His argument was that there was already a happy combination of the new elements and hereditary elements. He spoke early in the debate on 3rd February, following some of the constitutional heavyweights, and at some length—for over 20 minutes—and for once he was disappointed with his performance. 'You know', Dorothy wrote to John, 'how sensitive he is to an audience and atmosphere', and she went on to explain how he was put off by members coming and going for tea and by the unfamiliarly large gathering.[3] At one stage his memory failed and, speaking without notes, he felt he lost the thread. This did not deter him from speaking in a debate on the same subject four years later,[4] but, apart from that, and speaking in opposition to commercial broadcasting, he did not stray again from a topic related to medicine. Up to 1960 when, at the age of 78 he made his last speech, he spoke on nursing,[5] the manufacture of heroin,[6] which he opposed, doctors' pay,[7] the Princess Louise Hospital,[8] hospital services and merit awards,[9] and on the Report of the Royal Commission on Doctors' and Dentists' Remuneration 1957-1960.[10] Unhappy though Charles may have been about his speech on Life Peers in February 1953, he remained highly regarded as a speaker in the House, where it was observed that the benches would fill as he began to speak and empty when he had finished.[11]

Apart from writing to Dorothy when he was away, Charles was not given to writing chatty letters to his family. However, at this time, with John overseas, he sometimes added a scrawl at the end of one of Dorothy's weekly letters, mostly about public figures he was meeting, and giving snippets of political comments which were occasionally nominated as for John's eyes only. Dorothy's letters reflected her own very busy life. In early 1953 she wrote of acquiring robes for the coronation due in May, of attending luncheons, visiting exhibitions, and sitting on interesting committees like that of Bedford College. Charles's activities were more circumscribed. He enjoyed attending Foyles' literary luncheons[12] and went regularly to dinners of the Pilgrims, a group concerned with fostering Anglo-American friendship, where he met, or renewed acquaintance with, men of affairs far removed from medicine. After the dinner in March he wrote to John:

> 'At the Pilgrims Dinner last night I sat next to Ronald Storrs*. I told him you were in Israel, and he said he would like to meet you when you come back, so we might have him to a meal at Marshalls. . . . Almost everybody seemed to be at the dinner last night, and I spoke to Gaitskell** for a moment. Hartley Shawcross***, hearing we lived at Marshalls, said we must go to dinner. He lives fairly near.

> 'The speeches were quite dreadful.'

He went on to describe one speaker as a 'natural vulgarian' and the other as 'out of the same drawer'. He continued:

> 'On Tuesday I have promised to open a discussion at the Athenaeum on Voluntary Euthanasia, with the Lord Chancellor in the Chair. I have got to talk for 20 minutes, and the other speakers are confined to five minutes. We dine first, I can get all the material I want out of the two debates in the House of Lords.

> 'We see the Boat Race with the Waverleys† as hosts on board a Port of London craft. All this sounds gay enough, but there are many days when I only emerge for a short walk to Baker Street to buy a paper. The rest of the time I either do the book or do something about the Awards.'[13]

The Boat Race party on the Waverley's launch led in turn to new introductions and renewal of more acquaintances, including people Charles was to remain in touch with over a number of years, like Frederick Doidge, the New Zealand High Commissioner; William Haley, editor of *The Times*; the Oliver Franks's, now back from the Washington Embassy; and Pierson Dixon. But Charles felt he was in a rut. In his writing he had wandered from the main theme and

---

*Sir Ronald Storrs had been a British administrator in the Middle East.
**Hugh Gaitskell MP, was Chancellor of the Exchequer 1950-51.
***Sir Hartley Shawcross MP, was Attorney-General 1945-51.
†Sir John Anderson had been created Viscount Waverley.

was ploughing along, as he put it, with a chapter on Baldwin, which he thought would misfire. He felt he would like a complete change. Whereupon Dorothy arranged that they should go to Cornwall for Easter, where some 30 St Mary's students were paying their annual visit to play rugger against local teams. Dorothy, Charles, with Geoffrey and Jane, and Harold Boldero with his son Ned, joined two other families from the staff of St Mary's, the Dickson Wrights and the Kemps, staying at Treganna.[15] The weather was not very good but they enjoyed expeditions along the coast and saw four matches. Charles had his change.

Charles continued to call regularly on Churchill, either at Downing Street or, driven over by Dorothy from Marshalls, at Chartwell. Dorothy's letters, occasionally headed 'Outside No. 10' and written as she sat waiting in the car, reflected the time Charles might spend inside. Enjoyment of the coronation in May was associated with the delight of seeing John and his family *en route* for their new posting in Rio de Janeiro, and following the coronation, Charles modified his plans[16] so as to be able to go with Churchill at the end of June to a meeting in Bermuda with President Eisenhower and the French Prime Minister.[17] Then, on the evening of Tuesday 23 June, Churchill had another stroke. The first Charles knew of it was when he went to Downing Street on the morning of Wednesday 24 June. He had been woken soon after midnight by a call from the girl on the exchange at Number 10 asking him to go and see the Prime Minister at nine o'clock. When he arrived he learnt from Jock Colville and Christopher Soames*[18] that, after a dinner given on the previous evening for the Italian Ambassador, Soames noticed that his father-in-law was having difficulty in standing up and in speaking. He managed to convey to the Ambassador that Churchill was very tired and the guests left. The family escorted Churchill to his bedroom, where he seemed to feel and to be much better.[19] Jock, who had been at the dinner, had tried without success to contact Charles and so the message for him to come had been left with the Downing Street switchboard. Charles found Churchill alert, but very unsteady on his feet, with the left side of his mouth sagging. Was it, Churchill asked, a stroke? Charles explained that the circulation in his head was sluggish, and there was spasm of a small artery; it belonged to the same family as the incident in Monte Carlo in 1949.[20] Charles saw him again in the afternoon in consultation with Sir Russell Brain, the specialist neurologist who had succeeded Charles as President of the Royal College of Physicians. Between them they dissuaded Churchill from attending the House of Commons Question Time in the afternoon. Charles told him that he could not guarantee that he would not get up in the House and

---

*Christopher Soames married Mary Churchill in 1947.

use the wrong word.[20] On the following day, Thursday 25, Churchill's gait was worse and he was persuaded to move to the relative privacy of Chartwell. On the third day, Friday 26, Charles found his left hand and leg had become weak and this steady progression of the paralysis led him to tell Jock that he thought it unlikely that Winston would live through the week-end.[21] However, Saturday proved to be the nadir, and on Sunday Charles was able to tell the family that there was a distinct improvement. There were now nurses in the house, and Churchill was got into his chair at the head of the table before Max Beaverbrook, in an ebullient mood, came to lunch.[22] From then on progress on the whole was smooth, though Charles was kept busy coping with a variety of tiresome symptoms. After two months Churchill, who never gave up his office as Prime Minister, presided over a Cabinet meeting,[23] and in September he left for two weeks convalescence in the South of France, accompanied by Christopher and Mary Soames.

Charles was at his patient's beck and call throughout this illness, and during the first month he saw him daily. At the onset he was of course well aware how difficult it was to forecast events from hour to hour, let alone from day to day. Persisting disability, rapid recovery, or disastrous paralysis were equally unpredictable. His attitude was: 'There will be lots of people buzzing round, but we must sit tight until we know where we are. In a few days the position be plainer.' Sitting tight, as he put it, did not however prevent him from spending part of the second day, Thursday 25 June, at Lords, where the cricket turned out to be rather dull, or, with Dorothy, from dining on that evening with the Camroses.[24] Lord Camrose, proprietor of the *Daily Telegraph*, was one of three of Churchill's friends with powerful influence over the press (the other two being Bracken, who owned the *Financial Times* and Beaverbrook who owned the *Daily Express* and *Evening Standard*) to whom Colville had already written in what proved to be an almost completely successful attempt to prevent news of Churchill's condition reaching the newspapers. Colville had done this, despite Churchill's injunction not to let it be known that he was temporarily incapacitated, because he believed the truth would leak out unless defensive action were taken.[25] On Saturday 27 July, a statement was issued from Number 10 announcing the cancellation of the Bermuda conference, with an attached medical bulletin signed by Charles and Brain. The bulletin, which Charles drew up with the help of the patient, said that a disturbance of the cerebral circulation had developed, resulting in attacks of giddiness.[28] After he and Brain signed it Charles showed it to Salisbury* and RA Butler**,

---

*Lord Salisbury, Lord President in Churchill's government.
**RA Butler, Chancellor of the Exchequer in Churchill's government.

who between them were holding the fort in government on Churchill's behalf because Eden was in hospital in Boston, and they persuaded Churchill to agree to an alteration in the wording. Among other things they removed the reference to a circulatory disturbance. The resulting bland bulletin gave no diagnosis, and simply indicated that the Prime Minister was in need of complete rest.[28] Charles was cross about this. In writing to Beaverbrook two days later to thank him for some hospitality which he felt he had abused by wrangling over the bulletin he stated his position:

'The bulletin issue is simple enough:

(1) *Procedure* Where it is not possible or desirable in a bulletin to give the facts, it is, I think, better not to issue one (eg Monte Carlo). I thought at the time that it would have been better if we doctors had not come into it, leaving it to the political people to make their own explanations. After all, if doctors issue bulletins deliberately designed to mislead the public, bulletins would soon come into as much disrepute as the evidence of psychiatrists in murder cases.

(2) *Judgment* When Brain and I drew up the bulletin originally we felt that something must be said to explain his sudden retirement—people like Winston don't suddenly rest on doctors' orders for a month at a critical time without some good reason. The reason I wanted them to give was that he had had a disturbance of the circulation leading to attacks of giddiness. That is a much less damaging admission than to say he had a stroke, and would, I believe, have prevented all this talk about a stroke—as you know people everywhere are saying that he has had a stroke. Anyway it is too early to say whether what Butler and Salisbury concocted will turn out to be wise or not.'[27]

Discussing the bulletin in retrospect a month later when he was well on the road to recovery, Churchill said he was glad Salisbury had altered it. Charles conceded that the chance they had taken had come off but his objections stood.[29] The policy not to announce a diagnosis remained in place, and Churchill did not state publicly that he had had a stroke in 1953 until the occasion of a debate in the House of Commons two years later;[26] but he made no secret of it in private[30] and Charles thought the drama of the illness appealed to him.[31]

Ten days after the onset of the stroke, Dorothy wrote from Marshalls to John:

'I have had a very strange and odd week, standing by at Marshalls to act as chauffeur between there and Chartwell and to make odd meals at odd times for Daddy. He has stayed there off and on. At first he had an anxious and difficult time but now he tells me the news is excellent. The old man retains a great sense of humour, "At least" he says, "I have displaced Christie from the headlines."* . . . I am now going up to London for a Girton lunch and to call at C [Chartwell] with letters, clothes etc . . .'[32]

At the end of Churchill's second week at Chartwell, Dorothy wrote to John from Harley Street:

'Daddy came back home from Chartwell yesterday—he himself has had a horrid neuritis in his arm and neck all the week—a result of his old injury. It is slowly getting better but it has made him very tired and he has had bad nights. The other patient is making progress and is in great form.'[33]

After three weeks Dorothy commented to John:

'This as you can imagine is a bit of an effort but they provide transport if I don't want to go. We shall call in tonight on our way from Harley Street to Marshalls and go over from there on Saturday and Sunday. He is threatening to go to Chequers soon which will complicate our life considerably—it is about 70 miles from Marshalls.'[34]

Four weeks after the onset of his stroke, Churchill moved to Chequers to give the staff at Chartwell a much-needed rest.[35] Charles, his painful neuritis now better, continued to call on him on most days.[36] In August both Parkinson and Brain, who again saw him in consultation, took a gloomy view of his chances of being able to cope with his duties in the House as Prime Minister[37] but Charles was determined to continue to gain time for him, and this he did. His patient wanted to remain as Prime Minister and Charles did not dissuade him. At most, he saw it as his duty to offer pros and cons.[38] This is not to say that Charles never had doubts. The main hurdle Churchill had to confront was his first speech after his recovery, to be made at the Conservative Party Conference at Margate on 10 October 1953. Charles interrupted his own travels in connection with merit awards, returning from Truro to London on the night train 24 hours beforehand, in order to see if he was in good fettle.[39] 'The bother is', he confessed, 'that Winston has made me as windy as himself about his infernal speech'.[40] But doubts of this sort were, for Charles, exceptional, and when the time came for his patient to appear once more in public, Charles departed from the therapeutic nihilism of which Churchill was wont to accuse him. For the all-important Margate speech, Charles resolved to

---

*Christie's notorious murder trial.

redeem his 'rather negative reputation as a vendor of nostrums by inventing a pill which he will take an hour before he rises to address the meeting'.[39] The pill, which Churchill referred to as a 'Moran',[41] was tried out a few days in advance, when Churchill said it completely cleared away the muzzy feeling in his head and gave him great confidence. When Charles saw his patient in the evening after the speech, which by all accounts had been a great success, Churchill greeted him affectionately:

"The pill was marvellous", he said, putting his hand on my arm. "What was in it? Did you invent it? Now, Charles, I know you don't like medicines, but you see what good they can do. You must have given a lot of thought to this pill. I won't ask for it often, I promise. Perhaps once a month when I have a difficult speech in the House. Anyway, Charles what harm would it do if I took it more often?"'[40]

This was the start of an empirical programme of medication with pills given pet-names such as majors and minors with which Charles tried over the next few years to help his patient cope.

The close association which Charles had had with Churchill during his attack of pneumonia at Carthage in 1944, and during his stay at Lake Como in 1945, was renewed during the 1953 stroke episode.[43] This time, as Charles stayed at Chartwell, or was motored over there, he had to see more of the family, and he was involved with the visits of a number of Churchill's friends and political associates. Among these, in the first 10 days at Chartwell, were Max Beaverbrook, Brendan Bracken, Lord Camrose, the Prof, Norman Brook*, Harold Macmillan, and Monty. This situation contributed further to the extended role that Charles had already come to play as a medical advisor. Reflecting on Churchill's last years as Prime Minister, Mary Soames later wrote:[44]

'Lord Moran understood Winston thoroughly, and he was indeed fortunate he had as a doctor a man who understood not only the medical considerations and risks to his patient, but one who was also fully aware of the implications, with regard to the office he held, of his condition at any time. Lord Moran moreover understood the relationship between, and with, Winston's colleagues, and where one could expect loyalty, understanding and total discretion—and when one could not.'

Following Churchill's return to public life in October 1953 after his stroke, Charles usually saw him once or twice a week. He was

*Sir Norman Brook had succeeded Sir Edward Bridges as Secretary to the Cabinet in 1947.

concerned with his mood and morale, he helped him over hurdles such as making speeches, and acted as a sort of sounding board as Churchill havered over whether he should resign and let Anthony Eden succeed him. The friction between Churchill and Eden became a recurring theme in the 200 to 300 word notes that Charles jotted down each time he saw Churchill. Charles believed that no one else knew Churchill's views on Eden,[45] apparently unaware that the Prime Minister spoke with no less frankness to Jock Colville, another assiduous diarist in his entourage.[46]

Charles had given his patient clear advice about retirement when he was recovering from his stroke in August.

> 'We have taken a good many risks together. But now it's my job as your doctor to warn you bluntly that if you are not willing to think out a new way of being Prime Minister, then you would be wise to resign before October.'[47]

Being much about the place with his frequent visits to Number 10, Chartwell and Chequers, Charles was often approached on this and related subjects by people in Churchill's entourage. Colville might talk of the PM's tiresome procrastination, (and incidentally learn that Charles had given Winston a pill before the last Cabinet because he did not seem to be able to concentrate);[48] Soames might phone Charles, away in the north of England on merit awards business, because he was worried that Winston was breathless when bobbing up and down answering questions in the House;[49] and Soames, gallantly helping to hold the fort with Colville,[50] might take Charles aside and tell him it was time for the PM to pull out and that he, Charles was the only person who could persuade him to go.[51] Mrs Churchill was of like mind[52]. But so far as Charles was concerned, the test for retirement would be whether Winston was harming himself by continuing as PM, not family sentiment, or political considerations, or other people's estimates of his performance. In October 1953, when Soames complained that he could not get Winston to read important papers, Charles defined his attitude:

> 'If you and Jock and Norman Brook agree at any time that he is doing himself no good in his job, then I will try to get him to resign.'[53]

The postponed conference in Bermuda with Eisenhower and the French Prime Minister, M. Joseph Laniel, took place in December.[54] Dorothy, with the wives of the other travellers, saw the party off from Heathrow at midnight on 1 December in the BOAC strato-cruiser 'Canopus'. There was a small impromptu party, the airliner was floodlit on the tarmac, and Dorothy could not help thinking of the contrast with the furtive midnight departures during the war.[55] Charles, too, was in a reflective mood, surmising that this might be his last journey with Winston:

'We began life humbly enough, in an unheated Lancaster bomber, and end it, twelve years later, in high state in the strato-cruiser . . . messages no longer pass to the captain asking at what height we are flying . . . it is all one to us, pressurised at 5000 feet. Most of the seniors and quite a few of the juniors came to me last night for sleeping pills—this weak-kneed generation that needs dope for a few hours in the air.'

He might have added that the weak-kneed generation spent the long night sitting up. Churchill and Eden had beds and he and the Prof had lower berths, being, in age, by far the most senior members of the party after the Prime Minister, whose 79th birthday party Dorothy and Charles had attended on the previous night.[55]

Charles started his description of the passing scene with the lunch in 'Canopus'. He sat at a table for four, Churchill and the Prof on one side, Eden and himself on the other:

'After greeting Anthony cheerfully, Winston took up his book, *Death to the French* by CS Forester, and kept his nose in it through the meal. The Prof, who is getting deaf, could not hear what was said, so giving up the attempt to bring him in, I talked to Anthony.'[56]

In a letter to Dorothy written on the day after they arrived, Charles retailed this conversation, after first saying how he had spent the morning:

'The French have just arrived. I did not see them as I was demonstrating to Christopher and the Prof how short approach shots should be played, with astonishing accuracy! . . . I had a long and interesting talk [at lunch] with Eden who is very friendly. Many of his views are mine. He is much more discerning about people than PM is, listens to what you say and is interested and seems sensible about most things. "France is a geographical necessity but otherwise hopeless." "Alex no brains." Knew Pug was dying to come to Bermuda, and said it was such a bore!'[57]

Despite finding some common ground with Eden, Charles's overall estimate was that he 'lacked the hard core which in Winston is hidden by his emotional nature and magnanimity'.[56]

Charles enjoyed the comfort of the Mid-Ocean Club, where Churchill's inner circle stayed. The British delegation was small and Charles was involved in the official social activities. He liked the style of the Governor, Lieutenant General Sir Alexander Hood, a doctor, who had taken the post after serving in the war as head of the Army Medical Service:

'Hood has been a success here. He has an advisory Council of 3 and consults them on everything. He (not his ADC) telephones them and they like that. They like a soldier, who is some good at administration and handling men. It is really a sinecure for all purposes. PM, hearing he was a Dr said: "Would you like to be a Governor, Charles?" I think idea entered his head. But I doubt whether I really want to spend my remaining days in Jamaica or Bermuda: anyway it will be time enough to consider it if and when they offer me it.'[58]

Apart from his daily contacts with Churchill, who after a seven-hour meeting said 'Your pill worked wonders',[59] Charles had one other professional call when M. Laniel developed pneumonia.[60] The party flew home on 10 December, and a few days later Charles wrote to John:

'I should guess Eden will be PM within next few months. Ike said he thought Lord Salisbury would be a good Foreign Secretary (he had obviously been impressed by him), but Pug interposed that he was now in the Lords. I imagine this best kept to yourself as about seven of us were dining as Ike's guests and he was talking freely. Pug is apparently thinking of retiring from his Nato job* which astonishes me. Eden thought he was there for life. Winston burnt his hand this afternoon and came out of Cabinet to see me and Dunhill. Gather Egyptians are being very obstreperous. As WC says we can never do anything until they attack us. I think he'd rather like to do this . . .

'I wrote a short preface to a book on Annigoni's painting, which pleased him very much, and considering how little I know about painting was ingenuous. I think his portraits of women are very good but his landscapes aren't in my line at all.

I'm good friends with Mrs Woodham Smith, whose *The Reason Why* has had very good reviews. She sold 200 000 copies of *Florence Nightingale*. She is a born story teller. I gave Winston for his birthday *Royal Flush* which interested him. [An historical novel by Margaret Irwin] He likes that kind of book. Life have offered Winston 50 000 dollars every year for four years for serial rights of his *History of English Speaking Peoples*. It was written before war but needs some rewriting. This for your ear.'[61]

As 1954 began, Dorothy mentioned to John that M. Laniel had sent Charles two dozen of claret 'La Mission haut Brion—grand

---

*Ismay had become Secretary General of NATO in 1952.

premier cru—1948'. She had been advised that it was a very good wine for laying down and that it would mature in 20 years. 'I think', she added, 'we shall have to lay down a little for you and GH and try to exchange some for a more mature wine which Daddy can enjoy!'[62] Charles, in the same letter, told John that he and Charles Morgan, the author and playwright, had been the speakers at a city vintner's dinner. He had got hold of Sainsbury's cellar book and 'mugged up quite an effective little oration'. Morgan was 'very good in a precious, self conscious way . . . as I think you might tell from his books!' He then went on to write about Winston, first mentioned the recurrent theme, how he had talked of retiring but seemed to have settled down again. He also mentioned progress with his own book.[63] The background, which John already knew, was that Henry Laughlin, of Houghton Mifflin, whom Charles had met at Bernard Baruch's home in January 1952, had been as good as his word. He had visited England in the following July and he and his wife Becky had spent an evening at Marshalls. Charles had read parts of his book to him and Laughlin had been so impressed that on his return to Boston he had sent Charles a partially filled-in contract.[64] He had advised Charles to expand his material to carry more of his own interpretation. He also advised including conversations with people who, with Charles, had accompanied Churchill on his trips, and anything he might feel justified in putting in about Mrs Churchill and other members of the family. Laughlin suggested that Charles should get the book into final form, and add to it from day to day as the Prime Minister continued his career. Laughlin's enthusiasm was matched by an offer of £1000 now and £1000 on receipt of the manuscript. Charles had sent a non-committal response.[65] He referred to his difficulty in deciding how much could be said, and to his plan to write as if these considerations did not arise, and then to review the position. Laughlin had acknowledged this as a good plan.[66]

Whether or not influenced by Laughlin's advice in the summer of 1952, Charles had acted in accordance with it. Now (in January 1954) in his letter to John, he wrote:

'Whenever I see him [Winston] I jot down a few of the things he says: in this way I've compiled 36 000 words since September 1952. It's quite different from the accounts of the Conferences. I think the danger is it may be repetitive and trivial, but it is no trouble and the result will be eventually I'll have a very big book, perhaps 130 000-140 000 [words] from which I can cut out the duller parts.

'Why don't you keep a diary? Harold Nicolson has done so for years. Then if you ever write it is a mine you can dig in . . . I wish very much I'd done this long ago. I find now I notice things which previously (even during war) I never noticed.'

Nineteen-fifty-four unfolded with the now familiar routine of writing, Foyles lunches, Pilgrims dinners, Rugby football matches and merit awards travels. Sometimes the latter two activities could be combined, as in March when Charles contrived to make his Scottish awards meeting coincide with the Calcutta Cup, and he was invited to be the guest of the Scottish Rugby Football Union for lunch, the match and dinner.[67] The dinner was a wild affair with singing, throwing bread and squirting soda water, and Charles, now one of the older aficionados of the game, when called on to speak, performed the unlikely feat of so interesting his audience as to have them listen to him in absolute silence.[68] Dorothy planned what she envisaged as the grandest of their weekends at Marshalls for the beginning of July, when the United States Ambassador, Winthrop Aldrich and his wife, and the David Cecils had accepted invitations to visit.[69] Charles had come to know Lord David Cecil through Desmond MacCarthy, who was his father-in-law,[70] Cecil's book on Lord Melbourne was about to be published, and Charles was longing to talk books with him. But it did not work out like that. Churchill decided to cross the Atlantic again on 24 June,[71] and Dorothy was left to cope alone with the house party, feeling she could not put off the weekend because the Aldrichs had tickets to take them all to Glyndebourne.[72]

This trip involved an absence of two weeks, with a flight, again in 'Canopus', visits to Washington and Ottawa, and a return journey in the 'Queen Elizabeth'.[73] Washington was tiresomely hot, but Charles's bedroom in the British Embassy was air-conditioned and he spent his days in it except when visiting Churchill at the White House or attending social functions.[74] From his almost daily letters to Dorothy he seems to have had time on his hands, and his recording of the conversations of those around him reflected little of the high purpose that Churchill had had when the expedition set out, which was to try to take some of the heat out of the cold war.[73] At the back of his mind he remained fretful at missing the weekend at Marshalls, and very anxious that it should be a success. His letter exhorting Dorothy to open two bottles of claret and one of champagne[75] was reminiscent of his attempts to control details in London during his wartime travels overseas.

Three days before Churchill's 80th birthday, on 30 November 1954, Charles sent a letter to Brendan Bracken[76] which he had drafted two weeks earlier.[77] It began:

'My dear Brendan,

'You have been so good to me that I think I would like to give an account of my stewardship.

'It is now nearly fifteen years since, at your instigation, I first saw the Prime Minister. Since then he has had: (i) a heart attack in Washington . . .'

and Charles proceeded to list the various ailments with which he had contended, incidentally emphasizing the risk to himself that he took in concealing the 1941 heart attack. He ended the letter:

'It has been possible, with the exception of two attacks of pneumonia and some talk about his stroke, in June 1953, to keep all this from the public, and indeed from the political world. I cannot help taking a certain pride that these battle honours will not be known in my lifetime. I hope that you will think that, having induced the PM to see me, it has not worked out badly.
Yours ever'[76]

The response from Bracken was prompt and brief. No one, he said, had ever been a more faithful steward than Charles and he could take pride in this fact as the Boss, as he called Winston, entered his 81st year.[78] There are three noteworthy points about Charles's letter. In his book he later gave the impression that the sentiments expressed were put together on the morning of Churchill's birthday, 30 November,[79] which may be allowable artist's license. Secondly the letter indicated the intention on Charles's part not to make public in his, Charles's, lifetime the illness that Churchill had suffered, an intention which eventually he did not sustain. Finally, why did he write the letter? It appears to have come out of the blue, and its contents would not have been news to Bracken. It seems to be an invitation for a pat on the back. Perhaps what Charles was trying to say was that, with Churchill about to receive congratulations on reaching his 80th birthday, could there not be some acknowledgement of the dedication of his physician, which no one, if they stopped to think about it, could deny? Charles surely sometimes reflected on the fact that it was 12 years since he had received a public honour in the form of his barony.

On 30 November 1954, the day of the birthday, Charles made his regular morning visit to Number 10 an early one, bringing as a gift from Dorothy and himself specially bound copies of David Cecil's two volumes on Lord Melbourne, together with one of the Duke of Marlborough's letters written in French as a present from John and Geoffrey.[80] Charles was photographed on his arrival carrying a large box, and it had to be explained that it was not a gift but his academic gown which he had to wear at St Mary's in the afternoon, when the Queen Mother would be visiting. He was getting Winston's valet to press it and hang it out. Charles did not care for Graham Sutherland's portrait, which was presented to Churchill as a birthday gift from both Houses of Parliament. On the occasion of one of the early sittings at Chartwell, Sutherland had told Charles that he wanted to paint Churchill 'with a kind of four-square book', and Charles said he had tried to sound a warning note. 'Don't forget', he said, 'that Winston is always acting, try to see him when he has got the grease paint off his face.'[81] After seeing the finished version, Charles wrote:

'There is, to be sure, plenty of power and vigour and defiance in the coarse features that Graham Sutherland has drawn, but they do not belong to Winston Churchill.'[82]

For Charles, the Orpen portrait,[83] painted after the Dardenelles in the First World War, portrayed the man he knew. Charles was invited to contribute directly to Winston's birthday celebrations by taking part in a series of tributes on television, compèred by Pug Ismay.[84] Consistent with his policy about speaking publicly about Churchill, he declined.[80]

Dorothy and Charles both went to the party at Number Ten on the following day, and Dorothy wrote to John:

'The setting was beautiful—those gracious rooms, charmingly lighted. Winston was very affectionate and referred to your Marlborough letter which had pleased him. It must have made a deep impression for him to remember it in the 23 000 greetings and presents he has had. . . . All the family were there—I like Mary much the best of them. The Secretaries were buzzing round, rather subdued except for Jock whom nothing would subdue. Jane Portal* said they were all in disgrace over this extraordinary episode of the Woodford speech and the non-existent telegram. Daddy will talk to you about that. We have come to like Anthony Browne** very much—he is always sensible and very intelligent. Two enormous birthday cakes were on view. . . .'[80]

Charles was in a lot of pain[85] from an attack of shingles when Churchill eventually resigned as Prime Minister on 6 April 1955, but he stood by and saw him almost daily over the event until, six days after leaving Downing Street, Sir Winston and Lady Churchill left for a two-week holiday in Sicily.[86] For more than a week before Churchill's resignation, Charles fought a brusque action to try to persuade him that he should accompany them. Letters were exchanged in which various arguments and counter arguments were marshalled, Churchill's main point being that he did not wish his departure to be seen as if it were on health grounds, and Charles's main point being the potential hazards of the withdrawal of 'minors' or of their unsupervised use.[87] Churchill won, having decided that he could stop the minors before he left and that there would be no need for him to take them when abroad. Once he settled in at Syracuse he thoughtfully sent Charles a telegram assuring him all was well.[88]

---

*Jane Portal, one of Churchill's personal secretaries.
**Anthony Montague Browne, one of Churchill's Private Secretaries, who remained with him through his retirement.

Through the 10 years between Churchill's resignation as Prime Minister and his death in 1965 in his 91st year, Charles watched over his ups and downs, his periods of melancholy and withdrawal, and the times when some of life's interests returned. The slow decline was set against a background of increasing deafness and recurrent small strokes, which, one by one, left his patient increasingly impaired in mind and body. For several of these years Charles shared the task of providing a regular medical presence, and responding quickly to distress signals, with Dr John Roberts, who practised in Monte Carlo. This came about because Churchill spent many months in his last years abroad, mostly in the South of France. Dr Roberts, who was called in when Churchill had his first stroke in 1949,[89] provided support there for him for weeks at a time from 1956 to 1962. Churchill liked him; his reassuring air had a beneficial effect.[90] Roberts was more willing than Charles to try different treatments,[91] and this appealed to the patient, who was convinced that French medicine was much ahead of English.[92] Charles conveyed his disapproval of this approach directly to Churchill,[91] and in very specific terms when he discovered that Roberts was prescribing a white tablet, which Churchill thought was splendid,[92] which consisted of exactly the same barbiturate that was contained in the 'reds' which Charles had been prescribing for years.[93]

Quite apart from Dr Roberts, Charles's relationships with other doctors were not always easy where Churchill was concerned. He was resentful if consultants whom he called in were inclined to take charge,[94] and justifiably so because his intimate knowledge of his patient gave him a unique qualification for overall management. But as the years went by he was increasingly jealous of his position at centre stage[95] and in his last years was known to go so far as to identify to the press a distinguished senior colleague, who was fortunately also a friend, as his assistant, his senior registrar.[96]

A response to a call for help in February 1958 led Charles to visit Churchill at Roquebrune in the South of France, where Mr Emery Reves's house, La Pausa, stood high above the sea between Menton and Monte Carlo. Churchill stayed there altogether some 10 times, usually without Lady Churchill, who disliked the Riviera.[97] Before the war, Reves had been Churchill's European literary agent[98] and after the war he had acquired the foreign language rights in his *War Memoirs* and *History of the English Speaking Peoples*.[97] Charles's visit to La Pausa followed a telephone call from Dr Roberts to say that Churchill was feverish and coughing. Charles flew to Nice and on arriving at La Pausa found his patient had broncho-pneumonia.[99] He stayed for two weeks, during which the lady of the house, Wendy Russell (later Mrs Reves) was not only impressed with his devotion to his patient but also found him the most considerate of her guests.[100] For his part, Charles for once found conversation with a woman easy; he had found someone *sympathique*, whose main interest was his own, for Wendy could talk interminably of Churchill and his family. In recalling this, Charles wrote:

'After months in England, where the entries in my diary were little more than a dirge, he [Winston] would go off to France and return, perhaps in two months time, in better spirits, ready for engagements, prepared to make plans. Wendy's vitality, her high spirits, her unconventional habits and loving ways attracted him. I can see her dancing a few steps and Winston watching her with an affectionate smile. The world, with all its veneration, accepted the fact that his life was over. Wendy obstinately refused to pull down the blinds. I think Winston felt this and was grateful.'[101]

Charles did his best to persuade Churchill to take him with him when he visited Washington a year later, in May 1959, arguing he had it in mind to keep him in top form by regulating his use of 'minors',[102] but Churchill declined his offer. However, in March 1960 Charles and Dorothy were both invited to join the Churchills in a cruise to the West Indies in the yacht 'Christina', which belonged to Mr Ari Onassis, the Greek shipowner. Onassis's brother, a surgeon in active practice, was one of the other guests, and Charles was not seen as travelling in his professional capacity.[103] The party was small and oddly assorted, ranging in age from Anthony Montague Browne, Churchill's Private Secretary, and his wife Nonie, to the Churchills and the Morans. Dorothy kept a diary[104] which showed that the trip was not without its tensions:

Sun 20 March 1960:

'Meals have been a little uncomfortable. I am generally between WSC who has an ear machine in the ear on the other side, and Theodor who has no English. However we battle along. Clemmie talks all the time to Anthony [Montague Browne]. It almost seems at times that she is baiting Charles for all his bête-noirs come up, Roberts at Monte Carlo, Ismay etc. However Charles is not to be drawn and the awkward moments go by.'

Thursday 30 March

'I am worried by the relation between Charles and Clemmie. She really does try to bait him. At lunch she started on the old argument about heroin and said that no relation of hers should go to Stanford Cade* who had written to the *Times* that he never used it. Then in the evening she started on to me about the specialist

---

*Sir Stanford Cade, consultant surgeon to the Westminster Hospital.

obstetricians . . . Charles is proud and sensitive and incapable of hiding his feelings. Between them I feel a bit sad and uncomfortable.'

What with language barriers, deafness and other complications, mealtimes could present a challenge even to one so accomplished in conversation as Dorothy:

'. . . And meals too were generally disturbed by Toby the budgerigar whose cage was solemnly put on the table and the door opened and then he would fly round, perching on people's shoulders and pulling Theodor's moustache, and conversation became impossible as people kept saying "Toby, Toby".'

Dorothy summed up the trip as an unforgettable experience, but she was sad for Charles

'Clemmie is difficult. She made a great fuss for several days about a sore eye, and raved at Charles because he did not do anything for it and [said] that she would go ashore where any native doctor would put her right. Now that Winston is so old, she really is in charge in a way that she has never been before. This makes things very difficult. I often wished on the voyage that Charles had someone more understanding, someone who spoke the same language both literally and figuratively. However, with all this sun and warm air he is in much better shape and has lost his cough . . .'[104]

As Dorothy finished her diary for this trip on 2 April 1960, so too Charles ended the account of Churchill that he later published in his book. There was no point, he wrote, in continuing the story of Churchill when it had ceased to be of any historical significance.[105]

Chapter 22

Author at Work—With Interruptions

After Churchill retired in 1955, Charles's life became altogether more placid. His patient's illnesses no longer had the potential to become high matters of State, and there were no more threats of sudden journeys with the travelling circus. Also, some nice things happened. Geoffrey completed his exams as a chartered accountant, and in October 1955 married Jane Hebblethwaite. Then John and his family had a spell in England. And there was cricket to watch in the summer and rugger in the winter, and gradually the restlessness of the first post-war decade was replaced by a style of life more suited to an ageing physician. It was even noted that Charles showed signs of becoming a bird-watcher, keeping under observation a nest of flycatchers in a rose bush outside the north window of the book room at Marshalls.[1]

In 1956, Charles received a warning that he, like his patient, was not immortal; he developed a pain in the chest which he recognised as angina, and so had to climb the stairs more slowly when he visited Churchill in his bedroom.[2] At this time too, he and Dorothy decided to stop rattling about uncomfortably in their large house in Harley Street. Charles made his last entry in what in recent years had been a very sparsely filled case book,[3] and they moved to a flat in Bryanston Square. Charles was still receiving a salary as chairman of the merit awards committee, and concern for Dorothy's future, should he die, was again eased when Churchill renewed the deeds of covenant for the annuities which she, John and Geoffrey had been receiving.[4]

Also in 1956, Charles received his second invitation to speak at a medical gathering in the United States. He was bidden by the University of California at San Francisco to be the speaker at the annual medical graduation ceremony. The visit was arranged through the professor of medicine, Dr William J Kerr,[5] who had once been a house officer of Charles's friend Dr Roger Lee of Boston.[6] Charles set out on his own in May, in the 'Queen Elizabeth', with little enthusiasm. He had hated being out of touch with Dorothy during his wartime travels, when he wrote to her almost daily and handed his letters in to the Prime Minister's travelling office personally, always with the words—Make sure it goes in the Bag, please.[7] He tolerated his separations no better as he grew older, and no sooner was he at sea than he was worrying about sneezing and having a sore throat and about having left Dorothy with a cold. 'Don't take any risks' he begged her in a letter that could not be posted for several days. 'These virus things are very tricky'.[8] He also worried about leaving Churchill,[9] and to cap it all, he did not feel at home among what he described as the many wealthy industrialists in the first class accommodation, although he couldn't help wondering if any of them might conceivably be useful to Geoffrey.[8] On reaching New York he flew to Boston to spend a few days with the Lees. There he found the years had caught up with his host, who dropped off to sleep on all possible occasions, and snored before lunch when he took Charles to his club.[10] Charles was very hospitably received in San Francisco, where he was lodged in the Bohemian Club whose motto was 'Weaving Spiders Come Not Here'. He judged his speech on the history of the Royal College of Physicians, which he called 'Out of the Past', to have been a success but not a triumph because he lost his voice.[11] On his return journey he visited Concord to stay with the Laughlins and talk about his book.[12]

Marshalls continued to provide a centre for social contact with the wider world. Charles and Dorothy saw something of people who lived not far away, including Harold Macmillan and his wife Lady Dorothy, and Sir Hartley and Lady Shawcross; Sir Hartley had been Attorney General and had led the British prosecution at Nuremberg when Charles had been involved in the case of Rudolf Hess. In the visitor's book at Marshalls many names were recorded of people of distinction in various walks of life. They included the William Haleys, the Oliver Franks's, the Norman Brooks's, the David Cecils, the George Mallabys*, the Alexander Cadogans and the Ian Jacobs.[13] None were intimate friends in that Dorothy and Charles saw little of them apart from these visits, but they were people with whom, for Charles, conversation was always fascinating. Beyond doubt, too, both husbands and wives satisfied Dorothy's criteria for making people welcome, which were that she judged them to be genuine and intelligent and that they enjoyed Mozart, whose tunes she happily hummed around the house.

Few doctors were invited to Marshalls. Charles by now had no interest in talking medical shop; if he wanted to know what was going on in medicine, he always knew whom to ring up. Among the exceptions as a visitor was Sir John Richardson**, who became Dorothy's and Charles's physician. He and his wife Sybil developed an abiding friendship for the Morans, which was reciprocated. Sybil, a gifted painter and acute observer, did sketches of Charles and a painting of Dorothy. She was one of the few members of the female

---

*Sir George Mallaby, a senior civil servant.
**Sir John (later Lord) Richardson, physician to St Thomas's Hospital.

sex with whom Charles was socially at ease, and she for her part enjoyed his company and turn of phrase.[14] Recognising, like others, that in criticising people he was inclined to be malicious,[15] she also discerned a lot of straight wit and a Puckish humour. Some of his quips became lasting memories; 'I don't like that eye' he said, on getting a side view of a drawing she was doing of him, 'I don't think that's the kind of eye that would be nice for the grandchildren'.[14] Another medical exception among the visitors was Dr TA Kemp, who, with his wife Ruth, enjoyed a warm friendship with both Dorothy and Charles. Tom Kemp had been one of Charles's star students, had captained England at Rugby football and had been appointed to the staff of St Mary's after the war. He had come to know the Moran family well enough to wonder sometimes about Charles's and Dorothy's respective roles. To what extent was the conventional picture of the young Charles, stern, ambitious and ruthless, and the soft, warm-hearted Dorothy, really correct?[16] There was, perhaps, more softness in Charles and ruthlessness in Dorothy than met the eye.

It was in this period, in January 1958, when Charles was 75, that there occurred the second of what Dorothy called the three occasions on which he was at war with public opinion. The first, the great rugger row of the 1930s, was distant enough to have become a joke which enlivened many a meeting between St Mary's men and colleagues from other hospitals. The background to the latest war was the cost of the National Health Service. It had been a problem from the start, and the remuneration of doctors was one of the most troublesome questions. General practitioners had benefited in 1952 under the so-called Danckwerts award,[17] but this had given rise to the question of adjusting the pay of consultants and other hospital medical staff. Eventually, in 1957, a Royal Commission was set up under the chairmanship of an industrialist, Sir Harry Pilkington, to look at the whole question of doctors' and dentists' remuneration,[18] and quite early in its proceedings Charles indicated that he was ready to give evidence.[19]

In medical practice at this time, Moran was probably the best known name in England. Dawson had died in 1945, and Horder in 1955. Unlike them, Charles had held no royal appointment, but such was Churchill's stature in the popular mind that to be known as his doctor brought no less renown. To his fellow doctors, Charles was not seen as the fount of medical patronage in the way that Dawson had been, nor had he the clinical reputation of Dawson and Horder which had made it impossible for important people to die without benefit of the opinion of one of them. Nevertheless he was widely regarded as the Elder among consultants, and as very influential because of his chairmanship of the merit awards committee. Within the profession he was still seen as a controversial figure, although there had been little occasion since he left the presidency of the College for him to provoke controversy himself.

Ten days before Charles gave evidence to the Commission on 17 January 1958, the secretary sent him a list of topics so that he should have some idea of what was likely to be discussed.[20] The topics all related to consultants and the merit award scheme; there was no mention of general practice. Charles gave evidence, at a public hearing at Church House, Westminster, for some two hours in the morning and for at least as long after lunch.[21] As a performance, illuminating consultant matters and the details of the operation of the merit awards scheme, it was a *tour-de-force*; at the end of the day, when the chairman of the Commission asked his colleagues if there were any further questions, one of them said that he had none, but if Lord Moran would be prepared to reveal the secret of his endurance they would all be very grateful. It may be construed as a tribute to Charles's description of the merit awards scheme for consultants that one of the commissioners' eventual recommendations was that funds should be made available to recognise distinguished general practice by additional remuneration.[22] But that was not discussed when Charles was giving evidence. The subject of general practice came up almost incidentally in the afternoon in the course of an exploration of what constituted professional distinction among consultants. And almost at once Charles made a remark that was to dog him for the rest of his life. He was arguing that if there were 87 000 people on the medical register, the 7000 who were consultants were already a little out of the ordinary, and the merit awards went to those judged to be in the upper one third of this already special group. To illustrate the competitiveness of the process of becoming a consultant he used, as he had done in a debate on medical manpower eight years before in the House of Lords,[23] the climbing of a ladder as a metaphor. Whereas in the House of Lords he had been concise and clear, on this afternoon he was in one of his circumlocutory phases. Nevertheless he conveyed the notion that, to become a consultant, people had to climb a ladder, starting when they first went to medical school. Those who shone above their fellows and succeeded in getting house jobs and registrar posts reached the top of the ladder and became consultants. On the way up the ladder, people were constantly falling off. After a short rather confused discussion of the numbers Charles had quoted, the following exchange took place:

'*Chairman*: It has been put to us by a good many people that the two branches of the profession, general practice and consultancy, are not senior or junior to one another but they are level, do you agree with that?

'*Moran*: I say emphatically, no. Could anything be more absurd? I was Dean of St Mary's Hospital Medical School for 25 years and all the time I was on the staff we had an entry of about 80. It is probably more accurate to say by the end of that time we had 85, and earlier it was not so big. All the people of outstanding merit, with the few exceptions, aimed to get on the staff. There was no other aim and it was a ladder off which some of them fell. How can you say that the people who get to the top of the ladder are the same as the people who fall off it? It seems to be so ludicrous.'[21]

Having replied in this way, Charles was in trouble. He had originally used the metaphor of a ladder to illustrate the long and difficult climb from being a medical student to becoming a consultant, with the risk of falling off the ladder for any of a variety of reasons on the way up. By extending the use of the metaphor to cover the case not just of aspiring consultants, but of students and doctors generally, the inference had to be that general practitioners were doctors who had fallen off the ladder. And when the chairman commented that Charles was the first person to suggest that general practitioners were a somewhat inferior branch, Charles replied: 'I would not have done it except for your leading question'. It was no help to him then to mount a rearguard action, to complain that he was being drawn in public into a series of statements which were highly controversial and obnoxious to a very large number of his profession, to acknowledge that 'Perhaps if one had time to think one would put it differently', nor, before they left the subject, to say that he would be distressed if, in the course of these questions, and due to his giving quick answers, he was reported as saying that there was an inferior section of the profession.[21]

Dorothy, who was in the audience, realised as soon as Charles did that he was in trouble and dreaded the consequences.[24] The inevitable happened. 'General Practitioners Who Fall Off the Ladder' was one of the headlines on the following day,[25] which was a Saturday, and over the weekend outraged doctors and doctors' wives wrote letters, some to Charles and some to the newspapers. Charles put his own pen to paper too during the week-end, drafting a letter which he sent to the *Lancet* and *British Medical Journal*.[25] In it he explained his concept of a ladder in the training of those who aspired to be consultants, and the dangers of falling off on the way up, and he made the point that if there was not adequate reward for those who got to the top and became consultants, people would ask if the game was worth the candle. 'Alas', he wrote, 'I was met only by doubt whether there was in fact any such ladder, that all men of our calling are equal. If I had been more wise I should have left it there. . . .' He went on to say that in the quick exchanges that followed he had allowed himself to be drawn outside his argument, and that his argument for rewarding the man who had climbed the ladder had been taken as critical or even derogatory of those who had never even made the attempt. In a number of the letters published in the *British Medical Journal*[26] and sent personally to Charles, he was criticised for being wrong and for speaking in bad taste.[27,28] And in spite of the Chairman of the BMA Council saying that they should not be too hard on him for making a statement, which he had subsequently withdrawn, in the course of four or five hours of evidence, the Council passed a motion regretting that a statement so manifestly false should ever had been made.[29] But the letters were not all critical, some writers taking the view that the best response was to try to correct things in general practice which engendered the sort of comment that Charles had made.[30] Other writers conveyed privately, to him that he was quite right, everyone was not equal and he was to be commended for having had the courage to say so.[31] However, even some of his closest supporters thought he had dropped a brick,[32] and overall the comment that he had 'said more than he intended, though not perhaps more than he meant'[33] had a ring of truth about it.

Possibly the most revealing words in this sorry affair were Charles's own: 'If I had been wise I should have left it there'.[26] Given that he was appearing before the commission as an expert on consultant matters, and that his College's policy was that the many extra years of training undergone by consultants must be recognised, there was nothing to be gained and a great deal to be lost by his participating in an impromptu public discussion on whether consultants and general practitioners were senior or junior to each other. Having allowed himself be led on, Charles let his personal prejudices determine his responses. Despite his admiration for his general practitioner father, and his friendship with individual general practitioners, Charles had little regard for general practitioners as a group. He thought them rather lazy and as having committed the ultimate sin of having failed to try to excel. His family were inclined to see in this a reaction to his brother Lorton, who, as a general practitioner, was held up to them as gifted but idle, an Awful Warning.[34] As well as this rather negative reason for Charles's attitude, there was also a positive one. To him consultants, and especially consultant physicians, were the élite of the profession. In this attitude he was a true Victorian[35] and many of his generation were of like mind. The difference between Charles and most of the others was that he actually wanted to see something done to raise standards in general practice. As he had shown in parliamentary debates on the NHS, he wanted GPs to work in groups in health centres, as originally advocated by Dawson, to enable them to live more collegiate lives, and he wanted them to re-enter hospitals. Given that Charles was interrupted in the full flood of his enthusiasm for merit awards on that afternoon, and allowing for his prejudices, it was nevertheless out of character for him to be so politically inept. The fact was that eight years had passed since he had engaged in close and challenging debate of this sort. The set pieces to which he had more recently contributed in the House of Lords were very different from the debates of the 1940s in the Comitia of the RCP, and an examination by a Royal Commission was akin to the latter. He was out of practice, and he was eight years older.

For Charles, the public sequel to the ladder affair was on 27 April 1960 when the Royal Commission's report was debated in the House of Lords.[36] He introduced the subject with great lucidity, and in a 30 minute speech, made without a note, he contrasted the content-ment of consultants in the NHS with the discontent of general practitioners. He attributed the content among consultants to the fact that exceptionally good work received exceptional financial reward, and the discontent among general practitioners to the fact that this was not the case for them. The only way in which they could earn more was to increase the number of their patients to the permitted maximum of 3500, which was too many to care for properly. Charles strongly supported the Commission's idea of developing a merit award system for general practice, and he returned to his other theme of the need for general practitioners to be associated with hospitals. He also pointed, not for the first time, to the need for a standing review body to watch over conditions of service in medicine, where the government was now a monopoly employer. A notable feature of the debate was that speaker after speaker expressed admiration for the way in which Charles had carried out the very difficult task of chairing the merit awards committee. There was no mention of a ladder.[36]

It was not planned as such, but this was Charles's last major contribution to public discussion of the NHS and to debates in the House of Lords. The sadnesses that come with advancing years had so far touched him only lightly, but now in his later 70s he was starting to write obituary comments in *The Times* on some people younger than himself, as well as on contemporaries. Brendan Bracken died in August 1958 and Charles's note about him brought a letter from William Haley, *The Times*' editor who was a friend of both Charles and Bracken, saying what pleasure Charles's words had given him.[37] Charles had stressed Bracken's generosity:

'Most of us have random impulses of good nature, but with Brendan the desire to help was a steady driving force, impelling him almost every day of his life to search out some lame duck who needed help.'[38]

Aneurin Bevan died in July 1960; here was a Minister, Charles wrote, who did not live on borrowed thoughts.[39] And in December 1960, when the loyal Harold Boldero died, still in harness as Registrar of the Royal College of Physicians, and serving his third president, Robert Platt, Charles wrote:

'He had always subscribed to the code of a certain type of Englishman, and though a most kindly soul, he was slow to forgive any departure from his own fastidious standard.'[40]

In so far as Charles's activities through the 1950s and into the 1960s were a background to his preparation of the book that he longed to write, this period had its frustrations, for as Churchill survived set-back after set-back in health he came to feel that his subject was immortal[41] and that his ambition would never be fulfilled. Since meeting Henry Laughlin in New York in January 1952 he had had no reason to doubt that when he eventually completed his book he would be able to get it published and that its economic side would be bright,[42] and any doubts whether it should be published in Churchill's lifetime seem to have been finally resolved following the publication of the Alanbrooke diaries. Extracts from the diaries, with autobiographical notes of the Field Marshal, the soldier whom Charles had most admired, were published in a book in February 1957.[43] Charles was present at the launching, which took place before 1200 people at the Dorchester.[44] This was the first authoritative book written after the war questioning the widely held belief that Churchill had personally directed all the principal military decisions.[45] Given the adulation which Churchill still enjoyed, such questioning was not popular. At the launching, Alanbrooke, who was a very sick man, asked Charles to make his peace with Winston.[44] Charles was sensitive to the fact that the book would upset him, which indeed it did,[46] and a few weeks after its publication he wrote to Laughlin that with Winston aged 82 there was a feeling that Alanbrooke ought to have waited till after he was gone.[47] Thereafter, so far as Charles's own work was concerned, it was accepted that the publication would be after Churchill's death. But while the timing of publication was resolved, there were still many other problems. Charles was a compulsive writer. He couldn't not write,[48] so that through the 1950s, when he was not fully occupied with the merit awards, he spent much of each day writing and re-writing, forever touching things up or trying a new approach. The major change that came about in his early draft was scrapping the essays which were to have followed the story of the wartime conferences and Churchill's fall from power. Desmond MacCarthy's criticisms of the essays had been echoed by John,[49] so Charles incorporated material from them in the main text, and the last part of the book became instead an account of Churchill's second ministry from 1951 to 1955, and his long battle with declining health.

After MacCarthy died in 1952, John was the only reader of the developing drafts. Parcel after parcel came to him at his postings in the Middle East, Rio de Janeiro and then Washington. While he encouraged his father's enterprise and praised many passages, he continued to be a forthright critic.[50] Initially he had been concerned about the need for his father to give a balanced impression of his subject and to avoid ill-informed political judgments.[51] As the redrafting continued he criticised Charles's attempts to put in background that he knew only at second hand, and his attempts to highlight the clash of his and Churchill's temperaments. And he picked him up for making isolated rude remarks about people.[52] John also pointed to some passages as discursive and meandering, and, as time went by, full of repetition.[53] A constant complaint, echoed by later readers,[54] was that Charles kept mixing his tenses, moving from present to past and back again. This was the result, in part at least, of repeated rewriting in the course of which original notes and later comments became mixed up. Charles generally acknowledged John's criticisms and tried again. He continued to bemoan his lack of facility in writing, and was inclined to take the view that he would put everything in, and end up with a very large book from which he would then cut out the duller parts. He likened his creation to a shapely woman one and a half stone overweight.[54]

Another matter that bothered John after going through a draft of the 1945 to 1947 period was his father's handling of medical details, exemplified by the episode of Churchill's hernia in 1945. Charles's response was that such material would not be printable for a long time but Boswell would on no account have left it out.[55] John conceded that Boswell would have 'kept in the bits about hernias, trusses etc etc', but still maintained that they were not to his taste.[56] John agreed that the medical details were anyway not publishable for a long time, and suggested 40-50 years. John also criticised the inclusion of some of the material about the Churchill family which Charles considered necessary to portray Churchill's domestic background. In relation to both the medical details and the material on the family, John was insistent that what should be included must depend on whether the intention was to publish within five years or so, or later, or to publish an expurgated and then an unexpurgated edition, or to compromise. But Charles made no decision. He continued to include everything with the intention of cutting bits out when he had finished.[54]

As the apparently endless writing and rewriting continued, Charles was confronted with another problem. New information bearing on his story was steadily becoming available.[54] It was not just Alanbrooke's diaries. Churchill's own six volumes on the war were published between 1948 and 1954, there were memoirs by the other chiefs of staff, Montgomery and Ismay had their say, and so did Harry Hopkins and many others besides. As Charles read each new work he would go through his own script, correcting and expanding it and adding more of what he called the connective tissue, the explanatory material that put his original notes into context. He also used comments made over the years by the acute observers of people and affairs whom he met socially. After a weekend at

Marshalls, for instance, he would make a note of points made in conversation,[57] and some of these, with the names of the persons to whom they were attributed, found their way into his writing. With the incorporation of all this new material spread over a decade, it was not surprising that when the professional editing of his book came to be undertaken in the 1960s he had to admit that he sometimes did not recognise what he had written originally and what had been added later.[58]

Having spoken in 1951 in Churchill's presence at the Royal College of Physicians of his aspiration to 'add a postscript' to him,[59] Charles kept the progress of his writing very much to himself. When, in July 1955 Beaverbrook pressed him to get on with it and offered to buy his book from him, Charles did not tell him how far he had got 'lest it got back via Brendan to WC'.[60] And in May 1958, Bracken, in pressing Charles to write his memoirs,[61] still appeared unaware of the progress of the writing, for he told Charles that he should make the best possible arrangements in relation to taxation before he set to work. To this end Bracken introduced Charles to a solicitor whose advice he valued. Two months later when Charles had what Bracken referred to as 'a "book" yarn about Winston',[62] Charles quoted Bracken as saying 'If you are going to write about him, as of course you must . . . ,'[63] as though the writing was still something for the future. If Charles was coy about divulging his progress with his writing, except to John and to Laughlin, he had little reservation in letting his interest be known more widely. In an obituary note that he sent to *The Times* when Bracken died in August, two weeks after their book yarn, Charles wrote that Brendan had for a long time wanted him 'to write on a certain subject'.[64] In the publishing world, Laughlin had some time before engaged the interest of the English publisher, Collins, in Charles's project.[65] William Collins and his wife were guests at Marshalls in 1956 and 1958,[66] and in 1958 Collins wanted to know more details. Lord Kemsley[67] of *The Sunday Times*, and David Astor[68] of the *Observer* both expressed interest at this time in possible serial rights. News of Charles's project was around in America also, for in May 1958 Charles received a letter expressing interest from the New York publishers Simon and Schuster who referred to a recent statement in the *New York Herald Tribune* that Charles had nearly finished his memoirs.[69] Despite this flurry of interest, no final decisions were made about possible avenues for publication, and, for Charles, 1959 was yet another year of writing and revision and bemoaning the absence of literary advice.[70] Towards the end of the year he told Laughlin that the book was now in a form where all that had to be done was to cut out what was not publishable at that time. But no sooner had he written that sentence than he qualified it: 'But' he added, 'when I say the book is finished I think I shall go on working at it till the very last moment.'[70]

The summer of 1960 brought Henry and Becky Laughlin to Marshalls once more; they had become regular visitors over the years. On this occasion plans were made for having the book critically read.[71] Laughlin suggested that Craig Wylie, editorial associate to the Editor-in-Chief for Houghton Mifflin, should come and stay at Marshalls and go through the whole book, but when Laughlin phoned his partners in Boston they took the line that he himself was the man to do the job. Charles doubted whether Laughlin had the literary gifts, but accepted the proposal.[72] The following months were tiresome for Charles, who felt that he had spent much time revising already, and he was 78 and getting no younger.[73] Laughlin's advice was that the war diaries needed a good deal of cutting and revision, there was too much reliance on information Charles had accumulated since writing his original notes,[73] and Laughlin did not at all like a chapter Charles had written about Churchill and his father, Lord Randolph.[74] By the end of 1961 it was apparent to Charles that he not only had a large workload ahead of him but also he must make hard decisions on what to cut out. He hoped to be able to make these decisions about cuts himself, but he expressed the wish that, if he died before the book was published, his trustees should take the advice of his wife and two sons.[75] In any event he wished the suppressed material to be kept and, because he believed it to be of considerable historical interest, he hoped it could be incorporated in a new edition of the book or used in some other way in 20 or 30 years.[75]

As things turned out it was Dorothy, not Charles, who was to be struck down. In October 1961 she suddenly became gravely ill, and Sir John Richardson had her admitted to St Thomas's Hospital where she soon became unconscious.[76] A diagnosis was made of sub-arachnoid haemorrhage, a condition caused by the rupture of a blood vessel on the surface of the brain. Called to return to London on the night train from Newcastle, where he was on merit awards business, Charles had to face the fact that Dorothy's illness might well be fatal. In the ups and downs of the first weeks he was supported not only by Geoffrey and Jane, who were living in Stafford, but also by John and Shirley, who were home on leave. Then, when John returned to Washington, Charles established an unvarying routine. Every day, in all weathers, he took a bus from Marble Arch down Whitehall and walked over Westminster Bridge to St Thomas's Hospital. There he sat beside Dorothy's bed and read poetry out loud, hoping that perhaps some words might get through and counter the apparently permanent state of unrousable sleep in which she lay. He then got up, shed a few tears, and made his way back to the lonely emptiness of 25 Bryanston Square, sometimes getting a lift from Richardson, otherwise returning, as he had come, by bus.[77] Week by week and then month by month, Dorothy was kept alive by the skill and devotion of the nurses and all that they did was matched by the dedication of Richardson. He saw Dorothy daily, except when on rare occasions he allowed himself a weekend off, and gave Charles such support and comfort as he could, forgiving his infuriating habit of inviting, off his own bat, colleague after colleague to consult over his patient.[77] Through visits to Marshalls Richardson had not only become devoted to Dorothy but had also come to realise what a remarkable person Charles was. His regard for him did nothing but increase as he saw the love and attention that this little old, cold and lonely man gave to his stricken wife; it sometimes seemed to Richardson as beyond all logic and beyond all sense, but Charles's behaviour was such that no one at St Thomas's felt they could let up in their unremitting care. The Richardsons arranged that Charles should spend Christmas of 1961 with them, and they remembered him as having been a marvellous guest, who joined in with the children, and who then kept himself happy playing with the allocation of the last two most junior C merit awards. Charles left his host not only with a deep respect for his thoroughness but also shuddering as he thought of his own telephone bill.[77]

Only once in the early weeks of Dorothy's illness did Charles emerge into a wider world. Shortly before John returned to Washington in November, the Queen Mother opened Wilson House, a residence for St Mary's students named after Charles, the great Dean. John persuaded his father to attend. Arriving gloomy and preoccupied, Charles's mood briefly lifted when he met some old friends and proceeded to tell them just what needed doing at the hospital and medical school: 'To begin with you must get rid of the Matron, etc etc'.[76]

Charles was spurred on to continue his daily vigils when one day in February 1962 he discovered that his reading might be stirring old chords. 'Where fairies dance in a place apart' he read, and Dorothy said 'I will arise and go now, and go to Innisfree'.[78] But mostly the winter seemed awful.[79] Working on the book and visiting Dorothy did not fill the time, the days seemed interminable and the nights were worse.[80] Charles saw virtually no one except a loyal 'daily' who appeared at meal times. And he had to face a new problem, for cataracts in his eyes had reached a stage where he could not see at all to read with one eye and his vision was impaired in the other.[81] His eye surgeon foreshadowed operating in about a year's time. The only bright spot was news that John and his family were soon to return from Washington, which they did in April.

While Dorothy lay in St Thomas's, Charles had to pass another watershed in his life. His chairmanship of the merit awards committee finished at the end of May, when he was succeeded by Russell Brain. Although he had had 18 month's warning,[82] when the time came Charles was as reluctant to go as he had been when his deanship had ended at St Mary's in 1945 and his presidency of the College had ended in 1950. This time he complained that he was given no reason why the appointment should be terminated, and he supposed they had got his age wrong.[83] Perhaps he thought they should have waited because his 80th birthday was still six months away. The practical effect of his retirement from the committee was his loss of salary, which by then was 3000 guineas a year,[84] and the loss of his only occupation apart from his writing. Opinion at the Ministry of Health was that Charles had made the award system work as no one else at that time would have done,[85] and there was some sadness when his name did not appear in the Queen's Birthday Honours;[86] he declined an invitation from Harold Macmillan, who was then Prime Minister, to have his name submitted for the award of a GBE, which he told John was the sort of thing that is given to civil servants.[87] The consequence was that his achievements in establishing and administering the merit awards system came to an end without public recognition. It was perhaps some consolation to him to be nominated by Churchill in September for membership of the Other Club,[88] a dining club which Churchill and FE Smith (later Lord Birkenhead) had founded in 1911. He much enjoyed attending the dinners, although he did not shine in that sort of milieu. He had remained an un-clubable person.[89] Churchill's introduction of Charles to the Other Club was his second gesture, in his old age, of personal kindness to his doctor. During the previous year he had asked Charles, out of the blue, if he would like to be a Viscount. Charles's spontaneous reply was that he would far prefer Dorothy to be made a life Peer. Churchill was greatly annoyed and the matter was never referred to again.[90]

Through the summer of 1962, while Charles's daily pilgrimages continued, Dorothy remained unconscious, apparently fading gradually away. Then, one day late in September, a nurse tore out of Dorothy's room to the Sister in charge of the ward. Dorothy had just spoken. 'Would you think I was very greedy', she said, 'if I asked for more Charlotte Russe?' From then on Dorothy's unconsciousness gradually lifted.[90] Her intellect was unimpaired, and after a long spell of rehabilitation she was able to return to Bryanston Square in the following April (1963). It was not long before she started appearing on social occasions and people thought they were seeing a ghost. Here she was, apparently returned from the dead. Charles dedicated his book 'To Dorothy who has been given back to me . . .'

As Dorothy lay unconscious in St Thomas's, Charles's writing may have diverted him but it was not altogether relaxing. On the positive side arrangements were made for trustees to become the owners of the book and for John, in the event of Charles's death, to advise them.[91] Also on the positive side, Laughlin and Wylie in Boston, as well as John, made fewer criticisms of the post-war sections, which more directly reflected continuous diary entries than had the pre-war ones.[92] But the transatlantic dialogue caused endless irritations.

Charles complained of delays and lack of clarity in replies to his letters.[93] Some of the frustration may have been mutual, for Charles's letters were not always typed and his handwriting had not improved with age. When he received a letter referring to an enclosure that was not in the envelope, he exploded to John:

'I cannot fathom Henry [Laughlin]. I don't know whether he has gone senile. . . . The impression is that for a year or more nobody looked at the Post-war volumes. Then stung by my letter Henry rushed through them and made Craig Wylie go through them at the same pace. . . . Could you telephone Henry and first ascertain if the Post-war volumes are being done as carefully as the War books were?'[94]

Then there was a nagging worry when it appeared that no one knew where one of the volumes was and concern was confounded when Laughlin asked for more material to be copied. Charles was very sensitive about the fact that he had not yet deleted sections and comments, particularly about the Churchill family, which might cause offence.[94] For that reason he was anxious about having more copies made, let alone about losing existing ones. The worry about a possibly lost volume proved all too well justified; and it was not one volume but two that turned out to be missing.[95] Charles was sure he was not responsible for he kept his copies in the bank, apart from sections he was actually working on. Laughlin eventually traced the missing volumes to Castle Hyde in Ireland, a mansion belonging to his wife's family where he went from time to time for the fishing. For a man engaged in the enterprise Laughlin had undertaken, to go fishing was, to Charles's way of thinking, sheer frivolity, and when Laughlin indicated that, after a forthcoming fishing trip he would not be coming on to England,[96] Charles exploded again. 'Surely', he wrote to John, 'after his incredible behaviour he ought to see the two volumes are put in my hand even if he swims the Irish Channel to do it'.[97] Equanimity was not restored until Laughlin arranged for an associate returning from a skiing holiday in Europe to be handed the volumes when his flight stopped at Shannon; they were eventually returned to Charles via Boston and Washington in the diplomatic bag.[98]

In the summer of 1962, while it was accepted that Houghton Mifflin would publish Charles's book in the United States, no decision had been made about its publication in England. Charles now took the plunge, and Milton Waldman of Collins read it. The speed of his response contrasted strikingly with the leisurely pace across the Atlantic, and the verdict was that the book in its present form was a two-volume work and it needed reducing to one volume. When the cuts recommended were specified,[99] Charles's response was that Waldman did not know what he was trying to do, and he reiterated his position to John. He was writing a book that would be read in 50 years time; Churchill's well known victory sign, his hats and dressing gown and his cigar might bring him to life but they were not enough to make him of interest in 50 years.

'If he is to live as a great individual character, you must explain how he is different from other people and *why he dominated them.* How did he get his way with everyone? How did his mind work? What was he really like? It is more difficult to answer these questions than to paint his external ways vividly.'[100]

What Charles wanted to do was so much at variance with the Collins view that the book should recount his personal experience with Churchill, that no meeting of minds was possible. While this dialogue was going on, Charles received a note from Benjamin Glazebrook of Constable and Co. who had published *The Anatomy of Courage,* reminding him that they had an option which entitled them to first refusal of his new work.[101] Glazebrook and Laughlin came together, and the problem of an English publisher was solved.

Meanwhile, in September 1962, Charles was led to seek advice from Richard Church, a well known writer and publisher's editor of long experience, about necessary cuts. An excellent relationship was established at once.[102-104] In introducing himself, Charles wrote:

'Someone once said I had a legal mind and I certainly have a strong bias for the judicial handling of evidence. I feel that the decision [on cuts to be made] ought not to be made on an impression but that all doubtful passages should be marked and then we ought to be able to decide whether they really do add to the picture.'[105]

Church proceeded in a business-like way to do what Charles asked of him, and, over four months interspersed with letters and lunch at the Athenaeum, Charles received the precise and detailed advice that he had been hoping to receive for the past two years from Laughlin and Wylie. Material to be cut was clearly identified and as a result the book was significantly shortened. Charles's morale must incidentally have been raised by Church's frank commendation of what he saw as a remarkable piece of biographical history written in prose that he described as simple, direct and supple.[106]

In the spring of 1963, soon after Dorothy's return home, Charles himself became ill. He developed a pain in the chest, and when coronary thrombosis was diagnosed he put himself to bed for a month in accordance with the practice of the time.[107]

That summer, news of his writing received sudden publicity through a column in the *London Evening Standard.*[108] This brought both a flutter of letters from Fleet Street newspaper editors interested in serialising the book, and a letter from Anthony Montague Browne saying Sir Winston had seen the article, and could Charles let him know if there was any truth in the story.[109] Charles was seeing Churchill regularly at this time and there appears to have been no written response.

Despite all the advice he had received, New Year of 1964 found Charles still agonising over his typescript, which he now took for criticism to Professor TJB Spencer, a Shakespeare scholar at Birmingham University. Charles tried to convey to him the urgency which he felt.[110] He was, he said, 82, the one eye on which he depended was not as good as it was, and he had had a coronary. Spencer was busy with the 400th anniversary of Shakespeare's birth and the correspondence extended over more than 12 months. There may have been some comfort in Spencer's comment that this was one of the most remarkable books of our time,[111] but equally it must have been disconcerting to find that by seeking help from so many people he was beginning to receive conflicting advice. Spencer saw value in providing historical information and recommended including some passages which other advisors had said should be cut.[112,113] Charles also continued to worry about having included a detailed account of his patient's latter years. In January 1965 he wrote to Spencer:

> 'It is idle to deceive oneself that this will not bring down on my head a spate of criticism. My position in meeting such criticisms will be weakened by the fact that I am Winston's doctor. There will be talk of the Hippocratic Oath.'[113]

Acknowledging Charles's wish not to give pain or offence to people who were alive, Spencer expressed his belief that there was nothing unkind or mean about what Charles had written. He agreed that some of the comments could not be printed at present, but he urged Charles that all the material should be preserved and deposited, preferably in the British Museum. One day, when all concerned had passed from the scene, these facts should be put back into the book.[114]

The extent of Charles's predicament was brought home to him by other correspondence during 1964. A year after his enquiry on Churchill's behalf, Montague Browne wrote from Chartwell that in view of Charles's plans he thought it wise to let him know the situation regarding permission to quote Sir Winston and Lady Churchill's letters to him, and this Montague Browne did.[115] A few weeks later Charles received a letter from Lady Churchill referring to the earlier newspaper report indicating that Charles was writing a book about Winston and saying she would much like to read any part of the manuscript he would like her to see.[116] This letter led to a

conversation between Lady Churchill and Charles following which
Lady Churchill wrote to him:

'I am seriously disturbed by our conversation yesterday. I think
that you should have told me of your intentions; it was only
through the matter having been mentioned in the Press that I
found out you intended to write a book about Winston, and I
subsequently raised the matter with Jock.

'I had always supposed that the relationship between a doctor and
his patient was one of complete confidence.

'Had you been writing your own biography, with passing references
to Winston, it would have been understandable, though I would
have hoped that you would tell us what you intended to say. But
I do not see how you can justify your present course. An impartial
observer would, I think, consider that your career had been a
successful one and had not been damaged by your association with
Winston, and I think he has not shown himself ungrateful to you.

'. . . I do urge you to reconsider your intentions.'[117]

Charles, at this stage, wrote nothing in reply.[118]

Chapter 23

The Great Book Row

Although Dorothy's mind was clear after her long illness, she continued to use a stick for walking and to need help with dressing. To cope with this she sought living-in help, and in May 1964 Miss Marian Dean joined the household at 25 Bryanston Square. The stalwart Miss Dean, whose family roots were in Ilkley, over the moor from Charles's childhood home in Skipton, not only helped Dorothy but also drove the car and acted as secretary to Charles. With her arrival, visits to Marshalls became possible again.[1]

That summer brought another obituary comment from Charles in *The Times*;[2] Beaverbrook's death in June ended an association extending over 40 years, during which Charles had observed him, well and ill, in many roles. There had never been the sort of estrangement between them that was so liable to happen in Charles's relationships. From the start the two men had been useful to each other. While Beaverbrook had eased Charles's way to fame by making possible the rebuilding of the medical school at St Mary's Hospital, he had had good reason at the same time to be grateful for Charles's professional care. Beaverbrook's long and at times close association with Churchill had meant that when Beaverbrook and Charles were thrown together, as they often were during the war, Charles would speak freely about their mutual friend. They probably over-estimated each other's influence. If Beaverbrook had an exaggerated idea of his doctors', and particularly Charles's, abilities to extend a person's life-span, Charles equally seems to have had an exaggerated idea of Beaverbrook's ability to sway Churchill, although he was probably right if he assumed that anything he said to Beaverbrook might be passed on. Beaverbrook's character came in for a good deal of dissection in Charles's book and in other written fragments, but Charles chose for once to be influenced by the *de mortuis* principle in his public obituary comments. He portrayed Beaverbrook as, at bottom, a Puritan, apt to brood over any lapse from grace, and, for much of his life, lonely.[2] Charles and Beaverbrook had quite a lot in common.

In January 1965 Churchill's condition took a turn for the worse, and Miss Dean drove Charles to Hyde Park Gate two or three times a day[1]. The situation was kept quiet initially, but on 15 January the news was out, and Hyde Park Gate, which was a cul-de-sac, became packed with media people and their paraphernalia. From the steps of Number 28 Charles read out medical bulletins, for which he found it hard to find new words each day. The crowding soon

Figure 19. Lord Moran outside 28 Hyde Park Gate, 1965, reading a medical bulletin about Churchill's health to the waiting media. (Reproduced by kind permission of The Times.*) (CMAC PP/CMW/P.77)*

became so inconvenient that the reporters and photographers were asked to withdraw to the top of the street.[3] At Bryanston Square Miss Dean was busy answering the telephone,[1] which brought calls from royal Ladies-in-waiting, newspapers, and many others. One day a call came from a Chicago newspaper to say that if the President of the United States were gravely ill there would be a platoon of doctors in attendance and did Charles feel able to take responsibility all on his own? Then there were the cranks—a lady with a vision that Charles should apply 12 leeches to Churchill's head, and an American caller who said that if Charles would pay his fare he would share with him knowledge of the elixir of life. With calls at night coming directly to his bedside, Charles became very tired. Eventually, in the small hours of 24 January 1966, he was woken with news that the end was near. Miss Dean drove him through the bitterly cold night to Hyde Park Gate, where he remained until Churchill died soon after 8.00 am.[4] Impractical as ever, Charles had taken no steps to acquire a death certificate form so, after breakfast, Miss Dean had to drive him to St Mary's Hospital to obtain one. It was also in character that, hearing that Wendy Reves had not been invited to the funeral service, he took her to the lying-in-State in Westminster Hall and brought her home to dinner afterwards.[5] For the State funeral, Charles and Dorothy were seated in the chancel at St Paul's, and Charles attended the burial service in the country churchyard at Bladon.

Following Churchill's death, upwards of one hundred people wrote to Charles to say how greatly they appreciated the care he had given his patient.[6] Letters also came from bodies representing the media thanking him for the courteous way in which he had treated photographers and reporters.[7,8] Through this time Charles showed both at home and in public the equanimity that medical teachers of his youth regarded as a hallmark of the true physician. Professionally in his management of Churchill he appeared not to have put a foot wrong, and after Churchill died he received as a gift a gold watch which had been given to his patient by the physicians of Zürich.[9]

Charles, who was now 82, had one aim only, to see his book published. Although his trustees' agreements with Houghton Mifflin and Constable had been completed,[10] and publication fixed for the Spring of 1966, there was a lot of work still to be done. The main task was to decide what material still needed to be cut from the text, the decision having already been made to remove most of the references to members of Churchill's family. First, however, Charles had to have his cataract operation, and for this he went into Moorfields Hospital in April. The operation went well, but he was not allowed to read until June,[11] and so he was under great pressure to work between then and the end of July, when the publisher wanted the decisions made. Both Charles's operation and his age were reported in the Press, and among letters he received was a friendly one from Colville, who commented that Charles had always seemed to him sounder in sense and in limb than people 30 years younger.[12] It would have been a source of pleasure too that Anthony Montague Browne, who had been Churchill's devoted private secretary for the 10 years before his death,[13] and his wife Nonie, were among the first of the few guests to stay at Marshalls that summer.[14] Notwithstanding the concerns that Lady Churchill had expressed to Charles a year before about his writing about Winston, the relationships between Charles and the members of Churchill's staff who had been closest to him remained cordial.

In August a newspaper commentator remarked that it had taken 21 months after President Kennedy's* death for the first memoirs to appear, and asked how long it would be before books on Churchill appeared.[15] The scene depicted was one of rivalry between newspaper proprietors. The first volume of Randolph Churchill's life of his father was due in the Autumn of 1966 and the *Daily Telegraph* and *Sunday Telegraph* were said to be investing in it. The *Sunday Express* was said to have a plan for a book on the friendship between

*John F Kennedy, President of the United States of America 1961-1963.

Churchill and Beaverbrook, and The *Express* was also said to be concerned with articles by Sarah Churchill about her father. Charles's memoirs were mentioned in connection with Lord Thomson, owner of *The Sunday Times*. Three months later the timing, relative to each other, of the publication of Charles's and Randolph Churchill's books was described in a newspaper as a race in which Charles was said to be leading the field.[16] At this time the editor of *The Sunday Times* sent Charles an *aide memoire* summarising a midnight telephone call he had received from Randolph Churchill protesting that Charles's book should have waited for three or four years.[17] These reported rivalries added a new dimension to Charles's concerns as he struggled with the final trimming of his intended masterpiece, which, it had been decided, would first appear as extracts in both *The Sunday Times* and *Life*.

When Charles was confronted by the galley proofs of his book in August, there was no more time for prevarication. Despite the excisions he had made after consulting Richard Church in 1962 and Terence Spencer in 1964, he still agonised over the need for cuts. He made a last appeal for help and consulted the Oxford historian Robert Blake of Christ Church. Approached by Charles, Blake agreed to read the proofs,[18] and, within a week, having read half of the work, he wrote to say he was absolutely fascinated.[19] He asked Charles to list passages that he had doubts about and also mentioned two general matters. One was the importance of getting the agreement of living persons whose talks with Charles were being reported. Blake's other concern was the presentation of medical details, and he commented that Charles would know whether there were rules which forbade this. Two weeks later, having read the whole work, Blake sent Charles the forthright sort of advice that he so badly needed.[20] Charles had had two main queries. One was whether, in quoting Churchill's comments on Anthony Eden (in a section of the book headed 'That Other Eden', later changed to 'Winston and Anthony'), Eden had been dealt with too harshly. Charles's other query was about his extended chronicling of Churchill's declining health.[21] In thanking Blake for his comments Charles wrote:

'You have confirmed my misgivings in that I was courting trouble in the 1954 picture of Anthony Eden, and my detailed account of Winston's advancing decrepitude during the years 1955 to 1965.

'I need not tell you that when many years have been spent trying to paint a faithful portrait what it means in cutting out slices of it. It is not as if any danegeld can avert the wrath that will descend on me. Nevertheless I must pull myself together and try to take a wise course.'[22]

In this fatalistic mood Charles asked Blake's counsel on how to follow his advice and Blake responded promptly with suggestions, some of which Charles accepted and some of which he did not. As their correspondence extended Blake commented on how the book highlighted the conflict that can arise between recording historical truth and sparing people's feelings.[23] There was a particular sensitivity here because Blake had got to know the Edens while helping Anthony Eden over the first volume of his memoirs. Even if Charles omitted some of Churchill's more pungent expressions about Eden, difficulties could arise, and for this reason Blake asked not to be acknowledged in any prefaratory remarks.[24] In the event Charles accepted a few suggestions on the section on 'Winston and Anthony' after fighting a lively rearguard action. He also accepted Blake's advice that the last part of the book, 'The Long Farewell', which contained a lot of clinical detail, should be abbreviated, but he did not respond specifically to Blake's reiterated point that there might be comment on the doctor-patient relationship and that this was a matter on which Charles had to be the judge.[23] Charles's only response was that he rather dreaded the controversy that the book would raise.[25]

By November, when the second galleys had to be returned to Constable,[26] the final form of the work was settled. It would consist of one volume made up of two 'books' with titles and accompanying quotations suggested by John. Book One[27] was called 'This Star of England'. It covered the period May 1940 to February 1945 and the quotation from Shakespeare's *Henry V* on the title page read:

'Small time, but in that small most greatly lived
This star of England: fortune made his sword.'

Book Two was titled 'The Withered Garland' and it covered the period from April 1945 to January 1965. The accompanying quotation from *Antony and Cleopatra* was:

'O wither'd is the garland of the war,
The soldiers pole is fallen: young boys and girls
Are level now with men: the odds is gone.
And there is nothing left remarkable
Beneath the visiting moon.'

Even at this stage there were still several matters calling urgently for decisions. Charles was dismayed to find that the accuracy of some of the notes on people and places was in question. He needed help and didn't know where to find it.[28] Then Laughlin cabled from Boston to say that in the United States they were unhappy about the proposed title 'Winston Churchill—The Struggle for Survival'.[29] Charles at this time seemed to favour 'Winston Churchill by his

Physician Lord Moran', having apparently forgotten his earlier resolve that sales must not be promoted by advertising his role as a doctor in the title.[30] In the end, *Winston Churchill—The Struggle for Survival* was used by Constable, and Houghton Mifflin used *Churchill—Taken from the Diaries of Lord Moran.*

A more fundamental question calling for decision was whether there should be a Preface and what it should contain. Charles drafted one, intending that it should justify his writing the book when he was Churchill's doctor.[31] He saw it as falling into two parts, the first about why he kept a diary and what was in it, and the second about how he was persuaded to convert the diary into a book. He sent the draft to John, now posted to Cape Town, and John did not like it, mainly on the grounds that *'qui s'éxcuse s'accuse'*.[27] Blake on the other hand believed that some explanation was indeed needed of Charles's decision to publish his diaries about his patient.[23] Charles set to work at the beginning of January to polish what he had hastily prepared and on 19 January, the deadline for the printer, he added a quotation,[32] which he had just received from John, from Clarendon's Preface to the first edition of the *History of the Rebellion*:

'However, all things of this nature must be submitted, as this is, with great deference, to the judgment of the equal reader.'

The die was cast.

Having left so late a series of decisions that needed to be made, Charles found the weeks leading to the printer's deadline on 19 January heavy going.[33] So did Dorothy. She became anxious about Charles's health as well as what she saw as a looming controversy, and her worries were compounded by that hazard of an English winter, burst water pipes, which had to be coped with at Marshalls. Then, to cap it all, Dorothy's blood pressure was found to have risen and she was advised to rest all day. Consequently the trip that she and Charles had planned to make to South Africa before the book was published, to see John and his family, had to be cancelled.

While Charles hoped that his Preface would go a long way towards mitigating criticism, he knew that even among his friends there was still doubt about his writing about his patient,[33] and he was reminded of Lady Churchill's attitude when he asked her permission to illustrate his book with a photograph of the portrait of Churchill painted by Sir William Orpen.[34] Lady Churchill, in her reply, having commiserated over Dorothy's illness and the cancelled trip to South Africa, reiterated her regret that Charles should write about Winston.[35] Charles responded by dictating a long letter, starting with an allusion to Lady Churchill's earlier request that she might see the proofs, and then touching on several other points:

'Thank you for your letter.

'I suppose like most writing people I don't like anyone dipping into a book when it is only half written. It is the same kind of feeling that one has for serialisation, that the abbreviation often gives you only a poor idea of the book. I trust that when you have read my book in its final form you will not disapprove. It is not a book of gossip. Two historians who have read it take it very seriously.

'I think that you are bothered by the doctor/patient relationship. Before I decided to write the book I went to GM Trevelyan, the Master of Trinity and doyen of historians. He was a greatly respected figure in the academic world and had a reputation as a stickler for what was right and proper. I told him I was Winston's doctor and I asked him whether in his judgment this disqualified me from writing about him. He said at once: every aspect of a great historical figure like Winston is bound to come under review sooner or later. Everything about him will become known. He spoke of the extensive literature about the medical details of Napoleon, hardly any of it by doctors. We don't want that, he said. Let the facts about Winston be presented by some responsible person. Smuts took the same line, and Brendan sent for me, a few days before his death, and pressed me to write about Winston.

'There are times when it is not easy to be fair to Winston or to measure the size of the man without some knowledge of his medical background. To take only one instance. In 1953, five days after his stroke, at a time when most people would be thinking of one thing only, whether they would come through, Winston's mind was completely taken up with plans for getting back into political life. He decided that he must first take a number of hurdles: his first appearance in public, the first time he answered questions in the House of Commons, his first speech there, his first Cabinet, and finally his appearance at the Party gathering at Margate. I can think of nothing in his whole career, not excluding 1940, which brings home to one the extraordinary strength of his will-power as his fight in 1953 to get back into politics. At such times I felt very close to him, I loved his guts, he seemed invincible. I think this ought to be known. It is part of his story. Whatever political commentators may say of 1953 it was a pretty grim test of his courage, and he came through it triumphantly.

'When Winston allowed me to have Orpen's portrait photographed I had it framed and it has been on my mantlepiece ever since. I have come to like it very much. Orpen, I think, comes much nearer to the real Winston than Sutherland's portrait or the war pictures, and I shall be sad if I cannot illustrate my tribute to him with this understanding portrait.

'I am sending this by hand. I find that I have got behind and have allowed domestic worries to interfere with my search for illustrations that do justice to Winston. The Publisher has sent the page-proofs to the Printer, but I shall, of course, have Orpen's portrait excised if you still feel unable to allow me to use it.'[36]

A few days later Charles was notified that the copyright of the Orpen painting was vested in Randolph Churchill.[37]

In February, with the book at the printer and the publication date set for 23 May, Charles could at last make no more changes to the text. He now had to face up to media interviews arranged by his publishers, including one with Maurice Wiggins of *The Sunday Times*. This was to appear on 3 April as a preamble to the series of extracts from his book that would be presented in the following weeks. 'All this', Charles wrote to John, 'is not up my street but I imagine it has to be endured'.[38] Time now hung heavily on Charles's hands and he took to watching television in the afternoon until such time as Marian Dean went out to buy the *Evening Standard*. Miss Dean came in for the full repertoire of quips and quotations that had been a feature of life in Harley Street days years ago when the children were young. 'In such a night stood Dido with a willow in her hand upon the wild sea-banks' was the standard riposte when Miss Dean, setting out to buy the paper, commented that it was a wet night.

Dorothy's health improved enough for her to go with Charles for a three-week holiday in Portugal in March. Miss Dean made the arrangements and went with them. After spending two nights as guests at the British Embassy in Lisbon they settled at the Hotel Palacia at Estoril.[1] Charles, reflecting that he had read very few books in the last 25 years, resolved to catch up.[39] He had already started with *The Little Genius*, a short biography of Horder by his son, which Charles described as very judicial and fair-minded, and he stocked up with *Vanity Fair, Tono-Bungay* and a book by Fuller* on war strategy. The days passed at Estoril with blue skies, sun and invigorating fresh air, which Dorothy enjoyed, but Charles had a flare-up of eczema which had been bothering him for some months, and there was no escaping book affairs.[40] News came that Constable would publish a new edition of *The Anatomy of Courage* after the Churchill book appeared, and that Houghton Mifflin would publish a first American edition. Despite John Winant's enthusiasm, it had proved impossible to find a willing American publisher for *The Anatomy of Courage* in 1944. Charles recalled that the total sales had been 20 000 in the first year and had quickly dwindled to one or two hundred a year, and he doubted if the book would now

---

*Major General JF Fuller, author of many publications on warfare.

get a new lease of life*.[40] Galleys of the extracts from his new book that were to appear in *The Sunday Times* also came to him in Estoril.[41] He was not consulted about what of the original text was left in or cut out in these extracts, but having read the wartime ones he was fairly resigned to what had been done. Nevertheless, he dreaded what would appear when extracts were made of his last sections on 'Winston and Anthony' and 'The Long Farewell'. Would shortening and cuts make Churchill's contemptuous references to Eden, and the details of his own decline, stand out harshly? In the book they were cushioned by a good deal of other material but even so were strong meat for the reader.[41] By the end of March, when the holiday in Portugal was over, Charles had hardly opened *Vanity Fair*, *Tono-Bungay* or Fuller's book on strategy.

As Charles left Estoril, there was more writing on the wall. Norman Brook, who had retired as Secretary to the Cabinet in 1962, wrote to say that, at Henry Laughlin's instigation, Houghton Mifflin had sent him a set of galley-proofs of the book, and that, while he did not wish to challenge Charles's accuracy, he was disturbed to find statements recorded which he had made to Charles in confidence, and he asked Charles to delete or modify some of them.[42] Brook also drew Charles's attention to the fact that the last paragraph in his Acknowledgements, at the beginning of the book, would lead some people to believe that those whom Charles quoted had consented to the publication of the statements attributed to them. Brook suggested that some alteration in the wording might be desirable. The changes Brook suggested were not made. It was too late. Copies of the printed book were already on their way to various people.[43] So after 20 years in writing, the book had ended up in going to press with three very significant parts, the title, the Acknowledgements and the Preface, having been subjected, compared to the rest of the text, to the least critical discussion.

Back from Portugal, Charles was greeted at the beginning of April with the article about himself in *The Sunday Times*, which heralded the series of extracts from his book.[44] All remained quiet until the Thursday after the first extract appeared, when newspaper reporters began to ring up to talk about an editorial annotation in that week's *Lancet*.[45] It was headed 'A Question of Confidence' and in effect it rebuked Charles for writing publicly about the medical condition of his patient. The annotation contained an eminently quotable passage:

'A doctor, like a lawyer or a priest, does not readily recount his professional dealings with an identifiable person; and the public trust in the medical profession derives largely from its conviction

---

*Nevertheless an American re-issue by Avery Publishing in 1987 was still selling steadily in 1992. The Keynes Press, British Medical Association, published a new edition in 1984.

that what transpires between patient and doctor will not be bandied about. If this confidentiality is owed to the living, it is doubly owed to the dead.'[46]

Charles had an anxious evening speaking to the press without the *Lancet* article in front of him, for his copy of the journal was not delivered until the following day. Then he at first decided to do nothing, hoping that, having made his comments, the matter would fizzle out.[45] But attacks on him in the weekend papers led him to draft a letter for publication in *The Times*, which on the Saturday had printed the *Lancet* annotation in full. 'Our Medical Correspondent' had added a comment conceding that the *Lancet* was, generally speaking, correct, but identifying this as an exceptional case; much of the medical information was already known, and most doctors would feel that in this instance the *Lancet* was being 'a trifle pedantic and more than a little severe'.[47]

In his letter to *The Times*, which was published on the Monday,[48] Charles responded to the *Lancet* annotation by first submitting that the obligation of a doctor to observe conventions governing doctor-patient relationships, while absolute in the life-time of a patient, was not applicable to a great historical figure after his death. Lay accounts of illnesses were bound to appear and were liable to be inaccurate. They had already done so in this case. Secondly he cited GM Trevelyan's exhortations: 'This is history, you ought to get it on paper'; and 'It is inevitable that everything about this man will be known in time. Let us have the truth'. Thirdly he quoted Trevelyan as having argued that knowledge of Churchill's health might disarm criticism of his conduct of affairs, and Charles illustrated this proposition by giving an example. He wrote:

'It was exhaustion of mind and body that accounted for much that is otherwise inexplicable in the last year of the war, for instance the deterioration in his relations with President Roosevelt.'[48]

Charles ended his letter with what read like an afterthought: 'I may add that I told Sir Winston about what I proposed to do.'

Tuesday's *Times* brought a letter from Randolph Churchill[49] saying that he and his mother knew nothing of Charles having told Sir Winston about what he proposed to do, and that Charles had not said what Sir Winston's response had been; Charles had written against the wishes of Lady Churchill and had refused to show her proofs of his book; and he was at variance with the *Lancet* over obligations to patients who were dead. Further, Trevelyan had told Charles he ought to 'get it on paper', not 'You ought to publish it'; and 'certainly not within 15 months of his patient's death, and against the wishes of his family.' In a second letter a few days later Randolph Churchill wrote: 'I ask no more for my father than that he should be treated by his physician in the same way that the generality of the people in this country are treated by their local GPs'.[50]

For the next six weeks the correspondence columns of *The Times* became the forum for airing views on the affair. Colville joined in early to criticise Charles's statement that it was Churchill's health that accounted for the deterioration of his relations with Roosevelt in the last year of the war. It was, Colville observed, Roosevelt who was dying, not Churchill.[51] Colville's emphasis in fact accorded with the comment Charles had made when writing earlier on this topic, but somehow he had come to put things the other way round in the hurriedly written and as yet unpublished Preface to his book on which he drew heavily in writing his letter.

Most of the views expressed in *The Times* correspondence were critical of Charles. It was said that the mode and timing of the publication of the extracts that were appearing in *The Sunday Times* were wrong, and that Charles's writings should have been deposited in safekeeping for a considerable number of years; that it was questionable whether the eminence of a person should be taken into account when considering medical disclosures, and that Charles had erred in disclosing comments made in private conversations. In his defence it was said that the extracts from his book enhanced rather than detracted from Churchill's reputation and that he emerged as a greater man because more human. A plea was also made that judgment of what Charles had done should not be made until people had read the whole book.

Randolph Churchill's first letter made Charles realise that the question which stood out above all others was whether he had written with Churchill's knowledge and consent. It was a question that the historians he had consulted had raised, and John, months before, had advised him to answer it by describing how he had told Churchill that he was writing the book and to quote Churchill's reply.[52] So far all Charles had produced was the throw-away remark at the end of his letter to *The Times*, that he had told Sir Winston about what he proposed to do. Charles now set about drafting a letter describing what had taken place,[53] intending to send it to *The Times*, but he changed his mind and decided to wait until he responded to the correspondence as a whole. Instead, he wrote a letter to the Secretary of the BMA, Dr Derek Stevenson describing what had happened:

'Because all the facts are not known I was told yesterday that I had transgressed the convention which governs the patient/doctor relationship.

'I have always understood that this convention was designed to protect the patient from his doctor repeating what had passed between them without the patient's permission and approval, and perhaps in a manner injurious to a patient's reputation.

'Applying this to Sir Winston I thought it right to tell him that I was writing a book about him. He said at once "My dear Charles, I am sure I will like anything you write about me." With a grin "I hope you will not be too rough on my strategy".'[54]

Charles said that Brendan Bracken saw Winston about the book and then arranged for him to see Winston's legal adviser about the business side of it, and he added:

'I went to see Winston on several occasions when questions arose about the book and he was always most helpful and encouraging.'

Having touched on a number of other matters, Charles ended his letter:

'I do not write this for publication because I don't want to start a correspondence in the BMJ like the one that has appeared in *The Times*. But you are at liberty to quote from my letter as you think fit. I do not get about much these days and have little opportunity for explanation, but you must hear these matters discussed and I thought you would like to know my point of view.'[54]

Pressure on Charles to deal further with the matter of consent was suddenly eased at this stage by a letter in *The Times* written by Professor Sir Herbert Seddon,[55] a greatly respected surgeon, who had, among other things, treated Churchill when he had injured his spine in a fall in 1960[56] and when he had broken his hip in 1962.[57] Seddon forthrightly stated that he had evidence that Charles's book was written with Sir Winston's knowledge and consent and that satisfied him that no ethical problem had arisen. Seddon was not publicly pressed to enlarge on this statement, which held the suggestion that he could say no more without betraying confidences.

The publication of private conversations was the other major matter raised in *The Times* correspondence.[50,58] It too had been raised by those whose comments Charles had sought on the galley proofs. There was general as well as medical criticism. The latter came from Russell Brain personally to Charles[59] and simultaneously in a published letter.[60] Brain, who had just received a pre-publication copy of the book, pointed out that Charles had reported what had taken place at some of their consultations on Churchill and that these confidential matters had been published without his knowledge. Having made his point, Brain expressed the hope that what he called this unhappy controversy would not be allowed to obscure Charles's great services to Churchill, and that Charles's medical critics in particular would now feel that, their protest having been made, the matter should be allowed to rest. The flurry of new letters provoked by Brain's letter had scarcely settled when Charles received a personal note in similar vein from the editor of *The Times* himself, who, with his wife, had several times stayed at Marshalls and who was on first name terms. Haley had now received a pre-publication copy of the book and had found in it things that he had said privately to Charles as his guest.[61] He also complained that Charles, in the Acknowledgement section of the book, misleadingly implied that everyone quoted had given their consent. The extent of the disquiet on this score was emphasised further on 24 May, the day after the book was published, in a letter in *The Times* in which Norman Brook repeated points that he had already made privately to Charles, and complained in particular about the recording of statements he had made as Secretary of the Cabinet in reply to questions Charles, in his professional capacity as Churchill's doctor, had asked him.[62] Charles seemed quite puzzled by this fuss about reporting conversations, and wrote both to Haley[63] and to Sir George Clark,[64] whose opinion as a distinguished historian and friend he particularly valued. He explained that where, in a conversation, there had been criticism of Winston, he wrote asking permission to use it. 'Where', he wrote, 'in conversation, there was nothing but praise of Winston I was nothing like as careful because it did not occur to me that anyone could object to their praise of Winston being used in building up my portrait of him. This was my working rule and it is plain now that it has not worked as well as I had hoped'.[63] The replies Charles received to his letters were both to the effect that private conversations should not be printed without permission,[65,66] though Clark, on further reflection, proposed that publication without consent could be condoned if it did no harm to the person quoted.[67] Charles gained no support at all for his idiosyncratic working rule.

Charles sought to round off *The Times* correspondence with a letter published on 3 June.[68] This time he led with the question of Churchill's knowledge and approval of his writing his book, and gave virtually the same account of this that he had given to the Secretary of the BMA,[54] concluding with: 'When that is said what is left?' He then commented on his retentive memory which enabled him accurately to remember details of conversations, and he described his working rule about quoting conversations, saying that it did not occur to him that anyone would object to it. He defended the publication of his book so soon after Churchill's death on the grounds that a controversial book like this one should appear in the author's lifetime so that he might answer his critics, and he defended the length of his book, which some critics had complained about following its publication a week before, on the grounds that it was only by inclusion of the smallest details that Churchill could be shown to be different from other men. Charles neither covered all the criticisms levelled against him, nor did he concede that any of them might be valid. And he could not resist trailing his coat. In a last sentence he quoted Churchill as saying 'Generosity is always wise' and added 'When he went smaller men took his place and sought to speak for him'.[68] In these circumstances it was scarcely surprising that his letter was not the last word in the correspondence. Next day, a letter from Mr Anthony Moir, who had been Churchill's solicitor and to whom Bracken had introduced Charles, indicated that at Charles's interview with him in 1958 no mention had been made of a book to be solely based upon a part of Churchill's life, and no reference made to approval having been given by Churchill to any book.[69] A letter from Montague Browne followed, in which, ignoring Sir Herbert Seddon's affirmation, he suggested, in effect, that Charles's claims that he had obtained Churchill's approval for writing the book were unconvincing.[70] What failed to emerge in these letters was that what Charles had talked about to Bracken[71] and to Moir[72] was his Memoirs, that in the Churchill entourage it was known that he was preparing his Memoirs,[73] and that he kept a journal which was joked about.[74] In having referred to his writing as his Memoirs and then taken on the mantle of Churchill's Boswell,[68] Charles had inevitably laid himself open to some of the sort of criticism and questioning that appeared in *The Times* correspondence.

The furore precipitated by *The Sunday Times* extracts was greater than Charles and Dorothy had expected[75] and Dorothy at times felt shattered by it.[45,76] Charles had his ups and downs, and was particularly shaken by the medical criticism.[77] In days gone by he had rejoiced in controversy and had ridden out cheerfully to do battle with the Amalekites, but now he was a very old man, in his eighty-fourth year, carrying on without much help one side of a very public row which seemed endless.[78] Not having an office, and virtually unprotected at home, he had to cope with everything himself. The bedside telephone would ring in the small hours and a reporter would quote from a letter that was appearing in that morning's *Times* and ask him, half asleep, what he had to say about it. But, although he became very tired, and at times his zest for conflict left him, on the whole he was resilient[79] and was even heard to murmur at one stage that it was better than a quiet life—a sentiment which Dorothy emphatically did not share.[80] There was one moment of light relief two days after the book was published. Charles and Dorothy went to the church at Mickleham, where a memorial window to Beaverbrook was unveiled. From there they went to Cherkley, where Lady Beaverbrook gave a large buffet lunch, during which she seized on Charles and took him up to Anthony Eden and his wife (now Lord and Lady Avon) and said 'You know each other of course!' As Dorothy said, there was absolutely no comment.[81]

Charles's remark to the Secretary of the BMA that he did not get about very much was no understatement. Apart from an occasional formal outing such as the unveiling of the Beaverbrook memorial window, or a funeral, there was little to take him out, and there were seldom visitors at home. Increasingly remote, he believed all the fuss was the result of a deliberate campaign against himself and his book,[82] with doctors getting their own back over the part he had played in launching the NHS, and the Churchill family feeling aggrieved that his book was being published ahead of Randolph Churchill's first volume on the life of his father. Charles in his isolation did not seem to realise that, whatever might be the motives of the various players, whether he had done rightly or wrongly was being very widely discussed in the world outside 25 Bryanston Square,[82] including within his own family. Those of his grandchildren who were of an age to understand what was going on, between them probably reflected the spectrum of opinions in England, one believing grandfather had been rather naughty, one much enjoying the whole furore, and one saying he wasn't concerned because it wasn't reported in *Horse & Hound*.[83]

It is the tradition in most clubs that personal animosities are left outside and are not allowed to detract from the courtesies which members extend to each other. However, when at the height of the contretemps Charles attended the June meeting of the Other Club he was publicly upbraided by Christopher Soames. Charles described what happened in a letter written a few days later:

> 'At the Other Club on Thursday before dinner I was sitting talking to Colin Coote (late editor of the *Telegraph*) when I became aware of Christopher standing over me. "I am surprised to find you here among Winston's friends" he said.'[84]

But not all of Churchill's friends shunned him, and Lord Longford, who had been absent on that occasion, made a point of sitting next to him at the next dinner.[85] Nevertheless, Charles's attendances became less congenial to him and four years later, when the club's future was being reviewed, he indicated that he was unlikely to attend in future.[86]

As *The Times* correspondence drew to a close, a sort of coda was played in the *Daily Telegraph* following an article by Randolph Churchill headed 'The Churchill Controversy—Was He A Burnt-Out Case?'[87] At the same time the *British Medical Journal* carried letters which were mostly critical of Charles. No new points were raised, and the *BMJ* correspondence was interesting in the lack of letters over the signatures of the leaders of the profession. For one reason or another, Russell Brain's plea to allow things to rest seemed to have struck a sympathetic chord. Dr William Sargant recalled Brain telling him at this time that Churchill knew perfectly well that Charles was writing the book,[88] and this confirmation of what Seddon had written in *The Times* would, in so far as it was known, have been accepted without question.

All through *The Times* correspondence, which stemmed almost entirely from *The Sunday Times* extracts, Charles believed that his work would be much more favourably received when the book was published on 23 May, and people read the extracts in context. So he was disappointed when the reviews in Britain mostly, while disclaiming competence in medical ethics, nevertheless dwelt on the feeling that there had been an offence against good taste in the publication of the work so soon after Churchill's death and in the face of Lady Churchill's objection. For Charles this criticism tended to overshadow the many very good things that were also said, even by some of his sharpest critics, about his high performance as a writer, about the biographical interest of his work and, although there was some difference of opinion on this, about his contribution to knowledge of history. It is given to few biographers to have their works described, as this one was, as a literary masterpiece.[89] Ethical judgments apart, the one consistent criticism was that his book was too long. Charles had good reason to be pleased with the American reviews, which were mostly very enthusiastic and touched lightly, if at all, on medical ethics.[90]

By the end of June there were glimpses of the pleasanter side of being the author of a book that looked as if it might be a best seller. Charles had talks to prepare for literary clubs and luncheons[91,92] and his publishers planned for him to visit Holland, Sweden and Denmark in October. He agreed to go so long as press and radio interviews were restricted to historical aspects, for he believed that reference to ethics would only start a controversy again in the English press.[93] Another trip across the Atlantic was a possibility too when Charles tentatively accepted an invitation to speak at the University of Victoria, British Columbia—'an adventure and I wonder if he is up to it'—was Dorothy's comment.[94] Once the book was published, another pleasant happening was the arrival of letters from people who greatly liked what they read. They included Lord Casey,[95] who had been Minister of State in the Middle East during the war and was now Governor General of Australia, Lady Casey,[96] Sir Roger Makins,[97] Sir Compton Mackenzie,[98] Noel Coward[99] and the military historian Liddell Hart[100] who, while full of praise, took the opportunity to put Charles right on a few points of military history which he thought should be corrected in future editions. The commendations in such letters were much the same, that the book was an outstanding biography, a great contribution to history, that it was wonderfully written and that it did nothing but enhance Churchill's reputation.

Notwithstanding expressions of opinion of this sort, and the apparent acceptance by medical consultants of Russell Brain's proposal that things should be allowed to rest, the BMA's annual representative meeting held in Exeter in July took a course of its own. It spent two hours debating policy on professional secrecy and carried a motion by 597 votes to 3 confirming the Association's stated policy on professional secrecy and affirming that the death of a patient did not absolve the doctor from his obligation of secrecy.[101] In discussing consent for disclosure of matters covered by the notion of professional secrecy a distinction was recognised between the consent of the patient and, when the patient was dead, of some other person competent to give consent, but this subject was not explored in depth.[102] Delegates were instructed by the chairman, Dr Ronald Gibson of Winchester, not to mention any identifiable incident or practitioner in the debate, and the closest anyone came to doing so was when a speaker provided light relief by commenting that there was a lot more he could say, but he would be a 'proper Charlie' if he did so. The *Daily Telegraph* headlined its main article, which incidentally reminded its readers of the forthcoming serialisation of Randolph Churchill's biography, 'Doctors Disown Lord Moran'.[103] Things then became quiet over the summer months and for Charles and Dorothy Marshalls provided its usual solace. Since Dorothy's illness, weekends with men of affairs as visitors had not been resumed, and in any event the appearance in print of things that were said conversationally had led to a coolness in some of the relationships between Charles and the erstwhile guests. Come the autumn, after visiting Scandinavia to promote his book, accompanied by Dorothy and Miss Dean, Charles complained that he was unemployed[92] and leading a very hum-drum existence in one room

Figure 20. Charles and Dorothy at Marshalls in the 1960s. (Wellcome Institute Library, London; CMAC PP/CMW/P.29)

apart from half an hour's walk round Bryanston Square.[104] He read *War and Peace*. Russell Brain, whose letter to *The Times* had initially deeply upset Charles,[105] but with whom bridges had been built again, told Charles he had been reading *War and Peace* too; also that when visiting Copenhagen in July he had found copies of Charles's book on all the booksellers' counters.[106] Brain's death shortly afterwards drew from Charles his last pithy obituary comment in *The Times*. It was indeed an unqualified tribute in which Charles remarked on Brain's cool thought and complete absence from prejudice, and in which he summarised in the fewest possible words the essence of what many saw in the man: 'He was completely without vanity and when he had said what he had to say he would sit down'.[107]

The BMA's meeting in Exeter in July proved not to be the last word from that quarter. Charles learnt that a complaint had been made about him to the Association and it was to be considered by the central ethical committee. His position was that his book had been written with Churchill's knowledge and approval, but he believed the committee would be influenced by knowledge that Lady Churchill had not wanted him to write it.[108] At first Charles was inclined not to take the matter very seriously, but when he learnt that the central ethical committee meeting on 25 October had recommended to the Council of the Association that he should be expelled, he turned things over to his solicitor.[104] To begin with he was surprised, apart from anything else, that he could be expelled, for having paid his subscription for years by a banker's order, he had forgotten that he was still a member. The fact that Charles was involved in any way with the ethical committee would never have been publicly known had not an alert newspaper reporter noticed in November that one Charles McMoran Wilson was seeking an injunction to restrain the BMA from doing various things including acting on the resolution (the nature of which was divulged) of its central ethical committee.[109] 'Moran sues the BMA' was all over the papers. One immediate effect was more letters written by doctors to Charles saying they were on his side.[110]

With the lawyers pursuing their course, Charles set out independently to defend his position to those he thought would be the key players at the BMA meeting, and he was heartened, as he wrote, 'that so many have been willing to help and to try to undo the harm done by the Ethical Committee'.[111] The council meeting was due to be held on 3 January 1967 just before Charles and Dorothy set out for their postponed and much-looked-forward-to trip to South Africa. Charles decided that he would withdraw his legal proceedings against the BMA and would personally address the Council, and this he did.[112] People visiting him[113], and those close to him[114] at this time could not help noticing that he was liable to be confused and that he was more than a little forgetful, although like many very old people he retained a disarming capacity to appear totally on the ball for short periods, given the right cues. The proceedings of the Council, like those of its central ethical committee were, according to normal practice, affairs of complete confidence, but some ill-disposed person must have leaked them, and four days after the meeting there were again headlines in some papers which reported the original ethical committee's recommendation and that the Council had decided that Charles should be censured but not expelled from the BMA.[115] The exact nature of the complaint against Charles was not specified, the BMA remained silent and the news made little impact. Charles and Dorothy had left for South Africa by sea the day before, both with colds and very tired and with Dorothy overwhelmed at having to cope on her own. Left behind, Miss Dean had many anxieties about them, and was especially concerned that Charles would have forgotten much of the detail of the recent happenings and be unable to recount them to John.[114]

Charles's last word came in a statement that he issued to the press on his arrival in Capetown on 18 January, in which he said he would make no comment on the matter which had been in dispute between himself and the BMA except to confirm that it had been disposed of. He added:

'So far as the general controversy over my book is concerned I will only repeat that I believe that I was right to write it, that I wrote with Sir Winston's knowledge, and that I hope that my book, by describing what he was really like, can only enhance his reputation.'[116]

The visit to South Africa, with its rest and recuperation, was a total success. Charles reverted to form. The family observed that after he had spent a few days with his younger grandson William visiting a game reserve, William complained that he talked the whole time about Churchill; Charles complained that William just talked.[117]

Chapter 24

The Last Years

In its publication Charles's book had been as much an American as a British enterprise, and when he and Dorothy returned from South Africa they set off for the United States on a visit arranged by Houghton Mifflin. Accompanied and steered by Miss Dean, they flew to Boston, where they started their tour in the suite in the Ritz Carlton that Randolph Churchill had occupied a few weeks earlier[1] when the same publishers had been promoting the first volume of his biography of his father.[2] As well as being interviewed by the media and attending a reception in Boston to mark the publication of an American edition of *The Anatomy of Courage*, Charles gave eight lectures in three weeks.[3] His usual title, including that for the Eberhard Faber Public Lecture at Princeton, was 'Twenty-Five years with Churchill' but for the Gay Lecture at Harvard he chose 'In Defence of Medical Biography'. What he said on that occasion went unrecorded. It was certainly not a deep exploration of what is really a complex subject and his argument no doubt followed the line which he took in media interviews,[4] which was to assert that in the ordinary way a doctor should not write about a patient but in the case of a great historical figure who was dead, that did not apply. The over-riding consideration in Churchill's case was that the truth should be told. And with regard to the timing of publication he was adamant that it had to be in his lifetime, for if there were any attacks on the book he was the person to answer them. If the book had been published after his death, his son would have had to defend it, and that would have been wrong. Miss Dean worried about how Charles would cope with these questions,[1] but at interview he handled them with the sort of conviction that tends to discourage further questioning, his still finely resonant voice belying his age.[4]

Charles had one complaint about his trip. Houghton Mifflin believed that the programme they had arranged, with mostly more than one event a day during the three weeks and a tight travel schedule in the eastern states, would sufficiently extend their elderly, and in Dorothy's case physically limited, visitors. Charles did not see it in this light. He accused them of neglecting the promotion of his book in favour of Randolph Churchill's, and felt that he had not reached a truly national audience.[2] This led him to suggest returning for a major lecture tour, but he received no encouragement from those close to him. Although on set occasions he blossomed and appeared as an unusually vigorous 84 year old, there were

times when he was not only tired but also quite confused, and Miss
Dean was thankful when they returned home safely.

Back in England at the end of April, Charles at first longed for
more excitement, but the American visit really marked the end of
his life as a public figure. His last war with public opinion was over.
So far as his book on Churchill was concerned, he never had second
thoughts on his decision to publish. He was convinced that he had
done right, he accepted that he had lost some friends, and he was
confident that he had made a significant contribution to the historical
record. He persisted in seeing the controversy as localised to a few
doctors who were getting their own back for his actions over the
National Health Service, and to the Churchill family who he believed
would have preferred the book to have been written by Randolph.[4]
Charles lived long enough to see his book beginning to be used as
an important source for an understanding of the context in which
Churchill operated,[5] although not long enough to see it extensively
quoted in the major historical studies of Churchill in the 1980s.[6-8]
He also lived long enough to read a sensitive article by a highly
regarded member of his own profession, Sir Douglas Hubble,
comparing him as a diarist with James Boswell and pointing to their
shared attribute of social courage, by which he meant their readiness
on occasion to oppose their subjects' opinions.[9] Given Charles's
passionate love of writing, he was very pleased in his last years when
John, during a posting at the Foreign Office in London, not only
wrote a substantial life of Campbell-Bannerman,[10] one of England's
lesser known prime ministers, but also received the Whitbread
Award for it as the outstanding biography of 1973.

Marshalls continued to play an important part in Charles's and
Dorothy's lives. They had reached a stage when family and a few
valued old friends were what really mattered, and the visitors book
continued to reflect such visitors. The oldest friend of all, MVB Hill—
Hillo of the first war years—appeared regularly and was the one
guest for whom whisky was always provided before bed time. For
a few years, too, with the help of Geoffrey and Jane and Miss Dean,
Charles and Dorothy were able to pursue the sun with holidays in
Europe. But, despite money derived from the book, and assured
support within the family, Charles continued to worry about what
would happen to Dorothy when he died, and he persisted in living
frugally. He kept on attending the House of Lords into his nineties,
enjoying the interest, warmth and companionship that he found
there; but despite receiving the sitting fee, he still travelled by bus.
One day when there was a strike and buses were not running, he
arrived home exhausted having walked from Westminster to
Bryanston Square rather than take a taxi. This was of course
symptomatic of the situation, common in later life, when
idiosyncrasies of earlier years become exaggerated. Charles still left
all handling of money to Dorothy and had to ask her for some when

Figure 21. Charles with 'Hillo' (Colonel MVB Hill) at Marshalls in the 1960s. (Wellcome Institute Library, London; CMAC PP/CMW/P.30)

he went out. He had no idea about tipping and thought one shilling covered everything. For a long time he was reluctant to resign from the Athenaeum because he liked the old barber there. He continued to wear the same sort of knitted black tie that he had worn for years, which was increasingly expensive and hard to obtain. He remained inordinately fussy about having what he saw as good fresh food, and on the rare occasions when he went out to lunch he would foresee objectionable fare and ask for an indigestion tablet to take as a precaution. He continued to loathe wet weather, attributing his hatred to his memories of France in the first war, and never went out in it except when he and Dorothy were taken to Rugby matches at Twickenham, where the weather didn't seem to matter and there was always an enjoyable picnic in the car.[1]

Although Charles did not look forward to living through his nineties, he retained his sense of fun. Not long before his 90th birthday he enlivened a family dinner with a spine-chilling impression of Henry Irving as the murderer in *The Bells*—a play which he must have seen in about 1900.[11] To celebrate his 90th birthday on 10 November 1972 John and Shirley arranged a family party in their house in Hampstead. Dorothy wrote out a list of suggested guests, designed to reflect the different periods of Charles's life. Against School and Student days she wrote: no survivors. Against First War she wrote: Hillo. Together ran 1st RF [Royal Fusiliers].[12] St Mary's, the College, the Book and Sussex life all had their nominees and the only gap was in names reflecting the Churchill years. The abiding memories of the occasion were of Charles making a sparkling spontaneous speech on the theme of picking winners, and then of he and Hillo falling asleep in their chairs at the table before the pudding came. On the following day the Royal College of Physicians gave a lunch party for Charles and he had to make another speech. 'I used to make a lot of speeches', he wrote to his granddaughter Laura, 'and found them easy but now I am old I find it very difficult'.[13]

Old age was indeed slowly and relentlessly making life more difficult, although when Charles was 91 he and Dorothy travelled behind the Iron Curtain to visit John and Shirley, who were stationed in Budapest. In the following year Charles rather suddenly began to show signs of his great age and in 1975 he and Dorothy left Bryanston Square, sold Marshalls, parted regretfully from Miss Dean, and went to live with Jane and Geoffrey who had settled with their family of four children in a beautiful old house at Newton Valence in Hampshire. In earlier years, Charles had been particularly close to John, with whom there was a shared interest in words and writing. But he had always taken pride in Geoffrey's steady advancement in the business world, and now they were drawn together as Geoffrey tried to provide moments of relief from the tedium of extreme old age. Charles was also very fond of Jane, and her warmth and kindness went far to shelter him, and later Dorothy, in their last years. In the peaceful surroundings of the Old Manor House at Newton Valence Charles faded gently away and died on 12 April 1977 in his ninety-fifth year. He was buried in the adjacent churchyard, where Dorothy, whose mind and spirit remained vigorous to the end, was also buried six years later.

A memorial service was held for Charles on 22 April 1977 at All Souls, Langham Place. The congregation included members of his family and a remarkable cross-section of the elders of medicine, political life and the army but no representative of the Churchill family. Dr Tom Kemp, the St Mary's student to whom Charles had remained closest, read from *The Pilgrim's Progress* how Mr Valiant-for-truth was taken with a summons and how, when he passed over, all the trumpets sounded for him on the other side.

References

Abbreviations

C	Charles, when recipient of family letters.
CMW	Charles Wilson before his barony in 1943.
D	Dorothy Dufton, later Dorothy Wilson and, from 1943, Dorothy, Lady Moran.
FP	Family papers*.
GHW	Geoffrey Wilson.
JM	John Wilson after succeeding his father as the 2nd Lord Moran in 1977.
JW	John Wilson before 1977.
M	Charles Wilson after becoming Lord Moran in 1943.
Munk's Roll	*Lives of the Fellows of the Royal College of Physicians of London.* London RCP.
RCP	Royal College of Physicians.
SMH	St Mary's Hospital.

Chapter 1
Early Years

1 Giles J. Letter to Dr JF Wilson 21 December 1877 (FP).
2 M. Letter to Dr RG Rowley March 1967 (FP).
3 Autobiographical notes (FP).
4 Teale Dr F Pidgin. Letter to Dr JF Wilson 1 July 1866 (FP).
5 Albutt Dr F Clifford. Letter to Dr JF Wilson July 1866 (FP).
6 D. Letter to author, 16 November 1980.
7 Cope VZ. *The history of St Mary's Hospital Medical School.* London: Heinemann, 1954; p 11.
8 Peterson M Jeanne. *The medical profession in mid-Victorian London.* London: University of California Press, 1978: p 13.
9 St Mary's Hospital Medical School. Roll of pupils. Volume 2.
10 Cope VZ (ref: 1.7) p 178, 179.
11 Cope VZ (ref: 1.7) p 195, 196.
12 Munk's Roll. Vol 5, 1968; pp 175, 176.
13 Cope VZ (ref: 1.7) p 149, 150.
14 Munk's Roll. Vol 4, 1955; p 351.
15 SMH Gazette Vol 8, 1902; p 149.
16 SMH Gazette Vol 10, 1904; p 65.
17 SMH Gazette Vol 11, 1905; p 59.
18 SMH Gazette Vol 12, 1906; p 48.
19 SMH Gazette Vol 13, 1907; p 35.

---

*The present Lord Moran has placed his father's papers in the custody of the Contemporary Medical Archives Centre (CMAC) at the Wellcome Institute for the History of Medicine, where they have been catalogued with the help of a grant from the Wellcome Trust. Intending readers are advised to write in advance to The Archivist, CMAC, Wellcome Institute, 183 Euston Road, London NW1 2BN.

20 SMH Gazette Vol 13, 1907; p 32.
21 Moran Lord. SMH Gazette. Vol 71, 1965; p 219.
22 SMH Gazette Vol 13, 1907; p 46.
23 SMH Gazette Vol 14, 1908; p 50.
24 SMG Gazette Vol 11, 1905; p 101.

Chapter 2
Disenchanted Young Doctor

1 SMH Board of Management. Minutes. Vol 6, 1906-1911.
2 Autobiographical notes (FP).
3 Moran Lord. *Winston Churchill, the struggle for survival.* London: Constable 1966; p 169.
4 SMH Medical School Committee Minutes, Feb 1910.
5 SMH Gazette Vol 16, 1910; p 22.
6 SMH Gazette Vol 16, 1910; p 61.
7 SMH Gazette Vol 16, 1910; p 73.
8 SMH Gazette Vol 16, 1910; pp 87, 88.
9 SMH Gazette Vol 16, 1910; pp 94-96.
10 SMH Medical School Committee. Minutes, Oct 1910.
11 SMH Gazette Vol 16, 1910; pp 115-117.
12 SMH Gazette Vol 17, 1911; p 11.
13 SMH Gazette Vol 17, 1911; p 34.
14 D. Letter to author 3 June 1980.
15 M. ref: 2.3 p 169.
16 CMW. Letter to Dr & Mrs JF Wilson 4 Aug 1913 (FP).
17 CMW. Letter to Dr & Mrs JF Wilson 7 July 1913 (FP).
18 CMW. Letter to Dr & Mrs JF Wilson 9 July 1913 (FP).
19 CMW. Letter to Dr & Mrs JF Wilson 23 July 1913 (FP).
20 CMW. Letter to Dr & Mrs JF Wilson 11 Aug 1913 (FP).
21 Maurice, Dick. Six generations in Wiltshire. *British Medical Journal* 1988; **284**: 1756-8.
22 CMW. Letter to Dr & Mrs JF Wilson 19 Aug 1913 (FP).
23 CMW. Letter to Dr & Mrs JF Wilson 25 Oct 1913 (FP).
24 CMW. Letter to Dr & Mrs JF Wilson 27 Oct 1913 (FP).
25 SMH Medical Committee. Minutes, 10 Nov 1913.
26 SMH Board of Management. Minutes 13 Nov 1913.
27 SMH Medical Committee. Minutes 8 Dec 1913.
28 Munk's Roll. Vol 5, 1968. pp 157, 158.
29 Munk's Roll. Vol 5, 1968; p 67.
30 Munk's Roll. Vol 6, 1982; pp 273-5.
31 CMW. Letter to Dr JF Wilson 22 February 1909 (FP).

Chapter 3
The Army in France 1914-1918

1 Autobiographical notes (FP).
2 Commission (FP).

3 Daniel AW. Letter to Dr JF Wilson 8 Dec 1919 (FP).
4 D. Letter to author 16 Nov 1980.
5 Hart BH Liddell. *History of the First World War*. London: Pan Books, 1972; p 131.
6 Moran Lord. *The Anatomy of Courage*. London: Constable, 1945.
7 War Diary, 1st Battalion, The Royal Fusiliers. London: Public Record Office, Reference WO95, 1613.
8 Hill MVB. Letter to author 12 September 1980.
9 Herringham W. *A Physician in France*. London: Arnold, 1919; p 57.
10 M. ref: 2.3 p 165.
11 Hart BHL (ref. 3.5) pp 231-53.
12 Keegan J. *The Face of Battle*. Harmondsworth: Penguin Books, 1978; p 260.
13 Moran Lord. Wear and tear. *Lancet* 1950; i: 1099-101.
14 Citation of award of Military Cross (FP).
15 War Diary, 1st Battalion, The Royal Fusiliers. London: Public Record Office, Reference WO95, 2207.
16 Ministry of Defence. Letter to author 9 Oct 1981.
17 D. Letter to author 6 Sept 1980.
18 Munk's Roll. Vol 4, 1955; pp 334, 335.
19 Munk's Roll. Vol 6, 1982; pp 317-19.
20 Wilson CM, Mackintosh JM. Mustard gas poisoning. *Quart J Med* 1920; **13**: 201-40.
21 Pickering Professor Sir George. Personal communication, 24 April 1980.

Chapter 4
Reluctant Physician

1 Fisher HAL. *A History of Europe*. London: Arnold, 1936; p 1195.
2 D. Letter to author 3 June 1980.
3 Barcroft J. Letter to D 8 Aug 1919 (FP).
4 D. Letter to her mother Jan 1919 (FP).
5 D. Letter to her mother Feb/March 1919 (FP).
6 D. Letter to her father 25 March 1919 (FP).
7 Dufton SF. A smokeless Leeds. *Yorkshire Post* 20 Nov 1916.
8 Hardy WB. Letter to D 22 May 1916 (FP).
9 Barcroft J, Bayliss WM. Physiological Society. Notice of Annual General Meeting, 27 Jan 1917 (FP).
10 Barcroft Mrs. Letter to D 10 April 1919 (FP).
11 Ryle J. Letter to D 5 April 1919 (FP).
12 CMW. Letter to D March/April 1919 (FP).
13 Notice of demobilisation 4 April 1919 (FP).
14 CMW. Letter to D 5 April 1919 (FP).
15 CMW. Letter to D 11 April 1919 (FP).
16 CMW. Letter to D 7 April 1919 (FP).

17　Cope VZ (ref: 1.7) p 224.
18　CMW. Letter to D 22 April 1919 (FP).
19　CMW. Letter to D 16 April 1919 (FP).
20　CMW. Letter to Dr SF Dufton 18 April 1919 (FP).
21　CMW. Letter to D 19 April 1919 (FP).
22　CMW. Letter to D 20 April 1919 (FP).
23　Peterson M Jeanne. (ref: 1.8). Chap 5 pp 194-243.
24　CMW. Letter to D Sunday (FP).
25　CMW. Letter to D undated (FP).
26　CMW. Letter to D 2 June 1919 (FP).
27　CMW. Letter to D 20 May 1919 (FP).
28　CMW. Letter to D Tuesday (FP).
29　CMW. Letter to D Saturday afternoon (FP).
30　CMW. Letter to D Wednesday (FP).
31　CMW. Letter to D Friday (FP).
32　CMW. Letter to D 31 May 1919 (FP).
33　CMW. Letter to D 1 June 1919 (FP).
34　Dale HH. Thomas Renton Elliott 1988-1961. *Biogr Mem Fellows R Soc Lond* 1961; **Vol 7**: 53-74.
35　CMW. Letter to D Sunday (FP).
36　CMW. Letter to D Tuesday (FP).
37　CMW. Letter to D 6.40 p.m. (FP).
38　Marriage certificate 15 July 1919 (FP).
39　Wilson Dr JF. Letter to D 30 July 1919 (FP).

Chapter 5
St Mary's Hospital

1　Kettle Dr EH. Letter to CMW 30th July 1919 (FP).
2　Cope VZ. ref: 1.7 p 22.
3　Royal Commission on University Education in London. Final Report of the Commissioners. para. 247 London: HM Stationery Office, 1913.
4　Royal Commission on University Education in London (ref: 5.3) para. 248.
5　Müller Professor Friedrich von. Royal Commission on University Education in London. Minutes of Evidence, p 305 30 June 1911. London: HM Stationery Office, 1911.
6　Osler Sir William. Royal Commission on University Education in London. Minutes of Evidence, p 342, 21 July 1911. London: HM Stationery Office, 1911.
7　Royal Commission on University Education in London. (ref: 5.3) para. 275.
8　St Mary's Hospital Medical School Committee. Minutes. 2 June 1914.
9　Munk's Roll. Vol 4, 1955; pp 559, 560.

10 Newman G. *Some Notes on Medical Education in England.* London: HM Stationery Office, 1918.

11 Graham G. The formation of the medical and surgical professorial units in the London teaching hospitals. *Annals of Science*, 1970; **26**: 1-22.

12 CMW. Letter to D 8 May 1919 (FP).

13 Macfarlane G. *Alexander Fleming, the Man and the Myth.* London: Chatto & Windus—Hogarth Press, 1984: pp 53-5.

14 CMW. Letter to D Saturday afternoon (FP).

15 D. Letter to author 28 Aug 1980.

16 Maurice G. Letter to CMW 5 Oct 1919 (FP).

17 Pickering GW (ref: 3.21).

18 Broadbent JFH. Letter to CMW 10 Sept 1919 (FP).

19 St Mary's Hospital Medical School Committee Minutes, Vol 5.

20 Notes. *St Mary's Hospital Gazette* 1919; **25**: 119.

21 Editorial. The case for change. *St Mary's Hospital Gazette* 1919; **25**: 113-115. (MS in family papers).

22 Editorial Notes. *St Mary's Hospital Gazette* 1919; **25**: 119, 120.

23 SMH Medical Committee minutes, 26 Jan 1920.

24 SMH Board of Management minutes, 29 Jan 1920.

25 SMH Medical Committee minutes, 13 Oct 1919.

26 Cope VZ. ref: 1.7 p 142.

27 SMH Medical Committee minutes, 24 Nov 1919.

28 SMH Medical Committee minutes, 8 Dec 1919.

29 SMH Reports of Sundry Committee minutes, 15 Dec 1919.

30 SMH Medical Committee minutes, 15 Dec 1919.

31 SMH Board of Management minutes, 18 Dec 1919.

32 SMH Medical Committee minutes, 9 Feb 1920.

33 SMH Board of Management minutes, 15 Feb 1920.

34 SMH Medical Committee minutes, 16 Feb 1920.

35 Herringham WP. Letter to CMW 5 March 1920 (FP).

36 CMW. Letter to Sir Wilmot Herringham 8 March 1920 (FP).

37 Wilson CM, Wilson D. Determination of basal metabolic rate and its value in diseases of the thyroid gland. *Lancet* 1920; **ii**: 1042-5.

38 Wilson CM, Pannett CA. Influence of bile salts upon gastric functions. *Br J Exp Path* 1921; **2**: 70-4.

39 Wilson CM, Bourne AW. Relation of thyroid to female pelvic organs. *Lancet* 1922; **i**: 1038-43.

40 *The Times* 21 April 1920.

41 CMW. Letter. *The Times* 5 May 1920.

42 Wilson CM. The future of the Poor-law infirmary. *Lancet* 1920; **ii**: 1287-90.

43 *The Times*, 2 Sept 1920.

44 D. Letter to author 1 Aug 1980.

45 Wilson CM. Shell shock. Social significance of courage. Character in action. *The Times* 22 Sept 1920.

46 Wilson CM. Leaders and led. The nemesis of deception. Peace lessons from war. *The Times* 16 Oct 1920.

47 War Office Committee on Shell Shock. Typescript transcript of evidence, 1920 (FP).

48 Wilson CM. Some effects of the war on industrial unrest. A talk reported in *The Manchester Guardian* 26 May 1921.

49 D. Personal communication, 1981.

Chapter 6
Dean of the Medical School

1 SMH. Medical School Committee. Minutes 7 Dec 1920.

2 D. Letter to Lord Beaverbrook 20th October 1935 (FP).

3 Moran Lord. BE Matthews 1866-1946. *St Mary's Hospital Gazette* 1948; 48.

4 Appleton Miss LB. Personal communication 1981.

5 Secretary SMH. Memorandum to Secretary, SMH Medical School, 14 Jan 1941 (FP).

6 SMH Board of Management minutes 19 March 1921.

7 M. Interview with Dr Charles Newman recorded on tape at the Royal College of Physicians, 25 June 1970.

8 Autobiographical notes (FP).

9 SMH Medical Committee minutes, 4 April 1921.

10 SMH Medical School Committee. Minutes 20 June 1921.

11 Graham G. (ref: 5.11).

12 SMH Medical School Committee. Minutes 3 May 1921.

13 D to author. Personal communication, 1981.

14 M. Notes for Sir Zachary Cope (handwritten) in response to Cope's request of 6 Jan 1954 for comment on his draft of his History of St Mary's Hospital Medical School (FP).

15 CMW. Letter to D Saturday (FP).

16 Pickering GW. (ref: 3.21).

17 M. Letter to P. Dixon 15 Oct 1969 (FP).

18 Wilson CM. Clinical units: their purpose and achievement. *Lancet* 1921; ii: 33-7.

19 Albutt Clifford. Letter to CMW 8 July 1921 (FP).

20 Albutt Clifford. Postcard to CMW. Undated (FP).

21 Elliott TR. Letter to CMW 22 Nov 1921 (FP).

22 CMW. Letter to TR Elliott 23 Nov 1921. Wellcome Institute for History of Medicine. Contemporary Archive Centre GC/42.

23 Elliott TR. Letter to CMW 29 Nov 1921 (FP).

24 SMH Board of Management. Minutes 13 Oct 1921.

25 Parkes W. Letter to CMW 15 Oct 1921 (FP).

26 D. Letter to author 28 Aug 1980.

27 SMH Medical School Committee. Minutes. First report on medical clinical unit, 1921, by FS Langmead.

28 Brooks Dr WDW. Letter to author 3 Sept 1981.

29 Editorial. A glimpse of Germany. *St Mary's Hospital Gazette* 1923; **29**: 17-19.

30 Firkin, Professor B to author. Personal communication.

31 SMH Medical School Committee. Minutes 12 Dec 1935.

32 SMH Medical School. *The Dean's Report 1921-1922.*

33 Cattell J McK, ed. *Science and Education Vol 2. Medical Research & Education.* New York: The Science Press, 1913; p 454.

34 SMH Medical School Committee. Minutes 7 Nov 1922.

35 SMH Medical School Committee. Minutes 5 Dec 1922.

36 SMH Medical School. *The Dean's Report 1922-1923.*

37 SMH Medical School Committee. Minutes 3 July 1923.

38 SMH Medical School Committee. Minutes 2 Oct 1923.

39 SMH Medical School Committee. Minutes 14 July 1925.

40 SMH Medical School Committee. Minutes 1 April 1924.

41 SMH Medical School Committee. Minutes 2 March 1920.

42 Moran Lord. Annual address by the President, Royal College of Physicians, 1948, pp 7-8.

43. SMH Medical School Committee. Minutes 28 April 1924.

44 Cope VZ. (ref: 1.7) p 69.

45 CMW. Letter to Lord Beaverbrook 29 July 1931 (FP).

Chapter 7
Harley Street Years

1 SMH Board of Management. Minutes 3 July 1919.

2 Cope VZ. (ref: 1.7) p 66.

3 Merrington WR. *University College Hospital and its Medical School: A History.* London: Heinemann, 1976; p 124.

4 CMW. Notes, handwritten, circa 1930 (FP).

5 Beaverbrook Lord. Letter to M 18 Aug 1947 (FP).

6 D. Letter to author 29 July 1980.

7 Taylor AJP. *Beaverbrook.* New York: Simon & Schuster, 1972; p 255, p 364.

8 Moran Lord. (ref: 2.3) p 10.

9 Taylor AJP. (ref: 7.7) p 239.

10 D. Letter to author 1 Aug 1980.

11 Taylor AJP. (ref: 7.8) p 212.

12 D. Letter to author 22 Jan 1981.

13 Kenmare Lady Elizabeth. Letter to D Friday (FP).

14 *The Cork Examiner* 17 Sept 1928.

15 GHW. Personal communication.

16 CMW. Letter to Lady Kenmare 13 May 1929 (FP).

17 SMH Medical School Committee. Minutes 7 May 1929.

18 SMH Medical School Committee. Minutes 4 June 1929.

19 Cope VZ. (ref: 1.7). p 67.

20 Taylor AJP. (ref: 7.7) p 259.

21 Moran Lord. Friends & Contemporaries. Script for BBC broadcast 1 Sept 1968 (FP).
22 Autobiographical notes (FP).
23 M. (ref: 6.14).
24 CMW. Letter to Beaverbrook 18 Jan 1928 (FP).
25 Taylor AJP. (ref: 7.7) p 256.
26 CMW. Letter to Beaverbrook 8 May 1929 (FP).
27 Beaverbrook Lord. Letter to C 9 May 1929 (FP).
28 CMW. Letter to Beaverbrook 10 May 1929 (FP).
29 Herringham WP. Letter to C 12 May 1929 (FP).
30 CMW. Letter to Montagu Norman 24 May 1929 (FP).
31 CMW. Letter to Montagu Norman 16 May 1929 (FP).
32 Norman Montagu. Letter to CMW 4 June 1929 (FP).
33 CMW. Letter to Montagu Norman, 4 June 1929 (FP).
34 D. Letter to Beaverbrook 20 Oct 1935 (FP).
35 Beaverbrook Lord. Letter to D 23 Oct 1935 (FP).
36 JM. Personal communication 1981.
37 D. Letter to author 2 Aug 1980.
38 D. Personal communication.
39 Wilson CM. Treatment of coli bacillium by ketogenic diet. *Lancet* 1932; **ii**: 960-62.
40 Wilson CM. Treatment of chronic B. Coli infections of urinary tract by ketogenic diet. *Postgraduate Medical Journal* 1933; **9**: 96-9.
41 D. Letter to author 28 Aug 1980.
42 CMW. Case books (FP).
43 Cockburn Dr HD. Personal communication 1981.
44 Moran Lady Shirley. Personal communication 1981.
45 Hunt Dr TC. Personal communication 1981.
46 CMW. Letter to D 19 June 1919 (FP).
47 Pickering GW (ref: 3.21).
48 Beaverbrook Lord. Letter to C 25 Sept 1934 (FP).
49 Beaverbrook & others. Letter to C 17 Jan 1935 (FP).
50 Brooks Dr WDW. (ref: 6.28).
51 JM. Personal communication.
52 D. Letter to author 6 Sept 1980.
53 D. Personal communication.
54 D. Letter to Godfrey Maurice 9 April 1935 (FP).
55 D. Letter to TR Elliott 3 Nov 1922. Wellcome Foundation for History of Medicine. Contemporary Medical Archive Centre GC/42.
56 Macfarlane G. (ref: 5.13). p 67.
57 CMW. Note on Herringham (FP).
58 M (ref: 6.7).
59 D. Personal communication.
60 D. Letter to Godfrey Maurice 18 March 1936 (FP).
61 D. Letters to Godfrey Maurice 6 Aug 1934, 10 Aug 1935 (FP).

62 CMW. Letter to D 21 April 1934 (FP).
63 D. Letter to Godfrey Maurice 8 Sept 1935 (FP).
64 Maurice TR. Letter to author 26 March 1984.
65 D. Letter to Godfrey Maurice 31 Jan 1936 (FP).
66 JM. Personal communication.
67 D. Letter to Godfrey Maurice 23 Jan 1936 (FP).
68 D. Letter to Godfrey Maurice 5 Oct 1936 (FP).
69 CMW. Letter to Registrar University of London, 11 Aug 1937 (FP).
70 JM. Personal communication.
71 Pickering GW. Obituary: Lord Moran. *St Mary's Hospital Gazette* 1977; **83**: 12-14.
72 Wilson CM. (ref: 5.42).
73 Wilson CM. Pay bed and the future of the voluntary hospitals. *British Medical Journal* 1928; 1(suppl): 85-7.
74 Wilson CM. (ref: 6.18).
75 Moran Lord. Obituary: Lord Dawson of Penn. *Lancet*, 1945; **i**: 388-9.
76 Watson F. *Dawson of Penn*. London: Chatto and Windus, 1950.
77 JM. Personal communication.
78 Horder T. Medicine and old ethicks. *British Medical Journal* 1924; **1**: 485-9.
79 Editorial. The electronic reactions of Abrams. *Lancet* 1924; **ii**:866-7.
80 Editorial Note. *St Mary's Hospital Gazette* 1925; **21**: 32.
81 Horder Lord. Letter to CMW 29 Jan 1938 (FP).
82 M. (ref: 6.7).

Chapter 8
Choosing People

1 SMH Board of Management minutes 30 May 1929.
2 SMH Medical School Committee minutes 7 May 1929.
3 CMW. Letter to Dr John Freeman 24 March 1929 (FP).
4 Freeman J. Letter to CMW 26 March 1929 (FP).
5 Freeman J. Letter to CMW 1.30 Saturday (FP).
6 Freeman J. Letter to CMW Sunday (FP).
7 Keith A. Letter to CMW 27 May 1929 (FP).
8 SMH Board of Management minutes 24 July 1929.
9 Pickering GW. (ref: 3.21).
10 Cope VZ. (ref: 1.7) p 67.
11 Sargant W. In: Abse D, ed. *My Medical School*. London: Robson Books, 1978.
12 SMH Medical School Committee minutes 15 July 1930.
13 Verney H. Letter to Lady Kenmare 17 April 1930 (FP).
14 Graham Lady Helen. Letter to CMW 24 March 1931 (FP).
15 Graham-Little Sir Ernest. Letter to CMW 6 May 1931 (FP).
16 Baldwin S. Letter to Lt-Colonel HE Verney 28 May 1931 (FP).

17 *St Mary's Hospital Gazette* 1931; **37**: 73-5.
18 *The Times* 1 July 1931.
19 Programme. Foundation Stone Ceremony. 30 June 1931 (FP).
20 CMW. Manuscript pages (FP).
21 JM. Personal communication.
22 Brooks WDW. (ref: 6.28).
23 Nolan Cynthia. *A Bride of St Thomas*. London: Constable, 1970.
24 Brick E, Camp W. Football. *Encyclopaedia Britannica*. 1911; **10**: 617-25.
25 Cope VZ. (ref: 1.7) p 116.
26 Gathorne-Hardy J. *The Public School Phenomenon*. Harmondsworth: Penguin Books, 1979.
27 War Office Committee on Shell Shock (ref: 5.47).
28 Wilson CM. On the meaning of games to a medical school. *St Mary's Hospital Gazette*. 1922; **29**: 55-6.
29 Anonymous. Typescript (FP).
30 Pickering GW. (ref: 3.21).
31 CMW. Letter to D 24 February 1926 (FP).
32 Brooks WDW. (ref: 6.28).
33 SMH Medical School. *Dean's Report 1924-1925*.
34 SMH Medical School. *Dean's Report 1929-1930*.
35 CMW. Letter to Beaverbrook 29 July 1931 (FP).
36 SMH Medical School. *Dean's Report 1930-31*.
37 *Daily Mail* 28 September 1932.
38 Sargant W. *The Unquiet Mind*. London: Heinemann, 1967.
39 Typescript (FP).
40 Typescript recording the tribunal's decision (FP).
41 Law V. Letter to CMW 12 April 1933 (FP).
42 Munk's Roll. Vol 4, 1955; p 473.
43 Buzzard EF. Letter to John Freeman 9 December 1932 (FP).
44 Freeman J. Letter to EF. Buzzard 14 December 1932 (FP).
45 CMW. Letter to Dawson 9 March 1933 (FP).
46 Brown WL. Letter to CMW 23 May 1934 (FP).
47 CMW. Comment on a report of an inspection of the medical school 1932 or 1933 (FP).
48 CMW. Letter to Dawson 1 June 1931 (FP).
49 Dawson Lord. Quoted in Watson F. (ref: 7.76).
50 Elizabeth Duchess of York. Letter to CMW 24 June 1933 (FP).
51 Dawson Lord. Letter to CMW 6 December 1933 (FP).
52 CMW. Manuscript draft of letter to Sir Clive Wigram (FP).
53 CMW. Manuscript draft of letter to Sir George Newman (FP).
54 Programme for opening of the new Medical School and Pathological Institute, St Mary's Hospital. 12 December 1933 (FP).
55 D. Personal communication.

56 Medical news. *Lancet* 1934; **i**: 270.

57 CMW. Letter to D 21 April 1934 (FP).

58 Wilson CM. 'The student in irons'. *British Medical Journal* 1932; **1**: 485-7.

59 Greenwood M. *British Medical Journal* 1932; **1**: 541.

60 Munk's Roll. (ref: 42) p 592.

61 Ryle JA. *British Medical Journal* 1932; **1**: 587.

62 Ryle JA. (ref: 4.11).

63 Greenwood M. Letter to CMW 12 May 1932 (FP).

64 Wilson CM. *British Medical Journal* 1933; **2**: 887.

65 Wilson CM. Reform of the Medical Curriculum. *The Medical Press & Circular.* 1933; **88**: 210.

66 Cooke AM. *A History of the Royal College of Physicians of London.* Vol 3. Oxford: Oxford University Press, 1972; p 1066.

67 Heseltine M. Letter to CMW 14 June 1934 (FP).

68 Elliott TR. Letter to CMW 26 March 1932 (FP).

69 Wilson CM. Examinations as a path to freedom. *British Medical Journal* 1936; **2**:449-52.

70 Pickering GW. (ref: 3.21).

71 CMW. Letter to Crawford 31 July 1935 (FP).

72 CMW. Letter: Dear Sir 7 May 1936 (FP).

73 Dawson Lord. Letter to C 24 November 1935 (FP).

74 CMW to the author 1938.

75 CMW. Letter to Gardiner-Hill 11 August 1937 (FP).

76 Kemp Dr TA. Personal communication.

77 D. Letter to author 16 November 1980.

78 CMW. Letter to FRE Davis 23 February 1938 (FP).

79 Cockburn Dr HD. Personal communication.

80 Hartigan General IA. Letter to CMW 29 July 1935 (FP).

81 D. Letter to author 1 August 1980.

82 Goschen General Arthur. Letter to CMW 2 September 1935 (FP).

83 Pollock RV. Letter to CMW 16 November 1937 (FP).

84 CMW typescript: *The Birth of the Emergency medical Service* (FP).

85 CMW. Letter to Captain E Altham RN 9 August 1936 (FP).

86 Beaverbrook Lord. Letter to CMW 10 November 1936 (FP).

87 Taylor AJP. (ref: 7.7) p 367.

88 CMW. Letter to D Sunday 12 [November 1936] (FP).

89 Sargant W. (ref: 8.11) p 49.

90 EK to D. Tuesday (FP).

91 CMW. Handwritten drafts of letters to Lady Helen Graham 2 January 1937 & 31 May 1937 (FP).

92 JM. Personal communication.

93 CMW. Letter to D Monday 1937 (FP).

94 CMW. Handwritten draft of letter to Sir Wilfred Eady. 16 January 1938 (FP).

95 CMW. Letter to Brendan Bracken January 1938 (FP).

96   CMW. Letter to Beaverbrook 13 January 1938 (House of Lords Record Office, Beaverbrook Papers, C/249).
97   D. Letter to author 7 March 1981.
98   Pater JE. Letter to author 18 June 1981.
99   Dunn CL. *The Emergency Medical Services*. London: HMSO, 1952; p 44.
100 Sharpe Lady Evelyn. Letter to author 24 August 1981.

Chapter 9
Churchill's Doctor and President of the Royal College of Physicians

1   Cooke AM. (ref: 8.66) p 1061.
2   CMW to Dawson. Letter 1 January 1931 (FP).
3   Dawson Lord. Letter to CMW 2 July 1935 (FP).
4   Brooks WDW. (ref: 6.28).
5   CMW. Royal College of Physicians. A note on policy by Sir Charles Wilson. Typescript (FP).
6   CMW. Letter to 'Dear Eden' 27 March 1938 (FP).
7   CMW. Letter to D Monday 1937 (FP).
8   Phillips S. Letter to CMW 14 November 1938 (FP).
9   Illegible name. Letter to CMW 29 July 1938 (FP).
10 Cooke AM. (ref: 8.66) p 1072.
11 Cooke AM. (ref: 8.66) p 1198.
12 Hutchison R. Letter to CMW 13 April 1938 (FP).
13 Cooke AM. (ref: 8.66) p 1073.
14 Newman C. Personal communication.
15 D. Personal communication.
16 St Mary's Hospital and the emergency. Typescript page written after the Munich agreement of 30 September 1938 (FP).
17 Dunn CL. (ref: 8.99) p 44.
18 JM. Letter to author 11 November 1985.
19 Taylor AJP. *English History 1914 to 1945*. Harmondsworth: Penguin Books, 1970, p 555.
20 *The Times*. 24 November 1939.
21 Taylor AJP. (ref: 9.19) p 504.
22 D. Personal communication.
23 Deputy Senior Regional Officer, Ministry of Health. Letter to CMW 15 September 1939 (FP).
24 Dunn CL. (ref 8.99) p 55.
25 Gort Lord. Letter to CMW 12 Sept 1939 (FP).
26 CMW. Hospitals in war-time. Letter to *The Times* 6 December 1939.
27 Hunt Dr TC, Porritt Lord. Personal communications.
28 Group Officers of the ten London hospital sectors. Letter to CMW 16 June 1941 (FP).

29 Hart BH Liddell. *History of the Second World War*. London: Pan Books. 1973; p 114.

30 Pater JE. *The Making of the National Health Service*. King Edward's Hospital Fund for London, 1981; p 54.

31 Group Officers. (ref: 9.28).

32 D. Personal communication.

33 GHW. Personal communication.

34 Vaughan P. Cited by Grey-Turner E, Sutherland FM. *History of British Medical Association. Vol 2 1932-1981*. London: British Medical Association, 1982; p 34.

35 Cooke AM. (ref: 8.66) p 1085.

36 CMW. Letter to certain Fellow Royal College of Physicians 28 October 1940 (FP).

37 Buckley CW. Letter to CMW 31 October 1940 (FP).

38 CMW. Letter to Prof HP Himsworth 20 November 1940 (FP).

39 *Annals of the Royal College of Physicians*. 10 December 1940.

40 Cooke AM. (ref: 8.66) p 1086.

41 Pickering GW. letter to CMW 15 December 1940. RCP Box 17, File 2.

42 Cooke AM (ref: 8.66) p 1074.

43 Munk's Roll. 1982; **6**: 162, 163.

44 Ellis A. Letter to CMW 12 March 1941 (FP).

45 CMW. Letters to Prof Arthur Ellis 10 March 1941 & 11 March 1941 (FP).

46 CMW. Letter to Prof Arthur Ellis 22 March 1941 (FP).

47 Brooks WDW. (ref: 6.28).

48 Pyke Dr Charles. Memorandum, entitled Electing the President, from the Registrar, RCP, to Fellows of the College, 30 September 1985.

49 M. Note on presidential elections. 1941-1952 (FP).

50 D. Personal communication.

51 Grey-Turner E, Sutherland FM. (ref: 9.34) p 28.

52 Munk's Roll. 1968; **5**: 198-200.

53 Horder M. *The Little Genius*. London: Gerald Duckworth & Co. Ltd. 1966

54 M. (ref: 2.3) p 5.

55 Hill Mrs Kathleen. Letter to M 16 January 1966 (FP).

56 M. Letter to Brendan Bracken 10 November 1954 (FP).

57 Lysaght CE. *Brendan Bracken*. London: Allen Lane, 1979; p 177.

58 Soames Mary. *Clementine Churchill*. London: Cassell, 1979; p 252.

59 M. (ref: 2.3) p 72.

60 Colville J. *The Churchillians*. London: Weidenfeld & Nicholson, 1982; p 189.

61 Churchill Winston S. *The Second World War. Vol 2*. London: Cassell & Co Ltd, 1949; p 71.

62 CMW. Medical notes (FP).

63 *News of the World.* 28 December 1941.
64 Beaverbrook Lord. Letter to CMW 10 November 1936 (FP).
65 CMW. Letter to Beaverbrook 16 May 1940 (FP).
66 Beaverbrook Lord. Letter to CMW 16 May 1940 (FP).
67 CMW. Letter to Brendan Bracken 23 May 1940 (FP).
68 Colville J. (ref: 9.60) p 47.
69 Moran Lord. (ref: 2.3) p 6.
70 Ismay Lord. *The Memoirs of General the Lord Ismay.* London: Heinemann, 1960; p 214.

Chapter 10
1941—Moscow and Washington

1 Cooke AM. (ref: 8.66) p 1086.
2 Fraser F. Letter to D 26 September 1941 (FP).
3 CMW. Letter to Dr Letheby Tidy 21 September 1941 (FP).
4 CMW. Letter to Brendan Bracken 21 September 1941 (FP).
5 Ismay Lord (ref: 9.70) p 229.
6 Taylor AJP. (ref: 7.7) p 487.
7 CMW. Typescript headed: Moscow Conference. Medical Supplies Committee. Notes by Sir Charles Wilson. Dated 7 October 1941 (FP).
8 CMW. Script of talk on Russia (FP) (prepared for BBC. Weymouth A. Letter to CMW 28 Oct 1941 (FP)).
9 Dufton SF. Letter to CMW Saturday (FP).
10 Menu card of Dinner in honour of Lord Beaverbrook and Mr Averell Harriman. 13 October 1941. Cartoon on cover by Lowe (FP).
11 Beaverbrook Lord. Letter to CMW 16 October 1941 (FP).
12 Maisky, Mrs Agnes. Letter to CMW 6 November 1941 (FP).
13 Warburton F. Letter to CMW 12 November 1941 (FP).
14 Churchill Mrs Clementine S. Letter to CMW 26 November 1941 (FP).
15 CMW. Rough handwritten notes for address to RCP following visit to Russia (FP).
16 *Annals of RCP.* 30 October 1941.
17 Pickering GW. (ref: 3.21).
18 Elliott CA. Letter to CMW 28 November 1941 (FP).
19 Churchill Winston S. *The Second World War. Vol 3.* London: Cassell & Co Ltd, 1950; p 540.
20 Taylor AJP. (ref: 7.7) p 502.
21 Soames Mary. (ref: 9.58).
22 M. (ref: 2.3) p 11.
23 M. (ref: 2.3) p 12.
24 Mackenzie J. *Diseases of the Heart.* London: Henry Frowde, Hodder & Stoughton, 1910; p 164.
25 M. (ref: 2.3) p 16.

26 M. (ref: 2.3) p 17.
27 M. (ref: 2.3) p 18.
28 Churchill Winston S. (ref: 10.19) p 603.
29 Churchill Winston S. (ref: 10.19) p 613.
30 Soames Mary. (ref: 9.58) p 312.
31 Churchill Winston S. (ref: 10.19) p 612.
32 M. (ref: 2.3) p 21.
33 M. (ref: 2.3) p 23.
34 M. Draft of book. 53308 (FP).
35 M. (ref: 2.3) p 6.
36 CMW. Letter to Mrs Hill 27 March 1941 (FP).
37 Churchill Winston S. (ref: 10.19) p 556.
38 M. MS book (FP).
39 *Evening Standard.* 17 January 1942.
40 CMW. Handwritten note. 15 January 1942 (FP).
41 M. (ref: 2.3) p 23.
42 Fisher TWL. Letter to CMW 12 February 1942 (FP).
43 *Annals of RCP.* 29 January 1942.
44 CMW. Letter to Dr Roger I Lee 9 March 1942 (FP).
45 Dawson Lord. Letter to M 18 January 1942 (FP).
46 CMW. Letter to Brendan Bracken 9 April 1942 (FP).
47 CMW. Letter to Dawson 12 November 1941 (FP).
48 CMW. Letter to Prime Minister 26 March 1942 (FP).
49 Martin John. Letter to CMW 27 March 1942 (FP).
50 CMW. Letter to John Martin 31 March 1942 (FP).
51 Typescript note dated 3 July 1942, referring to 'two talks with Sir Charles Wilson' (FP).
52 CMW. Letter to D Wednesday 5.30 pm (FP).
53 CMW. Letter to D postmark 17 May 1942 (FP).
54 M. (ref: 6.7).
55 D. Letter to Dr H Boldero 11 February 1942 (FP).
56 Brooks WDW. (ref: 7.50).
57 Richardson Lord. Personal communication. 20 August 1981.
58 M. (ref: 9.49).
59 *Annals of RCP.* 30 March 1942.
60 Hartley DLB. The wartime brains you could trust. *The Times* 6 December 1980.
61 Wellington Maud. Letter to CMW 15 May 1942 (FP).
62 McDowall EB. Letter to CMW 20 April 1942 (FP).
63 Military Assistant to Commmander-in-Chief, Home Forces. Letter to CMW 26 April 1942 (FP).
64 CMW. Letter to General Bernard Paget 10 May 1942 (FP).
65 Paget General B. Letter to CMW 12 October 1942 (FP).
66 Quiller-Couch Sir Arthur. Letter to CMW 16 September 1940 (FP).
67 MacCarthy D. Letter to CMW 24 May 1942 (FP).

68 Desborough (Ethel) Lady. Letter to CMW 20 September 1942 (FP).

69 CMW. Letter to Desmond MacCarthy 12 December 1942 (FP).

Chapter 11
His Itinerant Patient

1 Gilbert Martin. *Winston S Churchill. Vol 7 Road to Victory.* London: Heinemann, 1986; p 53.

2 Gilbert M. (ref: 11.1) p 72.

3 Gilbert M. (ref: 11.1) p 126.

4 M. MS book p 21.

5 Jacob General Sir Ian. Personal communication. 3 March 1983.

6 CMW. Letter to Sir John Anderson 9 July 1942 (FP).

7 Typescript note (ref: 10.51).

8 Anderson J. Letter to CMW 9 July 1942 (FP).

9 Gilbert M. (ref: 11.1) p 155.

10 Gilbert M. (ref: 11.1) p 157.

11 Gilbert M. (ref: 11.1) p 158.

12 *Annals of RCP.* 30 July 1942.

13 CMW. Letter to Ernest Brown 1 August 1942 (FP).

14 CMW. Letter to Dr George Anderson 1 August 1942 (FP).

15 M. (ref: 2.3) p 49.

16 Gilbert M. (ref: 11.1) p 161.

17 Churchill Winston S. *The Second World War. Vol 4.* London: Cassell & Co Ltd, 1951; p 411.

18 Churchill Winston S. (ref: 11.17) p 412.

19 Alanbrooke Field Marshal the Viscount, cited in Bryant A. *The Turn of the Tide.* London: The Reprint Society, 1958; p 365.

20 Evans, Trefor C ed. *The Killearn Diaries* London: Sidgwick & Jackson, 1972; p 229.

21 M. MS 2.3 p 23.

22 M. (ref: 2.3) p 50.

23 Churchill Winston S. (ref: 11.17) p 412.

24 M. (ref: 2.3) p 51.

25 M. MS 2.3, p 37 (cf ref 2.3 p 70).

26 Clark Kerr Sir Archibald. Handwritten account of the Moscow conference. Public Record Office, reference FO 800/300.

27 M. (ref: 2.3) p 55.

28 M. (ref: 2.3) p 56.

29 M. (ref: 2.3) p 57.

30 Gilbert M. (ref: 11.1) p 188.

31 M. (ref: 2.3) p 58.

32 M. (ref: 2.3) p 59.

33 Gilbert M. (ref: 11.1) p 193.

34 M. (ref: 2.3) p 60.

35 M. MS 2.3 p 29.

36 Ross G. Operation bracelet: Churchill in Moscow 1942. In: Dilks D, ed.*Retreat from Power—Britain's Foreign Policy of the 20th Century.* Vol 2. London: MacMillan, 1981; p 113.
37 Alanbrooke. (ref: 11,19) p 384.
38 M. MS book p 30.
39 Reed J. Handwritten letter. Public Records Office, 800/300 53941.
40 Gilbert M. (ref: 11.1) p 206.
41 M. (ref: 2.3) p 68.
42 Cadogan Sir Alexander, cited in Gilbert M. (ref: 11.1) p 214.
43 JM. Personal communication.
44 James Dr GWB. Letter to M 4 December 1947 (FP).
45 M. (ref: 2.3) p 71.
46 Gilbert M. (ref: 11.1) p 261.
47 M. (ref: 2.3) p 76.
48 M. (ref: 2.3) p 72.
49 M. MS book p 39.
50 Notebook with entries by D (FP).
51 Coope Dr Robert. Letter to CMW 23 Nov 1942 (FP).
52 William-Olsson H. Letter to CMW 2 Oct 1942 enclosing typescript of talk (FP).
53 CMW. Letter to Desmond MacCarthy 12 Dec 1942 (FP).
54 Churchill Winston S. Letter to CMW 11 Dec 1942 (FP).
55 Beaverbrook Lord. Letter to CMW 5 Jan 1943 (FP).
56 Matthew Dr AW. Letter to CMW 1 Jan 1943 (FP).
57 Wollaston Sir Gerald. Letter to CMW 23 Feb 1945 (FP).
58 Gilbert M. (ref: 11.1) p 257.
59 Soames Mary. (ref: 9.58) p 330.
60 Churchill Winston S. (ref: 11.17) p 604.
61 Gilbert M. (ref: 11.1) p 293.
62 M. MS book p 40.
63 Gilbert M. (ref: 11.1) p 329.
64 JM. Personal communication.
65 M. MS book p 41.
66 Churchill Winston S. (ref: 11.17) p 622.
67 Moran Lord. (ref: 2.3) p 83.
68 Gilbert M. (ref: 11.1) p 319.
69 M. MS book p 42.
70 M. MS book p 46.
71 M. MS book p 43.
72 M. MS book p 44.
73 Gilbert M. (ref: 11.1) pp 335, 336.

Chapter 12
More of the Travelling Circus

1 Wollaston Sir Gerald (ref: 11.68).
2 JM. Letter to author 18 Jan 1987.

3 Maurice Dr TR. Letter to author 26 Jan 1984.
4 Secretary, Birmingham University. Letter to CMW 8 Feb 1943 (FP).
5 CMW. Letter to *The Times* 15 Feb 1943.
6 Dawson Lord. Letter to CMW 15 Feb 1943 (FP).
7 M. (ref: 2.3) p 88.
8 Peck J. *Dublin from Downing Street.* Dublin: Gill and Macmillan, 1978; p 77.
9 Miles D, quoted in Gilbert M (ref: 11.1) p 354.
10 Horder Lord. Letter to CMW 8 March 1943 (FP).
11 M. (ref: 9.49).
12 Cooke AM. (ref: 8.66) p 1204.
13 Berkeley Comyns. Letter to CMW 2 March 1943 (FP).
14 Jacob General Sir Ian. Personal communication March 1983.
15 Sargant W. Personal communication July 1981.
16 Gilbert M. (ref: 11.1) p 393.
17 M. (ref: 2.3) p 93.
18 M. MS book p 47.
19 Astley Joan B. *The Inner Circle.* Quality Book Club. London: Hutchinson & Co, 1972; p 91.
20 Pickering GW. (ref: 3.21).
21 Social insurance and allied services: report. (Chairman, WH Beveridge). London: HM Stationery Office, 1942
22 Pater JE. (ref: 9.30) p 44.
23 M. MS book p 48.
24 M. (ref: 2.3) p 94.
25 *Annals of RCP*, 29 April 1943.
26 M. MS book p 49.
27 M. MS book p 50.
28 M. (ref: 2.3) p 98.
29 JM. Letter to author 14 Sept 1987.
30 M. (ref: 2.3) p 99.
31 Assistant Accountant, Treasury. Letter to M 5 May 1943 (FP).
32 Gilbert M. (ref: 11.1) p 404.
33 Gilbert M. (ref: 11.1) p 441.
34 M. Letter to Barber 20 April 1943 (RCP Box 7 File 2).
35 Stopford J. Letter to M Feb 1943 (RCP Box 7 File 2).
36 Grey-Turner E, Sutherland FM. (ref: 9.34) p 40.
37 RCP papers (RCP Box 7 File 2).
38 Pater JE. (ref: 9.30) p 60.
39 Pater JE. (ref: 9.30) p 61.
40 *The Times* 2nd June 1943.
41 Churchill Mrs Clementine S. Letter to M 5th June 1943 (FP).
42 Evans Dr Geoffrey. Letter to M 2nd June 1943 (FP).
43 *The Times* 6 Aug 1943.
44 Astley JB. (ref: 12.19) p 107.
45 Colville Sir John. Letter to author 10 Sept 1981.

46 Peck Sir John. Letter to author 9 Feb 1983.
47 Gilbert M. (ref: 11.1) p 467.
48 Soames Mary. (ref: 9.58) p 338.
49 Soames Mary. (ref: 9.58) p 340.
50 M. Typescript early draft of book, p 332 (FP).
51 M. (ref: 2.3) p 111.
53 M. MS book p 57.
54 M. (ref: 2.3) p 109.
55 M. MS book p 55.
56 Ziegler P. *Mountbatten*. London: Collins, 1985; p 179.
57 Colville J. (ref: 9.61) p 192.
58 M. (ref: 2.3) p 114.
59 M. (ref: 12.50) p 348 (FP).
60 M. MS book p 56.
61 Gilbert M. (ref: 11.1) p 482.
62 Gilbert M. (ref: 11.1) p 483.
63 M. (ref: 2.3) p 115.
64 M. (ref: 12.50) p 350 (FP).
65 Gilbert M. (ref: 11.1) p 485.
66 M. MS book p 58.
67 Gilbert M. (ref: 11.1) p 491.
68 M. MS book p 59.
69 M. MS book p 63.
70 M. Letter to GHW 26 Aug 1943 (FP).
71 Martin JM. Memo to M, 9 Sept 1943 (FP).
72 M. MS book p 65.
73 Gilbert M. (ref: 11.1) p 506.

Chapter 13
Frustrations, Conflicts and Hard Decisions

1 Dawson Lord. Letter to M 17 Sept 1943 (FP).
2 *Annals of RCP* 28 Oct 1943.
3 M. *The Times* 8 Jan 1944.
4 Anderson Mrs Elizabeth. Letter to M 2 Nov 1943 (FP).
5 M. Letter to Beaverbrook 16 Oct 1943 (FP).
6 Taylor AJP. (ref: 7.7) p 546.
7 Beaverbrook Lord. Letter to M 29 Sept 1943 (FP).
8 Beaverbrook Lord. Letter to M 18 Oct 1943 (FP).
9 Harris HA. Letters to M between 26 April & 9 Nov 1943 (FP).
10 M. *The Times* 3 Nov 1943.
11 M. Letter to Dr Charles Symonds 18 Oct 1943 (FP).
12 M. Letter to Dr Desmond Curran 18 Oct 1943 (FP).
13 M. Letter to Col MVB Hill 19 Oct 1943 (FP).
14 M. Draft preface for a new edition of *The Anatomy of Courage*, 8 April 1966 (FP).
15 M. (ref: 2.3) p 125.

16 M. Letter to D 'Monday 5.30' 15 Nov 1943 (FP).
17 Gilbert M. (ref: 11.1) p 555.
18 M. Letter to D 18 Nov 1943 (FP).
19 M. Letter to D 19 Nov 1943 (FP).
20 M. Letter to D 20 Nov 1943 (FP).
21 M. Letter to D 26 Nov 1943 (FP).
22 M. Letter to JM 26 Nov 1943 (FP).
23 Brooks WDW. (ref: 6.28).
24 M. Letter to D 2 Dec 1943 (FP).
25 M. Letter to D from Teheran. Undated (FP).
26 M. (ref: 2.3) pp 133-144.
27 M. MS book p 80.
28 M. Letter to D 30 Nov 1943 (FP).
29 M. (ref: 2.3) p 139.
30 M. (ref: 2.3) p 140.
31 M. (ref: 2.3) p 280.
32 M. MS book p 79.
33 Churchill Winston S. *The Second World War Vol V*. London: Cassell & Co Ltd, 1952; pp 635-7.
34 M. MS book p 78, cf. ref: 2.3 pp 143, 144.
35 M. MS book p 81.
36 M. Letter to D 4 Dec 1943 (FP).
37 M. Letter to D 3 Dec 1943 (FP).
38 M. Letter to D 7 Dec 1943 (FP).
39 M. Letter to D 5 Dec 1943 (FP).
40 Jacob Sir Ian. In: Wheeler-Bennett, Sir John, ed. *Action This Day*. London: Macmillan, 1968; p 185.
41 Churchill Winston S. (ref: 13.33) p 372.
42 M. (ref: 2.3) p 146.
43 M. Handwritten draft of letter dated 8 Dec 1943 (FP).
44 Alanbrooke, Field Marshall the Viscount, cited in Bryant, A. *Triumph in the West*. London: The Reprint Society, 1960; p 93.
45 M. Letter to D 9 Dec 1943 (FP).
46 M. (ref: 2.3) p 147.
47 M. MS book p 83.
48 M. (ref: 2.3) p 148.
49 Churchill Winston S. (ref: 13.33) p 373.
50 M. Letter to D 13 Dec 1943 (FP).
51 M. Letter to D 14 Dec 1943 (FP).
52 Gilbert M. (ref: 11.1) p 606.
53 M. Letter to D 16 Dec 1943 (FP).
54 M. Letter to D 18 Dec 1943 (FP).
55 JM. Personal communication.
56 M. Letter to D 24 Dec 1943 (FP).
57 M. Letter to D 25 Dec 1943 (FP).
58 Soames Mary (ref: 9.58) p 346.

59   Colville J. *The Fringes of Power*. London: Hodder & Stoughton 1985; p 457.

60   M. Letter to D 30 Dec 1943 (FP).

61   M. Letter to D 28 Dec 1943 (FP).

62   M. Letter to D 4 Jan 1944 (FP).

63   JW. MS Dec 1944 (FP).

64   M. Letter to D 11 Jan 1944 (FP).

65   JM. Personal communication.

66   Pawle G. *The War & Colonel Warden*. London: George G. Harrap & Co. Ltd 1963; p 290.

67   M. Letter to D 14 Jan 1944 (FP).

Chapter 14
Self Perceptions

1   JW. MS Dec 1944.

2   M. *The Times* 3 March 1944.

3   *Annals of RCP* 27 Jan 1944.

4   Browne A Montague. Personal communication April 1984.

5   M. Letter to Dr TC Hunt, RCP Box 7 File 5.

6   M. Letter to Dr Leonard Parsons 9 Feb 1944. RCP Box 7 File 4.

7   Grey-Turner E, Sutherland FM. (ref: 9.34) p 38.

8   Parsons L. Letter to M 17 Feb 1944. RCP Box 5 File 4.

9   M. (ref: 6.7).

10   M. Letter to Dawson RCP Box 7 File 5.

11   *A National Health Service*. London: HM Stationery Office, 1944.

12   Cooke AM. (ref: 8.66) p 1093.

13   Ref: 9.49.

14   *Annals of RCP* 27 July 1944.

15   Cooke AM. (ref: 8.66) p 1094.

16   M. Letter to the Editor of *The Times* 21 June 1944 (FP).

17   Webb J. Letter to CMW 22 June 1944 (FP).

18   M. Letter to R Barrington-Ward 25th June 1944 (FP).

19   M. Letter to R Barrington-Ward 1 July 1944 (FP).

20   Churchill Mrs Clementine S. Letter to M 2 Feb 1944 (FP).

21   M. *The Times* 3 March 1944.

22   Gilbert M. (ref: 11.1) p 669 & following.

23   Alanbrooke (ref: 13.44) p 132.

24   Alanbrooke (ref: 13.44) p 95.

25   M. Letter to Beaverbrook 26 May 1944 (FP).

26   Bracken Brendan. Letter to M 5 April 1944 (FP).

27   Bond N. Letter to M 25 April 1944 (FP).

28   Planning committee: Report on medical education. RCP 27 April 1944.

29   M. The making of a doctor. Typescript for BBC broadcast 2 May 1944 (FP).

30   M. Letter to Beaverbrook 13 July 1944 (FP).

31 M. Letter to 'Dear Sir' 26 July 1944 (FP).
32 M. Handwritten draft of letter to Mr Kyllmann, 31 Aug [1944] (FP).
33 M. (ref: 2.3) p 162.
34 M. (ref: 2.3) p 163.
35 M. Letter to Prime Minister 9 Aug 1944 (FP).
36 M. (ref: 2.3) p 164.
37 Typescript dated 16 Aug 1944, headed Use of Mepacrine. Source not indicated (FP).
38 Gilbert M. (ref: 11.1) pp 887 to 921.
39 M. MS book p 101.
40 M. MS book p 99.
41 Soames Mary (ref: 9.58) p 357.
42 Gilbert M. (ref: 11.1) pp 937, 938.
43 Munk's Roll 1968; 5: pp 444, 445.
44 Gilbert M. (ref: 11.1) p 981.
45 M. (ref: 2.3) p 176.
46 M. (ref: 2.3) p 201.
47 M. (ref: 2.3) p 193.
48 M. (ref: 2.3) p 179.
49 Gilbert M. (ref: 11.1) p 954.
50 Gilbert M. (ref: 11.1) p 971.
51 M. MS book p 103.
52 M. MS book p 102.
53 M. (ref: 2.3) p 177.
54 M. MS book p 104.
55 Colville J. (ref: 13.59) pp 514, 515.
56 Gilbert M. (ref: 11.1) p 979.
57 M. (ref: 2.3) p 191.
58 M. MS book p 115.
59 M. MS book p 117.
60 M. (ref: 2.3) p 196.
61 Peck Sir John. Letter to author 1 Feb 1982.
62 M. (ref: 2.3) pp 197, 198.
63 Gilbert M. (ref: 11.1) p 1036.
64 *Annals of RCP* 26 Oct 1944.
65 Cooke AM. (ref: 8.66) p 1095.
66 Munk's Roll 1975; 6: pp 448, 449.
67 M. MS book, p 129 cf ref: 2.3 p 209.
68 Gilbert M. (ref: 11.1) p 1115.
69 Colville J. (ref: 13.59) p 538.
70 Gilbert M. (ref: 11.1) p 1116.
71 Colville J. (ref: 13.59) p 541.
72 Colville J. (ref: 13.59) p 545.
73 M. (ref: 2.3) p 238.
74 Newspaper cutting—unidentified (FP).
75 Gilbert M. (ref: 11.1) p 1135.

Chapter 15
The Anatomy of Courage and a New Diary

1   M. MS book 2 p 1.
2   Porritt, Lord. Personal communication Sept 1981.
3   M. MS book 2 p 2.
4   M. MS book 2 p 5.
5   M. MS book 2 p 6.
6   D. Personal communication.
7   Bracken B. Letter to D 2 Oct 1944 (FP).
8   Colville J. (ref: 13.59) p 546.
9   Cooke AM. (ref: 8.66) p 1095.
10 *Annals of RCP* 17 Jan 1945.
11 M. MS book 2 p 8.
12 M. MS book 2 p 9.
13 Cooke AM. (ref: 8.66) pp 1056, 1057.
14 *Annals of RCP* 25 Jan 1945.
15 M. MS book 2 p 11.
16 Moran, Lord (ref: 2.3).
17 Gilbert M. (ref: 11.1) p 1163.
18 Churchill Sarah. With father at the war. *Sunday Telegraph* 29 March 1981.
19 M. (ref: 2.3) p 216.
20 M. MS book 2 p 13.
21 M. Letter to D Wednesday (FP).
22 Gilbert M. (ref: 11.1) pp 1171-1227.
23 M. MS Book 2 p 22.
24 Gilbert M. (ref: 11.1) p 1175.
25 M. (ref: 2.3) p 223.
26 Bruenn Dr Howard G. Letter to author 11 March 1980.
27 M. (ref: 2.3) p 226.
28 M. MS book 2 p 23 (cf. ref: 2.3 p 223).
29 M. (ref: 2.3) p 230.
30 Ismay Lord. (ref: 9.70) p 387.
31 M. MS book 2 p 28.
32 Colville J. (ref: 13.59) p 515.
33 M. (ref: 2.3) p 227.
34 M. MS book 2 p 28.
35 M. MS book 2 p 54.
36 M. MS book 2 p 38 (cf. ref: 2.3 p 238).
37 M. (ref:2.3) p 127.
38 Typed abstracts from reviews (FP), quoting *Sunday Times Manchester Guardian and Spectator.*
39 Bracken B. Letter to M 1 March 1945 (FP).
40 M. Letter to D 11 & 14 Feb 1945 (FP).
41 M. Letter to D 9 Feb 1945 (FP).
42 M. (ref: 9.49).
43 M. MS book 2 p 49.

44 M. Letter to *Women's Journal* 5 May 1945 (FP).
45 M. MS book 2 p 72.
46 M. MS book 2 p 59.
47 M. (ref: 2.3) pp 250, 251.
48 M. MS book 2 p 57.
49 M. (ref: 2.3) p 251.
50 Colville J. (ref: 13.59) p 599.
51 Ref: 11.52.
52 Pamphlet: Centenary appeal for the reconstruction & extension of the hospital. May 1945 (FP).
53 M. MS book 2 p 83.
54 M. MS book 2 p 84.
55 M. MS book 2 p 86.
56 M. Draft titled Appeal on behalf of St Mary's Hospital, London, Sunday 1 July 1945 (FP).
57 Colville J. (ref: 13.59) p 610.
58 Pawle G. (ref: 13.66) p 388.
59 M. MS book 2 p 93.
60 M. MS book 2 p 91.
61 M. (ref: 2.2) p xv.
62 M. MS book 2 p 88.
63 M. MS book 2 p 94.
64 M. MS book 2 p 98.
65 M. Letter to D 25 July 1945 (FP).
66 M. MS book 2 p 102.
67 M. (ref: 2.3) p 277.
68 M. MS book 2 pp 107, 108.
69 M. MS book 2 pp 119-21.
70 M. MS book 2 p 121. (cf. ref: 2.3 pp 282, 283).
71 M. MS book 2 p 125.
72 M. (ref: 2.3) p 286.
73 M. (ref: 2.3) p 287.
74 Pawle G. (ref: 13.66) pp 402-4.
75 M. (ref: 2.3) p 288.
76 M. (ref: 2.3) p 289.
77 M. MS book 2 p 139.
78 M. MS book 2 p 141.
79 M. MS book 2 p 129.
80 JM. Personal communication.
81 M. MS book 2 p 142.
82 M. MS book 2 p 144 (cf. ref: 2.3 p 291).
83 Soames Mary. (ref: 9.58) p 392.
84 M. Letter to D 3 Sept 1945 (FP).
85 M. MS book 2 p 149.
86 M. (ref: 2.3) p 298.

Chapter 16
Public Figure

1 Churchill Mrs Clementine S. Letter to C 19 Sept 1945 (FP).
2 Gosse Dr AH. Letter to M 27 Sept 1945 (FP).
3 CMW. Letter to D 16 June 1919 (FP).
4 Huggett Professor A St G. Typescript: Reflections arising out of the meeting of the sub-committee on Terms of Office & Election of the Dean. 15 May 1945 (FP).
5 Brinton Dr DH. Personal communication Sept 1981.
6 Pickering GW. (ref: 3.21).
7 Editorial comment: London School of Medicine for Women. Lord Moran's philosophy. *British Medical Journal* 1945; **2**: 472.
8 M. Letter to DH Brinton 3 June 1945 (FP).
9 Brinton DB. Letter to M 22 Dec 1948 (FP).
10 M. Letter to Dr AG Cross 16 Sept 1954 (FP).
11 Carmalt-Jones Professor DW. Letter to M 17 Dec 1950 (FP).
12 Cope VZ. (ref 1.7).
13 M. Letter to Dr AG Cross 1 Oct 1954 (FP).
14 *The Times* 2 Oct 1945.
15 The Royal College of Physicians of London. Harveian Dinner. Speeches, Oct 18 1945. Pamphlet (FP).
16 King WL Mackenzie. Letter to M 21 Oct 1945 (FP).
17 Moran Lord. Commemoration of the science and art of healing in Canterbury Cathedral. *Lancet* 1949; **ii**: 22-3.
18 *The Times* 27 June 1949.
19 D. Letter to JW 26 June 1949 (FP).
20 Colville J. (ref: 9.60) p 192.
21 Typed pages headed Prevention of another war (FP).
22 M. (ref: 2.3) p 177.
23 Pater JE. (ref: 9.30) p 107.
24 Munk's Roll. 1955; **4**: 600.
25 Munk's Roll. 1982; **6**: 387-90.
26 M. MS book 2 pp 158-66.
27 Cooper RW. *The Nuremberg Trial*. London: Penguin Books Ltd, 1947; p 267.
28 War Crimes Executive. Letter to M 15 Jan 1946 (FP).
29 M. (ref: 2.3) pp 306-29.
30 JM. Personal communication.
31 M. (ref: 2.3) p 322.
32 Soames Mary. (ref: 9.58) p 406.
33 Gilbert M. *Winston S. Churchill. Vol 8. Never Despair*. London: Heinemann 1988; p 395.
34 M. Letter to JW 29 April 1948 (FP).
35 Castillo H. Pan-European movement. *Encyclopedia Britannica* 1961; **17**: 180.

36 Soames Mary. (ref: 9.58) p 407.
37 Taylor AJP. (ref: 7.7) p 593.
38 M. (ref: 2.3) p 333.
39 M. (ref: 2.3) p 334.
40 Churchill Clementine S. Telegram to Lord & Lady Moran, 8 Nov 1945. Letter to D 18 Nov 1947 (FP).
41 Churchill Clementine S. Letter to D 28 July 1949 (FP).
42 Churchill Clementine S. Letter to C 9 Feb 1942 (FP).
43 D. Letter to JW 11 April 1949 (FP).
44 M. Letter to Sir Godfrey Ince, Minister of Labour & National Service 28 Oct 1948 (FP).
45 Archbishop of Canterbury. Letter to M 27 July 1946 (FP).
46 Archbishop of Canterbury. Letter to M 27 Nov 1946 (FP).
47 M. Letter to Archbishop of Canterbury 3 Dec 1946 (FP).
48 *The Times* 4 June 1947.
49 M. Speech at Blundell's School 14 July 1949. Typescript (FP).
50 *La Montagne* 11 July 1947.
51 Buckler BC. Letter to M 16 Nov 1949 (FP).
52 JW. notes 4 Nov 1948 (FP).
53 M. Letter to Leslie Rowan 19 Nov 1946 (FP).
54 Williams D. In: Introduction to Moran, Lord. *The Anatomy of Courage.* London: Keynes Press edition. British Medical Association 1984; p x.
55 M. Letter to JW 31 Oct 1949 (FP).
56 Patient's letter to M 25 Nov 1947 (FP).
57 M. Statement of fees. (FP).
58 M. (ref 15.43).
59 M. (ref 16.53).
60 Rowan L. Letter to M 28 Oct 1946 (FP).
61 M. Letter to D 8 Oct 1947 (FP).
62 Peat HD. Letter to M 7 Nov 1946 (FP).
63 M. Letter to HD Peat 29 Nov 1946 (FP).
64 M. Letter to JW 11 April 1948 (FP).
65 M. Letter to JW 4 May 1949 (FP).
66 Churchill Winston S. Letter to M 29 April 1949 (FP).
67 Churchill Winston S. Letter to M 16 Sept 1949 (FP).

Chapter 17
The National Health Service Crisis

1 RCP papers. Box 3.
2 Hill of Luton Lord. *Both Sides of the Hill.* London: Heinemann 1964; p 91.
3 Hill Lord. (ref: 17.2) p 89.
4 M. Letter to Sir Arthur Rucker 20 Dec 1944. RCP papers, Box 1 File 1.
5 M. Letter to Dr Harold Boldero 8 Feb 1945. RCP papers, Box 2 File 1.

6 Pater JE. (ref: 9.30) p 177.
7 M. (ref: 6.7).
8 Profile—Aneurin Bevan. *The Observer* 29 April 1951.
9 Taylor AJP. (ref: 7.7) pp 334, 335.
10 D. Personal communication August 1980.
11 Foot M. *Aneurin Bevan* Vol 2. London: Paladin, 1975; p 123. First published by London: Davis-Poynter Ltd, 1973.
12 Pater JE. (ref: 9.30) p 107.
13 RCP papers Box 1.
14 Pater JE. (ref: 9.30) p 113.
15 Hill Lord. (ref: 17.2) p 86.
16 *Annals of RCP* 15 April 1946.
17 Pater JE. (ref: 9.30) p 105.
18 Pater JE. (ref: 9.30) p 108.
19 *Annals of RCP* 25 Oct 1945.
20 Ref: 9.49.
21 Pater JE. (ref: 9.30) p 117.
22 Rucker A. Letter to M 13 Feb 1946 (FP).
23 National Health Service Bill. Summary of the proposed new service. London: HM Stationery Office, March 1946.
24 *The Times* 17 April 1946.
25 Pater JE. (ref: 9.30) p 122.
26 Pater JE. (ref: 9.30) pp 124, 125.
27 *Annals of RCP* 16 May 1946.
28 *Lancet* 1946; **i**: 786.
29 Pater JE. (ref: 9.30) p 129.
30 *The Times* 9 Oct 1946.
31 *The Times* 18, 22 & 23 Oct 1946.
32 *The Times* 7 Nov 1946.
33 Webster C. *The Health Services Since the War.* Vol 1. London: HM Stationery Office, 1988; p 120.
34 Grey-Turner E, Sutherland EM. (ref: 9.34) p 45.
35 Webster C. (ref: 17.33) p 67.
36 Pater JE. (ref 9.30) pp 140, 141.
37 M. Letter to Aneurin Bevan 15 Dec 1946 (FP).
38 M. Letter to Dr TL Hardy 7 Jan 1947 (FP).
39 Hardy Dr TL. Letter to M 2 Jan 1947 (FP).
40 Pater JE. (ref: 9.30) p 142.
41 Foot M. (ref: 17.11) pp 162, 163.
42 Cooke AM. (ref: 8.66) p 1215.
43 M. Typescript, headed Digression (FP).
44 Pater JE. (ref: 9.30) p 143.
45 M. (ref: 9.49).
46 Holmes Dr JM. Letter to author 8 August 1980.
47 M. Letter to Aneurin Bevan 28 March 1947 (FP).
48 Bevan A. Letter to M 3 April 1947 (FP).
49 Pater JE. (ref: 9.30) p 150.

50 Pater JE. (ref: 9.30) p 153.
51 *British Medical Journal* 1948; **1**: 17–18.
52 *Annals of RCP* 29 January 1948.
53 D. Letter to JW 29 Jan 1948 (FP).
54 Pater JE. (ref: 9.30) p 156.
55 Webster C. (ref: 17.33) p 113.
56 Webster C. (ref: 17.33) p 114.
57 D. Letter to JW 6 March 1948 citing article in *The Economist* (FP).
58 Manuscript headed: Interview with Minister 10 March 1948. 12 noon (FP).
59 D. Letter to JW 13 March 1948 (FP).
60 D. Letter to JW 18 March 1948 (FP).
61 M. Letter to JW 29 March 1948 (FP).
62 D. Letter to JW 23 March 1948 (FP).
63 M. (ref: 9.49)
64 M. Letter to JW 11 April 1948 (FP).
65 *Annals of RCP* 22 March 1948.
66 Webster C. (ref: 17.33) p 116.
67 Bevan A. Letter to M 6 April 1948 (FP).
68 Foot M. (ref: 17.11) p 196.
69 Dain Dr HG. *British Medical Journal* 1948; **1**: 699.
70 M. Letter to Dr Hugh Clegg 9 April 1948 (FP).
71 *The Times* 8 April 1948.
72 Bevan A. Letter to M 10 April 1948 (FP).
73 Pater J. (ref: 9.30) p 175.
74 Webster C. (ref: 17.33) p 116.
75 Foot M. (ref: 17.11) p 197.
76 Webster C. (ref: 17.33) pp 118, 119.
77 Pater JE. (ref: 9.30) p 163.
78 Pickering GW. (ref: 7.71).
79 Brinton DH. Personal communication Sept 1981.
80 M. (ref: 9.49).
81 M. Letter to fellows of RCP 23 March 1950 (FP).
82 D. Letter to JW 19 Jan 1950 (FP).
83 D. Letter to JW 28 Feb 1950 (FP).
84 D. Letter to JW 14 March 1950 (FP).
85 Sheldon Dr JH. Letter to M 9 March 1950 (FP).
86 Fox Dr TF. Letter to M 3 March 1950 (FP).
87 M. Letter to JH Sheldon 14 March 1950 (FP).
88 Moran Lord. Annual Address delivered to the Royal College of Physicians of London on Monday April 3, 1950 by the President, Lord Moran MC MD (FP).
89 M. (ref: 9.49).

Chapter 18
Gracious Living

1 Fitz Dr Reginald. Letter to M 14 November 1949 (FP).

2 D. Letter to her mother 4 April 1950 (FP).
3 *The Times* 4 April 1950 (FP).
4 Churchill Mrs Clementine S. Radiogram to Lord and Lady Moran 5 April 1950 (FP).
5 Camrose Lord. Letters to M 3 March & 6 June 1950 (FP).
6 M. Letter to W Colston Leigh 19 Jan 1950 (FP).
7 Collins AP. Letter to M 14 April 1950 (FP).
8 Fletcher M. Letter to M 31 March 1950 (FP).
9 Longwell D. Letter to M 6 April 1950 (FP).
10 Graebner W. Letter to M 16 Feb 1950 (FP).
11 Gilbert M. (ref: 16.33) p 395.
12 Gilbert M. (ref 16.33) p 386.
13 Loveland ER. Letter to M 18 April 1950 (FP).
14 M. Letter to Dr R Fitz 23 Nov 1949 (FP).
15 M. Wear & Tear. *Lancet* 1950; **i**: 1098-101.
16 *Daily Telegraph* 24 April 1950.
17 Editorial. *New England Journal of Medicine* 1950; **242**: 801-2.
18 Kattwinkel Dr Egon E. Letter to M 18 April 1950 (FP).
19 Speeches made at the presentation of a portrait to Lord Moran. Pamphlet. Royal College of Physicians, 10 July 1951.
20 M. Letter to JW 29 Nov 1950 (FP).
21 du Mont N. Letter to D 19 Oct 1950 (FP).
22 D. Letter to author 25 May 1981.
23 Annigoni Pietro. *An Artists' Life, as told by Robert Waight.* London: WLT Allen 1977; p 74.
24 D. Letter to author 6 Sept 1980.
25 Churchill Mrs Clementine S. Letter to M 9 July 1951 (FP).
26 Portal Jane. Letter to M 29 July 1951 (FP).
27 JM. Personal communication.
28 M. On credulity. The Harveian Oration 1952. *Lancet* 1954; **i**: 167.
29 M. Letter to Dr T Fox 13 Feb 1953 (FP).
30 JM. Personal communication.
31 D. Letter to JW 4 March 1951 (FP).
32 D. Letter to JW 16 March 1951 (FP).
33 D. Letter to JW 16 Aug 1951 (FP).
34 D. Personal communication.
35 Visitors' Book for Marshalls (FP).
36 White JW. *Guests of the Unspeakable.* London: John Hamilton Ltd 1928.
37 M. (ref: 2.3) p 67.
38 M. MS book p 44.
39 Jacob Sir Ian. Personal communication.
40 Harley Mrs Judith. Personal communication.

Chapter 19
Work and Play—Merit Awards and Writing

1 *Annals of RCP* 30 Oct 1947.

2 Report of the inter-departmental committee on the remuneration of consultants and specialists. London: HM Stationery Office, May 1948.

3 Webster C. (ref: 17.33) p 252.

4 Webster C. (ref: 17.33) p 314.

5 Ref: 5.22.

6 M. (ref: 6.7).

7 M. Letter to My dear—(apparently Bevan) 1 Sept 1948 (FP).

8 Bevan A. Letter to M Oct 1948 (FP).

9 M. Letter to Bevan 30 Oct 1948, marked 'sent 12-11-48'.

10 Bridges Sir Edward. Letter to M 2 Nov 1948 (FP).

11 M. Letter to Bevan 6 Dec 1948 (FP).

12 *British Medical Journal* 1949; **1**: p 505.

13 Hill Dr Charles. Letter to M 28 Dec 1949 (FP).

14 M. Letter to Sir John Hawton 19 March 1955 (FP).

15 M. Letter to chairmen of medical committees of teaching hospitals 29 July 1949 (FP).

16 D. Personal communication.

17 M. *Lancet* 1954; **ii**: 141.

18 Sowry Dr GSC. Personal communication.

19 Richardson Lord. Personal communication.

20 Holmes Mrs Molly. Personal communication.

21 Holmes Dr JM. Letter to author 15 Sept 1980.

22 JM. Personal communication.

23 M. Letter to JW 16 Dec 1949 (FP).

24 Walshe Dr FMR. *British Medical Journal* 1949; **2**: 383.

25 M. (ref: 6.7).

26 D. Letter to M 9 Sept 1952 (FP).

27 Personal communications from Dr JM Holmes, Dame Janet Vaughan, Sir John McMichael.

28 D. Letter to JW 14 Jan 1950.

29 McMichael Professor Sir John. Personal communication Aug 1981.

30 M. Notebook (FP).

31 M. Letter to Sir Robert Platt 18 Dec 1959 (FP).

32 Moran Lord. *British Medical Journal* 1950; **1**: 497.

33 JM. Personal communication.

34 M. Letter to Dr RA Fawcus 16 Aug 1948 (FP).

35 D. Letter to JW 10 Aug 1948 (FP).

36 M. Letter to D 8 Oct 1947 (FP).

37 M. Letters to JW 1949-1951 (FP).

38 Boswell James. *The Life of Samuel Johnson*. Vol 2. Everyman Library. London: JM Dent and Sons Ltd 1906; p 614.

39 M. Letter to JW 19 Dec 1950 (FP).

40 M. Letter to D 25 July 1945 (FP).

41 M. MS book 2 p 54 2 May 1945.

42 M. MS book 2 p 144 1 Sept 1945.

43 M. MS book 2 p 188 10 Nov 1946.

44 M. Letter to Mackenzie King 12 April 1949 (FP).
45 M. Letter to JW 29 April 1948 (FP).
46 King WL Mackenzie. Letter to M 28 March 1948 (FP).
47 M. Letter to Lewis Douglas 6 Nov 1950 (FP).
48 M. Letter to JW 5 June 1949 (FP).
49 M. Draft essay entitled The President and the PM (FP).
50 JW. Letter to M 26 Aug 1949 (FP).
51 Lee Dr Roger. Letter to M 16 Jan 1951 (FP).
52 FW Hodson. Letter to M 1 May 1951 (FP).
53 M. Letter to FW Hodson 11 May 1951 (FP).
54 Clegg Dr H. Letter to M 2 Feb 1951 (FP).
55 M. Letter to Dr H Clegg 3 Feb 1951 (FP).

Chapter 20
Affairs of State

1 M. (ref: 2.3) pp 339-42.
2 M. (ref: 2.3) p 342.
3 M. Typescript, starting: '22.11.51. I shall now digress. . . .' (FP).
4 M. (ref: 2.3) p 343.
5 M. (ref: 2.3) p 344.
6 M. (ref: 2.3) pp 345-350.
7 M. (ref: 2.3) p 346.
8 D. Letter to Mr Churchill 19 Nov 1951 (FP).
9 Colville J. In: *Action this Day* Wheeler-Bennett J, ed. London: Macmillan, 1968: p 55.
10 Colville J. (ref: 20.9) p 111.
11 *Hansard.* House of Lords 26 March 1952.
12 M. Letter to various newspapers 17 March 1952 (FP).
13 M. Letter to Prime Minister 27 March 1952 (FP).
14 Churchill Winston S. Letter to M 11 April 1952 (FP).
15 Churchill Winston S. Letter to M 11 May 1952 (FP).
16 Gilbert M. (ref: 16.33) p 674.
17 M. Letter to Sir Alan Lascelles 13 Dec 1951 (FP).
18 Lascelles Sir Alan. Letter to M 14 Dec 1951 (FP).
19 M. (ref: 2.3) p 351.
20 M. (ref: 2.3) p 371.
21 M. Letter to D 11 Jan 1952 (FP).
22 M. Letter to JW 2 Feb 1952 (FP).
23 Lee Dr Roger I. Letter to M 7 March 1952 (FP).
24 Laughlin Henry A. Letter to M 1 Feb 1952 (FP).
25 Gilbert M. (ref: 16.33) p 468.
26 Gilbert M. (ref: 16.33) p 273.
27 Gilbert M. (ref: 16.33) p 695.
28 M. Letter to HA Laughlin 13 Feb 1952 (FP).
29 M. (ref: 2.3) p 372.
30 M. (ref: 2.3) p 374.
31 M. (ref: 2.3) p 375.

32 M. (ref: 2.3) p 376.
33 M. (ref: 2.3) p 377.
34 M. (ref: 2.3) p 381.
35 Colville J. (ref: 13.59) p 642.
36 M. (ref: 2.3) p 378.
37 Gilbert M. (ref: 16.33) p 704.
38 M. (ref: 2.3) p 379.
39 M. (ref: 2.3) p 382.
40 Seldon A. *Churchill's Indian Summer*. London: Hodder and Stoughton, 1981; p 34.
41 M. Letter to Prime Minister 13 Dec 1952 (FP).
42 M. Letter to Prime Minister 23 Dec 1952 (FP).
43 Churchill Winston S. Letter to M 29 Dec 1952 (FP).

Chapter 21
One-Patient Doctor

1 *Hansard*. House of Lords 3 Feb 1953.
2 D. Letter to JW 23 Jan 1953 (FP).
3 D. Letter to JW 3 Feb 1953 (FP).
4 *Hansard*. House of Lords 5 Dec 1957.
5 *The Times* 13 May 1953.
6 *Hansard*. House of Lords 13 Dec 1955.
7 *The Times* 5 April 1954.
8 *Hansard*. House of Lords 26 June 1957.
9 *Hansard*. House of Lords 2 July 1958.
10 *Hansard*. House of Lords 27 April 1960.
11 Obituary, *The Times* 13 April 1977.
12 D. Letter to JW 27 Feb 1953 (FP).
13 M. Letter to JW 20 March 1953 (FP).
14 D. Letter to JW 29 March 1953 (FP).
15 D. Letter to J 10 April 1953 (FP).
16 D. Letter to J 28 Jan 1953 (FP).
17 Gilbert M. (ref: 16.33) p 833.
18 M. (ref: 2.3) p 408.
19 Soames Mary. (ref: 9.58) p 434.
20 M. (ref: 2.3) p 409.
21 Soames Mary. (ref: 9.58) p 435.
22 M. (ref: 2.3) p 412.
23 Gilbert M. (ref: 16.33) p 875.
24 D. Letter to J 28 June 1953 (FP).
25 Colville J. (ref: 13.59) pp 668, 669.
26 Seldon A. (ref: 20.40) p 519.
27 M. Letter to Beaverbrook draft 24 July 1953 (FP).
28 M. (ref: 2.3) p 411.
29 M. (ref: 2.3) p 441.
30 Gilbert M. (ref: 16.33) pp 866, 965.
31   M. (ref: 2.3) p 638.

32   D. Letter to JW 4 July 1953 (FP).
33   D. Letter to JW 10 July 1953 (FP).
34   D. Letter to JW 17 July 1953 (FP).
35   Soames Mary. (ref: 9.58) p 436.
36   D. Letter to JW 18 July 1953 (FP).
37   M. (ref: 2.3) pp 459, 460.
38   M. (ref: 2.3) p 462.
39   M. (ref: 2.3) p 476.
40   M. (ref: 2.3) p 477.
41   Gilbert M. (ref: 16.33) p 901.
42   Gilbert M. (ref: 16.33) p 1114.
43   M. (ref: 2.3) pp 408-452.
44   Soames Mary. (ref: 9.58) p 431.
45   M. Letter to JW 17 June 1954 (FP).
46   Colville J. (ref: 13.59) p 694.
47   M. (ref: 2.3) p 463.
48   M. (ref: 2.3) p 521.
49   M. (ref: 2.3) p 522.
50   Colville J. (ref: 13.59) p 668.
51   M. (ref: 2.3) p 525.
52   M. (ref: 2.3) p 644.
53   M. (ref: 2.3) p 487.
54   Gilbert M. (ref: 16.33) p 916.
55   D. Letter to JW 4 Dec 1953 (FP).
56   M. (ref: 2.3) p 501.
57   M. Letter to D 'Thursday noon' [3 Dec 1953] (FP).
58   M. Letter to D 'Saturday 9.30' [5 Dec 1953] (FP).
59   M. (ref: 2.3) p 509.
60   M. (ref: 2.3) p 506.
61   M. Letter to JW 18 Dec 1953 (FP).
62   D. Letter to JW 1 Jan 1954 (FP).
63   M. Letter to JW 1 Jan 1954 (FP).
64   Laughlin H. Letter to M 14 Aug 1952 (FP).
65   M. Letter to Laughlin 16 Sept 1952 (FP).
66   Laughlin H. Letter to M 23 Sept 1952 (FP).
67   D. Letter to JW 12 March 1954 (FP).
68   D. Letter to JW 26 March 1954 (FP).
69   D. Letter to JW 7 May 1954 (FP).
70   Cecil Lord David. Letter to author 29 Dec 1983.
71   M. Letter to JW 17 June 1954 (FP).
72   D. Letter to JW 17 June 1954 (FP).
73   Gilbert M. (ref: 16.33) pp 996-1012.
74   M. Letter to D 'Saturday' (FP).
75   M. Letter to D 'Monday 10 am' (FP).
76   M. Letter to Bracken 27 Nov 1954 (FP).
77   M. Letter to Bracken, draft 10 Nov 1954 (FP).
78   Bracken Brendan. Letter to M 29 Nov 1954 (FP).

79 M. (ref: 2.3) p 614.
80 D. Letter to JW 2 Dec 1954 (FP).
81 M. (ref: 2.3) p 620.
82 M. (ref: 2.3) p 621.
83 M. (ref: 2.3) p 745.
84 D. Letter to JW 24 Nov 1954 (FP).
85 Churchill Winston S. Letter to M 31 March 1955 (FP).
86 Gilbert M. (ref: 16.33) p 1126.
87 Churchill Winston S. & M. Letters exchanged between 28 March & 3 April 1955.
88 Churchill Winston S. Telegram to M 15 April 1955 (FP).
89 Gilbert M. (ref: 16.33) p 485.
90 Gilbert M. (ref: 16.33) p 1243.
91 Gilbert M. (ref: 16.33) p 1219.
92 Gilbert M. (ref: 16.33) p 1230.
93 Gilbert M. (ref: 16.33) p 1231.
94 M. Letter to D (ref: 13.54).
95 Hunt Dr TC. Personal communication.
96 Richardson Sir John. Personal communication.
97 Soames Mary. (ref: 9.58) p 461.
98 Gilbert M. (ref: 16.33) p 187.
99 M. (ref: 2.3) p 732.
100 Reves Mrs Wendy. Personal communication.
101 M. Typescript (FP).
102 M. Draft of letter to Churchill 3 May 1959 (FP).
103 *Daily Express* 5 March 1960.
104 D. Typescript of a diary of a cruise in Mr Onassis's yacht 1960 (FP).
105 M. (ref: 2.3) p 770.

Chapter 22
Author at Work—With Interruptions

1 D. Letter to JW 24 July 1955 (FP).
2 M. (ref: 2.3) p 690.
3 M. Case books (FP).
4 Gilbert M. (ref: 16.33) p 1198.
5 Kerr Dr William J. Letter to M 25 Feb 1956 (FP).
6 Anon. Typescript obituary of Dr Roger I Lee (FP).
7 Minto Mrs Sheila. Letter to author 24 Feb 1983.
8 M. Letter to D 'Monday evening' (FP).
9 M. Letter to Dr Roger I Lee 17 April 1956 (FP).
10 M. Letter to D 'Saturday 5.30 p.m.' (FP).
11 M. Letter to D 8 June 1956 (FP).
12 M. Letter to D 30 May 1956 (FP).
13 Visitors' book Marshalls (FP).
14 Richardson Lady. Personal communication 20 Aug 1981.

15 Colville J. (ref: 9.60) p 191.
16 Kemp Dr TA. Personal communication June 1981.
17 Webster C. (ref: 17.33) p 198.
18 Webster C. (ref: 17.33) p 232.
19 Fuller WA. Letter to M 30 Dec 1957 (FP).
20 Fuller WA. Letter to M 6 Jan 1958 (FP).
21 Moran Lord. Evidence of Lord Moran taken before the Royal Commission on Doctors' and Dentists' remuneration, fourth day, Friday, 17th January, 1958. Report of the Royal Commission on Doctors' and Dentists' remuneration. London: HM Stationery Office, 1960; pp 171-207.
22 Report of the Royal Commission on Doctors' and Dentists' Remuneration (ref: 21) para. 348.
23 *Hansard*. House of Lords 18 Oct 1950.
24 D. Letter to author 29 Sept 1980.
25 *The Manchester Guardian* 18 Jan 1958.
26 Moran Lord. *British Medical Journal* 1958; (Suppl 25 Jan): 36.
27 Stathers D. *British Medical Journal* 1958; (Suppl 25 Jan): 37.
28 Barber G. *British Medical Journal* 1958; (Suppl 8 Feb): 75.
29 *British Medical Journal* 1958; (Suppl 8 Feb): 51.
30 Taylor C. *British Medical Journal* 1968; (Suppl 8 Feb): 62.
31 Letters to M Jan 1958 (FP).
32 Platt Dr Robert. Letter to M 16 Feb 1958 (FP).
33 Dowthwaite AH. *British Medical Journal* (Suppl 1 Feb): 48.
34 JM. Personal communication.
35 Peterson MJ. (ref: 1.8) p 230.
36 *Hansard*. House of Lords 27 April 1960.
37 Haley Sir William. Letter to M 21 Aug 1958 (FP).
38 *The Times* 13 Aug 1958.
39 *The Times* 14 July 1960.
40 *The Times* 8 Dec 1960.
41 M. Letter to JW Dec 1960 (FP).
42 M. Letter to JW 22 Aug 1955 (FP).
43 Bryant A. *The Turn of the Tide*. London: William Collins, Sons and Co. Ltd, 1957.
44 M. (ref: 2.3) p 715.
45 Bryant Sir Arthur. The making of *The Turn of the Tide*. In: Fraser D. Alanbrooke. London: William Collins Sons & Co Ltd, 1982. Hamlyn Paperbacks, 1983; p 562.
46 M. (ref: book) p 722.
47 M. Letter to HA Laughlin 7 May 1957 (FP).
48 Richardson Lord. Personal communication.
49 JW. Letter to M 3 March 1953 (FP).
50 M. Letter to JW 12 Dec 1952 (FP).
51 JW. Letter to M 26 Aug 1949 (FP).
52 M. Letter to JW 12 Dec 1952 (FP).

53 JW. Letter to M 3 March 1953 (FP).
54 M. Letter to HA Laughlin 7 Sept 1960 (FP).
55 M. Letter to JW 13 June 1955 (FP).
56 JW. Letter to M 17 June 1965 (FP).
57 M. Handwritten notes (FP).
58 JW. Letter to M 11 March 1962 (FP).
59 M. (ref: 18.19).
60 M. Letter to JW 31 July 1955 (FP).
61 Bracken B. Letter to M 13 May 1958 (FP).
62 Bracken B. Letter to M 4 July 1958 (FP).
63 M. (ref: 2.3) p 747.
64 *The Times* 13 Aug 1958.
65 M. Letter to JW 11 Sept 1955 (FP).
66 Ref: 22.13.
67 M. Letter to Laughlin 10 Dec 1958 (FP).
68 M. Letter to David Astor 2 Jan 1959 (FP).
69 Kaplan Justin D. Letter to M 8 May 1958 (FP).
70 M. Letter to Laughlin 1 Sept 1959 (FP).
71 M. Letter to JW Sept 1960 (FP).
72 M. Letter to Laughlin 7 Sept 1960 (FP).
73 M. Letter to Laughlin 14 Dec 1960 (FP).
74 Laughlin HA. Letter to C 21 Aug 1961 (FP).
75 M. Draft letter to 'My dear Talbot' 7 Sept 1961 (FP).
76 JM. Personal communication.
77 Richardson Lord. Personal communication.
78 M. Letter to JW 15 Feb 1962 (FP).
79 M. Letter to Laughlin 1 March 1962 (FP).
80 M. Letter to Laughlin 17 Jan 1962 (FP).
81 M. Letter to Laughlin 1 March 1962 (FP).
82 Powell Enoch. Letter to M 23 June 1961 (FP).
83 M. Letter to Sir Russell Brain 28 Aug 1961 (FP).
84 Godber Sir George. Letter to M 23 June 1961 (FP).
85 Godber Sir George. Letter to author 21 February 1983.
86 Godber Sir George. Letter to M 5 June 1962 (FP).
87 JM. Personal communication.
88 Churchill Sir Winston. Letter to M 26 Sept 1962 (FP).
89 Shawcross Lord. Personal communication 6 Feb 1985.
90 Richardson Lord. Personal communication.
91 M. Letter to Laughlin 1 March 1962 (FP).
92 Laughlin HA. Letter to M 11 Jan 1962 (FP).
93 M. Letter to Laughlin 17 Jan 1962 (FP).
94 M. Letter to JW 11 Feb 1962 (FP).
95 M. Letter to JW 19 Feb 1962 (FP).
96 Laughlin HA. Letter to JW 15 March 1962 (FP).
97 M. Letter to JW 22 March 1962 (FP).
98 Laughlin HA. Letter to JW 23 March 1962 (FP).
99 Waldman M. Letter to M 16 July 1962 (FP).

100 M. Letter to JW undated, apparently July 1962 (FP).
101 Glazebrook B. Letter to M 7 May 1962 (FP).
102 Church R. Letter to M 7 Sept 1962 (FP).
103 Church R. Letter to M 21 Dec 1962 (FP).
104 Church R. Letter to M 5 Dec 1962 (FP).
105 M. Letter to Church 'Wed Sept' (FP).
106 Church R. Letter to M 7 Sept 1962 (FP).
107 D. Personal communication.
108 *Evening Standard* 17 May 1963.
109 Montague Browne A. Letter to M 27 May 1963 (FP).
110 M. Letter to Prof TJB Spenser 21 Feb 1964 (FP).
111 Spencer TJB. Letter to M 21 Nov 1964 (FP).
112 M. Letter to Spencer 13 Jan 1965 (FP).
113 M. Letter to Spencer 19 Jan 1965 (FP).
114 Spencer TJB. Letter to M 9 April 1965 (FP).
115 Montague Browne A. Letter to M 6 April 1964 (FP).
116 Churchill Lady. Letter to M 18 June 1964 (FP).
117 Churchill Lady. Letter to M 30 July 1964 quoted in Soames Mary. (ref: 9.58) p 508.
118 Soames Mary. (ref: 9.58) p 508.

Chapter 23
The Great Book Row

1   Miss Marian Dean. Personal communication May 1987.
2   *The Times* 15 June 1964.
3   Soames Mary. (ref: 9.58) p 490.
4   Soames Mary. (ref: 9.58) p 493.
5   Reves Mrs Wendy. Personal communication.
6   Family papers.
7   Humi Julius B. Letter to M 18 Feb 1965 (FP).
8   Morgan K. Letter to M 19 Feb 1965 (FP).
9   JM. Personal communication.
10 Laughlin HA. Letter to M 30 March 1965 (FP).
11 M. Letter to JW 11 April 1965 (FP).
12 Colville J. Letter to M 21 April 1965 (FP).
13 Gilbert M. (ref: 16.33) p 1146.
14 Visitors' book, Marshalls (FP).
15 *The Observer* 22 Aug 1965.
16 *The Sun* 30 Nov 1965.
17 Aide memoire (FP).
18 Blake R. Letter to M 23 Aug 1965 (FP).
19 Blake R. Letter to M 29 Aug 1965 (FP).
20 Blake R. Letter to M 6 Sept 1965 (FP).
21 M. Letter to Blake 1 Sept 1965 (FP).
22 M. Letter to Blake 7 Sept 1965 (FP).
23 Blake R. Letter to M 22 Sept 1965 (FP).

24 Blake R. Letter to M 4 Jan 1966 (FP).
25 M. Letter to Blake 29 Sept 1965 (FP).
26 M. Letter to Blake 11 Nov 1965 (FP).
27 JM. Personal communication.
28 M. Letter to Blake 17 Nov 1965 (FP).
29 M. Letter to Blake 14 Dec 1965 (FP).
30 M. Letter to JW 15 Feb 1962 (FP).
31 M. Letter to Blake 13 Jan 1966 (FP).
32 M. Letter to Blake 19 Jan 1966 (FP).
33 M. Letter to JW 11 Jan 1966 (FP).
34 Soames Mary. (ref: 9.58) p 508.
35 Churchill Lady. Letter to M 21 Jan 1966 (FP).
36 M. Letter to Lady Churchill 24 Jan 1966 (FP).
37 Oswald Hickson Collier & Co. Letter to M 28 Jan 1966 (FP).
38 M. Letter to JW 21 Feb 1966 (FP).
39 M. Letter to JW 5 March 1966 (FP).
40 M. Letter to JW 18 March 1966 (FP).
41 M. Letter to JW 23 March 1966 (FP).
42 Normanbrook Lord. Letter to M 21 March 1966 (FP).
43 JW. Letter to M 11 April 1966 (FP).
44 *The Sunday Times* 3 April 1966.
45 D. Letter to JW 25 April 1966 (FP).
46 *Lancet* 1966; **i**: 920 (23 April 1966).
47 'Our medical correspondent', *The Times* 23 April 1966.
48 M. *The Times* 25 April 1966.
49 Churchill R. *The Times* 26 April 1966.
50 Churchill R. *The Times* 30 April 1966.
51 Colville J. *The Times* 27 April 1966.
52 JW. Letter to M 29 Jan 1966 (FP).
53 M. Draft letter 30 April 1966 (FP).
54 M. Letter to Dr D Stevenson 11 May 1966 (FP).
55 Seddon Professor Sir Herbert, *The Times* 17 May 1966.
56 Gilbert M. (ref: 16.33) p 1316.
57 Gilbert M. (ref: 16.33) p 1335.
58 Brogan C. *The Times* 29 April 1966.
59 Brain Lord. Letter to M 9 May 1966 (FP).
60 Brain Lord. *The Times* 10 May 1966.
61 Haley Sir William. Letter to M 17 May 1966 (FP).
62 Normanbrook Lord. *The Times* 24 May 1966.
63 M. Letter to Sir William Haley 20 May 1966 (FP).
64 M. Letter to Sir George Clark 19 May 1966 (FP).
65 Haley Sir William. Letter to M 24 May 1966 (FP).
66 Clark Sir George. Letter to M 25 May 1966 (FP).
67 Clark Sir George. Letter to M 8 June 1966 (FP).
68 M. *The Times* 3 June 1966.
69 Moir A. *The Times* 6 June 1966.
70 Montague Browne A. *The Times* 6 June 1966.

71 Bracken B. (ref: 22.61).
72 Moir A. Letter to M 3 June 1958 (FP).
73 Montague Browne A. Personal communication 10 April 1984.
74 Reves Mrs W. Letter to M 13 June 1966 (FP).
75 D. Personal communication.
76 D. Letter to JW 28 April 1966 (FP).
77 D. Letter to JW 9 May 1966 (FP).
78 JM. Personal communication.
79 D. Letter to JW 6 June 1966 (FP).
80 D. Letter to JW 23 May 1966 (FP).
81 D. Letter to JW 26 May 1966 (FP).
82 Haley Sir William. Letter to M 16 May 1966 (FP).
83 JM. Personal communication.
84 M. Letter to JW. 13 June 1966 (FP).
85 Longford Lord. Letter to author 7 Feb 1984.
86 Note: The Other Club. 21 Oct 1970 (FP).
87 *The Daily Telegraph* 16 June 1966.
88 Sargant W. Personal communication July 1981.
89 Grigg J. The *Guardian*.
90 M. Letter to JW 13 June 1966 (FP).
91 D. Letter to JW 27 June 1966 (FP).
92 M. Letter to JW 12 Oct 1966 (FP).
93 M. Letter to 'Dear Sir' 25 Aug 1966 (FP).
94 D. Letter to JW 27 June 1966 (FP).
95 Casey Lord. Letter to M 1 July 1966 (FP).
96 Casey Lady. Letter to M 22 July 1966 (FP).
97 Makins Sir Roger. Letter to M 5 June 1966 (FP).
98 Mackenzie Sir Compton. Letter to M 1 August 1966 (FP).
99 Coward Noel. Letter to M 26 May 1966 (FP).
100 Hart Sir Basil Liddell. Letter to M 1 Sept 1966 (FP).
101 *The Times* 6 July 1966.
102 *British Medical Journal* 1966; **2**: 44.
103 *Daily Telegraph* 6 July 1966.
104 M. Letter to JW 15 Nov 1966 (FP).
105 M. Manuscript note (FP).
106 Brain Lord. Letter to M 11 Oct 1966 (FP).
107 *The Times* 30 Dec 1966.
108 M. Letter to Rubinstein A 23 Oct 1966 (FP).
109 *Evening Standard* 28 Nov 1966 (FP).
110 Letters to M Dec 1966 (FP).
111 M. Letter to JW 21 Dec 1966 (FP).
112 Rubinstein A. Letter to JW 5 Jan 1967 (FP).
113 Gibson Sir Ronald. Letter to author 10 March 1981 (FP).
114 Dean Marian. Letter to JW 9 Jan 1967 (FP).
115 *Daily Telegraph* and *Daily Express* 7 Jan 1967.
116 *The Cape Argus* 18 Jan 1967.
117 JM. Personal communication.

Chapter 24
The Last Years

1 Dean Marian. Personal communication.
2 Wylie C. Letter to JW 25 April 1967 (FP).
3 Programme of American tour (FP).
4 Tape recording of interview 24 April 1967 (FP).
5 Koss S in a review of Pelling H. *Churchill.* (London: Macmillan, 1974) in *Times Literary Supplement* 26 July 1974.
6 Seldon A. (ref: 20.40).
7 Gilbert M. (ref: 11.1).
8 Gilbert M. (ref: 16.33).
9 Hubble D. Lord Moran & James Boswell: the two diarists compared and contrasted. *Medical History* 1969; **13**: 1-9.
10 Wilson J. *CB: A life of Sir Henry Campbell-Bannerman.* London: Constable, 1973.
11 JM. Personal communication.
12 D. Handwritten note (FP).
13 M. Letter to 'My dear Laura' 11 Nov 1972 (FP).

Index

441